The Economic History of China

D1478503

China's extraordinary rise as an economic powerhouse in the past two decades poses a challenge to many long-held assumptions about the relationship between political institutions and economic development. Economic prosperity also was vitally important to the longevity of the Chinese empire throughout the preindustrial era. Before the eighteenth century, China's economy shared some of the features – such as highly productive agriculture and sophisticated markets – found in the most advanced regions of Europe. But in many respects, from the central importance of irrigated rice farming to family structure, property rights, the status of merchants, the monetary system, and the imperial state's fiscal and economic policies, China's preindustrial economy diverged from the Western path of development. In this comprehensive but accessible study, Richard von Glahn examines the institutional foundations, continuities, and discontinuities in China's economic development over three millennia, from the Bronze Age to the early twentieth century.

RICHARD VON GLAHN is Professor of History at the University of California, Los Angeles. He has previously published three monographs on Chinese history, including *Fountain of Fortune: Money and Monetary Policy in China, 1000–1700* (1996) and *The Sinister Way: The Divine and the Demonic in Chinese Religious Culture* (2004), and a co-authored textbook on world history, *Crossroads and Cultures: A History of the World* (2012).

The Economic History of China

From Antiquity to the Nineteenth Century

Richard von Glahn

University of California, Los Angeles

CAMBRIDGE
UNIVERSITY PRESS

CAMBRIDGE
UNIVERSITY PRESS

University Printing House, Cambridge CB2 8BS, United Kingdom

Cambridge University Press is part of the University of Cambridge.

It furthers the University's mission by disseminating knowledge in the pursuit of
education, learning and research at the highest international levels of excellence.

www.cambridge.org
Information on this title: www.cambridge.org/9781107030565

© Richard von Glahn 2016

First published 2016
3rd printing 2019

Printed and bound in Great Britain by Clays Ltd, Elcograf S.p.A.

A catalogue record for this publication is available from the British Library

Library of Congress Cataloguing in Publication data
Von Glahn, Richard.
An economic history of China : from antiquity to the nineteenth century /
Richard von Glahn, University of California, Los Angeles.
   pages   cm
Includes bibliographical references and index.
ISBN 978-1-107-03056-5 (Hardback : alk. paper) –
ISBN 978-1-107-61570-0 (Paperback. : alk. paper)
1. China–Economic conditions–To 1644.
2. China–Economic conditions–1644–1912.   I. Title.
HC427.6.V66 2015
330.951–dc23   2015031124

ISBN 978-1-107-03056-5 Hardback
ISBN 978-1-107-61570-0 Paperback

In memory of Ken Sokoloff

Contents

Figures

Maps

Tables

Acknowledgments

For two decades I had the immense good fortune of having an office adjoining that of Ken Sokoloff, one of our most distinguished scholars of economic history. Through his unflagging good cheer, robust wisdom, and ecumenical knowledge of economics and history, Ken was a steadfast source of support for my own research and writing in Chinese economic history. One could not hope for a finer colleague, or imagine a finer person. His untimely death has been an enormous loss for the field of economic history – as numerous eulogists have already attested. I deeply regret that Ken did not live to see this book – which in ways large and small he encouraged and nurtured – appear in print. I can only acknowledge my appreciation by dedicating it to his memory, and to the ideals of scholarly community that he, more than anyone I have ever known, embodied.

R. Bin Wong and Jean-Laurent Rosenthal read drafts of each chapter and generously provided me with cogent advice and provocative criticism. I am beholden to them and to the student participants in the Cal Tech-UCLA Workshop on Chinese Economic History during the past several years – Xiang Chi, Xiaowen Hao, Yifei Huang, Sunkyu Lee, Guillermo Ruiz-Stoval, Dong Yan, and Meng Zhang – who also sacrificed their time and energy in reading and commenting on the entire manuscript. I have also keenly bene-fited from the comments and corrections provided by Lothar von Falkenhau-sen, Anthony Barbieri-Low, and Maxim Korolkov, each of whom read several of the early chapters of the book manuscript. I have not been able to address all of the issues raised by these readers, but their efforts have improved it significantly. Omissions are inevitable in a synthetic study like this, and no doubt errors have crept in as well; I assume responsibility for any shortcomings.

The immense debt I owe to the legions of scholars whose research has informed this study should be readily apparent, even if my references to their writings and ideas only imperfectly acknowledge their contributions. I have been extremely fortunate to receive the financial support of a fellowship from the National Endowment for the Humanities in 2010–11, which launched the writing of this book, and also a Guggenheim Fellowship in 2013–14 that enabled me to finish the writing in timely fashion. And finally, although words scarcely suffice for the task, I wish to express my gratitude to Kayoko and Erika for making this journey a joyous one.

Introduction

Until the 1960s, historians viewed China's history – and especially its economic history – through the lens of Western teleologies of historical change predicated on the progress of "freedom," leading either to capitalist democracy or socialist utopia. As I have written elsewhere, whether construed in Weberian terms as a peculiar type of "bureaucratic feudalism" or in Marxist categories as a species of the "Asiatic mode of production" genus, both Western and Asian scholarship portrayed imperial China as a static society whose periodic changes in regime barely caused a ripple on the stagnant pond of despotism.[1] The immobility of imperial Chinese society and economy typically was attributed to the parasitic nature of the imperial state and its dominant social class, the "gentry." Although the Chinese empire was believed to share the basic features of "oriental despotisms" in general, its unique longevity could be explained by the remarkable durability of the gentry's dominance over government office, landowning, intellectual life, and culture. In contrast, for example, to the dispersion of social power among monarchs, warriors, clerics, seigneurs, and urban corporations in medieval Europe, the gentry monopolized political, economic, and cultural authority and deflected challenges from any insurgent group, be they merchants, military officers, or disaffected intelligentsia. In the eyes of Marxist historians, the persistence of gentry rule perpetuated feudal property ownership and relations of production in which the rentier elite absorbed the surpluses generated by the peasant families under their dominion. American scholars balked at employing the category of "feudalism," given its Marxist associations, but their paradigm of "traditional" Chinese society essentially conformed to this depiction of economic inertia.

The most potent challenges to this image of an unchanging China were voiced by Japanese historians. Naitō Kōnan, writing in 1914, was the first to posit a fundamental transformation in Chinese government and society from the eighth to the twelfth centuries (what has become known as the

---

[1] For further elaboration of the historiography of imperial China discussed here, see von Glahn 2003a.

"Tang-Song transition") during which aristocratic domination dissolved and
was superseded both by a more autocratic state and greater autonomy for
village society. Naitō's disciple Miyazaki Ichisada, in his 1950 book *East
Asia's Modern Age*, likened the Tang-Song transition to the European Renais-
sance, both of which exhibited the secularization of society and culture and the
rebirth of rational philosophy on one hand, and the rise of cities, commerce,
and the free disposition of property and labor on the other, that have become
hallmarks of the modern world.[2] Japanese Marxist historians, in contrast,
interpreted the Tang-Song transition as the moment in which a feudal society
based on serfdom eclipsed the ancient slave-labor economy. In their view, in
contrast to genuine forms of feudalism – to be found in the medieval eras of
both Europe and Japan – Chinese feudalism proved resistant to further social
development because of the ineluctable tenacity of China's patriarchal
social institutions of family, lineage, village, and guild.

The crucial breakthrough in the conceptualization of China's premodern
economy came in the 1960s. Shiba Yoshinobu's magisterial study of the
commercial economy of Song China (tenth to thirteenth centuries) marked
a crucial departure from linear conceptions of history to study the facts of
economic life.[3] In meticulous detail Shiba reconstructed the innovations in
transport, agricultural and industrial productivity, markets, urban structure,
business enterprise, and credit and finance that stimulated an unprecedented
commercial efflorescence. As Shiba demonstrated, the Song period witnessed the formation of regional, national, and international markets for a
wide range of commodities, including staples such as grain, salt, and timber
and new consumer products (tea, sugar, porcelain) as well as luxury goods.
Although Shiba's study focused on private commerce and the formation
of commercial capital, he disavowed the idea that the rise of the market
economy heralded the emergence of a bourgeois social class. At the same
time Robert Hartwell published a series of provocative essays on the coal
and iron industries in Song China that offered further corroboration of the
importance of market demand for industrial development.[4] Hartwell's
study attested to prodigious iron and steel output by large-scale enterprises
utilizing technologies such as blast furnaces and coking far beyond anything
available in the West at the time. While primarily stressing the demand
for iron goods emanating from urban markets (and especially the Song
capital of Kaifeng), Hartwell also underscored the contributions of the
Song state – in providing domestic peace, a stable monetary system, transport
facilities, and predictable economic policies – in reducing risks and fostering
private investment.

[2] Miyazaki 1950.   [3] Shiba 1968.   [4] Hartwell 1962, 1966, 1967.

The fruits of the pioneering research by Shiba and Hartwell were gathered together into a far more ambitious interpretation of China's premodern economy proposed by Mark Elvin in his seminal study, *The Pattern of the Chinese Past* (1973). Elvin divided his analysis of Chinese history into three parts that surveyed (1) the main features of political economy from the early empires down to the fourteenth century, with a focus on the military and fiscal capacities of the imperial state; (2) what Elvin dubbed "the medieval economic revolution" of the eighth to thirteenth centuries, focused on technological and institutional changes that enabled unprecedented growth in agriculture, industrial production, commerce, and cities; and (3) the flattening of growth and technological stasis throughout the late imperial period (from the fourteenth century onward), resulting in what he described as "quantitative growth and qualitative standstill." Elvin concluded that the turning point in China's economic development came during the fourteenth century, pointing to three changes or reversals that deterred further investment, material and intellectual, in technological innovation: (1) the diminution of foreign contact and trade resulting from the Ming state's self-imposed maritime embargo, which cut off China from international trade, vitiated its navy, and hindered the development of national identity; (2) the "filling-up" of China's frontiers and closing of outlets for emigration, resulting in a worsening imbalance in the labor/land ratio that discouraged labor-saving innovations; and (3) the waning of philosophical interest in the natural world and efforts to gain mastery over it, thus precluding the emergence of "science." Despite important developments in the late imperial period (especially during 1550–1800), including the disappearance of serfdom, the growth of rural trade and industry, and increased scale of economic organization, China remained encased in a technological cul-de-sac that precluded a breakthrough to an industrial revolution.

Elvin's book was not intended as a comprehensive economic history, but it did advance a bold and novel thesis to explain long-term changes in the Chinese economy and its failure to generate the kind of transformative change wrought by the Industrial Revolution in the West. Equally importantly, however, Elvin established the idea of a "medieval economic revolution" in China that confounded the universal categories of Western social science and challenged commonplace assumptions about the primacy of the Western European historical experience. Historians of late imperial China responded to Elvin's contrast between the medieval economic revolution and the merely incremental pace of subsequent economic growth by asserting that from the sixteenth century onward China underwent a "second economic revolution" characterized by: the disappearance of bound labor; the ascendancy of private enterprise over state economic management; the growth of rural industries; the increasing spatial range of the market; higher levels of monetization in private trade and public finance; a greater volume of foreign trade; and dramatic increases in the size of the population and economic output.[5]

Nonetheless, despite the emerging consensus that the market exerted a growing influence on economic life from the Song dynasty onward, many scholars shared Elvin's conviction that China's late imperial economy remained trapped in some form of structural equilibrium that prohibited transformational growth. In contrast to the focus on commercial development in the studies by Shiba, Hartwell, and Elvin, scholars such as Kang Chao and Philip Huang emphasized the constraints imposed by the inherent limitations of a peasant economy dominated by small family farms.[6] Chao and Huang argued that the persistence of a peasant mode of production driven by family subsistence needs inhibited labor-saving technological innovation and the formation of capital-intensive farming. Access to land and market opportunities ironically reinforced, in Huang's words, an "involutionary" pattern of diminishing labor productivity and "growth without development." Kent Deng singled out the crucial importance of the "absolute" landownership rights of free peasant families as the key to a structural equilibrium that in his view was congruent with the development of the Chinese empire since its origins in antiquity. Deng postulated that the interlocking effects of Confucian ideology, the imperial state, and the landholding system promoted economic stability, a decent and at times affluent livelihood, commercial expansion, population growth, and military security, but the strength of this fundamentally agrarian system also deterred transformative change.[7]

This notion that China's economy was constrained by a peasant mode of production has been disputed by scholars steeped in the tenets of neoclassical economics who argued that farming families were inculcated with norms of diligence, thrift, and accumulation and responded positively to shifts in factor prices within smoothly functioning, competitive markets largely free from government interference. Although the constraints of premodern technologies – especially in transport – limited the potential for market-driven development, the growth of regional and international markets after 1870 (at least in some favored areas) because of improvements in transport, information, and technological diffusion generated rising real incomes and sustained economic growth before the onset of the Great Depression and the Japanese invasions in the 1930s.[8] The involution thesis also was challenged by Li Bozhong's contention that – in contrast to Elvin's depiction of technological stasis in the Ming-Qing era – Chinese farmers continually innovated by developing new agricultural technologies and investing

---

[5] Rowe 1985.   [6] Chao 1986; Philip Huang 1985, 1990.   [7] Gang Deng 1999.
[8] For a summary of this argument and the scholarship supporting it, see Myers 1991.

household labor in handicraft industries that boosted family incomes and rural prosperity throughout the late imperial era.[9]

The dispute over the nature of the Chinese rural economy ultimately hinged on the question of whether it should be understood primarily as a product of China's unique historical experience – the most crucial features of which were the predominance of small family farms and a distinct "peasant" mentality – or, conversely, as one governed by universal laws of economic behavior in which farming households responded affirmatively to market incentives, behaving much like entrepreneurial firms. In the 1990s, the search to transcend the apparent stalemate between these conflicting views gave rise to what has come to be known as the "California School" of Chinese economic history. Applying the analytical tools of comparative economic history to the study of China's late imperial economy framed within a world-historical perspective, the California School group challenged long-standing assumptions about the inherent superiority of Western institutions, culture, and government for the promotion of economic growth.[10] In his provocative study of the "Great Divergence" that led to the Industrial Revolution breakthrough in Britain but not elsewhere, Kenneth Pomeranz raised the question of whether institutional differences in fact produced divergent outcomes in economic performance.[11] Pomeranz contended that despite their different institutional matrices, the most economically advanced regions of the premodern world – including not only Britain and the Netherlands in Europe and China's Yangzi Delta, but also Bengal in India and eastern Japan – evinced fundamental similarities grounded in what Adam Smith identified as the motive forces of economic growth: the expansion of markets and the specialization of labor. Pomeranz thus repudiated Huang's involutionary model in contending that Chinese farming families and entrepreneurial firms alike responded efficiently to price-setting markets for land, labor, and capital. At the same time Pomeranz emphasized the limits to Smithian dynamics of economic growth and the intensifying constraints to further development, largely due to exhaustion of natural resources, that all of the leading economic regions of the world faced by the end of the eighteenth century. The breakthrough to modern economic growth came not from further

---

[9] Li Bozhong 1998, 2003.

[10] The term "California School" was coined by Jack Goldstone 2000. The seminal works in this vein of scholarship were Wong 1997 and Pomeranz 2000. Other notable expressions of this approach (whose analyses and conclusions nonetheless diverged in many respects) include Flynn and Giráldez 1995; von Glahn 1996a; Lee and Campbell 1997; Frank 1998; Li Bozhong 1998; Marks 1999; Goldstone 2002; and Sugihara 2003. Among other issues, the California School scholarship also challenged the common view that integration into the global economy since the sixteenth century had negative repercussions that impoverished the Chinese population and subjected China to domination by Western imperialism and capitalism. On this point, see in particular von Glahn 1996b, Frank 1998.

[11] Pomeranz 2000.

extension of Smithian market dynamics, but rather from Britain's unique advantages for resolving resource constraints through its colonial empire and for developing the revolution in energy (coal-powered steam technology) that was the true basis for the Industrial Revolution.

The tempestuous debate over the "Great Divergence" incited by the work of Pomeranz and other California School historians without doubt has been the most hotly contested issue as well as the most vitally creative catalyst for new scholarship in the field of comparative economic history during the past fifteen years.[12] The most important influence of the California School scholarship – and what will be its enduring legacy – has been its insistence on precision and consistency in comparing economic institutions and performance in Europe, Asia, and beyond. In response to – and the response overwhelmingly has consisted of efforts at refutation – Pomeranz's "Great Divergence" thesis, economic historians have focused intently on developing quantitative measures of economic performance to test its arguments. As a result, the recent wave of scholarship on the Chinese economy in comparative historical perspective has mostly been confined to issues and time periods for which quantitative measurement might be feasible (and yet still, as we shall see, severely hindered by the limitations of empirical evidence). As a result little of this scholarship examines Chinese economic history before the eighteenth century. Moreover, for reasons that defy ready explanation, the "Great Divergence" debate seems to have engaged economists more than historians, and the impetus for new research stimulated by it has largely come – apart from the California School scholars themselves – from Asian and European scholars rather than the North American academic community.

As welcome as the new attention to the economic history of China generated by the "Great Divergence" debate is, the narrow focus of recent comparative scholarship on particular institutions and quantitative measurement has caused scholars to lose sight of the Chinese economy as a whole and its historical development. Insufficient attention has been paid to the fact that the value of institutions always is context-specific; there is no set of institutions that is optimally valid under all historical circumstances – a point forcefully argued by Pomeranz, but often ignored. The purpose of this book is to tell the story of the Chinese economy in its own terms; or, perhaps I should say, to view the story of Chinese history through the lens of economic livelihood. Scholars and students of Chinese history as well as comparative economic historians presently lack access to even basic knowledge about Chinese economic history. General economic histories of China have been published in China – perhaps most authoritatively, the sixteen-volume *Comprehensive*

---

[12] For further discussion of the debates over the Chinese rural economy and the California School scholarship, see Chapter 9.

Economic History of China (中国经济通史) published by Jingji Ribao
Chubanshe (2nd edition, 2007) under the guidance of eleven editors – but
they remain encumbered by shopworn Marxist paradigms and fail to incorporate virtually any Western scholarship, and Japanese scholarship only intermit-
tently. Surprisingly, synthetic surveys of Chinese economic history rarely have
been attempted by Japanese scholars in the past half-century. Mention should
be made of a recently published volume edited by Okamoto Takashi, which
provides a cogent but highly abbreviated survey of Chinese economic history
from the Neolithic era to the advent of the recent economic reforms launched
in 1978.[13] But this work, with some exceptions, draws almost exclusively on
Japanese scholarship. Elvin's *Pattern of the Chinese Past*, now more than forty
years old, has served – and for the most part served well – as the basic point of
reference for Western scholars and students without command of the Chinese
or Japanese languages, but Elvin's book was not intended as a comprehensive
economic history of China, and much of its content has been superseded
by new knowledge.

This book, which spans nearly thirty centuries from the Bronze Age to
the dawn of the twentieth century, immodestly attempts to fill this void. As the
brief synopsis of recent debates over the premodern Chinese economy delineated above suggests, this field of study is riven by clashing interpretations,
and as the following chapters will show, consensus is elusive on many major
issues for virtually every period of Chinese history. Since this book is intended
to be a work of synthesis, I have striven to achieve balance and objectivity;
where I have waded into scholarly controversies and made my own interpret-
ative choices, I have tried to acknowledge differing opinions and to justify my
own judgments. My allegiance to the California School – as a matter of
method, not doctrine – will be self-evident, but I hope I have succeeded in
providing a fair hearing to opposing points of view.

My goal has been to write a coherent, synthetic narrative of the development
of the Chinese economy over the very long term based on the best available
scholarship. Of course, given the constraints of time, space, and resources,
omissions are inevitable, and worthy scholarship undoubtedly has been overlooked in places. I have not proposed an overarching theory of the Chinese
economy; my hope is that in this case, truly "le bon dieu est dans le détail."
But there is indeed a polemic that underlies this narrative. In the first place, this
study repudiates any linear, stadial notion of history or economic development.
Second, it disavows a fundamental tenet of neoclassical economics, namely
the idea that the market is *the* driving force in economic development and
the creation of wealth. Modern economic growth (and this was true of

---

[13] Okamoto 2013. Nearly half of the Okamoto volume is devoted to fifty-nine self-contained short
essays (one to three pages each) that provide valuable digests of specific topics and institutions.

premodern economic growth as well) principally derives not from the expansion of markets, but rather from innovations fostered by new knowledge and technology. The narrow attention economic historians have focused on the market has obscured the impact of other institutions – most notably, the state – in promoting economic development.

Needless to say, in the case of China, where the imperial state endured for two millennia, the presence of the state loomed especially large in the lives and livelihoods of its subjects. As noted above, the remarkable durability of the imperial state has induced Western social theorists to categorize China as a form of "oriental despotism" in which the stultifying effects of imperial rule imparted a profound inertia to political and economic institutions that defied the norms of economic behavior and economic history. This characterization of Chinese "despotism" has persisted in Western social science even in recent times.[14] Over the past several decades, Chinese historians have endeavored to counter this false image by delineating the dramatic expansion of the private economy since the mid-sixteenth century, the diminished role of the state in governing economic life, and even the possible emergence of a "civil society" in which the state granted substantial autonomy to local community leaders. In a different vein, the work of R. Bin Wong has rehabilitated our understanding of the late imperial Chinese state, refuting the caricature of a despotic and arbitrary government dedicated to the enrichment and opulence of the sovereign by elucidating the actual goals, capacities, and commitments of its leadership and the ways in which state actions – not necessarily deliberately – made positive contributions to economic growth.[15] Nonetheless, the conviction that late imperial China should be seen as a "patronage economy" that "obstructed innovation and also encouraged widespread corruption" remains widespread, even among scholars who specialize in the study of the Chinese economy.[16]

In the study of European history, growing numbers of economists and historians have begun to recognize that the consolidation of power in the hands of territorial states during the early modern period enhanced the state's fiscal and infrastructural capacity and encouraged state interventions to promote economic welfare that had positive effects on economic growth. Rather than dismissing the state as an invariably rent-seeking encumbrance continually interfering with the free play of market forces, this body of scholarship has

---

[14] See Mann 1986, Landes 1998, Macfarlane 2000, and Acemoglu and Robinson 2012 for influential examples.

[15] Wong 1997, 2012.

[16] Brandt, Ma, and Rawski 2014: 79. This is only one aspect of the imperial state analyzed by this group of authors, but in their view the patronage economy is one of the imperial state's legacies – and perhaps the main one – that persists in the People's Republic of China today. See ibid.: 106.

sought to recuperate the crucial importance of the early modern state in fostering or abetting economic developments that culminated in the emergence of capitalism and the Industrial Revolution.[17] The state did so through promoting and protecting new knowledge, investing in public goods, and incubating nascent strategic industries through policies that can be broadly described as "mercantilist" in the sense defined by Gustav Schmoller in 1884: "the total transformation of society and its organizations, as well as of the state and its institutions, in the replacing of a local and territorial economy by that of the national state."[18] Centralization of political power curtailed seigneurial and urban monopolies, privileges, and jurisdictional authorities that had hindered market integration, commercial competition, technological diffusion, and industrial investment.[19] War-making, despite the short-term devastation it inflicted, exerted crucial influence on state formation and long-term economic development.[20] Rather than simply an extension of Smithian dynamics of market expansion and labor specialization, economic growth in early modern Europe was nurtured by Schumpeterian principles in which it is not perfect markets, but rather imperfect markets, that spur innovation and economic growth. The quest for national sovereignty and geopolitical power led not only to an expansion of the fiscal capacity of the state, but also to the protection of property rights (including intellectual property through patents), investment in "infant" industries, greater mobility of skilled labor, the acquisition of new technologies, and the creation of trade networks that extended around the globe.[21]

We also see this Schumpeterian dynamic at work in Chinese history. The imperial state was not a monolithic entity. Just as the economy evolved over time, so did the state and its institutions. The dialectic between the fiscal operations of the state and the wider economy yielded divergent results under different historical circumstances and ideological commitments. From a Schumpeterian perspective, at times the Chinese imperial state galvanized economic growth by providing domestic peace, international security, and investment in public goods – education, welfare, transport systems, water control, and standardized market institutions – as well as creating an institutional infrastructure that enabled Smithian growth in agriculture and

---

[17] I am particularly influenced here by the work of Reinert 1999; Epstein 2000; Reinert and Reinert 2005; and O'Brien 2012. See also Vries 2015, which appeared too late for me to incorporate here.

[18] Schmoller 1967: 51. Regrettably, our understanding of the historical role of mercantilist ideas and policies has largely been shaped by one of mercantilism's most hostile critics, Eli Heckscher (1955). For a more historically grounded and balanced assessment of mercantilism, see Magnusson 1994.

[19] Epstein 2000.   [20] Findlay and O'Rourke 2007; Rosenthal and Wong 2011.

[21] Reinert and Reinert 2005; O'Brien 2012.

commerce. The state's role in creating demand (including war-making) also figured significantly in stimulating economic development. During the late imperial era, China's rulers embraced the Neo-Confucian ideological abhorrence (not unlike that of neoclassical economics) to state interference in the private economy. Although this commitment to light taxation and minimal state intrusion – a far cry from the "oriental despotism" imagined by Western social theorists! – had positive effects in encouraging Smithian dynamics of economic expansion, the weak infrastructural capacity of the state limited the potential for economic growth along Schumpeterian lines as was happening concurrently in early modern Europe.

That, at least, is a hypothesis that should be subjected to rigorous research and analysis. This study will, I hope, provide a new set of benchmarks for comparative economic history, but my principal intention is to present a coherent narrative of the development of the premodern Chinese economy. Above all, it is my fervent wish that this study can begin to do justice to a proper understanding of the lives and livelihoods – and the diversity, imagination, and industry – of the Chinese people over the past three millennia.

1   The Bronze Age economy (1045 to 707 BCE)

China's Bronze Age, beginning *c.* 2000 BCE, gave birth to the earliest states in East Asia and the technologies and institutions that made possible the mobilization of material and human resources on a large scale. The first state, Shang (*c.* 1570–1045 BCE), developed political institutions and a ritual order that enabled it to impose its dominion over much of North China's Central Plain, the alluvial floodplain of the Yellow River that became the heartland of early Chinese civilization. From *c.* 1200 BCE the Shang rulers began to use writing to record the divinations essential to the royal ancestral cult and the conduct of their government. Shang rule was overthrown by the upstart Zhou dynasty in 1045 BCE. The Zhou ecumene, centered in the ancestral Zhou homeland of the Wei River valley in the west, encompassed the entire Central Plain as well. The Zhou retained many features of Shang culture, including its ritual practices, writing system, and bronze metallurgy. But the Zhou also introduced new conceptions of divine authority and political sovereignty and developed a more formalized bureaucratic government to extend the reach of royal power.

If any civilization merits the appellation "Bronze Age" it is surely ancient China. Bronze ritual vessels occupied the central place in the political, social, and cultural order of the earliest Chinese states. The sheer quantity of surviving bronze artifacts from China's Bronze Age is without peer among ancient civilizations: more than 12,000 Zhou bronze ritual vessels exist today, and no doubt many yet remain undiscovered in tombs and caches. The scale of these artifacts also is enormous: one bronze cauldron from *c.* 1200 BCE weighs 875 kg., and archaeologists recovered more than 10 tons of bronze vessels from a single cache buried in the fifth century BCE.[1] Beginning in the late Shang period, but especially with the onset of the Zhou dynasty, the ruling elite began to inscribe bronze vessels for commemorative purposes. These inscriptions primarily signified the purpose for casting the vessel and commemorated the honors the maker received from the king that brought glory to

---

[1] Bagley 1999: 137.

his lineage and his ancestors.[2] Zhou bronze inscriptions – notably the "appointment inscriptions," which record the bestowal of offices, rewards, and duties by the king – also contain valuable information about the organization of the Zhou state and the self-conception and cultural practices of its rulers. More incidentally, the bronze inscriptions yield important insights into the economic livelihood and resources of the Zhou ruling class, subjects regarding which we know little for the Shang period. Therefore this study of China's economic history begins with the founding of the Zhou dynasty.

Much ink has been spilled over the nature of the early Chinese state, especially on the question of whether Shang-Zhou China should be defined as a slave society or a feudal society. Few scholars today – outside of China, where Marxian theories of historical development still hold sway – find any utility in these obsolete categories, but there is little consensus on how to define the Zhou state and society.[3] In my view, the Zhou can best be described as a *patrimonial state*.

The concept of a patrimonial state as an ideal type was central to Max Weber's sociology of the state. For Weber, the patrimonial state was a large-scale version of the patriarchal household (*oikos*) in which "the most fundamental obligation of the subjects is the maintenance of the ruler." In Weber's formulation, the ruler of the patrimonial state expands his authority beyond the personal retainers attached to his household through gifts of land and other means of control to "political subjects" – local lords, governors, and associations – who retain some degree of autonomy. Although Weber believed that the patrimonial state was compatible with a wide range of economic forms, including a market economy, he especially associated it with liturgic governance, by which he meant taxation in services and goods imposed on certain groups (classes, status groups, castes) in return for monopoly rights over their respective economic pursuits. Weber identified the patrimonial state with a wide variety of ancient societies (Egypt perhaps being the most salient), and also with the major Asian empires of more recent times in the Middle East, India, and China.[4]

---

[2] For an introduction to Zhou bronze inscriptions, see Shaughnessy 1991. Only about one hundred Shang vessels have inscriptions, whereas the vast majority of Zhou bronzes do. Chinese scholarship (e.g., Zhou Ziqiang 2007) continues to rely heavily on the corpus of late Eastern Zhou philosophical, ritual, and historical writings to interpret the economic history of the Western Zhou period. In my view these later texts, which are heavily prescriptive in nature, cannot provide reliable testimony for the Western Zhou and I have excluded them from my analysis.
[3] Recently Li Feng (2008: 23, 294–98) has proposed defining the Western Zhou as a "delegatory kin-ordered settlement state." While perhaps accurate in a descriptive sense, such a definition has limited utility for comparative analysis.
[4] Weber 1978: 2, 1006–69. Quotation is from p. 1014.

Although I borrow the nomenclature of the patrimonial state, I disassociate it from Weber's theory of the evolution of historical societies. I define the patrimonial state as one in which the monarch shares his sovereign authority with noble houses established by royal investiture and linked to the royal family through real or fictive kinship ties. Sovereign authority is transmitted through the patrilineal line of descent, typically through primogeniture. Junior lines of descent also have some share in the status, prestige, and wealth – the common patrimony – of these aristocratic lineages. Induction into this ruling class is sanctified by ritual practices derived from ancestor worship, the principles of family hierarchy, and the bestowal of ritually prestigious goods. In Chinese history – and also in later Chinese political theory, which frequently invoked the patrimonial state as an ideal type – the patrimonial state was antecedent to the emergence of the autocratic state from *c.* 450 BCE onward.[5] In contrast to Weber, for whom the late imperial Chinese state epitomized the patrimonial form of governance, I argue that the patrimonial state disappeared forever in China after the founding of the first unified empire in the third century BCE.

Economic life in Zhou China centered on the patrimonial ruling lineages who commanded the labor of farmers and artisans. The ruling lineages consisted of blood relatives sharing common residence and organized into hierarchically ordered statuses that were affirmed through regular feasting and rituals. In addition to lands, the Zhou king bestowed on his vassals and officers servile populations whose "most fundamental obligation," as in Weber's formulation, was providing for the maintenance of their lords. As an economic unit, we can speak of the lineage as a household comprising not only members of the lineage but also a wider group of officers, artisans, and servile dependents who participated in the lineage's administrative and economic activities. The structure of the lineage household of Zhou China differed from households in other ancient societies. The society of Early Dynastic Mesopotamia was organized into large temple and palace households encompassing priests, administrators, farmers, artisans, and shepherds that provided for the subsistence needs of its numerous members.[6] The Greek conception of the *oikos* or household – expressed most cogently in the *Oikonomikos* of Xenophon in the fourth century BCE – focused on the gentleman farmer

---

[5] In Chinese political theory, the early Zhou system was known by the term *fengjian* 封建, a term that in modern Chinese is used to translate "feudalism," which has led to unfortunate misunderstandings about the nature of Zhou society. *Fengjian* comprises two separate verbs: *feng*, "to demarcate a boundary," and *jian*: "to establish." Recent scholarship has suggested that in the Zhou bronze inscriptions *feng* signified awards of lands within the royal domain to aristocratic lineages, while *jian* was reserved for the founding of the regional domains in the old Shang territories. See Li Feng 2008: 47–49.

[6] Van De Mieroop 2004: 53–55.

and the management of the property and persons under his dominion.[7] The Zhou lineage household also differed markedly from the household institution – comprising the conjugal family and its dependents – created by the centralizing states of the Warring States era, which persisted throughout the history of imperial China. But the Zhou patrimonial lineage, like these other types of households, was a single unit of production and consumption whose members resided together. In the absence of markets, the lineage household was largely self-sufficient. But the Zhou ruling lineages also engaged in complex exchanges of property and people as well as symbolically invested prestige goods.

At present it remains unknown whether other institutions played a significant role in the economic life of the early Zhou period. Our evidence, both textual and archaeological, is restricted to the activities of the Zhou royal house and the ruling lineages within the royal domain. We must begin, then, by examining the structure and operation of the patrimonial state.

The patrimonial state of the western Zhou (1045–771 BCE)

Following its sudden and perhaps unexpected victory over the Shang *c.* 1045 BCE, the Zhou faced severe logistical obstacles in extending its rule over the former Shang territories. The Zhou's territorial base in the Wei River valley was located on the western fringe of the Shang ecumene, separated from the Central Plain by the rugged furl of the Taihang Mountains. Under the forceful leadership of the Duke of Zhou, regent to the child king Cheng, the Zhou developed a two-pronged strategy to impose its suzerainty. The Zhou homeland in the west was directly ruled by royal administrators and defended by the main royal military forces, known as the Six Armies. The twin capitals of Feng and Hao served as the centers of court life and ceremony, but Zhouyuan (also known as Qiyi), the ancestral home of the Zhou lineage 100 kilometers to the west, remained a major political center. Zhouyuan was the site of important royal temples and tombs, and many aristocratic lineages maintained residences there. In the east, in the old Shang territories of the Central Plain, the Zhou exercised only indirect control. The Zhou appointed at least two dozen – and perhaps forty or more – royal kinsmen and long-time allies to rule over new domains carved from the former Shang territories.

The bronze inscriptions and early literary evidence such as the "Announcement" chapters of the *Book of Documents* portray the Zhou kings as all-powerful yet magnanimous sovereigns, bearers of the Mandate of Heaven

---

[7] Finley 1973: 17–21. It is now recognized that Xenophon's definition of the *oikos* – centered on the conjugal family as the basic unit of production, consumption, and reproduction – simplified more complicated socio-economic realities. Cox 1998: 130–67.

who entrusted the weighty duties of government and justice to worthy kinsmen. Rulers in the eastern domains who were not related to the royal line by blood nonetheless were inducted into the king's circle of intimates through solemn rituals of fealty modeled on the forms of ancestor worship. Under the principles of patrimonial rule, the king shared his realm with this extended family of subordinate rulers: as long as they paid homage to the king and submitted to his will, they and their descendants would continue to enjoy the blessing not only of the king but also of Heaven – the supreme fount of sovereign authority. Most importantly, both rulers of domains and royal officers received lands and resources as the hereditary patrimony of their lineage. Many inscriptions on bronze vessels commemorate the gifts, honors, offices, and duties bestowed by the Zhou kings on individuals. These individuals in turn cast bronze vessels dedicated to their fathers and grandfathers both to glorify their ancestors and for the edification of their posterity.

The Zhou kings entrusted administration of the royal domain to a group of officials known as the Three Ministries – of Lands (revenue), Construction (public works), and Horses (military affairs and hunting).[8] A large staff of scribes and secretaries acted as the mouthpieces of the king, issuing royal orders, composing the king's speeches for major ceremonial events, and preserving the government's documentary records. Many of these scribes were persons of exalted social standing with close ties to the king, whom they served as personal advisors and emissaries. Real power often lay in the hands of high-ranking royal princes, however, rather than the ministerial officials. On occasion kings delegated full authority over the entire royal administration to a leading prince, a practice that commenced with the regency of the Duke of Zhou.

The rulers of the new domains – known as "archer lords" (*hou* 侯) – were strategically positioned around the perimeters of the Central Plain and in the Fen River valley (Map 1.1). The *Chronicles of Zuo*, a fourth century BCE historical work, describes the founding of the domain of Lu in the eastern part of the Central Plain as follows:

The portion given to the Lord of Lu [Bo Qin, the eldest son of the Duke of Zhou] included a grand chariot; a grand flag bearing an ensign of entwined dragons; the huang jade ornament of the Xia sovereigns; Fanruo, the bow of Fengfu; and six lineages of Shang – Tiao, Xu, Xiao, Suo, Changshao, and Weishao. The king ordered Bo Qin to take command of the lineage elders, assemble his kinsmen, and gather together all their dependents, to model himself on the Duke of Zhou and receive the king's mandate. In this way Bo Qin may perform the king's service in Lu, and thus make manifest the illustrious virtue of [his father] the Duke of Zhou. The king bestowed upon Lu lands and all the resources attached to them, along with the priests and wardens of the

---

[8] This description of the organization and evolution of Zhou royal government is based on Li Feng 2008.

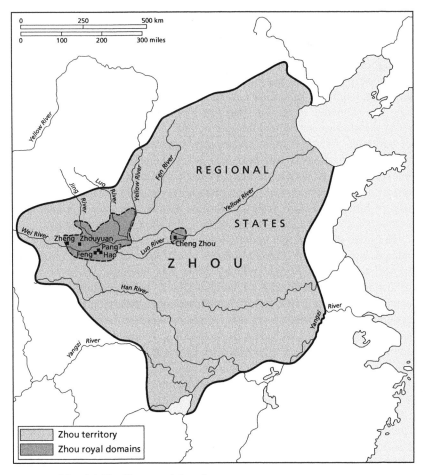

Map 1.1 The Zhou royal domains
Source: Li Feng 2008: 102, map 2.

ancestral temple, diviners, scribes, ceremonial dress and regalia, written records on bamboo slips, officers of state, and ritual vessels. Furthermore, the people of Shangyan were compelled to submit to the rule of Bo Qin, whose seat of government was placed at the site of the ancient king Shaohao's capital.[9]

In addition to receiving a territory and all the trappings of sovereign office, Bo Qin was assigned a portion of the defeated Shang population, who were

---

[9] ZZ 3A: 780 (Dinggong 4th year). My translation of this passage follows the interpretation advanced in Itō Michiharu 1987: 78–87. Shaohao was a legendary sovereign of remote antiquity, not a Shang king.

relocated to Lu and obliged to render service to their new master. The domain rulers gained full authority over their subjects and the fruits of their labor. They owed fealty to the Zhou king and often were called upon to provide military assistance, but there is no definitive evidence that they were required to pay tribute. A secondary capital known as Cheng Zhou, near modern Luoyang, extended the reach of royal power to the east. Another contingent of royal military forces known as the Eight Armies was stationed around Cheng Zhou to defend the eastern and southern frontiers of the Zhou realm.

The Zhou ruling class thus was bifurcated into two groups, the archer lords and royal officers. The archer lords were first and foremost military commanders, but held dominion over their territories, whose inhabitants were subject to their lord's juridical authority and demands for revenue. According to a bronze inscription commemorating the investiture of Ke as ruler of Yan, at the far northern edge of the Central Plain, the king conferred six groups of people as Ke's subjects. These six groups included long-time allies of the Zhou, former enemies relocated from distant areas, and local inhabitants, suggesting that the Zhou deliberately sought to foster new social communities in the old Shang territories.[10] The power wielded by the domain rulers over their subjects was not absolute, however. The Zhou kings also dispatched overseers, chosen from the most highly ranked royal kinsmen, to supervise the conduct of the archer lords, whom the king could – in theory at least – replace at will.

The second group within the Zhou ruling class consisted of royal officials. In lieu of regular salaries or stipends royal officers received benefices – grants of lands and servile laborers – to provide for their needs. Early Zhou bronze inscriptions typically record the king's award of lands and subjects along with ritual regalia and weapons. For example, in 981 BCE King Kang appointed a certain Yu, grandson of an illustrious high official said to have served the Zhou founders, to a major military office. Yu cast a bronze cauldron to commemorate his appointment in which he quoted extensively from the king's charge to him, including the detailed list of gifts bestowed by the king:

[The king spoke:] I award you a vessel of sacrificial wine, a hat, a cloak, a pair of knee pads, slippers, and a horse and chariot. I award you the flag of your late grandfather, Lord of the Nan lineage, to use in hunting. I award you four Elders from the Zhou domains along with 659 bondsmen ranging from charioteers to common men. I award you thirteen Elders of foreign origin who are royal servants along with 1,050 bondsmen. Order them to relocate immediately from their lands.[11]

---

[10] Li Feng 2008: 241–43.

[11] Da Yu *ding* (Ma Chengyuan 1988: #62). NB: bronze inscriptions will be identified according to the catalogue number given in Ma Chengyuan 1988. Translation modified from those in Cook 1997: 274 and Li Feng 2006: 127.

Yu received a total of 1,709 bondsmen under the leadership of local officers (of both Zhou and foreign origin) who formerly had been direct subjects of the king and now were transferred to Yu's authority and transferred to the lands possessed by his lineage. "Elder" here is most likely a kinship term signifying the head of a lineage, and the groups in question probably were entire lineages. The benefices obtained by royal officers like Yu became the hereditary patrimony of their lineage. These aristocratic lineages continued to maintain residences and ancestral temples at Zhouyuan in addition to their estates, which often were scattered across the royal domain.

Although members of aristocratic lineages often acceded to offices performed by their fathers and grandfathers, strictly speaking appointments were not hereditary. Instead, young men first had to prove their mettle as aides to senior officials before receiving royal appointments.[12] In the inscription quoted above King Kang commended Yu's past loyalty and accomplishments, saying that "day and night you have performed great services." As it turned out, the king's faith in Yu proved well-founded. Two years after receiving his appointment as a military commander, Yu cast another cauldron in which he commemorated his victory over a foreign enemy and enumerated the chiefs, men, horses, oxen, and chariots he captured as well as the severed ears taken as trophies from slain enemy soldiers. By the ninth century BCE royal officials commonly served in a series of both civil and military posts over the course of their government career.

During the first century following the conquest of Shang, the Zhou kings – secure in their ritual preeminence and with formidable military power at their disposal – exercised supreme authority over the ecumene. But in 957 BCE the Zhou suffered a calamitous military defeat inflicted by the rival state of Chu in the south in which the reigning king was killed and the royal Six Armies annihilated. This military setback heralded a decisive shift in royal fortunes. Henceforth the Zhou found itself largely on the defensive against its foreign adversaries. The royal government was reorganized into a more formal and bureaucratic institution. In addition to the Three Ministries, the Secretariat and the Royal Household emerged as distinct branches of government. The expanded duties of the separate Secretariat reflected a new emphasis on bureaucratic communication and record-keeping. Each branch of government developed a more or less formal hierarchy of offices.

Nonetheless, royal authority became more circumscribed. The king exercised effective control only over the royal domain in the west and the region around Cheng Zhou, leaving the eastern domains more independent of

---

[12] Li Feng 2008: 190–234.

royal control. At times the kings were forced to resort to military force to impose their will on recalcitrant archer lords.

The truncated reach of the Zhou kings' political power resulted not only from their waning military strength but also from the steady depletion of their economic base. The practice of bestowing lands and population on royal officers reduced the revenues at the command of the royal house. By the late tenth century BCE the Zhou kings no longer awarded entire territories to meritorious officials, but instead parceled out scattered small farms and the laborers who worked them. Despite the diminished resources at their disposal, the Zhou kings continued to make land grants, even to the extent of seizing lands from other lineages to do so. For example, King Li (r. c. 857–853 to 842 BCE), upon charging his subordinate Ke with an important military commission, presented Ke with seven parcels of land in different locations. Among these parcels were lands previously held by the Jing lineage. In earlier times members of the Jing lineage had held powerful positions in the Zhou government; apparently the family's stature and influence had declined to the point where the king could brazenly expropriate their possessions for his own purposes.[13] Another bronze inscription dated to King Li's time again shows the king transferring a local jurisdiction within the royal domain from one noble lineage to another.[14]

Although in these cases King Li seems to have been exercising his sovereign dominion over all landholdings, such assertions of royal prerogative no longer went unchallenged. In the mid-ninth century BCE the royal house was wracked by a series of succession disputes that further sapped royal prestige and authority. In 842 BCE a group of disgruntled nobles banded together to force King Li into exile.[15] For fourteen years, until Li's death in 828 BCE smoothed the way to restore the heir apparent to the throne, one of the rebel lords presided over the Zhou court. Royal authority briefly revived following the restoration of King Xuan (r. 827–782 BCE), but lapsed again in Xuan's later years after a series of military setbacks.

Later writers portray the principal adversaries of the Zhou at this time – the Xianyun people of the Ordos region, to the north of the Zhou homeland, and the Southern Huaiyi in the Huai River valley of central China – as rude "barbarians," nemeses of civilized culture. But the Xianyun and Southern Huaiyi possessed formidable military power and were capable of fielding

---

[13] Da Ke *ding* (Ma Chengyuan 1988: #297); Shaughnessy 1999: 328.

[14] Da *gui* (Ma Chengyuan 1988: #393); Li Feng 2006: 133.

[15] Later historians blamed King Li for his demise, portraying him as a tyrant who "monopolized wealth" (*zhuanli* 專利) and refused to heed the wise counsel of his advisors. See Li Feng 2006: 131–34. Shaughnessy (1991: 170) observes that the inscriptions on vessels cast by Li "reflect a royal personality at once arrogant and yet insecure, boastful of his achievements but apparently still striving to establish his legitimacy."

hundreds of chariots in battles with the Zhou, indicating substantial resources in men and materiel. The Southern Huaiyi already had launched offensives against the Zhou in the late tenth century BCE, but beginning with the reign of King Li the Zhou found itself locked in prolonged wars against the Xianyun that threatened its very survival.

The crisis in royal authority in the face of internecine strife and frontier invasion triggered a far-reaching transformation in the culture and ideology of the Zhou ruling class. During the first century after the conquest of Shang the inventories and decoration of the bronze vessels fundamental to conceptions of sovereignty and divine power remained largely unchanged, suggesting a strong continuity in ritual and political culture between the Shang and the early Zhou. Between 950 and 850 BCE, however, a transformation in the types, decoration, and use of bronze ritual vessels occurred on such a radical scale that archaeologists speak of it as constituting a "ritual revolution."[16] The dramatic changes in the types of vessels testify to a significant reconceptualization not only of ritual performance but also of the relationship between divine power and human authority. In addition, the adoption of highly standardized sets of vessels graded according to ritual rank both for use in sacrifices at ancestral temples and as elite burial goods reveals a new emphasis on sumptuary regulation to define social hierarchy. The remarkable homogeneity of the new ritual culture at a time of growing conflict within the Zhou ruling class also bespoke a concerted effort to articulate a coherent identity for Zhou civilization in opposition to the "barbarian" cultures that now threatened it with extinction.[17]

The growing emphasis on hierarchal order within the ruling class and a distinctive Zhou cultural identity did little to reverse the declining fortunes of the royal house, however. Partisan struggles at the court and military blunders led to a catastrophic defeat in 771 BCE at the hands of the Xianyun and their allies among disaffected Zhou nobles. The Xianyun sacked the capitals of Feng and Hao, killed the Zhou king, and forced the Zhou to abandon their homeland. Surviving members of the royal clan fled to Cheng Zhou, where a new king was installed. Historians regard the relocation of the Zhou capital to Cheng Zhou in the east as the crucial watershed that demarcated the Western Zhou (1045–771 BCE) from the Eastern Zhou period (771–256 BCE).

Although the Zhou dynasty survived, the power and prestige of the Zhou kings had suffered a mortal blow. Their economic base dwindled to a small

---

[16] Although the idea of a "ritual revolution" is now widely accepted, scholars differ in their assessment of when it occurred. Rawson (1999) dates the ritual revolution to the second half of the tenth century BCE, while von Falkenhausen (1999a, 1999b) – who speaks of a "ritual reform" rather than a "revolution" – places this transition in the first half of the ninth century BCE.

[17] Von Falkenhausen 2006.

territory in the immediate environs of Cheng Zhou. A number of aristocratic lineages closely connected to the royal family – most notably, the Zheng and Guo – followed the Zhou eastward and reestablished themselves in new domains on the Central Plain. The Zheng and Guo houses, long bitter rivals, continued to vie for supremacy at the Cheng Zhou court. In 707 BCE, the Zhou king launched a punitive campaign against Lord Zhuang of Zheng (r. 743–701 BCE), only to suffer a humiliating defeat. Zhuang subsequently wielded ruthless military force and intimidation to secure his position as the paramount political leader among the rulers of the Central States, foreshadowing the emergence of the "hegemon" (*ba* 霸) as a formal institution in the mid-seventh century BCE (see Chapter 2). Although the Zhou kings retained their ritual preeminence and continued to receive homage from the regional rulers, political and economic power tilted decisively in favor of the latter.

After the fall of the Western Zhou, various non-Zhou peoples occupied parts of the former Zhou homeland and settled in the Central Plain as well. Over the next several centuries – conventionally known as the Spring and Autumn period, spanning *c*. 720–481 BCE – conflicts between the Zhou peoples and their foreign neighbors intensified. Cultural boundaries became more rigid, fostering a distinctively Chinese (Hua 華) ethnic identity. The emergence of pastoral nomadism in the steppe grasslands along the northern frontiers of the Zhou ecumene during these centuries further sharpened this sense of cultural and ethnic distinction. But within the Zhou ecumene assimilation to the prevailing norms of Zhou high culture accelerated. Strong upstart states emerged on the margins of the Zhou ecumene, notably Qin in the former Zhou homeland and Chu in the Huai and Yangzi River valleys. Although Qin and Chu exhibited distinctive features in religious practices and material culture stemming in part from interactions with their non-Zhou neighbors, the ruling classes of these states emulated the elite culture of the Zhou world and modeled their political and social institutions on the prevailing Zhou traditions.

Political economy of the Western Zhou

Land and labor were the foundations of the Bronze Age economy and the major sources of wealth for the Zhou ruling class, but the two were not inseparably linked. The fundamental social and economic unit of the early Zhou was the *yi* 邑, a broad term that encompassed settlements ranging from simple villages to royal capitals. Originally *yi* may have designated kin groups, but over time their populations became more heterogeneous.[18] Various

---

[18] Itō 1975: 214–15.

numbers of dependent settlements (*shuyi* 屬邑) were attached to royal capitals (*dayi* 大邑) and the towns that served as seats of aristocratic lineages (*zuyi* 族邑, *zongyi* 宗邑). The estate of an individual lineage or landowner might encompass numerous settlements. One late Western Zhou bronze inscription, which records a royal command mandating the return of lands (apparently illegally occupied by the official's subordinates) to the rightful owner, identified the lands by the *yi* to which they were attached, thirteen *yi* in all.[19] Another inscription attests the transfer of a total of twenty-two *yi* from one domain to another.[20]

One of the few early Zhou "appointment" inscriptions recording the founding of a new domain commemorates King Kang's investiture of Ze as the ruler of Yi in the early tenth century BCE. Ze did not simply assume authority over an existing territory, however; at the same time the king assigned Ze overlordship of a disparate group of subjects, many of whom were transferred from elsewhere (ellipses indicate illegible graphs on the original vessel; X indicates a graph whose meaning and pronunciation is unknown):

[The king speaks:] I award you lands, including three hundred zhen [甽] fields; one hundred twenty...; thirty-five residential settlements [zhaiyi 宅邑]; and one hundred forty .... I also award you ... seven surnames[21] of the king's men [wangren 王人] residing at Yi; seven Elders of Zheng whose X-retainers number ... and fifty men. I further award you commoners at Yi numbering six hundred and ... six men.[22]

The unknown graphs in this inscription impede a full understanding of the text, but it is clear that the king's award consisted of three elements: arable lands, settlements, and people. "*Zhen* fields" probably referred to valley bottom arable lands, although the dimensions of such lands are unknown. In addition to the thirty-five residential settlements, the number 140 probably also denoted village settlements, although the distinction made here between types of settlements is unclear.[23] Finally, the award specifies three population groups. "King's men" referred to persons attached to the Royal Household. It seems that the king retained some residual authority or responsibility over these people even after they were assigned to the ruler of a domain or an aristocratic lord. As mentioned earlier, "Elders" probably denoted lineage heads. Thus the king transferred seven lineage groups from Zheng, a royal city in the Wei

[19] Guo Cong *xu* (Ma Chengyuan 1988: #424); translated in Li Feng 2008: 176. See also Itō 1975: 194–95.
[20] Sanshi *pan* (Ma Chengyuan 1988: #428).
[21] The missing graph here almost surely is a numeral, probably ten. Itō (1987: 98) thus reads "seventeen surnames" here.
[22] Yi Hou Ze *gui* (Ma Chengyuan 1988: #57). Translation modified from Li Feng 2008: 238–39. Li Feng's transcription, which differs from that of Li Ling (1998: 89), seems preferable.
[23] Itō 1987: 101.

River valley, to Yi, located in the Central Plain. Finally, the king confirmed Ze's authority over more than 600 commoner families who already were inhabitants of Yi. Initially, at least, each of these three populations apparently differed in the nature of their subordination to their new ruler, although we cannot say what these differences were. The founding of a new domain thus also created a new community with its own complex social order.

The extant bronze inscriptions are virtually silent about the internal organization of the domains of the Central Plain, but we are better informed about the royal realm in the west. Initially, the Zhou kings wielded direct control over much of the territory and population of the royal domain in the Wei River valley and the region adjacent to Cheng Zhou. Although the twin capitals of Feng and Hao constituted the political center of the Zhou state, the main royal ancestral temples and tombs remained at Zhouyuan. As noted earlier, the Zhou appointed various ministers to supervise revenue collection, construction projects, and military procurement. Several – perhaps many – persons served in these ministerial offices at any given time. Appointments to the office of Minister of Lands (Situ 司土), for example, typically conferred responsibility over specific territories, populations, or occupational groups. In one case, the king ordered the official he appointed as Minister of Lands "to take charge of the forests, mountains, and pastures in the outlying areas around Zheng."[24] This dispensation suggests that the Zhou state drew revenues from mines, forests, and stock-raising as well as from arable lands. However, the means by which the royal government extracted revenue from its subjects remains poorly understood.

A number of inscriptions make reference to local officials charged with the administration of territorial units known as *bang* 邦 and *li* 里. Li Feng suggests that the *bang* units generally were associated with aristocratic estates and the *li* units with territories under direct royal control, and that both units encompassed multiple *yi* settlements. But the term *li* sometimes was applied to aristocratic estates, and the relationship between the local administrators of these territories, known as *bangjun* 邦君 or *lijun* 里君, and the estate owners remains obscure. There are examples of the Zhou king transferring *li* units from one proprietor to another and appointing *bangjun* administrators with jurisdiction over aristocratic estates.[25] The terms *bang* and *bangjun* are relatively rare, however, and probably the aristocratic households themselves exercised direct control over local governance.

In addition, late Western Zhou inscriptions make frequent mention of appointments to offices managing the lands and populations of the "Five Cities" (Wuyi 五邑), either individually or collectively. Although

[24] Mian *fu* (Ma Chengyuan 1988: #252). Li Feng 2008: 168; Itō 1987: 130–31.
[25] Li Feng 2008: 180–88.

the Five Cities cannot be identified precisely, it seems likely that the term included cities often mentioned in connection with the royal domains such as Zheng, Pang, and Zhouyuan, and perhaps the capitals of Feng and Hao as well.[26] Quite possibly the Five Cities had become the main source of state revenues by this time.

The role of tribute in the political economy of the Zhou state remains obscure. References to tribute payments – primarily from foreign enemies such as the Southern Huaiyi—appear relatively late, mostly dating from the reign of King Xuan. In an inscription dated to 823 BCE the king appointed an official to supervise the storehouses at Cheng Zhou where the tribute goods received from "the four quarters of the world" (i.e., foreign states on the periphery of the Zhou ecumene) were deposited. The king also ordered the official to go to the land of the Southern Huaiyi and collect the tribute – in the forms of goods (which commentators generally believe consisted of textiles and agricultural products) and people – owed to the Zhou king. In addition, the inscription states that tribute received from the regional rulers was deposited at Cheng Zhou as well.[27] In a second inscription, probably dating from several decades later, the king decreed a punitive campaign against the Southern Huaiyi for failing to submit tribute.[28] Another inscription from this era depicts the king directing a royal official to take charge of the twenty storehouses at Cheng Zhou and to inspect a newly built storehouse.[29] These documents attest to the central place of Cheng Zhou in the royal fiscal administration in the late Western Zhou period, but it is impossible to estimate the significance of tribute as a form of revenue.

Beginning in the mid-Western Zhou period the Royal Household (*wangjia* 王家) emerged as a distinct institution apart from the Zhou state. The Royal Household was headed by one or several Stewards (Zai 宰), a title that in Shang times denoted a close companion to the king who accompanied him at hunts and banquets. The Stewards exercised broad authority over the affairs of the king's household, the lands and peoples directly subject to its rule, and the royal workshops. The Stewards often acted as the king's representative in court ceremonies and as the channel of communication between the king and his ministers. Stewards also were obliged to attend to the needs of the king's

---

[26] Ibid.: 166–69.

[27] Xi Jia *pan* (Ma Chengyuan 1988: #437). Ma Chengyuan's annotation of this inscription makes the interpolation that the Zhou imposed customs excises on goods brought by both foreign tributary subjects and the Zhou regional rulers, but in the absence of other evidence for the existence of markets at this time such an inference seems unwarranted.

[28] Shi Yuan *gui* (Ma Chengyuan 1988: #439). Translated in Li Feng 2008: 266. A mid-Western Zhou inscription (Guaibo *gui*; Ma Chengyuan 1988: #206) also mentions the submission of tribute by the Mei'ao, a defeated foreign polity on the western edge of the Wei River valley. See Matsui 2002: 47; Li Feng 2006: 184.

[29] Song *ding* (Ma Chengyuan 1988: #434). Translated in Li Feng 2008: 105–6.

consorts, who apparently had their own properties and retinues. By the late Western Zhou period the Royal Household had developed a separate administrative corps, complete with its own group of ministers and staff of secretaries, in which the office of Provisioner (Shanfu 膳夫) became especially prominent. Although the Provisioners probably originally were responsible for supplying the royal family with victuals and other necessities, their role evolved into serving as the king's confidant and advisor.[30]

Several inscriptions dating from the mid-Western Zhou period instruct officials to take charge of the "male and female bondservants and dependent laborers of the Royal Household attached to King Kang's Temple" (康宫王家臣妾附庸) or "the king's male and female bondservants and hundred artisans attached to King Kang's Temple."[31] The temple of King Kang, located at Zhouyuan, was one of the most important ritual sites of the Western Zhou, frequently mentioned as the place where the king conferred appointments and honors on his officials. The temple appears to have been part of the Royal Household, with its own retinue of servants, craftsmen, and agricultural laborers (the term *fuyong*, "dependent laborers," usually is linked to arable lands in other contexts) to supply its needs. Mention also is made of populations attached to the Royal Household located at a number of other cities. Thus the Royal Household, like the royal government itself, seems to have managed lands, workshops, and ceremonial centers that were widely dispersed across the Wei River valley.

In addition to the archer lords in the east, the Zhou kings created an aristocracy in the west through grants of lands and population within the royal domain. In contrast to the quasi-independent domains of the archer lords, however, the monarchy retained sovereign rights over the aristocratic estates carved out from the king's own lands. Over time the aristocratic lineages divided into collateral branches subordinated to the main line of descent in a clearly graded hierarchical order.[32] Kinship solidarity was reinforced by common residence, ritual life, and feasting. The economic organization of the aristocratic households – which included various types of bondsmen, including farmers, craftsmen, shepherds, and domestic servants – seems to have paralleled that of the royal household. Yet the lineage Elders often entrusted management of lineage affairs to outsiders. The aristocratic lineages developed their own administrative staff parallel to the royal government. In an inscription from 841 BCE, Bo Hefu, then ruling in place of the exiled King Li,

---

[30] Matsui 2002: 94–121; Li Feng 2008: 67–70, 90–93. Zhu Fenghan (2004: 333) observes that prominent royal kinsmen commonly occupied the office of Steward.

[31] Zai Shou *gui* (cited in Luo Xizhang 1998) and Yi *gui* (Ma Chengyuan 1988: #222). Li Feng 2008: 153–54; Matsui 2002: 96–97.

[32] According to von Falkenhausen (2006: 69–70), evidence for the splitting of lineages into collateral lines of descent appears from *c.* 900 BCE.

commanded a certain Shi Hui to assume his father's place and take command of "our family's servant chariot-drivers, hundred craftsmen, herders, and bondsmen and bondswomen" (僕馭, 百工, 牧, 臣妾). In another inscription from the same era a lineage elder lauds the service performed by the father and grandfather of the vessel-maker Ni to his family and appoints Ni to take charge of "the household servants and male and female bondservants of the common household (*gongshi* 公室; i.e., the main branch of the lineage) and the household affairs of the collateral branches (*xiaozi shijia* 小子室家)."[33] Like royal appointments, such service often became hereditary. Like royal officials, too, those who served as managers of aristocratic households received grants of lands and servants in lieu of a regular stipend. The important role of administrators in managing lineage affairs suggests that the junior branches did not become independent economic units; instead, family wealth and property remained under the control of the main line.[34]

The internal organization of the Royal Household and the aristocratic lineages probably differed more in scale than in kind. As the Shi Hui inscription cited above indicates, aristocratic lineages possessed diverse economic resources, including industrial workshops. A set of inscriptions dedicated by a certain Qiu Wei itemizes extensive lists of leather goods and chariot ornaments used to trade for lands, leading some scholars to speculate that this family specialized in the manufacture of these goods. It has also been suggested that it was the wealth gained from craft production that enabled Wei's family to ascend into the ranks of the aristocracy.[35]

Many aristocratic lineages, especially the most exalted ones, maintained residences at Zhouyuan in close proximity to the king, even though their landholdings may have been located some considerable distance away. The main line of the Jing lineage, a powerful presence at the court in the middle Western Zhou period, resided at Zhouyuan, but its estate was located near Baoji, far to the west. Collateral branches of the Jing family also resided in the royal cities of Feng and Zheng.[36] Although a "Jing domain" (Jing *bang* 井邦) existed down to the end of the Western Zhou, at least some branches of the Jing lineage had lost their privileged position and were unable to protect their landholdings from expropriation or forfeiture.[37]

By 900 BCE aristocratic landholdings were becoming widely dispersed. As noted earlier, as the lands at the disposal of the king diminished, royal land grants increasingly took the form not of entire territories but rather

---

[33] Shi Hui *gui* (Ma Chengyuan 1988: #384); Ni *zhong* (Ma Chengyuan 1988: #274). Cited in Zhu Fenghan 2004: 313, 319.

[34] Zhu Fenghan 2004: 328.   [35] Itō 1987: 219; Zhu Fenghan 2004: 326–27; Li Feng 2008: 169.

[36] See the reconstruction of the Jing lineage in Matsui 2002: 215–27.

[37] The expropriation of several Jing estates and their transfer to a new master is recorded in the Da Ke *ding* inscription (Ma Chengyuan 1988: #297). See Shaughnessy 1999: 328.

"fields" (*tian*), or individual tracts of land.[38] Although the dimensions of these "fields" were not specified, the practice of transferring fields and bondsmen in roughly equal proportion suggests that a "field" amounted to the amount of land that a single farmer could cultivate – generally said to be 100 *mu*, or 1.82 hectares (about 4.5 acres). These smaller parcels of land also became objects of exchange among aristocratic households. A bronze inscription from the late tenth century BCE records that the vessel was cast to commemorate – and, it seems, to serve as legal testimony of – an exchange of four fine horses for thirty fields.[39] In other cases lands were exchanged for a variety of goods, including jade ornaments, ritual vessels, carriages, equipage, and silks.

Transfers of fields in such transactions typically were described in terms of "relinquishing" (*she* 舍) property. Surveying the lands and having an official notary record the transfer of property and its boundaries were crucial procedures for establishing land claims. But such transactions did not confer absolute rights over land. The king retained residual – though not uncontested – rights to appropriate and reassign landholdings within the royal domain. Transmission of property through inheritance also involved complex ritual exchanges and the certification of royal officials. A set of inscriptions dated 867–866 BCE records the division of property by the head of the Shao lineage between his two sons. In addition to bequeathing his rank to his eldest son, Shao stipulated the division of his lands and retainers between the two heirs. The vessel-maker Zhousheng, the younger son (and a royal steward), affirmed his assent to his father's disposition by swearing an oath to support his brother, conveying gifts of jade, silk, and ritual bronzes to his father, mother, and brother, and casting these bronze vessels. The elder brother submitted the father's testament to the royal scribes for verification and subsequently delivered a notarized copy to Zhousheng.[40]

In addition, aristocratic lineages within the royal domain began to assert competing claims to land, leading to conflicts that required royal intervention. In a case dated to 913 BCE, Qiu Wei – the possibly parvenu leather manufacturer mentioned earlier – petitioned for redress when a local royal official, Li, reneged on his promise of "relinquishing" to Qiu five fields as he had previously promised. A group of five senior officials deliberated on

---

[38] In the Mao *gui* inscription (Ma Chengyuan 1988: #244), for example, the steward Mao received four separate parcels of land (*tian*) in four different *yi* from his lord.

[39] Pengsheng *gui* (Ma Chengyuan 1988: #210).

[40] The Fifth Year Zhousheng *gui* inscription (Ma Chengyuan 1988: #289) – notoriously difficult to decipher – has long been interpreted as a property dispute between two nobles (see e.g., Matsumaru and Takeuchi 1993: 29–33). But the recent discovery of the inscribed Fifth Year Zhousheng *zun* makes clear that the transaction in fact recorded the division of inheritance among two sons. See Xu Yihua 2007.

Qiu's complaint and ruled in his favor, commanding Li to surrender four fields as well as a residence in his settlement. Subsequently the Three Supervisors undertook a survey of the lands Li handed over to Qiu and established their boundaries. Li's lineage also was obliged to provide a feast for the Three Supervisors to compensate for their time and effort.[41] These procedures for arbitration by royal officials became the standard practice in land disputes

As Itō Michiharu and Li Feng have shown, the land boundaries described in the Qiu Wei inscription reveal a complex configuration of landownership in which fields belonging to different aristocratic lineages were interspersed in a mosaic-like pattern (Figure 1.1). This pattern of dispersed holdings of small parcels of land rather than contiguous manorial estates probably became typical in the Wei River valley in late Western Zhou times. Conflicts over land tenure and transactions also suggest some strong measure of economic competition. The decline of royal power in the late Western Zhou period was paralleled by shifting fortunes among the aristocratic lineages.

Production and labor

In contrast to the skilled proficiency of Western Zhou bronze workers and other artisans, agriculture still had not advanced beyond Stone Age technologies. North China has a dry climate, with highly irregular rainfall, and thus is prone to drought. The fertile loess soil of the middle and upper reaches of the Yellow River valley was easily worked; it is in this region that agriculture in East Asia, dating back at least to c. 7000 BCE, originated. The highly porous loess also was readily eroded by the flow of rivers, however. The Yellow River traverses this region, accumulating the great quantities of loess silt that give the river its name. The Central Plain, regularly inundated by the floodwaters of the Yellow River, developed thick alluvial deposits of loess soil carried down from the highlands to the west. But the Yellow River floods also turned much of the Central Plain into marshland. Farmers in the Central Plain thus faced very different conditions and problems compared with those inhabiting the Wei River valley.

[41] Fifth Year Wei *ding* (Ma Chengyuan 1988: #198). For translations of this inscription see Shaughnessy 1999: 327; Cook 1997: 271; Itō 1987: 188–89; Matsumaru and Takeuchi 1993: 10–13. The nature of the transaction remains obscure. The most plausible reading, in my view, is that of Matsumaru and Takeuchi, who suggest that Li bestowed the lands on Qiu in exchange for the latter's help in an irrigation project on royal lands. In Shaughnessy's translation, Li "sold" the lands to Qiu, but the text repeatedly states that the lands were "relinquished" (*she*) (on this kind of unilateral transfer of lands, see Li Ling 1998: 99). The main dispute concerned the amount of lands Li offered to Qiu.

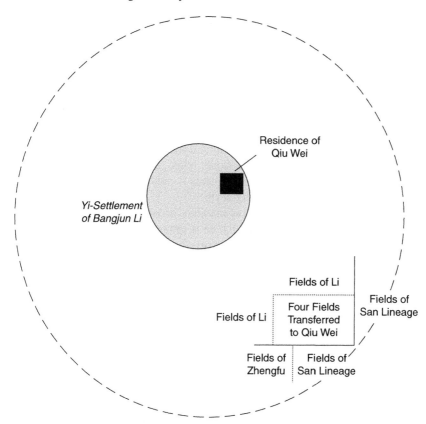

Figure 1.1 Configuration of landholdings recorded in the fifth-year Wei *Ding*
inscription
Source: Li Feng 2008: 177; based on Itō 1987: 192.

The principal foods crops of Bronze Age China were millet cereals and
soybeans, both originally domesticated in the loess soil region of the middle
Yellow River valley. Zhou farmers cultivated a variety of millets, of which
the "broomcorn" variety (*panicum milleium*) – either steamed or boiled
to make porridge – was considered the best-tasting. Millet is poorly suited
for making flour, however. Wheat – an import from West Asia – and rice
were still rare in North China at this time, and their consumption most
likely was confined to the ruling classes. Hemp was an especially versatile
crop: the seeds were eaten as a cereal food as well as pressed to make
cooking oil, and hemp fibers were woven into linen-like textiles. The most
important domestic animals were pigs, chickens, and dogs, which provided
the principal sources of meat. Beef and mutton were prominent in sacrificial

offerings, but less commonly consumed than pork. Alcoholic beverages were made by fermenting millet.[42]

We still know little about farming techniques in the early Zhou, but permanent cultivation of fields (with occasional fallowing) was widespread by that time.

There are a few references to irrigating fields, achieved primarily by diverting streams into adjoining farmlands. Large-scale irrigation works did not appear until much later. Bronze was too precious to be widely used for utilitarian purposes such as agricultural tools. Instead Zhou farmers continued to rely on tools made from stone, bone, and shells. Agricultural tools consisted primarily of digging implements – one- and two-pronged digging sticks and spades – and harvesting scythes.[43]

Little is known too about the organization of labor on royal or aristocratic estates. Scholars have relied heavily on a group of litanies recorded in the *Book of Odes* (*c.* 600 BCE) that portray the early Zhou rulers marshaling hundreds of farm laborers to till great landed estates. The following song describes the first Zhou king, at the time of the spring sacrifices to the gods, exhorting his overseers to commence work in the fields:

> Hark! King Cheng
> Has issued his command.
> Lead your husbandmen,
> Sow the hundred crops,
> Hasten to break ground on your private fields,
> Thirty li around.
> With earnest effort till the soil,
> By tens and thousands, working in pairs.[44]

In this and other songs in the *Book of Odes* royal officials directly supervise the agricultural work of numerous field laborers. According to a treatise dated to *c.* 300 BCE, "working in pairs" referred to two men digging furrows with spades side-by-side. The "working in pairs" cultivation technique gave rise to the standard unit of land measurement, the *mu*, originally defined as one pace wide and one hundred paces long.[45] This song also makes reference to "private fields," an issue that has been the subject of much scholarly dispute. A similar

---

[42] Chang 1977.
[43] For overviews of farming techniques and tools at this time, see Hsu and Linduff 1988: 351–55; Zhou Ziqiang 2007: 576–602. The most comprehensive survey of Chinese agriculture is Bray 1984, but Bray's book is not organized chronologically.
[44] "Yixi" 噫嘻 (Ode 277), in *ShJ*, 1: 770.
[45] "Kao gong ji, jiangren" 考工記。匠人, in *ZL*, 2A: 395. On the relationship of cultivation techniques to the *mu* measurement, see Li Xueqin 1982: 70.

reference appears in "Great Fields," a panegyric celebrating the blessings bestowed by the gods in the form of abundant harvests:

> Clouds fill the sky, brisk and chill,
> Gentle rains softly fall.
> The rain soaks our public lands (gongtian 公田),
> And then reaches our private fields.
> Here stand waves of unripened grain,
> There reapers have stacked the bundled sheaves,
> Here fallen kernels have been left,
> There ears of grain lie scattered on the ground
> For widows and orphans to glean.[46]

Although many commentators have argued that these "private fields" refer to lands cultivated by farmers for their own subsistence, it seems more likely that a distinction is being drawn between lands allocated to officials and those whose produce is reserved for the king.[47]

The songs quoted above, written from the perspective of the king and his officials, depict large latifundia farmed collectively by great numbers of servile laborers. In contrast, the song "Seventh Month" adopts the point of view of a humble farmer who recites the year-round cycle of farming and household tasks in which his family engages. This song's evocative portrayal of the rhythms of a farm family's working life merits quotation at length:

> In the seventh month, the Fire Star passes the meridian,
> In the ninth month, warm clothes are given out.
> In the days of our first month, the wind blows cold and shrill,
> In the days of our second month, our bones the air does chill.
> Without our garments of homespun hemp,
> How could we last to the end of the year?
> In the days of our third month, we take spades in hand,
> In the days of our fourth month, we make our way to the fields.
> Together with my wife and children,
> We bring food to those toiling in the south-facing fields
> The surveyor of fields is well-pleased.
> In the seventh month, the Fire Star passes the meridian,
> In the ninth month, warm clothes are given out.
> The spring days bring warmth,
> And the oriole begins to sing.
> The young women lift their deep baskets,
> And follow the narrow paths,
> Seeking the tender mulberry leaves.
> As the spring days lengthen,

---

[46] Datian" 大田 (Ode 212), in *ShJ*, 1: 680–81.
[47] On this point I concur with Zhou Ziqiang (1987), although I disagree with Zhou's larger argument about the Western Zhou as a slave society.

The plucked mugwort piles high.
The young lady's heart is wounded by grief,
For the moment the young lord whisks her away draws near.
In the seventh month, the Fire Star passes the meridian,
In the eighth month, the reeds and sedges grow thick.
In the silkworm month, the mulberry branches are stripped bare.
Taking axes and hatchets,
They lop off the high spreading branches,
And haul away the fresh leaves.
In the seventh month, the shrike screeches,
In the eighth month, the spinning begins,
Both the black yarn and the yellow;
Our brilliant reds, finest of all,
Are reserved for the young lord's breeches.
In the fourth month, the clover is in ear,
In the fifth month, the cicadas' chirping resounds,
In the eighth month, the harvest is gathered,
In the tenth month, the leaves have all fallen.
In the days of our first month, they go after badgers,
Taking the foxes and wild cats as well,
To supply our young lord with furs.
In the days of our second month, a great hunt is held.
All must attend the lord's carriage
Girded for battle.
The year-old shoats can be kept for oneself,
The full-grown boars must be offered to the lord . . .
In the sixth month, they feast on plums and wild grapes,
In the seventh month, they boil the greens and pulse,
In the eighth month, they knock down the dates,
In the tenth month, they reap the rice
For brewing the springtime wine
To toast the longevity of the elders.
In the seventh month, they eat melons,
In the eighth month, they cut down the bottle gourds,
In the ninth month, they gather the hempseed,
Pluck bitter herbs, and fell the foul ailanthus,
To feed our husbandmen.
In the ninth month, they prepare the threshing ground,
In the tenth month, the harvested grain is gathered in,
The early-ripening millet and the late,
The hempseed, beans, and wheat.
Oh, fellow husbandmen!
Our harvest is well secured,
Now we must set to putting the houses in repair.
In daytime we collect the rushes,
At night we twist them into thatch,
We climb to the roofs in haste,

Soon we must begin sowing our fields again.
The days of our second month echo with the sound of axes hewing ice,
In the days of our third month, the ice house is fully stocked.
Early in our fourth month, sacrifices of lamb and leeks are offered,
In the ninth month, the hoar frost sets in,
In the tenth month, the threshing ground is swept clean,
With a pair of wine flasks each toasts the other,
Saying, "Let's kill both lamb and sheep,
And go up to the hall of our prince,
We'll raise our cups of rhinoceros horn,
And wish him long life without end!"[48]

A pastoral idyll, this song nonetheless alludes to the manifold obligations that farmers owed their lord throughout the seasons: accompanying him on his hunts, repairing his buildings, stocking his ice-house, providing silk clothes. The vast disparity between the farmers and the landowners is readily apparent in the contrast between the coarse clothing and foods of the former compared to the fine silks and sumptuous larder of the latter. In contrast to the great armies of field workers described in "Great Fields" and other songs, though, here the scale of farm labor appears to be considerably smaller.

Based on the evidence of the *Book of Odes*, most scholars have concluded that collective labor under the direction of overseers was the norm in the Western Zhou period on "public" and "private" lands alike. Zhu Fenghan, citing evidence such as the "Seventh Month" song, has postulated that extended kinship groups – rather than gangs of slaves – were the basic units of production in agricultural work at this time. Zhu argues that commoner lineages farmed "private lands" to provide for their own subsistence, while submitting the produce of the "public lands" to the landowner. He further suggests that the commoner lineages apportioned the yield generated by communal work according to the labor contributed by each individual family; hence the widows and orphans in "Great Fields" must resort to gleaning, since they receive no share of the harvest.[49]

At this stage of knowledge Zhu Fenghan's hypothesis must be considered speculative. Unfortunately, archaeological study thus far has shed little light on the livelihood or social organization of the commoner population. One cemetery of commoner graves found near the capital of Feng provides some support for Zhu's analysis. The forty-five graves in the cemetery appear to be grouped into seven to eight clusters, perhaps comprising separate lines of descent within a larger lineage group. Each cluster spans the same time period, from the middle to the late Western Zhou. Most graves are small and contained only rudimentary mortuary goods. But one cluster of graves stands out as noticeably

---

[48] "Qiyue" 七月 (Ode 154), in *ShJ*, 1: 604–07.   [49] Zhu Fenghan 2004: 322–26.

larger; three of these graves contained bronze halberds, and one had two bronze ritual vessels, the only bronze vessels found in the cemetery. Zhu has plausibly suggested that this cluster belonged to the headmen of a commoner lineage who provided military service – considered a mark of distinction – in the Six Armies stationed at Feng.[50]

In contrast to the depictions of large latifundia in the *Book of Odes*, however, the inscriptional evidence from middle and late Western Zhou suggests that agricultural work was organized on the far smaller scale of the individual household. As noted earlier, some bronze inscriptions indicate that the size of a "field" corresponded to the amount of land a single laborer could farm. In one case one noble offered another five laborers and four fields as compensation for a theft of grain committed by his retainers. In another inscription a meritorious official received an award of five families and ten fields.[51] These ratios imply small-scale units of production such as family farms.

The question of the organization of labor necessarily leads to the problem of the nature of economic subordination in the Western Zhou. The term *chenqie* 臣妾, which I translate as "male and female bondservants," has been the subject of much dispute. Marxist scholars in China have long wrangled over whether *chenqie* denoted slaves or serfs, and thus differ in their views on whether the Western Zhou constituted a slave society or a feudal society. Later, in the Eastern Zhou period, the term *chenqie* does come to mean chattel slaves who could be bought and sold (see Chapter 2). However, the precise status of *chenqie* in the Western Zhou remains obscure.[52] Royal land grants and even transfers of land among aristocratic lineages commonly were accompanied by the transfer of *chenqie* as well, suggesting that these persons tilled agricultural lands on behalf of the owner. In some cases *chenqie* clearly were attached to the land they farmed, but in other examples *chenqie* were relocated from other places to their new home. Moreover, awards of *chenqie* attached to the Royal Household did not entirely dissolve those bonds. The king seems to have retained some residual authority over royal retainers (*wangjia* 王家, *wangren* 王人) even after he bestowed them on another.

In addition to *chenqie*, a number of other terms denoting servile statuses appear in Zhou bronze inscriptions, such as "servant" (*pu* 僕); "attached laborer" (*fuyong* 附庸); and "commoner" (*li* 鬲; *shuren* 庶人). Some inscriptions group these terms together, and given our present state of knowledge it is

[50] Ibid.: 421–23.
[51] Hu *ding* (Ma Chengyuan 1988: #242); Buqi *gui* (Ma Chengyuan 1988: #441). Cited in Li Ling 1998: 93.
[52] Yates (2002) takes an agnostic position, merely observing that we lack sufficient information to determine whether *chenqie* in the Western Zhou can be described as slaves or not. Li Feng (2008) uses the neutral terms "servant" and "retainer" to translate *chenqie*.

difficult to discern the distinctions among them, other than noting that *fuyong* denoted agricultural laborers attached to the land. To avoid categories such as "slave" and "serf" that inevitably entail specific modes of production, I prefer use the more neutral translation "bondservant" to represent all of these discrete terms.

The complexity of the relationship between agricultural laborers and the ruling classes is suggested by the Hu *ding* bronze inscription (dated to 899 BCE), which has been the focus of spirited debate. Hu, a diviner in the Royal Household, submitted a grievance to a high official, Jing Shu, accusing another noble, Xiaofu, of failing to make good on his promised exchange of five bondservants in return for horses and silk. Jing Shu negotiated a settlement in which Hu agreed to pay a hundred measures of bronze metal in lieu of the original payment in horses and silk. The five bondservants over whom Hu assumed overlordship remained on the lands which they previously tilled; thus the produce of the land was transferred to Hu as well. Apparently the bondservants remained in close proximity to Xiaofu, who is told that he must allow the bondservants "to live in the village (*yi*) in which they have lived, and farm the land which they have farmed." At the same time Jing Shu enjoined Hu not to stir up animosity between the bondservants and their former master, Xiaofu. The bondservants are also described as "the king's men" (*wangren*), suggesting that they had been members of the royal retinue before having been bestowed on Xiaofu. Their status as "the king's men" probably limited the authority that their new master Hu exercised over them, but in what way remains uncertain. At the conclusion of the transaction Hu provided a feast of mutton and wine along with gifts of silk to the five bondservants to signify his new status as their lord.[53]

This inscription is one of the rare instances that describe an exchange of persons for goods. The nature of the transaction is not as straightforward as the term "purchase" might imply. Hu is said to have "redeemed" (*shu* 贖) the bondservants in exchange for "compensation" (*chang* 償) in other goods.[54] Hu did not take physical possession of the bondservants, who continue to live and work in their original place of residence. Moreover, the seller, Xiaofu, relinquished not only the five men but also his claim to the produce of the land which they farmed – in effect, his claim to the land itself. The bondservants appear to have been living under multiple jurisdictions, and their fealty to their new master required reciprocation in the form of feasts and gifts. In this as in

[53] Hu *ding* (Ma Chengyuan 1988: #242). I follow the interpretation of the inscription presented in Itō 1987: 193–202. For an alternative interpretation that leads to different conclusions, see Matsumaru 1984. Ma Chengyuan's (1988: 169–72) reading is more consistent with that of Itō. For the date of this vessel, see Shaughnessy 1991: 284.

[54] According to Itō (1987: 206), this is the only instance in the Zhou bronze inscriptions in which *shu* has the meaning of "to buy."

other cases, the economic value of the bondservants lay in the product of their labor, not their labor itself. Nowhere in the bronze inscriptions do we find evidence of bondservants performing labor services on behalf of their masters.

The transactions in this and other middle and late Western Zhou inscriptions involved individual fields and households, in contrast to the territories and large groups of peoples that appeared in earlier appointment inscriptions. Over time, the fragmentation of estates into small parcels dispersed over considerable distances and the exchange of individual bondservants along with the land they worked probably weakened kinship bonds among the farming population while strengthening their attachment to their village. Subordination to the lord became personal rather than collective, even though the lord may have resided in a distant town. In contrast to Zhu Fenghan's emphasis on the primacy of kinship bonds among commoner lineages, Itō Michiharu contends that in the later Western Zhou period group identity was based on common residence rather than kinship.[55]

Mention has already been made of the inclusion of workshops and specialized craftworkers in both the Royal Household and the households of aristocratic lineages. Manufacture of utilitarian goods such as pottery took a variety of forms ranging from seasonal household work for domestic use or local exchange in rural areas to full-time specialized production in large workshops located in the capital cities under the supervision of royal officers. The "Seventh Month" song depicts rural women spinning silk yarn and weaving and dyeing silk fabrics for the use of their lord; no doubt they also made hemp clothes for their own families. Bronze ritual vessels exhibit remarkable homogeneity in design and decoration across the Zhou ecumene, suggesting that metallurgical knowledge was widely shared. Pottery artifacts, in contrast, display marked regional variation.

A number of bronze, bone, pottery, jade, and tile workshops have been excavated in the Zhouyuan region that presumably were attached to aristocratic households. Since the size of these workshops far exceeded the needs of even an extended lineage, some of their production was intended for exchange and wider distribution. The Yuntang bone workshop at Zhouyuan specialized in the production of one type of ornament (hairpins), further evidence that production was oriented for consumption beyond the aristocratic household.[56]

Artisans employed by the Royal Household and aristocratic lineages typically are grouped together with *chenqie* and other servile groups in the bronze inscriptions. Some inscriptions also mention the transfer of craft workers between aristocratic lineages. A recent study of a cemetery for the artisans attached to a workshop for the manufacture of *jue* 玦 earrings

---

[55] Itō 1987: 207–20.   [56] Sun Zhouyong 2008: 20–22, 106.

(a commonplace stone ornament) at Zhouyuan has revealed a steeply inclined hierarchy of status. One tomb contained a rich variety of bronze ritual vessels, lacquer and jade wares, and oracle bones as well as tools used in *jue* manufacture, indicating that the occupant was a high-ranking person, probably the supervisor of the workshop with the status of a household steward. None of the other artisan burials contained bronzes, although two classes of graves can be differentiated based on size, jade artifacts, and the quantity of plebeian grave goods such as ceramics. These distinctions most likely correspond to a differentiation between master craftsmen and journeymen workers. Only a few skeletons were sufficiently well-preserved to permit gender identification, but all of them were female. We can infer from the close proximity of artisans' graves and workshops to elite residences that artisans were not independent agents who freely disposed of their labor, but rather were attached to aristocratic households in some servile capacity.[57]

A large bronze foundry excavated near Cheng Zhou dating from the early Western Zhou period undoubtedly was a royal workshop. A few smaller bronze workshops also have been found near the Feng-Hao capitals, including one that specialized in the manufacture of chariot fixtures. Aristocratic households likewise had their own bronze foundries, although the workmanship of these private bronze casters generally was inferior. Qiu Wei's lineage probably cast its own commemorative vessels in addition to its leather-making enterprise. Despite the radical change in the types and iconography of bronze vessels accompanying the ritual revolution of the ninth century BCE, the Western Zhou did not witness any notable technological changes in bronze metallurgy. Zhou bronze-making artisans continued to use the Shang methods of piece-mold casting down to the sixth century BCE.[58]

The chariot was the most sophisticated industrial product of this era. In the post-conquest era the Zhou took up the Shang practice of burying chariots – complete with horses and drivers – as part of elite mortuary ritual. Archaeological finds of chariot burials have been concentrated around the Feng-Hao capitals, where the Zhou Six Armies were stationed. Few remains of chariots from the early Western Zhou have been discovered in the Zhouyuan region, but they become more numerous in the middle Western Zhou period. Manufacture of chariots drew on the combined skills of carpenters, bronze smiths, leatherworkers, and jade inlay and lacquer decorators. Chariots with intricately worked bronze fittings were highly prized emblems of noble status and frequently appear in the lists of gifts bestowed by the Zhou king. No workshops related to chariot manufacture have yet been identified, however.

---

[57] Ibid.: 95–100.   [58] Hsu and Linduff 1988: 311–18.

Accumulating wealth

The Western Zhou ruling class derived its wealth from gifts, land revenue, craft manufacture, and exchange with other aristocratic houses. Unfortunately, we lack reliable evidence to estimate the relative value of these forms of income in the household economy as a whole. Land and agriculture comprised the material base of the Western Zhou economy. But a wide array of prestige goods also endowed individuals and families with marks of status. Over the course of the Western Zhou we can see an incipient – but still incomplete – movement from a redistributive economy in which wealth circulated through royal largesse and gift-giving to a tenurial economy based on rights of permanent possession and exchange validated through contract.

The foundation of the Zhou state rested on the dispensation of gifts from the king to his subordinates, both the archer lords and royal officials. Most importantly, the king granted the lands and laborers that enabled the aristocratic lineages to establish their own independent economic base. In addition, the king bestowed the right to cast, inscribe, and use bronze vessels, the crucial mark of membership in the Zhou elite. Other gifts listed in the bronze inscriptions – and commonly found in elite tombs as well – included: cowries; bronze ritual vessels; sacrificial wine; bronze metal; carriages; horses; flags; weapons, armor, and other military accouterments; jade ornaments; and vestments. Possession and display of these goods expressed one's status, although an explicit hierarchy of rank does not seem to have existed before the ritual reforms of the ninth century BCE. It is possible that the formalization of strict sumptuary rules in mortuary practice that emerged from the ritual reforms represented a reaction to a breakdown in an implicit hereditary hierarchy within the Zhou nobility.

The gifts of cowries that commonly accompanied royal investitures in the early Zhou period represented a continuation of a Shang practice. Indeed, gifts of cowries constitute virtually the only form of prestation recorded in Shang oracle bone inscriptions. Cowry shells have been used as money in a number of premodern Asian and African societies. Cowries shared many of the intrinsic virtues of metallic currency – scarcity, durability, uniformity in size and shape, and countability – and, most importantly, were impossible to duplicate. Cowries served as a measure of value in the exchange of goods in the Western Zhou (see below), but not as a means of exchange.[59] The once common

---

[59] Ma Chengyuan (2000) argues that the inscription of the Kang *ding* (an early Western Zhou vessel acquired by the Shanghai Museum in 1998) records the purchase (*mai* 買) of a jade ornament with payment in cowries, ritual vessels, wine, and an ox. But this interpretation is doubtful. As Ma concedes, nowhere else in the Zhou bronze inscriptions does the *mai* graph appear to have the sense of "purchase." Kakinuma's (2011: 108–9) interpretation that this

assertion that cowries served as currency in Shang and Zhou times is now deemed fallacious.[60] The value imputed to cowries undoubtedly derived from their ritual uses in sacrifice and as mortuary goods, rather than any abstract notion of monetary value. Moreover, the prominence of cowries in gift-giving declined markedly over the course of the Western Zhou.

We lack contemporary evidence for the burden of land rent in the Western Zhou. According to the fourth-century BCE philosopher Mencius, in Shang and early Zhou times the ruler extracted a tithe of 10 percent of the yield of the land.[61] The *Rituals of Zhou*, which depicts the organization of the Zhou state in highly schematic and idealized form, claimed that noble lords turned over two-thirds of the revenue from royal land grants to the king, reserving only one-third for themselves.[62] But we have no way of verifying such claims, which must be regarded as dubious. Songs from the *Book of Odes* such as "Seventh Month" suggest that the farming population performed casual labor services for their lords, but in general they owed dues in agricultural and handicraft products, not labor. Monumental building, even at the behest of the Zhou kings, was rare at this time.

Markets did not exist in the Western Zhou. All of the exchanges recorded in bronze inscriptions consisted of personal transactions between aristocratic lineages. Land transfers often involved the intermediation of royal officers and local officials as well as complex exchanges of gifts. The late Western Zhou kings seem to have routinely reassigned tenurial rights to landholdings within the royal domain to new proprietors – although such royal interventions may not have gone uncontested. Even where there is evidence – for example, from the inscriptions on bronze vessels cast by Qiu Wei – of a conscious effort to acquire and accumulate landholdings we find ample testimony of the complexity of tenurial rights in the Western Zhou.

As noted earlier, it has been suggested that Qiu Wei was an upstart entrepreneur whose status derived not from royal appointment – he does not seem to have held any – but rather the wealth generated by the manufacturing workshops he controlled. Two separate inscriptions record transactions in which Qiu obtained lands from a nobleman named Ju. On one occasion Ju received from Qiu ceremonial attire and jade ornaments to be worn at a royal ritual in exchange for arable land, a total of thirteen fields in all:

Elder Ju's men obtained (*qu* 取) from Qiu Wei a jade emblem, the value of which was determined to be eighty strands of cowries. They relinquished ten fields of arable land. Ju also obtained two red tiger-shaped jades, two deerskin knee covers, and one

transaction is really an exchange of gifts and that cowries served as a measure of value rather than a means of exchange is more persuasive. On this point see also Li Yung-ti 2006: 9–11.
[60] Cook 1997: 262–65; Li Yung-ti 2006; Kakinuma 2011: 73–104.   [61] *Mencius*, IIIA.3.
[62] "Xiaguan sima 夏官司馬, sixun司勛," in *ZL*, 2: 257.

decorated leather apron, with a total value determined to be twenty strands. They relinquished three fields of arable land.

Qiu then reported the transaction to a group of five Elders, who assigned the task of verifying the transfer of lands to the Three Supervisors. Finally, several individuals (whose status is unspecified; perhaps they were Ju's men) and a kinsman of Qiu hosted a feast for the officials.[63]

In the first transaction, the parcels of land had an average value of 8 strands of cowries, while in the second transaction the average value is 6⅔ strands, suggesting some difference in the size or quality of the fields.[64] This inscription constitutes the one case in which the value of land was measured in cowries, and it is difficult to determine how common this practice might have been. Qiu's obligation to make a report to the five Elders and the role of the Three Supervisors in certifying the land transfer – which, as other inscriptions confirm, was a standard practice – suggest that this kind of land transaction required the approval of the king's representatives.[65] The provision of feasts for the royal officials involved in the transaction also seems to have been obligatory.

The second of Qiu's land purchases from Ju further demonstrates the complexity of land tenure at this time. In this case Ju obtained from Qiu a chariot and various chariot ornaments, mostly made of leather and animal skins. In return Ju "relinquished" to Qiu forest land in the Linzi *li* district. Qiu then "relinquished" a pair of horses to a certain Yan Chenda, a garment to Yan's wife, and a badger-skin cloak and boar-skin canopy to Shou Shang, an official under Yan's supervision. In this case the land survey and marking of the borders was carried out by Shou Shang and Yan's men, whom Qiu rewarded with a variety of gifts, mostly animal hides. Finally, Qiu's kinsmen prepared a celebratory feast for Yan's men, who gave gifts to Qiu's retinue in return.[66] Most scholars have concluded that Yan Chenda was in some capacity subordinate to the landowner Ju, perhaps as the local *li* administrator. Yan clearly had some rights over this forest land that required indemnification after Ju transferred ownership to Qiu. As Itō Michiharu has observed, the elaborate rituals of gift-giving undertaken by Qiu undercut a purely utilitarian view of this transaction as a land sale.[67]

---

[63] Wei *he* (Ma Chengyuan 1988: #193). For discussions of this inscription, see Zhao Guangxian 1979; Itō 1987: 190–91; Hsu and Lindruff 1988: 275–78; Cook 1997: 271–73; Li Yung-ti 2006: 6–9.

[64] Although Shang-Zhou inscriptions routinely measure cowries in "strands" (*peng* 朋), the amount of cowries in a strand has not been determined.

[65] On the routine practice of designating court dignitaries to serve as "committees of five" in adjudicating important civil matters, see Li Feng 2008: 84–85.

[66] Jiunian Wei *ding* (Ma Chengyuan 1988: #203). For discussions of this inscription, see Cao Wei 2002: 237–41; Itō 1987: 163–64; Li Ling 1998: 97.

[67] Itō 1987: 164.

One scholar has interpreted these events as symbolic of the changing fortunes of the aristocracy in the middle Western Zhou period: Ju, having fallen on hard times, was forced to sell his lands in order to obtain the proper regalia to attend royal ceremonies, while Qiu represented an upwardly mobile class of entrepreneurs enriched by craft manufacture.[68] This assessment surely exaggerates the power of wealth to transform the Western Zhou social order. Moreover, not all aristocratic lineages sought to capitalize on opportunities to expand their landholdings. In one case involving a theft of grain by a group of bondservants, the thieves' lord offered to make reparations in the form of lands and laborers, but the aggrieved noble insisted on payment in grain.[69]

Several inscriptions recording land transfers stipulate that at the conclusion of the agreement each party received a split tally (xi 析) to certify the transaction. Of course, the bronze inscriptions themselves served this documentary purpose. Late Western Zhou land exchanges also mention the practice of swearing oaths to ratify the agreement as irrevocable. Yet we must not conclude that land was freely alienable. Li Ling has described the land transactions that appear in Western Zhou bronze inscriptions as redemptions of debts rather than sales. Li contends that the language employed in the inscriptions – whereby one party "obtains" certain goods (usually having prestige value in ritual use or display), and then "relinquishes" lands as compensation – implied two actions separated in time rather than simultaneous exchange.[70] Nor were lands ever exchanged for cowries or any simulacrum of money. The role of royal officials in endorsing land transfers and performing tasks such as surveying the lands and marking their boundaries, as well as the oath-taking and ritual feasting that concluded such transactions, cautions us against thinking that aristocratic estates constituted private property in the strict sense. The principle function of exchange was the acquisition of prestige goods that displayed status; land and labor – rather than constituting the goal of exchange – typically were "relinquished" for this purpose.

Moreover, land as well as prestige goods and noble status itself was possessed by the aristocratic lineage, not an individual. Constance Cook observes that "the accumulation of prestige and wealth was an ongoing process passed down through the generations."[71] Royal sanction was crucial not only in the initial founding of lineage estates, but in reaffirming the succession of later generations to the status and offices of their forebears. To be sure,

---

[68] Zhao Guangxian 1979.   [69] Hu *ding* (Ma Chengyuan 1988; #242).
[70] Li Ling 1998: 99. Cook (1997: 282) likewise emphasizes the "inalienable" nature of land (which still "belonged" to the king) throughout the Western Zhou.
[71] Cook 1997: 278.

the fortunes of individual lineages rose and fell, and the progressive segmentation of lineages over time most likely fostered growing economic inequality among lineage branches. But the principles of the patrimonial order remained intact, and exchange mediated through a market had not yet emerged.

Conclusion

In the Western Zhou, the king, the archer lords, and royal officers all drew revenues from lands which they possessed as the common patrimony of their lineage. The concept of taxation did not yet exist. The Western Zhou thus can be categorized as a type of *domain state* in which the wealth and income of the ruling class derived from personal and familial rights to land and labor rather than the perquisites of office.[72] But over the course of the Western Zhou period royal authority became increasingly circumscribed. From the outset the Zhou kings had ceded control of the territories and populations of the old Shang heartland on the Central Plain to the archer lords. Within the royal domain in the west, the award of land grants to royal officials progressively diminished the monarchy's direct control over land, labor, and other resources. Nonetheless, the Zhou kings continued to exert considerable influence over the royal domain, at least indirectly. The Zhou government developed a more formal bureaucratic structure and exercised effective juridical authority, as the central role of royal officials in arbitrating disputes between aristocratic lineages demonstrates. The emergence of the Royal Household as an autonomous branch of the royal government perhaps enhanced the personal power of the king, but over an increasingly smaller dominion. At the same time the attrition of royal power was accompanied by growing instability within the ranks of aristocratic lineages. The patrimonial order of the Zhou aristocracy had been founded on lineage solidarity and the ancestral cult. Over time, kinship bonds loosened as genealogical connections became more distant. The fragmentation and dispersal of landholdings also contributed to social and economic differentiation within aristocratic lineages. Among both aristocrats and commoners alike, social identity increasingly focused on the territorial community – the settlement (*yi*).

After the debacle of 771 BCE and the loss of their homeland, the Zhou kings slid toward irrelevance, the titular figureheads of a defunct political order. Military and economic power devolved to the archer lords, now fully independent of royal control. We know little about the activities of the archer lords during the Western Zhou period, but they take center stage in the Eastern Zhou. Although the archer lords emulated some features of late Western Zhou

---

[72] The concept of "domain state" employed here is derived from Schumpeter's distinction between the princely domain and the tax state. See Schumpeter 1991; Musgrave 1992; Bonney 1999.

royal government, a new type of polity – the *city-state* – dominated the political, social, and economic landscape of the Spring and Autumn era. The city-state was engendered by a reorganization of the Zhou patrimonial order that removed the king from the apex of power. But the city-states also fostered political, military, and economic forces that would hasten the final demise of the patrimonial state.

2   From city-state to autocratic monarchy (707 to 250 BCE)

With the fall of the Western Zhou in 771 BCE, royal majesty faded into a long, sputtering twilight. The lords of regional domains, large and small, broke free from Zhou rule, although they continued to pay homage to the ritual preeminence of the Zhou kings. Many of the several hundred newly independent polities took the form of agrarian city-states, consisting of a capital city where the ruling lineages dwelled and adjoining rural settlements whose inhabitants worked the land under servile conditions. The largest territorial states were located on the periphery: Jin in the north, Qi in the east, Qin to the west, and Chu stretching across the southern perimeter of the Zhou ecumene (Map 2.1). The political world of the early Eastern Zhou period – known as the Spring and Autumn era (771–481 BCE), named after the chronicle of this age purportedly written by Confucius (551–479 BCE) – was wracked by chronic warfare. Many states perished, victims of internecine struggles as much as foreign attack. Even the most powerful states were not immune to these centripetal political forces. Jin, descended from the Zhou royal house, expanded northward from its original base in the lower Fen River valley through conquests of non-Zhou peoples. But powerful noble families brazenly asserted their own independence, and the Jin ruling house itself succumbed to a coup-d'état by a junior kinsman in 678 BCE. Despite its military might, Jin "was actually a congeries of semi-independent city-states that spent almost as much time fighting their ruler and each other as waging war with other states."[1]

The endemic disorder that afflicted the Zhou ecumene in the Spring and Autumn era was temporarily ameliorated by the advent of the institution of the hegemon (*ba* 霸), which first appeared in 667 BCE. The first hegemon, Lord Huan of Qi (r. 685–43 BCE), claimed to act in the name of the Zhou king to summon the rulers of the various states to assemblies, negotiate truces and succession disputes, and marshal the collective forces of the various states to pursue military campaigns against non-Zhou peoples. But the Qi rulers' assertion of hegemonic authority rested on their precarious military supremacy

---

[1] Lewis 2000a: 364.

44

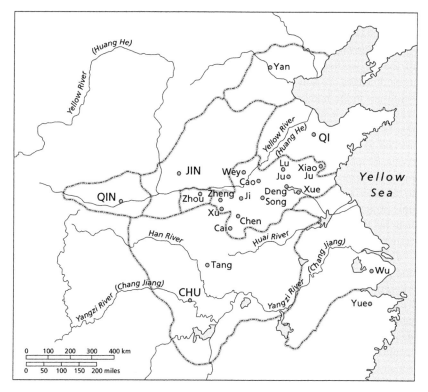

Map 2.1 Major states of the Spring and Autumn era, 771–481 BCE

and transient political alliances. By the end of the seventh century BCE the rulers of Jin had usurped the mantle of hegemon, although they likewise faced constant challenges to their nominal suzerainty, notably from the upstart southern state of Chu. By the time of Confucius no ruler could wield sufficient authority to win recognition as hegemon, and the institution lapsed into obsolescence.

The city-state polities, too, proved unstable. As in the Western Zhou, rulers lavishly bestowed grants of land and population on kinsmen and officials, and in so doing diminished the resources on which their authority depended. Powerful ministers eclipsed their sovereigns in government and diplomacy. Civil wars between rival ministers and factions often toppled hereditary rulers or reduced them, like the Zhou kings, to otiose pawns. Bureaucratic rank increasingly superseded aristocratic pedigree. During the fifth century a new political order arose, one founded on the centralization of power in the hands of an all-powerful monarch. Fewer than two dozen states survived into the Warring States era (453–221 BCE), of which seven formidable macrostates emerged as contenders for supremacy.

The Warring States period thus marked the eclipse of the patrimonial order of the early Zhou, in which rulers shared their authority with kinsmen and noble lineages, by a new type of polity that concentrated power and economic resources in the hands of an exalted monarch. The rise of the *autocratic state* was driven by a series of social, technological, and economic transformations that swept across the Zhou ecumene. The monarchs of the Warring States era needed to increase revenues and enlarge their armies to compete against their rivals. Stripping the nobility of their lands and offices, they granted proprietary rights to farmers in return for labor and military service and taxes paid directly to the ruler's treasury. From this time the conjugal household became the basic unit of agricultural production and taxation. Small-scale agriculture exemplified by the family farm would remain a distinctive feature of the Chinese economy throughout the imperial era.

Technological as well as political changes transformed the sources of wealth and power. The introduction of iron metallurgy triggered a military revolution. Mass production of iron weapons rendered obsolete chariot warfare conducted by nobles. Rulers instead fielded vastly larger infantry armies mustered from peasant conscripts. Warring States rulers also turned to an emerging class of merchants to assist them in gathering and centralizing control over economic resources. The invention of coinage facilitated long-distance trade and the accumulation of wealth. A sharp bifurcation in the ruling class emerged. Autocratic rulers entrusted bureaucratic office and military leadership to a rising professional administrative class whose members largely were drawn from the ranks of the lesser nobility (*shi* 士). Many hereditary noble families – shorn of their privileges, deprived of their lands, and excluded from office-holding – sank into poverty and political irrelevance.

The autocratic state that developed during the Warring States period laid the institutional foundations for the unification of China into a single empire. The Qin state, perched on the periphery of the Zhou ecumene, was by no means the pioneer in formulating centralization policies. But over the course of the fourth to third centuries BCE Qin dramatically outstripped its rivals in wealth and power. Qin's rapid ascent rested in no small part on a comprehensive body of administrative and criminal law that stifled dissent, imposed strict bureaucratic discipline, and enabled the state to mobilize men and materiel on an unimagined scale.

The heyday of the city-state

As we saw in Chapter 1, the settlement (*yi*) was the basic social unit of the early Bronze Age. Most of these settlements were no more than villages.

The last Shang capital at Anyang – an agglomeration of palaces, temples, workshops, elite residences, and farming communities stretching over 24 square kilometers – was forty-five times the size of any other settlement of its day.[2] During the Western Zhou the administrative functions of the state appear to have been dispersed throughout a network of royal cities without a single paramount center. In the Eastern Zhou period the new capital at Cheng Zhou retained symbolic importance as a ceremonial center, but politically it had been reduced to a hollow shell. The common feature of the new Spring and Autumn polities was the concentration of political and military power in the walled cities that served as the capitals for the multitude of independent ruling lineages. Thus the Spring and Autumn era marked the heyday of the city-state in China.

In the Shang and Western Zhou periods, cities formed around the nuclei of palace and temple compounds and elite tombs. These ritual centers spawned a host of satellite settlements that served as the residences of noble lineages, each with its own complement of farmers, craftworkers, and menial servants. At Zhouyuan, for example, archaeologists have discovered more than twenty elite settlement sites together with bronze, bone, pottery, and jade workshops scattered across an area of 15 square kilometers. The royal capitals of Feng and Hao as well as other Zhou cities display a similar pattern of dispersed settlements without any clear differentiation of urban space from agricultural activities. Most strikingly, the Western Zhou royal cities lacked the defensive walls that became the cardinal feature of the Chinese city beginning in the Spring and Autumn era.[3]

The surge of city-building in the Spring and Autumn period and the appearance of defensive walls as the defining characteristic of the Chinese city was driven by the need to fortify cities against attack. In the state of Lu – a relatively small state, but the best-documented one – no fewer than twenty cities were fortified between 770 and 480 BCE.[4] Unfortunately, archaeological evidence for Spring and Autumn cities remains scant. Virtually all of these cities were rebuilt on a larger scale in the Warring States era, leaving few remnants of their earlier configuration. Some Spring and Autumn state capitals – for example, in Lu, Qin, and Zheng – had walls 13–15 kilometers in circumference, but most cities of this era were much smaller.[5] As ministerial and noble houses waxed in power they too constructed walled towns (known as *du* 都, a word that later came to mean "capital city," but at this time designated the seat of a noble lineage) around their residences. Contemporaries were well aware of the perils of allowing noble lineages to build their own castle towns. In 722 BCE Ji Zhong, a minister in the state of Zheng, objected

---

[2] Li Feng 2008: 25. [3] Xu Hong 2000: 61, 81–2. [4] Ibid.: 166, appendix table 4.
[5] Ibid.: 128.

to his ruler's award of a walled city to his younger brother because the circumference of the city's walls exceeded one hundred *zhi* (4.5 kilometers). Ji Zhong warned that according to the regulations of the former kings, the walls of a *du* must not exceed one-third the size of the ruler's capital; if larger, the state will surely suffer harm.[6] The political history of the Spring and Autumn era repeatedly demonstrated the wisdom of Ji Zhong's admonition. In 626 BCE, an attempt was made to resolve a violent succession dispute among the three sons of the recently deceased ruler of Lu by granting each son his own walled city. These castle towns subsequently provided the descendants of the three brothers with the means to impose labor service on the local population, build up their military power, and wrest authority from the rightful ruler. From 562 BCE Lu was in effect carved into three parts.[7]

In fiscal terms, the city-state remained a type of domain state: the ruler and his subordinates derived their income from personal or lineage rights to the fruits of land and labor. Most Spring and Autumn polities created two grades of officials – ministers (*qing* 卿) and officers (*dafu* 大夫) – under the command of a prime minister. As in the Western Zhou, ministerial responsibilities were divided among revenue, public works, and military affairs; in the Spring and Autumn period it became standard practice to appoint judicial ministers as well. Officials received emoluments in the form of benefices (*caiyi* 采邑), usually measured in numbers of settlements (*yi*) and lands, and thus obtained their own independent base of territory, subjects, and resources. The size of settlements and benefices varied. The custom of the state of Zheng fixed the benefice of a prime minister at eight *yi*, but several inscriptions from Qi mention awards of 300 *yi* to meritorious generals and officials.[8] In the former case, *yi* most likely referred to a town and its surrounding rural hinterland, while in latter instance the *yi* probably were no more than small villages.[9] A fourth century BCE military manual defined a "one-chariot settlement" (that is, a *yi* obligated to provide the ruler's army with one war chariot) as consisting of ninety households.[10] Other documents suggest that the size of *yi* ranged from thirty to a hundred households.[11]

At the same time, noble lineages became internally differentiated by rank and wealth, an acceleration of a trend that had already appeared in the late

---

[6] Yingong 1st Year, in ZZ, 3A: 3.

[7] Du Zhengsheng 1990: 41; Yang Kuan 1998: 165; Lewis 1999: 598.

[8] Du Zhengsheng 1990: 112.   [9] Zhu Fenghan 2004: 491–92.

[10] *Sima fa* 司馬法, now lost but quoted in Du Yu's commentary on the *Zuozhuan*. See Du Zhengsheng 1990: 100.

[11] Du Zhengsheng 1990: 100–1. According to a text of uncertain date appended to the *Zhou shu* 周書 of *c.* 300 BCE, in order to facilitate agricultural work the outlying walled towns (*du*) and countryside villages (*bi* 鄙) should be no larger than 100 households. See "Zuoluo 作雒" in YZS, 1: 531.

Western Zhou period. Benefices in theory remained the property of the lineage as a whole, but it became common practice to apportion settlements and lands among the various branches. Junior branches of noble houses thus acquired a certain measure of economic independence.[12] Mortuary evidence indicates considerable inequality of wealth and status among the individual lineage branches, and in some cases junior branches had more lavish tomb goods than the senior ones.[13]

The nobility of the Spring and Autumn period defined itself by its monopoly over the "three great affairs" of war, sacrifice, and hunting, through which they displayed their awesome authority by taking life and spilling blood. Shared participation in the "three great affairs" imparted a collegial martial identity to the noble class that was reinforced by the common practice of blood oaths to forge bonds of fealty and political alliances.[14] At the same time ritual rank within the nobility became more strictly hierarchical and codified by elaborate sumptuary rules. Ritual performance shifted away from the renewal of intimate congress with the ancestors through sacrificial feasts and toward flaunting the lineage's rank and instilling solidarity among its living members.[15] Noble status was hereditary, but rank, wealth, and power were closely aligned with office-holding. Ministers and officers formed a new political class that vied with the rulers for control of the state – and often, as in the case of Lu mentioned above, succeeded. In the growing competition among noble houses for land and wealth, military force usually proved decisive.

As in the Western Zhou, noble lineages typically resided not at their rural estates but rather in and around the capital, in close proximity to the ruler. The population of the city-state was broadly divided into the citizens of the capital (*guoren* 國人) and the inhabitants of the countryside, including the lesser towns (*yeren* 野人). The citizenry did not encompass the entire capital population, however. Membership in the citizenry initially was restricted to members of noble lineages – including the lesser nobility, known as *shi* 士 – who performed military service on the ruler's behalf. Over time the citizenry expanded with the extension of liability for military service to include some commoners, but as a rule merchants, artisans, and farmers remained excluded.[16] Chinese society in this era has been aptly characterized as

---

[12] Zhu Fenghan 2004: 493–99.   [13] Von Falkenhausen 2006: 144.   [14] Lewis 1990: 17–36.
[15] Von Falkenhausen 2006: 294–97.
[16] Lewis (2000a: 369, 2006: 144–45), following in the footsteps of Masubuchi Tatsuo, emphasizes the inclusion of urban commoners in the citizenry. Chinese scholars (e.g., Si Weizhi 1978, Yang Ying 1996) have adopted an even broader definition of the citizenry that includes some farmers as well as merchants and artisans. Yoshimoto (1986), however, convincingly demonstrates that military service was the defining characteristic of the citizenry and that only in one instance

consisting of an "armed nobility based in the cities, surrounded by a country-side occupied by a servile peasantry."[17]

The urban citizenry often became a political force in the Spring and Autumn city-states. In times of crisis, such as military emergencies or succession disputes, rulers or ministers summoned assemblies of citizens to rally support for their actions. The citizenry often played a decisive role in partisan conflicts between the ruler and noble families, or between rival political factions. On occasion, collective action by the citizenry sufficed to depose a tyrannical ruler. The civil strife that afflicted the city-states vitiated the power of heredi-tary rulers and noble lineages alike – and ultimately subverted the citizenry as well, as the case of Zheng illustrates.[18]

Zheng's ruling lineage, one of the senior branches of the Zhou royal house, became an influential force in the early Eastern Zhou, in the immediate aftermath of the relocation of the royal capital to nearby Cheng Zhou. But throughout the seventh century BCE Zheng was plagued by intrigue, regicide, and frequent changes of regime. With the rise of the Qi, Jin, and Chu as the dominant contenders for hegemony, smaller states such as Zheng found themselves imperiled by extinction. Squeezed between the archenemies Jin and Chu, Zheng's leaders sought protection through alliances with either macrostate, changing sides as the balance of power shifted. Bloody conflict among Zheng's noble lineages and between the ministers and citizenry made its political predicament even more dire.[19] In 565 BCE the prime minister Zisi orchestrated the assassination of Zheng's ruler and replaced him with a more malleable substitute. Two years later Zisi's attempt to wrest control of some lands from five noble families provoked an insurrection. The revolt was suppressed, but not before Zisi was put to death by his enemies.

Among the allies of Zisi killed in the uprising was the father of Zichan (c. 581–522 BCE), a member of a minor branch of Zheng's ruling house. Over the next two decades the young Zichan skillfully navigated Zheng's turbulent political waters and propelled himself into a position of power. In 554 BCE Zichan was elevated to a ministership after Zheng's citizenry rose in rebellion and killed the prime minister who had succeeded Zisi. When Zichan led a victorious campaign against the neighboring state of Chen the Zheng ruler

---

were merchants and artisans included in the citizenry – precisely because they were required to perform military service.

[17] Lewis 2000a: 361. According to the *Rituals of Zhou*, the urban citizenry served as fighting men while the rural populace performed menial logistical tasks such as construction, carrying armor, and feeding horses. See Du Zhengsheng 1990: 39.

[18] The following synopsis of the career of Zichan of Zheng is based on the detailed study by Yamazaki (1978). See also Lewis 2000a: 369–70.

[19] Zheng also was perhaps the earliest case in which the leading noble lineages sought to distinguish themselves from the lesser nobility through ritual display and mortuary practices. See von Falkenhausen 2006: 361–62.

rewarded him with a carriage, ceremonial robes, and six settlements. Zichan refused the ruler's offer, however, insisting that his rank entitled him to only two settlements; in the end he was persuaded to accept three. Zichan's uncommon modesty won him the respect of the populace. In 543 BCE, after Zheng's citizenry deposed and executed yet another prime minister, a senior member of Zheng's ruling clan invited Zichan to take the reins of government. At first Zichan demurred, but he finally agreed to do so after receiving assurances that he would have full executive authority.

Possessing a prudent respect for the power of the citizenry, Zichan had worked assiduously to earn their support. Once securely in command of the state, however, he unveiled a bold political agenda that resurrected Zisi's abortive attempt to strengthen the government's control over resources. Zichan proposed to construct irrigation channels and divide arable lands into uniform units that would become the basis for assessing land taxes and military service while also extending liability for military service to a larger proportion of the population. In 536 BCE, Zichan promulgated a law code which he had inscribed on bronze cauldrons – the tangible symbols of sovereign authority – so that the laws would be publicly known and enforced without discrimination on commoners and nobles alike. According to the *Chronicles of Zuo*, the indignant citizenry at first reviled Zichan's reforms, but ultimately came to embrace Zichan for restoring Zheng to prosperity:

After a year under Zichan's administration of government, the people of Zheng sang of him:
We must take our gowns and caps and hide them away,
We must take our lands and fields and divide them into five portions,
Should any man seek to slay this Zichan, we will gladly join him!

But after three years the words of the song had changed:
We have sons and brothers
'Tis Zichan who has tutored them.
We have lands and fields
'Tis Zichan to whom we owe our bounty,
Should Zichan die
Who would take his place?[20]

Zichan retained the support of Zheng's citizenry and remained prime minister until his death in 522 BCE.

The urban citizenry also played an influential role in the usurpation of the rulership of Qi by the Tian clan. At the same time that Zichan assumed the prime ministership in Zheng, Tian Wuyu became the dominant figure at the Qi court through his magnanimity toward the citizenry, for example by

---

[20] Zhao 4th Year, in ZZ, 3A: 564.

lending grain on generous terms.[21] His son Tian Qi likewise gained the support of the Qi citizenry, enabling him to usurp control of the Qi government in 481 BCE and paving the way for the Tian clan formally to displace Qi's ancestral rulers in 386 BCE.[22]

Mark Lewis has likened Zichan to the tyrants or demagogues of the ancient Greek city-states who wooed popular support to seize power and then exercised harsh rule to maintain it.[23] Certainly, like the Greek tyrants, Zichan and Tian Wuyu were harbingers of a new political order that would concentrate power in the hands of the ruler and extinguish the city-states and their acrimonious politics. In the eyes of the later Legalist philosopher Han Fei Zi (c. 280–233 BCE), Zichan deserved comparison with the sage-rulers of high antiquity like Yu the Great, who is said to have rescued the world from the Great Flood.[24] But Han Fei Zi's contemporary and rival, the Confucian philosopher Xun Zi (fl. c. 310–c. 215 BCE), rendered a far more dour verdict: "Zichan gained the support of the people, but he never learned how to govern them."[25]

The rise of the autocratic state

During the sixth century BCE, the mounting tensions within the Zhou city-states burst, unleashing powerful torrents of political and social change. The precisely graded ranking of the nobility broke down. Stratification within the ruling class intensified, fomenting a vast disparity in wealth and power between the rulers and the rest of the nobility. A new political order arose, one founded on the centralization of power in the hands of all-powerful monarchs (Map 2.2). The next several centuries witnessed the destruction of the old noble lineages and the largely autarkic estate economies under their dominion. Rulers asserted direct control over the land, which they awarded to farming families in return for tax payments, labor duties, and military service. The nobility's hereditary rights to office were abrogated, and rulers instead established bureaucratic forms of government in which officials served at the ruler's pleasure. The advent of the Iron Age also posed a direct challenge to the status, privileges, and self-identity of the nobility. Chariot warfare conducted by nobles under strict rules of chivalry was supplanted by far more bloody conflicts fought by massive infantry armies conscripted from the agrarian population and equipped with iron

---

[21] Zhao 3rd Year; in ZZ, 3A: 598.   [22] Lewis 1999: 598.   [23] Lewis 2000a: 370.

[24] Chapter 50, "Xianxue" 顯學, in HFZ, 2: 1104. In this passage Han Fei Zi groups Zichan with historical (or legendary) figures who brought great benefits to the people yet suffered scorn and derision, thus showing the ignorance of the common folk.

[25] Chapter 9, "Wangzhi" 王制, in XZ: 168.

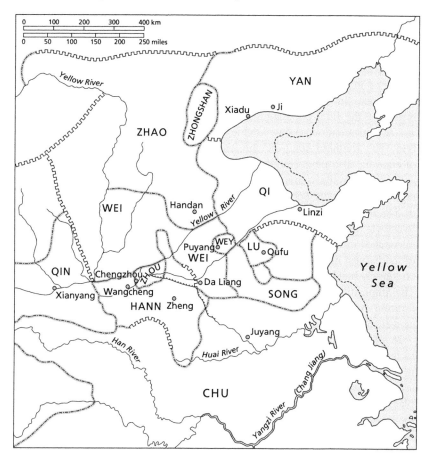

Map 2.2 Major states of the Warring States era, 481–221 BCE

weapons, including powerful crossbows. Skilled leaders of commoner origins rose through the ranks to take command of the new armies.

This transformation of the relationship between rulers and subjects began with the need to enhance the military power of the state and the corresponding development of written records to amass information about individuals, households, and property.[26] Initially, the main purpose of written registers was military conscription. A chronicle entry for 645 BCE states that the ruler of Jin, after a military defeat at the hands of Chu, awarded grants of land as

---

[26] This paragraph is based on Du Zhengsheng 1990: 22–25, 175–78; Hori 1996: 47–55; Yang Kuan 1998: 151–67.

compensation for military service. But this instance probably was a one-time expedient restricted to the citizenry, evidence of the ruler's weakness rather than strength.[27] The earliest efforts to broaden the basis of taxation and military service – in Lu in the 590s BCE and the reforms Zichan launched in Zheng in 543 BCE – likewise appeared in weaker states besieged by powerful adversaries. In both Lu and Zheng officials conducted land surveys and organized the rural population into units liable for military service, although we lack information on how land registration was related to military conscription. The southern state of Chu, the first to field infantry armies in place of chariots, also pioneered the development of bureaucratic tools to mobilize soldiers and military supplies. Chu's government conducted the first universal registration of able-bodied adult men for military service in 589 BCE, and in 548 BCE undertook a comprehensive survey of land, forest, mineral, and livestock resources. By 500 BCE population registers apparently had been introduced in Qi as well. By that time, too, a land tax amounting to 20 percent of the harvest had been implemented in most of the Jin state, whose territories effectively had been partitioned among the so-called "Six Ministerial Houses." The imposition of this land tax had been premised on grants of lands to farming households, and most likely required some form of registration as well.

In addition, expansionary macrostates such as Jin, Qin, and Chu also began to found new administrative towns known as *xian* 縣 in their borderlands and in newly conquered territories. Rather than award the *xian* towns, which at first served primarily military purposes, as benefices to noble lineages, rulers placed them under the jurisdiction of appointed governors. Often, however, the governors turned the *xian* under their control into personal fiefdoms, even though they had no hereditary rights of succession. In Jin, which was said to have forty *xian* in the late Spring and Autumn era, the ruler occasionally rewarded meritorious officials with grants of *xian* that became part of their hereditary benefice. But in 514 BCE the prime minister of Jin confiscated lands belonging to two nobles caught conspiring against the ruler and converted them into a total of ten *xian* directly controlled by the state[28] In the late Spring and Autumn period, ministerial houses also began to establish *xian* towns within their own large benefices. Not until the reforms of Shang Yang in Qin in the mid-fourth century BCE did *xian* become the basic units of a comprehensive system of territorial control directly subordinated to the central state.[29]

---

[27] Du Zhengsheng 1990: 177–78.   [28] Zhaogong 28th Year, in ZZ, 3A: 753.
[29] Du Zhengsheng 1990: 119–23. Jin also seems to have been the first state to create *jun* 郡 units, in the late Spring and Autumn period. *Jun* units were areas of strategic military importance, larger in area than *xian* but of lesser economic value, perhaps because they had smaller populations or poorer land. See ibid., pp. 123–24.

Following the partition of Jin into the three states of Wei, Hann, and Zhao in 453 BCE, the Wei kingdom pioneered the institutional reforms that became the hallmark of autocratic rule in the Warring States period. In 419 BCE Wei's armies inflicted a decisive defeat on Qin and annexed rich agricultural lands on the western edge of the Central Plain. It was around this time that Li Kui, the prime minister of Wei, instituted policies focused on agricultural improvement and enhancing the welfare of farming families. Wei was probably the most densely populated state of the time, and thus Li Kui emphasized intensification of farming by cultivating multiple staple crops (millet, wheat, hemp, and soybeans) to reduce risk of harvest failure, adopting more laborious cultivation techniques, and utilizing marginal lands by planting mulberries and other non-food crops. Li Kui also advocated a form of indirect price control by having the state purchase grain after abundant harvests when prices were low in order to boost the income of farmers, while protecting urban consumers by selling its stocks when grain was dear. This form of state intervention to smooth out oscillations in food prices became a cardinal feature of the political economy of the Chinese imperial state.[30]

Li Kui also is credited with instituting a law code and compiling perhaps the earliest treatise on law, the *Canon of Laws*. Although Li's law code does not survive, it is said to have served as the foundation for the imperial law codes of the Qin and Han empires.[31] Li Kui often is regarded as one of the forefathers of Legalism and progenitor of the doctrine of "enriching the state and strengthening the army" (*fuguo qiangbing* 富國強兵). Certainly, Li deemed the impoverishment of the agrarian population – the ultimate source of the state's wealth – as the greatest danger to the state. Thus he advocated that the ruler should impose only modest levies on farmers while curbing extravagant consumption through sumptuary regulation and inhibiting merchants from manipulating prices to the disadvantage of producers and consumers alike. Li – himself of commoner descent – displayed scorn toward the old nobility and warned that disparities in status, wealth, and knowledge undermined social order and the stability of the state.[32]

The full flowering of the autocratic state occurred in Qin in the mid-fourth century BCE, during the prime ministership of Shang Yang. The Qin reform agenda was powerfully shaped by the Wei precedent. In 385 BCE, a Qin prince who, thirty years earlier, at the age of ten, had been forced into exile in

---

[30] For Li Kui's economic policies, see Yang Kuan 1998: 188–92; Hu Jichuang 1962: 1, 265–78.
[31] Two articles incorporated into the Wei Code of 252 BCE have been preserved in the *Weili zhi dao* 為吏之道 manuscript found among the cache of Qin-era texts excavated at Shuihudi. About ten articles said to have been taken from Li's *Canon of Laws* were published in a late Ming historical work. The authenticity of this source is dubious, however. See Ikeda 2008a: 112–31.
[32] Li's political vision has been pieced together from highly fragmented sources by Ikeda (2008a).

Wei, returned to Qin and reclaimed the throne. Lord Xian (r. 385–362 BCE), as he became known, then introduced changes modeled on Wei institutions: appointing market inspectors to collect taxes on trade, establishing household registers for military service, introducing *xian* administrative units, and moving the Qin capital from Yong to Yueyang, a more centrally located site with ready access to the commercial networks of Wei and the Central Plain. Lord Xian's son, Lord Xiao (r. 361–338 BCE), continued his father's initiatives while seeking to recruit talented statesmen from abroad. One of those who answered his summons was Gongsun Yang (better known as Shang Yang, 390–338 BCE), a member of the ruling clan of Wey then serving as a household officer for the prime minister of Wei. Shang Yang, like Lord Xian before him, regarded the rich and powerful Wei state as a model for emulation.

In 356 BCE Lord Xiao appointed Shang Yang as a senior minister and gave him license to undertake sweeping administrative and legal reforms.[33] Shang immediately enacted a law code, ostensibly based on Li Kui's *Canon of Laws*, and introduced a new system of military rank – seventeen grades in all – that became the basis for recognition of accomplishment in warfare.[34] According to the *Book of Lord Shang*, a digest of Shang Yang's policies and political theories composed in the third century BCE, the rewards for killing one enemy soldier in battle included promotion of one grade in rank, a grant of 100 *mu* of arable land, 9 *mu* of land for a dwelling, and one servant farmer (*shuzi* 庶子).[35] Thus Shang Yang sought to create a system of merit based on service to the state that would supersede the privileges of the old nobility and provide the basis for the reallocation of land and wealth. He also organized the population into military-style units of five and ten households and established the principle of mutual responsibility, whereby all members of the group bore equal legal culpability for crimes committed by any of its members. Finally, the first phase of Shang Yang's reforms imposed severe legal penalties intended to curb exploitation by unscrupulous merchants. Like Li Kui, Shang Yang championed the well-being of farmers – who toiled at the "primary occupation" (*benye* 本業), the root of the state's wealth – over and above the "inessential occupations" (*moye* 末業) of artisans and merchants.[36]

---

[33] Lewis 1999: 612–16; Yang Kuan 1998: 201–11; Hori 1996: 33–38.

[34] The assertion that the law code enacted by Shang Yang in Qin was based on Li Kui's treatise is found only in much later sources, and has been rejected by some scholars (e.g., Cao Lüning 2002: 57–63). For a deeply researched argument in support of this assertion, see Ikeda 2008a.

[35] Chapter 19, "Jingnei" 境內, in *SJS*: 119; see also Yang Kuan 1998: 180.

[36] In the words of the *Book of Lord Shang*, "The ruler who wishes to enrich his state through agriculture ensures that within his territory the cost of foodstuffs remains dear, while multiplying the levies on non-agricultural activities and imposing heavy tariffs on the profits of trade." Chapter 22, "Wainei 外內," in *SJS*: 129.

Although Shang Yang's program aroused resentment and opposition from the noble lineages of Qin, Lord Xiao remained loyal to his protégé. In 352 BCE he elevated Shang to the office of chancellor, which combined the portfolio of prime minister with control of the military. Two years later, in 350 BCE, Shang launched a second and more sweeping series of institutional reforms.

One key goal of Shang Yang's policies was to establish the conjugal household as the basic unit of social and economic organization. Among the new laws introduced by Shang Yang in 356 BCE was the stipulation that the tax assessment on households with two or more adult males would be doubled. During the second phase of reform, Shang made it a crime for fathers and adult sons to live together. Moreover, Shang abolished the practice of primogeniture and instituted the requirement that all sons inherited equal portions of the father's estate. This set of decrees was intended to undermine the economic foundations of the old nobility by breaking up their landholdings and dividing them among numerous sons. Recently excavated household registers and legal statutes suggest that Shang Yang's draconian reforms were not fully implemented even under the Qin Empire.[37] But the principle of equal inheritance subsequently became enshrined in imperial law for more than twenty centuries and one of the cornerstones of China's family farm economy.

The new measures Shang Yang enacted in 350 BCE included a law that divided arable lands into standardized parcels separated by boundary ridges (known as *qianmo* 阡陌). This initiative clearly can be traced to Li Kui's policies in Wei and perhaps to the reforms of Zichan – about which we know little – as well. A recently excavated document dating from 309 BCE contains a portion of the Qin land statutes that provides some details about the *qianmo* practice. The law stipulated that the land was to be divided into parcels 1 pace wide and 240 paces long. Two of these parcels constituted a *mu* unit, and 100 *mu* (or 1 *qing*) became the standard land allotment that the Qin state provided to farming households. The parcels were to be marked off by boundaries such as ridges and roads, and landowners were required to perform annual maintenance to ensure that the parcels remained clearly demarcated.[38]

---

[37] For example, some undivided households appear in the Liye registers, and the Zhangjiashan corpus reveals that the eldest son received much more in terms of rank (and landholdings) than the other sons even in the early Han Empire. Personal communications from Maxim Korolkov and Anthony Barbieri-Low.

[38] Huang Shengzhang 1982; Li Xueqin 1982; Yamada 1993: 34–6; Hori 1996: 33–7. The Qin land parcel apparently was based on the prevailing practice in Zhao, where the *mu* unit was larger than in Wei or other states. The larger *mu* unit implied that farmers received larger land grants from the state. However, it is worth keeping in mind that land productivity in core states such as Wei and Hann undoubtedly was higher than in peripheral ones such as Zhao and Qin. According to the *Lüshi chunqiu*, the Wei state doubled the land allocations to 200 *mu* in the vicinity of Ye because the land there was less productive. See Zhu Honglin 2008: 223.

These standardized land units became the basis of a new system of land tenure and taxation in which the Qin government distributed lands to individual households in return for payments of grain, fodder, and straw as well as labor and military service. It seems likely that some form of this system of land tenure had been introduced by Zichan in Zheng nearly two centuries before, and already existed in Wei and the other Jin successor states (Hann and Zhao), and perhaps in other states as well. The extent to which Shang Yang was able to seize lands from noble lineages and reallocate them to ordinary farming households remains unclear. Allocation of land to farming households most likely was carried out on newly opened lands and in conquered areas where the local population was forcibly displaced by Qin colonists.[39]

Shang Yang pursued other centralization policies as well. In 344 BCE he ordered the Qin officialdom to adopt uniform weights and measures to ensure equity in tax collections. He also moved the Qin capital to a new site at Xianyang and began the construction of monumental palaces befitting the supreme dignity of the Qin ruler. The founding of the new capital separated the ruler and his government from the residences of the noble lineages, which remained clustered around the older capital at Yong. Shang Yang's reforms did not abolish the Qin nobility, however. Indeed, in 340 BCE, after a military victory over Wei, Lord Xiao bestowed noble rank on Shang Yang and rewarded him with a benefice of fifteen settlements.

After Lord Xiao's death in 338 BCE, however, Shang Yang's enemies quickly fanned the new ruler's suspicions about his chancellor's loyalty. Within a year Shang was arrested for treason and executed in gruesome fashion by being drawn and quartered. But his legacy endured. At the time of Shang's death the Qin state had become the most formidable military power of the Zhou ecumene, and already had embarked on the long march that would culminate with the founding of the first universal empire.

The institutions established by autocratic rulers in Qin and other states transformed the Zhou social order. Many of the old noble lineages disappeared, supplanted by a rising new nobility awarded rank in return for meritorious service to the state in government or warfare. The distinction between the citizenry of the capital and the inhabitants of the countryside had been largely erased. A new commoner (*shuren* 庶人) class emerged that was tied directly to the state by grants of land received in return for tax payments, statutory labor, and military service.[40] In the Western Zhou period, *shuren* had designated a servile class of farmers subordinated

---

[39] Personal communication from Maxim Korolkov.

[40] On the evolution of the category of *shuren*, see Si Weizhi 1978; Yang Ying 1996. I disagree with the analyses of Si and Yang on a number of issues, however, especially their contention

to noble households. The new institutional regime that began to coalesce from the sixth century BCE transformed *shuren* into independent farming families, although connotations of servile status persisted. Confucius, dismayed by the decay of the Zhou nobility, vehemently objected to giving *shuren* any voice in affairs of state.[41] But the Confucian philosopher Mencius, writing in the mid-fourth century BCE, readily acknowledged that *shuren* could and did serve in government. Nonetheless, although Mencius dismissed the distinction between urban and rural residence as obsolete, he still insisted on maintaining the proper social and political hierarchy between the ruling elite and non-official commoners.[42]

Other records from this era place the *shuren* on the same footing with merchants and artisans – below the lesser nobility (*shi* 士) and above a range of servile groups designated by general terms such as "menials" (*zao* 皂), "dependents" (*li* 隸), and "servants" (*chen* 臣) as well as by occupational categories such as drivers (*yu* 輿), stablehands (*yu* 圉), and herders (*mu* 牧).[43] What appears to distinguish *shuren* (a term that retained its sense of persons engaged in agriculture), merchants, and artisans from the servile classes was their independent means of livelihood. However, the lands received by *shuren* strictly speaking were not private property, but rather tenurial rights conditionally bestowed by the state in return for goods and services.

Although *shuren* no longer were considered a servile class, forced labor occupied a far more central place in the political economy of the autocratic state than in the city-states of the past. The burden of statutory labor service often was heavy, as the frequent protests – especially by artisans – against excessive demands for labor service demonstrate.[44] However, penal servitude supplied most of the labor force in government workshops. This practice may have begun in the Jin successor states, but it became a keystone of the legal regime instituted in Qin by Shang Yang. Shang Yang's reforms created a category of penal servitude imposed on men and women alike, collectively known as *lichenqie* 隸臣妾, that encompassed both convict laborers and government slaves (mostly war captives). In contrast to earlier times, when bondservants were attached to noble households, by the Warring States period the servile classes were largely wards of the state. Although Qin law established distinctions between convict laborers and government slaves, both groups were fundamentally defined by the unconditional surrender of their

---

that the urban citizenry (*guoren*) of the Spring and Autumn period included *shuren* (see above, note 16).
[41] *Analects* 16.2.   [42] *Mencius* 5B.2, 5B.7.
[43] See the *Chronicles of Zuo* passages cited in Si Weizhi 1978: 105; Yoshimoto 1986: 635.
[44] Si Weizhi 1978: 108.

labor power to the state.[45] Lack of a stable occupation itself became a crime: the *Book of Lord Shang* advocated that the idle should be enslaved by the state, while the *Wei Code* of 252 BCE stipulated that they should be impressed into the army and treated more harshly than honorable soldiers.[46] In the economy of the autocratic state, work became the defining mark of personhood, for free and unfree alike.

Economic transformation in the dawning Iron Age

The three centuries before the unification of China under the first empire, Qin, in 221 BCE, witnessed remarkable changes in economic livelihood. The major states contending for supremacy – notably Qin, Chu, and Qi – increasingly centralized control of land, labor, and goods. Bondservants liberated from the dominion of their lords acquired significant tenurial rights. The introduction of iron metallurgy and tool-making led to rapid improvements in the productivity of agriculture. Political centralization and the advent of a money economy spurred interregional trade, urban growth, and the rise of an independent merchant class. Some of these trends intensified under the imperial rule of the Qin and Han dynasties, while others atrophied.

Chief among the technological innovations of the Eastern Zhou period was the introduction of iron metallurgy. Evidence for the manufacture of iron dates back to the ninth century BCE, but the production of iron tools – chiefly spades and hoes, but also plows, sickles, knives, axes, and chisels – can be attested only from the fifth century BCE. At this time iron tools were cast in molds, and thus relatively small and light. For the rulers of the Warring States, equipping their large infantry armies with iron weapons took precedence over manufacturing agricultural tools. Moreover, iron tools required more refined metallurgical technology to reduce the amount of carbon and harden the iron. Nonetheless, over the course of the Warring States period the manufacture and use of iron tools became widespread, leading to greater efficiencies in agriculture and increases in total output. These advances in agricultural productivity on one hand enabled the rulers to feed ever more massive armies, and on the other hand favored smaller household-level units of production.[47]

Apart from the introduction of iron tools, other innovations in agricultural technology contributed to rising productivity in the Warring States period.

---

[45] Huang Shengzhang 2001; Yates 2002; Li Li 2007. Convict laborers generally were sentenced to three to six years of hard labor, terms that often proved to be life sentences. In general only war captives and certain classes of convicted criminals could be enslaved, but meritorious officials and soldiers often were rewarded with gifts of slaves and slave markets existed at least by the third century BCE.

[46] Yates 2002: 312.   [47] Emura 2005: 110.

It is difficult to determine when the use of ox-drawn plows was introduced, but plow oxen are frequently mentioned in Qin documents from the third century BCE. The earliest reference in historical chronicles to building flood-control dikes along the Yellow River dates back to 602 BCE. The Wei government organized large-scale irrigation projects in the region around modern Kaifeng when it relocated its capital to Da Liang in 362 BCE. In the third century BCE officials in Qin initiated major irrigation projects in newly conquered regions, such as the Zheng Guo Canal in Henan, which was said to have irrigated 40,000 *qing* (180,000 hectares). The Duyan irrigation works constructed by the Qin governor Li Bing *c.* 250 BCE transformed the Chengdu Plain in Sichuan into a fertile rice-growing region. Qin officials attributed their abrupt rise in power in the fourth–third centuries BCE to the greater efficiency of agriculture in their realm. Modern scholars are inclined to agree.[48]

The rise of family farm as the foundation of the Warring States economy is amply attested by economic policies that made the nuclear household the fundamental unit of taxation and services required by the state. As we have seen, Li Kui, the prime minister of Wei, advocated more intensive land-use and cultivation techniques in order to raise farm incomes and generate income for the state. Li's proposal for the state to intervene in grain markets to ensure stable prices was premised on his bleak assessment of the economic situation of ordinary farmers. According to Li, a typical farming household of five persons cultivated 100 *mu* of land that yielded a total harvest of 150 *shi* ("stones"; one *shi* was equivalent to 20 liters) of grain. The state collected a land tax of 10 percent, or 15 *shi*, and the family required 90 *shi* of grain for its own subsistence, leaving a surplus of 45 *shi*. At a market price of 30 coins per *shi*, the surplus was equivalent to 1,350 coins. Community ritual observances cost 300 coins annually, and clothing for five persons a total of 1,500 coins. Thus the household incurred an annual deficit of 450 coins, "not including expenses for unfortunate events like illness, death, and burial, or extraordinary exactions imposed from above."[49] According to Li Kui, then, the market occupied a vital place in the livelihood of ordinary farmers, who disposed of their surplus grain on the market and depended on this cash income to provide for many of their basic needs. But this reliance on the market, Li concluded, also necessitated intervention by the state to protect farmers from violent oscillations in prices.

Many scholars are skeptical about this depiction of the pervasive influence of the market in the agrarian economy of this era, especially since the speech attributed to Li Kui appears only in a historical work compiled long after his

---

[48] Hsu 1980: 99–100. Honda 2000a: 6.
[49] *HS* 24A: 1124–25; translated in Hsu 1980: 235–36; Swann 1950: 140–43.

time, in the first century CE.[50] Surely the scenario described by Li Kui was not typical of the Warring States world, but it may have been common in Wei, the most commercially advanced region within the Zhou ecumene. The Warring States era witnessed a concentration of wealth in the hands of rulers, their kin, high officials, and probably some merchants as well, and a sharpening economic polarization between this group and the lower elite. In contrast to Li Kui's gloomy assessment, however, archaeological evidence also suggests a broader distribution of wealth among the lower orders of society as the social boundaries between the lower elite and commoners blurred. In Qin, a radical transformation in mortuary customs around the time of Shang Yang's reforms testifies to a sudden change in the status of the nobility. In Chu, where documentation of mortuary practices for the lower social strata is most extensive, grave goods became increasingly homogeneous during the Warring States era, indicating an erosion of the privileges of the lower nobility and the growing importance of wealth as the measure of social status. The inclusion of at least a modest inventory of grave goods in the great majority of Chu tombs perhaps reflects a general increase in prosperity.[51] In the view of some scholars, the possession of bronze ritual vessels by a broader spectrum of Chu society and the greater variety, larger size, and more elaborate decoration of bronze artifacts testifies to a growing consumption demand emanating from the lower ranks of nobility and newly affluent commoners.[52] A similar convergence in mortuary goods, including the presence of weapons, in commoner and elite tombs in the Qi region likewise "indicates a continuum in life style from elite to at least some commoners."[53]

The emergence of money and markets in China was prompted by the need of rulers to amass resources across increasingly greater distances. Bronze currency in the shape of knives and spades first appeared c. 600 BCE, around the same time as the earliest coinage in the Mediterranean world. The physical shapes of these currencies derived from useful tools, and their adoption as signifiers of money perhaps reflects the growing economic value of practical utensils. The earliest spade currency apparently was issued in the name of the Zhou king, and shortly afterward was imitated by other core states of the Central Plain such as Jin, Zheng, Song, and Wey. By c. 500 BCE the eastern seaboard states of Qi and Yan began to issue a distinctively different knife-shaped currency, while Qin introduced the first round bronze coins, known as Banliang, probably around 335 BCE. The southern state of Chu had the

---

[50] Kanaya (1987: 147) argues that this passage dates from the late Warring States period, while Hu Jichuang (1962, 1: 277) suggested it was composed during the Western Han.

[51] For the Qin and Chu mortuary evidence, see von Falkenhausen 2006: 370–99. Von Falkenhausen himself is cautious about drawing inferences about socio-economic trends from this evidence at the present stage of research, however.

[52] Emura 2005: 104–07.   [53] Li Min 2003: 109–11.

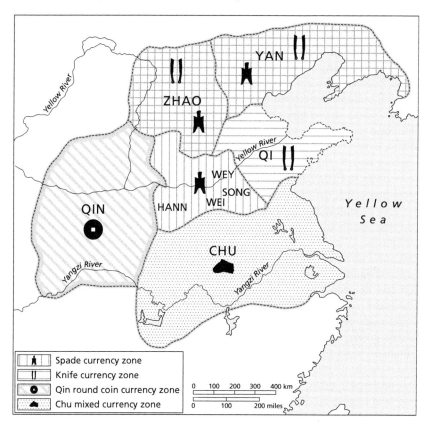

Map 2.3 The distribution of bronze currency types in the Warring States era

most distinctive monetary system, which included gold pieces and bronze imitations of cowry shells as well as spade-shaped bronze currency. Because of its multiple currencies, Chu pioneered in developing abstract units of monetary value that enabled conversions of values between different types of money. Chu's gold currency also served to some degree as an international currency, particularly in Qi and Qin.[54]

The distribution of currency types and monetary units reveals the contours of four zones of monetary circulation (Map 2.3). Both the Qi knife currency and the Qin Banliang coins were highly standardized, and neither circulated much beyond the state's borders. In addition, little bronze currency from

[54] For a general overview of pre-Qin currencies, see Yamada 2000: 29–51. For detailed analysis of regional types, see Emura 2011.

foreign states has been unearthed in the territories of the Qi and Qin states, which seem to have relied on Chu gold tokens for interstate exchange. By contrast, the Jin successor states and other core polities of the Central Plain issued many varieties of bronze currencies that circulated widely across state borders. The Jin successor states of Zhao and Wei also pioneered in issuing multiple denominations of bronze currency.[55] Although the Chu monetary system was unique, its bronze currencies – including a spade currency modeled on a Wei prototype – circulated in Wei and elsewhere in the Central Plain, indicating extensive commercial interchange between these regions. The density and diversity of currency at archaeological sites in the Central Plain – especially in Henan, the heartland of the Wei and Hann states – reinforces the conclusion that commercial exchange was concentrated in this region.[56]

The proliferation of currency accompanied the emergence of a class of private merchants on whom rulers depended to procure vital goods and resources. The wealth of merchants and the escalating demand for their services endowed them with a significant degree of independence. Fan Li, upon resigning as prime minister of Yue in 473 BCE, is said to have traveled to Qi and devoted himself to husbandry, earning a fortune of several hundred thousand coins. Subsequently Fan moved to Tao, the major commercial crossroads on the Central Plain, where he "established his business, storing away goods, looking for a profitable time to sell ... and in the course of nineteen years three times made a fortune of one thousand catties of gold." Bai Gui (fl. c. 370–300 BCE), a Wei merchant, reaped a great fortune from his dealings in grain, silk, and lacquer. Bai Gui's mercantile acumen prompted the Wei ruler to recruit him for high office. As prime minister of Wei, Bai Gui is said to have pursued strongly pro-commercial policies, such as reducing the customs duty on commercial goods from 10 to 5 percent.[57] Commercial success launched other merchants into political careers as well. Lü Buwei, a traveling merchant from Wey who made a great fortune trading at Handan, the capital of Zhao, attracted the attention and friendship of a Qin prince, the future King Zhuangxiang, who appointed him chancellor upon his coronation in 250 BCE. In 247 BCE, when King Zhuangxiang died suddenly and was succeeded by his 13-year-old son, Lü became regent and political tutor to the future first emperor of China.[58]

The Warring States rulers fully recognized the value of strategic economic goods in the incessant struggle for world conquest. A passage in the *Guan Zi* coined the term "shadow kings" (*yinwang* 陰王) for the rulers of Chu, Qi, and

[55] Wu Liangbao 2005: 59–60.   [56] Emura 2005: 125–31; Yazawa 2008.
[57] *SJ* 129.3257–59. For Bai Gui's proposal to reduce custom levies, see *Mencius* 6B.10. See also Hu Jichuang 1962: 1: 174–92, 278–84.
[58] On Lü Buwei and his controversial political career, see Knoblock and Riegel 2000.

Yan, arguing that the mineral wealth they possessed (gold in Chu, salt in Qi and Yan) could make them supremely powerful if only the rulers knew how to best utilize these resources. Should the Qi ruler put his subjects to work producing salt, for example, he could sell the salt to the interior states of the Central Plain, rich in grain but poor in salt, and reap a great profit in gold. Once in possession of sufficient stockpiles of gold, the ruler could control the prices of all goods, and thus never lack what he needed. But if the ruler did not know how to profit from the natural resources of his realm, they were as worthless as dirt.[59]

The emergence of merchant entrepreneurs reflected not only the rulers' need to amass resources but also growing regional specialization of production of goods such as iron, salt, lacquer, and silk. Rulers especially coveted the profits reaped by entrepreneurs in the iron and salt industries, whose great wealth "rivaled the fortunes of kings."[60] The rulers of Qin made mines and salt ponds – "the wealth of the mountains and marshes" in the argot of the day – part of the ruler's personal domain. But Qin, like other states, levied excise taxes on these lucrative industries rather than managing them directly. The *Guan Zi* warned against direct government management of iron mines. In the remote areas where mines were located, the convict and slave laborers usually employed in state-run workshops would run away, while imposing labor conscription for such onerous work would incur the enmity of free subjects. The author of the treatise advised the ruler of Qi to allow private entrepreneurs to operate iron mines and collect a share (30 percent) of the mine output.[61]

Regulation of trade was vital to both the state's economic welfare and its military security. The E Jun Qi bronze tallies, issued by the Chu central government to a local official in 323 BCE, offer unique insights into the regulation of domestic trade during the Warring States period. The tallies granted exemptions from internal customs duties along stipulated trade routes for up to 50 wagons and 150 boats, exemptions that had to be renewed annually. These trading expeditions apparently were conducted under government oversight and moved throughout the Chu realm, but the tallies do not specify what goods were involved, nor do they explain the nature of the state's proprietary interest in this trade. The wagon tallies, which were intended for routes along the northern frontier of the Chu state, specifically prohibited the transport of metals, leather, and arrows – that is to say, strategic goods of military value. However, the boat tallies, intended for use in the southern

---

[59] Chapter 80, "Qingzhongjia" 輕重甲, in *GZ*, 1: 1422–23; for a translation, see Rickett 1998: 456–57.
[60] *SJ* 129.3259.
[61] Chapter 81, "Qingzhongyi" 輕重乙, in *GZ*, 3: 1448. I follow Ma Feibai's (1979, 2: 577) emendation of the state's portion from 3/13 in the received text to the more logical 3/10. On Qin taxation of mining, see He Qinggu 2003a.

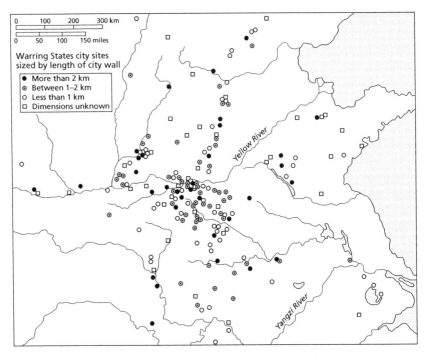

Map 2.4 Warring States cities, based on archaeological excavations
Source: Emura 2005: 68, figure 22.

portion of the Chu state, have no such provisions.[62] The tallies demonstrate
that the Chu state collected duties on domestic trade at customs stations along
major trade routes, a practice also attested for Qi. In Qin, by contrast, the state
tightly regulated border trade but apparently did not tax the movement of
goods within its territories.[63]

The city transformed

The most eloquent testimony to the economic transformation of the Warring
States period is found in the dramatic changes in the number, size, and structure
of cities. Archaeologists have identified more than 400 walled settlements
dating from this era, of which 114 encompass an area of at least 1 square
kilometer (Map 2.4). The spectacular urban growth of the Warring States period
is most apparent in the scale of the royal capitals. The longest walls of the
capitals of the seven largest states all extended more than 4 kilometers;

---

[62] For a translation and study of the E Jun Qi tallies, see von Falkenhausen 2005.
[63] Yamada 1993: 446–49.

Table 2.1 *City sizes in the Warring States period*
(all dates are BCE)

City	Recorded date of wall-building	State	Longest wall (m)	Area (km^2)	State capital
(1) Xiadu 下都		Yan	8,000	32	*
(2) Xianyang 咸陽	350	Qin	7,200		*
(3) Shouchun 壽春		Chu	6,200	26	* (241–224)
(4) Xinzheng 新鄭		Hann	5,000		*
(5) Handan 邯鄲		Zhao	4,880	19	* (from 386)
(6) Linzi 臨淄		Qi	4,500	20	*
(7) Ying 郢 (Ji'nan 紀南)	519	Chu	4,500	16	* (until 241)
(8) Lingshou 靈壽		Zhongshan	4,500		* (*c.* 380–296)
(9) Anyi 安邑	385	Wei		13	* (until 362)
(10) Liao 鄝		Chu	3,775		
(11) Qufu 曲阜		Lu	3,700	10	*
(12) Yong 雍		Qin	3,480	10	* (until 383)
(13) Xue 薛	323	Qi	3,300	7.36	
(14) Royal Zhou 周王城	510	Zhou	3,200		*
(15) Cai 蔡 (Shangcai 上蔡)		Chu	3,187		* (until 447)
(16) Quwo 曲沃		Jin	3,100		* (until 403)
(17) Song 宋 (Shangqiu 商丘)		Song	3,050		*
(18) Jiang 絳 (Xiangfen 襄汾)		Hann	2,700	5.0	
(19) Jinyang 晉陽		Zhao	2,700		
(20) Jiwangcheng 紀王城		Zou	2,530		*

Source: Xu Hong 2000.

the largest, Xiadu in Yan, stretched for 8 kilometers. Table 2.1 shows the twenty largest cities as measured by the length of their longest wall (note, however, that there are some important omissions in this list: for example, the site of Da Liang, established as the Wei capital in 362 BCE, has not been excavated). In addition to being far larger than their Spring and Autumn predecessors, Warring States cities exhibit marked changes in morphology. The cardinal feature of the Spring and Autumn city was a fortified enceinte enclosing the ruler's palace at the center of the larger walled town, a plan that emphasized the city's function as a defensive bulwark for the ruler. The royal cities of the Warring States period, by contrast, typically were partitioned by walls and canals into two (or more) zones: a palace sector distinguished by large mounds on which major palaces and temples were raised; and a plebeian sector for bronze, iron, jade, bone, and coinage workshops and the residents of artisans, merchants, and farmers who worked nearby fields.

The transformation of urban morphology in the Warring States era readily can be seen at Linzi, the capital of Qi. Linzi featured a small palace sector in its southwestern corner enclosed by walls and containing an iron foundry and mint that adjoined a much larger and older city crisscrossed by streets ranging from 6 to 20 meters wide, forming a grid pattern (Figure 2.1). Linzi's palace

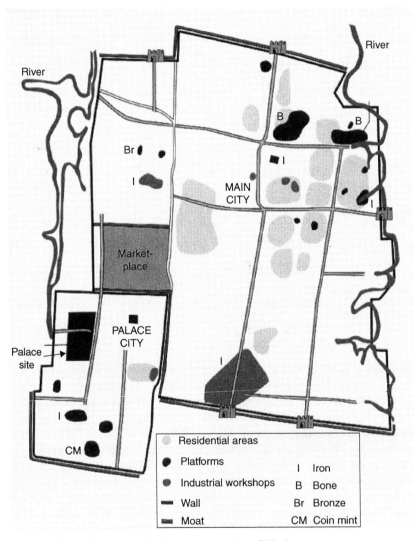

Figure 2.1 Archaeological reconstruction of Linzi

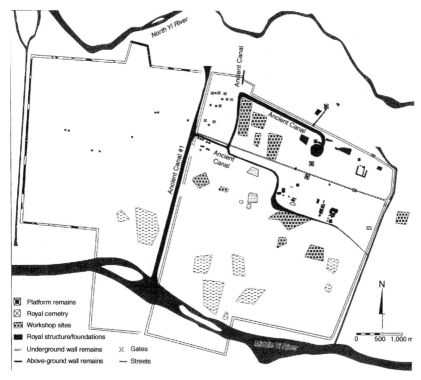

Figure 2.2 Archaeological reconstruction of Xiadu
Source: Chen Shen 2003: figure 12.1.

sector was a more recent addition, leading archaeologists to speculate that it
had been constructed by the Tian clan after they deposed Qi's ancestral
dynasty in 362 BCE. The workshops located within the palace sector undoubtedly were state-run enterprises, while smaller, privately operated workshops
were concentrated in the central, northeastern, and western portions of the
larger city.[64] This pattern also is seen in Xiadu in Yan, the largest of
the Warring States royal capitals, where large state-run foundries, mints, and
workshops clustered around the royal palace while smaller private workshops
were scattered throughout the plebeian residential areas (Figure 2.2). The
western walled sector of Xiadu was never occupied; apparently this enclosure
had been built in anticipation of future expansion of the city before Yan was
vanquished by Qin in 222 BCE.[65]

---

[64] Xu Hong 2000: 98–100.   [65] Chen Shen 2003.

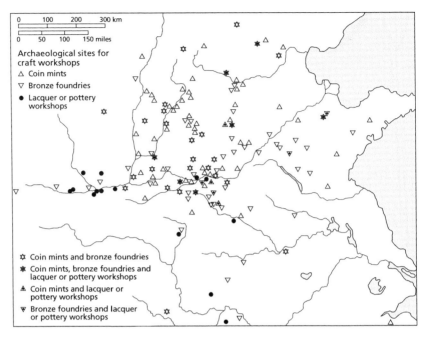

Map 2.5 Urban sites and economic activities in the Warring States period
Source: Emura 2005: 76, figure 23.

Even more significant than these large royal capitals, however, was the emergence of a dense network of smaller towns, more commercial in nature, in the southern portion of the Central Plain, especially in the states of Wei and Hann (roughly equivalent to modern Henan province). This region was the hub of the major trade routes and the most important iron-producing region. Archaeological evidence for the distribution of bronze and lacquer wares also is heavily concentrated in Wei and Hann as well as in the southern state of Chu (Map 2.5). Under Li Kui's regime, Wei had adopted policies intended to protect farmers from the vicissitudes of the market economy. But in the mid-fourth century BCE, during Bai Gui's tenure as prime minister, Wei pivoted toward a laissez-faire posture that allowed merchants considerable freedom from state control.[66] Subsequently Wei experienced vigorous commercial growth even as its military strength ebbed. In 289 BCE, when Qin recovered the Henei region it had lost to Wei in Li Kui's time, the Qin armies captured more than sixty walled towns. In 260 BCE, a Wei statesman boasted that the Wei territories east of the capital at Da Liang encompassed "seventeen large

---

[66] Emura 2005: 132–34.

xian cities, each with walls of a thousand *zhang* and a population of ten thousand households, along with thirty-plus small *xian* towns with marketplaces."[67] Unfortunately, this region has been repeatedly inundated by Yellow River floods and, as a glance at Map 2.4 shows, few Warring States cities have been excavated there.

The claim that many *xian* cities in Wei had populations of 10,000 households cannot be accepted at face value. Other sources suggest that the smaller towns had populations of around 1,000 persons, the larger cities 10,000 inhabitants, and the royal capitals perhaps many more – although the claim that Linzi numbered 70,000 households, attributed to a third-century BCE statesman, surely is an exaggeration.[68] Nonetheless, this depiction of a dense network of commercial towns blanketing the Wei territory appears to be valid. The leading commercial hubs all were located in the heart of the Central Plain (see Map 4.2). The city of Tao in Song, at the intersection of the principal east–west and north–south trade routes, was said to be "located at the center of the Subcelestial Realm, connected in the four directions to all of the states, a place where every sort of goods is exchanged."[69] Puyang, the capital of Wey, likewise prospered as a major crossroads of interstate trade.[70]

Archaeological research has confirmed the crucial role of Warring States cities as sites of mass production of industrial goods. Both bronze artifacts – especially weapons – and pottery commonly were marked with the name of the artisan who made them, a reflection of this shift toward mass production in large, state-run workshops. A third century BCE almanac for managing the organization of work throughout the year instructed that "goods must be inscribed with the name of their makers, so that their honesty can be scrutinized; if the craftsmanship is deficient, the maker must be punished, to eradicate such treachery."[71] Inscriptions on artifacts typically name the artisan, the workshop master, and the supervising official(s). Bronze ritual vessels cast in the state workshops in Wei specify the person who ordered vessel cast; the date of manufacture; the supervising official; the artisan; and the vessel's capacity and weight.[72] In many cases workshops were under

[67] Chapter 26, "Jian Tian Bing yu Liangnan zhang" 見田X於梁南章, in *ZGZH*: 165; see also Emura 2005: 78–87; Sahara 2002: 310.
[68] Emura 2005: 60. The figure of 70,000 households for the population of Linzi is recorded in *SJ* 69.2257. Linzi clearly was an impressive commercial metropolis in the eyes of contemporaries. In a speech to the Han Emperor Wudi (r. 141–87 BCE), a native of the Qi region claimed that Linzi had a population of 100,000 households and that in the numbers and wealth of its inhabitants the city surpassed the capital of Chang'an. See *SJ* 52.2008.
[69] *SJ* 129.3257. [70] Emura 2005: 93–94; Utsunomiya 1955: 110.
[71] "Mengdong ji" 孟冬紀, in *LSCQ*, 1: 516; for a slightly different translation, see Knoblock and Riegel 2000: 225. This passage also appears in Chapter 6, "Yueling" 月令, of the *Li ji*. See *LJ*, 2A:273–74.
[72] Huang Shengzhang 1974b.

the supervision of officials known as Sikou 司寇, originally an office charged with judicial and police duties. By this time Sikou often were appointed to supervise public works, since most of the artisans in state workshops were convict laborers.[73] Under the more centralized political regimes of the peripheral states, much industrial production was managed by the state. Although private workshops manufactured consumer goods, they did so under close supervision by state officials.[74]

In Qin, the manufacture and storage of weapons remained under the tight control of the central government. The inscriptions on Qin weapons often designate the area to which they were to be sent, often far from the place of manufacture. In the Jin successor states of Wei, Hann, and Zhao, by contrast, arms manufacture was decentralized. Arms workshops, which doubled as armories (*ku* 庫) for storing weapons, were found in many local cities – at least seventeen in the case of Wei.[75] The same pattern of regional variation is also found in coin manufacture. In contrast to the bureaucratic states of Qin, Chu, Qi, and Yan, where coinage was mostly restricted to central mints in the state capitals, many cities in the Jin successor states issued coins in their own name. Relatively few specimens from Wei, Hann, and Zhao designate capital cities; most of the coins issued by these states were cast in local mints, usually in the same cities that had weapons workshops. Moreover, the same mint cast many different types of currencies; the Hann city of Jinyang, for example, produced knife and spade currency and round coins, attesting to its connections to the Qi and Qin currency zones.

The evidence of coinage and weapons manufacture reinforces the conclusion that in contrast to the bureaucratic states of the periphery, where a high degree of central control over the internal economy prevailed, the cities of the Jin successor states enjoyed considerable political, military, and economic autonomy. In these cities, concentrated in the heartland of the Zhou ecumene, private commerce and an independent merchant class enjoyed greater freedom from state control.[76]

---

[73] Yang Kuan 1998: 107.

[74] For evidence of private enterprise in industries such as pottery, bone and stone ornaments, and iron tools in the states of Yan and Qin respectively, see Chen Shen 2003; He Qinggu 2003a.

[75] Huang Shengzhang 1974b: 40.

[76] Emura 2005: 116–37. Sahara (2002a: 152) disputes this view, arguing that the cities of the Jin successor states were primarily military cities under bureaucratic rule, but I find Emura's arguments more persuasive. Although defense and arms industries occupied a salient place in urban life and work everywhere, the Jin successor states can best be understood as leagues of allied cities markedly different from the centralized bureaucratic states in their political structure and economic life. For example, the Qin state created a parallel military field administration based on *jun* 郡 units (thirty-six altogether) – separate and superior to the *xian* units of its civil government – throughout its territories. The Jin successor states, by contrast, established only a few (three to six in number) *jun* as defensive buffers in frontier areas.

Cities also flourished as centers of trade as well as industry, although so far archaeological research has shed little light on the evolution of marketplaces as distinct urban spaces. In Spring and Autumn texts, the word *shi* 市refers to public gathering places within cities, the sites of festivals, citizen assemblies, and public executions, but with no mention of commercial activities.[77] By the mid-Warring States period, however, *shi* had acquired the meaning of urban marketplace; indeed, marketplaces had become synonymous with cities, as the frequent occurrence of the term *chengshiyi* 城市邑 ("settlements with walls and markets") attests. The practical value of commerce to the welfare of the state was cogently expressed in surviving fragments of the "Market laws" from the state of Qi:

In the realm of a true king there are no markets, nor does the hegemon need to set up shops and stalls. But a kingdom of middling size profits from commerce, and a small kingdom utterly depends on it. The market is the source of the hundred goods and the measure of the resources at the ruler's disposal. A kingdom of middling size able to profit from the market will become strong; a small kingdom able to profit from the market will remain secure. When the market flourishes, goods circulate; when goods circulate, the people ... [graph missing] and the wealth and possessions of the various states will arrive. When the wealth and possessions of the various states arrive, even a small kingdom will become rich.[78]

In contrast to the idyllic and peaceable times of the "true kings" of the early Zhou, in the fiercely competitive world of the Warring States the goods obtained from trade and the revenues generated by taxing commerce were vital to the state's survival. The value of commerce to the state was greatest in the smallest kingdoms, which lacked the manpower to field great armies.

Not surprisingly, autocratic monarchs kept a watchful eye on marketplaces, appointing inspectors to supervise the activities of merchants and to maintain order among potentially unruly urban crowds. At the Qin capital of Yong archaeologists have identified a rectangular walled area in the northwestern part of the city measuring 150 meters by 180 meters as a marketplace. Each wall had a single gate at its center, and the marketplace was internally divided by a grid of crisscrossing streets.[79] The "Market laws" of Qi prescribed that markets must be located in towns, and that the size of a marketplace be proportional to the size of the town; in the case of a royal capital, the market should be 400 paces square (roughly three times the size of the Yong market-place). Qi's "Market laws" also stipulated that the market should be enclosed

[77] Hori 1996: 211–14; Sahara 2002a: 307.
[78] Yinqueshan hanmu zhujian zhengli xiaozu 1985: 31.
[79] Yang Kuan 1998: 128. The date of the marketplace's construction is uncertain. Yong served as the Qin capital from 677 to 383 BCE, and remained an important city thereafter. Qin reportedly first instituted regulations for markets in 378 BCE.

by walls to restrict access, but with gates sufficiently large to permit the easy movement of goods. Shops should be arranged in orderly rows by trade, with the size of shops proportional to the dearness of its wares (more space was allowed for cheaper goods).[80] Unfortunately, we have no evidence, either textual or archaeological, for the organization of markets in the commercial cities of the Jin successor states.

Government inspectors routinely supervised commercial activities. Many Warring States pottery and lacquer artifacts are inscribed in ink with the graphs *shi* 市 ("marketplace") or *ting* 亭 (government post and police stations) – or the combination *shiting* 市亭 – which are believed to be marks of certification by local market inspectors responsible for ensuring the quality of goods.[81] A recently discovered cache of clay seals from the Chu city of Cai (no. 15 in Table 2.1) sheds additional light on government regulation of marketplaces. Many of these seals bear legends with the word *shi*, and attest to the existence of different types of markets, such as "night market" and "artisans' market." One unusual graph is believed to refer to private shops, and possibly attests to the presence of goldsmiths and shops selling fabrics and embroidery. A number of seals read "market container" or "Cai market container," presumably referring to the units of measurement in common use in Cai's marketplaces. The largest group of seals refers to "government storehouses" (*fu* 府), including "right storehouse"; "east (also west, north, and south) storehouse"; "east (also north) gate storehouse"; "customs storehouse"; and "grain storehouse." Other seals are inscribed with place-names, images of animals (perhaps trademarks), or the legends "trust" (*xin* 信), "honesty" (*du* 篤), and "pledge" (*zhi* 質). Although most of the seals came from Cai and elsewhere in Chu, a few seals are of Wei, Qin, and Qi provenance.[82] Taken together, the Cai seals testify to the city's vigorous commercial life, a multiplicity of markets, the presence of foreign merchants intermingled with local private traders, and also to the state's substantial involvement in the city's economy as a procurer of goods and regulator of market behavior.[83]

The emerging political economy of the fiscal state

Statesmen and philosophers of the Warring States period invariably defined agriculture as the "fundamental occupation" (*benye* 本業, *benshi* 本事), the staff of life for the people and the fount of wealth for the ruler. For proponents

---

[80] Yinqueshan hanmu zhujian zhengli xiaozu 1985: 32. See also Emura 2005: 160.
[81] Emura 2005: 117.   [82] Zhou Xiaolu and Lu Dongzhi 2005.
[83] Another group of seal specimens has now been identified as seals of government officials used to regulate the highly lucrative salt trade. See Zhao Ping'an 2004.

of the autocratic state, power stemmed from military strength, and increasing the population enabled the ruler to maintain larger armies. Thus the *Book of Lord Shang* asserted that "the security of the state depends on agriculture and war."[84] Statesmen such as Li Kui focused on the need to improve agricultural productivity through more intensive techniques of cultivation while protecting the farming population from the scourges of drought, flood, and the seasonal vicissitudes of the market. The older chapters of the *Guan Zi* likewise urged the ruler to increase the land under cultivation, ensure that agricultural tasks are not disrupted by untimely demands for labor and military service, and accumulate sufficient stocks of grain to support the people during times of dearth. In the oft-quoted words of this text, "the five grains and rice are the Masters of Destiny for the people."[85] But Confucian philosophers, too, insisted that the ruler must first provide for the material welfare of the people before he can train them to be moral subjects. In the words of Mencius, "this is the way of the common people: those with a secure means of livelihood (*hengchan* 恆產) will be steadfast in their hearts." Mencius further asserted that "benevolent government must begin with surveying and allocating lands. When boundaries are not drawn properly, neither the division of land according to the well-field system nor the levy of grain reserved for the ruler's emolument will be equitable."[86] According to Mencius, the "well-field system" (named after the Chinese graph for "water well," *jing* 井, which was seen as a visual representation of nine equal-sized plots of land) had been created by the sage-kings of yore to ensure the self-sufficiency of each household while providing the ruler with a modest share of the product of the land.

Just as there was common agreement on the primacy of agriculture as the mainstay of the economy, so too was there a growing awareness of the tension between the subsistence needs of the population and the demands of the autocratic state. Moreover, political leaders of the Warring States era began to recognize that left unchecked the market economy created inequalities of wealth inimical to both the power of the state and the welfare of the people. Initially, Chinese statesmen had expressed laissez-faire attitudes toward merchants and commercial activities. Zichan, explaining his refusal to assist a Jin minister in his efforts to obtain a jade ornament from a Zheng merchant, claimed that the ruler of Zheng had made a pact with city's merchants under which his government would not interfere with their business.[87] In a dialogue set in 523 BCE, the Qi minister Yan Ying criticized the Qi ruler for monopolizing the resources of mines, forests,

---

[84] Chapter 3, "Nongzhan" 農戰, in *SJS*: 22.
[85] Chapter 73, "Guoxu" 國蓄, in *GZ*, 3: 1259; see also Rickett 1998: 377.   [86] *Mencius* IIIA.3.
[87] Zhaogong 16th Year, in *ZZ*, 3A: 683–84.

and seas and allowing his palace women to commandeer goods from the capital's merchants without compensation. Subjects from outlying towns and rural areas who entered the capital had been summarily drafted into onerous labor service and forced to pay exorbitant customs duties. Surely, Yan Ying concluded, this predatory behavior would cause Qi's downfall.[88] Mencius, an arch critic of contemporary rulers' fixation on amassing wealth and power, claimed that in antiquity government officials merely supervised marketplaces to keep order, but did not interfere in the buying and selling of goods. Only when scoundrels began to hoard goods in order to manipulate prices did officials begin to tax commerce as a way of discouraging such despicable behavior.[89]

Mencius's conviction that the pursuit of profit inevitably sowed cupidity and deceit signaled an important shift in attitudes toward a merchant class that had now become a powerful force in economic affairs and in political life as well. Mencius's critique of the profit motive was widely shared across the philosophical spectrum, most emphatically by Mencius's staunchest adversaries, the Legalists. Statesmen such as Li Kui and Shang Yang deemed private commerce and the profiteering merchant class as threats to the commonweal embodied by the monarchal state. The Legalist philosopher Han Fei Zi concurred that the concentration of wealth in the hands of merchants undermined social order, above all because others would abandon the arduous work of husbandry to seek the easy profits of trade:

When office and rank can be bought, then none will despise merchants and artisans. When ill-gotten wealth and stocks of commodities fetch a good price in the marketplace, there will be no shortage of tradesmen. When jobbers and forestallers earn twice as much as farmers and enjoy greater esteem than soldiers or plowmen, then men of conscience and fortitude will be few and merchants and tradesmen will multiply.[90]

Thus Han Fei Zi deemed merchants to be one of the "five kinds of vermin" that the ruler must eradicate.

Nonetheless, even the Qin state sought not to stifle commerce but to regulate it. For example, Lü Buwei's blueprint for Qin's imperial rule stipulated that in mid-autumn, when farmers gather their harvest and put it up for sale, taxes on commerce should be lowered to encourage trade and the circulation of commodities:

In this month, adjust the levies at the border crossings and marketplaces to induce merchants and traders to come hither bearing goods and valuables, and in so doing benefit the people's livelihood.

---

[88] Zhaogong 20th Year, in *ZZ*, 3A: 706.   [89] *Mencius* IIB.10.
[90] Chapter 49, "Wudu"五蠹, in *HFZ*, 2: 1075–76.

When the various traders from the four quarters of the world
And those from the outlying provinces all arrive,
Then we will not lack for wealth and goods.
The ruler will not suffer a dearth of revenues,
And the hundred tasks all will be completed.[91]

Lü Buwei's advice here directly contradicted the *Book of Lord Shang*, which instead advocated onerous customs and market levies precisely to discourage commerce.[92] But numerous other contemporaries, including the Confucian Xun Zi and the authors of the *Guan Zi*, extolled the benefits of reducing customs duties and promoting foreign commerce.

Most representative, perhaps, of the emerging political economy of the Warring States era are the numerous essays incorporated into the *Guan Zi* treatise. The *Guan Zi* purports to record a series of Socratic dialogues between the first hegemon, Lord Huan of Qi, and his Machiavellian prime minister, Guan Zhong (*c.* 710–645 BCE), but the extant text dates from much later times. The older portions of the *Guan Zi* probably were composed at the Jixia Academy at the court of Qi during the last century of the Warring States era. These essays are eclectic in theme and spirit, representing a wide spectrum of philosophical principles. A more coherent set of economic doctrines – decidedly mercantilist and *dirigiste* in outlook – appears in the "Ratios of Exchange" chapters (chapters 68–85 of the received text), which most likely date from the first century of the Han dynasty. Although surely the work of several hands, the ideas in the "Ratios of Exchange" chapters are sufficiently consistent to consider them the product of a single author, who for the sake of convenience I will refer to as "Pseudo-Guanzi." We will examine the economic philosophy of Pseudo-Guanzi in the next chapter. Here I will confine my analysis to the earlier – and in many ways strikingly different – vision of political economy found in the older chapters, whose authors (again for heuristic purposes) I will refer to collectively as "Proto-Guanzi."[93]

The cardinal principle of Proto-Guanzi is the necessity for the ruler – as "shepherd of the people," to quote the title of the book's first chapter – to accumulate stores of grain and goods in order to provide for his subjects in times of dearth. The ruler must not only have the prudence to lay up stores; he must also have the magnanimity to share his wealth. Proto-Guanzi

---

[91] Chapter 8, "Zhongqiu ji" 中秋紀, in *LSCQ*, 1: 422; for a slightly different translation, see Knoblock and Riegel 2000: 192.

[92] Chapter 2, "Kenling" 墾令, in *SJS*: 17.

[93] This distinction between the economic philosophy of the later "Ratios of Exchange" chapters and that of the more eclectic older chapters is based on Kanaya 1987: 119–75, which I find to be the most perceptive analysis of the economic ideas in the *Guan Zi*. See also Hu Jichuang 1962, 1: 288–377; Rickett 1985, 1998. Chinese scholarship continues to portray the economic ideas of the *Guan Zi* in holistic terms. See for example Zhou Junmin 2003.

recognized the tensions and conflicts engendered by the emergence of the autocratic state and the market economy, as expressed in this terse formulation: "the rural areas compete with the marketplaces for inhabitants; private families compete with public storehouses for goods; gold competes with grain for value; the countryside competes with the court for suzerainty."[94] Production and exchange are both essential to the welfare of the state and the people, but the ruler must act to maintain the delicate balance between the two: if the profits of commerce exceed the returns from agriculture, farmers will abandon their lands; if the state imposes exorbitant taxes, the people will have no reserves in times of hardship. Seasonal and annual variations in the supply and demand for grain can cause ruinous gyrations in the price of foodstuffs, with potentially devastating consequences: cheap grain impoverishes producers, while dear grain imperils consumers. Thus – following in the footsteps of Li Kui – the wise ruler must intervene in markets to maintain price equilibrium.

Proto-Guanzi also enunciates what became the canonical conception of Chinese society as comprised of four functionally distinct classes: rulers (*shi* 士), farmers, artisans, and merchants. Each class has its proper and necessary role in society, but Proto-Guanzi insists that these occupations should be hereditary statuses passed from father to son, and indeed each class should dwell apart from the others. Interestingly, artisans are expected to reside at government workshops, while merchants occupy the marketplaces – further evidence of the prevalence of state-managed industry, in contrast to the more entrepreneurial world of commerce. This chapter also provides an archetypal statement of the behavior and activities of the merchant class:

Merchants observe outbreaks of dearth and starvation, scrutinize changes in the fortunes of states, study the patterns of the four seasons, and take notice of what goods are produced in each place. With this knowledge of prices in the marketplace, they gather up their stock of goods, load them on oxcarts and horses, and circulate throughout the four directions. Having reckoned what is abundant and what is scarce and calculated what is precious and what is worthless, they exchange what they possess for what they lack, buying cheap and selling dear . . . Marvelous and fantastic things arrive in timely fashion; rare and unusual goods readily gather. Day and night thus engaged, merchants tutor their sons and brothers, speaking the language of profit, teaching them the virtue of timeliness, and training them how to recognize the value of goods.[95]

---

[94] 野與市爭民, 家與府爭貨, 金與粟爭貴, 鄉與朝爭治. Chapter 3, "Quanxiu 權修," in *GZ*, 1: 52; for an alternative translation, see Rickett 1985: 94–5.

[95] Chapter 20, "Xiaokuang" 小匡, in *GZ*, 1: 402; cf. the translation in Rickett 1985: 327. A somewhat different version of this passage also is recorded in the *Guoyu*. See Chapter 6, "Qiyu" 齊語, in *GY*: 200–21.

Although this passage is remarkably free of moral judgment, in other places Proto-Guanzi inveighs against the unbridled pursuit of private commercial profit and its damaging effects on primary producers.

Ultimately, however, it is within the ruler's power to ensure the welfare and prosperity of his people. "If goods are plentiful and productive tasks properly regulated, there will be little need to seek blessings from Heaven," writes Proto-Guanzi in a chapter devoted to fiscal management. Although Proto-Guanzi repeatedly warns that extravagant and frivolous expenditures on the part of the ruler will impoverish the people and ultimately undermine the state, he advocates restraint, not austerity. The ruler must strike a balance between thrift and indulgence:

Gold is the standard of expenditures. The prince who discerns the fundamental laws of gold will understand the dangers of parsimony and prodigality. Knowing this, he will exercise moderation in his expenditures.

Now, parsimony in expenditure harms husbandry, while prodigality in expenditure harms trade. Parsimony causes the value of gold to fall, and when gold is cheap productive tasks remain uncompleted. For this reason, then, parsimony is harmful to husbandry. Prodigality in expenditure, by contrast, causes the value of gold to rise, and when gold is dear, the value of goods declines. For this reason, prodigality harms trade.

Thus goods remain unsold and the peoples suffer privation: such a state of affairs results from ignorance of the standard of expenditures. Production halts and yet the surfeit of goods grows: such a state of affairs results from ignorance of the need to moderate expenditures.[96]

Proto-Guanzi here denies that goods or money have value in themselves. It is the ruler, through his fiscal policies, that establishes their relative values. Meager revenue extraction and spending will reduce the demand for gold, and the resulting surplus of money in the market causes prices to rise. Conversely, excessive taxation and expenditure, by increasing the demand for gold, induces deflation and discourages production. Thus the inordinately frugal ruler is just as harmful as the extravagantly profligate one.

One chapter of the *Guan Zi*, entitled "On extravagance in spending" – a chapter sufficiently idiosyncratic that it must be considered a separate work – goes even further in stressing the positive value of state expenditures as a stimulus to economic prosperity. This chapter begins with the premise – also recognized by the Legalist Han Fei Zi – that population growth has the unfortunate consequences of raising land prices and fomenting competition among farmers, bringing ruin and unemployment to many families. But it is precisely the ostentatious lifestyles of the rich – for example, by building magnificent mausolea using the costliest materials and elaborate assemblages of grave goods – that will bring employment to the poor: "let the rich live in

---

[96] Chapter 5, "Chengma" 乘馬, in *GZ*, 1: 88–89; cf. the translation in Rickett 1985: 118.

luxury and the poor work for them." This text expresses rare enthusiasm for the contributions of commerce and conspicuous consumption to the economic vitality of the realm:

Itinerant merchants are no ordinary subjects. They claim no locality as their home, not do they serve any single prince. They sell goods to earn a profit, but they do not buy simply to acquire possessions. From the mountains and forests of the state they take what they can for profit; in the marketplaces of the capital they double the return on their investment. Thus when those on high spend extravagantly while those below live in luxury, the prince and his ministers each benefit. When those on high and those below treat each other as kinsmen, the prince and his ministers do not hoard their wealth for their private enjoyment. This being so, the poor will have work to do and food to eat.[97]

This uncommon defense of the economic benefits of public spending is not supported elsewhere in the *Guan Zi*, but it is at least consistent with Proto-Guanzi's critique of excessive frugality on the part of the ruler.

Leaving aside the chapter "On extravagance in spending," the basic tenets of political economy espoused by Proto-Guanzi were widely shared among contemporary philosophers and statesmen. Although Confucians repudiated the unvarnished goal of enriching the state to bolster its military might, they readily agreed that the ruler bore responsibility for the smooth functioning of markets so that his people would not lack the necessities of life. For example, Xun Zi described an economy in which the ruler manages resources for the benefit of all, ensuring the widest possible circulation of goods but extracting only modest revenues:

These are the laws of a true king: he establishes fair rates of taxation, regulates the people's livelihood, and disposes the myriad goods, thereby providing nourishment to all of his subjects. He assesses a tax of one-tenth of the produce of the land; his officials inspect goods at border crossings and marketplaces but levy no excises; he dictates the times when the mountains, forests, marshes, and fishing grounds will be closed or opened for the people's use without imposing excises on them; and his officials inspect arable lands and grade them according to their productivity. He determines tribute payments after taking into account the distances over which they must be conveyed. He ensures the free movement of goods and grains so that their circulation is not hindered or obstructed. Goods flow to where the need for them arises, and all within the four seas are like one family.[98]

But the quest to reap the benefits of private commerce both to provide for the people's livelihood and to satisfy the ruler's need for revenue proved difficult.

---

[97] Chapter 35, "Chimi" 侈靡, in *GZ*, 2: 652, 730; cf. translations in Rickett 1998: 311, 330.
[98] Chapter 9, "Wangzhi," in *XZ*: 175. Mencius (VIB.7) claimed that the former Qi hegemon, Lord Huan, allowed grain to be sold freely across state borders, but his descendants failed to follow his precedent.

Legalist philosophers, leery of the corrosive effects of private wealth and economic inequality, dissented from this embrace of even a well-regulated market economy. In their view, the sole means of securing the welfare of the people depended on first enriching the state, which in turn required that the state eradicate the self-interested aggrandizement epitomized by the entrepreneurial merchant.

The political economy of the Warring States era reflected a world in which codified law supplanted ritually governed norms and the patrimonial rights of the ruling elite had been transformed into the public powers of the state. A new political formation – the *fiscal state* – had eclipsed the domainal regimes of the Spring and Autumn city-states.[99] The emerging fiscal state was premised on the subordination of society – constituted by individual conjugal households – to the autocratic ruler through taxation, labor service, and military conscription. By centralizing control over economic resources and enhancing his military power, the ruler safeguarded his realm against foreign rivals, promoted the economic welfare of his subjects, and ensured that the public good would prevail over private interests. In addition, the state regulated market exchange, arbitrated disputes over exchange and property rights, and secured control over production of strategic goods. To be sure, Confucian philosophers abhorred "fiscalist ministers" (*julian zhi chen* 聚斂之臣) focused single-mindedly on amassing revenues without regard for its effects on the people.[100] Xun Zi predicted that if the ruler devoted himself solely to amassing revenues (*julian*) his state would surely perish.[101] But the Qin and Han empires fully embraced the principles of the fiscal state, and Confucian statesmen – with a few exceptions – would come to accept it as a pragmatic necessity.

---

[99] Although my use of the concept of fiscal state derives from Schumpeter's concept of the tax state (see references cited in Chapter 1, note 70), it is not equivalent to Schumpeter's concept, which Schumpeter identified with the modern, democratic nation-state. Recent scholarship (Bonney 1999; Yun-Casalilla 2012) largely continues to see the "fiscal state" as a modern product of the Western historical experience, despite ample evidence that its fundamental principles appeared in China as early as the Warring States period. See Deng 2012. The definition of "fiscal state" in the European scholarship is focused on the capacity to borrow through public debt and the constraints imposed on its power to borrow and tax. The former issue was irrelevant to the Chinese imperial state, and the latter was mediated through much different institutions.

[100] Confucius renounced his disciple Ran Qiu for abetting a tyrannical chief minister's efforts to "amass revenues" (*julian*) and thus make himself "richer than the Duke of Zhou." See *Analects* 11.17. The *locus classicus* for the term *julian zhi chen* is the Han-era Confucian treatise *The Great Learning*. See Chapter 42, "Daxue 大學," in *LJ*, 2A: 778. Following Robert Hartwell, I borrow the term "fiscalist" from *fiscalisme*, employed in early modern France to denote the state's interventions in industrial production for the purpose of generating greater revenues. See Heckscher 1955, 1: 178–84.

[101] Chapter 9, "Wangzhi," in *XZ*: 168.

Conclusion

The patrimonial state of the Western Zhou rested on a ritual order in which the king bestowed rank, office, and wealth according to kinship status and service to the royal house. As royal authority ebbed, regional domains asserted their independence from the Zhou kings, a trend already well underway before the fall of the Western Zhou in 771 BCE. Nonetheless, aristocratic status, kinship hierarchy, and ritual protocol continued to define the social order of the emerging city-state polities of the early Spring and Autumn era. Indeed, the culture of the ruling elite became increasingly homogeneous throughout the expanding Zhou ecumene during this period. But the constant warfare of the Spring and Autumn world unleashed new forces – including the militarization of society, the rise of the citizenry, and the devolution of power from hereditary rulers to their ministers and generals – that engulfed the lineage-based polities in perpetual internecine conflict. In the long-run, this endemic disorder spawned more centralized and bureaucratic regimes that absorbed many defunct city-states into expanding territorial states.

From c. 600 BCE, the centralization of power in the hands of powerful monarchies and the progress of territorial consolidation dramatically reshaped the economic and social structure of the Zhou ecumene. The Iron Age revolution had an equally convulsive impact on the social order. Iron metallurgy transformed the technologies of both destruction and production, further accelerating the centralization of state power. The rise of the autocratic state in the Warring States period was driven by the mobilization of men and materiel for war, which in turn required new techniques of political, economic, and legal control that fostered a direct relationship between the state and its subjects. These policies established the family farm as the mainstay of agricultural production and the conjugal household as the fundamental social unit that supplied revenues, conscript labor, and military recruits to the state. Agricultural production surged, and increasing numbers of people were employed in mining, logging, craft production, and transportation. Mass production in government-managed workshops supplied not only the state but also urban consumers with a wide range of goods. At the same time long-distance trade flourished, abetted by regional specialization of production, the emergence of an independent merchant class, and the introduction of bronze currency. Material wealth and political office superseded descent and rank as the basis for social distinction. Although Confucian traditionalists bemoaned the demise of the patrimonial state, already by the time of Mencius in the fourth century BCE a new calculus of economic livelihood – the fiscal state – had eclipsed the domainal regimes of the Spring and Autumn city-states. The ruler exercised unprecedented authority to extract economic resources in the name of the commonwealth. Yet he was also obliged to balance his determination to enhance the wealth and power of the state with the subsistence needs of his subjects.

By the late Warring States period, two distinctive patterns of economic development had emerged. In the thickly settled heartland of the North China Plain, central government authority weakened after the division of Jin into the three separate states of Wei, Hann, and Zhao in 453 BCE. In this region local cities and their merchant and artisan classes enjoyed considerable autonomy from their royal overlords. Private entrepreneurship stimulated industrial and commercial expansion. In the peripheral states of Qin, Chu, Qi, and Yan, by contrast, autocratic rulers established the bureaucratic institutions to control economic resources that became the hallmarks of the fiscal state. In these states industrial production was concentrated in state-managed work-shops and officials exercised much tighter control over trade. The latter pattern of strong state control of the economy would prevail after the formation of a unified empire under the Qin in 221 BCE.

3   Economic foundations of the universal empire (250 to 81 BCE)

Many of imperial China's political institutions and practices took shape during the reign of King Zheng of Qin (r. 247–210 BCE), first as king of Qin and ultimately as China's first emperor. The final triumph of Qin over its last remaining adversaries in 221 BCE owed much to the First Emperor's ruthless ambition and political acumen. The First Emperor vowed that his dynasty would last "for ten thousand generations," but the Qin state quickly fell into disarray after the emperor's death in 210 BCE. His successor was murdered in 207 BCE, plunging China once again into strife and war. It has become commonplace to conclude that the Qin fashioned a strategy for conquest but failed to develop a plan for governing; such an inference is mere shibboleth, however. The Qin also established the institutional infrastructure and political practices that made possible the creation of a unified empire over a vast territory.

The military triumph of Qin owed not to any advantage in arms or tactics but rather the state's mobilization of the entire society for warfare. The army served as the model for the organization of society. Qin officials enrolled the entire population into units of five households for purposes of taxation, military service, and public works construction. Social hierarchy was based on military rank. Generous rewards and promotions were doled out to meritorious soldiers and farmers. Local officials were held to exacting standards in the execution of their duties and faced harsh punishment for even slight shortcomings. In the words of the contemporary Confucian philosopher Xun Zi, the rulers of Qin "employ their people harshly, terrorize them with authority, embitter them with hardship, coax them with rewards, and cow them with punishments."[1]

As we observed in Chapter 2, the centralizing regimes of the Warring States era replaced patrimonial governance with a fiscal state. The fiscal state would remain the foundation of imperial rule, but it assumed different forms over the long arc of imperial history. The distinctive form of the fiscal state during

[1] Chapter 15, "Yibing" 議兵, in *XZ*: 317; translation from Watson 1967: 61–62.

the Qin and early Han empires can be categorized as a *military-physiocratic state* that fused a system of social ranking and obligations derived from military organization with an agrarian economic base. The Qin-Han rulers shared the physiocratic disdain – most cogently expressed by Legalist philosophers – for commerce as inherently sterile. Labor was considered the crucial resource, and the state mobilized slaves, convicts, and ordinary conscripts to work not only in its mines, workshops, and plantations but also on massive construction projects. The vital importance of labor also can be seen in a system of state extraction focused on labor services equally apportioned among all adults. Mobilization of labor in turn was predicated on the capacity of the state to penetrate local society through meticulous record-keeping on a scale scarcely imagined before modern times.

Although the Qin Empire barely lasted fifteen years, its legacy profoundly influenced its long-lived successor, Han (202 BCE–220 CE). The First Emperor of Qin was vilified from every quarter during the Han, yet the early Han emperors adopted many features of Qin government. As much as Legalist and Confucian statesmen differed on the proper role of government in economic life, both condemned the concentration of wealth in the hands of "aggrandizing" landowners and merchants. Legalists and Confucians also agreed that the legitimacy of the emperor to a significant degree depended on the economic well-being of his subjects. The Han, like the Qin, was committed to the smallholder family farm as the foundation of popular welfare. Many basic elements of Qin rule – including the establishment of the household as the basic social and fiscal unit, the use of merit ranks to award landed property, the legal tenet of mutual responsibility and shared liability among kinfolk and neighbors, and strict regulation of commerce and industry – became cornerstones of Han imperial governance as well.

Nonetheless, the early Han rulers distanced themselves from the excesses of the Qin regime. Professing to return to the benevolent rule of the ancient sage kings, they revived the principles of shared governance embedded in the patrimonial state. The first Han emperor, Liu Bang (Emperor Gaozu, r. 202–195 BCE), awarded sovereign rights over much of his territory to imperial kinsmen, in imitation of the early Zhou kings. The Huang-Lao philosophy of government, in which the supreme authority of the universal monarch is subject to the tenets of natural law, enjoyed great popularity in the early Han. Liu Bang's son, Emperor Wen (r. 180–157 BCE), consciously emulated the Huang-Lao ideal of a ruler who ensures the economic well-being of his subjects through personal frugality, minimal taxation, and refraining from disrupting their livelihood.[2] But Emperor Wu (r. 141–87 BCE)

---

[2] On the political and economic principles of Huang-Lao philosophy, see Peerenboom 1993.

repudiated Wen's laissez-faire policies and restored the highly centralized form of government that existed under the Qin Empire. Wu's regime enacted sweeping institutional reforms that empowered the state to seize control over much of private industry and commerce. This unprecedented intrusion of the autocratic state into economic life in turn provoked sharp conservative reaction, ultimately leading to the repeal of much of Wu's statist agenda.

Our knowledge of this era of Chinese history has been greatly amplified by the progress of archaeological research and the recovery of documents excavated from tombs. In the 1930s, a large cache of well-preserved administrative records dating from the mid-Han era were discovered at Juyan (Edsin-gol) in Gansu, the site of a major Han frontier garrison.[3] The Juyan manuscripts proved especially valuable because they offered a glimpse of local society and ordinary subjects – albeit for a frontier military colony that was hardly typical of the Han Empire as a whole – scarcely represented in the transmitted texts that have survived into modern times. With the rapid advance of archaeological investigation in recent decades, as many as 150 sites have now yielded specimens of writing, although the types, quantities, and legibility of these documents vary widely.[4] Among the caches of excavated manuscripts most important to the study of economic history are the Shuihudi documents, which include a corpus of administrative statutes placed in the tomb of a Qin local official who died c. 217 BCE;[5] the Zhangjiashan manuscripts, which preserve a portion of the "Statutes and Ordinances of the Second Year" issued by the Han court in 186 BCE;[6] and the Fenghuangshan manuscripts, among which the records of a local tax collector of the mid-second century BCE are especially illuminating. The excavated manuscripts not only provide us with new types of documentary sources, but they also cast new light on transmitted texts. For example, given the close affinities between the corpus of excavated Qin legal and administrative statutes and the *Rituals of Zhou* we can now recognize that the latter text – despite its later enshrinement in the Confucian canon – actually reflects the principles and forms of Qin imperial government.[7]

---

[3] The Juyan documents were written with brush and ink on wood slips or boards. More commonly during this era texts were written on silk or bamboo slips, but mulberry trees and bamboo did not grow in the arid northwestern region in which Juyan was located. The widespread adoption of paper for record-keeping in the first century CE had adverse consequences for historians: paper is more fragile than bamboo or wood and virtually no paper documents dating before the seventh century have survived. Loewe (1967) remains the most important study in English of the initial cache of Juyan documents.

[4] For an introduction to the excavated manuscripts from the Qin-Han period, see Giele 2010.

[5] For a translation, see Hulsewé 1985b.

[6] For brief introductions, see Li Xueqin and Xing Wen 2001; Loewe 2010a. A full English translation is in preparation (Barbieri-Low and Yates forthcoming).

[7] Li Xueqin 1999; Schaberg 2010.

Organizing imperial society: household registration, military service, and land tenure

Population registration was an essential building block for the construction of the autocratic state. The fundamental ethos of population registration under the autocratic state was summed up by the guiding principle of "register households in order to make the people equal" (*bianhu qimin* 編戶齊民). Civil registration became a crucial mechanism for eliminating the special status and privileges of the nobility and reducing the whole free population to common and equal status as subjects of the ruler.[8] Shang Yang's reforms compelled the division of kinship units into households composed of a married couple and their minor children.[9] The conjugal household became the basic unit of production, taxation, and social reproduction. Upon reaching adulthood, each son was to be given his share of the family patrimony in order to live apart as a separate household. Individual households were required to provide both statutory labor service and military service on a regular basis. Property rights were invested in the conjugal family as well, and property was transmitted through the patriline from fathers to sons, who formed separate patrilines.

The Qin state applied a military model of hierarchical organization and discipline to civil governance. Shang Yang's reforms – which, we must keep in mind, were based on existing practices in Wei and other Central Plain states – created a multitiered administrative hierarchy connecting subjects to rulers through a military-style chain of command. Even before Shang's time the Qin state organized its subjects into units of five families – which the Shuihudi manuscripts refer to as *wu* (伍) – that served as the basis for taxation and conscription.[10] As noted in Chapter 2, the entire *wu* group shared joint legal liability for the criminal actions of any of its members. The *wu* groupings were based on residential proximity rather than kinship connections.

No population registers from the Warring States era survive, but a speech recorded in the *Guan Zi* provides a revealing glimpse of the kinds of information deemed pertinent to proper governance:

Inquire about the orphans of those who died in war: are there any who do not have arable lands and dwellings? Inquire how many young and able-bodied men have not yet performed military service. Inquire about the widows of those who died in war: do they receive the grain allowances to which they are entitled?

---

[8] There were exceptions to this principle of equality. As we will see below, the Qin instituted a new social hierarchy based on military rank, and slaves and convicts constituted important categories of unfree persons.

[9] Under Qin law, the household was a co-resident group, including bondservants. However, co-residence itself did not confer legal status as a single household. See Hori 1996: 56–61, 75–76.

[10] Yates 1987.

... Make inquiries to determine the numbers of unmarried men, widowed women, and destitute or sick persons. Inquire about those exiled from the realm: to what clans do they belong? Inquire about the honorable families in the countryside: how many people do they support? Inquire about the poor townfolk; how many of them have gone into debt to feed themselves? Inquire how many families tend gardens to feed themselves. How many have cleared lands and cultivate them? How many officers (*shi* 士) cultivate land themselves? Inquire about the poor in the countryside: which lineages have they descended from?

... Inquire about the men and women who possess skills: how many can be usefully employed to make sturdy equipment? How many unmarried women remain at home engaged in domestic labor? How many merely depend on the state to fill their bellies? How many people are fed by the labor of a single individual? Inquire about the numbers of war chariots. How many privately owned draft horses are there, and how many privately owned carts?[11]

The full list of items about which officials should collect data runs much longer. Regardless of whether Warring States governments possessed the means to accumulate such detailed information about their subjects, knowledge of the productive capacity of the population, its consumption needs, and the resources available for waging war was an urgent priority. Noteworthy here, too, is the emphasis on maximizing the productive labor of women.[12]

The fullest description of the procedures for population registration has been preserved in the *Rituals of Zhou* – a prescriptive text, to be sure, but one that reflects the actual practices revealed by the excavated Qin-era documents. According to this text, local officials at the canton (*xiang* 鄉)[13] level were obliged "to apply the state's assessment rules and periodically investigate the numbers of individuals in each household; to distinguish the household's elderly and young, noble and base, lame and infirm, and its livestock resources; and to determine who is liable for labor service and who should be exempted."[14] Parallel passages add that the household surveys also

---

[11] Chapter 24, "Wen" 問, in *GZ*, 1: 486–87. For a full translation of this chapter, see Rickett 1985: 368–75.

[12] The *Guan Zi* treatise repeatedly underscores the economic value of women's labor, particularly in textile manufacture. See Chin 2014: 194–99.

[13] The canton (*xiang*) – in theory consisting of 1,000 to 5,000 households, but in actuality somewhat smaller, ranging from 300 to 2,000 households (Huang Jinyan 2005: 151) – was the basic unit of local government. Each *xiang* encompassed from ten to several dozen *li* settlements (which seem to have ranged from 10 to 100 households, with an average of 40–50 households). Whereas *xiang* were arbitrary administrative units, *li* denoted actual settlements (villages or urban neighborhoods). See Du Zhengsheng 1990: 108–15; He Shuangquan 1989: 179–80. The administrative functions of *xiang* under the Qin Empire encompassed management of state-owned lands, forests, pastures, granaries, and workshops; tax collection; assignment of labor services; policing and administration of justice; and supervision of agriculture and markets. See Hashimoto 2007.

[14] "Xiangshi" 鄉師, in *ZL*, 2A: 102. According to the *Rituals of Zhou*, children were recorded in the household registers once they reached the age of "teething" (defined as 8 months for boys,

registered weapons in the family's possession.[15] According to a sample form found among the Shuihudi manuscripts, Qin population registers listed the names, marital status, and service liability of the household head, his wife and children, and slaves. In addition, the register should contain information on the household's movable property ("clothes and utensils"), domestic animals, and the general dimensions of the dwelling (the number of gates and court-yards, and whether the roof was tiled or not).[16] Ages were not recorded, but the height of male children was. The Qin dynasty began to require that men report their age only from 231 BCE. Previously, liability for military service was determined by height rather than age, no doubt testifying to the limited reliability of birth records in the population registers prior to that time. The *Rituals of Zhou* states that military service was required of inhabitants of the capital who were 7 *chi* tall (161 cm) and under the age of 60 and rural inhabitants who were 6 *chi* (138 cm) and not yet 65 years old. In the Qin period the height requirement for military conscription was 7.1 *chi* (163 cm).[17]

The earliest extant specimens of household registration yet discovered were found among the Liye manuscripts, in the former territory of Chu, and date from the time of the Qin Empire. Of twenty-four registers from a single *li*, fifteen are sufficiently legible to determine the membership and structure of the household. The registers follow a standard format, recording the name of the *li* and the members of the household grouped according to labor service status (adult males; adult females; minor males; minor females; and persons exempt from service duty, such as elderly women and slaves). As we would expect, the conjugal family was the norm: in twelve of the fifteen cases, the households were conjugal families (in two cases including the widowed mother of the head of the household); in one case the household included an unmarried brother, while the remaining two households were joint families composed of two or three married brothers and their children. Although the Liye manuscripts do not provide all the information specified in the Shuihudi sample form, the differentiation of household members

---

7 months for girls), a reflection of the high infant mortality within the first six months of birth common to all premodern populations.

[15] Given the dramatic militarization of society during this period, the registration of weapons is hardly surprising. But the major polities adopted different policies toward private possession of weapons. In Chu, where weapons are wholly absent from tombs before the fifth century BCE, roughly half of all male tombs of the Warring States era contain weapons along with other artifacts that were the personal possessions of the individual. Qin tombs, by contrast, contain no weapons at all. Apparently the Qin officials kept weapons secured in state arsenals and distributed them to soldiers only when they were on active duty. See von Falkenhausen 2006: 384, 413.

[16] Du Zhengsheng 1990: 7.

[17] Ibid.: 17–21. The average height of soldiers recorded in the Han period military registers from Juyan was 168 cm (ibid.: 18).

by labor service status reflected the Qin state's overriding concern with mobilizing the labor power of its subjects.[18]

It is important to keep in mind that the concept of taxation (*fu* 賦) had originated in the obligation to perform military service, and the fiscal policies adopted by the Warring States regimes remained strongly imbued with the notion of taxation as a means of fortifying the military strength of the state. The Qin Empire apparently did not fully implement the Legalist principle – enunciated in the *Book of Lord Shang* – of imposing universal military conscription on women as well as men. But women comprised a crucial part of the labor resources mobilized by the state.[19] The household levy (*hufu* 戶賦) enacted in Qin by Shang Yang in 348 BCE imposed military service on adult males and conscript labor on all adults in addition to the land tax collected in grain. Unfortunately, the excavated Qin texts do not specify the tax obligations under the household levy except for payments of fodder. Generally speaking, the Warring States kingdoms collected a land tax amounting to 10 percent of the harvest. The excavated Qin documents suggest that the tax rate in grain was adjusted annually depending on harvest yields.[20] It is clear that some portion of the Qin household levy was collected in coin, but the origins of this practice remain unknown (it perhaps began with the issue of the Banliang coin by the Qin state *c.* 336 BCE).

Household registration also provided the basis for state land allocations. The practice of allocating lands to individual households had been widely adopted in the core states of the Central Plain in the late Spring and Autumn era. Shang Yang's reforms sought to deprive the hereditary nobility of its special status and privileges and instead create a new social hierarchy based on meritorious military service. He promulgated a steeply graded system of seventeen military ranks that entitled individuals to specific legal and economic prerogatives including allocations of arable land and dwellings, a practice known as *mingtianzhai* 名田宅.[21] The institution of land allocations (known more

---

[18] Chen Jie 2009; Lai Ming-chiu 2009; Washio 2009: 148–54. Liye was located on the remote periphery of Chu, in western Hunan, and the simplified contents of these registers may reflect its marginal location.

[19] A passage in *Mo Zi* dated to the Qin era famously depicts women taking up arms to defend a city, but there is no confirmation that the Qin actually conscripted women into military service. Later censure of Qin rule emphasized the harsh burdens of military service imposed on men and the conscription of women to perform corvée labor transporting tax revenues to the capital. See Zhang Rongqiang 2005: 31–32.

[20] Yang Zhenhong 2009: 173–81.

[21] Zhu Shaohou 1985: 16–24. The Han historian Sima Qian (*SJ* 78.2230) described Shang Yang's reform as "designating lands and dwellings according to the individual's military service, and allowing them to possess slaves and clothing according to family rank" (各以差次名田宅,臣妾衣服以家次). The quotas of lands and dwellings for each rank preserved in the Zhangjiashan manuscripts are believed to derive from the system in place under the Qin Empire. See Yang Zhenhong 2003, 2009: 126–86.

generally as *fentian* 分田) was implemented not only by Qin but also by the other major states of the Warring States era.

Civil registration served other purposes as well. The growing economic complexity and geographic mobility of the Warring States era posed a challenge to the autocratic state, which was premised on a rigidly immobile social order. The *Book of Lord Shang* emphasized that it is only by knowing the names of his subjects and fixing their residence that the ruler can gather the resources he requires and the people can obtain the lands and dwellings they need for their subsistence.[22] An article in the Wei Code of 252 BCE stipulated that transients without a stable domicile or occupation were prohibited from forming households or receiving land allocations from the state.[23] The Qin legal code deemed unauthorized change of residence a heinous crime punishable by convict labor servitude. Numerous treatises on political philosophy written in this period describe a world in which the state has spun a tightly meshed net of surveillance which scarcely anyone could elude.

Social stability required not only geographic immobility, but occupational immobility as well. In a speech recorded in several Warring States texts, Guan Zhong pronounces that "in ancient times, the sage-kings brought order to the world by grouping the citizens into three armies and organizing the rural inhabitants into units of five families; they fixed the people's dwelling places and ensured that all have their proper occupation." Guan Zhong then goes on to say that the capital should be divided into twenty-one districts, six to house merchants and artisans and fifteen reserved for officers and farmers who serve in the ruler's armies (here again we see that the discrimination against merchants and artisans was tied to their exclusion from military service). Artisans were to be assigned to government workshops, while merchants were required to conduct their business in designated market-places under the supervision of state officials.[24] This principle of fixed occupational statuses became central to the political economy of the Confucian philosopher Xun Zi as well. According to Xun Zi, social order required a clearly demarcated division of labor in which all individuals worked at an

---

[22] Chapter 15, "Laimin" 徠民, in *SJS*: 87. See also Du Zhengsheng 1990: 34; Cao Lüning 2002: 70.

[23] Most scholars have interpreted this passage as referring to itinerant merchants (e.g., Du Zhengsheng 1990: 182; Hori 1996: 55; Sahara 2002a: 312). Cao Lüning (2002: 64–72) disputed this consensus view and contended that the targets of this ordinance were rootless "vagrants" rather than merchants.

[24] "Qiyu" 齊語, in *GY*, 6.219; the same statement appears in the "Xiaokuang" 小匡 chapter of the *Guan Zi* (*GZ*, 1: 480); for a translation of the full passage, see Rickett 1985: 323–24. In another passage, Proto-Guanzi advises that officials must examine foreign visitors and take note of each person's name, "complexion," and occupational status: chapter 24, "Wen" 問, *GZ*, 1: 499.

occupation suitable to their talents and received their appropriate share (*fen* 分) of the wealth produced by society.[25]

Merchants, of course, epitomized the geographic and occupational mobility that the architects of the Qin state feared. For the most part Qin policies concentrated on regulating the activities of foreign merchants, not natives. The earliest evidence of legal discrimination against merchants dates only from after the founding of the empire. In 214 BCE the Qin enacted a deportation law that authorized the impressment of merchants and other kinds of transients into military service on the distant northern and southern frontiers. These frontier guard duties had aroused widespread resentment and resistance among the general population. The Qin state compiled "marketplace registers" (*shiji* 市籍) that listed merchants and tradesmen separate from the general population. Those currently enrolled on the marketplace registers – or whose parents or grandparents had been so registered – were subject to these deportation orders.[26] Scholars disagree on the question of whether marketplace registration was based on the current occupation of individuals or instead inherited from one's forebears, but certainly the trend was to treat it as a hereditary status. All persons who traveled away from their native place were required to carry passports, and itinerant merchants had to register with local officials to obtain permission to sell their wares. Social and economic restrictions on merchants became more stringent under the Han, when marketplace registers were used to requisition goods for official use and to impose a broader range of legal discriminations (for example, merchants and artisans at times were forbidden to hold government office, or to own arable land).[27]

The Zhangjiashan and Juyan manuscripts confirm that the Han essentially retained the Qin blueprint for population registration. The "Household Statutes" from Zhangjiashan specifies five types of registers compiled by local officials that listed household members, landed property, dwellings and gardens, and tax and service obligations. Local officials were obliged to record inheritances and transfers of property on these registers.[28] Annual household surveys were conducted in the eighth lunar month, and local officials relayed aggregate information to the central government through a procedure referred to as "submitted accounts" (*shangji* 上計) in the third lunar month.[29] The types of statistical information recorded in "submitted accounts" can be seen in the surviving specimen for Donghai 東海 commandery (in the lower Huai River valley of eastern China) for 13 BCE, shown in Table 3.1.

---

[25] This theme is enunciated most forcefully in the "Regulations of the King" and "Enriching the State" chapters of Xunzi's work. See Knoblock 1988: II: 85–138.

[26] Yamada 1979, 1988: 12–13; Shigechika 1990: 28–29; Cao Lüning 2002: 64–72; Sahara 2002a: 312–13; Barbieri-Low 2007: 126.

[27] Barbieri-Low 2007: 126–27; Yamada 1979.   [28] Zhu Honglin 2008: 243–56.

[29] Satō 1967: 2–7; Hori 1996: 62–63.

Table 3.1 *"Submitted account" for Donghai commandery, 13 BCE*

Population		
Local jurisdictions	38	18 counties 縣, 18 nobilities 侯國, 2 estates 邑
Total *xiang* 鄉	170	1,566 households per *xiang*
Total *li* 里	2,534	14.9 *li* per *xiang*
Households 戶	266,290	105 households per *li*
Individuals 口	1,397,343	5.25 persons per household
Males	706,064	50.2 percent of total
Females	688,132	49.8 percent of total
Revenue		
Total registered land (*qing* 頃)	512,092	192 *mu* per household
Land planted in wheat/barley* (*qing*)	107,380	40.3 *mu* per household
Total coin revenue (coins)	266,642,506	190 coins per capita
Total grain revenue (*shi* 石)	506,637	0.36 *shi* per capita
		0.047 *shi* per *mu* planted in grain

*At this time the word *mai* 麥 referred to both wheat and barley.
Sources: Lianyungang shi bowuguan 1996: 26; Gao Min 2004: 95–6.

The Han founder, seeking to reward the soldiers who brought him to victory, retained the Qin *mingtianzhai* land allocations based on military rank.[30] But the Han also broadened the award of ranks to include various kinds of meritorious service beyond military accomplishments and increased the number of ranks to twenty. The basic grant for households without rank – variously designated as *gongzu* 公卒, *shiwu* 士伍, and *shuren* 庶人 in the Zhangjiashan manuscripts – was 1 *qing* (100 *mu*) of arable land and one dwelling (defined as an area of 30 square paces).[31] Holders of merit ranks were eligible for far more generous allocations; for example, officers of the *gongcheng* 公乘 rank (thirteenth of the twenty ranks, and ordinarily the highest rank commoners could attain) were entitled to 20 *qing* of land, while the highest rank (*guanneihou* 關內侯) was allowed 95 *qing*. Under certain conditions – for example, purchased properties must be adjacent to one's existing landholdings – land grants

---

[30] Zhu Shaohou 1985: 25–29. In an effort to resettle the population displaced by war, Emperor Gaozu also awarded lands based on the head of household's previous Qin military rank. See Wang Yanhui 2006: 24.

[31] These terms encompassed a variety of statuses: *gongzu* denoted a modest status above a simple commoner (*shiwu*); *shuren* was a "freedman," formerly a bondservant, slave, or convict. *Shuren* remained a stigmatized status; only their children were deemed commoners. Anthony Barbieri, personal communication.

could be transferred or sold, but those who sold allocated lands forfeited eligibility for further grants.[32]

Thus both the Qin and Han apportioned land grants to individual households in one hundred *mu* units on the basis of ranks bestowed by the state. The hundred-*mu* tract of land – commonly known as *mo* 陌 – became in principle the basic unit of landownership and land taxation (with no adjustment for the size of the household). The recipients of land grants were defined as conjugal families: "one husband, one wife" (*yifu yifu* 一夫一婦), or – as some texts put it – a farmer and a weaver. These land grants conferred usufruct privilege rather than outright ownership, but the recipients also enjoyed rights of patrilineal inheritance.

Shang Yang's reforms had mandated that property be equally divided among heirs and that sons live apart in separate households. The principle of equal inheritance was by no means universal in the Han, as it would become in later custom and law. The father's successor (ordinarily the eldest son) inherited his merit rank – at a lower grade, however – and his landholding entitlement, although successors commonly divided the property with their brothers. Household division often occurred when sons married and established their own households; fathers could also dispose of their property through written wills, which were legally binding. The "Statutes and Ordinances" of 186 BCE tolerated brothers living together without division, but the principle of separate residence had long been established as customary practice. The Han state manifestly encouraged household division and the multiplication of independent farming families who would serve as the economic base of society and the fiscal foundation of the state. The *mingtian-zhai* allocations served to preserve and strengthen patrilineal succession through transmission of both property and status.[33]

The generous *mingtianzhai* quotas allowed to holders of merit ranks were maximum entitlements, and probably did not represent actual landholdings. The great majority of the recipients of land allocations undoubtedly were ordinary farming families.[34] Indeed, it has been argued that the "Statutes and Ordinances" of 186 BCE were intended to restore limits on landholding originally enacted by the Qin state.[35] Emperor Wen (r. 180–157 BCE) – enshrined

---

[32] Yang Zhenhong 2003. On the *mingtianzhai* system as reflected in the Zhangjiashan manuscripts, see also Zhang Jinguang 2007; Zhu Honglin 2008: 210–30; Ikeda 2008b: 487–511. For a brief introduction to the Han system of merit ranks, see Loewe 2010b: 297–99.

[33] Wang Yanhui 2006. Surviving household records from the Juyan garrison (dating from the late first century BCE) show that out of a total of forty-seven households, 67 percent consisted of conjugal families, and another 9 percent of conjugal families plus an elderly parent. In the remaining 24 percent of cases the household also included unmarried siblings , but there were no cases of married brothers living together. See ibid.: 28–29.

[34] Zhang Jinguang 2007.   [35] Yang Zhenhong 2003: 62–63.

in Confucian historiography as a model of magnanimity – subsequently removed restrictions on the amount of land and the number of slaves that individual households could possess.[36] Of course, local conditions – such as variations in population density, cropping regimes, and land productivity – also compelled modifications in the size of land allocations.

The land grant allocations, which combined state landownership with cultivation by individual households, laid the foundations for the development of the smallholder family farm economy. Warring States statesmen promoted this system not only because it fostered social stability by providing each household with a stable economic base, but also because they believed it would increase agricultural productivity. Lü Buwei's treatise on statecraft affirmed that individual tenure provided greater incentives for intensive effort than did collective farming, under which individuals tend to withhold their labor.[37] Similarly, Confucian scholars lauded the industry and thrift of smallholder farming families in the Central Plain heartland, where there were no great disparities in wealth and all could satisfy their consumption needs, in contrast to frontier regions that depended on commerce and consequently suffered debilitating economic inequality.[38] Nonetheless, within several decades after the founding of the Han dynasty the economic forces set in motion by the land allocation system caused its collapse.

The public sector in the Qin economy

The Legalist philosophy that governed the Qin imperial state was imbued with the notion of purposeful government: the state existed to provide for the security and material welfare of its subjects. Although there is increasing evidence of the persistence of private industry and commerce under the Qin Empire, the state exercised direct control over most productive assets – including foundries, workshops, mines, forests, pastures – and also a substantial portion of the agricultural economy. The state bureaucracy correspondingly expanded to accommodate these managerial functions. The treatise on statecraft attributed to Lü Buwei enumerated twenty departments believed necessary for the government to carry out its duties: in addition to five departments devoted to calendrical sciences and prognostication, others would assume responsibilities over slaves, clothing, maps, bows, chariots, carts, boats, oxen, palaces, wine, wells, markets, mortars (for grinding grain), physicians, and shamans.[39]

---

[36] *HS* 29A.1142.
[37] Book 17, "Shenfen" 審分, in *LSCQ*: 1029; Knoblock and Riegel 2000: 405. See also Hori 1996: 31–32.
[38] Chapter 3, "Tongyou" 通有, in *YTL*, 1: 42.
[39] Book 17, "Wugong" 勿躬, in *LSCQ*: 1077–78; Knoblock and Riegel 2000: 420.

The prominence of prognostication and medicine reflected contemporary rulers' obsession with oracles, omens, and personal immortality; the other portfolios enhanced the state's capacity to capitalize on its productive resources and build up its military might. Unfortunately, no formal description of the actual structure of the Qin central government has been preserved. But the public sector's dominance over economic life has been fully confirmed by excavated texts, notably the administrative statutes included in the Shuihudi manuscripts.

Shang Yang's reorganization of the Qin government transformed the office of chamberlain (*neishi* 內史) into that of an exchequer with broad jurisdiction over state finances, second in authority only to the chancellor (*xiang* 相), who managed diplomacy and military affairs. The rapid territorial expansion of the empire in the mid-third century BCE presented daunting logistical challenges, however. During Lü Buwei's tenure as chancellor, the Qin established an institution known as the Lesser Treasury (Shaofu 少府) to supervise the government workshops that supplied luxury goods to the king and his palace retinue. This type of Privy Purse has been attested for the states of Zhao, Hann, and Chu as well.[40] Around 227 BCE King Zheng and his chancellor Li Si restructured the Qin central government, replacing the chamberlain with two new offices: the imperial secretary (*yushi dafu* 御史大夫), who headed the state bureaucracy and in effect served as vice-chancellor, and the exchequer of grain tribute (*Zhisu neishi* 治粟內史), who took charge of grain revenues and state-owned arable lands. At the same time the jurisdiction of the Lesser Treasury – under the direct control of Li Si – expanded to include comprehensive authority over fiscal administration and tax collection. The Lesser Treasury became a sprawling administrative complex of treasuries, workshops, and storehouses that collected revenues in gold and coin, managed the state's parks, pastures, and forests, and supervised public works.[41]

Qin's march to power proceeded through the conquest and control of cities. The Qin conquests of Zhao, Hann, and Wei between 257 and 226 BCE reversed the trend toward growing independence and prosperity of the urban merchant classes of the Central Plain heartland. Major cities became the seats of newly established commanderies and bastions of bureaucratic rule. King Zheng reportedly ordered the forced relocation of 120,000 households of merchants and other wealthy persons to populate his capital at Xianyang, a measure intended to stifle the independence of the merchant class of the Jin successor states.[42] The Qin also employed relocation as a device to harness the talents of accomplished entrepreneurs and exploit its newly acquired resources. For example, rich iron foundry industrialists from the mercantile cities of Zhao

---

[40] Sahara 2002a: 130–35.   [41] Yamada 1987, 1990.   [42] Emura 2005: 210.

and Wei were stripped of their assets and wealth and dispatched to develop new iron production centers in conquered territories in Chu and in the former Shu kingdom in Sichuan.[43]

The militarization of society under Qin rule extended to production and trade. Market development in Qin was closely linked to military procurement. Under the Qin Empire, the arsenal, treasury, and granary became the economic nuclei of urban centers.[44]

Industrial production remained highly centralized at the capital under the empire as it had been since Shang Yang's day. The standardization of weights and measures, enacted to facilitate uniform tax collection, also probably originated with Shang Yang's administration. The Shuihudi manuscripts provide ample testimony of strict official supervision and control of urban marketplaces. Market supervisors determined the hours markets could be open for business, inspected the quality and price of merchandise, and ensured strict compliance with currency regulations.[45]

The activist agenda of the Qin state, reflected in its many projects to build roads, canals, and defensive fortifications (including city walls and the Great Wall along the empire's northern frontier), required enormous amounts of labor. Those who violated the stringent Qin legal code typically were sentenced to one to six years of hard labor. The language of Qin legal statutes indicates that male convict laborers mostly were employed in construction projects such as wall-building, while female convicts were assigned tasks such as husking and grinding grain. The Qin also relied heavily on statute labor duties levied on adult men and women. Conscript labor, like convict labor, was largely devoted to building projects. Both convict and conscript laborers bore full responsibility for the equipment "loaned" to them by the state, and harsh punishments were meted out for lost or broken tools.[46]

The Qin state also took an active role in agricultural development. The Qin kings had been virtually unique in offering public lands to induce immigration and settlement within their territories. One of the earliest discussions of farming practices appears in an encyclopedia organized in the form of an annual calendar of work and social activities issued *c.* 239 BCE by Lü Buwei in his capacity as chancellor of Qin. The chapters on agriculture in Lü's treatise focus on methods of field and soil preparation and the proper seasons for planting different crops, along with advice such as encouraging a rotation

[43] See the accounts of the Zhuo, Cheng, and Kong families recorded by Sima Qian, who celebrated the abilities of these entrepreneurs to remake their personal fortunes (despite the Qin state's antipathy for private wealth) but slighted their contributions to the growth of the industrial economy. See *SJ* 129.3278–79; Wagner 2008: 140–44.
[44] Sahara 2002a: 153.
[45] Hulsewé 1985a: 227–33; Cao Lüning 2002: 130–42; Sahara 2002a: 312–13.
[46] Hulsewé 1985a: 226–27.

of millet and wheat to preserve soil fertility.[47] While the family farm remained the mainstay of the Qin economy and the state's principal source of revenues, the Qin government also operated large-scale farms worked by convict laborers.

Already in Shang Yang's time the Qin rulers claimed for themselves the produce of non-agricultural lands, including mines, forests, and wildlife. The state leased mining rights to private entrepreneurs, who paid an excise tax to the state. The Qin state guarded its productive assets with meticulous scrutiny and harsh legal sanctions. For example, the death penalty was decreed for those who engaged in unlawful hunting in state-owned game reserves. Qin laws likewise prohibited private citizens from cutting timber (except for coffins), blocking springs and watercourses, burning grasses, or taking eggs during the spring and summer months in public forests and pastures.

Government initiative was especially conspicuous in stock-raising. Local administrators managed stud farms for breeding draft animals such as oxen and horses that were loaned to individual households in addition to raising horses for the imperial armies. Administrative statutes dictated the amount of feed for state-owned livestock depending on the type of animal and the amount of work they did; imposed fines on local officials who allowed animals in their charge to forage on private lands; and laid out detailed procedures for buying, selling, transporting, and recording the deaths of state-owned livestock. When crossing fords or passing customs stations, the owners or caretakers of horses and other livestock were required to show papers verifying ownership. The importance of draft animals in the Qin political economy is reflected in the land tax system, which required payments of hay and fodder as well as grain.[48]

The Qin state also maintained large stockpiles of grain that were disbursed as salaries for officials and soldiers and rations for convict laborers. The statutory requirements obliged commandery-level administrators to maintain stocks of 10,000 bushels (about 200,000 liters) of grain, while the granaries at the capital at Xianyang amassed 100,000 bushels.[49] Qin administrative laws demanded special diligence for proper maintenance of granaries; local officials were fined if inspectors found roof leaks or three or more rat holes (with three mouse holes deemed equivalent to one rat hole) in granaries under their purview.[50] There is no mention of disbursing grain for poor relief or emergency food rations, however, or even rations for statutory laborers.

---

[47] For a brief discussion of the chapters on husbandry in *Lüshi chunqiu*, see Hsü 1979: 7–9; see also the references to this text in Bray 1984.

[48] Ikeda 2008b: 452–53, 460–68, 494–95, 497–98.   [49] Hulsewé 1985a: 222–24.

[50] Hulsewé 1981: 17.

As the passage from the *Guan Zi* quoted above suggests, the poor piled up debts trying to feed their families. In addition to loans of draft animals, seed, and tools, the Qin state also lent coin, grain, and even slaves to its subjects. In the Warring States era, emergency loans of grain and money were regarded as a form of public philanthropy, with little expectation of repayment.[51] But just as the Qin state demanded compensation for losses of livestock and broken tools, it firmly insisted that the loans it issued must be repaid. The Qin state also actively policed private lending. Qin law prohibited the collection of interest on private debts and outlawed the practice of placing wives and children in debt bondage.[52] References to private lending at this time are infrequent, however. The Qin state itself acted as the principal source of credit for both productive purposes and consumption needs.

As in other spheres of economic regulation, Qin monetary policy tightly yoked private enterprise to public imperatives. The issue of the Banliang coin *c.* 336 BCE was tantamount to a declaration of economic independence.[53] The Qin rulers intended to make the round Banliang coins, strikingly different in shape and weight from the knife and spade currencies of the Central Plain, sovereign within their domains. The Shuihudi administrative statutes include detailed regulations on the use of official currencies and harsh punishments for counterfeiting or using the currencies of other states. The virtual absence of currency issued by other states at archaeological sites in the original Qin homeland testifies to the efficacy of Qin officialdom in imposing these controls.

The Han historian Sima Qian described the pre-imperial Qin monetary system as a tripartite combination of Banliang bronze coin, gold pieces, and bolts of hemp cloth. But in fact the Qin chiefly relied on Banliang coin as a means of exchange. Hemp cloth primarily served as a form of payment to the state – the stipulated size of these bolts of cloth sufficed to make a uniform for one soldier – rather than as a means of exchange in private commerce.[54] Although there are some references to the use of cloth as means of payment in the Shuihudi legal statutes, they disappeared altogether in the Han laws of 186 BCE.[55] Gold was probably incorporated into the Qin monetary system

---

[51] Okada 1990.

[52] According to the *Rituals of Zhou*, the state should assume the responsibility to enforce payment of private debts, and it is likely that the Qin state adopted this practice as well. See Zhu Honglin 2008: 151–54.

[53] On the Qin monetary system, see Inaba 1978, 2007; Yamada 2000: 43–75; He Qinggu 2003b; Shi Junzhi 2009; Kakinuma 2011: 170–90; Emura 2011: 374–98.

[54] This conclusion is based on the uniforms portrayed on the terracotta soldiers interred in the tomb of the First Emperor. See Cao Lüning 2002: 132.

[55] Many of the fines recorded in the Shuihudi manuscripts are expressed in multiples of eleven (e.g., 22 coins, 660 coins) that clearly were derived from the official exchange rate between coins and cloth (1 bolt of cloth was valued at 11 coins). This practice shows that the bolt of cloth

only after 278 BCE, when Qin conquered the Chu capital of Ying (Jiangling).[56] Ying was located in the main gold-producing region of China at that time, and housed the principal mint for Chu's gold currency. Apart from awards made to soldiers and meritorious subjects, however, gold seems to have had little place in Qin fiscal administration.[57]

As the empire expanded, it introduced its coin into newly subjugated territories. But the rapid pace of conquest overtaxed the Qin state's capacity to replace existing currencies with a uniform monetary standard. In many areas, especially in the Central Plain, the Banliang coin made few inroads and the spade and knife currencies of defunct states remained in circulation.[58] The statutes on currency among the Shuihudi manuscripts insisted that both public officials and private traders accept all coins "whether of good or bad quality" and prohibited the practice of shroffing (rejecting certain types of coin).[59] The political and social chaos that ensued following the First Emperor's death unleashed widespread counterfeiting, forcing the Second Emperor to institute a recoinage which reduced the weight of the Banliang coin by half or more.[60] The sudden collapse of the Qin Empire impeded progress toward the establishment of a universal currency, but the Han dynasty took up where the Qin rulers left off. The Han founder preserved not only the Banliang coin, but also the basic fiscal framework of the Qin state.

Early Han fiscal and monetary policies

Liu Bang, a general of commoner origins, defeated his principal rivals and declared his own Han dynasty as the successor to Qin in 202 BCE. During the civil wars Liu had sought to buttress the loyalty of his allies by awarding them titles as "kings" and conceding to them control over the territories they conquered in Liu's name. Once installed as emperor, however, Liu transferred nearly all of these territories to members of his family, who were granted hereditary rights of rulership. These satrapies (*wangguo* 王國) represented a

---

was used as a unit of account, but it does not confirm that cloth was actually used as a means of exchange. Most scholars (e.g., Yamada 2000: 70–75; Cao Lüning 2002: 131–34; Zhu Honglin 2008: 180) concur that cloth was not used as a means of exchange under the Qin and Han empires. Kakinuma (2011: 283–302) insists that cloth did function as money, but I find his arguments on this point unpersuasive.

[56] Inaba 2007: 247–55.

[57] There is some evidence from the former Chu region that imperial Qin began to use gold as a money of account, a trend that probably reflected the importance of gold in this region. See Yates 2013: 305–11.

[58] Emura 2011: 73.   [59] Hulsewé 1985b: 52–53.

[60] Coins issued under the First Emperor generally weighed around 8 g, but after the recoinage launched by the Second Emperor in 210 BCE Banliang coins weighing 3–4 g, or as little as 2 g, began to circulate. See He Qinggu 2003b: 318–24. The Han soon reduced the official weight standard of the Banliang coin to 5.2 g. See Yamada 2000: 87–88.

partial reversion to the patrimonial system of the early Zhou, under which the king shared authority with royal kin by awarding them autonomous domains. Within the territories over which he exercised direct control Liu largely preserved the political institutions, legal and administrative statutes, and bureaucratic ethos of the Qin Empire.[61] From its inception, then, the Han state was beset by an abiding tension between the autocratic and the patrimonial forms of rulership.

Under the hybrid administrative system of the early Han, more than two-thirds of the empire's territory was governed by imperial kinsmen who exercised considerable independence, including fiscal autonomy, from the court (Map 3.1). In addition, the Han emperors frequently awarded nobilities (*houguo* 侯國) to imperial kinsmen, meritorious officials, and personal favorites. These nobilities entailed rights to a share of the revenue collected from a specified number of households – ranging from several hundred to ten thousand or more – in a local jurisdiction as well as responsibility for law and order among them. A total of 788 nobilities were created between 201 BCE and 5 CE, but the number in existence at any one time was considerably less. Although nominally hereditary, nobilities could be forfeited for a variety of reasons. In 112 BCE Emperor Wu voided more than 100 nobilities founded a century earlier.[62]

The central government retained control over many of the commercial and urban centers of the Central Plain. The fledgling Han state, in dire need of revenues, sought to expropriate the wealth concentrated in this core region. In 198 BCE Liu Bang forcibly transferred many aristocratic families of the former Warring States to the region around the capital at Chang'an. In addition, a thousand households whose wealth was valued at more than 3 million coins were dragooned to serve as tomb guardians at the mausoleum of Liu Bang's father. Sumptuary restrictions were imposed on merchants, whose offspring were forbidden to enter government service.

In contrast to Qin, the chief priority of the early Han state was not imperial expansion but rather internal consolidation and recovery from wartime devastation. Much land had been abandoned in the course of the civil wars. It has been proposed that the population of the Han Empire *c.* 200 BCE was roughly 15–18 million, perhaps less than half of the peak population (estimates range from 25 to 40 million) at the founding of the Qin Empire.[63]

---

[61] For a concise overview of the organization and operation of the Han government, see Loewe 2006.

[62] On the Han system of nobilities, see Loewe 2006: 49–51. For sample data on the numbers of households attached to nobilities, see Ge Jianxiong 2002: 329–30, table 7-1.

[63] Higo 1990; Ge Jianxiong 1999. These figures should be regarded with some caution, since they are chiefly derived through backward projections from the Han imperial census of 2 CE, the earliest extant national census.

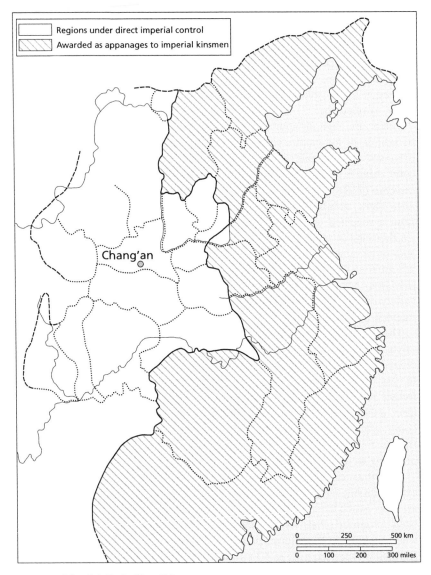

Map 3.1 Early Han China

Liu Bang demobilized his armies by awarding *mingtianzhai* land grants to his soldiers and officers. Taxes collected in grain and fodder were assessed not on total landholdings but on the acreage under cultivation, with adjustments for the quality of the land and harvest conditions.

First month, *siyou* day, fourth year of Yongguang era (40 BCE)

Passport 符傳 for Zhang Pengzu 張彭祖, commander of Yanshou unit, Tuotuo [Company]

Wife: Adult female [name missing], age 42, from Wansui *li* in Zhaowu county
Two Sons:
    Fu, adult, age 19
    Guangzong, minor, age 12
Daughter: Nüzu, minor, age 9
Wife of Fu: Nanlai, age 15

All of dark complexion

Figure 3.1 Juyan passport
Source: Juyan manuscript no. 29.2; see text and translation in Loewe 1967, 1: 113, 115. (NB: my translation differs from Loewe's.)

Liu Bang set the grain levy at one-fifteenth of the harvest, probably a reduction from the Qin rate.[64]

In 203 BCE, even before his final triumph over the rival warlord Xiang Yu, Liu Bang instituted the *suanfu* 算賦 poll tax collected in coin at a rate of 120 coins per adult (in addition, children age 7–14 were assessed at 20 coins per head). The poll taxes and labor service levies – the main sources of government revenue during the Han dynasty – required extensive documentation of the age and gender of all members of the household. Thus population registers carefully recorded liability for poll taxes and labor service (which varied by age) in addition to military service (which varied by age and gender), as can be seen in the passport for Zhang Pengzu, an officer stationed at Juyan, a garrison town on the northwestern frontier (Figure 3.1).

The *suanfu* poll tax also was coupled to labor and military service. Unfortunately, the standard historical sources offer no explanation of how the Han labor and military service systems operated, and interpretation of the fragmentary evidence remains highly disputed. Recently excavated texts such as the Zhangjiashan manuscripts have filled some of the gaps in our knowledge, but many issues remain unresolved, especially since the Han system did not clearly differentiate military conscription from labor service obligations. In the early Han adult males generally served two-year long tours of military duty: one year on guard duty at the capital and one year on

---

[64] On land taxation in the early Han, see Yamada 1993: 60–70.

assignment either at a frontier garrison or within the conscript's home commandery.[65] The Han raised the age of liability for military service from the Qin standard of 17 to between 20 and 24 years, depending on the person's merit rank, with the highest ranks exempt from military conscription altogether. In 155 BCE the privileged status of the higher merit ranks was voided, however, and "all males were registered for military service at age 20."[66]

Adult women as well as men were subject to labor conscription, but not military service. In an effort to promote population recovery, expectant and nursing mothers were granted a three-year exemption from labor service. By the same token, the state effectively compelled young women to marry by imposing a substantial penalty (a five-fold increase in the *suanfu* levies) on unmarried women of 15 to 30 years of age.[67]

Men and women did not shoulder equal labor service obligations, however. Men were obliged to perform "rotation duty" (*gengzu* 更卒) – one month of corvée labor every five months, undoubtedly the most onerous part of the *suanfu* levy – such as dike and road building or transport of grain and other government goods. "Rotation duty" – an extension, it seems, of military conscription – often entailed work away from home, while women's labor assignments were confined to the locality.[68] But the burden of labor service was by no means equally distributed among men, either. Labor service registers from Nan commandery (western Hubei) dating from *c*. 139 BCE reveal a strong disparity between the number of adult males registered for labor service rotations and the number of men actually conscripted; at least half, and perhaps two-thirds, of adult men received exemptions (Table 3.2). The sharp anomalies in the gender ratios for adults (62 percent female) and minors (61 percent male) among Nan's registered population is not well understood, but they probably reflect different ages for service liability based on gender (everyone became liable for *suanfu* levies at age 15, while men were registered for military service at age 20) and more concerted efforts on the part of men to evade military duty.[69]

Apart from these exceptions, the early Han state maintained the principle of equal apportionment of the *suanfu* burden on all adults regardless of

[65] Du Zhengsheng 1990: 32; Lewis 2000b: 34–36; Watanabe 2010: 108–11.
[66] *HS* 5.141. Zhang Rongqiang (2005: 34) has suggested that women were exempted from conscript labor service from this time, but I am not persuaded.
[67] For the exemptions and penalties for women, see Yamada 1993: 178–83.
[68] This reading of the conflicting evidence regarding the nature of *gengzu* and women's labor service obligations, offered by Washio (2009: 58–65; 164–65), makes the most sense to me.
[69] Thus far only a small portion of the excavated documents for Nan commandery from the Songbai site – near the former Chu capital of Ying – have been published. For a preliminary assessment, see Yang Zhenhong 2010.

Table 3.2 *Service and exemption registers for Nan commandery, c. 139 BCE*

Adult males	使大男	20,362	21.5%
Minor males	小男	25,334	26.7%
Total males		**45,696**	**48.2%**
Adult females	大女	32,640	34.4%
Minor females	小女	16,534	17.4%
Total females		**49,174**	**51.8%**
Total registered population		**94,870**	
Conscripts	卒	7,344	48.7%
"Liable for service"	可事	1,828	12.1%
Exempt elderly	免老	2,033	13.5%
Disabled	罷癃	2,190	14.5%
Privileged exemptions	復	1,683	11.2%
Total		**15,078**	

NB: The above figures include data from seven counties and three nobilities in Nan commandery; the data for the remaining six counties and one nobility are incomplete.
Source: Yang Zhenhong 2010: tables 1, 4.

wealth, income, gender, or occupation.[70] Here, too, we see the implementation of the principle of equality expressed in the *bianhu qimin* formula: the Qin and early Han states imposed uniform taxes on all adults irrespective of their actual wealth or income.[71] A surviving register of households and *suanfu* duties from Dongyang county (near Yutai in modern Jiangsu) from *c.* 119 BCE shows that precisely half of the registered population (and an average of 2.27 persons per household) was liable for *suanfu* levies, further confirmation that this tax obligation was imposed equally on women as well as men (Table 3.3).[72]

Under the direction of Xiao He, Liu Bang's chancellor during 198–193 BCE, the Han reversed the trend of the Qin Empire toward highly centralized fiscal administration. The Lesser Treasury (Shaofu), which dominated Qin state finances under Li Si, was reduced to serving once again as the Privy Purse, providing for the needs of the imperial household. The exchequer (*Zhisu neishi*) regained principal authority over financial administration. Each of these departments had its separate streams of revenue: income from the land tax, the *suanfu* levies, and state-owned lands was assigned to the exchequer, while "the yield of the mountains and marshes" (i.e., mineral and timber resources), commercial taxes, the poll tax on children, foreign tribute, mint

[70] For the most thorough study of the *suanfu* tax, see Yamada 1993: 137–262; a brief overview can be found in Ma Daying 1983: 59–66.
[71] Yamada 1993: 49–54, 140–42, 190–91.
[72] A total of 2,055 persons (5 percent of the total population) were exempted from the *suanfu* tax in Dongyang, probably because of advanced age, high merit rank, or other imperial dispensations. The dating of this text to *c.* 119 BCE is based on Yamada 2007: 2.

Table 3.3 *Population and* suanfu *registration, Dongyang county,* c. *119 BCE*

Xiang 鄉	Households 戶	Individuals 口	Liable for *suanfu* levy 事算
1. Du (Canton seat)	2,398	10,819	5,055
2. Dong	1,783	7,795	3,689
3. Yangchi	1,451	6,328	3,169
4. Qu	880	4,500	1,890
5. Huanyongbei	1,375	6,354	3,285
6. Huanyongdong	1,282	5,669	3,689
Reported total	9,169	40,970	20,009
Actual total	9,169	41,469	20,777
Average per *xiang*	1,528	6,912	3,463

Source: "Jibu" 集簿 ms, reproduced in Tianchangshi wenwu guanlisuo 2006: 15–16.

seigniorage, and revenues from the emperor's personal lands were deposited in the Lesser Treasury. When military emergencies or natural disasters demanded an urgent government response, the exchequer frequently had to turn to the Privy Purse for an infusion of funds.[73]

As in the Warring States period, much industrial production was controlled directly by the state. The Han employed mostly wage labor and conscript artisans at its weapons and luxury goods workshops, while relying almost exclusively on unfree labor (convicts and labor conscripts) in the mines and foundries. Convict laborers also were put to work in state-run dyeworks, mints, salterns, tileworks, and construction projects in addition to cutting fodder, harvesting timber, and transporting tax grain. The imperial workshops, many of which were located within the palace precincts, were attached to the Privy Purse, but the arsenals at Chang'an fell under the jurisdiction of the capital superintendent, who was charged with public security. The great majority of the artisans engaged in luxury goods crafts such as silk and lacquer manufacture were women. The Zhangjiashan manuscripts indicate that the quotas for conscript artisans preferred women over men or children by a ratio of two to one. Slaves also comprised an important part of the labor force in imperial workshops. Most government slaves were family members of convicted criminals who had been confiscated along with the convict's property. Slaves – many of them women with handicraft skills – were considered too valuable to waste working in the perilous mines and foundries, and thus enjoyed a status and level of comfort superior to convict laborers.[74]

[73] On the institutional structure of early Han fiscal administration, see Yamada 1987; Loewe 2006: 29–32.
[74] Barbieri-Low 2007: 107–14, 212–56.

As noted earlier, during its brief lifespan the Qin Empire was unable to unify the currency under its Banliang coin standard. The Han, having inaugurated the *suanfu* poll tax paid in coin as one of its main sources of revenue, had an even greater need for a standard currency. Initially, the Han adopted a policy of free coinage in an effort to displace the heterogeneous Warring States currencies still in circulation with the Banliang coin that the Han inherited from the Qin. However, many of the privately cast Banliang coins were substandard, mere thin loops of metal derisorily nicknamed "elm-pod coins," resulting in rampant inflation. In 186 BCE, during the regency of Empress Lü (188–180 BCE), the court issued new laws – some portions of which have been preserved in the Zhangjiashan cache of manuscripts – intended to strengthen government control over economic activities. In addition to restoring the state's exclusive right to mint coin, the new rules mandated a much heavier Banliang coin (weighing 5.2 g). However, the new coin increased the tax burden of the populace, cost the state more to mint, and in any event quickly disappeared into melting pots. In 182 BCE the state relented and reduced the standard for the Banliang coin by more than half (to 2.4 g). Yet this concession still failed to halt counterfeiting and the price inflation it engendered.[75]

Shortly after Empress Lü's death, Emperor Wen – who as noted earlier embraced the principles of frugal governance espoused by the Huang-Lao philosophy – returned to more liberal economic policies. In 175 BCE Wen reinstituted free coinage, in exchange for which private coiners paid license fees to the imperial state, and allowed private development of mineral resources, such as salt and iron, over which previous rulers had claimed sovereign proprietary rights. Among those who took advantage of these opportunities were Liu Pi, the Prince of Wu (capital at Yangzhou), whose territory contained rich copper mines, and Deng Tong, a Chang'an-based merchant who leased mining and minting rights to local merchants in Sichuan. Coupled to a new, slightly heavier, Banliang standard (2.6 g), the privately issued coins appear to have restored some stability to the money supply and reined in inflation.[76]

In 170 BCE, the imperial counselor Chao Cuo proposed a program of encouraging settlement along the northern and southern borders of the empire to build a stable revenue base and alleviate the fiscal burden of transporting food and other supplies to remote frontier army camps. In addition, Chao recommended that the emperor reward individuals who delivered specified quantities of grain to the frontier armies with merit ranks. Chao's policies apparently proved a great success, so much so that in 167 BCE Emperor Wen was emboldened to abolish the grain levy altogether, expecting that the grain yield from state-owned lands would suffice for the consumption needs of the

[75] Yamada 2000: 73–88.   [76] Ibid.: 89–93.

imperial retinue at the capital. But Chao's warnings that Wen's lenient approach to governance had weakened imperial authority and fanned the embers of sedition among the more powerful princes such as Liu Pi went unheeded.

Wen's policies saddled the central government with substantial deficits and diminished the control it exercised over the satrapies. Wen's successor, Emperor Jing (r. 157–141 BCE), almost immediately reinstated the grain levy, although he lowered it to one-thirtieth of the harvest, half the rate established by Liu Bang. Under the guidance of Chao Cuo, Jing sought to reassert imperial prerogatives, provoking the Rebellion of the Seven Princedoms under the leadership of Liu Pi in 154 BCE. The rebellion was suppressed, but Chao Cuo was accused of deliberately inciting the insurgency and executed. Despite Chao's death, the defeat of the rebel princes provided Emperor Jing an opportunity to repeal Wen's laissez-faire policies. In 145 BCE he revoked the fiscal autonomy of the satrapies, whose inhabitants henceforth owed their *suanfu* taxes and conscript labor services to the central government. Private coinage was rescinded, and counterfeiting was made a capital crime. At the same time Jing gave more favorable treatment to merchants, for example by relaxing the prohibition against merchants holding government office.

Emperor Jing's policies strengthened the hand of the central government in economic affairs. The surge in revenues from the princely domains enhanced the stature of the exchequer, which now had much greater resources at its disposal.[77] The empire enjoyed a considerable measure of peace and prosperity: by the time of Jing's death in 141 BCE, China's population had reached a new peak, estimated at 44–50 million persons. Yet population growth and growing inequities in the distribution of wealth gradually undermined the institutional principles of the Han fiscal order, which were premised on uniform taxation of all adults. In addition, beginning in 133 BCE the Han court's tense relations with the Xiongnu confederation of steppe nomads on its northern frontier erupted into prolonged armed conflict. Costly wars against the Xiongnu would lead to even greater government intrusion into economic life than the First Emperor of Qin had envisioned.

Local society in the early Han

Excavated manuscripts and other evidence from the Fenghuangshan tombs, dating from 160s–150s BCE, offer a unique glimpse at local social structure in

---

[77] The name of the exchequer's office was changed in 143 BCE from exchequer of the grain levy (*Zhisu neishi* 治粟內史) to grand director of agriculture (Danongling 大農令), and subsequently to grand superintendent of agriculture (Dasinong 大司農) in 104 BCE.

the early Han. The Fenghuangshan tombs were located near the city of Jiangling, on the north bank of the Yangzi River, in modern Hubei province. Formerly the capital of the Chu kingdom, Jiangling remained a major metropolis and prominent commercial entrepôt during the Han dynasty. One tomb, whose occupant has been identified as Zhang Yan, contained a variety of manuscripts pertaining to both local fiscal administration and Zhang's private business activities. The fiscal documents include records of land tax payments, distributions of seed from government stores, and labor service duties, but archaeologists believe that they concern urban residents who derived only part of their income from agriculture.[78]

Zhang Yan appears to have served as the community headman (*lizheng* 里正) of Ping *li*. Some Warring States texts specifically associate *li* with urban populations – for example, the Qi capital of Linzi was said to number 300 *li* – but certainly by Qin-Han times the term was applied to both rural villages and urban residential neighborhoods.[79] The *li* mentioned in the Fenghuangshan manuscripts most likely were located in or adjacent to the city of Jiangling. *Li* numbered as few as twenty and as many as fifty or more households, and it its generally believed that they corresponded to actual village or neighborhood communities rather than being artificial bureaucratic units.[80] The Qin state inaugurated the office of *lizheng* headmen, who were chosen from among the affluent members of the community and entrusted with responsibilities for tax collection, public security, and agricultural improvement.[81] The *lizheng* thus served as the lowest level of the state's administrative apparatus. Zhang Yan not only collected taxes and assigned labor service duties for Ping *li*, but was involved in the administration of at least four other *li* as well. The tax records reveal the meticulous accounting of monthly collection of the *suanfu* poll tax, commutation of the hay and straw taxes into coin payments, and fulfillment (or not) of labor service requirements. In one set of documents adult individuals from three to five households were combined into groups of ten on labor service rosters and assigned duties – one man and one woman at a time – in rotation; but in another set the households were grouped into

---

[78] From the time of their publication these documents have evoked contrasting interpretations, as can already be seen in the first wave of Chinese scholarship devoted to them: Huang Shengzhang 1974a, 1977; Qiu Xigui 1974, Hong Yi 1974. Whereas Qiu, and Sahara (2002b), have concentrated on Zhang Yan's role as a local administrator, Huang, Hong, Yamada (1981), and Suzuki (1990) have all placed equal emphasis on Zhang's private commercial dealings.

[79] Du Zhengsheng 1990: 102–10. Du's assertion that *li* always designated urban groups clearly is incorrect, but Hori's (1994: 271–74) argument that regardless of urban or rural residence *li* designated agricultural communities also must be rejected.

[80] Du Zhengsheng 1990: 104; Zhu Honglin 2008: 228–29.

[81] In the Shuihudi manuscripts the title of this office is given as *lidian* 里典, since *zheng* violated the taboo against using the First Emperor's personal name. On the organization and function of *li* units in the Qin and early Han see Iio 2007.

pairs for assessing labor services. *Lizheng* like Zhang Yan appear to have exercised broad discretion in tailoring the bureaucratic taxation system to the local social milieu.[82]

The Fenghuangshan documents make no direct mention of Zhang Yan's personal assets, but he held a merit rank that he probably purchased for a substantial sum.[83] His personal documents also included a contract through which a group of ten persons established a business partnership with Zhang as the head of the enterprise. Each member agreed to contribute 200 coins to the partnership and travel together to engage in trade. The contract stipulated fines for members who failed to make the journey (apparently substitutes were hired), did not provide their share of merchandise, misappropriated goods belonging to another, or did not attend meetings convened by the headman. The cost of lost or damaged goods was borne by the partnership as a whole. Other documents specify the cost and quantity of trade goods – including bamboo boxes, hemp yarn, vinegar, and charcoal – and the individuals to whom they were entrusted. One document records "expenditures" over a four-month period of 1,828 coins.[84] Although this enterprise appears to have been humble in scale, it testifies to Zhang Yan's diverse sources of income, which probably included landholding as well as commercial ventures and his role as a local tax collector.

It seems likely that some of the "partners" in this commercial enterprise supplied labor rather than capital, and indeed may have been indigent casual laborers. The document from Fenghuangshan that has received the most attention is a list of disbursements of seed from government stores to twenty-five households in Zheng *li* (Table 3.4). The list enumerates the number of persons capable of field work and the mouths to feed – in other words, the productive capacity and consumption needs of each household – along with the amount of arable land and the amount of seed allocated (at a uniform ratio of 1 *dou* per *mu*). The high ratio of 2.8 able-bodied workers per household suggests that all family members other than the very young and infirm adults were expected to work at agricultural tasks. Most strikingly, these households possessed on average only 25 *mu* of land, far below the 100 *mu* standard for state land allocations, and surely well below the minimum required to meet their subsistence needs. The consensus among scholars is that this

---

[82] Sahara 2002b: 429.
[83] Suzuki 1990: 52; Yamada 1981: 185. According to rules for sale of rank established in 186 BCE, this rank was awarded to those who delivered 4,000 *shi* of grain to the frontier, the cost of which at this time was in the range of 60,000–120,000 coins excluding transport expenses. See Ding Bangyou 2009: 94.
[84] Yamada 1981: 183–86; Suzuki 1990: 51–55. In addition, ten documents record daily assignments of merchandise to individuals with values ranging from 50 to 800 coins (averaging 236 coins).

Table 3.4 *Seed loan roster for Zheng* li

Household*	"Capable of fieldwork" 能田 (persons)	"Mouths" 口 (persons)	Landholdings (*mu*)	Landholdings per fieldworker (*mu*)
(1) Sheng	1	1	8	8.0
(2) Yang	1	3	10	10.0
(3) Guniu	2	4	12	6.0
(4) Ye	4	8	15	3.75
(5) Yanzhi	2	2	18	9.0
(6) ?	2	3	20	10.0
(7) Li	2	6	23	11.5
(8) Man of Yue 越人	3	6	30	10.0
(9) Buzhang	4	7	37	9.25
(10) Sheng	3	5	54	18.0
(11) Lü	2	4	20	10.0
(12) Gui	2	6	20	10.0
(13) Young slave 小奴	2	3	30	15.0
(14) Tuo?	3	4	20	6.67
(15) Anmin?	4	4	30	7.5
(16) Qingjian	3	6	27	9.0
(17) ? – slave – 奴	4	7	23	5.75
(18) ? – slave – 奴	3	–	40	13.33
(19) ?	4	6	33	8.25
(20) Gongshi 公士	3	6	21	7.0
(21) Pian	4	5	30	7.25
(22) Merchant Zhu 朱市	3	4	30	10.0
(23) ? – slave – 奴	3	3	–	–
(24) ?	2	3	20	10.0
(25) Gongshi Merchant 公士市人	3	4	32	10.67
Total: 25 households	71	112	603+	8.87

*The designations for households include personal names, merit ranks, and statuses.
Source: Qiu Xigui 1974: 51–52.

list – representing nearly half of Zheng *li*'s total of fifty-three households – attests to growing concentration of landownership and the immiseration of a substantial portion of the population in the Jiangling region.[85]

This depiction of a sharp polarization between rich and poor draws support from other evidence obtained from the Fenghuangshan tombs. Among the unique finds at Fenghuangshan, three tombs contained wooden figurines of servants at work that are inscribed with each servant's task – and in one tomb,

---

[85] In addition to the specialized studies cited in footnote 78 above, see Watanabe 1986: 21–23.

Table 3.5 *Servant figurines in the Fenghuangshan tombs*

	Tomb 8	Tomb 167	Tomb 168
Riders and grooms	5	1	5
Attendants	6	2	3
Domestic workers	10 (F)	12 (F)	14 (F)
Agricultural workers	7 (M)	7	8 (M)
	8 (F)		8 (F)
Boatmen	6	–	–
Oxcart drivers	–	2	1
Total	42	24	39

Source: Sahara 2002b: 408, table 1

their names as well (Table 3.5). The figurines thus represent the household's actual servile workforce. Although fieldworkers – evenly divided among men and women – comprised less than half of the entire servile workforce, the masters surely possessed substantial landed estates.[86] The occupant of Tomb 168, Ying Sui, held the same merit rank as Zhang Yan; we also know that he lived in an urban district and perhaps operated a private mint during the period of free coinage under Emperor Wen.[87] Zhang Yan's tomb, in contrast, contained only three servant figurines. By the standards of Ying Sui and the unnamed occupant of Tomb 8, Zhang Yan was a person of moderate affluence, occupying an intermediate position in the economic hierarchy between the majority of commoner households and the truly wealthy. Other tombs at Fenghuangshan comparable to that of Zhang Yan in size and construction – but lacking mortuary goods – suggest the existence of a stratum of middle income households in Jiangling society.[88]

Moreover, given that the *li* administered by Zhang Yan almost surely were urban communities, the small landholdings indicated in Table 3.4 should not be taken as conclusive evidence of the poverty of the farming population. As the Shuihudi manuscripts demonstrate, the disbursement of seed to farm households – apparently regardless of their need – was an important responsibility of local officials, one of the various ways in which the state subsidized the agrarian economy. The Jiangling region was primarily a rice-growing region, and thus farmers there required less land than cultivators of millet

---

[86] The occupant of Tomb 167 was female, which may explain the higher proportion of domestic workers relative to agricultural laborers.

[87] Ying Sui's tomb contained a scale specifically designed for measuring the weight of coins, which Huang Shengzhang (1977: 45) has cited as evidence that Ying was engaged in minting coin. Jiangling (the former Chu capital of Ying) had housed the principal mints of the Warring States Chu kingdom.

[88] Suzuki 1990: 57–62.

and wheat in North China. The list in fact encompasses a diverse population: two heads of households (nos. 20, 25) are identified as *gongshi* 公士 (the lowest of the twenty merit ranks, entitled to 150 *mu* of land); four (nos. 13, 17, 18, 23) as "slaves" (*nu* 奴, which perhaps means manumitted slaves, since slaves were ineligible to be heads of households); and two (nos. 22, 25) as merchants. Rather than reading this document as an index of endemic poverty, it is more likely that it testifies to the diversity of economic livelihood in the Jiangling region. A substantial portion of Jiangling's urban population cultivated at least some land, while even marginal persons with few or no assets engaged in trade. Over the course of the following century, however, Han society became more starkly polarized between a small elite of magnate families and a vast pool of destitute householders who had little choice but to surrender their independence to the great landowners.

Fiscal centralization under Emperor Wu

The reign of Emperor Wu (r. 141–87 BCE) marked a crucial watershed in the evolution of Han government and institutions. Wu embarked on a concerted effort to restore the supremacy of the emperor and the central state, stripping the princedoms of their political as well as fiscal autonomy. Wu also adopted an aggressive strategy against the Xiongnu nomad confederation. Abrogating his predecessors' policy of appeasing the Xiongnu with substantial gifts and trading opportunities, Wu repeatedly mounted military campaigns to secure the northern frontiers and project Han power far into Central Asia. After inflicting a major defeat on the Xiongnu in 121 BCE, the Han established a series of garrisons stretching more than a thousand kilometers along the trade corridor that would become known as the Silk Road. Wu also dispatched armies to seize control of territories on the empire's southern and northeastern borders, annexing the northern half of Vietnam and a large portion of the Korean peninsula. But Wu's military triumphs exacted enormous economic costs.

In addition, like his predecessors, Emperor Wu was embroiled in rancorous conflicts with his imperial kinsmen, culminating in an abortive revolt by the princes of Huainan and Hengshan in 122 BCE. Wu was especially disturbed by what he – and others – saw as collusion between the rulers of satrapies and wealthy merchants to amass landholdings. Decades before, Chao Cuo had warned that many farming families teetered on the brink of starvation and insolvency and were compelled to sell off their land allocations to redeem their debts.[89] But Chao's strategy to protect farmers by encouraging policies

---

[89] Chao's memorial to Emperor Wen was given a prominent place in the official history of the Han dynasty. See *HS* 29A.1130–34.

to raise grain prices had little effect, and the "aggrandizement" (*jianbing* 兼併) of landholdings by nobles and wealthy merchants escalated unchecked.[90] Even the historian Sima Qian – an admirer of free enterprise – conceded that "at this time the net of the law was slack and people became rich, using their wealth to lord it over the less fortunate, to the point where aggrandizers without title or office brutally imposed their will on the inhabitants of the countryside."[91]

Desperately in need of additional revenues to defray the costs of war and conquest, Wu recruited a brain trust of merchants to devise a new fiscal strategy. Given the plight of family farms, raising the *suanfu* levy or land taxes was out of the question. Beginning *c.* 120 BCE the emperor's advisors crafted a reorganization of the fiscal administration that led to a consolidation of the central government's revenues in the hands of the exchequer and ad hoc agencies – such as the Superintendent of Waterways and Parks (Shuiheng duwei 水衡都尉), established in 115 BCE – created to carry out the new fiscal initiatives. Wu was persuaded to repudiate Wen's legacy of minimalist government and impose onerous new taxes on the wealthy, revamp the currency, place the lucrative salt and iron industries under state monopoly, and allow state trading agencies to intervene aggressively in commercial exchange.

The first step taken by the new leadership was to broaden a tax originally levied solely on merchants into a universal tax on commercial enterprise. Under the new policy (known as *suanmin* 算緡), anyone engaged in commerce or moneylending was assessed a tax of 120 coins (one *suan*, the basic unit of the *suanfu* poll tax) for each 2,000 coins of assets (i.e., a rate of 6 percent); artisans were taxed at half that rate. Additional assessments were levied on boats and carts. Those accused of evading the tax were subject to criminal penalties and confiscation of their property, which could include enslavement of their family members. Moreover, the law forbade merchants from possessing lands allocated under the *mingtianzhai* system or obtaining government office. While the law served to separate merchants into a distinct occupational class subject to legal discrimination, it also was intended to discourage anyone other than professional merchants from engaging in commercial activities. Penalizing wealthy families for investing in trade and moneylending as well as preventing merchants from acquiring landholdings would help to curb the growing problem of "aggrandizement."[92]

Second, Wu inaugurated a state monopoly on the production and sale of iron and salt in order to capture the profits of what were regarded as the most

---

[90] Zhu Shaohou 1985: 63–72.   [91] *SJ* 30.1420.   [92] Yamada 1993: 220–38.

lucrative private industries. The emperor transferred his claims to "the yield of the mountains and marshes" to the office of the exchequer, which promptly seized iron and salt production facilities and turned them into state enterprises (Map 3.2). The Han state already had an elaborate procurement system to obtain raw iron for its workshops and arsenals; these officials now assumed control of the production and sale of iron in the private market as well. In most cases the former foundry and saltern owners were recruited as managers of the new state operations. In 98 BCE the Han also created a

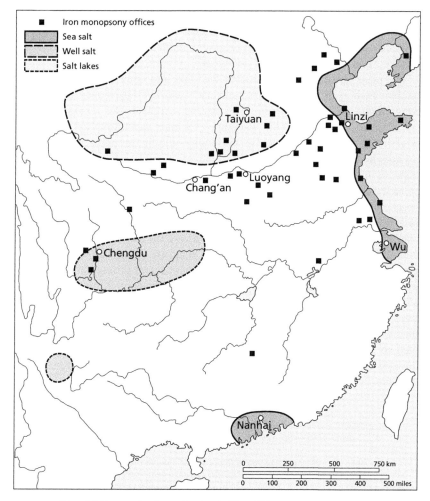

Map 3.2 Iron and salt production in Han China

state monopoly on wine, but this initiative proved far more difficult to enforce and was rescinded in 80 BCE.[93]

Third, Wu's fiscal advisors issued a new, heavier bronze currency, the Wuzhu coin, to replace the heterogeneous array of Banliang currencies in circulation. When first introduced in 118 BCE, the new coins were cast in provincial mints and varied significantly in weight and fineness. In 113 BCE, the minting of Wuzhu coins was consolidated at the capital under the aegis of the Superintendent of Waterways and Parks. From this time forward the state produced substantial quantities – estimated at more than 400 million coins per year for the remainder of Wu's reign – of fine Wuzhu coins (weighing 4.0–4.5 g). Although roundly reviled for his short-lived experiments with a variety of fiat currencies – including a deer-hide "bill" that was valued at 400,000 coins – Wu succeeded in creating a unified currency and a monetary standard that would endure for centuries.[94]

The most far-reaching intrusion of the state into commerce resulted from implementation of the "equitable delivery" (junshu 均輸) policy devised by Sang Hongyang. Sang, the son of a Luoyang merchant, was a mere 32 years old when he was recruited into the emperor's inner sanctum of fiscal advisors in 120 BCE because of his prodigious facility with figures and accounts. After his appointment as director of national accounts in 116 BCE, Sang sought to improve the efficiency of military logistics by redistributing tax revenues collected in richer regions to the deficit-ridden frontier territories. He also began to tap revenues from the salt and iron monopolies for this purpose. In 110 BCE, upon being promoted to exchequer, Sang launched an ambitious plan to merge the equitable delivery system with the salt and iron monopolies into what became known as the "balanced standard" (pingzhun 平準) system. Under the balanced standard policy, government agents throughout the empire used public funds, including monopoly revenues, to smooth out price fluctuations by buying up goods when prices were low and selling them when prices were high. Goods accumulated in government storehouses at the local level then were forwarded to the capital in lieu of suanfu tax payments and distributed to the palaces and imperial workshops. Most of the goods procured through the balanced standard mechanism were silk and hemp textiles, commodities that were relatively inexpensive to ship over long distances.[95]

[93] On the iron, salt, and wine monopolies and estimates of their revenues, see Ma Daying 1983: 114–34; Yamada 1993: 485–521; on the iron monopoly see also Wagner 2001b, 2008: 171–248.

[94] Yamada 2000: 99–105; for discussion of the deer-hide and other fiat currencies issued by Wu, see ibid., 126–30. For data on extant specimens of Wuzhu coins, see Zhao Ming and Ma Liqing 2007: 119–20.

[95] Scholars disagree whether the balanced standard system was largely a means of reallocating tax revenues among regions (Watanabe 1989) or instead a direct intervention of the state in

Table 3.6 *Estimated government revenues in the Western Han*
(all figures in millions of coins)

Revenue source	Central government	Local governments	Privy Purse	Total
Land tax 田租	1,000	6,000		7,000
Fodder tax 芻稿	80	1,200		1,280
Suanfu 算賦	2,071	2,071		4,143
Salt and iron monopolies	3,800			3,800
Other	100			100
Commercial excises and mining levies 山澤/市井			1,300	1,300
Poll tax on minors 口錢			287	287
Mint seigniorage			154	154
Gold tribute from nobility 酎金			19	19
Imperial clan lands			300	300
Miscellaneous			600	600
Total	7,051	9,271	2,660	18,982

Source: Yamada 1993: 653–58.

The fiscal system constructed by Emperor Wu's advisors came to rely heavily on indirect taxation, as can be seen in the estimates of state revenues compiled by Yamada Katsuyoshi based on the census and land registration data from 2 CE (Table 3.6; Yamada converted tax revenues in goods to monetary values). According to Yamada's calculations, roughly half of total revenues – especially in-kind receipts of grain and fodder – were retained at the local level. Most of the central government's income – and nearly half of total revenue – was collected in the form of coin. Yamada's estimate of total monetary revenues (9.26 billion coins) averages to 154 coins per capita, consistent with the recently excavated revenue account for Donghai commandery, which recorded cash revenues of 190 coins per capita in 13 BCE (Table 3.1). The salt and iron monopolies – which generated more than half of the central government's revenue and 20 percent of total revenues – clearly had become vitally important to the Han state. Indirect levies paid in coin also provided the vast majority of the revenues of the Privy Purse, now controlled by Sang Hongyang as exchequer.

Sang Hongyang's policies initially achieved significant success. "Within a year's time," wrote Sima Qian, "the granaries of the Grand Treasury

commerce in order to generate new revenues (Yamada 1993: 522–31). I believe it was intended to do both. On the interrelationship between the balanced standard system and the iron and salt monopolies, see Kakinuma 2011: 309–50.

[at Chang'an] and Sweet Springs Park [on the outskirts of the capital] were full, the frontier camps had surpluses of grain and other goods, and the equitable delivery offices held five million bolts of silk. Taxes on the people had not been increased, yet revenues sufficed to meet the imperial government's expenses."[96] Sang enjoyed the full confidence of the emperor, and continued to direct state fiscal policy for the remainder of Wu's lifetime and under his successor as well.

The fiscal system devised by Emperor Wu's advisors in fact deviated from the original principles of the military-physiocratic state in fundamental ways. Their policies centered on mobilizing economic resources rather than military manpower. Cognizant of the value of commerce and industry as sources of wealth, Sang Hongyang and his coterie sought not to suppress trade but rather to manipulate the terms of exchange and the money supply to ensure an inflow of goods and wealth into the hands of the state. The state assumed monopoly control of the most lucrative industries as well as the production of strategic goods and shifted revenue extraction toward indirect taxes paid in money rather than in-kind taxation of agricultural produce and labor. Emperor Wu's regime thus can be classified as a *mercantilist* fiscal state.[97] But in contrast to the mercantilist states of early modern Europe, which deployed state power to support and protect the privileges of the domestic merchant class, Chinese mercantilists aspired to supplanting private commerce with state-run institutions managed by enterprising merchants recruited to government service.

Many contemporary statesmen and scholars denounced Sang Hongyang's fiscal policies as an unwarranted government takeover of industry and commerce. Sima Qian quoted the imperial counselor Bu Shi fuming that "Sang Hongyang has government officials squatting in the market stalls trading in goods and scrambling for a profit!" Sima himself obliquely likened Wu's regime to the Qin Empire under the First Emperor, when "the wealth of the whole world was exhausted to serve the ruler, and yet he was not satisfied."[98]

Without doubt, the emperor's spendthrift ways and the mounting costs of frontier defense imposed an intractable burden on the state's fiscal capacity. The newly conquered frontier territories produced negligible revenues, but exacted huge costs. Maintaining political and military control was impossible without a massive infusion of resources from other areas. Wu's fiscal and logistical policies thus gave rise to a spatially differentiated imperial economy in which men and materiel were transferred from the densely populated

[96] *SJ* 30.1441.
[97] A digest of mercantilist doctrines can be found in Vaggi and Groenewegen 2003: 15–22; for more detailed analysis of mercantilist policies in early modern Europe, see Schumpeter 1954: 335–76; Heckscher 1955. For a revisionist interpretation of mercantilism in early modern Europe that emphasizes its positive effects on economic development, see O'Brien 2012.
[98] *SJ* 30.1442–43.

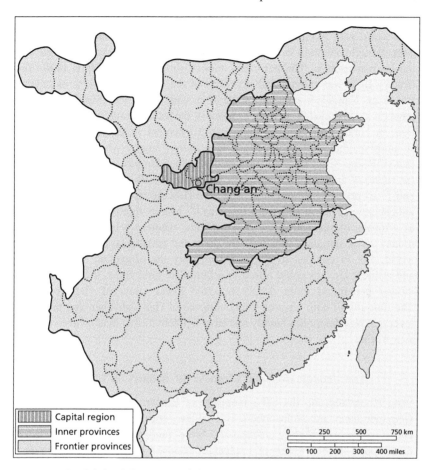

Map 3.3 Spatial structure of the Han Empire

agrarian heartland to the garrisons responsible for colonial dominion and defense along the empire's far-flung borders. This new economic geography was articulated by a three-fold division of the empire into: (1) the capital region (*sanfu* 三輔, the three commanderies around Chang'an, which shouldered the primary responsibility for provisioning the court and the capital): (2) the "interior provinces" (*neijun* 內郡); and (3) the "frontier provinces" (*bianjun* 邊郡), a spatial structure that would remain an abiding feature of imperial China's political economy (Map 3.3).[99]

---

[99] Iida 2004; Watanabe 2010: 165–99.

The success of the Wuzhu coin as a uniform monetary standard provided the Han world with a reliable means of payment. Despite the increased output of coin, though, the Han economy remained considerably less monetized than the Roman Empire. The per capita money supply of Han China in the first century BCE was roughly half the level of the Roman Empire in its heyday. Based on Yamada's estimate of the Han state's revenues (Table 3.6), state payments consumed 30 percent or more of the total amount of coin in circulation, in contrast to probably less than 10 percent in the case of Rome.[100] In addition, the composition of the Han money supply wholly differed from that of Rome. Coin in circulation in the Roman Empire *c.* 160 CE consisted (in value) of approximately 60 percent gold coins, 30–35 percent silver coins, and 5–10 percent bronze coins, while the Han money supply was comprised almost entirely of low-value bronze coins.[101] Money figured more significantly as a means of state payment in Han China, whereas a larger portion of the money stock remained available for trade and private savings in the Roman world. But in contrast to Rome, where only the oligarchic senatorial elite and affluent citizens could afford to accumulate gold coins, the circulation of money penetrated more deeply into the lower strata of Han society.[102] The ubiquity of coin inspired the confidence of Han statesmen that the state's leverage over the money supply served as a potent tool to manage the economy as a whole.

The struggle over Wu's legacy: the debates on salt and iron

Sang Hongyang and the other members of Emperor Wu's fiscal brain trust were merchants, not philosophers. But the theoretical principles underlying the command economy they inaugurated were fundamentally consistent with those found in the "Ratios of Exchange" chapters of the *Guan Zi*, which as noted in Chapter 2 diverge from the older sections of the treatise. These chapters by anonymous authors – who for the sake of convenience I refer to collectively as Pseudo-Guanzi – probably were composed during the second and first centuries BCE. Although they do not specifically refer to Wu's initiatives, they articulate a similar vision of state management of the economy. The political economy of Pseudo-Guanzi – centered on maximizing exploitation of agricultural, mining, and manufacturing resources; maintaining a favorable balance of trade; and amassing reserves of gold and bronze coin

---

[100] Scheidel 2009: 204.   [101] For the Roman data, see ibid.: 177–78.
[102] Gold coins remained almost entirely in the hands of the wealthy elites of the Roman Empire. Silver coins achieved wide distribution (geographic and social) through trade and army payments, but the production and circulation of bronze currencies were highly localized. See Katsari 2011: 167–78, 207–8; von Reden 2010: 86–91.

that enable the state to control prices and consumption – likewise can be categorized as a form of mercantilism.[103]

First of all, Pseudo-Guanzi depicts the ruler as enmeshed in a constant struggle not only with rival states, but also with merchants, moneylenders, and those who live off the revenues of noble estates. These groups are depicted as parasites voraciously exploiting the populace for their own private gain through the instrument of the market. The ruler is expected to take action to protect farming families from the inequities of the market-place, equalize the supply of and demand for goods, and level gross disparities in the distribution of wealth. To accomplish these goals the ruler must arm himself with both knowledge and tactics. Pseudo-Guanzi especially emphasizes the necessity of compiling accurate data about population, resources, and productive capacities in order to make proper judgments about, for example, the price level or the size of the money supply. This feature of Pseudo-Guanzi's thought recalls Sang Hongyang's widely acknowledged genius for compiling and analyzing fiscal data.[104]

Pseudo-Guanzi, like Wu's advisors, sought to raise revenues while providing tax relief to primary producers. Warning of the debilitating effects of labor and military service, Pseudo-Guanzi advocates avoiding direct taxation and instead extracting revenues from manufacturing and trade. Taxes discourage production and consumption, but used strategically they can also yield benefits, for example to suppress the usurious practices of moneylenders and grain forestallers. Pseudo-Guanzi also envisions a large role for the state in industrial production. The five-point outline presented in the "Stabilizing State Finances" chapter stipulates that the ruler must (1) monopolize the resources of "the mountains and marshes"; (2) manufacture consumer goods as well as weapons; (3) generate revenues from the production and trade of salt and iron; (4) issue currency; and (5) set aside hills and marshes unsuitable for agriculture as pasture for horses and cattle.[105] Here and elsewhere Pseudo-Guanzi asserts that salt and iron are immune from the normal laws of supply and demand: because the demand for these goods is inelastic, the ruler can extract substantial revenues from them that will lessen, if not obviate, the need for direct taxation.

But salt and iron were rare exceptions to the principle that supply and demand determine the price of goods. Above all, the price of grain – which

---

[103] On the economic philosophy of the "Ratios of Exchange" chapters of the *Guan Zi*, see von Glahn 1996a: 28–33; Kanaya 1987: 152–75; Hu Jichuang 1962: 238–377; Ma Feibai 1979. The recent study by Tamara Chin (2014) is essential for understanding the philosophy and rhetoric of the "Ratios of Exchange" chapters.

[104] On the crucial importance of mathematical calculation for fiscal and monetary strategy in the *Guan Zi*, see Chin 2014: 40–48.

[105] Chapter 79, "Guozhun" 國准, in *GZ*, 3: 1394. Cf. the translation in Rickett 1998: 444–45.

Pseudo-Guanzi repeatedly refers to as the "master of destiny" of the people – is subject to the rule of the market. Grain prices oscillate violently not only because of natural disasters such as drought, flood, and pests, but also because of the actions of forestallers and regraters (in Pseudo-Guanzi's language, *jiyu zangxian zhixu zhi jia* 積餘, 藏羨, 跱蓄之家) who accumulate stocks of grain, create shortages that artificially drive up prices, and profit handsomely by selling their stores to desperate consumers. Apart from legislation forbidding hoarding, the ruler must wrest control of the economy by building up his own grain reserves, which can be released into the market when consumers suffer from high prices. The enlightened monarch can manipulate markets to his own advantage, for example by raising the price of grain or other commodities to stimulate production and to encourage foreign merchants to import the goods the ruler desires. Indeed, Pseudo-Guanzi repeatedly touts the benefits of high grain prices, which bolster the income of farming households. At other times, however, Pseudo-Guanzi advocates circumventing the market altogether, for example by having the state lend seed, tools, capital, and food rations to indigent households and offer advance purchase contracts to farmers and women weavers.

In addition, the ruler wields a uniquely powerful weapon that he alone possesses: the ability to issue currency. If grain is the master of destiny, currency is the "universal medium" (*tongshi* 通施) through which the price of grain and all other goods can be controlled. The fundamental issue in Pseudo-Guanzi's philosophy of money is not – as it was for the Greek philosophers – how to determine a just price for the exchange of goods, but rather how the ruler can overcome the inevitable cycles of dearth and plenty to satisfy the subsistence needs of the people. Like other contemporary statesmen, Pseudo-Guanzi recognized that the values of money and commodities were related in inverse proportion to their quantities. But Pseudo-Guanzi further emphasized that unlike grain and other goods, the supply of money is directly subject to the ruler's control. Although money possesses no intrinsic value and cannot itself satisfy utilitarian needs for food, clothing, and shelter, through his monetary and fiscal policies – increasing or decreasing the money supply and intensifying or relaxing taxation – the ruler can manipulate the exchange value of money and by extension commodity prices. This leverage over exchange values enables the state to dictate the terms of trade, and thus manage all economic activities:

If wealth issues from a single source, the state will be invincible. If wealth issues from two sources, the state's military strength will suffice to defend its borders. If wealth issues from three sources, the ruler will find it impossible to raise an army. If wealth issues from four sources, the state is doomed. The former kings, knowing this to be true, therefore prevented the people from accumulating excess wealth and sealed off the paths to profit. Supply and demand remained the prerogative of the ruler, and wealth and poverty were subject to the ruler's will. Thus the people worshiped the ruler like the sun and the moon, and cherished the ruler as they would their fathers and mothers.[106]

In a world of incessant change, however, the ruler cannot rely on a single fixed strategy. He must be ever vigilant in discerning the appropriate responses to changing economic conditions.

Although the "Ratios of Exchange" chapters make no reference to the equitable delivery and balanced standard policies enacted by Wu's fiscal advisors, they are rooted in the same economic logic. In contrast to the older sections of the *Guan Zi*, which stress strategies for accumulating grain reserves and recognize the positive roles that merchants play in enabling the smooth functioning of markets, the "Ratios of Exchange" chapters dwell on monetary policy as the key to managing the economy and regard not only the merchant class but the wealthy elite as enemies of the common welfare. Pseudo-Guanzi explicitly rebuts the argument in favor of conspicuous consumption by the wealthy found in the idiosyncratic "On Extravagance in Spending" chapter (see Chapter 2).[107] Amid the constant clash of economic forces, it is the ruler alone who can create the balance (*heng* 衡) and stability (*zhun* 准) – two of Pseudo-Guanzi's favorite watchwords – necessary to enrich the people and the state. In underscoring that the ruler's "ability to manage" (*nengli* 能理) the economy requires not only knowledge of theoretical principles but also reliable data on population and resources, Pseudo-Guanzi hews closely to Sang Hongyang's convictions.[108]

Overt criticism of Wu's fiscal policies was muted during the emperor's lifetime. But soon after Wu's death in 87 BCE dissident officials sharply questioned the morality of state interference in the economy and the effect it had on the livelihood of the people. Reform of civil service recruitment during Wu's reign – enacted with the emperor's blessing – had opened the way for the rise of a new political class steeped in Confucian moral philosophy. Subsequently this group rose to dominance within Han officialdom. In 81 BCE the legacy of Wu's fiscal policies became the subject of a formal debate convened by Wu's successor, Emperor Zhao (r. 87–74 BCE). Sang Hongyang – still a senior statesman at the Han court – was called upon to defend prevailing policies such as the salt and iron monopolies against an array of sixty-odd "learned men" summoned to the capital to present their grievances. A digest of

---

[106] Chapter 73, "Guoxu" 國蓄, in *GZ*, 3: 1262. Cf. translation in Rickett 1998: 378.
[107] Chapter 76, "Shanzhishu" 山至數, in *GZ*, 3: 1322–51. For a translation, see Rickett 1998: 406–20.
[108] On the importance of the ruler's "ability to manage" the economy, see chapter 81, "Qingzhong yi" 輕重乙, *GZ*, 3: 1453. Cf. translation in Rickett 1998: 472. In *The Salt and Iron Debates*, Sang Hongyang argues that only those who have the "ability to manage" (*nengli*) their household and ensure the material security of their family can be entrusted with governing the empire. See chapter 17, "Pinfu" 貧富, in *YTL*, 1: 220.

the debate between Sang and his Confucian detractors has been preserved in dialogue form in a work entitled *The Salt and Iron Debates*, composed perhaps a decade or two after the actual event.[109]

In the *Debates*, Sang Hongyang initially defends Wu's fiscal policies as necessary responses to the Xiongnu menace and the rising costs of war and defense. But Sang quickly dispels the idea that these policies were simply emergency expedients, and instead insists on the ruler's right and responsibility to manage the economy for the benefit of the commonwealth in much the same language as Pseudo-Guanzi:

The true king should monopolize natural resources, regulate custom barriers and marketplaces, ensure that the tasks appropriate to each season are fulfilled in a timely manner, and govern the people by controlling the ratios of exchange. In good years of bountiful harvests the ruler stores up goods to provide for times of scarcity and want. In bad years of meager yields the ruler disburses money and goods, circulating his accumulated surplus in order to make up for shortfalls.[110]

Beyond this affirmation of mercantilist principles, Sang justifies his policies by pointing to their achievements: rationalization of the offices of imperial finance; the establishment of a sound, unified currency; strengthening of the agricultural base of the empire through water control projects, diffusion of advanced farming technologies, and sponsorship of agricultural colonies on frontiers; and equalization of the tax burden among different regions. He also upholds the managerial role of the state by extolling the virtues of systematic, long-range planning in contrast to the short-term, survival-oriented decision-making of individual households.

Moreover, Sang Hongyang underscores the crucial role of the state in achieving economic justice. He repeatedly urges the ruler to take decisive action to "place a yoke on the noble princes," "expel the rich and great merchants," and prevent "untitled power mongers" (*haomin* 豪民) from dominating the trade in vital goods such as salt and iron for their personal profit.[111] Sang unequivocally champions a redistribution of wealth from the rich to the poor, but he also emphasizes the need to redress regional imbalances in goods and resources. The wealthiest cities of the empire owe their prosperity not to their agricultural bounty but rather to their favorable geographical location at the crossroads of trade routes. Interregional

---

[109] On the salt and iron debates, see Loewe 1974: 91–112; Kroll 1978–79. For a serviceable but far from satisfactory partial translation, see Gale 1931. For a lucid analysis of the philosophical views and rhetorical styles of the antagonists in the *Salt and Iron Debates*, see Chin 2014.

[110] Chapter 2, "Ligeng" 力耕, in *YTL*, 1: 28.

[111] Chapter 2, "Ligeng"; chapter 14, "Qingzhong" 輕重; and chapter 5, "Jingeng" 禁耕; in *YTL*, 1: 27, 1: 179, and 1: 68 respectively.

exchange can enrich all only if the ruler intervenes to direct the flow of goods and ensure that the benefits of trade are shared equally.[112]

In response, the "learned men" – mostly middle-level officials – reiterated conventional bromides about agriculture as the source of all wealth, the immorality of the profit motive, and the virtues of frugality. In their view, the state was profiting at the expense of its subjects, and the emphasis on increasing revenues distracted officials from their proper duties as guardians of the spiritual and material welfare of the people. The critics also reproach government officials – no doubt with some justification – for abusing their augmented powers over markets, goods, and taxes to the detriment of hapless farming families. Rebuffing mercantilist doctrines, Sang's critics espouse a physiocratic vision of society founded on self-sufficient farming families shielded from the economic uncertainties and moral corruption of the market-place. But in appealing for a return to the laissez-faire regime of Emperor Wen they abetted the interests of the great landowners and noble lineages.

The court debate of 81 BCE did not fundamentally alter the Han state's fiscal regime. Emperor Zhao was persuaded to retain the salt and iron monopolies, although he rescinded the wine monopoly. The most substantial changes addressed the mounting burden of labor and military conscription, which even Sang Hongyang recognized as a drag on agricultural productivity. The obligation of "rotation duty" was reduced from once every five months to once per year. It also has been argued that the state commuted a substantial portion of conscript labor service to a money payment at this time; although the evidence for this claim is circumstantial, it is compelling.[113] In subsequent decades the Han eliminated most of the conscription for guard service at the capital, drastically reduced the assignment of men from the "interior provinces" to frontier garrisons, and allowed those who were summoned to military service at frontier garrisons to hire substitutes.[114] These reforms further institutionalized the functional differentiation between the interior and the frontier zones within the imperial political economy. In 30 CE the Han government would halt military conscription in the interior provinces altogether, a radical repudiation of the farmer-soldier ideal that had been the keystone of the Qin

---

[112] Chapter 3, "Tongyou," in *YTL*, 1: 41–43.

[113] Watanabe (2010: 94–100) argues that beginning in Zhao's reign in-person labor conscription (*gengyao* 更徭) was replaced by a new *gengfu* 更賦 system, which he interprets as a payment in coin. In spite of the lack of definitive confirmation for the monetization of labor services, Watanabe's analysis provides the most persuasive interpretation of the conflicting evidence on this issue and has been gaining acceptance (see e.g., Washio 2009: 73; Shi Yang 2012: 199).

[114] Iida 2004: 17–21. On the hiring of substitutes for frontier garrison duty, see Xie Guihua 1989. As Xie demonstrates, men from the interior provinces typically hired substitutes from their native county (and almost always of the same merit rank status) and paid them a standard wage. In this sense, at least, the hiring of substitutes can be seen as payment of a money tax in lieu of personal service.

empire-building project. Thereafter the Han court relied on transported convicts, nomad mercenaries, and emergency levies of frontier inhabitants to defend its Great Wall frontier.[115]

In the decades after the salt and iron debates the conservative reaction against Wu's fiscal strategies swelled. The anti-statist ideology and physiocratic principles enunciated by Sang Hongyang's critics were widely embraced by the rising class of Confucian statesmen. These officials viewed the emperor essentially as a paragon of moral behavior whose activities should be largely confined to his ritual duties. They rejected not only the strong imperial controls over commerce and industry enacted by Emperor Wu (and the Qin Empire before him), but also the market economy itself. Under the aegis of Emperor Yuan (r. 49–33 BCE) the political ideology of this group became deeply insinuated in government policy and institutions. The Privy Purse was forced to surrender most of its revenue to the finance ministry, constricting the emperor's fiscal authority. In 44 BCE the Confucian minister Gong Yu went so far as to advocate restoration of a barter economy by abolishing metallic money altogether. Gong's proposal was deemed impractical, but ritual reforms enacted in 44 and 31 BCE focused on reducing government expenditures and especially the voracious consumption habits of the imperial household.

Meanwhile, as the state retreated from the activist agenda of Sang Hongyang and his coterie, the concentration of landownership and wealth intensified. Over the next several decades an ascendant political class of Confucian statesmen fashioned themselves into a new oligarchic elite that became known as the "magnate clans" (*haozu* 豪族). The political triumph of the magnate clans also set in motion important economic changes, most notably a reorientation of wealth and investment from commerce to landed estates.

Conclusion

The Qin and Han empires presided over a crucial transition from military conquest to bureaucratic rule. The dynastic founders were dedicated to the idea that the enlightened ruler provides for the common welfare through interventions to promote agricultural production and facilitate the circulation of goods. The *mingtianzhai* system of land grants originally derived from the Qin model of a militarized society in which rank was based on accomplishments in war. The Han sought to foster a new meritocracy based more on civic virtue than military valor. But Emperor Wen's laissez-faire policies, coupled with the

---

[115] Lewis 2000b.

growing dominance of the rentier nobility, undermined the static economic order on which the *mingtianzhai* landholding system was premised. Merchants reaped new fortunes – especially in the Central Plain cities that had been the commercial heartland of the Warring States era – while landownership became increasingly concentrated in the hands of powerful lineages. Ultimately the shift from military rule to bureaucratic governance resulted in the formation of a new ruling class based on political office, noble rank, and landholding.

The imperial state's capacity to regulate the economy was closely tied to its ability to provide public goods and tax economic activity. The Qin Empire epitomized a command economy in which the state owned non-agricultural productive resources, managed much industrial manufacturing (using mostly unfree labor), and tightly supervised markets. The Legalist model of the military-physiocratic fiscal state focused more on mobilizing labor power than on collecting the fruits of labor. The value extracted by the state in the form of labor conscription was significantly greater than the burden of taxes on arable land. The Qin issued currency in the form of bronze coin less to facilitate market exchange than to provide an efficient means of collecting revenue as well as paying and provisioning its armies. As the Qin state expanded, culminating in the formation of a unified empire in 221 BCE, the problem of imposing the state's will on the thriving merchant classes of Chu and the Jin successor states of the Central Plain grew more acute. Under the empire, the Qin leaders adopted punitive measures intended to curb what they regarded as profiteering by merchants.

The Han founder, Liu Bang, initially retained many features of Qin fiscal policy, including the discrimination against merchants and the heavy reliance on conscript labor service. But apart from craft industries – in which the state continued to play a leading role – the Han withdrew from direct administration of the economy. Like the Qin, the Han state deemed the conjugal household the primary unit of economic production and assessed uniform taxes in money and labor service on all able-bodied adults. But as socio-economic inequality worsened and many farming families lost their independent means of livelihood, this presumption of parity became meaningless.

The exorbitant costs of foreign wars and imperial conquests in the remote frontiers of Inner Asia, Korea, and Vietnam propelled Emperor Wu to reverse the laissez-faire policies of his predecessors and embark on an audacious strategy of state usurpation of industry and commerce. But Wu's mercantilist policies also reflected a desire to rectify growing economic inequality. The failure of Wu's efforts to control the commercial economy and put fiscal administration on more sound footing presaged a withdrawal of the state from direct control of the economy under his successors, even though the salt and iron monopolies were retained. As the state's economic leverage diminished, the stratification of private wealth intensified.

Moreover, rather than reversing the trend toward the concentration of wealth, Wu's policies ironically had reinforced it. Heavy-handed efforts to extract revenue from the wealthy through measures such as the *suanmin* levy did not lead to the demise of the great landowners. On the contrary, the brunt of these exactions was borne by households of modest wealth. Farming families found it increasingly difficult to maintain their independence, and many fell into ruinous debt and were forced to sell off their lands. The *mingtianzhai* system of land allocations disappeared. As the economic polarization between rich and poor widened, the original Han fiscal system – premised on a basic equality of labor and land among farming households – proved increasingly unworkable. The resort to indirect taxation favored by Wu's advisors became increasingly indispensable to the state's fiscal solvency. Eventually the Han would abandon the principles of equity and universality that had been hallmarks of state-building since the Warring States era.[116]

---

[116] Yamada 1993: 239–42.

4 Magnate society and the estate economy (81 BCE to 485 CE)

The early Han state largely preserved the imperial order erected by the Qin Empire. The imperial government supported a smallholder agrarian economy through land grants, public investments in agricultural technology and infrastructure, and regulation of the marketplace to protect producers and consumers alike. Emperor Wu enlarged the regulatory role of the state and reorganized its fiscal structure for the purposes of military expansion and administrative control of a far-flung empire stretching into Central Asia, Korea, and Vietnam. But in the post-Emperor Wu era, in the face of swelling costs and the philosophical rejection of its mercantilist principles by a thoroughly Confucianized officialdom, this apparatus of imperial control no longer could be sustained. As the state retreated from Wu's fiscal policies, economic inequality sharpened.

In the early years of the first century CE, the statesman Wang Mang's brazen attempt to reestablish an aggressively interventionist imperial state went so far as to usurp the throne in the name of returning to the golden age of ancient Zhou. But the political and economic chaos that ensued, followed by Wang's overthrow and the swift restoration of the Han dynasty, further discredited state activism. The decision in 30 CE by the first Eastern Han (25–220 CE) emperor to end military conscription marked a key watershed in the abdication of the Qin-Han imperial order. The principle of service to the state as the foundation of social order had been abrogated, and instead increasing numbers of people became subject to the rising class of magnate landowners.

Nonetheless, domestic peace nourished economic growth. The intensification of agriculture through new technologies and the great expansion of arable land supported a growing population that numbered 60 million people on the eve of Wang Mang's coup-d'état. Trade and money remained vital to the manorial economy that reached full flower during the Eastern Han period. But over the course of the second century CE the imperial state, wracked by partisan conflict, weakened and collapsed. The final dismemberment of the Han Empire by competing warlord regimes in 220 CE ushered in a Period of Disunion that would last for nearly four centuries.

The centuries of disunion were characterized by the privatization of power – military, political, and economic. This devolution intensified after North China was overrun by nomad conquerors in the early fourth century, forcing the Chinese court to take refuge in the distant southern frontier of the Yangzi River Delta (the region known as Jiangnan, "South of the River"). Many aristocratic families followed the court in its flight to the south. But incessant warfare, factional strife, and frequent changes of regime stymied the consolidation of oligarchic control of government at the southern courts. By the fifth century political power and the perquisites of office largely had gravitated into the hands of military leaders and other men of humble birth. Nonetheless, the aristocracy – both the eminent émigré clans and the less-exalted indigenous elite – still dominated local society in the south. Much of the agrarian population was reduced to abject servitude. At the same time the recentering of the Chinese empire, even in the debilitated condition of the refugee courts, gave unprecedented impetus to economic development in the south, above all in Jiangnan. Magnate landowners established great latifundia, transforming vast tracts of wilderness into fertile rice paddies. Trade and industry flourished, stoked by the consumption demand of the court and the aristocracy. Despite the military and political frailty of the southern dynasties, during this era Jiangnan began its inexorable rise as the new economic heartland of the Chinese world.

Agricultural transformation in the Han period

The Han period witnessed significant advances in agriculture. The proliferation of sturdy iron tools and more intensive farming techniques engendered steady growth in agricultural production and population. The quality and quantity of iron plowshares increased dramatically, and plow cultivation attained a level of efficiency unmatched anywhere else in the ancient world.[1] Large-scale irrigation projects and new farming techniques expanded the range of cultivation in the arid regions of northern China. The imperial state played a crucial role in propagation of new farming techniques across the empire. But ultimately the new developments in agriculture favored large-scale enterprise and hastened the rise of the estate-based agrarian economy.

Cropping patterns and food consumption underwent the most momentous transformation since the Neolithic era. Millet remained the most important crop, but cultivation of wheat and barley spread in the north, as did rice in the

---

[1] The earliest textual reference to the use of plow oxen is found in the Shuihudi manuscripts of the late third century BCE (Hulsewé 1985a: 221). Most scholars have concluded that the use of oxen to draw plows began c. fifth century BCE, but Bray believes it likely dates from a much earlier time. See Bray 1984: 130–79.

south. Wheat depended more on irrigation than did millet, and thus was first adopted in well-watered areas such as the Central Plain. Land-use data for Donghai commandery along the eastern seaboard show that wheat and barley were the predominant crops in this region (see Table 3.1). During Emperor Wu's reign the state launched numerous irrigation projects in the Guanzhong region (the modern provinces of Shanxi and Shaanxi) surrounding the capital at Chang'an to provide farmers with a more secure water supply. Officials also encouraged the cultivation of wheat, which yields twice as much grain per acre as millet. In the late first century BCE the agronomist Fan Shengzhi observed that wheat and barley were widely planted in Guanzhong and produced bountiful harvests. The proliferation of wheat largely came at the expense of legumes, notably soybeans, long a staple food in North China. It is estimated that the proportion of land devoted to the cultivation of legumes declined from 25 percent in the Eastern Zhou period to 8 percent in the Han. Moreover, legumes increasingly were consumed in the form of condiments such as soy sauce and bean paste.[2] Apart from changes in staple foods, the Chinese diet also was augmented by new crops such as watermelon, cucumber, shallot, garlic, pepper, sesame, grapes, and alfalfa introduced to China via the Central Asian trade routes.[3]

By the founding of the Han dynasty, three principal agricultural regimes had emerged in China. The fertile loess soils of Guanzhong were easily worked, but because of the arid climate they were susceptible to evaporation and erosion. Light plows and hoes sufficed for tilling the loess soil. In this region the main preoccupation of farmers was careful timing of plowing, harrowing, and weeding to preserve soil moisture. The heavier alluvial soils of the Central Plain, by contrast, were subject to frequent flooding and required proper drainage. Here farmers developed more sophisticated tools such as ox-drawn moldboard plows and seed drills that enabled deeper tilling and more efficient use of seed. Ridge-and-furrow cultivation, a technique designed to cope with irregular rainfall that typically utilized plows drawn by pairs of oxen, originated in the Central Plain. The three-crops-in-two-years rotation (typically millet, winter wheat, and soybeans or millet) probably was pioneered in the Central Plain as well.[4]

Rice cultivation entailed very different farming methods. Han texts make reference to farmers in the south "tilling with fire and weeding with water," which some scholars have mistakenly interpreted as a form of swidden agriculture. Wet-rice cultivation already had a long history in China, and Han rice farmers undoubtedly were cultivating their crops in permanent irrigated fields. Most likely this phrase referred to burning of stubble after

---

[2] Peng Wei 2010.   [3] Hsu 1980: 89.
[4] Bray 1979–80: 4–5; Hsu 1980: 111–16; Yoneda 1989: 6–9.

the harvest, which was then plowed into the soil as fertilizer, and the flooding of fields to inhibit weeds. The practice of transplanting rice seedlings is already mentioned in an agricultural treatise of the second century CE.[5] By the third century plows specifically modified for wet-rice agriculture were in use in South China.[6] Still, much of the territory south of the Yangzi River was a frontier region of low population densities and less intensive forms of cultivation. In the Han period the major water control projects in South China took the form of building seawalls to protect farmland in coastal areas from inundation by salt water rather than irrigation works.[7]

The Han state largely focused its agricultural development initiatives in the Guanzhong region, which supplied the capital and the frontier armies with over 100,000 metric tons of grain each year. During Wu's reign government officials took an active role in propagating more intensive farming techniques in Guanzhong and the garrison colonies of the northwestern frontier. The development of large-scale irrigation projects under government initiative allowed farmers in these regions to adopt techniques such as the ridge-and-furrow fields and moldboard plows of the Central Plain. But by the late first century BCE the Han state no longer was making significant investments in agricultural development and Guanzhong farmers mostly reverted to less intensive farming methods.

Cho-yun Hsu calculated that a typical farming family required substantial income in cash (at least 25 percent of total income) to pay the poll taxes and meet other basic expenses.[8] Some of this income may have come from work such as processing foodstuffs, gathering fuel, textile manufacture and other domestic handicrafts, making and repairing tools, and construction. Rural women were expected to devote time to making cloth and clothing for the household. The notion of a gendered division of labor in which "men till and women weave" already was well-established before Han times. In the same vein a court historian writing in the first century CE portrays an idealized domestic economy in which "during the winter months women dwelling in the same neighborhood gather in the evening so that they can save expenses for heating and lighting, equalize the level of their skills, and harmonize practices and customs."[9] Since raising silkworms had to be done in the spring and early summer, the most labor-intensive season for agricultural work, sericulture was largely relegated to women. Nonetheless, while low-skilled tasks such as reeling silk or spinning yarn from hemp fibers fell within the province of "women's work," both men and women engaged in weaving and finishing cloth.

Settlement archaeology remains in its infancy in China, but recent excavations at the Sanyangzhuang site, on the Central Plain just west of the Han-era

---

[5] Bray 1979–80: 6–7; Hsu 1980: 121.   [6] Watanabe 1986: 187; Fang Gaofeng 2009: 18–22.
[7] Honda 2000b: 43–45.   [8] Hsu 1980: 79.   [9] *HS* 24A.1121.

course of the Yellow River, confirm the trends outlined above.[10] The Sanyangzhuang area was inundated by a catastrophic flood and abandoned early in the first century CE, and thus the site preserves the agrarian landscape of the late Western Han era. Farmers here practiced ridge-and-furrow cultivation using ox-drawn plows with large iron shares. Mulberry cultivation and remnants of looms testify to domestic textile production. The courtyard-style farm compounds at Sanyangzhuang were dispersed among cultivated fields rather than gathered into nucleated villages. The material remains from a dozen of these compounds varied only modestly, suggesting that a rough equality in economic well-being prevailed among members of the community.[11]

Although the family farm remained the basic unit of agricultural production, over the long term a trend toward concentration of landownership arose. The *mingtianzhai* merit rank system of land allocations, intended to strengthen a stable smallholder agrarian base, ultimately was transformed into a tool of aggrandizement that facilitated the formation of great landed estates. The higher merit ranks permitted substantial landholdings, from 2,000 *mu* (rank 13) to as much as 9,500 *mu* (rank 1), far in excess of the typical family farm of 40–50 *mu*. As early as 178 BCE the imperial adviser Chao Cuo warned that many farmers had fallen into destitution and were compelled to sell their *mingtianzhai* landholdings to repay their debts. Chao asserted that merchants and the wealthy not only profited from the distress of the poor, but also benefited from the sale of merit ranks in return for contributions of grain to military stores.[12] Emperor Wu's prohibition against merchants obtaining *mingtianzhai* lands did little to stem the concentration of landholding, and apparently expired after Wu's death. Wu's regime also tried to resettle landless families by offering tenancies on state-owned land (*jiatian* 假田) along the northern frontier and in other sparsely populated regions. But these lands, too, tended to gravitate – either by default or usurpation – into the hands of powerful landowners.[13] The merit rank system permitted legal acquisition of substantial estates, but complaints about accumulation of landholdings beyond the statutory entitlements steadily mounted during the first century BCE .[14]

The new farming techniques promoted by the state in Guanzhong and frontier areas required substantial investments in tools, livestock, and water control. The Han state's retreat from the activist policies of Wu's reign

---

[10] See the preliminary report in Kidder *et al.* 2012.

[11] It should be noted that although Sanyangzhuang is the best preserved of the six or seven Han village sites thus far studied, the nucleated settlement pattern appears to have been more common. Strikingly, none of these sites had an encircling wall, which according to documentary evidence was a basic feature of rural as well as urban settlements in this time. See Bai Yunxiang 2010.

[12] *HS* 24A.1132–33; transl. in Hsu 1980: 162.   [13] Zhu Shaohou 1985: 116–42.

[14] Yu Zhenbo 2004a: 36–38.

exposed many farmers to greater risks. Without the support and subventions provided by the state, households who could not survive on their own resources fell into debt, lost their land, and found themselves reduced to tenant farming or wage labor.[15] Moldboard plows required the use of oxen and teams of 3–6 workers – resources beyond the means of most farming families, and thus necessitated some degree of cooperative labor.[16] In addition, wheat – made into flour rather than eaten as porridge like millet – required more elaborate milling equipment. Water-powered grain mills – said to have "raised productivity a hundred-fold" – are first mentioned in the early first century CE, and proliferated along with the expansion of wheat cultivation.[17] Tenant farmers were obliged to rent oxen from their landlord and to pay fees to grind their grain in the landlord's mill.

Changes in agricultural production thus accelerated the trend toward the formation of large landed estates. Moreover, the rising oligarchy of magnate clans (*haozu*) benefited from the withdrawal of Wu's interventionist policies and the state's new tolerance of the concentration of wealth and landholdings. By the end of the first century BCE the family farms that had been the economic foundation of the first empires were increasingly eclipsed by a new landholding elite.

The rise of the estate economy

Imperial largesse – in the form of generous *mingtianzhai* allocations and the award of nobilities to meritorious officials and imperial kinsmen – figured importantly in the formation of great landed estates during the first century BCE. Yu Zhenbo has estimated that wealthy families with assets of 1–3 million coins probably owned 30–100 *qing* (3,000–10,000 *mu*) of arable lands, exactly the range of landholdings permitted to holders of government office under the *mingtianzhai* system.[18] Award of a nobility entitled the recipient only to the revenue from the land and did not confer actual ownership. But the holders of these nobilities also possessed substantial private estates. For example, Zhang Yu (d. 5 BCE), a favorite of Emperor Cheng, was granted the highest merit rank (*guanneihou*) and received a nobility of 600 households in 33 BCE, which was further increased to 1,000 households upon his retirement from the office of chancellor in 20 BCE. In addition, Zhang purchased 400 *qing* of private

---

[15] Bray 1979–80; Bray 1984: 591–96.   [16] Yoneda 1989: 16–17.

[17] Amano 1979: 860–62. The quotation is taken from Huan Tan's (*c.* 43 BCE –28 CE) *New Treatise*. See *XL*, cited in *TPYL*: 829. 3699b.

[18] Yu Zhenbo 2004a: 37. Yu's calculation is based on the assumption that landholdings amounted to one-third of the total assets of rich families and an average value of 100 coins per *mu* of arable land.

landholdings.[19] Utsunomiya calculated that Liu Xiu (6 BCE–57 CE), who became the founding emperor of the restored Han dynasty in 25 CE, accumulated private landholdings of 250–300 qing in addition to inheriting a nobility of 467 households (equivalent to the revenue from roughly 200 qing of arable land).[20]

The proliferation of great estates was especially conspicuous in Nanyang (Henan), the region where Liu Xiu's ancestral nobility was located. Liu Xiu's maternal grandfather, Fan Zhong, was said to have "wasted nothing in the management of his properties, and when putting his slaves to work, ensured that each was employed at a task suited to his skills. Thus he succeeded in inducing superiors and inferiors to work together cooperatively. Fan doubled his fortune every year, bringing more than 300 qing of land under cultivation." As his death drew near, Fan forgave the debts owed to him by burning the contracts for outstanding loans totaling several million coins.[21] The clan of Liu Xiu's wife, the Yin, reportedly owned 700 qing of land and numbered more than a thousand retainers.[22] Nanyang enjoyed robust economic prosperity in the Han, especially after the construction of major irrigation works in the 50s–40s BCE, and recorded the most dramatic population growth of any commandery between the censuses of 2 and 140 CE. It is likely that the adoption of more advanced agricultural techniques here favored the concentration of landholdings. As the case of Fan Zhong suggests, the formation of great estates also was abetted by the loss of smallholdings due to debt forfeitures.

The magnates who amassed such estates consisted largely of senior officials, imperial kinsmen, and the consort families, the kinfolk of empresses who held great power at the imperial court. Alarmed statesmen and social critics repeatedly warned that the rise of these great landed estates resulted from the growing impoverishment of the populace. But attempts to regulate the size of landholdings, such as a proposal in 7 BCE to limit the landholdings of a single family in Guanzhong to 30 qing, were thwarted by officials allied with powerful landowners.

Han commentators were deeply conscious of profound inequalities in wealth and social standing. According to Sima Qian, the poor suffered derision and often labored under servile conditions: "as for the common folk, those

---

[19] HS 81.3348–49.
[20] Utsunomiya 1955: 375–402. Utsunomiya's findings are briefly summarized in Hsu 1980: 50–51. Since the nobilities generated only land tax revenue (at the rate of 1/30 of the harvest), private landholdings (which would yield rents of 50 percent) generated substantially greater income.
[21] HHS 32.1119. On Fan Zhong, see also Wilbur 1943: 212–13; Gao Min 1986: 55–6; Inaba 1984: 95–8, 105–07.
[22] Utsunomiya 1955: 391–93.

whose wealth is ten times their own despise and slight them; those a hundred times wealthier fill them with fear and awe; those a thousand times wealthier put them to work; and those ten thousand times wealthier subject them to servitude."[23] Yet Sima and others frequently spoke of an intermediate stratum of "middling families" (*zhongjia* 中家) interposed between the wealthy "great families" (*dajia* 大家) and the destitute poor (*pinjia* 貧家).[24] Watanabe Shinichiro has estimated that middle-income families – perhaps half of the total population – possessed on average 100 *mu* of land, moveable assets worth 5,000 to 15,000 coins, and perhaps one or two slaves as well, or total wealth valued at 20,000–40,000 coins.[25] Others have suggested that the wealth of a typical smallholding family was more modest, amounting to 40–50 *mu* of land and assets in the range of 10,000 coins, while poor families had meager assets worth fewer than 5,000 coins.[26] By contrast, Han authors commonly referred to wealthy families as having assets in the range of 1 to 3 million coins. Sima Qian estimated the annual income of holders of nobilities and rich merchants at 200,000 coins.[27] According to Hsu Cho-yun's estimates, the annual salary of a minister of state was equivalent to more than 120,000 coins; that of a middle-rank official about 40,000 coins; and a typical farming household about 20,000 coins.[28]

The widening gulf between rich and poor provided the catalyst for the ambitious attempt at radical reform of state and society launched by Wang Mang, scion of a great clan who became regent to a child-emperor in 1 BCE. Wang sought to reinvigorate strong imperial rule through a wholesale reorganization of Han social and political institutions. Wang's political vision was inspired by *The Rituals of Zhou*, a canonical text which purports to be a detailed blueprint of the administrative organization of the ancient Zhou kingdom. After the child-emperor died in 6 CE Wang stalled nomination of a successor, and three years later – in the name of restoring the golden age of the Zhou – he anointed himself emperor of his own Xin ("New") Dynasty. Wang then launched a draconian program of reform, reorganizing the bureaucracy to strengthen the central government's control over local officials and abolishing the Han nobility and its hereditary rights to land revenues. Invoking the ancient doctrine that all land and wealth is the property of the ruler, he

[23] *SJ* 129.3274.
[24] Watanabe 1986: 20–21. In the eyes of Confucian critics, not only "the rich" but even "the middling sort" enjoyed a luxurious lifestyle in the time of Emperor Wu. See chapter 19, "Sanbuzu" 散不足, in *YTL*, 1: 348–400.
[25] Watanabe 1986: 26.   [26] Ōkushi 1985: 1188.
[27] *SJ* 129.3272; translated in Sima Qian 1993: 448. Sima Qian's estimates are based on a nobility drawing income from 1,000 households and merchants who earn a 20 percent return on capital investments of 1 million coins.
[28] Hsu 1980: 52–53, 76.

confiscated the landholdings of many estate owners and redistributed them to the poor. At the time of his accession Wang also banned the sale of land and slaves, but he was forced to rescind this prohibition three years later.[29]

Wang Mang was equally assertive in expanding state control of commerce and money. While still regent he had introduced two new forms of bronze currency with purely nominal values that circulated concurrently with the existing Wuzhu coin. In keeping with Wang's atavistic ideology, the key-shaped design of some of these coins grafted the form of the ancient knife currency onto the standard round coin. After declaring himself emperor, Wang proscribed the use of the Wuzhu coin and created a bewildering array of new currencies by recoining old Wuzhu coins. Other measures adopted by Wang Mang broadened the reach of the state monopolies on commodities, subjected trade and moneylending to strict regulation, and nationalized gold stocks. Such policies drove sound coin and gold out of circulation, unleashing rampant inflation and severely disrupting commerce and industrial production. Coins deposited in tombs and hoards during this era consist overwhelmingly of Wang's new currencies, suggesting that much of the existing stock of Wuzhu coins had vanished into the melting pot.[30]

Wang Mang's ambitious agenda directly challenged the political, social, and economic power of the magnate families and other estate owners, provoking fierce opposition. Government officials resisted implementing policies that threatened the vested interests of their kinfolk. Political chaos bred economic distress, antagonizing all ranks of society. In the end popular insurrections combined with the determined resistance of the landowning class toppled Wang's government. In 23 CE rebel forces seized the imperial palace and put Wang to death. Two years later, Liu Xiu (Emperor Guangwu, r. 25–57 CE) reestablished the Han dynasty, but moved the capital from Chang'an to Luoyang, near his ancestral nobility in Nanyang.

The relocation of the capital to the Central Plain inaugurated a new phase – designated the Later or Eastern Han (25–220 CE) – in the history of the Han dynasty. Most importantly, the restoration of Han rule solidified the social and economic dominance of the magnate families. Apart from Guangwu, the emperors exercised little personal authority; beginning from 88 CE, all of the Eastern Han emperors ascended the throne as children and abdicated or died before age 40. Military power devolved to the provincial level, where governors mustered their own standing forces, in effect creating private armies.[31] Consort families and eunuch cabals repeatedly usurped the power of the imperial office, plunging the court into incessant partisan strife. As the state's

---

[29] For an overview of Wang Mang's reign, see Bielenstein 1986: 224–40. On Wang's fiscal policies, see Yamada 1975.
[30] On Wang Mang's monetary policies, see Yamada 2000: 143–86.   [31] Lewis 2000b: 69–74.

capacity to intervene in the economy diminished, economic and social inequality intensified. Many more families fell into poverty, lost their independent means of livelihood, and were compelled to accept humble station as tenants, bondservants, or hired laborers.

Throughout the Eastern Han, condemnation of the growing concentration of wealth and landholdings swelled. By the second century CE mention of "middling families" disappears from political discourse; instead, social commentators such as Wang Fu, Cui Shi, and Zhongchang Tong depicted a starkly polarized social order in which the upper class had made itself lords of their inferiors.[32] These critics objected less to the disparities in wealth, perhaps, than to the subrogation of the state's control over the labor power of the populace; no longer liable for labor and military conscription, imperial subjects instead were in thrall to the private purposes of the magnate families.[33]

The evidence for tenurial relations and the concentration of landholdings in this period is almost wholly anecdotal, and it is impossible to measure the proportion of lands held by the great landowners. But there also is evidence for the persistence of villages of independent farms. A stele inscription dating from 72 CE records the establishment of an association (*dan* 僤) by twenty-five fellow villagers (with seven different surnames) in Yanshi (Henan), through which they raised funds to purchase 82 *mu* of land. The income from this land was intended to defray the group's collective obligations for serving as village headmen (*fulao* 父老), whose duties included superintending tax collection, public security, communal labor projects, and ritual ceremonies.[34] Each household subscribed 2,460 coins, which suggests that they occupied the upper end of the "middling families" stratum – constituting perhaps a quarter of the total village population. In this case the village community appears to have maintained a significant degree of independence from local magnates.

The formation of great estates during the Eastern Han resulted less from imperial dispensations such as *mingtianzhai* land grants than through purchases or debt forfeitures.[35] A stele inscription recovered from the tomb of Wang Xiaoyuan (d. 108 CE) in Pixian, Sichuan, although only partially legible, attests to the crucial role of the market in the formation of landed estates. This inscription has been identified as a land division testament in

---

[32] Utsunomiya 1955: 316–18; Tada 1964: 18; Watanabe 1986: 86. On this group of social critics, see Balazs 1964b.

[33] Ebrey 1986a: 626.

[34] Ning Ke 1982; Yamada 1993: 391–403. Another inscription dated 182 CE records the formation of a *dan* association by rural inhabitants to defray the costs of hiring substitutes to perform conscript labor service. See Ning Ke 1982: 23–24.

[35] Gao Min 1986: 41–42; Yamada 1993: 207.

which Wang apportioned his holdings among his heirs.[36] The inscription lists at least a dozen farms – ranging in size from 8 to 260 *mu*, with ten farms together totaling 1,255 *mu* – along with the name of the cultivator and the assets (oxen, buildings, and slaves) attached to them.[37] The document specifies the value of each asset, but using different language. Buildings and slaves usually were "valued" (*zhi* 直) at a certain number of coins, but *zhi* here probably referred to a standard value for assessing the *suanfu* tax rather than a market price. In contrast, nearly all of the land was assessed in terms of a debenture (*zhi* 質) or sale (*gu* 賈) value.[38] These notations suggest that Wang's lands were mostly acquired either through purchase or possessory loans, in which the creditor assumed control of real property in lieu of interest payment.

It appears that Wang Xiaoyuan possessed a sizable estate composed of separate farms cultivated by tenants, perhaps nominal owners who had pledged their lands to Wang in exchange for loans. This pattern seems to be generally true of the Han era. Magnate landowners rarely exercised direct control over agricultural production. More commonly, they leased lands to tenant farmers under sharecropping arrangements in which the landowner received 50 percent (or more, if the landlord supplied seed, tools, and/or draft animals) of the harvest. Although our sources remain mute about the terms of tenancy, tenant households most likely remained independent economic units. Moreover, hired laborers seem to have enjoyed rising wages and a greater measure of social respectability in the Eastern Han.[39] In Wang Xiaoyuan's day, tenant farmers and hired laborers were not yet subjected to the servile conditions that began to appear in the last decades of the Han.[40]

The most detailed account of the management of a landed estate in the Eastern Han is found in the calendar of annual work and ritual activities entitled *Monthly Instructions for the Four Classes of People* compiled by

[36] Although initially believed to be a register of properties, Zhang Xunliao and Liu Panshi (1980) have persuasively argued that the Pixian inscription must be a property division testament. This interpretation has been accepted by Yamada (1993: 202–07). For the text of the Pixian inscription, see Xie Yanxiang 1974.
[37] Some scholars believe that the slaves (a total of thirty-two, divided among six properties) transferred along with arable lands were fieldworkers, but this conclusion seems unwarranted. The slaves were allocated in groups of five (plus one group of seven) without regard to the size of the farm. The individual farms were fairly modest in size and were unlikely to require such large pools of labor. Moreover, six of the sixteen legible names of slaves are female and almost certainly domestic workers.
[38] On the implications of this nomenclature, see Ōkushi 1985.
[39] Shi Yang 2012. Shi emphasizes that although the laws proscribing private ownership of slaves were routinely flouted by magnate families, they effectively eliminated slaveholding by commoners, who instead turned to hired laborers. Moreover, under the Han migrant laborers were no longer treated as criminals subject to legal penalties as they were under Qin law.
[40] Tada 1964, 1965.

Cui Shi (c. 103–c. 170 CE).[41] Cui, a member of a prominent family of scholars, became embroiled in the factional struggles at the Luoyang court and was forced out of government office in 159 CE.[42] Cui vented his political frustrations in an acerbic treatise, *On Politics*, in which he decried the wretched conditions of the poor and the haughty disregard of the magnate families and imperial officials. "The great families amass fortunes measured in hundreds of millions of coins and landholdings equal to a hereditary prince," Cui wrote, "while the lower classes, with no land of their own, endure intractable hardships; fathers and sons, heads bowed, are enslaved in service to the rich."[43] Cui himself seems to have been a man of modest means, by the standards of his peers. Paying for his father's funeral expenses left him penniless, we are told, and Cui launched a brewing business to supplement his income from farming.

Addressed to the gentleman landowner, Cui's *Monthly Instructions* offers detailed guidance on estate management. In addition to cultivating millet, wheat, barley, legumes, and sesame, Cui's estate produced a wide range of processed foods such as fermented sauces, vinegar, pickles, yeast, and wine. The estate operated its own mill for grinding wheat flour and manufactured silk and hemp textiles, candles, and dyestuffs. Supervision of agricultural work and brewing was entrusted to overseers. Cui also mentions a wide range of tasks performed by women, who tended mulberry orchards, reeled and wove silk, and sewed clothes. In many respects the estate described by Cui resembles the contemporary tomb mural (dated to c. 145–180) of a manor from the Ordos region, along the great bend of the Yellow River, depicted in Figure 4.1. Adjacent to the manor house are horse stables, pens for sheep, pigs, and fowl, and gardens worked by farmers with hoes. At upper right farmers plow fields using teams of oxen, while women gather mulberry leaves at upper left. The three squares at lower left represent ponds in which hemp was soaked to soften the fibers. Other murals in this tomb depict granaries, tilt-hammers used to hull grain, oxcarts laden with harvest foods, and a brewery.[44]

Cui Shi gives no inkling of the size or status of the labor force on his estate. Scholarly opinion is divided; some suggest that Cui employed tenant farmers, while others believe he relied on hired laborers or slaves, or both. Given the harsh denunciations of the servile conditions of the poor and dispossessed he voiced in *On Politics*, it seems unlikely that Cui himself used slaves as

[41] For studies of Cui's *Monthly Instructions*, see Yang Liansheng 1934; Nishijima 1966: 49–57; Amano 1967; Ebrey 1974; Zhu Shaohou 1985: 101–06.

[42] Opinion differs on when Cui wrote the *Monthly Instructions*. Wang Guoding proposed that Cui wrote it in retirement in the final years of his life, while Shi Shenghan argued that he wrote it much earlier, in the 140s. Both scholars agree, however, that Cui was living in Luoyang at the time he composed the treatise, and that it reflects the economic environment of the capital region. See Amano 1967: 363–64.

[43] *ZhL*: 48.   [44] Wang Zhongshu 1982: 60.

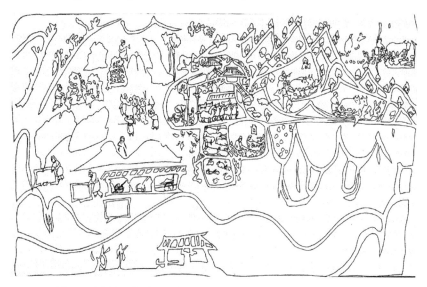

Figure 4.1 Mural of Han Manor, Holingor, Inner Mongolia
Source: Neimenggu zizhiqu bowuguan gongzuodui 1978: 21, figure 38.

fieldworkers. Clearly Cui expected the landowner to devote personal attention to the operation of his estate, but he also delegated supervision of the brewery and agricultural work to overseers. Most likely Cui exercised some degree of patriarchal dominion over the farmers, whether tenants or hired laborers, as well as domestic workers and servants.

Like most works of its type, the *Monthly Instructions* preaches the virtues of thrift, industry, and resourcefulness. Cui by no means envisioned his estate as self-sufficient, however; he specifies the proper seasons for buying and selling a wide range of goods to supply domestic needs and earn additional income. In addition to its brewery business, the estate was expected to earn income from the sale of millet, beans, sesame, and a variety of finished silk goods, while purchasing wheat, bran, glutinous rice, hemp cloth, thread, and charcoal. For many of these items Cui advised buying in one month and selling in another to take advantage of seasonal price changes. Judicious resort to market opportunities did not contradict Cui's ethic of frugality and self-reliance.

By Cui Shi's time, the central government was rapidly losing effective control over local society. Men like Cui retreated from the partisan strife that paralyzed the capital and carved out a place for themselves as leaders of local communities. The breakdown of social order and the ensuing spread of violence can already be glimpsed in Cui's *Monthly Instructions*, which urged landowners to maintain weapons and the defensive walls surrounding their manors in good repair and to conduct military exercises regularly. When the Han state crumbled after the Yellow Turban rebellion in 184, private power fully eclipsed public authority. Local magnates mustered militias from among their kinfolk, tenants, and neighbors to shelter their families and property from roving bandits. Dependent upon local magnates for protection, tenants and laborers were reduced to the condition of bondservitude. After the demise of the Han dynasty in 220, the magnate families coalesced into a tight-knit aristocracy, and a full-blooded manorial order came into being.

Population trends

The Han historian Ban Gu repeatedly asserted that the wars and economic turmoil caused by Emperor Wu coupled with natural disasters reduced the population of the Han Empire by half. Modern scholars tend to concur with Ban's estimate, suggesting that during the half-century of Wu's reign the population fell from approximately 44–50 million to 22–25 million.[45] Although fragmentary data from a group of nobilities indicates an absolute decrease during Wu's reign, such a dramatic decline seems unlikely. Subsequently the population grew steadily during the last century of the Western Han. The earliest surviving national census, from 2 CE, recorded a population of 12.2 million households and 59.6 million individuals. The next extant national census, from 57 CE, counted only 21 million persons, reflecting the great disorder and population losses of the Wang Mang era – and also, perhaps, the growth of private clientage. By 105 the registered population had recovered to 53 million, but leveled off thereafter. The final Han census of 157 reported a population of 10.7 million households and 56 million persons.

The 2 CE census reveals that nearly half of the entire population of the Han Empire was concentrated on the Central Plain, where population densities far exceeded any other region, including the environs of Chang'an (Table 4.1; Map 4.1). After the relocation of the capital to Luoyang in the Eastern Han, the population became even more concentrated in the Central Plain. During the Eastern Han era the Nanyang region south of Luoyang and the Jiangnan region in the Lower Yangzi River Basin achieved the highest rates of population growth. But the population of the south still lagged far behind that of the north.

Newly excavated documents have yielded robust demographic data that amplifies our knowledge of the Han population but also raises questions about the accuracy of aggregate population statistics. For example, the population register for the West canton of Nan commandery (modern Jiangling, Hubei)

---

[45] Higo 1990: 119–22, 129: Ge Jianxiong 2000: 375–95.

Table 4.1 *Regional population densities in Han China, 2 CE*

Region	Population (2 CE)	Persons/sq. km
(1) Capital Region (Sanfu)	2,436,360	45.1
(2) Central Plain Macroregion	26,201,340	70.4
(3) Nanyang Macroregion	9,266,019	43.0
(4) Lower Yangzi Macroregion	5,333,272	13.2
(5) Sichuan Macroregion	3,105,848	8.4
(6) Middle Yangzi Macroregion	1,697,172	3.5
(7) Northern Frontiers	6,740,746	6.6
(8) Southern Frontiers	2,514,518	2.6

Source: Liang Fangzhong 1980: 18–9, table A.4.

for 139 BCE shows that local officials indeed gathered precise figures on population changes in their annual reports to the central government (Table 4.2). But at the same time the register shows a conspicuous under-reporting of males – and especially adult males – that no doubt resulted from evasion of military service. The low number of persons per household (3.7, compared to the more typical range of 4.8–5.2) suggests that in this case many males eluded registration altogether.

A similar under-reporting of males appears in the household-level data from Changsha (Hunan) dating from the 230s CE, shortly after the fall of the Han dynasty. The Zoumalou cache of documents includes nearly 500 house-hold registers from a single county within the territory of the Wu kingdom, which retained the Han fiscal system.[46] Although the overall gender ratio (107 males to 100 females) matches the expected ratio for premodern popu-lations, the number of females age 14 and below is only two-thirds that of males, while males age 20–59 (liable for military conscription) are only 88 percent the number of females (Table 4.3). In addition, nearly 10 percent of all persons – overwhelmingly (80 percent) males – were noted as suffering from physical infirmities, presumably ones that disqualified them from labor service.[47] The Zoumalou registers also record improbably high numbers of persons age 60 and above. Nonetheless, the ability of the fledgling Wu kingdom to conduct household registration amid the chaos and civil wars of the Three Kingdoms era inspires confidence in the fiscal capabilities of the Han state.

In the view of some demographic historians, however, the new evidence for Han population registration displays significant distortions that call into

---

[46] The most comprehensive study of the Zoumalou documents – based only on the first collection of the three sets of documents published thus far – is Yu Zhenbo 2004b.

[47] Ibid.: 134–41. The exact meanings of the categories of infirmities are uncertain.

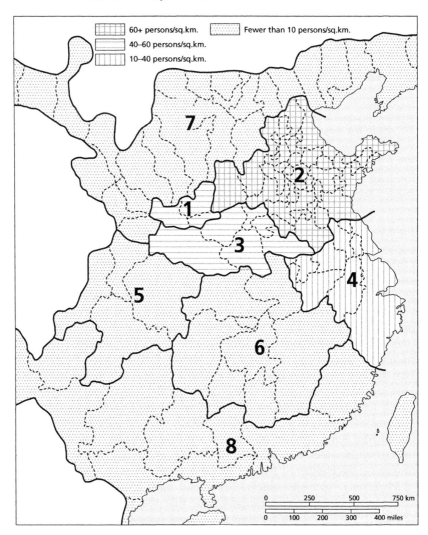

Map 4.1 Regional population densities in Han China, 2 CE

question the reliability of national population figures.[48] Yet taken collectively the new data suggests that the Han registers provide accurate information on the numbers of households and persons, even though the ages of males and the elderly often were altered to evade military and labor service and to obtain

---

[48] E.g., Gao Dalun 1998. For a rebuttal of Gao's critique, see Ge Jianxiong 2000: 323–27.

Table 4.2 *West Canton register of households and persons, 139 BCE*

Households	1,196	
Newly added households	70	
Terminated households	35	
Net increase in households	*45	
Adult males	991	Total males: 2,036
Minor males	1,045	
Adult females	1,695	Total females: 2,337
Minor females	642	
Newly added individuals	86	
Terminated individuals	43	
Net increase in individuals	43	
Total individuals	4,373	Net increase in this year: 0.99%

*Clearly a calculation error has occurred; probably should read "35."
Source: "Ernian Xixiang hukou bu 二年西鄉戶口簿," cited in Yang Zhenhong 2010: 1.

Table 4.3 *Population figures from Zoumalou (Changsha) registers, c. 235*

Age	Males	Females	Gender ratio	Total	(a) % of total
Under 6	229	182	126:100	411	16.5
7–14	298	170	175:100	468	18.7
15–19	88	83	106:100	171	6.8
20–29	194	212	92:100	406	16.3
30–39	180	229	79:100	409	16.4
40–49	84	110	76:100	194	7.8
50–59	88	81	109:100	169	6.8
60–69	72	83	87:100	155	6.2
70+	57	59	97:100	116	4.6
Total	1,290	1,209	107:100	2,499	

Source: Yu Zhenbo 2004b: 123, tables 5.1, 5.2.

the special honors granted to the aged. Correcting for these distortions, the age profile of the Han population is highly consistent with that of the still over-whelmingly agrarian society depicted in the first modern census conducted by the newly established People's Republic of China in 1953 (Table 4.4).

Commerce, cities, and foreign trade

With the founding of the Qin and Han empires, the state's demand for goods increased prodigiously. The Han central government included a large number of industrial agencies (of which the Shangfang Bureau was the most important) and also assigned local officials' responsibility for the manufacture or

146 	The Economic History of China

Table 4.4 *Age distributions in Han population registers*
(all figures are percentages)

	Nan (139 BCE)	Donghai (13 BCE)	Changsha (c. 235 CE)	1953 Census
6 and below		18.8	16.5	20.6
14 and below	44.0*		35.2	36.3
15–59	(51.7)*		54.0	56.4
60+	2.14**		10.8	9.6
	(4.3)			
60–70			6.2	7.3
70+			4.6	2.3
80+		2.43		0.34

*Nan figures only distinguish "minors" and "adults"; probably the "minor" category included males up to age 20, while the "adult" category included females age 15–20.
**Males only.
(Figures in parentheses): estimates based on doubling the 60+ population figure for males.
Sources: Gao Dalun 1998: 115–17; Ge Jianxiong 2000: 234–35; Yu Zhenbo 2004b: 123–25; Yang Zhenhong 2010: 3–4.

procurement of goods such as weapons, clothing and textiles, bronze wares, gold and other metals, ships, lacquer wares, mortuary goods, and a host of sundry artisanal products. The three state-run textile factories established at Linzi in Shandong each had several thousand artisans producing high-quality silks for the imperial household.[49] The creation of the salt and iron monopolies further enhanced the powerful influence of the imperial state in production and exchange during the Western Han period. Government workshops relied heavily on conscript and convict laborers supervised by a few master craftsmen. In a diatribe of 44 BCE denouncing the spendthrift excesses of the imperial court, the statesman Gong Yu complained that the government employed more than 100,000 convict laborers in its workshops, mints, and mines.[50]

Nowhere was the intrusion of the state into the economy felt more strongly than in the iron industry.[51] Iron manufacture had quickly reached a high level of technological sophistication in the late Warring States period, by which time

[49] Originally (e.g., Satō 1962: 145–47) it was believed that the passage which cites these figures referred to factories in three different cities. Recent scholarship instead favors the view that all three factories were located in Linzi. See Wang Zijin 2005.

[50] On the Han state's extensive use of conscript and convict labor in industrial production, see Barbieri-Low 2007: 212–56. For Gong Yu's estimate of convict laborers, see ibid.: 220.

[51] The following synopsis of the iron industry under the Han state monopoly is based on Wagner 2001, 2008: 171–248.

cast iron was produced in blast furnaces. Han ironworks took two forms: blast furnaces used to smelt iron from ore, and foundries in which raw iron was either cast into tools and weapons in a cupola furnace or converted to wrought iron in a fining hearth, a process that resulted in stronger products. The establishment of the iron monopoly in 119 BCE led to a consolidation of the industry in state-run ironworks. The census of 2 CE lists forty-eight local iron monopoly offices, chiefly in Shandong, northern Jiangsu, along the Hebei–Shanxi border, and in southern Shanxi (see Map 3.2). Most of the state ironworks were located near cities rather than the mines, suggesting that control of production took priority over considerations of cost. The state probably recruited supervisors and master craftsmen from the ranks of formerly private merchants and artisans, but unskilled tasks were performed by convict laborers.

During the era of the iron monopoly, smaller bloomery furnaces – the only iron smelting technology available in Europe before the twelfth century – seem to have disappeared entirely. Even after the Eastern Han government rescinded the iron monopoly in 88 CE iron manufacture remained confined to large-scale blast furnaces and foundries. The blast furnace technology and the economies of scale achieved by the state ironworks in the Han apparently rendered the bloomery technology economically obsolete. When small-scale ironworks reappeared in China during the Song dynasty they were operated using small blast furnaces rather than bloomery techniques.

The Eastern Han government gravitated away from direct state supervision of craft manufacture to procurement of goods from private artisans and merchants, or simply collecting taxes from these groups in lieu of goods.[52] One notable contribution of state workshops in the Han was the development, if not the invention, of papermaking. In 105 CE Cai Lun, the director of the Shangfang workshops, presented the emperor with fine paper made under his direction. Although Cai Lun's product achieved great renown and was widely emulated, he appears to have refined papermaking techniques already in existence.[53] Inscriptions on Han lacquer wares and bronze mirrors not only identify the artisan but in many cases claim that these pieces were made in imperial factories such as the Shangfang workshops, evidence of the cachet of the imperial trademark (often purloined by private manufacturers) in the marketplace.[54]

Despite the large role of the state in industrial production in the early Han period, private enterprise also flourished, especially under the laissez-faire

---

[52] Yamada 1998: 726.

[53] Tsien 1985: 38–41. The oldest paper artifacts have been traced back to the second–first century BCE, but the earliest specimens of paper with writing date from the time of Cai Lun. See ibid.

[54] Barbieri-Low 2007: 142–52.

policies of Emperor Wen. Sang Hongyang, himself born into a merchant family, lauded the entrepreneurial skills of merchants who "exercised their own intelligence in buying and selling, shipped goods to wherever they brought the greatest return, and profited from the differences in prices from one place to another."[55] The historian Sima Qian described private entrepreneurs in a wide range of industries, such as breweries, foodstuffs, leather and silk goods, dyeworks, lumberyards, potteries, bronze foundries, carriage-making, and lacquer wares. Some sense of the scale of commercial enterprises can be gleaned from Sima's assertion that farmers, traders, and craftsmen who have capital of 10,000 coins can expect a return of 2,000 coins in profit in a year; likewise, merchants with capital of one million coins can make a profit of 200,000 coins annually, an amount "equivalent to the income of a hereditary nobility." Speaking of the great tycoons of his day, Sima Qian singled out iron smelters and dealers in salt, fish, and other goods who accumulated fortunes amounting to 20 million or even 100 million coins.[56] But these enormous sums still were dwarfed by the wealth of the great estate owners of the Eastern Han, whose assets were measured in billions of coins.[57]

The commercial enterprises celebrated by Sima Qian all seem to have been family businesses; there is scant evidence for business partnerships apart from the small peddling operation headed by Zhang Yan discussed in Chapter 3. Otherwise, references in Han texts to "pooling funds" are confined to cases of collective payments for boats and pack animals rather than sharing investment risk. However, a rare trove of legal documents concerning a commercial dispute in 27 CE suggests that agents were routinely employed in commercial dealings. A military officer stationed at the frontier garrison of Juyan, Master Li, engaged a professional commercial agent, Kou En, to transport and sell a consignment of 5,000 fish in Lude, a journey of ten-odd days. Li obtained grain and a pair of oxen supplied by two local civil officials to pay Kou's expenses and salary; Kou was to receive one ox and 27 bushels of grain for his services. Li and Kou negotiated in advance that Li would receive a payment of 400,000 coins from the sale of the fish. However, the sale netted only 320,000 coins, even after Kou sold one of the oxen. Disgruntled, Li filed a legal suit demanding full payment of the agreed price as well as compensation for the sale of the ox. The judicial investigation revealed that Li had seized sundry goods, meat, and barley (valued at 24,600 coins in total) which Kou had brought back to Juyan; moreover Li had never paid Kou's son (whom he hired to catch the fish) a hundred days' wages valued at 80,000 coins. The dispute essentially hinged on whether Kou was merely a hired agent entitled to wages or an independent contractor who was obliged to deliver

---

[55] Chapter 17, "Pinfu," in *YTL*, 1: 220.
[56] *SJ* 129.3271–74; transl. in Sima Qian 1993: 447–50.   [57] Yamada 2000: 210.

the payment stipulated in his agreement with Li. The investigating official deemed Li's suit entirely without merit, and shortly afterward Li was removed from his post. It is not clear, however, whether the dismissal was based on legal principles or censure of Master Li's unseemly conduct as a public official.[58]

The Kou En case and other Juyan documents reveal that frontier officials regularly engaged in trade on their private account. The nature of the partnership between Master Li and the two civil officials is unclear; the latter may have been coerced to assume some of the capital costs of the venture, rather than true partners. No doubt many purveyors preferred to engage commercial agents like Kou En – who was far from his home in Yingchuan, Henan – to undertake the transport and sale of their goods in distant markets. The practice of buying and selling on credit (known as *shimai* 貰買, 貰賣), with payment deferred on terms specified by contract, also frequently recurs in the Juyan documents.[59]

In the Kou En case, both Kou and his son tendered their services in return for wage payments, which was a common practice in Han times. Cui Shi also makes reference to a magistrate – "if he does not have a slave" – needing to hire a valet who is paid "a monthly wage of 1,000 coins, plus 500 coins for fodder and meat, and 500 coins for charcoal, salt, and vegetables" in addition to a grain ration.[60] Like official salaries, wages typically were paid half in coin and half in grain. Most commonly hired labor was engaged by the day or month, but indentured labor (*baoyi* 保役) – terms of one to as many as fifteen years are mentioned – also was practiced. Although indentured labor often took the form of debt bondage, it did not lead to permanent servitude.[61]

Yamada Katsuyoshi argues that in the wake of the decline of large-scale state workshops in the Eastern Han, artisans gravitated toward the production of luxury goods for the magnate class. In his view, individual artisans became subject to a greater degree of personal subordination to their private patrons.

---

[58] This summary is based on Kong Xiangjun 2012, which proposes a new and more persuasive reading of this cache of depositions and reports compiled by a judicial official in Juyan. The case also is discussed in Scogin 1990: 1362–65; Helen Wang 2004: 52–53. Ding Bangyou (2009: 318–19) notes that the negotiated sale price of 80 coins per fish was vastly higher than the ordinary price (10 coins or less) for fish recorded in other Juyan documents. But all of the monetary sums cited in these documents are extremely high, reflecting the hyperinflation that resulted from Wang Mang's radical monetary experiments. At this time various local coinage issues, including large quantities of substandard coins, were circulating in the frontier region. See Helen Wang 2004: 48–49.

[59] For examples from the Juyan documents, see Xu Yueyao 1989: 55–56; Sumiya 1994; Helen Wang 2004: 53–54. On the use and nature of contracts in land sales, purchases of goods, and other transactions in the Han period, see Scogin 1990.

[60] *ZhL*: 41.

[61] Satō 1962: 287–90. On *bao* 保 (or 葆) as a designation for indentured labor, see Qiu Xigui 1979: 109–10.

But the evidence for this hypothesis is thin, and others question Yamada's claims for the decline of commerce and handicraft industry in the Eastern Han.[62] The dismantling of imperial workshops may well have diminished the role of women in industrial production, however. Although women comprised the great majority of the artisans in the state-run textile and lacquer workshops, they probably had fewer opportunities in private employment.[63] The evidence for prices and wages, limited as it is, does not support Yamada's argument for a decline in the economic position of hired laborers in the Eastern Han, however. Generally speaking, the normal range for grain prices in the Eastern Han (150–200 coins per *hu*) was roughly twice the range in the Western Han (80–110 coins per *hu*), while monthly wages appear to have risen at least three-fold.[64] This apparent trend of increasing real wages has been cited as evidence for the higher economic and social status of wage laborers in the Eastern Han and the concomitant disappearance of slave labor.[65]

The practice of lending money at interest (using language derived from animals giving birth to offspring) is well attested for the Warring States period.[66] No formal credit institutions existed during the Han dynasty, but frequent references to debts and the pervasive – if illegal – practice of debt bondage indicate that moneylending was a staple feature of the Han economy. The scholar Huan Tan (*c.* 43 BCE –28 CE), a sympathizer of Wang Mang's reforms, bemoaned the debilitating effects of usury, writing that "the rich merchants of today dispose of great quantities of land and money in making loans. The sons and brothers of middling families undertake indentured labor on their behalf, hastening to and fro with the diligence of menial servants, collecting payments comparable to the income of a hereditary noble."[67] As the example of Wang Xiaoyuan cited above suggests, possessory loans (*zhi* 質) were a crucial means whereby magnates expanded their landholdings. Wang Mang's reforms created a credit system under which the state offered interest-free loans for sacrificial rituals and funerals in addition to low-interest loans (3 percent per month, with a maximum of 10 percent per year) for poor farmers. Presumably these interest rates were modest compared to prevailing rates in the private market. Yet calculation problems in Han mathematics

---

[62] Yamada 1998. Gao Min (1989) argues against Yamada's hypothesis, and implicitly so does Kakinuma (2011).

[63] On women artisans in the Han, see Barbieri-Low 2007: 107–14, who notes that the vast majority of inscribed Qin-Han lacquer wares bear names of women and children.

[64] For grain prices, see Ding Bangyou 2009: 10–11, 162–89; Yu Yaohua 2000: 235–57; for wage rates, see Shi Yang 2012. The Han *hu* was roughly equivalent to 20 liters.

[65] Shi Yang 2012. Shi merely cites the high nominal wages in Eastern Han without considering the effects of price changes on real wages, but as I show here the price data supports the hypothesis of rising real wages.

[66] Yamada 2000: 245.   [67] *HHS* 28A: 1014–15.

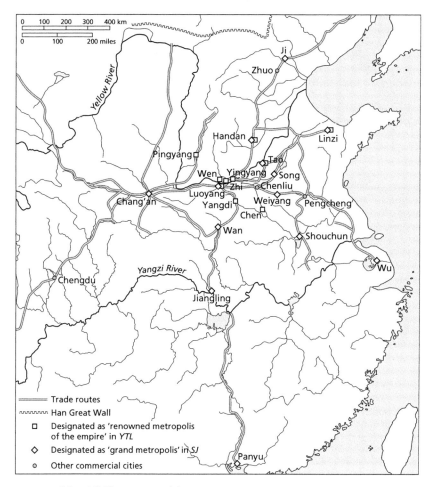

Map 4.2 Han commercial centers

treatises also use monthly interest rates of 3 percent, at least for short-term (a month or less) loans.[68]

Utsunomiya Kiyoyoshi identified more than twenty major cities in the Western Han period with estimated populations in the range of 30,000 to 100,000 inhabitants (Map 4.2).[69] Most of these cities were concentrated on the Central Plain; only two were located south of the Yangzi River. Following

---

[68] Ye Yuying 2005: 42–43. Ye suggests that Han officials in fact were successful in curbing usury.
[69] Utsunomiya 1955: 112–17.

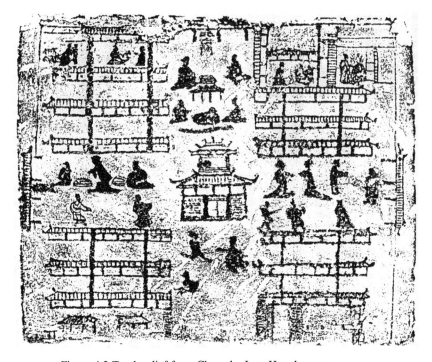

Figure 4.2 Tomb relief from Chengdu. Late Han dynasty

Qin precedents, the Han closely supervised urban marketplaces, which were placed under the supervision of a variety of government inspectors.[70] The marketplaces were enclosed by walls and gates; all shops in a given trade were confined to the same street within the marketplace; and the officials signaled the opening and closing hours by striking a great drum mounted in their watchtower at the center of the marketplace (Figure 4.2). As noted in Chapter 3, the Han government compiled registries of merchants separate from ordinary commoners and prohibited them from owning land or holding office. Emperor Wu used these registers to impose special taxes on merchants and to conscript them into military service at frontier garrisons.

It is difficult to determine to what extent such punitive measures, or the system of state regulation of marketplaces, stifled private commerce. Certainly the establishment of the salt and iron monopolies deprived merchants of the most lucrative sources of profit. Moreover, archaeological research indicates that many cities shrank in size and population over the course of the

---

[70] On government supervision of marketplaces, see Xu Yueyao 1989; Sahara 2002a: 281–323.

Han dynasty.[71] There is also corresponding evidence for a ruralization of the Chinese population compared to earlier times, resulting in a substantial increase in the number of small village communities.[72] The ultimate result of Wu's fiscal policies, it has been suggested, was to cause capital and investment to drain away from commerce to agriculture.[73] According to Yamada, declining mint output on top of Wu's *dirigiste* interference disrupted private commerce and the circulation of coin even before Wang Mang's catastrophic attempt to introduce a wholly new monetary system. The failure of Wang's reforms led to the withdrawal of sound Wuzhu coin from circulation and the disappearance of the use of gold as money altogether. The proliferation of debased counterfeit coin and the shift toward taxes collected in commodities such as grain and silk in the Eastern Han period reflected an increasingly emaciated urban and commercial economy.[74]

Other scholars, however, have argued that the post-Emperor Wu era witnessed not a withering of the money economy, but rather a reorientation of commercial activity away from major urban centers to local markets.[75] Wang Fu's (*c.* 78–163) statement that "the empire encompasses a hundred commanderies, a thousand counties, and ten thousand markets and towns (*shiyi* 市邑)" often has been cited as evidence for the broad distribution of marketplaces across the countryside in the mid-Eastern Han era.[76] Yet corroboration of this thesis remains elusive. We know little about the operation of local markets,

---

[71] Apart from the capital of Chang'an, virtually all major Han cities were significantly smaller in scale and residential occupation than their Warring States predecessors. See Emura 2005: 265; Pirazzoli-t'Serstevens 2010: 185. Sahara (2002a: 30–31) – who stresses the military rather than commercial character of cities in this era – contends that the decline of urban population in the Han resulted from the reduced need to station large garrisons in cities rather than the contraction of private commerce.

[72] Underhill *et al.* 2008: 21–24.   [73] Yamada 1993: 238; Emura 2005: 264–71.

[74] Yamada 2000: 143–222. Following in the footsteps of Miyazaki Ichisada and Lao Gan, Yamada suggests that much of China's gold was exported via the Central Asian trade routes. See ibid.: 133–35. There is scant evidence for such a drain of gold abroad, however.

[75] Tada 1965; Shigechika 1990; Kamiya 1994.

[76] Chapter 12, "Fuchi" 浮侈, in *QL*: 120. Huang Jinyan (2005: 153) goes farther, confidently asserting that every *xiang* and *li* (over 72,000 in the Western Han, and roughly 40,000 in the Eastern Han) had markets that operated with a high degree of autonomy. Sahara (2002a: 303–5) likewise emphasizes that periodic markets were common in much of rural China, but in his view the stringent government regulation of urban marketplaces also was applied to rural markets, which he locates at the sites of local constabularies known as *ting* 亭. As we saw in Chapter 3, under the Qin the phrase *shiting* 市亭 designated artifacts produced in government workshops. Kamiya (1994) concurs with Sahara's identification of *ting* as the sites of rural periodic markets. Challenging the common view that commerce declined after Emperor Wu's time, Kamiya instead asserts on one hand that rural markets proliferated in the late Western and Eastern Han and on the other hand that local officials exercised a significant measure of control over these markets. Observing that the number of *ting* in the Eastern Han (12,442 in 153 CE) was of the same magnitude as Wang Fu's estimate of *shiyi*, Kamiya concludes that *shiyi* designated rural rather than urban marketplaces.

but estate owners routinely engaged in handicraft production as well as marketing their agricultural surplus. Cui Shi, as we have seen, sold wine and cloth in addition to various foodstuffs, while Fan Zhong planted catalpa trees on his estate to supply the raw material for lacquer ware manufacture. Magnate landowners often wielded monopolistic control over local markets. Complaints of politically connected magnates "cornering the market" (*guque* 辜榷) by preventing the entry of competitors into local marketplaces were frequently aired beginning in the late first century BCE.[77] The rise of great estates during the Eastern Han gave further impetus to this crucial shift in the locus of economic activity. Commerce remained a vital part of economic life, but goods circulated through local markets in the countryside rather than accumulating in urban emporia.

Few Chinese merchants ventured beyond the empire's frontiers during the Han period. Despite the often-cited lament of Pliny the Elder (23–79 CE) about the debilitating drain of gold out of the Roman Empire to pay for imports of Chinese silk, the notion of a "silk road" in Han times is largely a myth. Although Roman merchants from Egypt and Syria sailed to India to obtain Chinese silks as well as cotton, spices, and gems, few if any Roman goods reached China in Han times. Imports to China chiefly consisted of exotic luxury goods from Western Asia and India such as coral, gemstones, pearls, and aromatics. Organized trading caravans appear to have emerged only in the third century CE, after the demise of the Han Empire. Tribute, plunder, and gift-giving rather than commerce accounted for most of the widespread distribution of Han goods such as silk yarn and cloth, lacquer wares, and bronze mirrors throughout Central Asia.[78]

The rise of pastoral nomadism in the steppe grasslands of Eastern Eurasia in the first millennium BCE transformed China's northern frontier into more sharply differentiated ecological and economic zones. The steppe inhabitants largely abandoned sedentary life – perhaps because of an increasingly arid environment – in favor of reliance on animal husbandry to meet their needs for food, clothing, shelter, and fuel. The sixth–fourth centuries BCE witnessed the formation in eastern Eurasia of the classic steppe nomad culture in which warrior aristocracies achieved political supremacy. The spread of iron metallurgy enhanced the military power of the nomads, who subjugated settled populations along the northern frontier and organized themselves into confederations to conduct diplomatic and commercial intercourse with Chinese states.[79] Archaeological remains of nomadic cultures in the Ordos region display a distinct shift by the late fourth century BCE: fewer weapons, more

---

[77] Kamiya 1994: 662–66.   [78] On this point see the meticulous research of Raschke (1978).
[79] State formation among steppe nomads usually has been attributed to the nomads' chronic need for access to the products of sedentary societies, which fostered the rise of warrior rulers,

iron artifacts of all types, and hoards of gold, silver, and bronze wares that attest to the accumulation of treasure as a mark of elite status. Finds of bronze and gold belt buckles and other ornaments made in Qin workshops using animal designs borrowed from the pan-Eurasian nomad culture attest to the manufacture of goods specifically for trade with the nomadic peoples.[80]

From its inception the Han Empire was bedeviled by a powerful confederation of steppe nomads known as the Xiongnu.[81] Xiongnu raids on Han territories commenced in the year of the dynasty's founding, and from as early as 198 BCE the Han sought peace on the northern frontier by offering the Xiongnu gifts of silk and grain. Beginning in Emperor Wen's reign, the Han inaugurated a system of tributary diplomacy under which it sent annual payments of millet, gold, and silk yarn and cloth to the Xiongnu in exchange for a cessation of raiding and nominal recognition of Han imperial sovereignty. The Han also established markets along the frontier where the Xiongnu could barter with Chinese merchants. The stigma of "buying peace" incited Emperor Wu to abrogate the truce with the Xiongnu in 133 BCE and embark on his campaigns of conquest in the "western regions." Sang Hongyang envisioned that the imperial government would reap lucrative profits from foreign trade, but instead the enormous expenditures on distant garrisons and fortifications drained the Han treasuries. Wu's successors reverted to the tributary system arrangement. Although the Xiongnu confederation split into two groups in the late first century BCE, the onerous burden of tribute payments on state finances persisted. In the late first century CE the cost of the tributary system reportedly consumed 7 percent of total government revenues.[82]

Trade conducted at the Chinese garrisons and frontier trading posts was largely limited to local exchange of staple goods. Significant long-distance exchange across Central Asia did not emerge until the second century CE, the heyday of the Kushan kingdom (c. 30–260 CE), centered in Afghanistan.[83] The Kushan rulers, descended from nomad warriors, actively encouraged commerce. Kushan became the crossroads of trade routes that extended eastward to China and southward to India and across the Arabian Sea to the Roman world. The Kushan royal treasury at Begram contained imported bronzes, glass, and alabaster sculptures from the Roman Empire, Indian

strategies of predation, and the resolution of violent confrontations through tributary and commercial exchanges. See Khazanov 1989; Barfield 1989. Di Cosmo (2002: 167–74), in contrast, emphasizes not the contrasting modes of economic livelihood between nomadic and sedentary peoples but rather the political interrelationship between nomadic polities and sedentary states.

[80] So and Bunker 1995: 53–67; Di Cosmo 2002: 83–87.
[81] On Han relations with the Xiongnu confederation, see di Cosmo 2002: 161–311.
[82] Yü 1967: 64.
[83] On the role of Kushan as the key intermediary in trans-Eurasian exchange during this period, see Liu Xinru 1988.

ivories, and Chinese lacquer wares.[84] The Kushan also minted a prodigious amount of gold coin (the first gold coins in the Indic world, perhaps reminted from Roman ones), but merchants in Central Asia preferred Chinese silks rather than coin as their medium of exchange. No Kushan coins have been found in Han territories. The Han state shipped large quantities of coin to frontier regions to pay its soldiers, but these coins did not circulate beyond the garrison towns. As early as 30 CE the rulers of the oasis city-state of Khotan issued bronze coins that imitated Kushan currencies yet also bore inscriptions in Chinese designating their weight in Chinese units. Although these coins reveal that the Khotanese reckoned values both in terms of Kushan and Han coins, given their limited spatial range they do not seemed to have figured in long-distance trade.[85]

Economic retrenchment during the Period of Disunion

Imperial governance essentially collapsed after the outbreak of the Yellow Turban rebellion in 184. Although the Han dynasty lingered on, power devolved into the hands of the military leaders who raised personal armies to suppress the rebellion, chief among them the notorious Cao Cao. Following Cao Cao's death in 220 his son Cao Pei declared the founding a new dynasty, Wei, to succeed the Han. His rivals immediately proclaimed their own independent regimes, Shu in the southwest and Wu in the southeast, ushering in the Three Kingdoms period.

The Jin dynasty, which supplanted the Wei in North China in 265 and reunified the country in 280, made an ambitious effort to reassert centralized control over the empire and its economy. But the Jin court was riven by internecine conflict and beset by hostile enemies among the steppe nomads on its northern frontier. In 311 nomad invaders sacked the Jin capital of Luoyang, forcing the court to flee to the southeast. In 317 the Jin court reestablished itself at Jiankang (modern Nanjing), on the south bank of the Yangzi River. For much of the fourth century North China remained a battleground ravaged by marauding armies, both Chinese and non-Chinese. Some measure of order was restored by the chieftains of a Xianbei confederation of nomad warriors, who established their Northern Wei kingdom in 386. By 439 the Northern Wei extended its rule over nearly all of North China. For nearly three centuries, however, China was split between a series of Chinese-ruled dynasties in the south and non-Chinese conquerors in the north.

---

[84] On the Begram hoard, see Raschke 1978: 632–34; Mehendale 1996. Mehendale contends – unpersuasively, to my mind – that the Begram hoard was not a royal treasury but a merchant storehouse.
[85] Helen Wang 2004: 37–8.

The magnate families' dominance over society and the economy intensified during these centuries. Local warlords and rich landowners formed private militias of military retainers (*buqu* 部曲) and constructed fortified villages to defend their property and dependents. Refugees displaced by war and independent farming families often pledged themselves as private clients (*ke* 客) of these local magnates and took refuge in their fortresses. As the threat of warfare receded, many of the military retainers became agricultural laborers. Private clientage essentially became a form of bondservitude. The clients paid half or more of their harvest to their lord, but contributed no taxes or labor service to the state.[86]

To shore up its base of support the Wei kingdom created a new institution for recruiting government officials, the Nine Ranks system, that granted the most powerful magnate families hereditary rights to office. Similar policies were adopted by successive dynasties in both the north and the south. The Nine Ranks system also divided the population into noble (*shi* 士) and commoner (*shu* 庶) households, laying the legal and institutional foundations for rigid social stratification. *Shi* families acquired a broad range of privileges, such as legal immunities and exemption from certain taxes and conscript labor, that defined them as a distinct aristocratic class. This aristocracy dominated social and economic life in both north and south throughout the Period of Disunion.

The social and political turmoil that ravaged China in the wake of the Yellow Turban rebellion radically altered the priorities of the warlords competing for the imperial mantle. Their main concern was not the concentration of landownership, but rather population losses and land abandonment. In 196, after civil wars had left the capital cities of Luoyang and Chang'an in ruins, Cao Cao set a puppet emperor on the Han throne while maneuvering to bolster his personal power. He assigned tracts of abandoned lands to both soldiers and civilian households, who in effect became tenants of Cao's warlord regime. These agricultural colonies (*tuntian* 屯田) provided crucial revenues that enabled Cao to consolidate his control over North China. But after the founding of the Wei dynasty Cao's successors routinely rewarded generals and officers with allotments of *tuntian* lands and the households that worked them, which in effect privatized these resources.[87]

Cao Cao also jettisoned the Qin-Han principle of uniform taxation of individuals in favor of graduated taxation based on household wealth. In so doing Cao completed a trend that had been long underway. From the Wang Mang era onward, the imperial state often resorted to irregular requisitions (*diao* 調) to raise funds for military campaigns. In contrast to the regular

---

[86] Tang Changru 1990.   [87] Fujiie 1989: 119–40; Gao Min 1986: 109–20.

suanfu poll taxes paid in coin, these levies were assessed on households graded according to wealth and commonly paid in various types of fine cloth. Over the course of the Eastern Han such irregular levies became increasingly routinized. In 198 Cao made the *diao* assessment the centerpiece of his new "household levy" (*hudiao* 戶調) tax plan.[88] Under the *hudiao* system households paid taxes in grain and cloth, but not in coin. Thus, in addition to shifting the basis of taxation from the individual to the household, the *hudiao* system also accelerated the retreat from the use of coin in state finance. Guangwu, the first Eastern Han emperor, had resumed minting Wuzhu coins, but coinage was largely relegated to local officials, and mint output soon faltered. Circulating coin was debased by clipping and counterfeiting. The trend toward state payments in high-value silks reflected the depreciating value of coin.[89] The Wei kingdom and the succeeding Jin dynasty ceased coinage altogether, and bolts of silk cloth became the new monetary standard.

The ruler of the rival Wu kingdom, Sun Quan, preserved the Han *suanfu* taxes paid in coin, but Sun too utilized *tuntian* land allocations to resettle displaced populations and rebuild a firm revenue base for the state.[90] Unlike Wei, however, the Wu state often placed *tuntian* lands under the jurisdiction of local civil administrators rather than the military. From the evidence of the Zoumalou manuscripts from the Changsha region (dating to the 230s), many of the households assigned *tuntian* lands were refugees, criminals, prisoners of war, government slaves, and indigents over whom the state wielded considerable coercive power. Indeed, these groups seem to have been forcibly settled on *tuntian* lands and compelled to pay a much higher land tax in grain than ordinary landowners. In contrast to Cao Cao's regime, whose reforms were intended to simplify and reduce the taxes borne by farming families, the Wu state retained the onerous tax structure erected during the Eastern Han. In addition to the *suanfu* poll tax paid in coin, Wu officials collected land taxes in grain, cloth, and coin as well as a profusion of irregular *diao* levies.[91]

Upon formally superseding the Cao family's Wei dynasty in 265, the Sima clan's Jin government attempted to restore more uniform taxation while retaining the principles of Cao Cao's *hudiao* system. The Jin eliminated the

---

[88] Tang Changru 1955; Yang Jiping 2006: 43–6; Watanabe 2010: 239–54. The term *hudiao* appears only in later sources, however.

[89] Yamada 2000: 204–22.   [90] Gao Min 1986: 120–25; Fang Gaofeng 2009: 28–33.

[91] Yu Zhenbo 2004b: 25–31, 89–91; Jiang Fuya 2008: 56–7. According to Gao Min (2006: 26–27), the *suanfu* rate under Wu was only slighter higher than during the Han (130 rather than 120 coins per adult). But the Wu state assessed much heavier land taxes in addition to a wide range of *diao* levies. The third of the Three Kingdoms, Shu Han, also retained the Han fiscal system before being absorbed by the Wei-Jin state in the 260s, but little information on Shu Han fiscal policies has survived.

distinctions between *tuntian* and ordinary landholdings, placed both under the jurisdiction of the civil administration, and standardized land taxes and labor services.[92] After conquering Wu and reestablishing a unified empire in 280, the Jin court conducted a census as a first step toward rebuilding the fiscal system. The census of 280 recorded only 2.46 million households, however, less than a quarter of the 10.68 million households registered in the last national Han census in 157. Population losses from a century of civil war certainly exacted an enormous toll. But the reduced figures also reflected the disappearance of much of the population into private clientage. The Nine Ranks system created by the Wei in 220 granted generous legal and economic privileges to aristocratic families, including exemptions from labor service. By submitting themselves to the lordship of aristocratic patrons, commoners sheltered themselves behind this barricade of privilege and vanished from the tax registers.

The Jin attempted to reverse this trend by introducing a new fiscal system (*zhantian ketian* 占田課田) that adjusted the rates for tax payments in grain and silk according to the household's landholdings and the age and gender of its members. Inhabitants of distant areas and non-Chinese subjects were assessed taxes at lower rates. The new system did not allocate lands to farm families as often has been supposed, but rather imposed standardized tax rates based on the maximum amount of land that an able-bodied man was deemed capable of cultivating (50 *mu*).[93] Its purpose, then, was to generate revenues more than to ensure the economic independence of cultivators. The Jin state did attempt to restrain the growth of latifundia by imposing quotas for private clients and landholdings, up to a maximum of fifty client households and 5,000 *mu* of land for the highest-ranking officials. The extent to which these policies were implemented remains unclear, but it is unlikely that they had much effect in curtailing private clientage. Under Jin rule, the hereditary privileges of aristocratic families mediated through the Nine Ranks system became more deeply entrenched.

The state's ability to control land and resources diminished even further with the displacement of the population during the mass exodus to the south after 311. The Eastern Jin period (317–420) marked the zenith of the great clans' supremacy. The Jin court at Jiankang accommodated the irredentist

---

[92] Fujiie 1989: 141–54.

[93] The little – and long outdated – English-language scholarship on the *zhantian ketian* (e.g., Liensheng Yang 1961: 135–39; Balazs 1964a: 104–05) abides by the once-common presumption that it imitated the "well-field" ideal of equal landownership and allocated lands to farm families based on the demographic structure of the household, thus anticipating the equal-field policies enacted by the Northern Wei state in the fifth century. It is now widely recognized that the *zhantian ketian* policy was a taxation system, not a landownership system. See, e.g., Gao Min 1986: 190–99; Jiang Fuya 2005: 140–49; Watanabe 2010: 207–28.

yearnings of refugees from the north (as well as their own) by creating "sojourner" (*qiao* 僑) jurisdictions in the south separate from the regular local governments as caretakers of the refugee population. In some cases these "sojourner" units provided lands for refugee families and fulfilled most of the functions of local government; but often they exercised merely nominal authority over widely scattered émigrés who were given provisional registration that entailed few or no obligations to the state. Jin officials periodically attempted to conduct "residence resolution" surveys (*tuduan* 土斷) to incorporate refugee households into the regular taxpaying population, but these efforts at best produced transient results.[94] Only in 413, when the warlord Liu Yu took command of the enfeebled Jin state, was a forceful effort made to implement "residence resolution." Liu abolished both separate registration for émigré households from the north as well as many of the sojourner jurisdictions. Liu also issued prohibitions against the illegal occupation of wilderness areas by magnate clans.[95]

In 420 Liu Yu ratified his seizure of power by declaring himself emperor of his own Song dynasty (420–479). Liu's coup d'état marked a crucial turning point in the relationship between the southern dynasty courts and the magnate families. The emperors of the Song and succeeding dynasties maintained a firmer grip on the armed forces and recruited commoners (like Liu himself) as military commanders. But persistent rivalries among the generals undermined the central government's authority and left it vulnerable to repeated military coups. Although stripped of their military and administrative powers, the magnate families continued to hold sway over local society and economic life.

Settlement and economic development in Jiangnan under the southern dynasties

Despite this political chaos, South China experienced a greater measure of economic prosperity than the north during the centuries of divided rule. The Jiangnan region, long a sparsely populated frontier, became the economic heartland of the southern dynasties. Much of Jiangnan consisted of low-lying swamps, but the region was ideally suited for rice cultivation. Aristocratic families who accompanied the Jin court to the south quickly laid claim to vast expanses of wilderness. Complaints denouncing the enclosure of uncultivated lands, traditionally regarded as communal resources, by private landowners were legion. Magnate estates typically ranged in size from several hundred to tens of thousands of *mu*, and the richest landowners were said to employ thousands of private clients to cultivate their holdings. In an essay addressed to

---

[94] Crowell 1990; Chen Mingguang 1997: 110–20.   [95] Fujiie 1989: 240, 253.

his sons on the virtues of frugality, the scholar Yan Zhitui (531–91) counseled that a household of twenty persons should require no more than twenty servants and 10 *qing* (1,000 *mu*) of fine arable land for its upkeep.[96] Yan's figures undoubtedly defined the minimum threshold for the landed estates of magnate families.

Landed estates generally included scattered properties farmed by tenant households in addition to a large consolidated landholding around the owner's manor (*bieshu* 別墅) worked by bondservants. Yet even the manorial lands appear to have been divided into separate plots worked by individuals or small teams of farmhands (including bondservants and indentured laborers) rather than under the direct supervision of the landowner. This pattern of small-scale cultivation was especially prevalent in the rice-growing regions of Jiangnan.[97]

As already noted, in the third century the Wu kingdom, imitating its Wei rival, had established civilian and military agricultural colonies both on the Jiangnan plain and throughout the Yangzi River valley. Following the move of the Jin court to Jiankang, however, most of these lands were seized by aristocratic landowners. During this period reclamation efforts largely were concentrated to the north and west of Lake Tai and along the southern shore of Hangzhou Bay. Reservoirs constructed on elevated ground provided irrigation for lower-lying rice fields. On the coastal plain of Shaoxing a dike had been constructed along the foothills in late Han times to capture the run-off from upland streams, forming a lake extending more than 50 kilometers from east to west. A series of sixty-nine sluice gates regulated the flow of water from the lake to the rice fields lying between the lake and the seacoast (Map 4.3). In the early fifth century these lands were regarded as unmatched in productivity and commanded high prices. Private estate owners in adjacent areas imitated this example, mobilizing their bondservants to build dikes and ponds to irrigate their lands.[98]

Although many émigré aristocrats from the north settled in the Shaoxing region, the indigenous magnate clans dominated the local economy.[99] An earnest official appointed as a county magistrate in Shaoxing in the early Eastern Jin period exposed thousands of client households illegally hidden from tax registration by their magnate masters within two months of his arrival. But the elite families accused of tax evasion were deemed too eminent to suffer disgrace, and instead the magistrate was abruptly recalled.[100] Typical of the Shaoxing magnates was Kong Yingfu (d. 465), whose estate was said to

---

[96] Chapter 13, "Zhizu" 止足, in *YSJX*: 317.
[97] Tang Changru 1954, 1990; Watanabe 1986: 132–72.   [98] Honda 2000b: 47.
[99] On the salience of Shaoxing's leading magnate clans in the local economy, see Liu Shufen 1992: 255–315.
[100] Tang Changru 1990: 120–21; Liu Shufen 1992: 289.

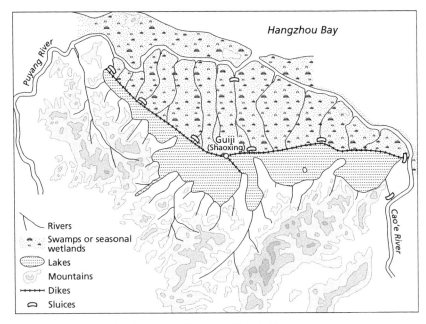

Map 4.3 Irrigation on the Shaoxing Plain in Han times
Source: Chen Qiaoyi 1962: 191, figure 3.

"measure 33 leagues around, encompassing 265 *qing* of land and water strad-
dling two mountains, as well as nine fruit orchards." Around 457 Kong
proposed that the court resettle landless households from Shanyin, the metro-
politan county of Shaoxing, on homesteads in less populated areas farther east,
in modern Ningbo. Kong's plan aroused a fierce storm of protest among court
officials, who raised numerous objections: there was sufficient land in Shanyin
for the indigent, if they were truly industrious; homesteading in virgin wilderness areas would pose even greater subsistence risks; the costs of relocation
would far exceed the meager revenues that the government could expect from
impoverished farmers working marginal lands. But fear of losing leverage over
the local labor supply undoubtedly was at the heart of the matter. In the end, we
are told, the Song emperor assented to Kong's plan, which proved a success.
But Kong made many enemies; shortly afterward he himself was accused of
illegal enclosures and temporarily dismissed from the civil service.[101]

According to an investigation of 488, nearly half of Shanyin's 20,000
taxable households possessed assets worth fewer than 3,000 coins. The same

---

[101] *SoS*, 54.1532–33. See also Watanabe 1986: 188–89.

report charged that the truly affluent aristocrat households evaded taxes and labor service, while the poor and destitute had been reduced to servitude and vanished from the tax rolls. The household median of a mere 3,000 coins in assets suggests that small cultivators in Shaoxing were decidedly less well off than the "middling class" of the Han.[102]

In addition to its agricultural bounty, Shaoxing also flourished as a center of industry and commerce. Hundreds of pottery kiln sites dating from Warring States and Han times have been found in Shaoxing, and during the Southern Dynasties the Yue ceramics produced in this region achieved an unrivalled reputation for beauty and craftsmanship. During this period, too, Shaoxing emerged as the most important center for the manufacture of bronze wares, especially the bronze mirrors that since Han times had become a prized luxury good. The talents of Shaoxing's bronze mirror artisans were in great demand, and some migrated to other parts of China or even to Japan – where Chinese mirrors were valued as the most politically potent of prestige goods – and established foundries there. Shaoxing also developed a thriving paper industry that used local mulberry wood and rattan as raw materials.[103]

Land reclamation and the development of irrigation dikes and ponds in the Yangzi Delta also created a network of waterways that facilitated transport and commerce throughout the region. A series of shipping canals connected major cities such as Yangzhou, Suzhou and Shaoxing with the capital at Jiankang. In the fifth–sixth centuries Jiankang became the hub of regional and international trade.

At its peak in the early sixth century Jiankang was said – undoubtedly with exaggeration – to number 280,000 households.[104] Unlike the fortified cities of the north, at Jiankang only the imperial palaces were enclosed by walls, while the mansions of officials and aristocrats, marketplaces, artisan workshops, and the humble homes of the working population sprawled across the surrounding countryside. Jiankang reportedly had more than a dozen major marketplaces under official supervision, including markets for grain, salt, cloth, shellfish, and livestock, as well as over a hundred smaller markets. Despite the claim of a Tang historian, when commenting on the commercial prosperity of Jiankang at this time, that "the petty folk engaged in trade, while the gentlemen depended on their official salaries for income," aristocratic families and imperial princes were deeply involved in commerce and

---

[102] To be sure, contemporaries characterized this period as one of very low prices compared to earlier times. However, the price of rice at this time (normally 100 coins per *hu*, according to Yu Yaohua 2000: 357–58) was roughly comparable to the Western Han, when the assets of middling households were far greater. See above, pp. 135–36.

[103] Liu Shufen 1992: 210–16; 2001: 46.

[104] On urban and economic development in Jiankang during the Southern Dynasties, see Liu Shufen 1992: 3–192; Liu Shufen 2001.

moneylending.[105] Magnate families often acted through agents recruited from among their clients rather than engaging directly in trade. The growth of commerce was hampered by persistent shortages of money, however. The Three Kingdoms states issued only token amounts of new coin, and the Jin ceased coinage altogether. Under the *hudiao* system, the state collected revenues mainly in cloth and grain. But private commerce relied on coin rather than cloth as a means of exchange.[106] The southern dynasties recommenced minting coin beginning with the Song in 430, but the demand for money far outstripped the supply of new coin, resulting in chronic shortages and the proliferation of privately cast coins. Archaeological evidence confirms that the vast majority of circulating coins were Han Wuzhu coins or – much more commonly – ersatz imitations of Wuzhu coins.[107]

The growth of commerce in Jiangnan under the southern dynasties altered the fiscal strategy of the state. Departing from the Jin *zhantian ketian* system, an attempt to revive the Han principle of taxing people, the Song court returned to taxation based on property (measured in arable lands, mulberry trees, and dwellings). Given their limited control over either land or people, however, the southern dynasties relied heavily on revenues from a variety of commercial taxes, including transit and sales taxes and excises imposed on shops and inns, collected in coin. In addition, the regular *hudiao* levies were increasingly paid in coin. According to a 476 report on tax arrears in the two largest provinces, approximately 38 percent (by value) of the delinquent payments were denominated in coin, in contrast to 47 percent in grain and 15 percent in cloth. In 479, the first year of the Qi dynasty (479–502), 69 percent of the revenues in three Middle Yangzi provinces was paid in coin, compared to 21 percent in grain and 10 percent in hemp cloth.[108] In the 480s the Qi court formally codified the increasingly common practice of paying taxes in coin, stipulating that henceforth the property tax on households would be collected half in coin and half in cloth. A major motivation for this change was the sharp appreciation in the value of coin and falling prices for grain and hemp cloth, which eroded state revenues. In 488 the Qi government disbursed 50 million coins to purchase silks, hemp cloth, rice, beans, barley, and sesame in eleven

---

[105] Quotation from *SS*, 31.887.
[106] Wang Yichen 2007: 106–27. Kakinuma (2010) argues that we should not overlook the monetary importance of cloth in state payments, gifts, and other uses, but he concedes that coin predominated in market exchange.
[107] Miyazawa 2000: 57–58.
[108] Chen Mingguang 1997: 155, 163; Watanabe 2010: 284. It is not clear whether these ratios reflected the total proportions of taxes levied in grain, coin, and cloth, but scholars have tended to accept this inference.

provinces in an attempt to reverse this deflationary trend, which also adversely affected the incomes of farming families.[109]

The rulers of the Song and Qi dynasties had asserted greater personal control over state finances, but often abused these powers through profligate spending. The founder of the Liang dynasty (502–57), Emperor Wu (r. 502-49), instead opted to strengthen bureaucratic authority by establishing a new Grand Exchequer (Taifuqing 太府卿) with broad authority over fiscal and monetary matters, including the Privy Purse.[110] Wu also was persuaded by arguments that taxation of household property discouraged investment in productive resources and reverted to the principle of taxing individuals at uniform rates. Still, the Liang state, like its predecessors, relied primarily on indirect taxation of commerce to raise revenues. Despite Wu's intentions, however, his reforms proved unsuccessful in curbing private clientage, the entrenched disparities between rich and poor, or even lavish imperial expenditures.[111] In the early decades of the Liang, privileged groups – the imperial clan, aristocrats, and high-ranking military officers – enjoyed a sumptuous lifestyle that in the eyes of contemporary critics exceeded all precedent. This "consumption boom," as one historian has put it, was made possible by the vigor of the money economy.[112]

Among the southern dynasties, the Liang made the most concerted effort to reestablish a bronze coin monetary standard, but failed. Emperor Wu immediately began minting a new Wuzhu coin, as well as an official version of the so-called "distaff coins" (nüqian 女錢), the private coins in common use. But mint output fell far short of meeting market demand. After his effort to restore a sound bronze currency foundered, in 523 Wu reversed course and resorted to minting iron coins to resolve the chronic shortages of currency. The flood of iron coin sparked a financial panic and rampant price inflation. It became common practice to bundle coins into "strings" (guan 貫) nominally comprising 100 coins, but in fact containing only 70–90 coins, varying from region to region. By the end of the Liang dynasty these "short strings" contained a mere 35 coins; iron coins had become defunct, and people often made recourse to using grain and cloth as substitutes for coin.[113]

It has been argued that the commercial efflorescence of the Liang actually undermined the economic foundations of the magnate class. Aristocrats forsook their rural villas for the cultural glamor and luxurious pleasures of the capital, living off official stipends while neglecting stewardship of their landed

---

[109] Watanabe 2010: 270–71; Chen Mingguang 1997: 147–51; 164–65; Fujiie 1989: 147–50.
[110] Watanabe 2010: 266–68.   [111] Chen Mingguang 1997: 215–26.
[112] Kawakatsu 1982: 386.
[113] Kawakatsu 1982: 359–66; Miyazawa 2000: 46–48, 60. At this time the guan ("string") referred to units of 100 coins (also known as mo 陌), not 1,000 coins as was true during the Tang and after.

estates. The monetary turmoil resulting from the issue of iron coins further depressed agricultural incomes while also eroding the value of government salaries, paid mostly in coin. This hypothesis remains speculative, however. What is more certain is that the mortal blow to the preeminence of the great aristocratic clans was struck by the Hou Jing rebellion of 548–52. The rebellion severely weakened the Liang dynasty (which collapsed five years later), left Jiankang in ruins, devastated family fortunes, and drove the scions of august lineages into ignominious refuge in distant regions, or even into exile in the north. The rulers of the Chen dynasty (557–89) that succeeded the Liang eagerly welcomed the surviving remnants of the great clans, but only to swathe their court in an aura of nostalgic grace. Genuine power was entrusted to low-born officials and generals.[114]

Conclusion

Following the long and tumultuous reign of the Han emperor Wu, the Qin-Han imperial order steadily eroded. Ironically, privileges granted by the state to its officials became the foundation of the new manorial order that concentrated wealth and power in the hands of magnate landowners. This privatization of power intensified in the final decades of the Eastern Han, and especially during the ensuing Period of Disunion. Magnates assumed leadership of local communities and responsibility for public security and social welfare. The rise of the manorial economy was accompanied by a shift in population and economic activity from the cities to the countryside, a trend perhaps encouraged by the Han state's punitive measures aimed at wealthy merchants. But the retreat from state regulation of commerce in the Eastern Han allowed greater scope for local magnates to flex their muscles in the marketplace. Economic domination by the magnate clans reached its peak in the century after the sack of Luoyang in 311 and the flight of the Jin court to Jiangnan.

As the Zoumalou manuscripts show, to the very end of the Han the imperial state retained substantial capability to extend its reach into local society. But the Zoumalou population registers also reveal concerted resistance to the state's demands, especially military conscription. In the post-Han era rulers repeatedly attempted to reestablish a stable revenue base – — through the *tuntian* farmer-soldier colonies created by Cao Cao and the rulers of the Three Kingdoms; the *zhantian ketian* taxation system of the Jin; and the fiscal reforms enacted by the founder of Liang in the early sixth century. But these efforts failed to loosen the magnates' control over land and labor, and often were subverted by the rulers' own self-enrichment.

[114] Kawakatsu 1982: 407–35.

Already in the Eastern Han deepening economic inequality forced the state to retreat from the principle of uniform taxation of all subjects. Instead, beleaguered officials adopted new expedients to base taxation on the actual wealth of households. In addition, the collection of revenues in coin was gradually replaced by payments in cloth and grain. But this shift to in-kind taxation did not portend the disappearance of the money economy, as often has been supposed. Coin was indispensable to private trade, and the demand for money intensified with the growing prosperity of the southern dynasties in the fifth and sixth centuries.

This renewed economic vigor resulted from the rise of the Jiangnan region as the heartland of the southern regimes. Few of the benefits of this resurgence accrued to the state, however. Magnate landowners spearheaded the development of rice agriculture in the south, laying claim to wilderness lands and mobilizing the labor needed to bring them under cultivation. Private clientage remained the mainstay of the manorial order that flourished under the southern dynasties.

Commercial vitality enabled the southern courts once again to collect a significant share of taxes in coin. But the renewed importance of coin in state finances should not be taken as a sign of a sturdy fiscal system. Instead, it reflected the desperate straits of regimes beset by soaring military costs in the face of mounting pressure from the powerful Northern Wei state in the north.[115] The census conducted by the Song in 464 counted only 907,000 households and fewer than five million people (less than half the population for South China in the Han census of 140 CE), a telling indication of the state's feeble control over labor and resources.[116] Instead, it was the foreign-ruled Northern Wei state that would develop the new institutions to build the formidable military machine that made possible the reunification of China in the late sixth century.

---

[115] Watanabe 2010: 289.
[116] Figures from Liang Fangzhong 1980: 22 (table A.6), 47 (table A.16).

5   The Chinese-nomad synthesis and the reunification of the empire (485 to 755)

During the Period of Disunion the economies of North and South China diverged in crucial ways. The devastation inflicted by repeated nomad invasions gravely disrupted agricultural production and commerce in North China. This anarchic warfare finally came to a halt after Tuoba Gui, a chief of the Xianbei steppe nomads, conquered much of the Central Plain in 398 and laid the foundations for the Northern Wei dynasty (386–534). Under Northern Wei dominion North China enjoyed a degree of political stability that eluded the more transitory Chinese-ruled dynasties in the south. Eventually the Northern Wei leaders turned away from the political and cultural traditions of the steppe and sought to refashion their state in the image of a Chinese empire. In so doing the Northern Wei promoted a synthesis of Chinese and nomadic institutions based on bureaucratic rule and a caste-like social order of hereditary occupational statuses that succeeded, at least in the short run, in reviving agricultural production. The political economy of the Northern Wei in its mature phase (after 485) recapitulated the military-physiocratic principles of the first empires: like the Qin–early Han rulers, the Northern Wei leaders sought to magnify the state's military might through equitable allocation of lands, uniform taxation in goods and labor, and universal military conscription. In contrast to the south, however, commercial development was muted and monetary circulation remained feeble.

The Northern Wei also fostered the formation of a hybrid Xianbei-Chinese ruling class through intermarriage between the Xianbei nobility and the leading Chinese aristocratic clans. Although a few favored Chinese clans were admitted to this ruling elite, in general the social power of Chinese local magnates in the north atrophied over the course of the Northern Wei dynasty. Xianbei military domination and the equal-field landholding system inaugurated by the Northern Wei did not deprive local magnates of their privileges or wealth, but they bolstered the state's control over the common people.[1] The institutional infrastructure erected by the Northern Wei state survived

[1] Chen Shuang 1998: 189–202.

168

the fall of the dynasty in 534 and its division into rival regimes. The success of Yang Jian, founder of the Sui dynasty (581–618), in reinstating unified imperial rule over both North and South China in 589 can be attributed in no small degree to the political and institutional achievements of the Northern Wei.

At the same time the founders of the Sui and Tang (618–907) dynasties looked back to the great empire of Han as their political model. They restored centralized bureaucratic government, rule by codified law, and Confucian schooling, ritual practices, and moral norms. Yet they also embraced the multiethnic society and cosmopolitan culture of North China – including the Buddhist faith, which became deeply implanted in both north and south during the Period of Disunion. Indeed, Yang Jian, a fervent Buddhist, promoted Buddhism rather than Confucianism as the common core of beliefs, values, and social practices that would inspire unity among the disparate peoples gathered under his dominion. The Sui and Tang rulers envisaged an even more grand universal empire than had the Han emperors centuries before, one that far exceeded the horizons of the Zhou ecumene to encompass the world of the steppe nomads and beyond. The Tang rulers enhanced their supreme dignity as emperors by also laying claim to the title of khan ("lord of the steppe" in the Turkish language). Yang Jian and Wu Zetian, the woman monarch who briefly supplanted the Tang dynasty in the late seventh century, consciously emulated the "wheel-turning kings" (*çakravartin*) of Buddhist lore, fighting righteous wars to propagate the true faith – not unlike the Roman Christian emperors of Byzantium and the Franks, or the Islamic caliphs. Aggressive imperial expansion ultimately would cause the downfall of both the Sui and Tang empires. Yet the might and wealth of the Sui-Tang empires at their peak deeply impressed China's neighbors. Japan, the Korean states, and even (briefly) Tibet imitated the Sui-Tang imperial model, and to a greater or lesser degree adopted the Chinese written language, Sui-Tang political institutions and laws, Confucian ideology, and the Buddhist religion. It was during this era that East Asia – a community of independent national states sharing a common civilization – took shape in forms that have endured down to modern times.[2]

Despite its apparent supremacy within East Asia, the Tang state was bedeviled by institutional rigidities that diminished its fiscal and logistical capabilities. The equal-field system of the Northern Wei was premised on a static and uniform society of smallholding farmers insulated from the vicissitudes of the market. Imposing the equal-field system on South China, with its large disparities in wealth and landholdings and burgeoning commercial sector, proved

---

[2] On the formation of East Asia as a distinct civilization in world history during this era, see Holcombe 2001.

impossible. Population pressure and growing inequities in the burden of taxes created a large, rootless class of landless "vagrants" who evaded the net of state surveillance and control. The Tang fiscal administration relied heavily on in-kind direct taxation and made little effort to capture revenues from commerce and industry. Unable to issue an adequate supply of bronze coin, the Tang state was forced to create an immense and costly transport network to collect and deliver grain and cloth revenues. Ultimately, the catastrophic An Lushan rebellion in the mid-eighth century spelled the doom of the institutional heritage of the Northern Wei and compelled the Tang leadership to construct a wholly new paradigm of fiscal governance.

Recovery and stabilization under the Northern Wei

The consolidation of Northern Wei rule over North China restored some measure of order in the Chinese heartland, although the Xianbei monarchs relied on military clientage rather than a civil bureaucracy to govern local society. Tuoba Gui's (Emperor Daowu, r. 386–409) singular achievement was to sever the nomad warriors under his command from their tribal allegiances and transform them into a hereditary military caste loyal to the Northern Wei regime.[3] During the first century of their rule the Xianbei dynasts lived in an uneasy condominium with the native Chinese aristocracy. The Xianbei entrusted leading aristocratic families with broad discretion to exercise both civil and military authority within their home jurisdictions. In 398, Daowu forcibly relocated a mixed population of 360,000 from the Central Plain as well as 100,000 skilled artisans to the environs of his new capital at Pingcheng, in the grasslands just within the Great Wall, to feed the capital's inhabitants and supply the Xianbei court.[4] Tensions periodically erupted into overt hostility when the interests of Xianbei herdsmen and Chinese farmers collided. By the mid-fifth century the population of the Central Plain had recovered to the extent that pressure on the land started to intensify. At the same time the Northern Wei rulers began to recruit leading figures among the Chinese aristocracy into their government, much to the dismay of the Xianbei nobility (Map 5.1).

As the Han dynasty disintegrated, and especially after the sack of Luoyang in 311, local magnates had taken responsibility for the defense and welfare of local communities. Many people sought refuge in the fortified settlements (*wubao* 塢堡) raised by the magnates, rendering service as armed retainers (*buqu* 部曲). Leagues of fortresses formed under the leadership of paramount commanders, who sometimes sealed their alliances through formal oaths and

---

[3] Graff 2002: 69–72; Lewis 2009: 79–81.   [4] Hori 1975: 102.

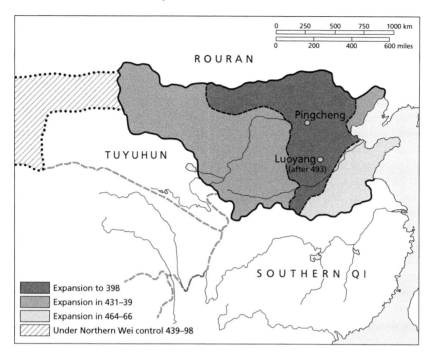

Map 5.1 Expansion of the Northern Wei state

covenants. When hostilities ceased, the retainers remained in thrall to the local magnates, to whom they owed fealty and tribute. Membership in the local village community (*cun* 村, a neologism coined at this time) superseded imperial subjecthood.[5] The forces mobilized by these local magnates typically included both kinsmen and private clients or bondsmen unrelated by blood. Although the precise nature of kinship organization at this time remains uncertain, there is little doubt that the power of local magnates rested heavily on clan loyalties. For example, Li Xianfu, a junior member of the eminent Zhaojun Li clan, was said to have mobilized several thousand of his kinsmen to settle in the foothills of the Taihang Mountains in southwestern Hebei, where they brought "fifty or sixty square leagues" under cultivation. Despite Li

[5] Miyakawa 1956; Hori 1975: 132–33; Liu Shufen 1992: 368–73; Fan Zhaofei and Zhang Mingming 2011. Tanigawa (1985: 100–10) challenges the conventional view that the magnates exercised tyrannical rule over local society, instead arguing that the social structure of this time was strongly "communitarian" and that the aristocracy exercised suasive moral leadership based on shared ethical-religious values. I am not in the least persuaded by Tanigawa's arguments. For a recent critique of Tanigawa's communitarian thesis, see Chittick 2009.

Xianfu's modest position in the clan hierarchy – his elder brother had inherited their father's rank and office – the settlers recognized him as their "clan chief" (*zongzhu* 宗主).[6]

Initially, the Xianbei rulers of the Northern Wei depended on entrenched magnates like Li Xianfu to maintain order at local level. Many local magnate leaders were formally appointed as governors of their native regions. Thus Northern Wei patronage both strengthened solidarity within magnate clans and deepened their control over local society, especially in Hebei and Shanxi.[7] But this arrangement left the Northern Wei state unable to raise revenues and soldiers, needs that became increasingly urgent after the seizure of Shandong and Huaibei from the Song in the 460s. In keeping with nomad traditions, in the wake of their conquests the Xianbei liberally awarded large numbers of war captives as bondservants (designated as *tongli* 僮隸 or *lihu* 隸戶) to meritorious generals, officials, and nobles. Under Northern Wei rule, such menial persons comprised a substantial portion of the agricultural labor force to a far greater degree than in the past.[8] The Northern Wei also imposed hereditary menial status on war captives with specialized skills who were pressed into service to the state as clerks, entertainers, salt makers, weavers, and other artisans, collectively known as "miscellaneous (service) households" (*zahu* 雜戶).[9] Magnate families also harbored craftsmen and entertainers as private clients. Since much of the population was subsumed under the households of Chinese aristocrats and Xianbei nobles, the burdens of corvée labor fell on a relatively small number of independent farmers. More-over, in 473 the Northern Wei reintroduced military conscription of its Chinese subjects to supplement its Xianbei warriors, now thinly stretched over a vast territory. But these impositions also encouraged smallholder farmers to evade them by becoming private clients of privileged magnates.[10]

It was against this background that the Northern Wei court, under the autocratic rule of the Empress Dowager Wenming (438–90), undertook a

[6] *BS* 33.1202. See also Fan Zhaofei and Zhang Mingming 2011: 18. Yang Jiping and Li Qing (2003) have challenged – but not to my mind refuted – the veracity of this account of Li Xianfu's role. On the role of clan chiefs in local governance in the Northern Wei, see Li Ping 2000: 365–407.

[7] For case studies of these effects, see Ebrey (1978: 52–61) and Holmgren (1983) on the Boling Cui clan in central Hebei, Mao Hanguang (1990a) on the Hedong Xue in southern Shanxi, and Chen Shuang (1998: 81–134) on the Fanyang Lu clan of northern Hebei.

[8] Wang Yi-t'ung 1953; Hori 1975: 178–79.

[9] Hori 1975: 377–88. Although the Northern Wei imposed hereditary status on such groups, who were denied the freedom to change their occupation or employer and forbidden to marry free subjects, their legal status remained separate and superior to that of slaves. "Miscellaneous households" were still recognized as families and not treated as chattels, whereas slaves had no social existence apart from their bondage to their masters. See Pearce 1991.

[10] On the need to increase the armed forces as a motive for creating the equal-field system, see Sagawa 1999.

series of bold initiatives aimed at remaking the Northern Wei into a centralized bureaucratic empire in the Chinese mold.[11] Acting in the name of her grandson Emperor Xiaowen (r. 471–99) – who continued her policies after her death – Wenming sought to create a unified ruling class by encouraging intermarriage between the Xianbei nobility and select Chinese aristocratic clans. She also encouraged the Xianbei to adopt Chinese language, dress, and customs. In 493 Xiaowen moved the Northern Wei capital from Pingcheng to the traditional Chinese capital of Luoyang in the Central Plain. More than a symbolic gesture, the relocation of the capital epitomized a reinforced commitment to building a settled agrarian empire.

While Wenming wooed Chinese aristocrats to participate actively in the Northern Wei government, she also was determined to solidify the fiscal foundations of the state. In 485 the court introduced a new land allocation policy known as the equal-field (*juntian* 均田) system.[12] Over the next few years the new policy underwent various adjustments; most importantly, it was coupled to efforts to compile accurate population registers and to integrate village society into the state administration through what became known as the "Three Elders" (*sanzhang* 三長) system. The 485 land law also was accompanied by a revised tax code – one still based on the *hudiao* system of Wei and Jin – in which the amounts of grain, cloth, and labor service owed to the state were directly proportional to the land allocation the household received. In addition, the state reserved one-tenth of the land to found new garrison colonies (*tuntian*).

The regulations governing the equal-field allocations preserved in the historical records most likely were issued in 492 (Table 5.1).[13] Each household was entitled to lands in proportion to its labor power, divided into two types of tenure based on land use: (1) arable land for cereal cultivation and (2) lands to support textile production, which would take one of two forms: "mulberry lands" in silk-producing areas and "hemp lands" in regions where sericulture was infeasible. The state assigned 40 *mu* of arable land and either 10 or 20 *mu* (depending on the crop) to support textile production for each adult male in the household, and half those amounts for adult females. Households possessing slaves and plow oxen were entitled to substantially larger allocations.

---

[11] On Empress Dowager Wenming's domination of the Northern Wei court from 476 until her death in 490 and her pro-sinification policies, see Li Ping 2000: 194–280; Holmgren 1983.

[12] The literature on the equal-field system is vast. For a comprehensive review of the Japanese scholarship, see Sagawa 2001a. My analysis is based chiefly on the classic study of Hori Toshikazu (1975), as amended by Sagawa (1999, 2001b). The most important study in Chinese is Yang Jiping 2003.

[13] For an exegesis of the legal statutes governing the equal-field system, see Gao Min 1987. But I agree with the consensus among Japanese scholars that these statutes were issued in 492, not in 485 when the equal-field system was first enacted as Gao maintains.

Table 5.1 *Land allocations under the Northern Wei equal-field system*

Land type		Free subjects (*liangmin* 良民)		Slaves* (*nubi* 奴婢)	Oxen**
		Adult males	Adult females		
Arable land (*lutian* 露田)	Standard allocation (*zhengtian* 正田)	40 *mu*	20 *mu*	Same as free subjects	30 *mu*
	Supplemental allocation (*beitian* 倍田)	40 *mu*	20 *mu*		30 *mu*
Mulberry fields (*sangtian* 桑田)		20 *mu*			
Hemp fields (*matian* 麻田)		10 *mu*	5 *mu*		
Dwelling allocation		1 *mu* per 3 persons		1 *mu* per 5 persons	

*Unlimited.
**Up to four oxen.
Source: WS 110: 2853–54; adapted from Hori 1975: 167, table 1.

The arable land allocations would be doubled or tripled in areas where the land was less fertile or the population sparse. In principle, the arable lands and hemp lands reverted to the state for reallocation upon the death of the house-holder; mulberry lands, however, were granted in perpetuity and passed on to the householder's heirs because of the long-term investment and care mulberry orchards required. Sale of these land grants was forbidden, although subleasing was permitted under some circumstances. Land allocations would be adjusted annually to account for changes in the composition of the household and its number of oxen.

The equal-field system was part of broad-based effort to curtail private clientage and restore the state's authority and control over the populace. In the course of refining its equal-field policies, the Northern Wei delineated a strict legal distinction between "free subjects" (*liangren* 良人, literally "good people") and persons of menial status (*jianren* 賤人), a category restricted to slaves (*nubi*) and convicts (along with family members of convicts who were impressed into menial service to the state). By this definition, private clients and even "miscellaneous service households" were deemed free subjects eligible for equal-field allocations. Over the next several decades the Northern Wei enacted a series of laws intended to delimit the category of menial persons and wrest control of private clients from the grasp of magnate landowners.[14]

---

[14] Hori 1975: 380–86; Takenami 1984; Pearce 1991: 120.

Although the equal-field system was reminiscent of the egalitarian division of lands envisioned in Mencius's "well-field" system, its immediate goals were more practical: to maximize the amount of land under cultivation and ensure a stable revenue base for the state. The allocation of lands based on the labor power of the household rather than its consumption needs served more to secure revenues than to guarantee a minimum level of subsistence. The land grants for mulberry and hemp cultivation were premised on the substantial tax obligations that households paid in the forms of cloth and yarn. Ultimately, the equal-field policy had multiple objectives: increasing the amount of land under cultivation; curbing tax evasion and restoring private clients to the tax rolls, especially for the purpose of military conscription; raising revenues that would enable the state to begin to pay regular salaries to its officials; and accumulating grain stores at the local level for famine relief, a priority that took on special urgency after a catastrophic famine in 487–88. But the policy stopped well short of ushering in radical changes in landholding, or creating universal state ownership of land such as Wang Mang had envisioned.[15] Although the aggressive attempts to rectify the household and land registers reasserted the state's control over small cultivators, the generous allocations granted to owners of slaves and oxen left large landholdings intact. Indeed, the equal-field policy may well have prompted magnates to replace private clients – free subjects entitled to equal-field allocations – with slaves as their agricultural labor force.

The equal-field system obviously posed a direct challenge to the great landowners. Although the land allocations were supposed to be administered through the new network of village officials created by the Three Elders system, implementation of these policies ultimately depended on the cooperation of the aristocrats who dominated the state bureaucracy. It is unlikely, therefore, that the 485 land law encroached on the existing landholdings of powerful aristocratic families. Instead, the lands allocated under the equal-field system probably consisted of abandoned fields or uncultivated wilderness. Land allocations most likely were carried out in less populated areas where land remained relatively abundant.

The only direct evidence for the operation of the equal-field system comes from land and household registers compiled at the frontier garrison town of Dunhuang in 547, during the Western Wei dynasty.[16] These documents depict the equal-field system functioning according to its original design, with lands

---

[15] On this point, see Hori 1975: 173–75. Most Chinese scholarship – for example Yang Jiping 2003 – remains wedded to the notion that the equal-field system aimed (but failed) to create universal state ownership of land.

[16] The scholarship on these documents is voluminous. I have relied on Hori 1975: *passim*; Ikeda 1979: 37–56.

regularly repossessed from deceased householders and redistributed to new ones. But these registers also reveal significant deviations from the statutory allocations: most households received half or less of the amount of land to which they were entitled. These shortfalls are not surprising, however, given that Dunhuang was an oasis town with limited arable land. The deficits were confined almost entirely to the allotments for grain cultivation, the portion which reverted to the state upon death; in contrast, Dunhuang's inhabitants received nearly all of the statutory allocations of hemp lands to which the household obtained permanent allodial rights and could transmit to heirs (Table 5.2). It seems likely that local officials intended to provide full allotments of arable lands eventually; but the priority on providing hemp lands testifies to the importance of cloth – and the labor of the women who manufactured it – to the state's fiscal system.[17] Households with greater labor power received larger portions of their arable land entitlements, confirming that the goal of maximizing utilization of land and labor took precedence over equalizing landownership. Nonetheless, the award of full (but far smaller) allocations to elderly, lame, or minor males reflected a concern for providing a minimal level of subsistence.

The successful implementation of the land allocation and repossession policies in a distant region far from the capital suggests that the Northern Wei largely succeeded in instituting the equal-field system throughout its domains. We must keep in mind, however, that Dunhuang was a key military garrison, and military conscription was an especially crucial component of the equal-field system there. It is likely that the Northern Wei and its successors diligently monitored the operation of the equal-field policy in such areas.

The adoption of the equal-field system was part of a concerted effort by Empress Dowager Wenming and her advisors not only to stabilize state revenues but also to assert greater central control over them. The census and cadastral surveys carried out to establish the Three Elders system of village administration were said to have doubled the registered population to more than 5 million households.[18] Based on this population estimate, Watanabe Shinichirō has proposed the reconstruction of the Northern Wei's revenues and expenditures shown in Table 5.3. Information on expenditures is limited to disbursements of the regular *diao* cloth revenues, but is still useful for showing how those revenues were shared among different levels of

---

[17]   On these points see Ikeda 1979: 47–50. The Western Wei had regained control of the Dunhuang region only three years before, in 544, the same year that it launched an effort to reestablish the equal-field system that had fallen into abeyance after the collapse of the Northern Wei. The fact that the tax obligations of these households were based on the composition of the household (and by extension the amount of land to which it was entitled) rather than the actual amount of land at their disposal lends support to Ikeda's inference.

[18]   *TD* 7.40a.

Table 5.2 Register of equal-field land allocations in Dunhuang, 547

	Number of households	Individuals	Oxen		Quota 應受田	Actually received 已受田	Total	Per household
						Land allocations (in *mu*)		
Full allocation 足	6	6 lame, aged, or minor M	1	Arable lands 正田	80	80	116	19.3
				Hemp lands 麻田	30	30		
				Dwelling 宅園	6	6		
Three-quarters allocation 三分未足	6	11 adult M 9 adult F	3	Arable lands	370	244	531	88.5
				Hemp lands	155	135		
				Dwelling/garden	6	6		
Half allocation 二分未足	13	18 adult M 1 lame/aged M 15 adult F 1 slave F	2	Arable lands	570	170	848	65.2
				Hemp lands	265	250		
				Dwelling/garden	13	13		
One-quarter allocation 一分未足	7	8 adult M 8 adult F	0	Arable lands	220	–	?	?
				Hemp lands	110	–		
				Dwelling/garden	7	7		
No allocation 無田	1	1 aged F	0	Arable lands	10	0	0	0
				Hemp lands	5	0		
				Dwelling/garden	0	0		
Total	33	37 adult M 30 adult F 7 lame, aged, etc. M 1 slave F 1 aged F	6	Arable lands	1,250	500+	947+	
				Hemp lands	565	415+		
				Dwelling/garden	32	32		

Source: British Library manuscripts, Stein no. 613; reproduced in Ikeda 1979: 44.

177

the fiscal administration. A budget plan adopted in 488 apportioned state expenses as follows:[19]

Central government	39%
Local governments	20%
Official salaries (central and local)	30%
Famine relief reserves	11%

To the best of our knowledge, this scheme marked the first time that the imperial government established fixed budget allocations for local government and famine relief expenses. In the Han, local governments had to make do with whatever funds remained after they forwarded their revenue quotas to the central government. Although local officials now retained a fixed proportion of the revenues they collected, expenditure of those resources still required authorization by central government officials.

As can readily be seen in Table 5.3, the Northern Wei collected revenues only in grain and cloth. In marked contrast to the southern dynasties, which shifted to raising substantial revenues in bronze coin precisely at this time, coin played no part in the Northern Wei fiscal administration. The Northern Wei did begin to mint its own version of the Wuzhu coin in 495, but circulation of this new coin remained confined to the environs of Luoyang. In outlying areas local trade was conducted using old Han coins and sundry coins issued by southern dynasties. The government converted a portion of official salaries denominated in cloth to coin payments, but its efforts to legislate minimum standards for coin and fixed exchange ratios between cloth and coin were stillborn.[20]

Military conscription, of course, was integral to the equal-field system. The Three Elders administrative system grouped males liable for military service into units of fifteen men who served one-year terms of active duty in rotation (i.e., once every fifteen years). According to the Dunhuang register of 547, this rotation had accelerated to once every six years. In contrast, the households assigned to the *tuntian* agricultural colonies – reportedly 10 percent of the population – shouldered an onerous tax assessed in grain, but they were exempt from military service as well as all regular and irregular levies. The state thus relied on the equal-field system to recruit soldiers and laborers, while

[19] Watanabe 2010: 308. We should keep in mind that this budget probably applied only to the "regular levies," and other revenues remained outside the central government's fiscal administration. For example, the military silk levy (item I.3 in Table 5.3) went directly to army commanders; most likely this was true of *tuntian* grain revenues (item I.4) as well.
[20] Miyazawa 2000: 62–66, 2007: 125–29. A hoard dating to Northern Wei times excavated at Anyang (Hebei) contained 2,885 coins, of which 55 percent were Eastern Han issues and 43 percent sundry post-Han coins; 60 percent of the latter had been substantially clipped (ibid.: 128).

Table 5.3 *Estimated state revenues and expenditures in the Northern Wei*

Revenues		(a) Expenditures	
(1) Regular levies 常調,五調		(1) Central government	1.75 million bolts
(a) Grain 粟調	9 million bushels	(a) Military	
(b) Silk and hemp cloth 絹布調	4.5 million bolts	(b) Ritual and ceremonies	
(c) Yarn 綿麻調	36 million ounces	(c) Palace expenses	
(2) Irregular levies 雜調	?	(d) Gifts and awards	
(3) Military levy 兵調 (silk)	4.5 million bolts	(e) Salaries and stipends	
(4) *Tuntian* revenue 屯田 (grain)	30 million bushels	(f) Reserves	
(5) Clerical grain subsidy 僧祇粟	?	(2) Official salaries	1.05 million bolts
(6) Salt excises 鹽稅	300,000 bolts	(3) Local government	700,000 bolts
(7) Commercial taxes 市稅	?	(4) Reserves (local)	1 million bolts
(8) Rent on state lands	?		

Source: Watanabe 2010: 298, table 13.

depending on the *tuntian* colonies – located near military camps – to supply food for the army.

The deliberate sinification of Northern Wei government and society pursued by Empress Dowager Wenming and Emperor Xiaowen bred discontent among the Xianbei tribal garrisons based in the steppe, who clung to their pastoral warrior traditions. In 523 the steppe garrisons revolted. The ensuing civil war led to the collapse of the Northern Wei dynasty in 534 and the division of North China between two rival successors, the Eastern Wei and Western Wei dynasties. In the 550s each of these regimes was supplanted by new dynastic houses: the Northern Qi (550–77) in the east, and the Northern Zhou (557–81) in the west. The western regimes ruled over less populous and less productive territories inhabited by a heterogeneous mix of Xianbei and Tibetan nomads and Chinese farmers. The eastern regimes, based in the Central Plain, had greater resources at their disposal, but in this region the great aristocratic clans held sway, eclipsing the more diffuse stratum of local magnates. The successor states in both east and west retained the government institutions of the Northern Wei, but adapted them in different ways.

In the Central Plain, especially in Hebei and Henan, the Chinese aristocratic clans reached the apogee of their power in the decades after the fall of the Northern Wei. Song Xiaoyou, once a Qi fiscal official himself, harshly condemned the subversion of the land laws under the negligent stewardship of the Northern Qi: when the state opened lands for settlement, "by petition or lease the powerful magnates gained all of the fertile and well-watered lands, while the common folk were left without even a scrap of hillside." Public lands around the capital of Ye were distributed as gifts to the Xianbei nobility, Su further complained, and lands allocated to defray the expenses of officials became their personal property.[21] The land laws enacted by the Northern Qi in 564 made a half-hearted gesture toward reform, but in fact ratified the privileged entitlements enjoyed by officialdom and the nobility. Land allocations for slaves were limited for the first time, yet at such generous levels – from 60 to 300 slaves, depending on the official's rank – that they abetted rather than constrained rampant aggrandizement. The new laws raised the tax liabilities for slaves, but only to a level half that of free subjects. For the first time the allocations for mulberry orchards were explicitly designated the "hereditary property" (yongye 永業) of the recipients. Above all, officials blithely allowed debt-ridden famers to sell off their land grants, hastening their descent into poverty.[22] As a result the Northern Qi condoned legally sanctioned inequities in landownership based on official status. These disparities would persist in the equal-field policies of the Sui and Tang empires.

In 542, Yuwen Tai, the de facto leader of the Western Wei, lost most of his army in a disastrous campaign against the Eastern Wei, forcing him to turn to the local militias controlled by powerful magnates to shore up his military strength. Over the next decade Yuwen Tai also gradually built up a new military organization known as the fubing 府兵 or "garrison militias" into a professional soldiery.[23] Although local leadership of the fubing units often was hereditary, over time the allegiance of the soldiers to their commanders weakened and the militias came under direct central control. Yuwen Tai also revived the equal-field system as a means of conscripting soldiers to supplement the fubing militias. Groups of six families rotated the duty of providing one conscript for a year-long tour of military service; the other five families

---

[21] TD 2.15c, citing Song's now-lost Guandong fengsu ji 關東風俗記. Song's book, composed after the conquest of the Northern Qi by the Northern Zhou, predictably blamed the dynasty's fall on the excesses of its rulers, but Tang historians held it in high regard. See Chen Shuang 1998: 152–54.

[22] Sagawa 2001b: 20–25. For the text of the 564 Northern Qi land laws, see SS 24.677–78.

[23] The relationship of the private militias to the fubing armies remains in dispute. One school of thought holds that the fubing were formed by amalgamating the private militias, while another contends that the fubing was a new institution created through direct conscription of the registered populace. The most comprehensive study of the fubing system and its complex evolution is Kegasawa 1999; on the early development of the fubing, see also Mao Hanguang 1990b; Graff 2002: 107–16.

supplied the person on active duty with food, weapons, clothing, and a horse.[24] The Dunhuang household register from 547 demonstrates that this system was operating effectively only three years after the Western Wei regained control of the Dunhuang region.[25]

After Yuwen Tai's death in 556 his kinsmen formally set aside the Western Wei and established their own Northern Zhou dynasty. By that time their armies had gained the upper hand against their rivals in the east. Although the Xianbei rulers of the Northern Zhou were closely allied to – and intermarried with – the Chinese aristocratic clans of Guanzhong, they took more forceful steps to use the equal-field system to support smallholder farmers. They eliminated land allocations based on possession of slaves and oxen and reduced the obligation for military service to once every twelve years. In contrast to the Northern Qi, the Northern Zhou land laws favored small-holder families rather than the office-holding class.[26]

Over time the *fubing* militias were transformed into a hereditary military caste (*junren* 軍人) that grew dramatically as greater numbers of Chinese were recruited into its ranks. The *fubing* soldiers were transferred from the civil registration system to military registers and directly subordinated to the authority of the central government. It seems likely that the Chinese *fubing* soldiers – but probably not the Xianbei units – also were expected to be part-time farmers and provide for their own subsistence. Although organized on different principles, the *fubing* militias bore some resemblance to the *tuntian* military-agricultural colonies pioneered by Cao Cao. Both systems were designed to reduce direct government expenditures on the military by making the fighting forces self-sufficient. Under the Northern Zhou dynasty, the ranks of *fubing* soldiers swelled to 200,000 men. When Yang Jian, a general descended from the hybrid Chinese-Xianbei aristocracy fostered by Empress Wenming, deposed the Northern Zhou child-emperor (his own grandson) in 581, he had at his disposal a formidable army that soon enabled him to reunify China under a single monarch.

State-building in the reunified empire: Sui and Tang

After his coup-d'état in 581, Yang Jian declared the establishment of his own Sui dynasty. Less than a decade later, in 589, Yang (Emperor Wen, r. 581–604) succeeded in conquering the south and reestablishing unified rule over the Chinese world. Wen undertook an aggressive program of institutional reform and state-building in order to concentrate political power in his own

---

[24] Kegasawa 1999: 76–144; Watanabe 2010: 339–41.   [25] Ikeda 1979: 45–50.
[26] Sagawa 2001b: 27–30. On the shift in the balance of military power from east to west over the course of the sixth century, see Graff 2002: 97–116.

hands. At the same time he retained many of the basic institutions inherited from the northern dynasties, including the equal-field system of landownership and the *fubing* militias. But in a striking parallel to the first empire of Qin, the Sui regime collapsed during the reign of its second emperor. In 618 the Sui was supplanted by a new dynasty, Tang. The Tang imperial family, too, was descended from the old Chinese-Xianbei aristocracy of North China, and like the Sui perpetuated the political style of the northern dynasties.

The Sui faced formidable problems in restoring a unified empire in the mold of the Qin and Han. In contrast to Qin-Han times, China now was a multiethnic and multicultural society, and Confucian traditions had receded with the rise of Buddhism as the dominant religion. Regional diversity had intensified during nearly three centuries of political fragmentation. Aristocratic families had become deeply entrenched as the ruling class in both north and south.

Emperor Wen relied heavily on the support of the aristocratic families of northwestern China – warriors rather than learned courtiers – who had dominated the Western Wei and Northern Zhou courts. At the same time he faced hostile resistance from aristocratic families in the Central Plain and the south. The Sui quickly moved to abolish the Nine Ranks system, the formal basis of the aristocracy's privileged status, and the hereditary rights to office it entailed. Under the new law code, hastily compiled in 583, the legal discrimination between aristocrat and commoner was replaced with the ancient distinctions between officials and ordinary subjects. The emperor strengthened the central government, establishing the executive organs – the Three Departments (Sansheng 三省) of the Chancellery, the Secretariat, and an all-powerful Department of State Affairs – and the Six Ministries (Liubu 六部) bureaucracy that would remain the standard structure of central government administration throughout later Chinese imperial history. The profusion of local jurisdictions created during the Period of Disunion was radically reduced. In contrast to the previous practice, whereby local magistracies became virtual satrapies of powerful magnate families, the Sui regularly rotated local officials every two or three years and deprived them of their military staff. Thus magistrates became bureaucratic appointees with purely civil authority.[27]

The Sui dynasty's political and social base in northwestern China was relatively weak economically. The most productive agricultural areas were the Central Plain and the Jiangnan region. The inaugural Sui census in 589 tabulated only 4.1 million households, far fewer than the combined 6.9 million households recorded in the Northern Zhou and Northern Qi censuses of the late 570s. When the Sui conducted an empire-wide census in 609 the registered population had rebounded to 9 million households and

---

[27] On the founding of the Sui and the political and institutional changes instituted by Emperor Wen, see Wright 1978.

46 million persons, and the amount of registered arable land had increased by an impressive 280 percent.[28]

The Sui retained the equal-field system, but introduced some modifications. Raising revenues by ensuring that farming families had access to land superseded restoring abandoned fields to cultivation as the state's chief priority. Extra land allotments for households owning slaves and oxen were eliminated, a change that adversely affected the great landowners. Following Northern Qi practice, the Sui eliminated allocations for women and unmarried men and instead made the conjugal household, or "bed" (*chuang* 床), the basic fiscal unit of the equal-field system. The male head of the household assumed full liability for tax payments and labor service obligations. These changes undoubtedly were intended to strengthen the authority of the patriarchal family. In an effort to inculcate loyalty among its officials, the Sui awarded substantial land grants based on bureaucratic rank.[29] Most importantly, Wen sought to merge the *fubing* militias with the equal-field system. Following the demobilization of the armies after the conquest of the south, the garrison militias were assigned to local jurisdictions and received lands allocated through the equal-field system. In addition, the Sui also conscripted ordinary taxpaying males for military service, chiefly as frontier guardsmen. Although exemption from military conscription could be purchased with a money payment in cloth, Wen's policies stemmed from a desire to revive the Qin-Han imperial ideal of the farmer-soldier.[30]

The Sui intended to extend the equal-field system to the entire empire, but it is unlikely that its land allocation procedures were widely applied in the territories of the former southern dynasties. Rice agriculture required heavy investments of capital and labor to build and maintain irrigation systems, and periodic reallocation of lands would greatly diminish the incentive for making such investments. Moreover, the development of the south's agricultural potential had largely come at the initiative of powerful landholding families who had staunchly resisted any attempts by the emperors of the southern dynasties to restrict their landholdings.

Emperor Wen and his son, Yang Guang (Emperor Yang, r. 604–18), actively commandeered the wealth of the empire for investment in what they perceived as the public good. Enormous resources were concentrated at the Sui capital of Daxingcheng, near the site of the old Han capital of Chang'an. Wen demolished the old city and built a new and much grander one to the southeast of the former site. Immense stocks of grain were held at granaries at the capitals of Daxingcheng and Luoyang, "enough to last for fifty years."

[28] Liang Fangzhong 1980: 38 (table A.13), 69 (table A.21).
[29] Hori 1975: 171–72, 193–226, 235.
[30] Watanabe 2010: 357–58, 377–83; Graff 2002: 138–41.

The Sui expanded the welfare mission of the state by developing the first empire-wide system of local famine relief granaries. Wen also began to construct a system of transport canals to ensure a stable food supply for the grain-deficient capital region.

After his father's death, Emperor Yang developed Luoyang, a more centrally located hub of land and water transport, as a second capital.[31] Through a massive levy of corvée labor that mobilized more than two million men, Yang also constructed the series of canals that became known as the Grand Canal to link Luoyang with the agricultural heartlands of Jiangnan and the Central Plain. The canal project was combined with an equally ambitious program of road and bridge building. The completion of the Grand Canal enabled the central government to funnel the abundant surpluses of rice from Jiangnan to the capital and the *fubing* armies stationed in its vicinity. The canal and road system also enhanced military control of key regions on the periphery of the empire. But the enormous costs of these projects undermined popular support for the dynasty.

The Sui rulers also sought to reclaim distant territories of the old Han Empire such as northern Vietnam (conquered by Wen in 602) and the Korean peninsula. The split of the Turkish Empire in central Asia into two contending regimes in 582 mitigated military pressure on the northwestern frontier. Yang was determined to retake Korea, but the political terrain of northeast Asia had changed dramatically since Han times. The Korean peninsula was divided among three states – Koguryŏ, Paekche, and Silla – that had coalesced after the demise of Chinese rule in the third century. Koguryŏ, whose territory extended from the northern half of the peninsula northward into Manchuria, boasted the most powerful military of the three Korean states. Yang launched repeated offensives against Koguryŏ in 612, 613, and 614, but each ended in ignominious defeat. Confronted by a restive populace and escalating conflicts among his officials, Yang withdrew to Yangzhou in 616. Two years later Yang was murdered by a descendant of the royal house of Northern Zhou, and a new ruling dynasty, the Tang, swept into power.

Li Yuan (Emperor Gaozu, r. 618–26), founder of the Tang dynasty, descended from the same hybrid Xianbei-Chinese aristocracy as Yang Jian and his predecessors dating back to the Northern Wei. Although the early Tang rulers relied heavily on the support of the mixed-blood Guanzhong aristocrats, they also embraced Confucian tenets of civil governance to a much greater degree than did the Sui monarchs. Like their predecessors, too, the Tang emperors deemed themselves heirs to the martial traditions and ecumenical culture of the steppe as well as China's political and literary traditions. A remarkably

---

[31] Xiong 1993.

cosmopolitan cultural style flourished at the Tang capital of Chang'an. But the volatile internecine strife that plagued the Tang court hampered political unity: the second Tang emperor, Li Shimin (Emperor Taizong, r. 627–49), assassinated the crown prince and forced his father to abdicate, while the Empress Dowager Wu Zetian set aside the Li dynasts and ruled as Buddhist matriarch of her own Zhou dynasty (690–705) for fifteen years. Wu Zetian's controversial regime further exacerbated tensions between the coterie of mixed-blood aristocrats who dominated the court, the great aristocratic clans of the Central Plain, and a rising group of locally prominent scholar-official families largely based in the old southern dynasty territories.[32]

The Tang, like the Sui before it, preserved the basic fiscal institutions of the northern dynasties with additional modifications. The equal-field system of land tenure was renewed as the law of the land, although as noted above it probably was not enforced in the rice-growing regions of the south. Population growth and the pressure it placed on the land also hindered full application of land allocations even in North China. In practice adult males received the full entitlements of 80 *mu* of personal share lands (*koufentian* 口分田, which reverted to the state upon the death of the holder) and 20 *mu* of permanent tenure lands (*yongyetian* 永業田, intended for the cultivation of mulberry orchards and fiber crops) only in sparsely populated regions (*kuanxiang* 寬鄉). In "congested regions" (*xiaxiang* 狹鄉) such as Guanzhong and the Central Plain they obtained only half of the standard allocations. Population registers from the frontier oasis towns of Dunhuang and Turfan dating from the period 690–769 reveal that equal-field land grants in fact were reallocated as required by statute. Dunhuang households received their full allotment of permanent tenure lands, but only a fraction of the statutory quotas of personal share lands, indicating a shift toward *de facto* private ownership.[33] By contrast, in Turfan – classified as a "congested region" – even permanent tenure lands were surrendered to the state upon the death of the head of the household. Moreover, land allocations in Turfan were exceedingly small – only 10 *mu* for adult males, less for households headed by women or minor and elderly males.[34] The limited land available for equal-field allocations spurred frequent recourse to leasing state-owned and monastic lands, and even the nominally illegal practice of offering tenancies on personal share lands.[35] Although Turfan was exceptional in some respects, the operation of the equal-field system there undoubtedly had much in common with "congested regions" in the North China heartland.

---

[32] On the divisions and conflicts within the early Tang ruling class, see Twitchett 1973.
[33] Niida 1937: 756–92; Twitchett 1963: 6–9.
[34] Nishijima 1966: 672–715; Ikeda 1988; Xiong 1999.   [35] Hori 1975: 278–326.

In 624 the Tang introduced a taxation system premised on the equal-field system of land tenure known as *zu-yong-diao* 租庸調 after its three principal components: a land tax paid in grain (*zu*), a tax levied on households paid in cloth (*diao*), and a requirement of labor service assessed on adult males (*yong*).[36] In contrast to previous practice, in which the conjugal pair of husband and wife was the unit of taxation, the Tang shifted the basis to adult males (*kekou* 課口 or *ding* 丁) between the ages of 21 and 59. Since in theory each adult male possessed an equal amount of land, the rate of taxation was uniform: two *shi* (119 liters) of grain, two *zhang* (6.22 meters) of cloth (increased by 20 percent if paid in hemp or ramie rather than silk), and twenty days of statutory labor. Labor service often was commuted to an additional payment of cloth, as was the *zu* grain tax in the southern provinces. Although the *zu-yong-diao* taxes were levied on individual adult men, taxes were paid by the head of the household. Women were exempt from paying taxes, although presumably they produced most of the cloth that was the principal item of taxation. The Tang state relied far less on servile occupational castes (*zahu*) for goods and services compared to the northern dynasties. Instead, at any given time approximately 300,000 persons with the requisite skills were called to "specialized service" (*seyi* 色役) duty on a rotating basis (several months per year) to staff local government offices, working in an array of capacities from secretaries and bailiffs to cooks and grooms. Military conscription likewise was considered a form of specialized service that entailed exemption from regular statutory labor.[37]

In addition to the *zu-yong-diao* taxes, the Tang also had separate land and household taxes levied on household assets. The land tax (*dishui* 地稅), collected in grain, constituted the primary tax levy in the south, where the equal-field system was not implemented. Grain collected from the *dishui* in the south, amounting to as much as four million *shi* (23.8 million liters) a year, originally was stockpiled locally for famine relief, but by the eighth century these payments were merged with the central government's general revenues. For the purposes of the household tax (*hushui* 戶稅) the state ranked households according to nine grades of property and collected a tax paid in coin earmarked for local government expenses. This tax was relatively modest – in the 740s the average assessment was 240 coins per household, generating no more than 5 percent of the revenue collected from the *zu-yong-diao* taxes – but it was the only tax paid by townsmen who did not own arable land.

---

[36] The following synopsis of the early Tang system of direct taxation is based on Twitchett 1963: 24–34.

[37] Twitchett 1963: 30–31; Watanabe 2010: 409–12. In some cases specialized service obligations could be discharged with payment in goods or coin.

Greater ease of transport between north and south following the completion of the Grand Canal and the thriving traffic across the overland Silk Road stimulated long-distance trade throughout the early Tang period. However, the development of the monetary economy was constrained by persistent short-ages of bronze coin. In 621 the Tang introduced a new standard currency, the Kaiyuan tongbao 開元通寶, which replaced the various Wuzhu coins issued by successive dynasties since early Han times. But the central government itself had little direct control of coinage; instead, most mints were operated by local authorities, especially imperial princes in the early Tang and later local prefects. Despite this lack of central oversight, the Tang mints managed to produce highly standardized coin until the upheavals of the mid-eighth cen-tury. Still, the quantity of coin issued, averaging roughly 200 million per year, fell far short of market demand. As a result counterfeiting of coin was more prevalent during the Tang dynasty than at any other time in Chinese history.[38] Textiles – including silk, hemp, and ramie – comprised the chief form of currency and the *de facto* monetary standard of the early Tang fiscal adminis-tration. Textiles were cheaper to transport than bronze coin, but most import-antly they were more stable in value. The Tang government collected most of its revenues in textiles, which were used to pay officials and soldiers as well as supply its armed forces with uniforms.[39]

The Tang retained the *fubing* garrison militias as the core of its armed forces. By the mid-630s some 350 garrisons had been established, mostly concentrated in Guanzhong and at the capital of Chang'an (Map 5.2). By the early eighth century the number of garrisons had increased to 633, with a total complement of roughly 600,000 soldiers.[40] *Fubing* soldiers had to supply their own provisions and equipment, but as a form of specialized service (*seyi*) they were exempt from the standard *zu-yong-diao* levies. *Fubing* service typically required a time commitment of 72–75 days per year (including travel to and from the garrison). Scholars remain sharply divided over whether *fubing* service was lighter or heavier than the taxes and statutory labor borne by ordinary subjects.[41] But it seems likely that *fubing* service conferred a certain degree of prestige, as well as affording the opportunity to earn honorific ranks that entailed additional land allotments. Moreover, the Tang state utilized not only *fubing* troops but also conscription of ordinary subjects – several hundred thousand men for year-long tours of duty – to man the stockades and signal

---

[38] Miyazawa 2008: 144–53; see also Twitchett 1963: 66–77.   [39] Cartier 1976; Trombert 2000.
[40] For a brief overview of the Tang *fubing* system, see Graff 2002: 189–91. For more details, see Kegasawa 1999: 267–319.
[41] Earlier Japanese scholarship generally asserted that the burden of *fubing* service was roughly equal to the *zu-yong-diao* obligations of ordinary subjects. Kegasawa (1999: 306–09), in contrast, contends that *fubing* duties entailed a relatively lighter burden. Yet Zhang Guogang (2006: 183) argues that *fubing* service was more onerous than the *zu-yong-diao* obligations.

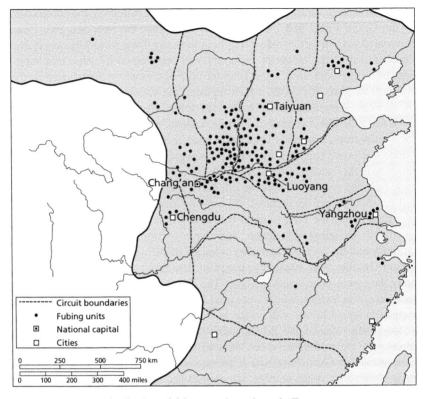

Map 5.2 Distribution of *fubing* garrisons in early Tang

posts along the frontiers.[42] Most ordinary subjects were liable for just twenty days of labor service (*yong*) annually, an obligation that often was commuted to a payment in cloth, especially in the southern provinces. In addition, at times of emergency the Tang state imposed extraordinary corvée levies (*zayao* 雜徭) that might require much lengthier terms of service. Those mustered for extra-ordinary labor duty received partial or complete exemption from *zu-yong-diao* obligations if their services were required for more than forty days.[43]

The imperial infrastructure of the Tang exhibited a basic continuity with the Han, displaying a clear division between revenue-generating regions in the Central Plain and the Yangzi River valley on one hand and the revenue-absorbing regions of the capital and the frontiers on the other (Map 5.3). As in the Han, the fiscal administration of the Tang Empire was highly centralized,

---

[42] Watanabe 2010: 357–64, 397–99.   [43] Ibid.: 403–07.

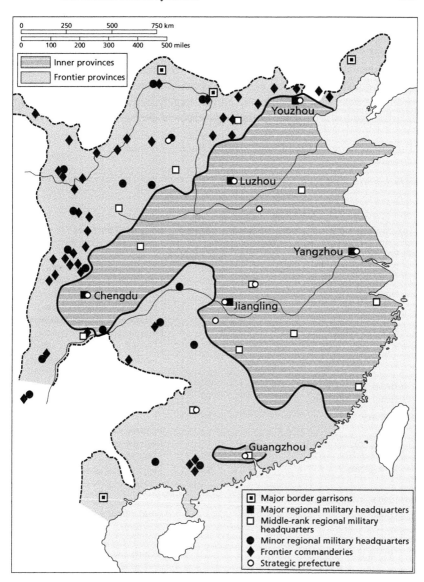

Map 5.3 Revenues and logistics in Tang China
Source: Watanabe 2010: 433, map 8.

with virtually all decision-making authority vested in the Ministry of Revenue, and especially in the Department of Public Revenue (Duzhisi 度支司). As Table 5.4 shows, in-kind payments in grain and cloth comprised 90 percent of the state's revenues, of which less than 10 percent was collected in coin. Most revenues in grain and coin were retained at the local level; transfers of revenues, especially to the frontier armies, largely were made in silk and hemp textiles, again affirming the central importance of cloth as a means of payment.

Table 5.4 *Income of the Department of Public Revenue, c. 742–55*
(all figures in millions)

Tax receipts	Revenues			Designated purposes
	Grain *(shi)*	Cloth (bolts)	Coin (strings)	
(1) Capital				
Grain	3.0			Converted to silk and hemp, deposited in capital treasuries
Grain	3.0			Converted to rice and soybeans, for imperial commissariat and kitchens of official departments
Grain	4.0			From Jiangnan; designated for famine relief granaries, official salaries, and other central government expenses
Hemp, silk, silk floss		13.0		Deposited at Chang'an
Hemp, silk, silk floss		1.0		Deposited at Luoyang
(2) Military				
Grain	1.9			Regional military commands
Hemp, silk, silk floss		11.0		Regional military commands, for purchase of grain for army
Bronze coin			0.6	Supplemented provision of army rations
(3) Local governments				
Grain	5.0			Local official salaries; transport expenses
Grain	8.9			Local famine relief granaries
Bronze coin			1.4	Salaries and administrative expenses of local governments; horse purchases for post stations
(4) Miscellaneous				
Hemp, silk, silk floss		2.0		Salaries for remote/small prefectures; transport expenses
Totals	25.8	27.0	2.0	
Share by value*	55%	35%	9%	

Sources: TD 6.34a-b; Twitchett 1963: 153–56; Watanabe 2010: 441–43; *Trombert 2000: 108.

The Tang did not establish regular budgets for local governments, although in practice a large portion of grain revenue (the *zu* tax) was retained by local officials to meet their administrative expenses.[44] Much of the revenue generated at the local level was transferred directly to the regional military headquarters (*dudufu* 都督府) – 43 in all – that managed military logistics. This transfer of revenues perhaps was the most onerous cost borne by the fiscal administration. Of the eight million men mustered for labor service each year, approximately half were employed in transport of tax receipts in grain and cloth. Tang statutes expressly prohibited local officials from hiring private transport for tax goods, or converting in-kind tax receipts into coin. There is evidence that local officials did not always adhere to these rules. Nonetheless, the Tang fiscal administration, following the pattern established by the Northern Wei, relied almost entirely on its own resources and management, allowing no recourse to market mechanisms.[45]

Agricultural and industrial development

During the Period of Disunion, the maturation of the agricultural innovations of the Han era improved the efficiency of dryland agriculture in North China. The three-crops-in-two-years rotation (usually combining winter wheat with millet, soybeans, or rape turnips) appears to have been widely employed.[46] Green fertilizers – particularly legumes, such as adzuki beans, that fix nitrogen in the soil – complemented animal and human manure.[47] Hand tillage was increasingly displaced by animal power. The invention of a curved plow-beam and withers harness made it possible to draw heavy plows with a single ox.[48] Ox-drawn harrows with iron tines also came into common use.[49] These advances widened the productivity gap between farmers who owned plow oxen and those who did not. Northern Wei officials, recognizing this disparity, repeatedly issued decrees to promote cooperative sharing of animal and human labor power. In the mid-fifth century, for example, the government proposed an exchange whereby those who lent their oxen to neighbors should be compensated by weeding, at a ratio of 7 *mu* of weeding for 20 *mu* of plowing.[50] The considerable advantages of owning oxen naturally favored

---

[44] Ōtsu 1986; Watanabe 2010: 430–38. For an overview of the organization of the Tang fiscal administration, see Twitchett 1963: 98–106. On local officials' lack of fiscal autonomy in the early Tang, see also Twitchett 1969–70.
[45] Watanabe 2010: 438–50.
[46] Yoneda 1989: 199–291. Nishijima (1966: 249–78) disputed Yoneda's claims about the widespread use of this crop rotation system at this time, but Yoneda's views have prevailed. See Bray 1984: 464.
[47] Bray 1984: 293–94. [48] Ibid.: 180. [49] Ibid.: 223–38.
[50] *TD* 1.12c. See Elvin 1973: 45; Watanabe 1986: 177.

the great estate owners. The great majority of smallholders did not own oxen; the 33 households surveyed in the Dunhuang registry from 547 possessed a total of just 6 oxen (Table 5.1).

Our knowledge of the advances in agriculture during this era largely derives from the comprehensive treatise on agronomics compiled c. 534 by Jia Sixie, who served as a local official in Shandong.[51] In over ninety chapters Jia recorded in exacting detail the practical aspects of managing a large estate, including cultivation of field and garden crops, animal husbandry, maintaining orchards and fish ponds, sericulture, brewing, and the preparation of processed foods and condiments. An interpolated chapter – believed to have been added by a Tang editor – advises that 300 *mu* of arable and a pair of oxen should suffice to maintain a family, an indication that the farm activities described in the work were typical of a landed estate, not a family farm. In his preface Jia apologizes for his simple prose, stating that his work was written not for learned men but for "domestic bondservants" (*jiatong* 家僮) – a term that often denoted field laborers. It was common to employ capable bondservants as stewards and overseers, however, and perhaps Jia was referring to supervisors of this sort.[52] Jia makes no mention of the composition of farm labor. Only once does he allude to hired labor – mentioning a "daily wage of 10 sheaves of firewood, with each sheaf worth 3 coins" – although occasionally he notes the price of slaves in various commodities.[53] Most likely an estate of this size relied chiefly on servile rather than hired labor. We perhaps encounter an estate similar to Jia's ideal in a pastoral panegyric written c. 570 by Xiao Zihuan, a scholar of royal descent, in which he expressed his contentment with a modest estate consisting of "a fruit orchard in the rear . . . and a vegetable garden in front . . . two *qing* [200 *mu*] of fields to supply food for the table, ten *mu* for sericulture and hemp cultivation, three to five servant girls who can be tasked with the weaving, and four or more domestic bondservants (*jiatong*) who can undertake the plowing and weeding." In addition to raising chickens, pigs, and sheep, Xiao mentions cultivating millet, soybeans, and mallow.[54]

Although Jia Sixie's preface spouted conventional platitudes about disinterest in commercial profit, his treatise affirmed that farms located near towns and marketplaces could reap handsome returns. Land planted in rape turnips (an important source of oil seeds, also made into pickles) yielded three times the income of cereal crops; melons and mallow (a popular vegetable, esteemed for its medicinal properties, that could be harvested three times a year) likewise

---

[51] On Jia Sixie's treatise, see Bray 1985: 55–59. A convenient digest of the agricultural practices described by Jia can be found in Lewis 2009: 118–25.
[52] "Preface," in *QMYS*, 1: 9.   [53] Chapter 46, "Zhong yu baiyang" 種榆柏楊, in *QMYS*, 2: 303.
[54] *ZS*: 42.758. Xiao Zihuan, son of the last emperor of the defunct Liang dynasty, took refuge in the north and was warmly received by the rulers of the Eastern Wei and Northern Qi dynasties.

earned a greater return than cereals; and timber from elms and poplars was even more profitable than vegetables, although arboriculture required long-term investment and was incompatible with cereal farming.[55] Planting one *qing* of land in safflower – used not only to make cooking oil but also for candle wax, dyestuffs, and axle grease – could generate an income of 300 bolts of hemp cloth. Harvesting one *qing* of safflower required a hundred pairs of hands but was practicable "if you gather children and bondservants together in groups of tens or a hundred to share the work of picking the safflower, as long as one divides the income obtained fairly, giving half to those who do the labor."[56] Jia proposed not a single model of the estate economy, but rather a range of alternatives that a landowner might pursue depending on the local ecology and accessibility to markets.[57]

Notably absent from Jia Sixie's treatise, however, is the use of skilled labor for the production of luxury goods. Mulberry cultivation and raising silkworms are discussed at length, but no mention is made of weaving. The chapter on lacquer is devoted to instructions on the proper care of lacquer wares, not their manufacture. Processing of raw agricultural products was limited to brewing wine and pickling and fermenting foods and condiments. The market-oriented activities of the estate remained confined to agricultural staples and processed foods for everyday consumption.

How prevalent was the kind of managerial estate described by Jia Sixie? Surely the answer varies by region. Inventories of religious donors for several villages in northern Shanxi in the mid-sixth century portray communities consisting of a heterogeneous mix of modest families with no significantly large or wealthy landowners and little evidence of kinship solidarity.[58] By the end of the sixth century the use of servile labor in agriculture was falling sharply. In 577 the Northern Zhou emancipated all enslaved war captives within its realm as well as all private and state slaves in the conquered Northern Qi territories, although the practical effects of these decrees are unknown. The reduction and eventual elimination of land allocations for slaves in the equal-field policies of the Northern Qi and Sui states removed a valuable incentive for maintaining a servile workforce. With the restoration of imperial order, the need for private militias disappeared, and land rather than labor became the scarce resource.[59] In Dunhuang, a region where large private

---

[55] Yoneda 1989: 23–28.
[56] Chapter 52, "Zhong honglanhua zhizi" 種紅藍花梔子, in *QMYS*, 2: 330–31.
[57] Yoneda 1989: 37.
[58] Hou Xudong 2005: 231–64. Hou also suggests that village solidarity was weak; the villages he studied were divided into a number of separate religious associations that perhaps were rivals for villagers' allegiance. But it remains unclear how representative these cases were.
[59] Hori 1975: 190–97: Wang Yi-t'ung 1953: 360–61. Tang Changru (1990: 130–34) argued to the contrary that slaves' personal subjugation to their masters intensified during the Northern Zhou

landholdings were virtually non-existent, slaves comprised only about 2 percent of the population recorded in eighth-century household registers.[60]
The prominence of mills for grinding grain and pressing oil – both water
mills and ox-powered rotary mills (*nianwei* 碾磑) – as valuable economic
assets is a striking feature of this period. Large-scale watermills first began to
appear in the third–fourth centuries, and frequently receive mention in inventories of assets from the sixth century onward. The proliferation of mills,
especially during the sixth century, testified to a decisive shift from millet
(usually eaten as porridge) to wheat (ground into flour and made into noodles,
cakes, and dumplings) in the diet of northern Chinese and in the agricultural
economy as well. Mills became important sources of income for estate owners,
who in addition to milling their own flour and pressing vegetable oils earned
fees by leasing their mills to small farmers. At the same time, watermills
triggered new conflicts over water rights, particularly in parched North China.
On several occasions in the eighth century the Tang government, inundated by
complaints from commoner farmers, was forced to destroy mills owned
by members of the imperial household that were siphoning off water needed
for irrigation.[61]
The obligation to pay a substantial portion of household taxes in cloth as
well as technological innovations engendered major advances in textile production during the Period of Disunion. All households were expected to
engage in the manufacture of cloth: silk and hemp in northern regions, ramie
and other bast fibers in the south. As Map 5.4 shows, during the Northern Wei
silk manufacture was concentrated in the core economic regions of the Central
Plain, while hemp production prevailed in peripheral areas. Bast fibers from
plants such as hemp, ramie, and kudzu are long and must be spliced together
by hand before being twisted into yarn, in contrast to short-fiber cotton and
wool, which are spun into yarn. Women in farming families wove cloth at
home using simple, compact "waist looms" (so-called because the tension in
the warp is maintained by a belt fastened around the weaver's waist). Silk
fabrics took much longer to weave, some 8–16 days per bolt in contrast
to two days for a bolt of bast fibers (the standard bolt was roughly 12 meters
in length and 56 cm wide). Women's work in spinning and weaving
contributed more than half of the household's tax payments under the equal-
field system, in addition to meeting the family's own clothing needs and

and Sui, but he agrees with Hori that by Sui-Tang times the most important source of labor for
the great estates was the swelling pool of landless – but legally free – displaced person known as
"floating clients" (*fuke* 浮客), who presumably worked as tenant farmers.
[60] Ikeda 1973: 139. Ikeda observed that there was a much higher ratio (perhaps as much as 20
percent) of slaves in Turfan population registers; he attributed the disparity to Turfan's much
greater dependence on commerce, which fostered greater economic stratification.
[61] Nishijima 1966: 233–49; Amano 1979: 860–62, 905–07; Gernet 1995: 142–50.

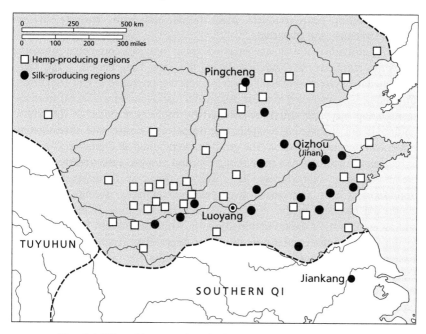

Map 5.4 Silk and hemp regions in the Northern Wei

perhaps generating additional income from sales of cloth in the market. The great estates could afford more sophisticated equipment such as the draw looms required for producing complex weaves. Anecdotal lore from this period makes frequent mention of the weaving skills of upper-class women, whose work presumably was motivated more by notions of gender and social status than by economic considerations.[62]

Scholarly opinion remains divided over whether the draw loom was developed independently by the Chinese during the Han dynasty or imported along with weft-faced weaving from Central Asia around the fifth century. In any event, during the Northern Wei, weft-faced weaving techniques superseded the warp-faced weaves of Han for manufacturing figured silks. Striped and chessboard designs using warps and wefts of different colors also appeared during this period, most likely influenced by similar designs that were highly popular in India, along with foreign decorative

[62] Bray 1997: 191–202.

motifs featuring pearl roundels, plant motifs, and exotic animals such as lions, elephants, and pheasants.[63]

While individual merchants amassed great fortunes, commerce remained subject to cumbersome regulation during the early Tang period.[64] The Tang continued the system of official urban markets that prevailed in Qin-Han times. Commerce was restricted to a few designated marketplaces walled off from the surrounding city and strictly supervised by officials responsible for setting trading hours, inspecting weights, measures, and coins, and investigating fraudulent business practices. The government required all domestic merchants to register as members of a trade (*hang* 行), and grouped each trade together in the marketplace. Nonetheless, the scale of commerce in major cities was impressive. Chang'an boasted two great marketplaces: foreign merchants conducted business in the Western Market, the terminus of the Silk Road and an emporium of exotic imported goods, while the Eastern Market catered to the needs of the capital's multitude of upper-class residents. Chang'an's Eastern Market reportedly had 220 *hang*, while the Southern Market at Luoyang enclosed more than 3,000 shops and over 400 inns within its walls.[65] In addition to housing traveling merchants, innkeepers provided them with brokerage services and storehouses for their goods.

International trade in the heyday of the Silk Road

Despite the political fragmentation and constant warfare of the Period of Disunion, China's international trade flourished. It was during this period that the overland Silk Road reached its peak of prosperity as the main artery of trans-Eurasian trade (Map 5.5). The spread of Buddhism from India to East Asia and the formation of far-flung steppe empires stimulated economic as well as cultural exchange across the Central Asian caravan routes. Diplomatic and commercial exchanges with India surged. More than fifty tribute missions were exchanged between Indian princes and the Tang court before 750.[66] Maritime commerce with Southeast Asia and the Indian Ocean world began to develop at this time as well. International trade facilitated transfers of technology and promoted new patterns of consumption. Chinese silk-making techniques spread to Iran, the Byzantine Empire, and India, while knowledge of sugar cultivation and refining passed from India to China. By the late eighth century black pepper from southern India had become a staple of Chinese

---

[63] Liu Xinru 1988: 72–75; Li Wenying 2012.
[64] On markets and state regulation of commerce in the early Tang, see Twitchett 1966.
[65] On the marketplaces of Chang'an, see Xiong 2000: 165–94. For Luoyang, see Xiong 1993.
[66] On Sino-Indian diplomatic and commercial relations – primarily mediated by Buddhism – during the Tang period, see Sen 2003.

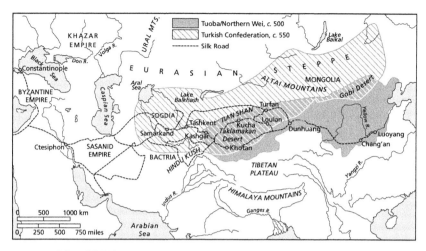

Map 5.5 Silk Road trade routes

cuisine and silver plate graced with Persian designs a fixture on the dining tables of the wealthy.

Silk, of course, was the principal commodity of trans-Eurasian trade. Exports to the Byzantine Empire and the Mediterranean world consisted mostly of raw silk or yarn, which was dyed and woven in Constantinople to suit Western tastes in garments and furnishings. After sericulture began to develop in the eastern Mediterranean from the sixth century onward imports of Chinese silk declined.[67] Yet the demand for fine Chinese silk yarn and fabrics continued unabated in Iran and India even after the emergence of indigenous sericulture and silk-weaving industries. Imports to China consisted primarily of luxury goods such as coral and pearls from the Indian Ocean and the Red Sea, Roman and Indian glass, jade, gems, perfumes, and incense. Nearly all of these items were connected to Buddhist worship and used either in religious rituals or for decorating shrines and monuments.[68]

After the fall of the Han dynasty, foreign merchants settled in the old garrison towns along the northwestern frontier. Oasis settlements spanning the Central Asian trade routes became thriving towns inhabited by cosmopolitan groups of merchants. In the fourth and fifth centuries merchants generally preferred the southern route around the Taklamakan Desert, through Loulan and Khotan (Map 5.5). Dozens or even hundreds of merchants banded together

---

[67] On the transfer of sericulture technology and development of the Byzantine silk industry, see Liu Xinru 1996: 73–91. Sericulture was introduced to Byzantine-ruled Syria sometime in the fifth century: see Muthesius 2002.

[68] Liu Xinru 1988: 54–64, 93–5.

to organize camel caravans for the arduous trek through the deserts and mountains of Central Asia. A fourth-century document from Khotan, for example, describes a caravan of 319 beasts of burden transporting 4,326 rolls of silk, among other goods.[69] Merchants also supplied textiles, furs, salt, wine, grain, and metal wares to the oasis towns and the pastoral nomads of the steppe.

By the end of the fourth century merchants from Sogdia, the gateway to Iran and Afghanistan, had become the dominant force in the Silk Road trade.[70] The central position of the Sogdians was further solidified after the formation of the nomadic empires of the Hephthalites and the Turks during the sixth century. Sogdian merchants forged alliances with the Turks and entered the administration, army, and diplomatic service of the Turkish khan. The Hephthalites and Turks extracted heavy tribute from sedentary rulers – the Sasanid rulers of Iran dispatched mule trains of silver coin to the Hephthalites, while the Northern Qi and Zhou rulers paid an annual tribute of 100,000 bolts of silk to the Turks in the late sixth century. The nomad chiefs in turn entrusted this tribute to their Sogdian agents to acquire the goods they coveted. Under the umbrella of Turkish protection, the route across the northern perimeter of the Taklamakan via Turfan, Kucha, and Kashgar became the main conduit of the Silk Road trade. A commercial tax register dating from the early seventh century shows Sogdian merchants at Turfan buying and selling silk, silver, gold, perfume, saffron, brass, medicines, and cane sugar.[71]

The spread of Sogdians throughout the commercial networks of the Silk Road took the form of a trade diaspora, in which kinship and patronage ties as well as common religion and language linked together far-flung merchant colonies.[72] Many Sogdian immigrants settled in the major oasis towns, such as Turfan and Dunhuang. Sogdian residents of Turfan included innkeepers, winemakers, leatherworkers, butchers, tanners, artists, and camel-shoers as well as caravan traders. Large communities of Sogdians also inhabited the leading commercial centers of northern China. The Northern Wei rulers built a special market for foreign traders in a merchant enclave located outside Luoyang's city wall. The Sogdian silk merchant He Tuo, who arrived in China in the mid-sixth century, joined the entourage of a Chinese prince and amassed a great fortune. His eldest son and nephew became experts at cutting gemstones, and the Sui Emperor Wen placed the nephew in charge of the imperial jewelry workshop. The He family also is credited with introducing the techniques of glassmaking to China.[73] The dominance of Sogdians over Silk Road

---

[69] De la Vaissière 2005: 188.
[70] The following paragraphs are primarily based on de la Vaissière 2005.
[71] Skaff 1998: 89–93.   [72] Skaff 2003. On the concept of trade diaspora, see Curtin 1984.
[73] On the He family, see de la Vaissière 2005: 144–45.

commerce fed stereotypes about their immense wealth and shallow morals. The Chinese Buddhist pilgrim Xuanzang, who passed through Samarkand in 630, derided the Sogdians as "greedy and deceitful," snidely observing that "fathers and sons scheme for profit, because everyone, noble and commoner alike, regards wealth as the measure of distinction."[74]

Amid the incessant tumult of the eastern steppe from the third to the fifth centuries coins disappeared from the Central Asian oasis towns; instead textiles and carpets were used as means of payment. In the fifth–sixth centuries the substantial booty of silver tribute the Hephthalites extracted from the Sasanids began to flow eastward to finance trading caravans to China. During 502–640, when Turfan was the capital of the independent Gaochang kingdom, Sasanid silver coins became the region's primary monetary standard and were widely used in trade, wage payments, and tenancy contracts for orchards and vineyards (rents for arable lands were paid in grain). After the Tang took control of Turfan in 640 Sasanid silver coins (and imitations of them minted by the new Arab rulers of Iran) continued to predominate, but silk became increasingly important as a means of exchange. Chinese officials and soldiers stationed at frontier garrisons received their pay in silk, which they could readily trade for the necessities of life. The Sui and Tang governments adamantly refused to accept Sasanid silver coins as legal tender in China proper, although foreigners were permitted to make some payments in silver coin. In the eighth century silver coins disappeared from the Turfan economy, displaced by silk and even Chinese bronze coins, attesting to Turfan's increasing incorporation into the Chinese economy as well as the slow attenuation of the Silk Road trade.[75]

Trade with the Indian Ocean world developed in the first century CE with the emergence of a thriving commercial kingdom known as Funan, located in the Mekong River Delta. Chinese records of the third century portray Funan, where Indian and Sasanid ships came to trade, as strongly influenced by Indian culture. Customs duties were paid in gold, silver, pearls, and perfumes. Copper and tin from Thailand supplied Funan's workshops. Indian pepper, Arabian frankincense, and exotic tropical products such as ivory, camphor, spices, and medicinal plants were carried to southern China by Chinese, Malay, and Iranian merchants. Funan began to decline in the fifth century, when ocean-going traders shifted to the faster route through the Straits of Melaka between the Malay Peninsula and Sumatra.[76] In 413 the Chinese pilgrim monk Faxian returned from Sri Lanka along this route via Java, "traveling in the company of many merchants aboard a large vessel with a capacity of over 200 men and provisions for 50 days."[77] By the seventh century the Srivijaya princes of

[74] XYJ: 1.8.   [75] Thierry 1993; Skaff 1998; Helen Wang 2004: 78–88.
[76] Hall 2011: 33–66.   [77] FXZ: 5.145.

Sumatra had become the principal intermediaries in China's trade with Southeast Asia and the Indian Ocean.[78] Direct contact between Chinese and Japanese rulers began in the third century CE with the exchange of envoys between the Wu kingdom in southeast China and the Wa queen Himiko.[79] Diplomatic ties intensified during the fifth century, but there is little evidence of significant trade between China and Japan at this time. Archaeological findings show that virtually all of the goods imported to Japan before the seventh century arrived via Korea.[80] Although the Chinese bronze mirrors that became prized prestige goods among the ruling elite of Japan were replicated in Japan itself, it is likely that these imitations were manufactured by immigrant Chinese craftsmen.[81] During the Sui and Tang dynasties, trade between China and Japan was largely confined to luxury goods obtained through the exchange of tribute missions.[82] "Tang goods" (*karamono* 唐物) bestowed enviable prestige; the term encompassed not just luxury wares made in China but also products of the Silk Road trade. The treasures sealed up in Emperor Shōmu's (r. 724–49) Shōsōin Repository included silks, wood and lacquer furnishings, Buddhist ritual paraphernalia, writing cases, and medicines from China, but also Byzantine glass, Iranian silverware, and a famous zither ornamented in mother-of-pearl portraying a Sogdian astride a camel playing the same instrument.

The economic impact of Buddhism

Buddhist missionaries arrived in China during the first century CE, following the overland Central Asian routes between India and China. Initially Buddhism had only a slight impact in China. In the fifth and sixth centuries, however, Buddhism became a major force in Chinese religion and society, and in China's economy as well. Through official and private patronage the Buddhist church came into possession of substantial landholdings. Buddhist monasteries also earned considerable income from loans and commercial enterprises in addition to the charitable donations and gifts obtained in exchange for religious services.

The great expansion in monastic foundations occurred during the late fifth and early sixth centuries. Before Emperor Xiaowen moved the Northern

---

[78] Hall 2011: 103–33.
[79] On the elusive figure of Himiko as the first documented ruler of Japan, see Kidder 2007. The early diplomatic exchanges between China and Japan are studied in Wang Zhenping 2006.
[80] Farris 1998: 68–97.
[81] The provenance of the bronze mirrors excavated from third–fifth century mound tumuli in Japan remains a controversial subject. See Farris 1998: 42–46; Kidder 2007: 160–85.
[82] On tribute trade between China and Japan during the Sui-Tang era, see von Verschuer 2006: 1–22.

Wei capital to Luoyang in 493 the city contained around 100 Buddhist monasteries and shrines. By the time the Northern Wei fell in 534 the number of Buddhist foundations in Luoyang had soared to 1,367.[83] The monk Falin (570–640) claimed that during the Northern Wei period alone 47 great state monasteries were established along with 839 temples founded by nobles, officials, and aristocratic families and more than 30,000 shrines built by commoners.[84] A similarly prodigious expansion of the Buddhist church took place in the south, especially during the reign of Emperor Wu of Liang (r. 502–49), who achieved lasting renown as one of the great patrons of Buddhism.

Confucian critics fumed over what they regarded as the pernicious economic costs of Buddhism: the extravagant expenditures on temples, icons, and rituals; the burden of monks who depended on the labor of others for their material support; and the rampant abuse of monastic exemptions from taxation. Yet at the same time the wealth that flowed into the Buddhist church stimulated many forms of economic activity. As already noted, many of the goods imported to China during the heyday of the Silk Road were connected with Buddhist devotion. Buddhism also fostered the emergence of craftsmen and merchant networks that supplied monasteries and lay devotees with a wide range of devotional objects. The construction of temples, the maintenance of monastic properties, and religious festivals required the services of architects, carpenters, masons, brickmakers, bronze craftsmen, sculptors, gold- and silversmiths, and many other artisanal trades.

The number of ordained clergy probably did not exceed 200,000, or less than 1 percent of the total population, at the end of the sixth century. But it has been estimated that at that time as much as 5–6 percent of the population of North China was able to evade taxation through false registration as clergy.[85] Following Indian precedents, Buddhist monks in China adopted rules and institutions that established religious foundations as legal entities. Such corporate entities had never existed in China, where the household had been the only legally recognized property-owning unit. The monk Daoxuan, who compiled the monastic regulations widely used in China, deemed not only sanctuaries, devotional objects, sacred books, and monks' quarters but also the lands, servants, and livestock attached to monasteries to be part of the "permanent endowment" (*changzhu* 常住) that belonged to the clergy (*sangha*) as a whole.[86] This permanent endowment thus was immune from the regular fission of private property caused by equal inheritance laws. Monastic codes restricted the property of individual clergy to the indispensable accoutrements of their vocation (robe, alms bowl, staff, and objects of

[83] Tang Yongtong 2006, 2: 451.   [84] Cited in Gernet 1995: 4.   [85] Ibid.: 10–2, 39–40.
[86] Ibid.: 66–73.

daily use).[87] But in fact many monks and nuns acquired personal property in the form of land, draft animals, carts, tools, and gold and silver objects that gave them a certain degree of economic independence.[88]

State patronage and private donations endowed monasteries with substantial landholdings and other assets, including agricultural laborers. In 469 the Northern Wei assigned some of the revenues from *tuntian* agricultural colonies to Buddhist monasteries. Beginning in 476 the government designated certain war captives, government slaves, and convicts as "*sangha* households" (*sengqihu* 僧祇戶) and "donated" them to the Buddhist church. The *sangha* households – who in essence became hereditary bondservants – cultivated lands belonging to the monasteries as well as providing other menial services.[89] In the south, too, making gifts of bondservants to monastic institutions was a common practice.

The landholdings of larger monasteries generally were in the range of 1,000–4,000 *mu*; significant holdings, to be sure, but dwarfed by the largest private estates. Figures from the eighth century suggest that monastic estates comprised only about 2 percent of the total cultivated land in the empire, though these landholdings were heavily concentrated around the Tang capitals of Chang'an and Luoyang.[90] More precise data from the twelfth–thirteenth centuries shows that Buddhist monasteries owned 17 percent of the arable fields and 25 percent of non-arable lands in Fuzhou (Fujian), an area in which Buddhist institutions were especially strong. In Ningbo and Taizhou prefectures in Zhejiang the share of arable land owned by monasteries was considerably smaller, in the range of 4–5 percent.[91] Like private owners of large estates, the monasteries also possessed commercial assets such as flour mills and oil presses that generated a major share of their income. Dunhuang's monasteries leased their facilities to millers and oil pressers, who paid either a fixed annual rent or a share of the flour and oil they produced.[92]

Buddhist monasteries also played an innovative role in the development of credit institutions. It is possible that the practice of issuing loans secured by pledges of property was introduced to China by Buddhist monasteries in imitation of Indian precedents. The earliest evidence for pawnshops making loans of money (*kuzhiqian* 庫質錢), either in coin or cloth, in exchange for goods deposited as security has been traced to Buddhist monasteries in South China in the fifth century. These loans generally seem to have been directed toward well-to-do clients, most likely benefactors of the monastery.

---

[87] On the personal possessions of Buddhist clergy, see Kieschnick 2003: 83–156.
[88] Gernet 1995: 78–93, 131–34. On the commercial and financial activities of Buddhist clergy, see also Trombert 1995.
[89] Gernet 1995: 100–12.   [90] Ibid.: 138–40.   [91] You Biao 2003: 110, 116–17.
[92] Gernet 1995: 142–52.

Monasteries often designated some of their permanent assets as "inexhaustible treasuries" (*wujincang* 無盡藏) whose funds, including grain as well as money, were lent at interest to both rich and poor supplicants.[93]

Monasteries also figure as the principal creditors in the cache of surviving loan contracts from Dunhuang dating from the ninth century.[94] In many of these instances monasteries lent grain and seed to poor farmers, including their own "*sangha* household" tenants (known as *sihu* 寺戶 in Dunhuang), to tide them over until the next harvest. Typically the monasteries charged no interest on loans (usually issued in the spring and falling due after the harvest) to *sangha* households, an indication perhaps of their ethical responsibility to perform charitable works. But compassion had its limits: if the borrower failed to repay on time the debt was doubled. Private creditors and monastic loans to independent farmers demanded 100 percent interest on such loans – a rate that violated the letter of the law (which capped interest charges at 6 percent per month) – but abided by the legal requirement that total interest could not exceed 100 percent of the principal. Interest payments from loans comprised as much as a third of the income of Dunhuang's larger monasteries.[95]

Loan contracts often specified seizure of (movable) assets as the penalty for failure to repay debts, but by the tenth century seizures were replaced by other remedies such as guarantors or collateralization. Collateral loans took two forms: either the collateral was a pledge of goods to be surrendered in the event the loan was not repaid (known in later Chinese law as *diya* 抵押), or the creditor took possession of the collateral and had free use of it until the debt was repaid. In the Dunhuang contracts the term *dian* 典 was applied to both types of loans, but later *dian* (along with a variety of cognate terms, such as *dianmai* 典賣) came to designate the latter type, often translated as "mortgage." In a few Dunhuang contracts an impoverished landowner conveyed the usufruct rights to a parcel of land for a period of two or more years – in one case twenty-two years. In this type of loan the creditor received cultivation rights in lieu of repayment of the principal and interest.[96] Land was inalienable under the equal-field system, but as that system began to disintegrate desperate expedients of this sort often led to loss of landholdings and poverty.

The economic power of the Buddhist church suffered a devastating shock in 845, when Emperor Wuzong (r. 840–46), motivated by anti-Buddhist zealotry and urgent need to raise war funds, issued orders to confiscate the vast

[93] Ibid.: 161–71.
[94] This paragraph and the next are based on the meticulous analysis of these contracts in Trombert 1995.
[95] Gernet 1995: 178.   [96] Trombert 1995: 173–78.

properties and wealth held by Buddhist monasteries and clergy. Reportedly, some 4,600 monasteries and over 40,000 shrines and sanctuaries were seized by state authorities and hundreds of thousands of monks and nuns forced to return to lay life. Although the proscription against Buddhism was repealed after Wuzong's death a year later, many Buddhist establishments had suffered irreparable harm. In some areas – notably in regions remote from the capital, such as Fujian and Anhui – Buddhist monasteries retained substantial land-holdings. But the role of Buddhist institutions in economic life waned in the aftermath of the 845 proscription.[97]

Demise of the Northern Wei institutional heritage

Over the course of the first century of Tang rule the equal-field landholding system and the *fubing* militias gradually weakened and collapsed. These institutions – created by the nomad-ruled states of North China to resettle the population and stabilize the state's resources of men and materiel at a time of profound economic upheaval and population loss – had imposed rigid uniformity on Chinese society and economy. The restoration of domestic peace under Sui and Tang rule unleashed dynamic economic forces that eroded the foundations of the equal-field system, while incessant wars along the empire's vast frontiers inflicted mounting hardship on the *fubing* soldiery and military conscripts. The Tang fiscal system relied heavily on taxes levied in grain and cloth on agricultural producers, and made no effort to capture revenues from the non-farm sectors of the economy. These problems, already evident in the second half of the seventh century, spiraled out of control during the eighth century.

The operation of the equal-field system was encumbered by the growing scarcity of land, especially in long-settled North China, in the face of steady population growth. In the densely populated regions of Guanzhong and the Central Plain farm families received only half or less of their nominal entitlements of lands. The weight of taxation fell heavily on North China's small farmers, who were liable for the uniform *zu-yong-diao* levies regardless of the actual amount of land they cultivated. This burden forced impoverished families to relinquish or abandon their landholdings. Many of these landless persons became bondservants absorbed into the households of great land-owners or they migrated to the less populated south, where land was relatively abundant and not subject to the strictures of the equal-field system. Consequently, aristocrats, officials, and Buddhist monasteries – beneficiaries of generous tax exemptions – amassed great estates, notably around the two

---

[97] For an effort to quantify the wealth of the Buddhist church and its fiscal impact, see Ch'en 1956.

capitals of Chang'an and Luoyang. By the eighth century "vagrant households" (*futaohu* 浮逃戶), as Tang statesmen referred to them, had become an acute fiscal as well as social problem. Many registered households no longer submitted tax payments and labor service, and officials tried to shift their obligations onto the rest of the local community. Efforts to redress the vagrancy problem, such as the program of allodial rights and tax amnesties for unregistered squatters who occupied abandoned lands (designated as "guest households" [*kehu* 客戶]) enacted in 724–27, achieved some success, increasing the registered population by about 12 percent. But it was estimated that 20 percent or more of the population still remained unregistered even after this reform.[98]

Although the Tang had no serious rivals for military supremacy in East Asia, from the 650s the court became entangled in intractable conflicts with the Tibetans in the west, the Eastern Turks to the north, and the Khitans and the Korean Koguryŏ kingdom in the northeast. The annexation of Turfan, Kucha, and other remote oasis towns in the 640s left the Tang frontier guards spread perilously thin across a defensive perimeter extending to the borderlands of Iran. Hostile confrontation with Koguryŏ erupted in the 660s into a pan-East Asian "world war" pitting the Tang and its ally, Silla, against both Koguryŏ on one hand and an alliance between the Paekche kingdom and Yamato Japan on the other. The Tang-Silla triumph in 668 extinguished Koguryŏ and Paekche and inflicted a humiliating defeat on Japan, but quickly soured when the Tang generals tried to occupy the Koguryŏ territories. By 675 Silla had repulsed the Tang forces and achieved uncontested control over the peninsula. By this time the balance of military power in the northwest too had shifted. The Tang found itself in the position of having to raise large expeditionary armies and augment its border guards to meet aggressive challenges from the Tibetans and the Turks. Increasingly frequent mobilization of *fubing* units impelled many soldiers to shirk summonses to duty. The breakdown of the equal-field system further undermined the viability of the *fubing* militias. By the turn of the eighth century the Tang began to turn instead to conscription of ordinary subjects into military service for increasingly lengthy tours of duty – up to four years by 717.[99]

Decisive action to resolve the deepening contradictions in the fundamental Tang institutions was hindered by factional struggles at the court. In 736, however, the chief minister Li Linfu secured dominance – some would say dictatorship – over the Tang government and launched a broad-gauged series

[98] On the problem of vagrancy, see Nakagawa 1962; Tang Changru 1961; Twitchett 1963: 12–6, 27–8; Dong Guodong 2002: 152–82.
[99] On the breakdown of the *fubing* system, see Kurihara 1964; Graff 2002: 205–9. On the increasing length in tours of duty for conscripts, see Watanabe 2010: 367–68.

of reforms. Seeking to restore the Tang to sound fiscal footing, Li's administration (1) replaced the hundreds of *fubing* garrisons with new professional armies organized into ten regional commands; (2) created a new logistical system for grain transport that absolved local officials of the responsibility to muster corvée labor while relying more heavily on market purchases of foodstuffs to provision the armies; (3) converted most statutory labor obligations to money payments, while also eliminating 220,000 special service (*seyi*) positions; and (4) streamlined the budget-making process and granted local authorities greater flexibility in meeting their tax quotas.[100] This rationalization of the fiscal administration helped shore up the state's revenue base: the registered population – only 6.16 million households in 705 – rose to 7.1 million households in 726 and 8.7 million households in 742, an increase of 41 percent in the span of thirty-seven years.[101] But these reforms also tacitly acknowledged the stark reality that the equal-field land system and *fubing* militias were defunct.

Conclusion

By the sixth century, the economic landscape of China had changed radically compared to Qin-Han times. None of the states of the Period of Disunion could wield the kind of control over the economy exerted by the Qin and early Han empires. Despite efforts, most notably by the Northern Wei, to assert the state's prerogatives over the allocation of lands, the concentration of landholdings in the hands of aristocratic families endured. The gulf between rich and poor widened along with the growing social and legal distinctions between aristocrats and commoners. Buddhism emerged as a powerful economic force. The major Buddhist monasteries – whose clergy were mostly drawn from the ranks of the aristocracy – became great landowners in their own right and exercised considerable influence on economic activities ranging from money-lending to handicraft production. Most significantly, South China's share of the national economy grew substantially during this era. Although the majority of China's population still resided in the traditional heartland of the Yellow River valley, a momentous shift had occurred that ultimately would lead to a recentering of the Chinese economy on the rice-growing regions of the south, especially the Jiangnan region in the Yangzi River Delta.

[100] On Li Linfu's regime and reform agenda, see Twitchett 1979: 409–20; Watanabe 2010: 453–61. On the replacement of the *fubing* with professional armies, see Graff 2002: 205–14; on the decentralization of the budget-making process, see Twitchett 1969–70: 91–2; Ōtsu 1986: 1856–59.
[101] Dong Guodong 2002: 97, table 2–2.

The founding of the Tang dynasty by Li Yuan in 618 in some respects was merely the culmination of a series of coups-d'état among leading figures of the hybrid Chinese-Xianbei aristocracy that had ruled the succession of short-lived dynasties since the fall of the Northern Wei. But the Tang dynasty would endure for nearly three centuries. During its first century the Tang dynasty presided over a peaceful and prosperous empire at home while exercising political and cultural influence on its neighbors far surpassing that of even the Han dynasty. Heirs to the traditions of the steppe as well as China, the Tang imperial house cultivated a cosmopolitan vision of empire that encouraged an unprecedented growth of foreign trade. The Tang capital of Chang'an was the largest city in the world, boasting perhaps more than one million residents. The outbreak of the devastating An Lushan rebellion in 755 brought a swift end to the golden age of Tang, however. While the dynasty survived the ensuing eight years of civil war, the rebellion crippled the central government and forced a fundamental transformation of its political and economic institutions. The An Lushan rebellion thus marked a momentous new departure in the evolution of the Chinese economy, as well as in Chinese political institutions, intellectual traditions, and social life.

6   Economic transformation in the Tang-Song transition (755 to 1127)

The outbreak in 755 of the An Lushan rebellion, led by a disgruntled frontier general of Sogdian descent who turned against the imperial court, dealt a shattering blow to the Tang dynasty. The reigning emperor was forced to flee Chang'an, which was seized by An Lushan in 756 and later sacked by a marauding Tibetan army, and seek refuge in the southwest. By the time the rebellion was quelled in 763 the rich agricultural heartland of the Central Plain lay in ruins and hundreds of thousands had perished. The Tang was restored to power only through the crucial support of Uighur mercenaries and by ceding effective control of most of the northern provinces to regional warlords. The Tang polity emerged from the rebellion only a shadow of its former self, its basic institutions irreparably broken.

The period from 750 to 1250, which scholars commonly refer to as the "Tang-Song transition," is widely recognized as the crucial watershed in the economic history of imperial China.[1] Over the course of this period the rice economy of the Yangzi River valley supplanted the traditional heartland of the Central Plain as the Chinese economy's center of gravity. The shift of population from north to south inaugurated a series of profound transformations in agricultural productivity, technology, industrial growth, transport,

---

[1] The concept of a "Tang-Song transition" as a crucial turning point in Chinese history derives from the work of the early twentieth century Japanese scholar Naitō Kōnan, who posited that the Tang-Song era marked the beginning of a precocious "modern age" in China (and indeed in world history). Naitō's hypothesis was reconceptualized with an explicit focus on economic history by his student Miyazaki Ichisada (1950). On Naitō's ideas and their influence, see Miyakawa 1955; Fogel 1984; von Glahn 2003a: 37–42. The Tang-Song transition concept, particularly as formulated by Miyazaki, has remained central to Japanese scholarship on Song history (see Satake 1996; Maruhashi 2001). The Tang-Song transition paradigm also has been highly influential in Western scholarship, as can be seen in the seminal studies of Mark Elvin (1973) and Robert Hartwell (1982) (for an analysis and critique of Hartwell's model, which stands as the most comprehensive analysis of the socio-economic changes engendered in the Tang-Song transition, see Luo Yinan 2005). The Tang-Song transition paradigm has had far less impact among historians in the PRC, where it conflicts with official historiographic dogma on the periodization of Chinese history. Since the late 1990s, however, historians in China have gradually incorporated some features of the model in their work. For a notable application of the concept to economic history, see Lin Wenxun 2011.

finance, and international trade. Sustained economic growth fueled unprecedented demographic expansion. By 1100 the empire's population reached 100 million, far surpassing the peak levels (roughly 60 million) of the Han and Tang. The new foundations of the Chinese economy laid during the Tang-Song transition would endure throughout the rest of China's imperial era.

The extraordinary sweep of economic change during the Tang-Song transition bespoke fundamental institutional transformations. Following the collapse of the equal-field system, private ownership of land became the rule. Progressive taxation based on household assets of villagers and towndwellers alike replaced the principle of uniform taxation that underlay the Tang *zu-yong-diao* tax regime. The abolition of statutory labor obligations for most of the population and the long-term decline in personal bondage eliminated key constraints on the allocation of household labor. The steady trend toward monetization of taxation – and the sharply reduced scale of tax payments in cloth in particular – likewise allowed households greater freedom to invest their labor and resources as they saw fit. Sustained population growth, rising agricultural surpluses, rapid development of water transport, and urbanization expanded the reach of markets, encouraging greater specialization of labor. A vast increase in the money supply, new forms of financial intermediation, and more reliable mechanisms for pooling capital, enforcing contracts, and resolving commercial disputes lowered transaction costs. Still, the fiscal policies of the state exerted a powerful impact on all spheres of economic activity, which brought both benefits and costs to the economy as a whole.

These changes took place at a time when the imperial might of the Chinese empire had greatly diminished. The Song was founded by military men, survivors of the incessant warfare that wracked North China throughout the first half of the tenth century. When Zhao Kuangyin (Emperor Taizu, r. 960–76) declared the founding of his Song dynasty in 960, the northern portion of the Central Plain, including the region around modern Beijing, remained in the hands of the Khitan Liao kingdom. Conquest of the independent states in South China and reunification of the empire was not achieved until 979. The Liao, who inflicted humiliating defeats on Song armies in 979, 986, and 1004, and the Tangut kingdom on the northwestern frontier continued to pose ominous threats to the Song. A tense truce along the northern borders was purchased at the cost of maintaining an enormous standing army and forfeiting substantial indemnities of silver and silk. In 1127 an upstart Manchurian kingdom, the Jurchen Jin, overwhelmed the Song defenses and captured the Song capital of Kaifeng. Once again North China fell under the rule of foreign conquerors. The Song dynasty reconstituted its government at a new southern capital, Hangzhou. The vigorous economy of South China played a vital role in the survival of the Song dynasty until it was finally overwhelmed by the Mongol onslaught in the 1270s.

Economic consequences of the An Lushan rebellion

In the course of the An Lushan rebellion, whose aftershocks reverberated for decades afterward, millions of families in North China had been uprooted. Many migrated to the south, settling in Jiangnan and the still largely frontier areas of the Middle Yangzi River valley. This shift in population, a dramatic acceleration of a trend underway since the steppe nomad invasions of the fourth century, marked a key turning point in the demography of China. Before the An Lushan rebellion approximately two-thirds of the population lived in the dryland farming regions of North China, with the densest concentration in the Central Plain heartland. By 1100 that ratio had reversed: two-thirds of the population inhabited the rice-growing regions of South China, and only one-third lived in the north, a distribution that has remained roughly constant down to the present (see Maps 6.1 and 6.2).

Among the principal casualties of the An Lushan rebellion were the equal-field land allocations and the *zu-yong-diao* tax system that was integrally

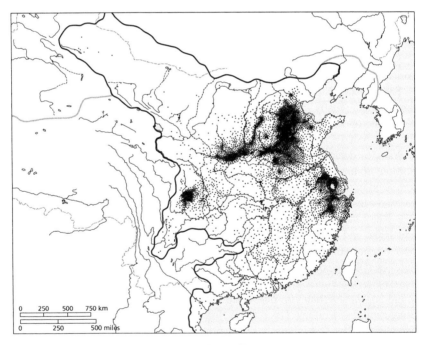

Map 6.1 Population of Tang China, 742
Source: Chen Zhengxiang 1982.

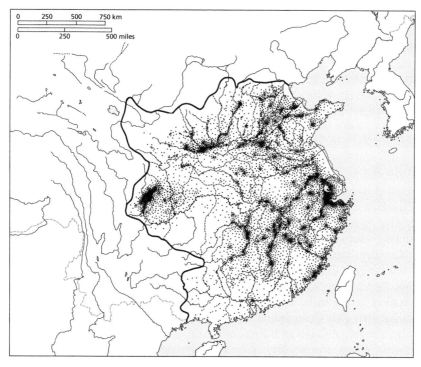

Map 6.2 Population of Northern Song China, 1102
Source: Chen Zhengxiang 1982.

linked to it. After the turmoil of the rebellion the registered population fell by more than three-fourths, and the regional military governors who held sway in the northern provinces either refused to submit the tax revenues ordinarily forwarded to the central government (*shanggong* 上供) or were excused from doing so (Map 6.3). The fiscal base of the central government was reduced mainly to the southern provinces where the equal-field system had never taken root. The household tax (*hushui*) became a major source of revenue, but indirect taxes on consumption and trade, most importantly on salt, emerged as the mainstays of imperial fiscal administration.

In the 720s, when the Tang fiscal system had begun to show serious signs of strain, the court appointed a number of plenipotentiary commissioners, offi-cials with special expertise in fiscal matters, to deal with problems such as vagrancy, tax evasion, transport of tax grain, and coinage. At that time proposals were floated to restore the monopolies on salt and iron that existed during the Han, but no action was taken. In 758, after experiments conducted on the local level for several years, the court established a monopoly on the production and sale of salt under the authority of a newly established Salt Commission.[2] All salt producers were made state employees and compelled to deliver their salt to government directorates (*jian* 監), which sold salt to wholesale merchants at a substantial markup. Liu Yan, who occupied the post of salt commissioner from 760 to 779, transformed the Salt Commission into a supremely powerful organization. Salt revenues rose ten-fold over the course of Liu's tenure as salt commissioner, and by 779 provided the central government with more than half of its annual income. Liu Yan also gathered mining, coinage, and the transport of tax grain from the south to the capital under the purview of the Salt Commission. Subsequent salt commissioners enacted additional consumption taxes on wine and tea, though these levies generated only modest revenues.[3]

The virtually unchecked power wielded by Liu Yan provoked great dismay among other officials. In 779 a bitter rival of Liu, Yang Yan, took office as chancellor determined to wrest control of the state's fiscal administration away from the Salt Commission and return it to the Finance Ministry. Yang also launched a sweeping reform of the tax system that sought to restore direct taxation as the main source of state revenue. Although Yang's attempt to abolish the Salt Commission was aborted, the new tax system he created would endure throughout the rest of the imperial era.

Yang Yan's reform acknowledged that the equal-field system of landownership was defunct, and along with it the *zu-yong-diao* taxes that had been the centerpiece of the Tang fiscal regime. Yang's plan formally abolished the *zu-yong-diao* assessments while incorporating the household (*hushui*) and land (*dishui*) levies into a new tax structure that came to be known as the twice-a-year tax (*liangshui* 兩稅). In keeping with the procedures for the existing *hushui* levy, households were ranked into nine property grades and assessed a tax measured in coin. Given the endemic shortage of coin, however, the household tax generally was commuted to commodities, primarily cloth. The land tax as before was assessed in grain. The household tax was collected in late summer and the land tax after the autumn harvest; hence the name twice-a-year tax.[4]

In essence, the twice-a-year tax was simply a rationalization of what had become the status quo. But it marked a fundamental and lasting change in economic philosophy. The principle of equity that underlay the equal-field

---

[2] The actual title, Commissioner of Salt and Iron Monopolies (Que yantie shi 榷鹽鐵使), harked back to the salt and iron monopolies of the Han, but in the Tang this office was solely charged with control of the salt market. No effort was made to restore a state monopoly on iron.

[3] Twitchett 1954, 1963: 49–53. The data on salt revenues is from ibid.: 264, n. 20.

[4] Twitchett 1963: 39–43.

system and earlier measures to restrict the concentration of landholding was abandoned, never to be resurrected in any serious way before the land collectivization policies carried out by the communist leadership of the People's Republic of China in the 1950s. Instead, the state and its cadre of Confucian officials, conceding the reality of the uneven distribution of landownership, focused on implementing a progressive land tax based on the amount of land under cultivation. In addition, the new tax system eliminated the universal statutory labor service owed to the central government. Local officials continued to conscript taxpayers for *ad hoc* public works projects (*zayao*) and assigned village officer duties to the highest-ranked – that is to say, most affluent – households. Coupled with the cessation of universal military conscription in the 730s, the suspension of regular labor service duties had the salutary effect of freeing up considerable labor resources for private purposes.

The twice-a-year tax was an instant success from the perspective of fiscal planners. In its first year of operation it generated greater income than the central government's revenue from all sources, including the salt monopoly, in the previous year. But as time wore on the provincial governors became increasingly independent of central government control and forwarded less revenue to the capital. In general, only about one-third of revenues collected at the local level were transmitted to the central government, although these proportions varied by region (see Table 6.1 for actual figures from a Yangzi Delta prefecture). The remainder was divided between provincial governors and prefectures. The military governors controlling the Central Plain were largely independent of the imperial government and forwarded little revenue to the capital. Nearly all of the central government's revenues were obtained from the southern provinces, especially in the Lower Yangzi Basin and Sichuan (Map 6.3). Although the average tax receipts generated by the twice-a-year tax (4.3 *guan* per household) were essentially unchanged from the *zu-yong-diao* levy (4.2 *guan* per household), total per capita revenues increased by 60 percent, driven largely by consumption taxes on tea, liquor, and above all salt.[5]

The twice-a-year tax, intended more as a measure to increase state revenues than to promote equity, contained several serious flaws. By focusing exclusively on cultivated land as the basis of taxation, it failed to capture revenues from urban real estate and commerce. The central government assigned permanent tax quotas to local prefectures regardless of the actual amount of land under cultivation, which led to significant disparities in the tax burden among

---

[5] On the reorganization of the Tang fiscal administration after the An Lushan Rebellion and its economic effects, see Watanabe 2010: 467–561.

Table 6.1 *Suzhou prefecture tax revenues, c. 861*

Cantons	194	
Households	143,261	
Revenues (*guan* 貫)*	692,885	
Average tax burden per household (*guan*)	4.84	
Central government (*shanggong* 上供)	306,830	44%
Provincial governor (*liushi* 留使)	207,720**	30%
Prefecture (*liuzhou* 留州)	178,349	26%

*Revenues from the twice-a-year tax, salt, liquor, and tea excises, and other taxes.
**Emending what appears to be a clerical error.
Source: WDJ: 1–3.

different regions. Commutation of the household tax into cloth also created inequities due to regional and temporal variations in the price of cloth.[6] The shift to taxes paid in money rather than in kind resulting from the institution of the salt monopoly and the twice-a-year tax further exacerbated the shortage of currency. Lack of coin was a principal cause of the deflationary trend that began in the 780s and lasted until the middle of the ninth century. Deflation in effect increased the real cost of taxes denominated in coin, spurring commutation of the household (summer) tax to payments of silk and other textiles. By 821 the summer tax had been converted entirely to payments in textiles.[7] The Tang court also attempted to make compulsory the use of silk as means of payment in large commercial transactions. Counterfeiting flourished in the early ninth century, as did the use of short strings of fewer coins to represent the token value of a full string of coin (coins usually circulated in strings of 100 coins at this time), a practice that had appeared earlier in South China during the Liang dynasty. The imperial proscription of Buddhism and confiscation of monastic properties in 845 provided some short-lived relief. Large quantities of bronze statuary, bells, and other religious paraphernalia were melted down to provide raw material for minting coin. At least twenty-three local mints were established to issue new coin. But the interdiction against Buddhism was rescinded within a year and the confiscation of monastic property halted. The sudden spurt in minting ceased as well.[8]

Despite the limited supply of coin, commerce thrived in the post-An Lushan era. Many of the constraints on merchants and trade weakened along with the waning influence of the central government. The largely autonomous provincial governors built up their own fiscal administrations and

[6] Twitchett 1963: 43–48. On the problem of trying to establish commutation rates that fairly matched constantly fluctuating market prices for textiles, see Shimasue 1990.
[7] Shimasue 1990: 338–44.   [8] Twitchett 1963: 67–69, 76–83; Miyazawa 2007: 154–63.

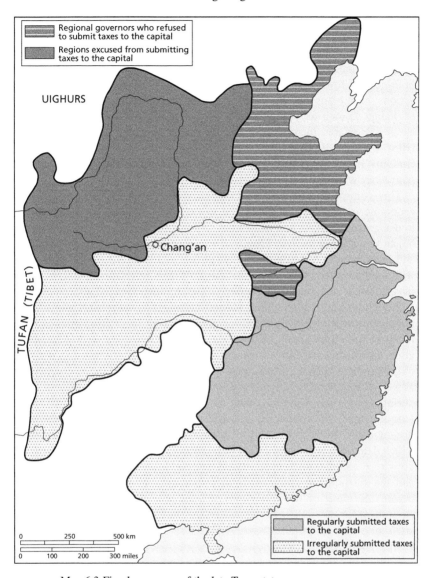

Map 6.3 Fiscal resources of the late Tang state

readily recruited merchants to staff them. Provincial capitals became magnets for tax and tribute goods as well as private commerce. Yangzhou, at the intersection of the Grand Canal and the Yangzi River, emerged as the most prosperous entrepôt in the south, a center of shipbuilding, textiles, leather making, and iron and bronze metallurgy as well as the largest salt market and a major port for overseas trade.[9] Chengdu prospered as a center of fine silk manufacture, papermaking, and a rapidly growing tea trade. Merchants in Chang'an and other cities began to develop credit and banking services. Safe-deposit firms (*guifang* 櫃房) provided financing for commercial transactions and loans to the government in military emergencies. Bills of exchange known as "flying cash" (*feiqian* 飛錢) were issued by a state agency to enable merchants to transfer funds from the capital to outlying cities without carrying away precious coin.[10] As we saw in Chapter 5, Buddhist monasteries played an important role in providing credit to wealthy patrons as well as the desperate poor.

This commercial efflorescence was vividly etched in the physical and economic morphology of cities and towns. The confinement of commerce to designated markets and residential segregation inside self-enclosed wards began to wither in the late Tang, and vanished altogether in the Song. Shops and marketplaces burst onto the main streets and lined the canals within and without the walled cities, while faubourgs of inns, warehouses, and the shops of wholesale merchants and brokers mushroomed outside the city walls. Although no longer under close official surveillance, merchants and artisans in the same trade often clustered together, creating specialized marketplaces for gold and silver smiths, silk goods, and booksellers as well as butchers, grain merchants, and lumber dealers. Night markets proliferated in defiance of government curfews. Marketplaces and fairs sprang up in the countryside as well. Rural markets typically were held periodically, perhaps once or twice during the ten-day Chinese week, and catered mostly to a local clientele. Larger temple fairs attracted worshipers and merchants alike from more distant areas. Most famous of all were the "silkworm fairs" of Chengdu, which date from at least the late eighth century. By Song times these fairs had grown so popular that they rotated among fifteen sites within Chengdu and the surrounding counties. Held in the early months of the New Year before the onset of the sericulture season, the silkworm fairs showcased equipment for raising silkworms and reeling and weaving silk. Local farmers could also buy agricultural tools, seeds, carts, lumber, medicines, and other sundry goods at the fairs.[11]

China's international trade also experienced momentous change in the wake of the An Lushan rebellion. The Arab conquests in Central Asia – including

---

[9] On Yangzhou's commercial prosperity in the Tang (and its subsequent decline), see Quan Hansheng 1972.

[10] The most comprehensive study of these financial institutions and "flying cash" bills is Hino 1982: 15–230. See also Miu Kunhe 2002: 15–27.

[11] Katō 1952b, 1952d; Twitchett 1966: 230–43.

Sogdiana – and Tibetan depredations in the Gansu Corridor disrupted the Sogdian trade network and Silk Road trade in general. The markets at Dunhuang, starved of coin, reverted to grain and wool as means of exchange.[12] Most decisively, trade with India and the Islamic world via maritime routes gradually eclipsed the overland caravan traffic.[13] By the beginning of the eighth century the Srivijayan princes of Sumatra had established way-stations at Palembang and other ports where ships traveling to and from China awaited the seasonal shift in the monsoon winds. Muslim merchants, both Arab and Persian, dominated these trade routes. Arab geographers of the mid-ninth century describe a thriving trade between Siraf in the Persian Gulf and the southern Chinese port of Guangzhou (Canton), where foreign merchants reportedly vastly outnumbered native Chinese.[14] The Belitung shipwreck, an Arab vessel that sank off Sumatra c. 825–50, is believed to have embarked from Yangzhou and was making intermediate stops at Southeast Asian ports before heading for its final destination of Siraf. The vessel's cargo principally consisted of 60,000 ceramic pieces – nearly all lead-glazed wares from Changsha – in addition to lead ingots, gold and silver plate, bronze mirrors, and jars of spices.[15] Over the next several centuries maritime trade through Southeast Asia boomed, and China's international trade underwent a permanent reorientation away from the overland Silk Road.

The An Lushan rebellion thus signified a major turning point in Chinese economic history. Some of these changes, such as the transition from a fixed head tax to a progressive land tax as the basis of the fiscal system, were triggered by the rebellion itself. Landholding was no longer subject to the constraints of the equal-field system, but at the same time the aristocratic families that had dominated landholding since late Han times also became exposed to the vicissitudes of the market economy. Private enterprise flourished in both agriculture and commerce. Although some sectors of the economy – most notably the salt industry – became subject to direct control by the state, the system of regulated urban markets began to break down and in general merchants enjoyed greater freedom. The most important change, however, was not a direct result of the rebellion but an acceleration of a trend that had been long underway: the shift of population to the southern rice-growing regions, which had far greater productive potential than the arid north.

---

[12] On the demise of the Sogdian trade network after the Arab occupation of Sogdiana, see de la Vaissière 2005: 261–330. Although some scholars (e.g., Zheng Binglin 2004) portray post-An Lushan Dunhuang as a vibrant center of Silk Road trade, in fact commerce at Dunhuang had become localized (Hansen 2012: 196). Moreover, Dunhuang's external trade became oriented more toward Turfan and Central Asia rather than China (Trombert 1995: 106).
[13] Sen 2003: 142–96.   [14] Heng 2009: 23–36.   [15] Guy 2010; Hsieh 2010.

Rise of the rice economy

Following the demise of the equal-field system, private ownership of land became the rule throughout China. Even after the restoration of a unified empire by the Song no effort was made to reverse this basic economic fact. The Song state generally sold off lands that came into its possession (as a result of lack of heirs, for example), and in 1082 state-owned lands amounted to only 1.4 percent of total registered land.[16] The privatization of landholdings spurred the commodification of landed property, and the rapid expansion of rice agriculture accelerated the formation of competitive markets for land and agricultural products.

A trend toward concentration of landholdings emerged in the late Tang period, most notably in the areas of North China devastated by the An Lushan rebellion. Contemporary sources frequently remark on the formation of landed estates (*zhuangyuan* 莊園) by imperial kinsmen, officials, and wealthy families. It was once thought that the proliferation of *zhuangyuan* gave birth to what Mark Elvin described as a manorial social order, similar to that of medieval Europe, "based on the enserfment of much of the peasant population and exerting a dominant influence over most of the rest."[17] The current consensus, however, rejects the equation of *zhuangyuan* with manorial serfdom, and instead recognizes wide variation in the nature of landholdings and tenurial relations across – and within – regions. *Zhuang yuan* typically were comprised not of large tracts of contiguous landholdings, but rather dispersed plots acquired in piece-meal fashion. In most cases *zhuangyuan* were worked by tenant farmers and hired laborers. This was particularly true in the south, since rice agriculture was more suited to intensive small-scale farming.

It is difficult to determine the prevalence of tenancy, especially since many small landholders also rented some of the land they farmed. Tenant farmers usually were economically independent of their landlords. Although there was wide variation in the terms of tenancy across regions, contractual tenancy largely superseded personal bondage except in lightly populated frontier regions in the interior, such as Hunan and Sichuan.[18] The most common form of tenancy was sharecropping, in which the tenant owed half of the harvest (or 60 percent if the landowner provided seed and tools) in kind to the landowner. Bondservitude generally took the form of indentured labor by indebted persons, commonly known as "tenant servants" (*dianpu* 佃僕).

[16] Zhang Jinpeng 2003: 203–04.
[17] Elvin 1973: 69. Elvin's analysis drew on the scholarship of Katō Shigeshi (1952e) and Sudō Yoshiyuki (1954c).
[18] Yanagida 1973; Golas 1980: 299–309; McDermott 1984; Kusano 1996.

Such bondservants were bound to their masters, not the soil, for lengthy periods of time, but under terms governed by contract and imperial law. The Song repealed older laws that had subjected tenants and hired laborers to the arbitrary control of landowners. Nonetheless the servile character of hired labor and tenancy was not wholly effaced. For example, landlords retained the right to choose marriage partners for hired laborers and bondservants, and tenants were subject to various legal discriminations in disputes with their landlords.[19] Although tenant servants were prominent in newly settled regions of South China such as Jiangxi and southern Anhui, they were uncommon in the more densely populated regions of the Yangzi Delta and Fujian.[20] As a rule, coercive labor arrangements entailing a high degree of personal bondage were confined to the frontier regions of South China where labor was in short supply.[21]

Agriculture in North China reached an optimum level of efficiency during the Tang dynasty.[22] Wheat decisively displaced millet as the dominant food grain. Cereal cultivation was complemented by a variety of winter crops – soybeans, snow peas (an import from West Asia), broad beans, rape, and clover (for animal fodder) – utilized in the increasingly common two-crops-in-three-years rotation.[23] Even the larger landholdings of *zhuangyuan* estates were divided among small household units of production rather than operated under unitary management. Ōsawa Masaaki suggests that in the late Tang a typical North China *zhuangyuan* comprised 240–300 *mu*, the maximum amount that could be cultivated with two oxen, and a total workforce of ten or so farmers. But the estate workers (*zhuangke* 莊客) most often were tenant farmers who, although subject to certain kinds of personal subordination to the landowner (for example, providing sundry labor services when the latter demanded), were responsible for their own subsistence.[24] Li Bozhong has calculated that on average a farm family in North China with an ox could cultivate 77 *mu*, or, if the family shared an ox with others, only 50 *mu*, generally regarded as the minimum amount of land required to meet subsistence needs.[25] Data from tenth-century tax registers in Dunhuang – where population pressure on the land was less intense than in the Central Plain – indicate an average of 68 *mu* per household, but this figure obscures significant variations (Table 6.2). Dunhuang's agrarian economy was divided into three

---

[19] Takahashi 2001.   [20] McDermott 1984: 24–30.   [21] Von Glahn 1987: 48–58.
[22] On the agrarian regime in North China during the Tang, see Ōsawa 1996: 79-124; Zhang Guogang 2012.
[23] Most scholars (e.g., Li Bozhong 1990: 253; Zhang Guoguang 2012: 36) concur with Yoneda (1989) that the two-crops-in-three-years rotation was widespread in the Tang (practiced by two-thirds of farm households, according to Li). But Ōsawa (1996: 91–94) has reservations, suggesting it was not widely used before the Song, or perhaps even later.
[24] Ōsawa 1996: 106.   [25] Li Bozhong 1990: 256–58.

Table 6.2 *Landholdings in tenth-century Dunhuang*

Amount of land (*mu*)	Number of households	Percentage of total households	Total land (*mu*)	Percentage of total land	Average land per household (*mu*)
Less than 20	29	15.8	383	3.1	13.2
20–130	136	73.9	6,686	53.6	49.2
130–400	14	7.6	3,979	31.9	284.2
More than 400	3	1.6	1,422	11.4	474.0
Total	184		12,469		67.8

Source: Yang Jiping 2003: 434, appendix table 24.

Table 6.3 *Labor intensity of principal crops*

Crop	Labor-days required to cultivate 100 *mu*	Index (wheat = 100)
Rice	948	536
Millet	283	160
Wheat	177	100
Soybeans	192	108

Sources: TLD, 7: 222–23; Ōsawa 1996: 98.

strata: a small number of large landowners possessing 300–400+ *mu*; a broad middle stratum that owned enough land to meet their own needs; and a substantial minority (perhaps 20–25 percent of the entire population) whose meager landholdings obliged them to seek other means of subsistence through tenancy, hired labor, or non-agricultural employment. This depiction of rural society in Dunhuang most likely was broadly true of North China in general.

The fundamental force behind the rapid pace of commercial and urban growth during the Tang-Song transition was the maturation of the rice economy in the Yangzi River Basin. Irrigated rice cultivation was far more labor intensive than dryland crops (Table 6.3). But the higher productivity of intensive rice cultivation, including continuous planting without fallowing, yielded at least five times as much food per unit of land as wheat or millet. Many of the advances in rice cultivation – such as improved tools, transplanting, irrigation techniques, frequent weeding, and the double-cropping of rice with winter dryland crops (usually wheat) – already appeared by the late Tang era, but their use was confined to upland valleys above the flood plains

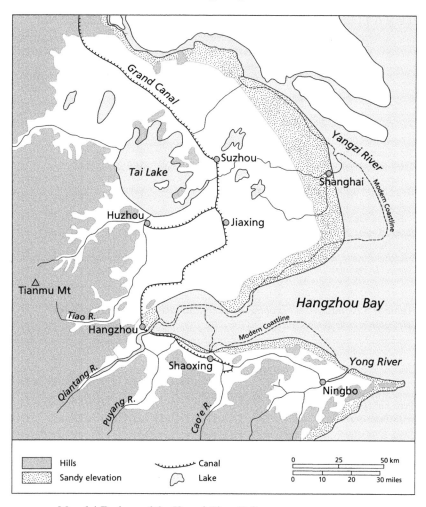

Map 6.4 Ecology of the Yangzi River Delta

(see Map 6.4).[26] Nonetheless, already in the Tang the intensification of rice agriculture had produced substantial increases in yields compared to the Period of Disunion. According to Li Bozhong, in the Tang most rice farming households possessed an ox, although interplanting rice and winter crops was still rare.[27] Even though farms were much smaller than in the past, Li calculates that by the late Tang Jiangnan household income from rice agriculture had

---

[26] Shiba 1988: 179–93; Ōsawa 1996: 253–82.   [27] Li Bozhong 1990: 129–57.

Table 6.4 *Cultivated land and grain output in Jiangnan rice agriculture*

	Period of Disunion (without ox)	Tang		
		Without ox	With ox	Double-cropping rice and wheat (with ox)
Average cultivated land per household (*mu*)	77	22	31	23
Total grain output (*shi*)	55	66	93	92
Total grain output (hectoliters)	32.5	38.9	54.9	54.3
Grain output per *mu* (liters)	42.1	177	177	236
Value of grain output in bolts of silk tabby (*pi*)	19.8	23.8	33.5	33.1
Index of value (Period of Disunion = 100)	100	120	169	167

Source: Li Bozhong 1990: 212, table 6–14.

Table 6.5 *Estimated net income of Jiangnan rice-farming households*
(all figures in bolts of silk)

	Fixed capital costs	Variable capital costs	Total income	Net income	Net after-tax income
Period of Disunion (without ox)	0.5	27	29.8	2.3	−2.9
Early Tang (without ox)	0.3	27	35.4	8.1	3.4
Early Tang (with ox)	8.5	27	45.1	9.6	4.9
Middle Tang (without ox)	0.3	27	37.0	9.7	2.8
Middle Tang (with ox)	8.5	27	47.5	12.0	5.1
Late Tang (with ox, single cropping; sericulture)	8.5	27	47.9	12.4	5.0
Late Tang (with ox, double-cropping; sericulture)	8.6	27	47.5	13.4	6.0

NB: Before the late Tang, income from cloth production was derived from ramie fabrics; in the late Tang, from silk.
Source: Li Bozhong 1990: 227, table 6–18; 244, table 6–25.

risen 70 percent compared to the Period of Disunion (Table 6.4). Including cloth manufacture, Li finds that net household income increased by more than five-fold (Table 6.5). To be sure, Li's calculations are based on stylized contemporary estimates, rather than actual output data, and reflect best practices that probably were utilized by only a minority of farm families. Moreover, the difference in net income per labor day was considerably lower (a 250 percent rather than 540 percent increase for a family with an ox practicing single-cropping). Given the greater labor intensity and longer work-year of families that combined rice agriculture and sericulture, it is not surprising that the twice-a-year taxation system shifted from extraction of labor services to payment in goods. Since the spring planting season for rice coincided with the peak season for highly labor-intensive sericulture tasks, this combination also encouraged a gendered division of labor, with women performing almost all of the sericulture work.[28]

The most significant development in Song agriculture was the expansion of rice cultivation through the reclamation of the marshlands of the Yangzi Delta and the building of terraced fields on hillsides in the mountainous regions of the interior. Farmers in the upland alluvial valleys of Zhejiang, Anhui, and Jiangxi pioneered many of the innovations in rice cultivation. Irrigation ponds, terraced fields, and labor-intensive techniques such as deep tilling and frequent weeding were first adopted in these areas.[29] The introduction of Champa rice, a hardy, fast-ripening seed variety from Southeast Asia, shortened the growing season and reduced the risk of crop failure. Over the course of the Song, however, the impetus for the expansion of the rice economy gravitated to the lowland plains of the Yangzi Delta. In this region the main priority was not storing irrigation water but rather draining marshes and lakes to make the land suitable for agriculture. Construction of polders (diked enclosures) – initially to drain swamps, and then to provide irrigation to rice fields – required substantial investments of labor and capital. The Wu-Yue kingdom in the tenth century and Wang Anshi's administration in the eleventh invested heavily in such land reclamation projects. It has been estimated that polder projects reclaimed at least 35 million acres of land in the two circuits of Liangzhe and Jiangdong during the last half century of the Northern Song alone.[30] The proliferation of polder fields in the Yangzi Delta continued in the Southern Song, but the initiative for land reclamation came from private landowners rather than the state.[31]

The rapid advance of polders not only greatly expanded cultivated land in the delta, but also radically altered the delta's ecology, as the example of Jian Lake in Shaoxing illustrates. Jian Lake had been artificially created as a source of irrigation water in the Han dynasty (Chapter 4). In the early eleventh century farmers along the lakeshore began to build diked enclosures to convert the lake bed into arable land. By the 1060s some 700 *qing* of land had been reclaimed in this fashion. At the end of the twelfth century, when more than 2,000 *qing*

---

[28] Ibid.: 203, 208.   [29] Ōsawa 1996: 253–82.   [30] Mihelich 1979: 193.
[31] Shiba 1988: 203–22; Ōsawa 1996: 236–52.

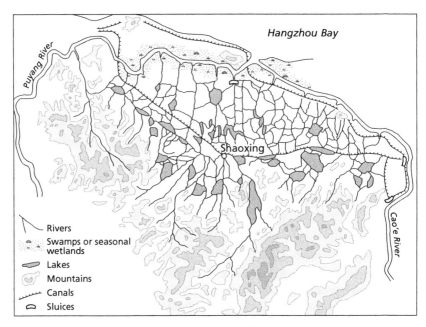

Map 6.5 Land reclamation of Jian Lake in Shaoxing
Source: Chen Qiaoyi 1962.

were under cultivation, the lake had been reduced to scattered marshes amid a vast expanse of rice paddies (Map 6.5; cf Map 4.3).[32] The depletion of lakes and increased sedimentation resulting from erosion in upstream areas rendered the coastal plains more vulnerable to flooding. Efforts to expedite the discharge of water to the sea by dredging channels and straightening rivers had contrary results, increasing the pressure on dikes and allowing ocean tides to surge inland. Moreover, the polders remained prone to water-logging that reduced fertility and inhibited double-cropping with winter dryland crops. During the Song, the yields from polder lands were no greater than the more intensively cultivated upland rice fields.[33]

Despite the trend toward concentration of landholdings following the demise of the equal-field system, great estates became increasingly rare

[32] Honda 2000b: 51. On the struggle to preserve Xiang Lake, an artificial lake constructed in the western part of Shaoxing in the early twelfth century as an irrigation reservoir, from such encroachment, see Schoppa 1989: 9–27.
[33] Adachi 1985; Shiba 1988: 137–39; Li Bozhong 2003: 147–53. On ecological change and agricultural development in the Hangzhou-Shaoxing region, see Shiba 1998.

during the Song dynasty. Rice agriculture was more suited to small-scale farming. Under the household ranking system established by the Song in 1033, approximately 10–15 percent of all registered households were classified as "upper households" (*shanghu* 上戶) owning more than 100 *mu* (5.6 hectares) of land, while 50–60 percent were registered as "lower households" (*xiahu* 下戶) with average landholdings of less than 25 *mu*. The remaining one-third of all households owned no land.[34] Although the superior households accounted for 80 percent of total landholdings, landownership was much more broadly dispersed than in the past. A survey conducted in Wenzhou prefecture (Zhejiang) in the thirteenth century found that only 1.5 percent of landowning households owned more than 400 *mu* (the largest single holding amounting to 2,600 *mu*), while 85 percent of landowners owned between 30 and 150 *mu*.[35] The average amount of farmland per household in rice-growing regions in the twelfth century ranged from 30–40 *mu* in lowland areas to around 10 *mu* in the rugged upland regions. Farm size, including lands worked by tenant farmers, in Song Jiangnan probably was in the range of 30–40 *mu*.[36] Conjugal families numbering 5–6 persons constituted the basic unit of agricultural production.

The transformation of Chinese agriculture during the Tang-Song era was more gradual and incremental than Mark Elvin's formulation of a "revolution in farming" suggests.[37] The productivity of polder fields in Song Jiangnan probably did not much surpass the high levels already achieved in the Tang, and many of the best practices described in Song agricultural handbooks were not widely employed before Ming-Qing times.[38] Nonetheless, the shift from millet and wheat to rice as the principal food crop dramatically raised aggregate grain output and made possible the doubling of China's peak population levels between the eighth and twelfth centuries. The number of registered households tripled between 980 and 1110 alone, although registered acreage grew at a far more modest pace, roughly 50 percent from 1000 to 1080 (Figure 6.1). Most importantly, the progressive commercialization of agriculture favored specialization of production, both across the empire and within the household. Wholesale merchants, brokers, hostellers (*didian* 邸店), commission agents, and retail shopkeepers constructed regional and national markets not only for grain and other foodstuffs but also for salt, tea, timber, textiles, lacquer, paper, and pottery.[39]

---

[34] These estimates are based on the data assembled in Yanagida 1986: 192–97.
[35] Qi Xia 1999, 1: 286–87.   [36] Liang Gengyao 1984: 101–11; Li Bozhong 2003: 162–65.
[37] Elvin 1973: 113–30.
[38] Li Bozhong 2003: 147–53. However, Li's caution about the limited productivity of rice agriculture in Song Jiangnan relies on questionable assumptions about the relationship between land rents and harvest yields. For an important critique of Li's analysis, see Ge Jinfang and Gu Rong 2000.
[39] Shiba 1968: 167–84, 391–420; Shiba 1970: 67–80, 165–80.

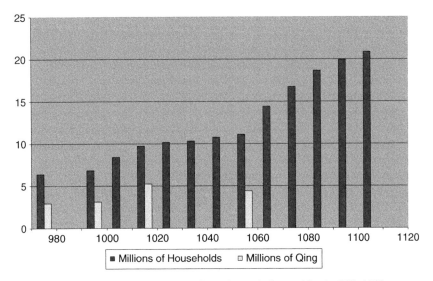

Figure 6.1 Northern Song registered population and lands, 980–1110
Sources: Population: Wu Songdi 2000: 346–48, table 8-1; Land: Shiba 1988: 228.

The return to mercantilist fiscal policies

After the final collapse of the Tang dynasty in 907, China once again was divided into northern and southern political spheres. In the north, a series of five successive dynasties rose and fell during the period 907–960 (thus this period is generally known as the Five Dynasties era). Amid this instability, actual power devolved to dozens of local warlord regimes. In the south, however, a relatively stable multistate system of seven regional kingdoms emerged, the last of which submitted to Song rule only in 978. In sharp contrast with the expansive, cosmopolitan empires of Sui and Tang, the rulers of this era focused on building a political base at the local and regional levels. The multistate system in South China fostered a regional pattern of economic development. This framework of regional states was preserved in the structure of the Song dynasty's territorial administration and later in the provincial units of the Ming and Qing dynasties.

The preeminence of military rule that prevailed during the late Tang continued in the Five Dynasties period. Already before the An Lushan rebellion the *fubing* system of soldier-farmer militias had seriously decayed, forcing the Tang to rely on large professional armies to defend its frontiers. The power of the Five Dynasties' rulers likewise rested on standing armies. Provisions of food and clothing and pay (in coin) for several hundred thousand troops consumed the lion's share of state revenue. Cadastral surveys conducted by the northern regimes of Later Tang (in 929) and Northern Zhou (in 958) extended the reach of the central government's fiscal authority at the local level.[40] As in the late Tang, shortages of coin compelled government officials to commute the summer tax portion of the twice-a-year tax to in-kind payments in cloth.[41]

The emergence of independent regional states stimulated robust economic growth in southern China. Regional specialization in the production of tea, salt, timber, paper, copper, silver, and textiles accelerated as the various states sought to capitalize on their comparative advantages in resources. Although political fragmentation and hostile relations posed obstacles to interregional trade, the rulers of these states also depended on commerce to obtain vital supplies – notably iron, salt, sulfur, and alum – as well as now-indispensable consumer staples such as tea.[42] The southern states developed cordial trading relations with the remote foreign states on the northern frontier, the Tanguts and the Khitan Liao, principally based on the exchange of tea for war horses. The coastal kingdoms of Wu-Yue, Min, and Southern Han actively promoted overseas trade with the Khitan, the Koryŏ kingdom in Korea, and Japan as well as Southeast Asia.[43] The direct role of the Southern Han state in maritime trade is evident in the cargo of the Intan shipwreck, which sank near Java c. 920–60. The ship, of Southeast Asian construction, carried Chinese and Southeast Asian ceramics; incense; copper and tin ingots and gold jewelry of Southeast Asian origin; Southern Han lead coins; and nearly 190 kg of silver ingots. Inscriptions indicate that the silver ingots had been deposited in the Southern Han state treasury as payment for salt excise levies, and presumably disbursed to purchase aromatics, spices, and other exotic goods the vessel had delivered to Guangzhou.[44]

The tenth century also witnessed the first flourish of private maritime commerce between China and Japan. Diplomatic exchanges between the Tang and Japanese courts had ceased after 838. Subsequently Japan's contact with the continent was mediated by Chinese and Korean merchants. Ningbo and other Zhejiang ports dominated the trade between China and Japan at this time, displacing Yangzhou and rivaling Guangzhou as the major emporia of maritime commerce.[45] Green-glazed Yuezhou 越州 stoneware from Shaoxing

---

[40] Sudō 1954a.
[41] For a synopsis of the fiscal administration and policies of the Five Dynasties' regimes, see Hino 1980: 87–124.
[42] Miyazaki 1943: 83–117. For an overview of economic policies of the southern regimes, see Clark 2009.
[43] On state promotion of maritime trade in the Wu-Yue (Yangzi Delta) and Min (Fujian) kingdoms, see Hino 1984: 17–248; Yamazaki 2010b.
[44] Twitchett and Stargardt 2002. The vessel also may well have carried perishable goods such as textiles.
[45] Yamazaki 2010a.

(near Ningbo) was by far the most common type of Chinese ceramics imported to Japan in the ninth–tenth centuries, followed by cream-colored Xingzhou 邢州 (southern Hebei) wares and the Changsha pottery found on the Belitung shipwreck.[46] Apart from ceramics, Chinese merchants brought textiles, books, and exotic goods from Central and Southeast Asia to Japan; their principal return cargo was gold from Mutsu in northern Japan.

The rulers of the South China states adopted explicitly mercantilist policies intended to strengthen their national economies and prevent the drain of hard currency – copper coin, gold, and silver – to neighboring rivals.[47] The northern courts, lacking any domestic supplies of copper, suffered from critical short-ages of money. Northern rulers repeatedly issued bans against the export of coin and non-monetary uses of copper. When the Later Tang vanquished the Former Shu state in Sichuan in 934, the victors brought back great quantities of gold and silver and six billion copper coins to Luoyang.[48] A new proscription against Buddhism enacted by the Northern Zhou in 955 was a thinly disguised ruse to seize bronze statues and other religious ornaments held by monasteries and private devotees for use as raw material for coinage. Even states with ample copper supplies such as Wu-Yue and Southern Tang ultimately resorted to minting iron coins to discourage the export of coin abroad. Other southern states such as Min, Southern Han, and Chu issued even cheaper lead coins. These monetary policies contributed to a pattern of regional monetary autarky that persisted after the Song reunification.

The precarious military situation of the Song cast a long shadow over fiscal policy. From the outset the Song emperors sought to reverse the centrifugal trends of the late Tang by recentralizing military power and economic resources in the hands of the central government. Most fiscal matters came under the purview of a new Finance Commission (Sansi 三司), an autonomous agency – comprised of the three departments of revenue (Duzhi 度支), salt (Yantie 鹽鐵), and census (Hubu 戶部) – that reported directly to the emperor rather than the chancellors. First created by the Later Tang in 930, the Finance Commission institutionalized the shift toward functional specialization in the central government fiscal bureaucracy that originated with the proliferation of plenipotentiary commissioners in the mid-Tang period. The structure of the Finance Commission encouraged the development of professional expertise in fiscal matters and the emergence a distinct career track within the Song bureaucracy for officials who acquired such knowledge and

[46] Kamei 1992: 120.
[47] Miyazaki 1943 remains the classic study of fiscal and monetary strategies in this era. See also Elvin 1973: 150–55; Miyazawa 2008.
[48] Hino 1980: 46–47.

experience.[49] The Song also divided the empire into regional circuits (*lu* 路) – a total of twenty-one in 979 – to coordinate policymaking between the central government and the empire's 300-odd prefectures.[50] The various circuit intendants – supervising military, fiscal, judicial, and educational affairs – reported to different authorities at the court. Fiscal Intendants (Juanyunshi 轉運使), acting as arms of the Finance Commission, were chiefly responsible for the allocation and transportation of locally generated revenues, above all for provisioning the armies.[51]

Since the Great Wall no longer served as a bulwark against invasion, the Song was forced to maintain large standing armies of professional soldiers along its long borders with the Tanguts and Khitan kingdom of Liao. In the early Song some 400,000 soldiers manned the garrisons along the northern frontier. Defeat in war with the Liao in 1004 forced the Song to pay large annual indemnities of silver and silk to the Liao rulers. During the Song offensive against the Tangut Xixia kingdom in 1040–44 – which ended in another devastating defeat and indemnities owed to Xixia as well – the Song armies swelled to 1.4 million soldiers. In the 1060s–70s, 700,000–800,000 troops were stationed in the northern border circuits of Hebei, Hedong, and Shaanxi.[52] Supplying these frontier armies imposed heavy fiscal and logistical burdens. Military expenditures consumed more than 80 percent of the central government's budget. The Song retained the twice-a-year tax system, but also sought to capture some of the profits generated by the rapidly expanding commercial economy to meet the ever-increasing costs of national defense.

Logistical considerations had figured significantly in the Song founder's choice of Kaifeng, the northern terminus of the Grand Canal, as his capital. Kaifeng became the hub of a system of waterways and roads that facilitated the delivery of goods from all corners of the Song realm. In the eleventh century state-operated convoys each year carried 4.89 million *shi* (464 million liters) of grain obtained as tax revenue from South China to Kaifeng. But nearly all of this grain was allocated to officials and soldiers stationed in and around the capital. Feeding the armies on the frontier required an additional 25 million *shi* (2.37 billion liters) per year, only half of which could be supplied by land tax revenues from the northern provinces. The remainder had to be obtained through the market through what was known as the "harmonious purchase" (*hedi* 和糴) policy. Most *hedi* grain was obtained locally in the northern

---

[49] Hartwell 1971. As Twitchett (1954) has shown, this professionalization of the fiscal bureaucracy was already underway in the Salt Commission of the late Tang.

[50] The number of circuits varied over time. On the spatial organization of the Song state and its transformation over time, see Mostern 2011.

[51] On the role of fiscal intendants in the Song, see Bao Weimin 2001: 13–45; Lamouroux 2003: 107–11.

[52] Shiba 1988: 236.

provinces, but each year the government purchased 2–3 million *shi* of rice in the south to provision the frontier armies.[53]

Like its predecessors, the Song relied heavily on profits from commodity monopolies to augment the relatively static income generated by direct taxation. In addition to the lucrative salt monopoly, the Song retained the monopoly on commerce in tea in the Huainan region that had been established by the Southern Tang. In 965 the Song created a Commodity Monopoly Bureau (Quehuowu 榷貨務) to sell licenses that enabled merchants to purchase tea in Huainan and market it in designated market regions. Like the Southern Tang, the Song initially used the tea monopoly as a weapon in its economic warfare with rival states. After the conquest of Wu-Yue in 978, however, the purpose of the tea monopoly changed along with the strategic goals of the Song leaders, now focused on recovering the region around modern Beijing from the Liao. Under the "frontier delivery" (*ruzhong* 入中) policy, the state offered lucrative incentives to entice merchants to provision the frontier armies. In 985 the Song began to tender exchange vouchers, known as *jiaoyin* 交引, as payment for shipments of grain, fodder, money (coin and silver), and other supplies to the frontier. These vouchers could be redeemed at the capital for coin, exotic imports such as incense and ivory, or the coveted licenses to procure and market tea and salt.[54]

The tea monopoly encountered intractable obstacles.[55] The government was unable to maintain a balance between its stocks of tea and the tea licenses it issued, resulting either in spoilage of unsold tea or lengthy delays for merchants seeking to redeem their licenses. Merchants often inflated the values of the supplies they delivered to the frontier, deflating the state's revenue. Above all, a monopoly on tea production proved impossible to enforce, since tea was widely grown by small producers across all of South China. In 1059 the government abandoned the monopoly and allowed free trade in tea. The salt monopoly, in contrast, was more successful, primarily because the state could more easily control the sources of supply.

Although the salt and tea monopolies were staple sources of revenue, in the early decades of the eleventh century they yielded less revenue than other indirect levies on trade (Table 6.6). Commercial taxes (on the shipment and sale of goods) became a major source of income, generating 20–25 percent of

---

[53] Ibid.: 234–44. In principle – as the designation "harmonious purchase" implies – the state purchased grain at market prices, but in times of emergency the government might provide little or no compensation. From the late Northern Song onward "harmonious purchases" increasingly became a form of confiscatory taxation.
[54] On *jiaoyin* exchange vouchers and their use in the frontier delivery system, see Miu Kunhe 2002: 47–90.
[55] On the shifting fiscal strategies employed in the operation of the Song tea monopoly, see Lamouroux 1991.

Table 6.6 *Coin revenues in the Northern Song*
(in millions of *guan*)

	997	1021	c. 1044	1064	c. 1077*
Salt	3.00	3.00	7.15	11.23	22.30
Tea	2.86	3.30	1.50**	1.18	0.77
Liquor	3.26	11.59	17.10	12.86	12.93
Subtotal for state monopolies	9.12	17.89	25.75	25.27	34.70
Commercial taxes	4.00	12.04	19.75	8.46	8.05
Coinage	?	?	?	?	5.95
Twice-a-year tax	?	?	?	4.93	5.59
New policies	–	–	–	–	18.00
Total coin revenues***	16.93	29.93	45.50	36.82	72.29
Total revenues (coin equivalent)	35.59	57.23	?	60.00	89.33
Percentage of total revenues in coin	48%	52%	–	61%	81%

*Figures variously from 1076, 1077, and 1078; does not include revenues from Green Sprouts
loans and maritime customs (because revenue data for these categories is not divided into coin
and non-coin portions).
**Figure from 1034; 1054 figure was 1.28 million.
***Total revenues also included additional revenues apart from the above categories.
Sources: Wang Shengduo 1995, 2: 691, appendix table 1.6; 2: 705, appendix table 4; 2: 709–13,
appendix table 7; 2: 748-49, appendix table 22; Guo Zhengzhong 1990: 676–77, table 44; Jia
Daquan 1981: 53–54; Miyazawa 1998: 56, table 4.

the state's cash revenues.[56] A new liquor monopoly produced nearly as much
revenue as the commercial taxes. The state directly operated breweries in
major cities while licensing private producers in smaller towns and rural areas
who paid franchise fees to the state. A network of revenue depots (*changwu*
場務) blanketed the empire, collecting revenues from commercial taxes and
the liquor monopoly. In 1077, a total of 1,993 commercial tax stations and
1,861 liquor revenue depots were in operation.[57] Another revenue device
employed by the Song court was a system of loan advances to finance
purchases from silk producers (*heyumai* 和預買). The state made cash
advances to families engaged in sericulture who repaid the loans with finished
silk cloth. The amount of silk obtained through advance purchases rose from
1 million bolts in 1005 to 3 million in 1047.[58]

After the rapid escalation of frontier defense costs during and after the
Tangut war in the 1040s, the Song leadership desperately sought to increase
its revenues. The most successful innovation was decoupling the salt licenses

[56] On the commercial tax system, see Guo Zhengzhong 1997: 123–233.
[57] Qi Xia 1999, 2: 1142; Li Huarui 1995: 151.
[58] Sogabe 1941a; Shimasue 1990: 354–57. The advance purchase system was also employed in
tea cultivation; see Smith 1992: 68.

Table 6.7 *Principal state revenues in the Northern Song*

Revenues	997	1021	1065	1086
(all figures in millions)				
Coin (貫)	16.93	29.93	36.82	48.48
Silks (絹紬 only) (匹)	4.23	10.97	8.75	1.51
Grain (石)	21.94	29.83	26.94	24.45
Value in silver	**997**	**1021**	**1065**	**1086**
(figures in 1,000 kg)				
Coin	794	1,112	1,381	1,818
Silks	203	350	473	74
Grain	322	362	689	1,298
Total	1,319	1,824	2,543	3,190

Sources: Revenues from Wang Shengduo 1995, 2: 687–92, appendix tables 1.1, 1.4, 1.6, 1.8; silver equivalents derived from Peng Xinwei 1965: 503–09.

from the frontier delivery system in 1048. Merchants could simply purchase salt licenses outright, without undertaking the delivery of military supplies, and were given more flexibility to choose where they could market their salt. By purchasing grain on the market, the state avoided the problem of bloated costs that the frontier delivery system had entailed, and thus economized on military expenditures. Moreover, the salt licenses could be redeemed for money rather than salt, and thus served as a negotiable bill of exchange. The utility of salt licenses as financial instruments greatly enhanced their appeal, spurring the formation of a secondary market for trading salt licenses in Kaifeng. By the beginning of the twelfth century virtually the entire salt trade was in the hands of private merchants operating under state license. Government income from the salt monopoly rose, and the military procurement system was placed on sounder footing.[59]

Total government income rose substantially over the first half of the eleventh century (Table 6.7). Cash revenues soared amid the Tangut war in 1040–44, and by the 1060s payments in coin comprised 60 percent or more of the state's total income. Although the creation of the office of Finance Commissioner in 1003 unified the fiscal administration under a single executive, the Finance Commission's control over state finances increasingly was usurped by the emperor and his coterie of eunuchs. Emperors Zhenzong (r. 997–1022) and Renzong (r. 1022–63) greatly enlarged the sources of income garnered by the Privy Purse, and thus at their personal disposal. In addition to the emperor's traditional claims over "the mountains and

---

[59] On the operation of the Song salt monopoly, see Chien 2004; Guo Zhengzhong 1990.

the marshes" (income from mining and coinage) and domestic and foreign tribute, the Song emperors appropriated significant shares of revenues from maritime customs and commodity monopolies, and also required the Finance Commission to remit a portion of its annual receipts to the Privy Purse. Consequently, the Privy Purse's share of total revenues rose from 10 percent c. 1000 to 23 percent in the 1050s (Table 6.8). Originally the Privy Purse had been intended to serve as an emergency reserve in preparation for times of war and famine. The Finance Commission incurred chronic budget shortfalls – and massive deficits during the war years of the 1040s – that required regular infusions of revenue transferred from the Privy Purse. The Finance Commission's dependence on subsidies from the Privy Purse impeded central-ized control and coordination of the state's fiscal regime.[60]

Monetization of revenue collection required an ample supply of coin. In addition, commercial expansion intensified the demand for a reliable means of exchange. One of the main priorities of the early Song leadership was to restore a standard currency to replace the heterogeneous and cheaply made currencies that proliferated during the Five Dynasties interregnum. Currency unification proved impossible, however. The Song preserved the iron currency zone in Sichuan inherited from the Later Shu state, and from the 1040s created another separate currency zone along the northwestern frontier where a mix of iron and bronze coins as well as salt licenses served as currency.[61] The inconvenience of transporting bulky iron coins – a pound of salt cost 1½ pounds of iron coin in Sichuan – prompted merchants in Chengdu to issue their own paper bills of credit, known as jiaozi 交子. Like the state's "flying money," jiaozi bills were issued in varying amounts but could be transferred to third parties. In 1005 local authorities in Chengdu attempted to rein in the reckless issue of jiaozi by creating a standardized format for the bills and restricting their issue to a consortium of sixteen Chengdu merchants. Finally, in 1024 the government stepped in and took over the issue of the jiaozi bills. By fixing the value of the bills in standard denominations of iron coin with a three-year term of circulation, the state transformed the jiaozi into the world's first genuine paper money. But the circulation of jiaozi remained confined to Sichuan.[62]

In the rest of the empire bronze coin prevailed as the principal form of currency. The Song succeeded in dramatically increasing the money supply. By the early eleventh century the annual output of bronze coin was five to six

---

[60] Cheng Mingsheng 1984; Hartwell 1988; Lamouroux 2003.
[61] On monetary policies in Sichuan, see Schifferli 1986; Miyazawa 1998: 419–51; Gao Congming 1999: 243–80; for the special monetary zone on the northwestern frontier, see Miyazawa 1998: 377–418; Gao Congming 1999: 123–64; Lamouroux 2007.
[62] On the origins and development of paper money in Song China, see von Glahn 2005.

Table 6.8 Decennial averages of central government revenues, 960–1059
(in thousands of silver kg)

	Privy Purse						Finance Commission	Total
	Mining and coinage	Tribute and customs	Hemai 和買	Commodity monopolies	Other	Total		
960–69	16.7	6.7	0	0.9	64.5	88.9	664.9	753.6
970–79	16.9	10.3	0	1.5	59.5	88.1	664.9	753.0
980–89	15.0	14.7	0	78.4	46.3	154.4	1,093.1	1,247.5
990–99	30.7	10.2	0	79.5	50.7	171.1	1,354.3	1,535.4
1000–09	116.4	20.4	0	96.5	41.6	274.8	2,482.2	2,756.9
1010–19	116.3	18.8	27.8	118.1	18.8	299.7	2,488.2	2,787.9
1020–29	97.4	15.1	69.5	362.7	17.1	561.8	2,522.1	3,081.8
1030–39	97.4	17.1	69.5	385.7	17.1	591.2	2,520.4	3,111.6
1040–49	99.6	18.6	100.7	441.3	26.2	686.4	1,817.9	2,504.3
1050–59	62.7	26.0	104.2	463.9	4.2	661.0	2,888.5	3,749.5

Source: Hartwell 1988: 34, table 1; 62, table 5.

Table 6.9 *Issue of bronze currency in Northern Song*
(figures in millions of coins)

Period	Average annual coinage	Total output for period	Accumulated output*
976–82	70	490	490
983–96	300	4,200	4,690
997–99	800	2,400	7,090
1000–15	1,250	18,750	25,840
1016–48	1,000	33,000	58,840
1049–73	1,600	40,000	98,840
1074–85	4,500	54,000	152,840
1086–1125	2,800	109,200	262,040

*These figures do not account for the existing stock of coin or the loss of coin due to wear, melting, etc.
Source: Gao Congming 1999: 103.

times greater than the Tang average, and at their peak *c.* 1080 Song mints cast 6 billion coins per year, the highest recorded output in Chinese imperial history. There is a general consensus that during the Northern Song the state minted approximately 260 billion coins (see Table 6.9), but opinion differs sharply on the function of coin in the Song economy. Miyazawa Tomoyuki contends that the use of coin in the private market remained limited and local. In his view, coin functioned chiefly as a means of tax payment, and most coin remained stored in state treasuries. Miyazawa postulates that *c.* 1077, when the state's coin revenues reached their peak of 73 million *guan*, only 30 million *guan* of coin was circulating in the private market; thus coin figured far more significantly in revenue extraction than in commerce.[63] Gao Congming, while acknowledging the importance of what Miyazawa calls "fiscal trade" (state procurement and long-distance transport of goods, primarily for military supplies), arrives at the virtually opposite conclusion. Based on the earlier work of Qi Xia, Gao estimates that the total volume of private trade *c.* 1077 was 150 million *guan*, in contrast to average state revenues in coin of 60 million *guan*.[64] I am inclined to agree with Gao that the money supply was sufficiently large and elastic to meet the demands of both commerce and the state.[65]

---

[63] Miyazawa 1998: 498.
[64] Gao Congming 1999: 311–12. Qi Xia (1999, 2: 1156) derived his estimate of the volume of commodity trade of 143 million *guan* (175 million *guan* including the Sichuan iron coin region) from the 1077 commercial tax data. Zhang Jinpeng (2003: 76), based on the same data, proposes that the volume of market trade was in the range of 70–100 million *guan*.
[65] For further analysis of the contrasting views of Gao and Miyazawa, see von Glahn 2004.

Wang Anshi's new policies

The Tang-Song transition also witnessed crucial changes in the nature and composition of the political elite. The old aristocracy, whose fortunes fell along with those of the Tang court in the wake of the An Lushan rebellion, largely disappeared after the Song instituted rigorous merit-based civil service examinations as the principal means of recruiting government officials. The examination system also fostered a rejuvenated political culture imbued with a reawakened Confucian commitment to improve both the spiritual character and the material welfare of the people.[66] During the Northern Song period many leading officials expressed bold confidence in using the authority and institutions of the central government to engineer transformative social change. The humiliating military defeat inflicted by the Tanguts in the 1040s and the chronic deficits in the state budget resulting from, in Sogabe Shizuo's words, a "perpetual wartime fiscal regime" intensified the urgency of appeals for action.[67] The opportunity for radical reform came two decades later with the ascension of a young monarch, Emperor Shenzong (r. 1067–85), who swiftly promoted an ambitious and brilliant statesman, Wang Anshi (1021–85), to the position of chief minister in 1070. Wang immediately embarked on a program of sweeping institutional reforms known as the New Policies (*xinfa* 新法).[68] Above all, Wang implemented far-reaching changes in fiscal policy, seeking to free up productive energies in an economy undergoing rapid monetization by converting labor services to cash payments and pumping vast amounts of currency into the economy. The New Policies on one level were consistent with the trends toward monetization of fiscal administration and growing state intervention in the markets that had been underway since the An Lushan rebellion. Yet Wang Anshi also displayed a commitment to mercantilist principles of fiscal governance unseen since the time of Emperor Wu of the Han.

Under Wang Anshi's leadership, fiscal management – literally, "regulating wealth" (*licai* 理財) – displaced ethics, ritual propriety, and literary mastery as the defining feature of the art of government. Wang aimed to strengthen frontier defense while reducing the burden of military expenditures on the state budget; increase the state's income from monopoly commodities and foreign trade; streamline taxation by reducing or eliminating in-kind payments and labor services; and revitalize the agrarian base of society through state investments (the central government initiated over 11,000 irrigation and flood control projects), making low-cost loans to farmers, and expanding the reach

---

[66] On the transformation of political culture in the Song, see Bol 2008; Kuhn 2009.
[67] Sogabe 1941b: 3.
[68] The following synopsis of Wang Anshi's New Policies is based on Smith 2009; Qi Xia 1979. See also the massively detailed study by Higashi (1970).

of public relief in rural areas. Above all, Wang saw himself as the defender of family farms and small shopkeepers against rapacious rentier landowners and the great merchant houses, whom he castigated as "aggrandizers." Wang feared that unbridled market exchange created imbalances in the distribution in wealth and was vulnerable to manipulation by merchant cartels. To forestall such inequities he advocated state intervention in commerce and moneylending. Wang created new state agencies to manage wholesale trade at the capital and provide credit for retail businesses, turned private brokers into government agents, tightened the state's control of foreign trade, and extended the existing monopoly on salt production to include much tea cultivation as well.

When Emperor Shenzong proposed restoring the equal-field system as a means of resolving economic equality, Wang Anshi curtly dismissed the prospect of seizing lands from the wealthy as impractical.[69] Instead, Wang attributed the distress of family farms to their predicament of perpetual indebtedness and lack of access to capital for investment. The centerpiece of Wang's plan for reinvigorating the smallholder economy was his "Green Sprouts" (*qingmiao* 青苗) program, which sought to free family farms from the usurious moneylending of "aggrandizers" by providing them with low-cost loans in coin at the beginning of the spring planting season. Borrowers were required to join mutual-responsibility groups of 5–10 households, and could repay the loans in grain rather than coin if they wished. The Green Sprouts loan program was intended to be self-financing, and thus charged interest (usually 20 percent per annum) to keep the program solvent. However, as with many of the New Policy initiatives, the imperative to generate revenues eventually obscured the original goal of promoting economic welfare.

Wang Anshi's Hired Service (*muyi* 募役) program replaced conscription for local government service duties with professional clerical staff paid from the proceeds of a new tax assessed not only on affluent landowners, but also on groups previously exempt from the service obligation, such as the families of officials and townsmen. In addition, most village officer posts were abolished and subsumed into newly established local militias (*baojia* 保甲). Initially, the *baojia* militias were intended to relieve the professional soldiers who manned local garrisons and thus economize on military expenditures. *Baojia* headmen soon began to serve concurrently as village officers in charge of civil matters such as household registration, tax collection, and famine relief in addition to their public security duties. Although remuneration for *baojia* headmen was quickly discontinued, the tax created for this purpose remained on the books; the income it generated was simply merged into general revenues.[70]

[69] Qi Xia 1979: 193–99.   [70] McKnight 1971: 31–37, 73–94.

Determined to recruit a cadre of loyal officials committed to his goals ("united in one mind and common moral purpose"), Wang Anshi proposed a new civil service examination curriculum centered on public policy and current affairs that deemphasized literary skills such as poetry composition.[71] Wang also sought to circumvent a sclerotic bureaucracy by creating a host of new, task-oriented state agencies headed by upstart officials liberated from many of the constraints of civil service protocols – a political style dubbed "bureaucratic entrepreneurship" by one modern historian.[72] In its brief existence during 1069–70, Wang's Finance Planning Commission (Zhizhi Sansi tiaoli si 制置三司條例司) – filled with hand-picked sympathizers of low official rank – became the incubator for many of his reform proposals. Subsequently Wang bypassed the Finance Commission, which staunchly opposed his fiscal innovations, by delegating the drafting of the New Policies to an obscure office, the Exchequer of Imperial Lands (Sinongsi 司農寺). Implementation of the New Policies was entrusted to a new corps of circuit-level officials such as the Intendants for Ever-Normal Granaries, Husbandry, and Water Control (Tiju changping nongtian shuili shi 提舉常平農田水利使) and to ad hoc institutions such as the State Trade Bureau (Shiyiwu 市易務) in Kaifeng and the Tea Marketing Agency (Chachangsi 茶場司) in Sichuan. The dynamic role Wang Anshi envisioned for the state in managing the economy necessitated a substantial expansion in the size of the bureaucracy, which increased from 24,000 officials in 1067 to 34,000 by 1080. To deter peculation, Wang also boosted the salaries of public officials, increasing the budget for civil service personnel ten-fold.

Wang Anshi's principles of "bureaucratic entrepreneurship" – recruiting men with fiscal and managerial expertise, granting them long-term appointments unfettered by regulatory surveillance, and allowing wide latitude for experimentation – were most cogently articulated in his initiatives for direct government intervention in private commerce and finance. The State Trade Bureau (STB) originally was intended to eradicate what Wang perceived as monopolistic price manipulation by merchant cartels and usurious moneylenders. In addition to seizing control of wholesale marketing in Kaifeng and other cities (itinerant merchants were obliged to sell their stock to the bureau's agents), the STB engaged in a wide range of fiscal operations, such as trading in salt certificates, supplying the court and government agencies with the goods they requisitioned, and provisioning frontier armies. The STB also extended credit to petty retail shopkeepers such as fruit-sellers and butchers. Soon it branched out into more generalized financing, offering low-cost loans (the interest rate varied from 12 to 20 percent per annum) of coin, goods, and

[71] Quotation from *XCB*: 213.5169.   [72] Smith 1992: 111–18.

precious metals to individuals or groups. To ensure the solvency of this loan program, borrowers were obliged to provide guarantors and to pledge collateral as security. The bureau recruited not only "officials knowledgeable about finance" but also merchants to serve as the examiners who determined the creditworthiness of borrowers and authorized loans, a circumvention of civil service prerogatives that provoked heated protest. The repeal of the New Policies abolished the STB and direct government intervention in wholesale commerce, but the bureau's credit operations were spun off to a separate Collateral Lending Office (Didangsuo 抵當所) that endured into the Southern Song period.[73]

When the Tea Marketing Agency (TMA) was first established in Sichuan in 1074, its purpose was to generate revenues for procuring war horses from Central Asia and provisioning armies stationed on the northwestern frontier. Initially the TMA had no exclusive rights to the tea grown in Sichuan and simply bought tea in the private market at competitive prices. After tea production surged in tandem with rising TMA purchases, the TMA successfully lobbied to obtain monopsony rights to Sichuan's entire tea output. Like the STB, the TMA diversified into a wide range of commercial and financial enterprises, including lending grain to tea cultivators and trading in commodities such as silk, paper, furs, and medicines. The TMA proved a resounding fiscal success, generating several million *guan* in annual profits as well as supplying the military with 15,000–20,000 horses a year. Following the loss of North China in 1127, however, the economic logic of the TMA, notably its role in horse procurement, atrophied. The agency still retained its control over Sichuan's tea industry, but "bureaucratic entrepreneurship descended into confiscatory taxation."[74]

From the outset the New Policies aroused fierce opposition. Orthodox Confucians condemned the intrusion of state power into the private economy both on principle and because of the deleterious effects of Wang's initiatives. Perhaps the most vilified initiative was the Green Sprouts program. Critics charged that local officials forced farmers to borrow money from the state, turning the loan program into a regressive tax. It seems that fiscal goals indeed superseded commitments to social welfare. Revenues from the Green Sprouts loan program – which in its early years yielded roughly 3 million *guan* annually, or a net profit of 27 percent on its capital – were appropriated to finance flood control and famine relief and to provision frontier armies.[75] Despite the lower interest rates, defaults – even after repeated deferrals – were common, and by the 1080s the program began to suffer deficits. The state's injection of new credit into the rural economy

---

[73] Kumamoto 1983; Miyazawa 1998: 91–137.   [74] Smith 1992; quotation from p. 245.
[75] Smith 1993: 97.

apparently reinforced rather than remedied the perpetual cycle of indebtedness that afflicted many farming families.

Certainly the New Policies increased government revenues substantially, by at least 18 million *guan* annually. Tax receipts in coin rose by nearly 40 percent, primarily as a result of the monetization of labor services and the income generated by the Green Sprouts program; commercial sources, apart from the Sichuan tea monopoly, yielded only modest revenues. Although we lack complete figures for national accounts, estimates suggest that money payments reached a peak of 81 percent of central government revenues during the New Policies era, compared to 48 percent *c*. 1000 (Table 6.6). At the same time tax receipts in cloth, a staple of state finance since the Eastern Han, virtually disappeared (Table 6.7). From this time forward silver essentially replaced textiles in the Song fiscal system, and silk ceased to serve any monetary functions.[76]

The New Policies leaders also succeeded in maximizing control of fiscal resources by bringing the Privy Purse within their purview while sharply constricting the authority of the Finance Commission. After Wang Anshi's retirement in 1076, Shenzong himself took control of the reform agenda. In 1082 the emperor initiated a sweeping restructuring of the state bureaucracy that restored the Tang model of central government organization centered on the Six Ministries (Liubu 六部). Both the Finance Commission and the Exchequer for Imperial Lands were dissolved and replaced by the Ministry of Revenue (Hubu 戶部). At the same time Shenzong created the Yuanfeng Treasury (元豐庫) to mobilize funds in preparation for a new offensive against the Tanguts, one that would end in another ignominious defeat.[77] More broadly, the Yuanfeng Treasury became the depository for the revenues generated by the New Policies in addition to various commodity monopolies. Robert Hartwell's reconstruction of central government finances for 1093 indicates that the income of the Yuanfeng Treasury was equal to that of the Ministry of Revenue (Table 6.10). Thus the new Ministry of Revenue, like the Financial Commission before it, exercised only partial control over fiscal resources.

Wang Anshi's reforms did, however, transfer a greater share of revenues collected at the local level to central government agencies. At the local level the fiscal reorganization provided local government with more secure funding and replaced most labor service requirements with a money tax. In order to meet this escalating demand for cash, Wang Anshi's administration also accelerated mint output, which soared to an annual average of 4.5 billion coins during the New Policies era (Table 6.9). Despite this growth in the money

[76] Gao Congming 1999: 17; Wang Wencheng 2001: 148.   [77] Hartwell 1988: 70.

Table 6.10 *State income and expenditures in 1093*
(in thousands of silver kilos)

Revenues		Percent of total	Expenditures		Percent of total
(1) Privy Purse					
(內藏庫)					
Precious metals	15.60	0.5	Defense	19.35	0.6
Domestic tribute	6.44	0.2	Relief	12.03	0.4
Coinage	223.50	6.4	Patronage	0.59	< 0.1
Maritime customs	10.30	0.3	State subsidy	34.41	1.0
Foreign tribute	2.26	0.1	Liao/Xixia tribute	23.86	0.7
Hemai 和買	92.45	2.7	State funerals	15.42	0.5
Other	67.67	2.0	Palace expenses	119.14	3.5
Subtotal	421.76	12.1	Subtotal	224.79	6.6
(2) Yuanfeng treasury					
(元豐庫)					
Alum monopoly	21.97	0.6	Defense	16.33	0.5
Salt monopoly	301.98	8.7	Hired service pay	263.54	7.7
Xiezhou salt	63.98	1.8	State subsidy	0.39	< 0.1
Wine monopoly	503.92	14.4	Grain transport	17.09	0.5
Hired service levy	395.93	11.3	Monopoly costs	115.43	3.4
Breweries and ferries	143.65	4.1	Brewery and ferries	71.86	2.1
Subtotal	1,431.42	41.0	Subtotal	484.64	14.2
(3) Tea marketing agency (茶場司)	192.70	5.5			
Tea monopoly	192.70	5.5			?
(4) Ministry of Revenue (戶部)					
Twice-a-year tax	1,107.45	31.7	Civil salaries	43.56	1.3
Commercial taxes	328.02	9.4	Military salaries	1,133.23	33.2
Head tax	5.94	0.2	Relief	71.66	2.1
			Transfer to Privy Purse	16.16	0.5
Subtotal	1,441.41	41.3	Subtotal	1,264.61	37.1
(5) Unidentified agencies			Unidentified	1,437.06	42.1
Totals	3,490.23			3,411.09	

NB: Not all sources of state revenue are accounted for.
Source: Hartwell 1988: 71, table 8.

supply, many of Wang's critics complained that the state's monetization of taxes resulted in severe shortages of currency – "coin famines" (*qianhuang* 錢荒), in the idiom of the day – and falling rural incomes.

Following the deaths of Wang Anshi and Shenzong in 1085, Wang's enemies came to power and began to dismantle his reforms in the name of fiscal austerity. In 1093, however, proponents of the New Policies regained control of the court and revived the reform agenda. But incompetent leadership, a deteriorating military situation, and factional struggles at the court resulted in increasingly erratic fiscal policies and predatory taxation that inflicted enormous damage on the economy. The rapid collapse of the Song state in the face of the Jurchen invasion in 1126 was widely blamed on the fiscal mismanagement and private venality of Wang Anshi's self-anointed disciples. The refugee court that reconstituted Song rule in South China after the fall of Kaifeng in 1127 repudiated Wang Anshi's political philosophy and repealed most of the New Policies. But the powerful presence of the fiscal state endured.[78]

The great leap forward in economic productivity

The Song period witnessed unprecedented progress in market growth and economic productivity. Wet-rice agriculture became the mainstay of the national economy, but the cultivation of cash crops such as tea, sugar, mulberry (for silkworms), and indigo also expanded rapidly. The vast timber resources of South China were harvested to supply the burgeoning construction, shipbuilding, lacquer ware, and paper and printing industries. Iron and coal production, chiefly centered in the north, also experienced prodigious growth. Regional ceramics industries, invigorated by the invention of true porcelain and soaring demand in overseas markets, flourished. In the ceramics and silk industries as well as in agriculture we see a steady shift in the centers of production from north to south. The ready availability of water transport and the growth of maritime trade also contributed to the rise of industry and commerce in South China. The monetization of the economy expanded through vigorous growth in the money supply and the development of new credit and financial institutions. Finally, this commercial efflorescence stimulated urbanization and transformed the character of cities. Market towns sprang up in the countryside, while the walled cities became thriving hubs of commercial activity in addition to their traditional administrative and military functions.

---

[78] For a forthright affirmation of the emergence of a "fiscal state" based on indirect taxation, monetized taxes, and professionalization of fiscal administration in Song China, see William Liu 2015, which appeared too late for me to address its arguments here.

Tea-drinking boomed during the Song period, and tea became recognized – along with rice, salt, soy sauce, cooking oil, vinegar, and charcoal – as one of the seven indispensable items of household consumption.[79] At this time roasted tea leaves usually were pressed into bricks for ease of storage and transport. Fragments of these bricks were crushed or ground into a fine powder before brewing. Preparation of tea using loose leaves steadily gained in popularity, but did not fully displace powdered tea until the Ming period. Tea houses frequented by all social classes became a fixture of urban social life. The profusion of varieties of tea and gradations of quality encouraged connoisseurship and branding for diverse consumer markets. For example, the most prized variety of tea from Raozhou in Jiangxi fetched 500 coins per *jin* (0.59 kg), while the cheapest Raozhou teas sold for a mere 37 coins.[80] The avid thirst for tea among Central Asian nomads willing to pay top prices was the principal reason for the lucrative profits generated by Sichuan's Tea Marketing Agency. Cross-border trade absorbed one-third of Sichuan's tea output before 1104, when the frontier markets were opened to tea produced in the southeastern provinces.[81]

Tea cultivation spearheaded the settlement of the interior upland valleys of South China, where the rugged terrain was ill-suited for rice agriculture. In Fujian, for example, tea production rose from 230,000 kg at the beginning of the dynasty to 1.9 million kg in 1084. Most tea cultivation was carried out by rural households who typically harvested 60–300 kg a year, but in some areas large private and state-run plantations employed up to 100 men and women laborers and produced as much as 30,000 kg.[82] Over the course of the Song dynasty tea-picking became recognized as women's work, and male labor essentially disappeared from this industry.[83] Tea production, like the salt industry, became a significant source of government revenue and was subject at times to complex and burdensome regulation. But a monopoly on tea production, which was widely dispersed among tens of thousands of small cultivators, proved difficult to enforce. Still, we also see a high degree of regional specialization in tea production. A mere five prefectures generated 55 percent of the total tea output (excluding Sichuan) of more than 16 million kg in 1162 (Map 6.6).[84]

---

[79] Shiba 1968: 184–85.   [80] Mizuno 2000: 89.
[81] The loss of its monopoly in the trans-border trade sharply curtailed the profitability of the Tea Marketing Agency. See Smith 1992: 195–96.
[82] Smith 1992: 65.   [83] Lu Weijing 2004.
[84] Mizuno 2000: 92, table 1; total tea production figure for southeastern China based on adjustment by Zhang Jinpeng 2003: 138. Zhang (ibid.: 140) suggests that tea production in Sichuan was roughly equal to the entire southeast.

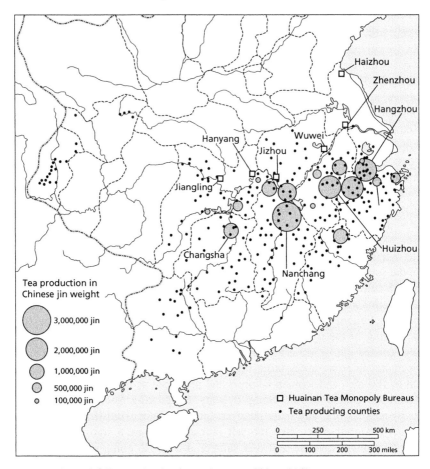

Map 6.6 Tea production in southeastern China, 1162
NB: No data for Sichuan.
Source: Mizuno 2000: 95, table 3.

Among the other southern crops that became important commercial goods during the Song period we can include sugar, indigo (for making dyes), tung oil (used to waterproof ships) and fruits such as oranges and other citruses, longan, and litchi. Crystallized sugar was widely used as a preservative for southern fruits, which had become popular delicacies in the cities of northern and central China. Chinese techniques for sugar extraction and refinement were efficient but labor-intensive. At least 10–20 laborers were needed to operate a sugar mill, using rotary mills – probably adapted from oil presses – powered by oxen to extract juice from sugar cane. A treatise of 1142 devoted to the Sichuan sugar industry claimed that in some counties of Suining prefecture 30 percent of households cultivated sugar cane and manufactured sugar candy. But the scale of these operations remained small – Suining's candy-makers produced at most several tens of jugs per year, with some households producing only one or two. Because the crystallization process was slow and subject to vagaries of weather, many growers merely extracted juice from sugar cane to sell to candy-makers. Most likely, sugar milling was confined to private and monastic estates with ample capital and labor resources that leased their facilities to small growers. Even after the adoption of more sophisticated extraction and crystallization technologies in the Ming dynasty, China never developed the kind of plantation economies that accompanied the rise of sugar production in the West.[85]

During the Song period industrial enterprise also attained unprecedented levels of output and organizational sophistication. Coal and copper mining, iron metallurgy, alum making, shipbuilding, salt processing, papermaking and printing all experienced exponential growth, leading to larger scales of operation and managerial innovations. Textile manufacture, previously confined mostly to domestic needs and tax payments, became reoriented to production for the market. The formation of national markets for luxury goods such as fine silks, paper, lacquer, and porcelain encouraged regional specialization of handicraft production.

Technological innovation and market demand drove the expansion of iron production.[86] Most iron mines were located in North China, where by Song times deforestation had sharply reduced the availability of charcoal as fuel for foundries. The invention of a coking process using bituminous coal produced the fuel needed for large blast furnaces employing the direct decarbonization (Bessemer technique) steel-making process. Coking and steel-making operations required substantial capital resources but also yielded significant economies of scale. The thirty-six private foundries at Liguo in northern Jiangsu employed an average of 100 wage laborers engaged in mining, coking, smelting, and refining tasks, and together produced nearly 7,000 tons of iron and steel per year. Total annual output of iron and steel in the late eleventh century has been estimated at roughly 125,000 tons.[87] Many of the major iron-producing areas, including Liguo, were close to the capital of Kaifeng, the largest urban market, whose population possibly reached 750,000 in the late eleventh century. Kaifeng's state armories and workshops alone employed more than 13,000 ironworkers engaged in

---

[85] Shiba 1968: 215–19; Daniels 1996: 88–93; Mazumdar 1998: 126–33.
[86] Hartwell 1962, 1966, 1967; Wagner 2001a, 2008: 278–325.
[87] Hartwell 1967: 104–06. Hartwell's method of calculation has been questioned, but it is generally agreed that his estimate is basically sound. See Wagner 2001a, 2008: 300.

manufacturing swords, armor, lances and other weapons as well as saws, hammers, stoves, nails, boilers, locks, lamps, and needles among numerous sundry utensils. While large-scale ironworks produced bar and cast iron for government armories and urban iron-finishing workshops, small rural forges employing seasonal labor continued to supply local blacksmiths and farmers with tools and utensils.

The sharp decline in silk and hemp as items of tax payment and the growth of consumer demand led to major changes in the structure of the textile industry.[88] New fashions in dress favored lightweight silk gauzes, which required more complex looms, over the heavy polychrome fabrics and tabbies that predominated in the Tang. Government factories and the private workshops that catered to this segment of the market employed male workers, and the production of fancy textiles largely became the preserve of highly trained male artisans. Rural women working at home still produced tabby weaves. North China remained the center of silk production both in terms of technical skill and output until the Jin invasion and the conquest of the north in the 1120s. During the Southern Song period the refugee capital of Hangzhou became the nucleus of the national economy, and the region around Hangzhou rapidly achieved dominance as the new center of China's sericulture industry. In his treatise *On Husbandry* (1149), Chen Fu – a native of the Yangzi Delta – observed that rural inhabitants in the western part of the delta, an area less favorable to rice cultivation, depended on silk manufacture as their main, if not sole, source of income:

The middle-income households of Anji county in Huzhou rely entirely on sericulture to make a living. A family of ten persons raises ten frames of silkworms, obtaining 12 jin of cocoons from each frame. Each jin of cocoons yields 1.3 ounces of silk thread. It takes 5 ounces of thread to weave one small bolt of silk tabby, which has a market value of 1.4 piculs of rice. The prices of silk tabby and rice usually move in tandem, so it is eminently feasible to provide for the family's annual needs for food and clothing by means of sericulture. One month of intensive labor is superior to a full year of diligent toil [in agriculture].[89]

The renowned quality of Anji's silk goods – not only simple tabbies, but also more complex silk fabrics such as gauzes (*sha* 紗) and twill weaves (*ling* 綾) –made this specialization possible. But many rural households abandoned silk weaving to concentrate on raising silkworms and reeling raw silk for sale to urban weaving workshops. A gazetteer of Huzhou published in 1201 recorded that rich families raised as many as several

---

[88] Bray 1997: 206–12.
[89] *NS*: xia.18. Chen's figures translate into a household income from sericulture equivalent to 43.7 piculs (*shi*) of rice, compared to contemporary estimates that the minimum consumption requirement for a family of five was 18 *shi* of rice per year (see Chapter 7).

hundred frames of silkworms in addition to hiring weavers, which suggests large workshops with dozens of artisans.[90] Chains of contractors, brokers, wholesale dealers, and long-distance merchants linked raw silk producers in the countryside with urban manufacturers and consumers.

Similar developments in technical refinement and market growth spurred industrial development in porcelain, paper manufacture, and printing. During the late Tang–early Song period Chinese craftsmen perfected the technique of making true porcelain, in which the pigments and glaze as well as the vessel body were vitrified. Regional styles of ceramic production flourished in all parts of China, but the southern city of Jingdezhen (Jiangxi) achieved particular distinction for its lustrous bluish-white (Qingbai) porcelains. Like metallurgy, porcelain manufacture featured a complex specialization of labor and substantial capital investment. Some kilns and ceramic workshops were operated as joint-capital enterprises. Jingdezhen was said to have numbered more than three hundred kilns in the Song period, which would have employed a labor force of 12,000 skilled workers, and probably an equal number of unskilled laborers.[91] Smaller ceramic centers exhibited a similar concentration of kilns, capital, and skilled labor. Yonghezhen in Jizhou prefecture (Jiangxi) emerged as a center of pottery manufacture in the mid-tenth century, and was formally recognized as a town by the Song state at the turn of the eleventh century.[92] A Song local historian boasted that Yonghezhen's "six boulevards and three marketplaces" (a poetic metaphor for a bustling metropolis) were home to a population of several thousand households. In the twelfth century Jizhou's dark-glazed wares briefly gained international repute, but subsequently they were eclipsed by Jingdezhen's porcelains.[93]

Porcelain and celadon wares displaced silks as China's chief export during the Song period, and surging demand in overseas markets reshaped the geography of ceramic manufacture. Fine porcelains from Jingdezhen, Dingzhou (Hebei), and Longquan (Zhejiang) were in great demand within China, but relatively few of these wares (except for Longquan products) were exported. Instead, new centers of ceramic manufacture developed in coastal

---

[90] *WXZ*: 20.5b.

[91] Ho (2001: 269) estimates that each kiln represented forty to forty-five workers directly engaged in ceramic manufacture (potters and kiln workers), while So (2000: 194) asserts that each kiln supported a minimum of 100 households employed in all aspects of pottery manufacture, merchandising, and transport.

[92] The Song state accorded the designation of "market town" (*zhen* 鎮) to commercial centers that lacked a county magistrate and appointed Town Supervisors (Jianzhen 監鎮) to take charge of public security and collection of commercial taxes. See Chen Zhiping 1993.

[93] Otagi 1987: 272–74. Archaeological surveys have identified twenty-four Song-Yuan era kilns in Yonghezhen, suggesting that the ceramic industry there was less than one-tenth the size of Jingdezhen's. See Liu Yang and Zhao Ronghua 2001: 11.

areas where potters had ready access to export markets, first in Guangdong and then in Fujian. In the late eleventh century, nearly fifty large-scale kilns manufacturing sophisticated ceramic wares abruptly appeared on the outskirts of Quanzhou, where a Maritime Customs Superintendency (Shibosi 市舶司) was established in 1087. Initially the Quanzhou potters imitated the prestigious Qingbai wares of Jingdezhen, but by the mid-twelfth century they produced their own distinctive styles that achieved great popularity in overseas markets, especially in Japan. The Quanzhou region ceramic industry required a high degree of specialized skills, managerial expertise, and capital resources as well as informed knowledge of overseas markets. The success of Quanzhou potteries in dominating foreign markets – older centers in Guangdong and Shaoxing atrophied, and their wares disappeared from the export trade – attests to the intense competition faced by entrepreneurs in this industry.[94]

The invention of woodblock printing dates back to the early Tang period, but before the Song printing was mostly confined to the reproduction of Buddhist texts and ephemera such as calendars, almanacs, and religious charms. The institutionalization of the civil service examinations and the proliferation of schools during the Song period created a booming market for books. The Song government itself issued authorized versions of the Confucian classics, histories, administrative handbooks, and legal manuals as well as medical works and technological treatises. During the Southern Song schools and private commercial firms became major forces in publishing. Commercial firms printed inexpensive editions of many of the same types of books issued by government agencies, but also published works that received scant attention from the state, such as poetry, memoirs, and informal writings. Kaifeng and Sichuan dominated the printing industry in the Northern Song period, but in the Southern Song Hangzhou and Fujian emerged as the new centers of printing and publishing.[95]

Rising consumption of consumer goods such as silk, liquor, tea, porcelain, and books attested to the commercial efflorescence of the Song era. The dramatic surge in the money supply, innovations in finance and credit, and advances in the technology, management, and financing of water transport all nourished the growth of the market economy.[96] Government procurement

---

[94] Ho 2001; So 2000: 186–201. Archaeological evidence from Japan attests to the abrupt rise of the South Fujian ceramic industry in the late eleventh century, and its dominance (trailed by Longquan wares) in the Japanese market by the late twelfth century. See Tanaka and Satō 2008. Billy So's comparative analysis of the Fujian and Guangdong ceramic industries (Su Jilang 2004) concludes that Fujian potters were better capitalized, had lower costs, and reaped higher profits than their competitors in Guangdong.

[95] Chia 2003.   [96] Shiba 1968: 49–132, 1970: 4–40; Elvin 1973: 131–78.

figured significantly in stimulating production and trade, but the state fulfilled a large and growing proportion of its needs through purchases in the market. Zhang Jinpeng has estimated the volume of commodity circulation in the Northern Song (converted into rice equivalents) at 148 liters per capita, more than twice (69 liters per capita) the most commonly cited estimate for commodity trade in the early nineteenth century.[97] Although there are reasons to believe that the nineteenth-century estimate is too low, the conclusion that during the Song purchasing power in the private economy probably reached its highest level in the history of imperial China seems irrefutable.

After the loss of North China in 1127 and the relocation of the capital to Hangzhou, the Jiangnan region permanently eclipsed the Central Plain as China's economic heartland. Yet the Lower Yangzi Basin had already emerged as the most dynamic commercial region in the Northern Song, as the geographical distribution of commercial tax revenues in 1077 shows (Map 6.7). The primacy of the imperial capital of Kaifeng as by far the largest commercial center – with commercial tax revenues five times greater than the next largest city, Hangzhou – is readily apparent. But apart from Kaifeng, commercial activity was concentrated in the southeast, especially along the Grand Canal corridor from Chuzhou to Hangzhou. Nine of the fifteen cities with the highest commercial tax revenues in 1077 were located in the Lower Yangzi Basin. The breadth of commercial activity is also noteworthy. Kaifeng's share of total commercial tax revenues was 5.2 percent, and the twenty-seven other cities with commercial tax revenues exceeding 30,000 *guan* together accounted for 15.2 percent of the total. Of the additional ninety-nine cities and towns that collected commercial taxes in the range of 10,000–30,000 *guan*, fifty-six were prefectural capitals, while forty-three were county seats (*xian*) or market towns (*zhen*).[98] The 520 market towns included in the 1077 data generated 29 percent of total commercial tax revenues.[99] In contrast to the salience of cities as seats of political power in the past, in Song cities commercial activity became the lifeblood of urban society.

The commercial tax data perhaps can serve as a proxy for the size and distribution of urban populations, but we lack direct evidence to measure the degree of urbanization in the Northern Song. Prefecture-level data from the Southern Song reveals wide regional variation in urbanization rates ranging

---

[97] Zhang Jinpeng 2003: 312–13. The nineteenth-century estimate for the volume of domestic trade – which is more conjectural, a projection based on estimates of per capita consumption rather than on actual data like the 1077 commercial tax receipts – is from Wu Chengming 1985: 253, table 2.

[98] Guo Zhengzhong 1997: 224–29, tables 3-21, 3-22.   [99] Shiba 1975: 27.

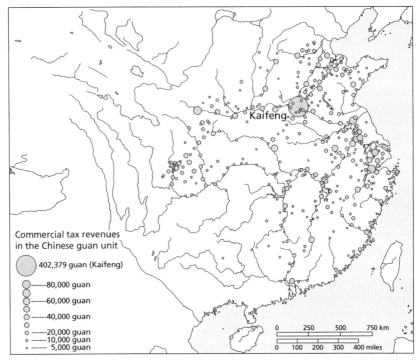

Map 6.7 Distribution of commercial tax revenues, 1077
Source: Chen Zhengxiang 1982.

from 3 percent in an upland interior area like Huizhou (Anhui) to 25 percent in
the booming maritime trade center of Quanzhou (Fujian). The imperial capitals
of Kaifeng and Hangzhou of course represented exceptional cases. Nearly
175,000 civilian households (46 percent of the prefectural total) were classified
as urban residents in Hangzhou in the mid-thirteenth century, to which must be
added the families of approximately 10,000 officials and 100,000 soldiers.
Including the capital's suburban non-agricultural population, Hangzhou's
total population may have been as large as 1.5 million persons.[100] Although
some scholars have postulated that the proportion of towndwellers in the
Southern Song reached as high as 20 percent of the total population, a more
likely estimate would be in the range of 12 percent.[101] The degree of urbanization in the Southern Song thus was roughly equal to that of early modern

[100] Shiba 1988: 320–21.   [101] Wu Songdi 2000: 614–19.

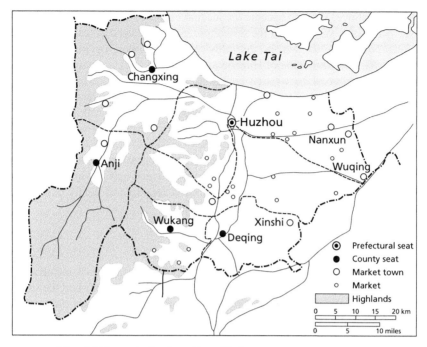

Map 6.8 Towns in Southern Song Huzhou
Source: Shiba 1988: 384.

Europe, for which Jan de Vries has proposed urbanization rates of 9.6 percent in 1500 and 13 percent in 1800.[102]

Commercial growth was the primary force driving urban development in the Song, but the effects of commercialization on urbanization varied. The rugged terrain of Huizhou was poorly suited to agriculture, which constricted urban growth. Although Huizhou flourished as an exporter of tea, lacquer, lumber, and paper to Hangzhou and other Jiangnan cities, the prefecture numbered fewer than 4,000 urban households (3 percent of the total) in 1227, roughly half of whom lived in the city of Huizhou.[103] In the Yangzi Delta prefecture of Huzhou, in contrast, a fertile agricultural base sustained a dense network of cities and towns, although we lack data on the size of its urban population.

---

[102] De Vries 1984: 72–3.
[103] Data from Shiba 1988: 396; Wu Songdi 2000: 616, table 13-3. The figure for the Huizhou city population (1,931 households) is from 1172, but the total prefectural population in 1172 (122,014 households) is virtually identical to that for 1227 (124,941 households, of whom 3,887 were urban households).

As noted above, Huzhou became the leading center of silk manufacture in the Southern Song, and much of the sericulture industry as well as tea and ceramic production were located in the hilly western portion of the prefecture (Map 6.8). The population of Huzhou and its eleven market towns was evenly distributed between the western highlands and the eastern lowlands. But the largest market towns (Xinshi, Nanxun, and Wuqing) – which had commercial tax revenues far greater than the average county seat – as well as numerous smaller towns were concentrated in the eastern lowlands, which generated substantial rice surpluses, enjoyed ready access to water transport, and developed a highly skilled urban workforce. In the post-Song era commercial and urban growth became concentrated in the eastern half of Huzhou, while the western portion of the prefecture regressed into a poor, lightly populated hinterland.[104]

Conclusion

The Tang-Song transition engendered far-reaching institutional changes in both the public and private sectors that transformed the economy and the state. More competitive factor markets for land, labor, and capital, new productive resources, and rising public and private demand provided the impetus for sustained economic growth. Nearly universal private landownership, monetization of tax payments, and the release of most of the population from statutory labor obligations fostered a more rational allocation of economic resources. Growth in the money supply and the proliferation of both public and private financial intermediation lubricated trade and investment. Marked increases in the output of staple foods, textiles, shipbuilding, and metallurgy resulted not so much from new knowledge but rather the application of existing technologies on a much wider scale, and especially the transfer of these technologies to the far richer resource base of South China. The great leap forward in food production made possible by the shift to wet-rice agriculture, rising consumption of new comestibles such as tea and sugar, and vigorous demand from the shipbuilding, paper, printing, and lacquer industries for the products of South China's ample forests all contributed to commercial growth, rising incomes, and the diversification of consumer demand. Market expansion fostered regional specialization, especially for high-quality silks, porcelain, paper, lacquer wares, and tea, but also for cheaper versions of these goods intended for mass consumption.

The relationship of the state to the private economy changed as well. The weakening of state control over land and labor in the aftermath of the

[104] Shiba 1975: 33–37, 1988: 365–89.

An Lushan rebellion compelled the Tang court to resort to indirect taxation, especially consumption taxes, in a desperate effort to boost revenues. This trend accelerated during the tenth century, after the final collapse of the Tang dynasty. Warfare among rival regimes, especially in South China, promoted mercantilist fiscal and monetary strategies for strengthening state power. The Song dynasty restored firm state control over the population and resources, but from the beginning the Song also faced dire threats to its existence from strong nomad-based states on its northern frontiers. The Song leadership chose to continue to rely chiefly on indirect taxation of commerce to meet the escalating costs of provisioning massive standing armies of professional soldiers. State income from land taxes remained static throughout the eleventh century, even as the population tripled and registered lands increased by 50 percent. The New Policies enacted by Wang Anshi and his followers were dedicated to the twin goals of capturing greater revenues from an expanding commercial economy and alleviating the economic inequality that commercialization entailed. Despite some promising initial achievements, in the long run the New Policies failed to achieve durable success in meeting either of these objectives.

Notwithstanding the repeal of the New Policies in the Southern Song period, the reconstruction of the imperial state during the Tang-Song transition marked a dramatic departure from the original conception of the military-physiocratic state formulated under the Qin-Han empires. At times – during the tenth century interregnum, and again under the New Policies regime – state fiscal policy revived the mercantilist principles of Pseudo-Guanzi and the interventionist policies devised by Emperor Wu of Han's coterie of advisors. Like Sang Hongyang, Wang Anshi and his acolytes were charged with the odious sin of fiscalism, of wielding state power to usurp the wealth of the people for their own power-mongering ends. But the fundamental feature of the military-physiocratic fiscal state, the presumption of economic equality established through state land allocations and ratified by uniform taxation and conscription imposed on all adults, was irreparably defunct. Landownership had become thoroughly privatized, and the principle of progressive taxation embedded in the twice-a-year tax system conceded to the reality of sizable disparities in land and wealth. Song fiscal administration adhered to some of the interventionist policies of Emperor Wu's mercantilist regime, such as the state monopoly on trade in salt and Wang Anshi's State Trade Bureau, modeled after Sang Hongyang's "balanced standard" system. But, in contrast to the Qin-Han states, the Song revenue system relied heavily on indirect taxation, and its fiscal policies for the most part sought to harness market forces rather than suppress them. Thus the *ruzhong* policy offered merchants incentives to deliver provisions to frontier armies in lieu of an inefficient state-run procurement and transportation system. A significant share of the profitability of the salt monopoly derived from the utility of salt certificates as negotiable financial instruments in the private economy. The lucrative liquor monopoly – further evidence of the central place of consumption taxes in the Song fiscal regime – combined state-run breweries with franchising of brewing and sales rights in places where small economies of scale favored private entrepreneurship over government operations. This legacy of maximizing revenues in concert with market growth continued to prevail during the Southern Song, when the dynasty faced equally dire challenges to its survival.

7   The heyday of the Jiangnan economy (1127–1550)

The Jin conquest of North China in 1127 once again sundered China in two, just as in the Period of Disunion that followed the nomad invasions of the early fourth century. For the next two and a half centuries North China was ruled by foreign conquerors, first the Jurchen and then the Mongols, while the refugee Song court retained control of the southern half of the empire. The military and fiscal dilemmas that had bedeviled the Northern Song leadership persisted unabated throughout the Southern Song. Yet ambitious programs of state-led reform, exemplified by Wang Anshi's New Policies, lost favor after the debacle of 1127. During the Southern Song period, the ascendant Neo-Confucian political philosophy stressed moral rejuvenation and community-based reforms under local leadership rather than state-driven institutional transformation. Nonetheless, the turn toward monetization of taxes and procurement of military provisions through market mechanisms continued and even intensified during the Southern Song. In any event, in the early thirteenth century the state's ability to manage its fiscal affairs abruptly deteriorated. The outbreak of renewed war with the Jin and civil war in Sichuan in 1205–08 utterly bankrupted the central government, forcing it to resort to ruinous fiscal and monetary policies. The Mongol conquest of the Jin in 1234 only heightened frontier tensions. After the Mongol invasions of the Southern Song began in earnest in 1257, the Song leadership again attempted radical reforms, such as an ill-fated program of confiscating lands from great landowners in the Yangzi Delta, with disastrous results. In 1276 the Mongols under the leadership of Qubilai, grandson of the great khan Chinggis, seized the Song capital of Hangzhou, and in 1279 the Mongols deposed the last Song emperor.

The loss of the Central Plain and the relocation of the Southern Song capital to Hangzhou reinforced the preeminence of Jiangnan as both the agricultural and commercial heartland of the Song Empire. Swelled by refugees from the north, Jiangnan's population grew by nearly 50 percent between 1102 and 1223, in contrast to an estimated 9 percent increase for the Southern Song territories as a whole.[1] Market towns and trade networks sprang up in the wake of the rapid advance of rice paddy polders across the plains of the Yangzi Delta, linking rural producers of grain and silk to Hangzhou and other major cities. Urban growth and rising consumption demand in both the towns and the countryside of Jiangnan stimulated long-distance trade and regional specialization. Jiangnan's dominant position as the dynamic center of trade and industry within the Chinese economy would endure, irrespective of the rise and fall of dynastic houses, down to the nineteenth century.

Fiscal policy in the Southern Song

After the Jin conquest of North China, the Song state faced an even more dire military predicament. Sheer survival necessitated drastic fiscal measures. However, disenchantment with the failure of the mercantilist agenda of Wang Anshi and his successors undermined faith in the transformative power of the state. Instead, a new political and intellectual climate developed in which Confucian-educated leaders at the local level favored private initiatives focused on small-scale reforms: broadened access to education, infrastructural improvements such as roads, bridges, and water control projects, and famine and debt relief for the farming population.[2] Despite this philosophical shift, the stark challenge of the costs of war forced the imperial government to pursue even more radical efforts to mobilize revenues.

While the war with the Jin lasted, the court relinquished its fiscal powers to its generals. Only after Emperor Gaozong (r. 1127–62) and his prime minister, Qin Gui, negotiated a truce in 1141 that conceded Jin rule over North China could the Song leadership attempt to rebuild its fiscal infrastructure. The loss of the north dramatically changed the political economy of the empire and the logistics of defending its borders. As in the past, the Song defensive perimeter stretched from east to west over a vast territory. The marshy plains of the Huai River valley, utterly lacking natural defensive barriers, now formed the main battlefront between the Song and Jin armies. The Song stationed most of its armies in large camps on the southern bank of the Yangzi River, with smaller numbers at forward bases near the actual border. Far-off Sichuan – already a distinct fiscal and monetary region in the Northern Song – was even more remote from the new capital at Hangzhou and remained beyond the effective control of the central government. The court had lost control of nearly half of the Northern Song territory (reduced from 320+ to 170 prefectures), although

[1] Wu Songdi 2007: 183–84, tables 5.1, 5.2. In 1223, Jiangnan (i.e., Liangzhe circuit, encompassing southern Jiangsu and Zhejiang) comprised 21.7 percent of the total Southern Song population.

[2] Schirokauer and Hymes 1993; Bol 2008: 246–56.

perhaps only a third of its population. Most importantly, the exiled regime at Hangzhou retained control of the richest regions of the empire.

After the truce with the Jin was ratified in 1141, Gaozong and Qin Gui moved quickly to restore civilian rule. Through adroit political maneuvering reminiscent of the Song founder, Qin Gui succeeded in forcing the top generals to surrender their commands – and, in more draconian fashion, imprisoned and secretly executed Yue Fei, the leading champion of the irredentist cause to retake the north. But the general Wu Jie established a virtual satrapy in Sichuan, where he and his descendants exercised full military and fiscal powers until 1207. Along with restoring civilian control over the military (outside Sichuan), Qin Gui entrusted the provisioning of the armies to three General Commissariats (Zonglingsuo 總領所) at key transport junctions along the Yangzi River (Map 7.1). A fourth General Commissariat was added in Sichuan in 1149, but this office was firmly under the thumb of the Wu family generals.

The court achieved its main objective of preventing the fragmentation of the empire into regional warlord regimes, the fate that befell the Tang. But centralizing control over fiscal resources proved elusive. Since the 1120s an array of emergency revenue streams had been created to meet the escalating costs of war. Chief among them was a variety of revenues collected in coin (chiefly from liquor excises) under the collective rubric "frontier supply and defense funds" (*jingzong zhiqian* 經總制錢). In the early 1130s the court assessed a surtax known as the "monthly sequestration funds" (*yuezhuangqian* 月樁錢) – collected on a monthly rather than annual basis – on local governments, which invented a multitude of new fees, stamp taxes, and liquor levies to satisfy these demands from above.[3] Both the frontier supply and defense funds and the monthly sequestration funds were funneled directly to the General Commissariats and the Privy Purse and remained outside the purview of the fiscal intendants. After the cessation of hostilities in 1141, these *ad hoc* levies were retained as part of the routine tax obligations borne by local jurisdictions.[4]

The bifurcation between the Privy Purse and the Ministry of Revenue that emerged in the Northern Song persisted in the Southern Song as well. In addition to its traditional revenues, the Privy Purse captured a share of the

---

[3] Sogabe 1941b: 37–48; Bao Weimin 2001: 138–50.
[4] The burden of these taxes varied significantly across regions. For example, the monthly sequestration funds levy was a major source of revenue in Jiangxi, Jiangdong, Hubei, and Hunan circuits, but not collected at all in Liangzhe (Jiangsu and Zhejiang). Surtaxes on silk production were levied in silk-producing regions, but not elsewhere. Salt monopoly revenues were especially prominent in Guangdong and Fujian, which did not forward rice tribute to the capital or the armies. For details on the whole range of new supplementary taxes and regional variations in their fiscal impact, see Bao Weimin 2001.

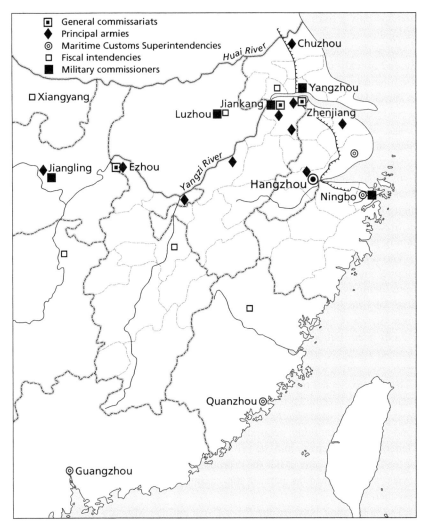

Map 7.1 Military procurement in the Southern Song
Source: Nagai 1992: 1249, map 3.

new taxes. The court also diluted the authority of the Ministry of Revenue by assigning some fiscal responsibilities to other circuit-level offices, including the Judicial Intendants (提點刑獄司) and the Tea and Salt Intendants (提舉茶鹽司; or in some circuits the Ever-Normal Granary Intendants [提舉常平司]). For example, the frontier supply and defense funds were placed under the authority of the Judicial Intendants rather than the Fiscal Intendants to ensure direct transmission of these revenues to the Privy Purse and the General Commissariats. Regional fiscal authorities controlled nearly 60 percent of state income – and, through transfers of funds from other agencies, more than 70 percent of expenditures. Only a mere 17 percent of total revenue was under the direct control of the Ministry of Revenue (Table 7.1).

The General Commissariats derived their revenues directly from local jurisdictions, bypassing the Fiscal Intendants and the Ministry of Revenue. The Huaidong General Commissariat, based at Zhenjiang, drew resources from multiple sources (Table 7.2; Map 7.1).

In the 1160s the Huaidong commissariat supplied provisions for 68,000 troops, 50,000 of whom were stationed at forward bases. Most of the commissariat's grain income was derived from twice-a-year tax revenues in Jiangdong and Jiangxi circuits, but at least 20 percent was procured through market purchases – the so-called "harmonious purchases" (*hedi*) – in Jiangxi. The commissariat's cash income, in contrast, largely came from Liangzhe circuit, primarily from salt monopoly revenues (60 percent of the total). Adjusted for inflation (largely caused by currency depreciation), the revenues of the Huaidong commissariat remained stable throughout the Southern Song.[5]

As the Huaidong General Commissariat data reveals, the shift from in-kind payments to money taxes became even more dramatic during the Southern Song. At current rice prices, cash revenues comprised 75–87 percent of the commissariat's total income in the second half of the twelfth century. Empire-wide grain receipts from the twice-a-year tax fell from 25–30 million *shi* per year in the eleventh century to 6 million *shi* in the late twelfth century.[6] As already noted, Southern Song policymakers created numerous supplementary taxes paid in money, such as the frontier supply and defense and monthly sequestration levies. These supplementary taxes amounted to roughly half of the statutory twice-a-year tax assessments. Because of the fragmented fiscal structure of the Southern Song state, it is difficult to achieve a full accounting of government revenues and expenditures for this period. Cobbling together scattered data from the mid-late twelfth century, we find that the combined revenues from the supplementary taxes and the commodity monopolies equaled the peak cash income (73 million *guan*) of the entire empire in the New Policies era (Table 7.3).[7] However, adjusted for the rise in grain prices, real per capita tax revenues during the first century of the Southern Song remained no higher than the level of the New Policies era.[8]

---

[5] Nagai 1992.   [6] Wang Shengduo 1995: 580.
[7] Other reports from *c.* 1185–90 estimated total government revenues in the range of 82 million *guan*. See Guo Zhengzhong 1985: 182–83. Deflating the Sichuan revenues as in Table 7.3 would yield approximately 75 million *guan*, nearly identical to the calculation in Table 7.3.
[8] Liu Guanglin 2008: 226–27. In fact, real per capita revenues reached their peak in the first half of the eleventh century, not during Wang Anshi's regime.

Table 7.1 *Government revenues, 1172*

	Privy Purse		Ministry of Revenue			Regional/local fiscal authorities	
	Revenues	Percent of total		Revenues	Percent of total		Revenues	Percent of total
(1) Neicang Treasury 內藏庫	134.37	6.1	(5) Zuocang Western Depot 左藏西庫	371.98	16.8	(7) Fiscal Intendants	611.21	27.6
Frontier supply and defense funds	88.67	4.0	Land tax	99.53	4.50	Land Tax	362.02	16.4
Domestic tribute	0.21	< 0.1	Wine monopoly	159.17	7.2	Salt monopoly	249.20	11.3
Coinage	5.68	0.3	Head tax (身丁錢)	20.36	0.9			
Maritime customs	33.88	1.5	Grand Ceremonial (Dali 大禮) tax	2.01	0.1	(8) Militia Treasuries	120.72	5.5
Other	5.93	0.2	Monopoly profits	90.94	4.1			
						(9) General Commissariats 總領所	525.93	23.8
(2) Court	109.71	5.0	(6) Military Bonus Treasury 犒賞酒庫	12.26	0.5	Breweries and ferries	46.62	2.1
Harmonious purchases (和買)	109.21	4.9	Wine monopoly	12.26	0.5	Monopoly profits	181.88	8.2
Other	0.50	< 0.1				Frontier supply and defense funds	230.37	10.4
						Monthly sequestration funds	67.06	3.0
(3) Zuocang Southern Depot 左藏南庫	178.81	8.1						
Breweries and ferries	69.23	3.1						
Other	109.59	4.9						
(4) Monopoly Revenue Bureau 権貨務	148.23	6.7						
Total Income		25.9			17.3			56.9

Table 7.2 *Revenues of the Huaidong General Commissariat*, c. *1164*

Revenue	Tax category	Geographic source
Rice (*shi*)		
600,000	Twice-a-year tax	Jiangdong, Jiangxi circuits
150,000	*Hedi* purchases	Jiangxi circuit
?*	*Hedi* purchases	Liangzhe circuit
Total: 750,000+		
Money (*guan*)		
3.6 million	Salt monopoly	Liangzhe circuit
1.8 million	Frontier supply and defense funds, silk commutation levy (*zheboqian* 折帛錢)	Suzhou, Changzhou, Zhenjiang prefectures (all in Liangzhe circuit)
1.56 million	Monthly sequestration funds	Jiangxi circuit
Total: 5.96 million		

*Emergency requisitions of *hedi* purchases were made in Liangzhe.
Source: Nagai 1992.

Table 7.3 *Central government cash revenues in the Southern Song*
(all figures in millions of *guan*)

	Sichuan* (c. 1142)	Southeast circuits (c. 1185)	Southeast circuits (variable dates)
Shanggong portion of twice-a-year tax	2.0	2.0	
Liquor excise	2.0		6.3 (c. 1160)
Salt monopoly	1.9		27.0 (1169)
Tea monopoly	0.5		4.2 (c. 1175)
All monopoly revenues and *hedi/hemai* income		44.9	
Frontier supply and defense funds (*jingzong zhiqian*)	1.2	14.4	
Monthly sequestration funds (*yuezhuangqian*)	N.A.	4.0	
Paper money service fees	0.2	N.A.	
Total	7.8	65.3	

*Sichuan figures have been deflated by 50 percent because Sichuan revenues were calculated in *qianyin* paper money, which was worth roughly half of the bronze coin/*huizi* paper money in circulation in the southeast circuits.
Sources: Guo Zhengzhong 1983: 179, table 6, 181, table 8; Wang Shengduo 1995: 703, appendix table 4, 706, appendix table 6, 716, appendix table 7.

Table 7.4 *Cash outlays in Fuzhou prefecture, Fujian, c. 1182*
(figures in thousands of *guan*)

Prefectural budgeted expenditures		700.0
Revenues forwarded to central government		542.9
Shanggong silver*	251.2	
Shanggong coin	6.0	
Frontier supply and defense funds	245.8	
(*jingzong zhiqian*)		
Other	39.9	
Total expenditures		1,242.9
Income		660.0
Deficit		−582.9

*Payment made in silver, expressed here in equivalent in coin.
Source: Bao Weimin 2001: 264, table 6–7.

Ironically, the proliferation of revenue demands imposed by the central government resulted in greater autonomy for local jurisdictions. Local officials often turned to non-statutory levies to meet their tax quotas, or found ways to reduce spending. Fiscal accounts from Fuzhou prefecture (Fujian) from *c.* 1182 shows that statutory taxation supplied only 53 percent of the cash revenues needed to meet its budgeted expenditures (Table 7.4).[9] In response, the prefecture sharply reduced its expenditures, for example by filling only 83 percent of its full quota of military and police personnel.[10] The apportionment of the tax burden among the local populace was determined less by the decisions of policymakers in Hangzhou than by local magistrates obliged to negotiate among competing stakeholders.[11] Although the Song may have been more successful in implementing progressive taxation based on household wealth, regional imbalances in tax liabilities grew increasingly stark.

The fiscal distress of the Southern Song state, together with a steep decline in the output of its mints, led to greater reliance on paper money in both payments to the state and private commerce. Copper production, which had soared in the eleventh century, fell by more than 90 percent as the major mines became depleted. Shortages of currency prompted local officials and money-changers to issue negotiable bills, but these notes circulated only in the capital and a few other areas. In 1161, amid renewed warfare with the Jin, the Hangzhou court introduced a new paper money known as *huizi* 會子 in the southeastern provinces separate from the existing paper money circulating in Sichuan (where the original *jiaozi* bills had been replaced by a new paper

---

[9] Deficits of similar magnitude were also reported for other local jurisdictions in many parts of South China at this time. See Bao Weimin 2001: 166–68.
[10] Liu Guanglin 2008: 232.   [11] Bao Weimin 2001: 106–16.

Table 7.5 *Volume of* huizi *paper currency in circulation in the Southern Song*

Issue number	Term of circulation	Quantity of notes (millions of *guan*)	Total volume of notes in circulation at time of issue (millions of *guan*)
1	1168–71	10	10
2	1170–73	10	10
3	1171–80	10	10
4	1173–83	10	10
5	1180–86	10	20
6	1183–89	18	28
7	1186–95	23.23	[41.2]*
8	1189–98	?	[46.5]
9	1195–1204	30	[53.2]
10	1195–1204	?	[60.0]
11	1204–11	36.33	83.9
12	1204–11	47.58	83.9
13	1207–11	55.48	139.4
14	1211–34	112.63	232.4**
15	1211–34	119.80	232.4**
16	1231–40	133.55	365.9
17	1234–64	139.86	273.4
18	1240–76	?	?

*Numbers in brackets are estimates based on the assumption that the quantity of issues no. 8 and 10 were the same as the previous issues, no. 7 and 9 respectively.
**Beginning with issue no. 14 the Song government abandoned the principle of fixed terms of expiry and instead repeatedly issued the same notes over an extended period of time. Thus the figures in this column for issues no. 14–15 indicate the total volume of notes issued over their lifetime (1211–34), not when they were first issued.
Source: von Glahn 2005: 77, table 4.1.

money, *qianyin* 錢引, in 1107). For several decades the government managed its paper money prudently, restricting the quantity in circulation, requiring tax payments in *huizi* as well as coin, and periodically buying back excess notes using its silver reserves. Heartened by public confidence in the *huizi* bills, the court established two additional paper monies in Huainan and Hubei-Hunan, dividing the empire into four distinct monetary regions.[12]

In the early thirteenth century, however, fiscal exigency caused the Song court to begin to issue paper money in excessive quantities, resulting in substantial depreciation (Table 7.5). A disastrous Song offensive launched against the Jin in 1206 and the abortive attempt by the Wu warlord in Sichuan to declare independence from Song rule once again triggered a surge in military expenditures. The state quadrupled the volume of *huizi* in circulation,

[12] On the origins and development of Song paper monies, see von Glahn 2005.

from 60 million to 230 million *guan*. The market value of *huizi* soon fell to 60 percent of its face value, and at their nadir in the 1240s *huizi* bills were discounted by as much as 75 percent.[13] Nonetheless, *huizi* and *qianyin* largely displaced bronze coin, at least in larger transactions, in both public and private finance. Nearly all records of land sales from 1215 onward were denominated in paper money.[14] Silver – in the form of ingots rather than coin – also became an important component of the money supply at this time. As Table 7.4 shows, silver comprised 46 percent of the revenues Fuzhou prefecture forwarded to the central government. About 30 percent of the salaries of officials and soldiers were disbursed in silver, and the Song required that a minimum of 24 percent of the purchase price of salt and tea monopoly certificates be paid in silver.[15] The slackening demand for bronze coin as a means of exchange fueled the boom in the export of coin to foreign markets, principally Japan, beginning around 1170, shortly after the *huizi* paper money was introduced (see below).

Echoing Confucian critics of the time, modern historians often have characterized the Southern Song as a predatory state whose profligate spending and voracious demands for revenue impoverished farming families and sharpened economic inequality, culminating in the ignominious Mongol conquest.[16] These judgments primarily cite the proliferation of new taxes, mostly imposed on commerce and consumption, and the severe depreciation that resulted from wanton over-issue of paper money in the thirteenth century. However, efforts to quantify the burden of taxation have not supported claims that fiscal and monetary policies caused havoc to the private economy.[17] Dour assessments of fiscal mismanagement generally have overlooked the fact that in the mid-eleventh century the Song state turned the twice-a-year tax assessments into fixed quotas per canton, regardless of actual population or farm income.[18] Subsequently the twice-a-year tax revenues remained essentially unchanged, or even declined, over the remainder of the dynasty, despite the substantial increases in population, cultivated land, and total agricultural output. Robert Hartwell's reconstruction of central government revenues – the most thorough

---

[13] Ibid.: 76–81.

[14] See the data presented in Zhu Ruixi 2006: 129–44. In addition, virtually all of the land sales contracts from 1215 onward cited in the legal casebook *Enlightened Judgments* denote payments in paper money. See McKnight and Liu 1998, *passim*.

[15] Von Glahn 2013: 22. On the expansion in the use of silver as money in the Southern Song, see Wang Wencheng 2001.

[16] On the predatory character of the Southern Song state, see Smith 1992; Bao Weimin 2001; Zhang Jinling 2001. Liang Gengyao (1984) focused instead on the debilitating effects of rural economic inequality.

[17] Liu Guanglin (2008) has exposed flaws in Bao Weimin's (2001) analysis of local taxation in the Southern Song and persuasively refutes at least in part Bao's claims of onerous increases in the real tax burden.

[18] Shiba 1988: 152–61; Bao Weimin 2001: 246–50.

attempt to quantify the burden of taxation – suggests that the state's share of total output remained roughly constant from 1077 to the end of the Southern Song.[19] Studies focused on rural households also have challenged claims that state exactions impoverished the rural economy. Nagai Chiaki's simulation of household income and tax expenditures in Jiangnan indicates that farm families cultivating 20 *mu* of high-yield rice paddy (or 40 *mu* of low-yield lands) could discharge their tax obligations and readily maintain a comfortable level of subsistence.[20] Since it is generally accepted that the average farm size in Southern Song Jiangnan was 40 *mu*, most farm families possessed adequate resources to meet their needs.[21] A recent analysis of rural living standards in Suzhou likewise concludes that the average farming family achieved an income well above the minimum level of subsistence.[22] But natural disasters such as flood and drought as well as inefficiencies in markets encumbered by slow and uneven modes of transport periodically triggered food shortages and famine crises.

Wide seasonal oscillations in grain prices encouraged the practice of regrating, whereby merchants stockpiled grain purchased cheaply after the autumn harvest to await the inevitable surge of prices in the spring and summer months when household food supplies ran low. One thirteenth-century magistrate reported that his single county alone numbered more than thirty grain stockpilers.[23] In contrast to both the Tang and Ming-Qing periods, during the Song state-run "ever-normal granaries" (*changping cang* 常平倉) played only a minimal role in regulating the food supply and grain prices. At their peak in 1076 ever-normal granaries possessed only a fifth of the grain and money assets compared to the maximum levels in the Tang.[24] Philanthropically minded patricians, inspired by Neo-Confucian ideals of community-based social welfare, founded "community granaries" (*shecang* 社倉) to lend grain to the indigent on more favorable terms than pawnbrokers offered. But these institutions rarely endured for long, falling victim to the penury that afflicted their clientele.[25] Local magistrates often ruefully concluded that the operation of the market was more effective in resolving food shortages than either government intervention or private charity.[26]

Trade, enterprise, and finance

Advances in the commercialization of agriculture and specialization of production during the Song were fostered by the expanding reach of markets, both at the local and national levels. National markets formed for both staples and

---

[19] Hartwell 1988: 78–79. See also Liu Guanglin 2008: 224–26.   [20] Nagai 2000: 129–33.
[21] Li Bozhong 2003: 162–63, which relies on data from Liang Gengyao 1984: 100–4.
[22] Geng Yuanli 2007.   [23] Jiang Xidong 2002: 266, 272.   [24] Nishioku 2004: 341.
[25] von Glahn 1993.   [26] Hymes 1993.

Table 7.6 *Commercial tax revenues in Southern Song Jiangnan*
(figures in *guan*)

| | | 1077 Commercial tax revenue | Southern Song commercial tax revenue | | |
			Revenue	Date	Percent change
Hangzhou 杭州	Prefecture	183,814	420,000	1265–74	+228
Zhenjiang 鎮江	Prefecture	37,503	206,298	1208–24	+550
Changzhou 常州	Prefecture	64,953	135,784	?	+209
Shaoxing 紹興	Prefecture	66,207	105,314	1201	+159
Ningbo 寧波	Prefecture	26,947	76,192	1227	+283
Huating 華亭	County	10,618	48,464	1193	+456
Jiangyin 江陰	County	4,272	41,907	1228–33	+981

Source: Liang Gengyao 1997: 483–85.

luxury goods. The surpluses generated by the rice economy and specialized rural production of goods such as silk yarn, tea, and indigo stimulated regular trade between town and country. Periodic markets sprang up in the countryside. These markets were held every three, six, or ten days to cater to the needs of rural inhabitants. Some of these markets grew into permanent towns of several hundred households, including brewers, butchers, blacksmiths, and other tradesmen. As we saw in Chapter 6, commercial growth fostered urban development, especially in the Jiangnan region. Although we lack empire-wide commercial tax data for the Southern Song, commercial taxes in Jiangnan cities rose sharply compared to the Northern Song (Table 7.6), attesting to the robust vitality of the regional economy. Sustained growth in urban population led to a corresponding increase in the concentration of purchasing power in the cities.

For the great majority of the population, consumption remained largely focused on foodstuffs. Wu Zimu, describing city life in late Song Hangzhou, declared that rice, firewood, vegetable oil, salt, soy sauce, vinegar, and tea were the "seven items indispensable to the daily life of every household."[27] Fang Hui, a contemporary of Wu, observed that villagers bringing rice to trade at a market town in the Yangzi Delta purchased incense, candles, spirit offerings, cooking oil, salt, soy sauce, vinegar, flour, noodles, pepper, ginger, and medicines.[28] Consumption by the urban middle and upper classes was far more varied than that of rural inhabitants. The Northern Song capital of Kaifeng numbered more than 6,400 merchant, artisan, and professional businesses in a hundred different trades (*hang*), and in thirteenth-century

[27] Cited in Shiba 1968: 184–85.   [28] Cited in von Glahn 2003b: 182.

Hangzhou a total of 414 *hang* – evidence of meticulous specialization of handicrafts and retail trade – catered to the needs of the court, the imperial government, and a city population of more than one million people.

Nevertheless merchants lacked honored status or any legal entitlement to economic privileges. The *hang* groups, created at the instigation of the state, existed primarily to fulfill government requisitions for goods and services (such as appraising the value of tax goods, auditing accounts, and assaying precious metals). The *hang* provided only weak organization and leadership to the merchant community. State officials repeatedly intervened to prevent *hang* from restricting entry into a trade or fixing prices.[29] The economic and social solidarity fostered by guild institutions in medieval Europe and elsewhere were conspicuously absent in Song China, despite accusations that the great merchants in trades like tea and salt acted as cartels.

Cities became hubs of finance as well as commerce. Major commercial centers boasted a broad array of specialists in financial and credit services, including goldsmiths and silversmiths, moneychangers, pawnbrokers, and dealers in bills of exchange and commercial paper such as salt and tea certificates. By the late eleventh century merchants commonly settled accounts through assignment transfers on bank deposits. Merchants also negotiated consignment contracts (*she* 賒) to obtain goods on credit. In 1092 the prefect of Hangzhou asserted that "as a rule cash is scarcely used in private trade in recent times. Instead retail shops rely on guarantees provided by trustworthy and wealthy individuals to make purchases on consignment from traveling merchants. Year after year they redeem the old debts and make new purchases."[30] The growing use of paper money and silver in the Southern Song century intensified the demand for moneychangers who dealt in gold, silver, bronze coin, and paper instruments and accepted deposits of funds. Deposit banks played only a modest role in finance, however, since they did not lend money either to the government or private clients. Despite the growing frequency of transfer banking, banks – in the sense of institutions providing long-term credit – did not emerge before the nineteenth century.

The Chinese state assumed only a minor role in the formal regulation of commerce. Private contracts were the primary means of establishing ownership rights and business obligations. Government endorsement of land sale contracts – for a hefty stamp tax that rose from 4 to 12 percent or more over

---

[29] Onodera 1966; Miyazawa 1998: 139–204. The views of Quan Hansheng (1935) and Katō Shigeshi (1937), who likened the *hang* institution to the guilds of medieval Europe, are no longer considered tenable. Nonetheless, Chinese scholarship continues to emphasize the corporate character of *hang* and their independence from state control. See Yang Dequan 1982; Qi Xia 1999, 2: 1102–16.

[30] "Jiao jin yingzhao suolun sishi zhuang" 繳進應詔所論四事狀, in *SDPQJ*, 2: 503. On *she* consignment sales – which required the intermediation of a broker – see Katō 1952c.

the course of the Southern Song – provided an important measure of valid-ation. Contracts did not require official verification to be legally binding, but because of the central importance of contracts in establishing property rights most buyers were willing to pay the stamp tax to certify land transactions. Much civil litigation centered on enforcement of contracts in matters such as marriage, adoption, inheritance, employment, property transfers, and busi-ness transactions. Although magistrates generally honored private contracts, they voided those that violated imperial law or the norms of kinship practices.[31]

The crucial importance of contracts in business dealings in turn created a demand for intermediation. Brokers (*yaren* 牙人, *shikuai* 市儈, *zangkuai* 駔儈) – some licensed by the state, others working in the shadows of legality – offered a wide range of intermediation services such as negotiating sales of goods and real property, notarizing contracts, registering deeds, acting as guarantors, hiring laborers and servants, making tax payments, handling con-signments of goods, and operating inns and warehouses. Officially licensed brokers also acted as commission agents for the state, for example in managing the tea monopoly in Sichuan, procuring rice through the "harmonious purchase" system of compulsory sales, and determining the value of cargoes of imported goods for the purpose of assessing customs duties. Farmers often marketed their crops through brokers. In addition, brokers negotiated advance sale contracts (also known as *she* 賒) whereby merchants would make pay-ments to farmers and weavers in exchange for future purchases at pre-arranged prices. Over the course of the Song dynasty brokers became more tightly regulated by the state, which was particularly determined to curb the growing practice of proprietary trading. In the Southern Song references to brokers buying and selling goods on their own account abruptly multiplied, as did complaints of the monopolistic leverage brokers wielded to the disadvantage of free trade. The brokerage system facilitated trade, but at the same time it revealed the limitations in the capacity of markets to integrate producers and consumers.[32]

The Song state's interventionist commercial policies and its heavy reliance on taxes levied on trade and consumption hardly stifled the spirit of commer-cial enterprise. Contemporaries recognized that just as money must circulate to fulfill its economic and social functions, so too capital must be put to work through investment. A Song statesman observed in 1126 that the rich mer-chants of Kaifeng never allow their capital to remain idle, but rather keep it constantly employed by investing in wholesale merchandising, moneylending,

[31] Hansen 1995: 78–104.
[32] Shiba 1968: 391–407, 1970: 165–73; Miyazawa 1998: 205–78; Lamouroux 2002; Li Weiguo 2007.

and trading voyages.[33] In his *Precepts for Social Life* (1178), the retired official Yuan Cai extolled the virtues of compound interest, observing that investing in a pawnbrokerage could double one's capital in the span of three years. Kinfolk who jointly invested in family businesses earned sufficient returns to temper the quarrels and dissensions over money and inheritance that often tore families asunder.[34] Commercial profit readily evaded the twice-a-year tax system, which was premised on a purely agrarian revenue base. Thus from the time of Wang Anshi's New Policies, local officials generally assessed twice-a-year taxes on calculations of household assets (*wuli* 物力, *jiaye* 家業) rather than landownership alone. A memorandum of 1169 identified pawn-brokerages, wholesale merchandising (*tingta* 停塌), commercial real estate (*fanglang* 房廊), retail stores, and leasing oxcarts and ships as lucrative sources of income that should be subject to twice-a-year taxation.[35] In the late twelfth century owners of pawnbrokerages and commercial real estate in Jiankang (Nanjing) reportedly had investment capital measured in tens of thousands of *guan*, while those in the prefecture's smaller cities "merely" had assets of 6,000–7,000 *guan* and invested capital of 2,000–3,000 *guan*.[36] But even the latter would have qualified as first-rank households (with assets of 6,000 *guan*) under the twice-a-year tax system, a category that probably comprised just 1 percent of the total population. At this time fewer than half of all households held assets worth more than 38.5 *guan* (the dividing line between the fourth and fifth household ranks, with the latter exempt from most extraordinary taxes).[37]

Business enterprise largely remained wedded to the family institution. The household was the fundamental social and economic unit under Chinese law. Property belonged to the household, not individuals. Business enterprises had no legal existence apart from the household of their owners, and thus naturally took the form of family firms. From the Song dynasty onward various kinds of partnerships were created to pool capital and dilute risks. Lacking standing as legal entities, the financing and operation of partnerships – like all business transactions – was governed by contracts.

The close relationships between long-distance merchants and local brokers and commission agents undoubtedly provided impetus for the formation of partnerships. Partnerships also emerged from the practice of merchants travel-ing together as groups in caravans and maritime voyages. Partnerships could

---

[33] Cited in Shiba 1968: 118; Shiba 1970: 32 erroneously dates this passage to 1137.
[34] Cited in Ebrey 1984b: 199–200.   [35] Cited in Shiba 1968: 114.
[36] Wang Zengyu 1985: 72. One legal suit recorded in the late Song legal casebook *Enlightened Judgments* concerned a pawnbrokerage that had capital assets of 3,608 *guan* and a monthly income of 35 *guan*, and thus earned a 12 percent annual return on total assets. See *QMJ*, 1: 230–32; McKnight and Liu 1998: 261.
[37] Yanagida 1986: 66–7, 109.

take a variety of forms. Most commonly, a passive investor entrusted funds to a merchant or agent in exchange for either a fixed rate of return or an equal division of the profits. In long-distance and maritime trade, such *commenda*-style partnerships generally took the form of single ventures; once the voyage or trading season was concluded, the partners divided their profits and dissolved the partnership. But this arrangement also was employed to hire managers – in many cases chosen from trustworthy household bondservants – on a permanent basis to operate pawnbrokerages and other commercial enterprises.[38] Joint-capital enterprises, in which merchants pooled their capital resources, sharing risks and dividing profits in proportion to their share of the subscribed capital, also existed. Joint-capital partnerships were common in commercial sectors with especially high risks (e.g., overseas trading voyages) or high capital requirements (e.g., the salt and tea trades and pawnbrokerages).[39] In addition, groups of investors often formed joint-capital firms to obtain brewery franchises. The government sold brewery franchises at auction in return for fixed annual payments to the government, an arrangement that was fraught with risk.[40] Despite these innovations in partnership arrangements, however, there is no evidence for permanent companies of merchants during the Song.

As noted in Chapter 6, a decisive shift in China's international trade away from the overland Silk Road to maritime routes already was well underway by the tenth century. With the northern frontiers of the Song controlled by enemy states, Silk Road trade declined precipitously. Nonetheless the Song conducted cross-border trade with the Liao, Xixia, and Jin at supervised "mutual trade" (*hushi* 互市) depots. Much of this trade consisted of an exchange of Chinese tea for steppe horses. The Southern Song also exported grain, medicines, plow oxen, and exotic goods from the South Seas to the Jin in return for silk, leather, and ginseng. Heavy excises and controls on exports prompted substantial smuggling of contraband goods including bronze coin, precious metals, iron and leather wares, and books.[41]

Maritime trade continued to grow during the Northern Song with the full encouragement of the government. During the twelfth century – before restrictive measures and high tariffs were applied in the 1160s – the state reaped 1–2 million *guan* annually in maritime customs revenues.[42] Flourishing maritime trade stimulated Chinese industry, especially the manufacture of ceramics,

---

[38] Shiba 1968: 441–51, 1970: 190–96; Jiang Xidong 2002: 46–52.

[39] Shiba 1968: 458–61, 1970: 199–200. In another case recorded in the *Enlightened Judgments*, a private investor deposited 100 *guan* in a pawnbrokerage in return for 20 percent annual interest. See *QMJ*, 1: 336–37; McKnight and Liu 1998: 333–34.

[40] Jiang Xidong 2002: 54–5.   [41] Shiba 1983.

[42] On maritime customs revenues, see Huang Chunyan 2003: 169–76. The progressive liberalization of Song maritime trade policies down to the 1160s is traced in Heng 2009: 38–59. Hartwell

which surpassed silk goods as China's main export. The ports of Ningbo
and Quanzhou along the southeast coast eclipsed older ports to the north
(Yangzhou) and south (Guangzhou) as the paramount centers of
overseas trade.

Maritime trade also received a boost from technological innovations, such
as the use of the maritime compass and the construction of so-called "Fuzhou
ships," whose deep keels and double-thickness hulls provided added stability
for open ocean voyages.[43] A 300-ton Fuzhou ship could make the voyage from
Ningbo to Japan in five to seven days. The long voyage between China and
Arabia, Persia, or India was broken up into several stages that corresponded to
the seasonal shifts in the monsoon winds. Chinese merchants usually disposed
of their cargoes at the Srivijayan ports in Sumatra and the Malay Peninsula
rather than continue on into the Indian Ocean. Most imports from the Indian
Ocean and Southeast Asia were luxury goods such as frankincense and other
aromatics, ivory, coral, cinnabar, aromatic woods, and pepper. By the late
thirteenth century cotton fabrics from India became a leading import commodity as well.[44]

Trade with Japan developed at a rapid pace, especially during the Southern
Song period. Chinese merchants imported bulk goods such as timber and
sulfur as well as large quantities of gold from Japan, while exporting ceramics,
silk, iron, books, and especially bronze coin. In the late twelfth century, as the
use of paper currency proliferated in China, exports of bronze coin to Japan
reached enormous proportions and led to the adoption of Song coin as the
monetary standard within Japan. The drain of bronze coin abroad alarmed
Song statesmen. Although the Song government enacted more restrictive
policies toward maritime trade after 1160 in an effort to interdict the export
of coin, these measures did little to inhibit smuggling.[45]

During the first century of the Song the port of Quanzhou in Fujian emerged
as a prime destination for foreign traders from the Nanyang (the "South Seas"
of Southeast Asia and the Indian Ocean), rivaling Guangzhou as a center of
overseas trade.[46] According to an inscription written in 1095, two convoys of
twenty ships each arrived at Quanzhou from the Nanyang each year. A 1206
report on foreigners trading at Quanzhou listed merchants from Arabia,

(1989: 462–65) argues that the shift in Song policy toward an anti-trade stance after 1160 was
prompted by the surging illegal export of Chinese coin abroad.
[43] Shiba 1968: 58–60, 1970: 6–7. Zhou Qufei, writing in 1178, claimed that ships engaging in
trade in Southeast Asia could carry several hundred men and stores for a year's journey. Marco
Polo, who visited China a century later, reported that sea-going Chinese ships could hold 4,000
to 12,000 quintals of cargo, equivalent to 224 to 672 tons. See Needham 1971: 464, 466.
[44] On Chinese trade with Southeast Asia and the Indian Ocean in this period, see Wade 2009;
Heng 2009.
[45] von Glahn 2014.   [46] This paragraph is based on So 2000.

Srivijaya, Angkor, Brunei, Java, Champa, Pagan, Korea, and various Philippine chiefdoms. Maritime trade stimulated local industries in Quanzhou city and its hinterland such as ceramics, sugar, wine, and salt, all of which became export commodities. Maritime trade thus promoted cross-sectoral prosperity, regional commercial integration, and urban growth.

In the thirteenth century, however, Quanzhou's foreign trade waned. Disruptions in overseas markets – Angkor's subjugation of Champa, the Mongol invasions of Korea in the 1220s, and the demise of the Srivijaya confederation – undoubtedly contributed to the downturn. More importantly, however, Quanzhou's decline can be attributed to the rise of Ningbo in concert with Japan's growing importance as China's main overseas trading partner. A large community of Ningbo merchants settled in Hakata, Japan's principal port, and developed networks of personal and economic alliance with the aristocrats, religious establishments, and courtier warlords that dominated Japanese society and economy. The robust growth of Ningbo's foreign trade during the twelfth and thirteenth centuries was due in no small measure to the strength of this merchant network.[47] The Sinan shipwreck – a Japanese vessel laden with 28 tons of Chinese coin as well as ceramics and other cargo that sank off the coast of Korea in 1323 on its return from Ningbo – attests to the importance of the Ningbo-Hakata connection. The vessel had been commissioned by the Tōfukuji monastery in Kyoto to obtain coin and goods from China to finance the rebuilding of the monastery after a devastating fire in 1319. The actual outfitting of the vessel at Ningbo appears to have been undertaken by Chinese merchants based in Hakata who acted as agents for the monastery.[48]

The impact of foreign trade on the Song economy was largely concentrated in the coastal areas around major ports such as Ningbo, Quanzhou, and Guangzhou. But the scale of this trade was still significant. Robert Hartwell has estimated that maritime trade generated 1.7 percent of Song China's gross domestic product (GDP) by 1100.[49] By comparison, it has been estimated that international trade comprised approximately 4 percent of GDP for Europe as a whole in the late eighteenth century, and probably around 10 percent for countries strongly oriented toward maritime trade such as England, the Netherlands, and Portugal.[50] The extension of China's commerce outward

---

[47] Von Glahn 2014. Other scholars (So 2000; Schottenhammer 2001) have attributed the decline of Quanzhou's foreign trade to structural changes in the local economy and the adverse effects of the export of bronze coin. In my view the export of coin caused no harm to the Chinese economy, and indeed far more coin was exported from Ningbo than Quanzhou.

[48] Kawazoe 1993.

[49] Hartwell 1989: 453. It's worth noting that Hartwell's estimate of Song gross domestic product (GDP) is considerably higher than that of other scholars. On the problems of estimating GDP in premodern China, see Chapter 9.

[50] Bairoch 1976: 79; O'Brien 1982: 4–5.

via maritime trade complemented the growing penetration of the market into the agrarian economy exemplified by the commodification of land.

The land market

Much of South China was still a frontier in the twelfth century. In the interior, timber cutting, mining, and tea cultivation spearheaded settlement and economic development. As we have seen, rice farming initially was concentrated in the valleys above the flood plains. The development of poldering and other water control technologies transformed the Yangzi River Delta and the lacustrine plains of the Middle Yangzi region into fertile rice-growing regions. Lightly populated interior provinces such as Jiangxi and Hunan produced rice surpluses that were exported to other regions. But it was in Jiangnan, the most densely settled and urbanized region, that the prosperity of rice agriculture made land a highly profitable investment.

Apart from the newly reclaimed polder fields in the delta marshlands, large landholdings were rare in Jiangnan. Some families possessed extensive landholdings of 1,000 or more *mu*, but such cases were rare.[51] The intensive labor rice farming required and the inherent limitations of irrigation technologies favored small units of cultivation. Farming families, whether landowners or tenants (or both), on average cultivated 40 *mu* of arable land, but typically they worked several separate plots rather than a single contiguous farm. Tenancy and sales records suggest that many parcels of rice paddy in the Yangzi Delta were 1–2 *mu* (or less) in size, with the largest parcels (a small proportion of the total) in the range of 10–20 *mu*. In some cases even small landholdings of 10–15 *mu* were comprised of 8–10 parcels farmed by three different tenants.[52]

Wealthy Jiangnan landowners invariably engaged tenant farmers rather than attempt to organize and coordinate cultivation of numerous scattered plots of land. Confucian patricians extolled the mutual economic interdependence of landlords and tenants as the cornerstone of social order. In his treatise on household management Yuan Cai urged his peers to display

[51] McDermott 1984: 18.
[52] Yanagida 1963: 101–04. The great majority of land sales mentioned in the *Enlightened Judgments* legal casebook involved parcels of 10 or fewer *mu* (in one case, a mere 0.66 *mu*). Several cases concerned much larger estates: in one, the estate of a high official was said to yield an income of 1,300 *shi*, which probably was equivalent to 400–650 *mu*; in another case the yield was 290 *shi*, suggesting an estate of 100–150 *mu*. But these figures reflected the size of the entire estate, not individual parcels. See *QMJ*, 1: 135, 141; McKnight and Liu 1998: 164, 171. The few surviving Southern Song land sales contracts also mostly referred to land sales of 1–10 *mu*, or even smaller parcels. See Zhu Ruixi 2006: 130–41.

solicitude and magnanimity toward the tenant farmers upon whom their economic fortunes rested:

The household's plowing and planting are the product of the toil of tenant farmers. How can you not value them? When members of your tenants' families give birth, get married, build houses, or die, you should give them generous gifts. If during the farming season they need to borrow, do not charge much interest. During years of floods and droughts, check the extent of the damage and quickly make reductions or exemptions from the rent owed.

Make no unfair demands on your tenants and do not impose labor duties at unreasonable times. Do not let your male relatives or managers harass them at their whim. Do not raise the annual rent because of something an enemy of theirs has said. Do not force them to take loans in order to collect high interest from them. Do not let greedy thoughts arise when you see they have their own fields.

If you look after your tenants and cherish them as though they were your relatives, you will be able to rely on their strength for your food and clothing, and you will be able to raise your head without shame.[53]

Needless to say, Yuan Cai's exhortations imply that all too often landlords failed to treat their tenants with dignity and compassion. Indeed, his comments reveal that landlords bore little responsibility for the welfare of their tenants. Although Yuan admonished landlords to reduce rents when harvests were poor, hard-pressed tenants often were obliged to borrow money and grain from their landlords or pawnbrokers.[54] From other evidence, the "labor duties" required of tenants generally was confined to the repair of irrigation dikes and channels, work for which compensation was expected.[55] Tenants had little security of tenure. Song officials condemned the arbitrary transfer of tenurial rights from one tenant to another (known as *chandian* 剗佃), to little avail. But magistrates did not hesitate to use penal force against tenants who failed to meet their rent obligations, and readily assented to the removal of tenants in arrears.[56]

Authors of manuals on household management, steeped in Confucian doctrines, exalted the moral as well as economic virtues of landholding. Yet they fully recognized the instability engendered by the market economy. "Poverty and wealth are not permanent circumstances," Yuan Cai wrote, "No house or field has a permanent owner. When you have money you buy; when you lack it, you sell."[57] Yuan counseled his peers to be frugal in spending, to invest wisely in land, moneylending, and business ventures, to diversify their assets,

[53] *YSSF*, xia: 15b–16a. Translation modified from Ebrey 1984b: 302–03.
[54] Yuan Cai deemed monthly interest rates of 2–6 percent, or 30–50 percent for grain lent until the harvest season, as reasonable. But he also reported that in some areas interest rates reached twice those levels or more. See *YSSF*, xia: 23a; Ebrey 1984b: 315–16.
[55] McDermott 1984: 29.   [56] Yanagida 1963: 105–06, 117.
[57] *YSSF*, xia: 22a; translation from Ebrey 1984b: 314.

and never become dependent on the goodwill and honesty of those with whom one does business. Yuan was unusual in his frank advocacy of increasing the family's income to solidify its economic foundations. Other writers were overwhelmingly concerned with preservation, not expansion, of the family's wealth. They focused on self-reliance, careful budgeting, and economizing on expenditures. But even among these writers one finds a palpable anxiety that landholding alone was insufficient to ensure the family's economic well-being; salaries from office-holding or teaching provided crucial supplements to household income.[58] Entrepreneurs who gained their fortunes in trade or finance bought land less as a source of income than as a secure investment to balance more speculative ventures. The competition for access to land undoubtedly was most intense among those near the bottom of the rural social order, the fifth-rank households – more than half of the total population – who owned 20 or fewer *mu* of land.[59]

As we have seen, throughout the imperial period the household (*hu* 戶) – usually defined as a conjugal couple and their children – was the basic unit of production, consumption, and taxation in Chinese society. Strictly speaking, however, property ownership inhered not in the household but in the patriline (*jia* 家) – the family conceived in terms of its ritual identity, linked to its ancestors in the past and its descendants in the future. The patriline constituted the crucial unit of biological and economic reproduction across time. The head of the household had broad rights to dispose of property as he saw fit, subject to two important conditions: he must abide by the legal obligation of equal inheritance and the deep-rooted cultural commitment to preserving the patrimony, the material foundation of the patriline's welfare, for future generations. The sale of arable land – the most fundamental means of ensuring the continuity of the patriline – was sanctioned only as a last resort. Individuals could own property – for example, dowries, salaries and wages, and businesses created without using family property – which they could dispose of freely. But real property and businesses built up through investment of family assets were deemed a common patrimony that was subject to strong legal and customary rules.[60]

---

[58] McDermott 1991.

[59] Yanagida 1986: 192–214. Yanagida (1995) has argued that many farming families could not make ends meet solely from the lands they owned or rented and were obliged to earn additional income from casual employment in handicraft manufacture, peddling, fishing, transport, and various kinds of unskilled or semi-skilled labor.

[60] On the concept of patriline and its role as an economic institution, see Ebrey 1984a; the transmission of property is discussed in Ebrey 1984b: 101–20. Kishimoto (2011: 69–70) describes land ownership rights in similar terms but with less precision than the concept of patriline.

The government's vested fiscal interest in and ideological commitment to preserving the patriline militated against the alienation of landed property, a predisposition fully reflected in the laws governing property rights. Transfers of property rights in land generally took three forms. The most common type was the conditional sale (*dianmai* 典賣), in which the seller transferred the use of the land to the buyer but retained the right to redeem the land upon repayment of the original sale price within twenty years. Alternatively, the owner would relinquish all claims to the land in an irrevocable sale (*juemai* 絕賣). Since a conditional sale conveyed only usufruct rights, the prices of conditional sales were far lower than irrevocable sales. A third type of land transaction, known *didang* 抵當, should be understood as a type of securitized loan. Under the *didang* arrangement, the seller retained possession and use of the land, but forfeited ownership rights if he failed to repay the principal and interest on the loan (through the payment of "rent") by the specified deadline. In 1027 the Song state outlawed the practice of *didang* as well as repayment of cash debts by transfer of landownership rights in an effort to protect lands against debt seizures. Seeking to deter *didang* transactions, the Song state mandated that sellers quit the land and surrender usufruct rights to the buyer. But this deeply engrained customary practice persisted in defiance of the strict letter of the law.[61]

Rising land prices encouraged the original owner (or his heirs) to seek redemption of lands relinquished through conditional sales years or decades before and to challenge the validity of irrevocable sales. The sharp increase in land prices in the thirteenth century – in large part due to the depreciation of paper money – spawned numerous lawsuits over redemption rights.[62] In adjudicating such disputes, magistrates assigned principal weight to sales contracts, and secondarily considered who actually cultivated the land and paid the taxes assessed on it. Official land registers – principally dating from the comprehensive cadastral survey conducted by the Song government in 1142, after the Song-Jin truce was declared – were regarded as obsolete compared to contracts.[63] But contracts that violated dynastic law were deemed void. In contrast to Ming-Qing jurisprudence, Song magistrates commonly invoked

---

[61] On property transfers in Song law and social practice, see Dai Jianguo 2001, 2011; Aoki 2006, 2013.

[62] No fewer than twenty-five cases included in the *Enlightened Judgments* involved disputes over redemption rights. In many of these cases, the suits were filed not by the original seller or his patrilineal descendants, but rather by kinfolk and neighbors who had rights of first refusal in conditional sales (subject to a three-year statute of limitations). See Kishimoto 2007: 221–30, 2011: 75–78. In principle, buyers were obliged to obtain quitclaims from the seller's kinfolk and neighbors in order to secure their title to the land. See Dai Jianguo 2011: 102.

[63] On the 1142 cadastral survey, see He Bingdi 1988: 11–37. Although local cadastral surveys were carried out by individual prefectures and counties in the twelfth and thirteenth centuries, no empire-wide survey was conducted after 1142 until the Ming survey of 1387.

legal statutes and precedents in adjudicating land disputes. At the same time they also gave consideration to "the body of local customary precedents" (*xiangyuan tili* 鄉原體例) in matters such as what was deemed a fair price in land sales.

In inheritance claims as well as in property disputes Song judges upheld the interests of the patriline and the preservation of its patrimony as the highest priority. Generally speaking, magistrates regarded the widow of a deceased head of the household rather than his agnatic kin as the best representative of the patriline's interests. Widows did not have a right of heirship, but they often acted as placeholders in the transmission of property, managing the estate until minor heirs reached the age of majority. Widows did retain full control over their dowry, and could take their personal property with them in the event of remarriage. Many thirteenth-century magistrates, steeped in Neo-Confucian patrilineal ideology, objected to remarriage on ethical grounds, but nonetheless upheld widows' legal rights to remarry. Unmarried daughters were entitled to an inheritance share half that of sons, a concession stripped away in later law codes that were firmly bound to Neo-Confucian mores.[64]

The prevalence of conditional sales with the right of redemption, reinforced by the staunch support of the Song state, encumbered the alienability of property rights to some degree. However, magistrates fully abided by the laws that governed conditional sales, especially the statutes of limitations on redemption rights. Moreover, as the price differentials between conditional sales and irrevocable sales clearly show, the market effectively took into account differences in the security of property rights. Conditional sales in effect divided property rights into two tiers of ownership, each of which acquired a life of its own. The holders of ownership and usufruct rights could freely transfer (through sale or bequest) those rights to third parties without requiring the consent of the other. This two-tiered separation of property rights, already common in the late Song, subsequently became known as "one field, two masters" (*yitian liangzhu* 一田兩主). The multiple and over-lapping rights in land engendered by this system clearly hindered absolute control of real property. Yet this system yielded other efficiencies. By fostering separate markets for owners of what become known as subsoil and topsoil rights, it enabled investors to acquire a proprietary interest in sturdy assets without the need to assume the burden of working the land, while at the same time enabling farmers of modest means to gain security of tenure.

According to the principle – dating back to the Warring States period – that all land belonged to the emperor, the state could exercise eminent domain rights to confiscate private landholdings. Such seizures were rare, but one

---

[64] On the unusual strength of women's property rights in the Song, see Birge 2002: 64–142.

occurred in the twilight years of the Southern Song. In response to the Mongol invasions of the late 1250s, the Song court vastly increased the quotas for compulsory grain sales (*hedi*) to obtain rations for its soldiers. To pay for these purchases the state resorted to wanton printing of *huizi* notes, causing the value of paper money to plummet. In 1263 Prime Minister Jia Sidao enacted a "public lands" law (*gongtianfa* 公田法) under which landowners were compelled to sell one-third of their holdings beyond 200 *mu* to the state. In this way the state received the rental income from the land rather than only collecting tax income. The public lands policy was confined to only six Jiangnan prefectures, but roughly 10–20 percent of the arable lands in this region became state property and generated sufficient income to replace most of the *hedi* purchases and allow the government to reduce the issue of paper money substantially. Although a fiscal success, Jia's initiative failed to reverse the dynasty's political fortunes. In 1275, on the eve of the Mongol capture of Hangzhou, Jia was dismissed and the lands restored to their former owners.[65] Ultimately Jia Sidao's public lands policy – which earned him the everlasting scorn of Confucian historians – is notable chiefly as an exception to the security of private landownership that characterized Chinese law and social practice in the late imperial era.

The economic consequences of Mongol rule in China

The Mongol conquest, which marked the first time all of China fell under the dominion of foreign rulers, had far-reaching repercussions on Chinese society, economy, and government. The Confucian scholar-official class was reduced to political impotence, though it still retained its social and cultural prestige. Qubilai (r. 1260–94) and his successors, who ruled as the Yuan dynasty (1271–1368), departed sharply not only from Chinese political traditions, but also from the practices of earlier foreign conquest dynasties. In contrast to the Khitan and Jurchen, who had been largely sedentary peoples prior to their conquests of Chinese territories, the Mongols were pure pastoral nomads. The subjugation of Chinese to Mongol political and social dominion was especially acute in North China, where the Mongols had supplanted the Jin in 1234. South China, in contrast, was far less directly affected by Mongol rule. Consequently the Mongol conquests further enhanced the position of the Jiangnan region as the economic center of the Chinese world.

Mongol society was governed by the principle of personal servitude. According to the testimony of Chinese envoys who visited Mongol camps in the early 1230s, members of the Mongol tribes were obligated to deliver tribute

---

[65] Sudō 1954b. It is not clear to what extent the original owners were able to regain their property, especially amid the chaos of wartime.

in the form of a percentage of their herds to the khan. In addition, the Mongol nobility imposed levies of food, horses, equipment, cloth, and labor services on the population under their dominion. Understood as a form of personal servitude, these requisitions collectively were known as *qubchir*. The *qubchir* was an irregular levy, collected whenever the ruler or master deemed necessary.[66]

Upon annexing the former Jin territories in North China in 1234, the Mongols sought to impose their own social institutions on their new subjects, who became known as the "Han people" regardless of their actual ancestry. In the world of the steppe, vanquished peoples became the slaves of the conquering chiefs. Since it was impossible to relocate the former Jin subjects to the steppe, Chinggis's successor as great khan, Ögödei (r. 1229–41), instead created a system of appanages (*touxia* 投下) by awarding swaths of Jin territory and their inhabitants to his kinfolk and other Mongol nobles. Slightly more than half of the former Jin population became subject to appanage holders, with the remainder under the direct rule of the khan. Within these appanages personal rule by the nobles replaced bureaucratic governance.[67] As in other parts of the Mongol realm, the appanage holders resorted to tax-farming to extract revenues from the sedentary agricultural populations under their dominion. Tax collection privileges were granted to merchants known collectively as *ortoq*. The *ortoq* merchants, mainly Uighurs and Muslim foreigners, also served as commercial agents for their Mongol overlords, investing their booty in trade ventures and moneylending. Under the Mongol great khans the *ortoq* dominated both fiscal administration and private commerce.[68]

The Mongols conquered the Jin only after twenty years of bloody struggle that once again devastated North China. Initially the Mongols had considered turning the plains of northern China into pasture for their livestock, but ultimately they were dissuaded from this course of action. Still, the agricultural economy was in a shambles and North China had suffered severe population losses. The registered population of North China declined by two-thirds between the Jin census of 1209 and the inaugural Ming census of 1393.

Pastoral social traditions emphasized control of people rather than land. The Mongols divided the "Han people" into numerous occupational classifications – ranging from broad categories such as civilians, soldiers,

---

[66] Schurmann 1956b remains the best exposition of the Mongol tribute system; see also Allsen 1987: 144–88.

[67] On the appanage system under Mongol rule, see Li Zhi'an 1992; Sugiyama 2004: 28–61. On the creation and administration of appanages in Chinese territories, see Endicott-West 1989b: 80–103.

[68] On the crucial role of the *ortoq* merchants in the Mongol-ruled economy, see Otagi 1973; Allsen 1989; Endicott-West 1989a; Uno 1989.

and artisans to highly specialized ones such as physicians, clergy, Confucian scholars, diviners, and *ortoq* merchants – for the purposes of household registration and taxation. These occupational statuses were intended to be hereditary. Military households, who comprised approximately 15–30 percent of the population in North China, were required to provide one able-bodied soldier at all times. The Mongols especially desired the services of skilled artisans. Many artisans were transported to the Mongol capital (initially at Qaraqorum in Mongolia, and from Qubilai's time at Dadu), where they became servile dependents of the khan, his government, or noble families. In addition to those attached directly to the government, a much larger group of artisan households was obliged to meet government requisitions for goods or short-term labor service at the local level.[69]

The tax system devised in 1236 by Ögödei's advisor Yelü Chucai, a former Jin official of Khitan ancestry, replaced the twice-a-year tax retained by the Jin with a combination of land and poll taxes.[70] Civilian, artisan, and clergy households were assessed taxes to be paid in grain, silk, and silver. Although in principle religious orders were required to pay taxes, the Mongols avidly patronized Buddhism and Daoism and granted numerous exemptions to individual clergy. Grain figured only modestly as a staple food in the pastoral livelihood of the Mongols, and thus the grain tax was relatively light. Instead, the major portion of taxes was collected in the forms of silk and silver, along with requisitions of bows, quivers, armor, and weapons. Statutory labor services – assessed on all households, whether landowners or not – also became a heavy burden. In the 1240s the Mongol rulers of eastern Turkestan converted the *qubchir* levy into a tax paid in silver. This precedent became the basis of the *baoyin* 包銀 levy, collected in silver, imposed on the former Jin population soon after Möngke's ascension as Great Khan in 1251.

The *baoyin* tax was assessed on households (rather than individual adult males, as was the common practice for the *qubchir*), initially at a standard amount of 6 *liang* (225 g) per year. This rate proved unsustainable, and in 1255 it was reduced to 4 *liang*, half to be paid in silver and half in silk yarn. Even at this reduced rate the *baoyin* levy was an onerous burden (4 *liang* of silver at this time was worth 190 liters of rice, or about one-half of the annual consumption of an adult male). Many households borrowed silver from the *ortoq* merchants, only to default on their debts, lose their land, and abscond. Wang Yun, one of Qubilai's Chinese advisors, reported in 1261 that the *baoyin* levy raised 60,000 *ding* (112.5 metric tons) of silver each year. Approximately 20 percent of this amount was retained in China to defray the administrative costs of the Mongol government. The remainder was delivered to the Mongol

court at Qaraqorum. The Mongols in turn entrusted their silver revenues to the
ortoq merchants to finance trading expeditions to western Asia. Demand for
silver in West Asia and beyond caused a steady drain of silver from China to
the Islamic world. One scholar, extrapolating from Wang Yun's statement,
estimates that 90 million *liang* (3,375 metric tons) of silver were exported from
China to Central and West Asia during the first thirty years of Mongol rule.
Although this figure surely is too high, by the time that Qubilai was elected
Great Khan in 1260 North China was suffering from severe shortages
of silver.[71]
   Qubilai immediately launched a substantial reorganization of Mongol government aimed at concentrating power in his hands and recentering the Mongol
Empire on China, its richest prize. Qubilai appointed regional governors
throughout North China who usurped most of the tax-gathering powers of
the appanages, introduced a unified paper money system in place of local
(appanage) paper currencies, and greatly increased the khanate's revenues by
instituting a range of commodity and commercial taxes. In 1262 he decided
to move his capital from the Mongolian steppe to China and began construction on a grand imperial city in the Chinese style at Dadu, the site of modern
Beijing. In 1271 Qubilai formally assumed the trappings of a Chinese
emperor and adopted the Chinese dynastic name of Yuan.[72]
   Mongol authority was rooted in military power. The provincial governments
(*xingsheng* 行省) of the Yuan state were little more than armies of occupation.
Although the Yuan created numerous bureaucratic agencies as well as a
Mongol-derived system of overseers (*darughachi*), chains of command were
inconsistent and responsibilities often overlapped. The Mongols relegated
most of the tasks of civil government to the local level.[73] In keeping with Jin
and Song precedents, village leaders bore the major burden of local administrative duties, including tax collection, labor service, and jurisdiction over
police and criminal matters. In addition, in 1270 the Mongols conducted a
census of the "Han lands" that served as the basis for a parallel system of local
administrative units known as *she* 社. The *she* heads assumed responsibility
for promoting agriculture, maintaining village schools and granaries for famine
relief, and adjudicating civil disputes. But there is little evidence to suggest that

[71] On the evolution of the *baoyin* tax from the *qubchir* levy, see Abe 1972; Allsen 1987: 163–71.
   On the flow of silver from China to Western Asia and beyond, see Blake 1937; Otagi 1973;
   Kuroda 2009. The estimate of silver exports of 90 million *liang* is from Otagi 1973, 1: 26. In my
   view (von Glahn 2013: 31), a more reasonable estimate is 29 million *liang*, or 1,100 tons.
[72] For a brief survey of Qubilai's administrative and fiscal policies, see Rossabi 1988: 70–75,
   119–27.
[73] For local governance in the Yuan with special attention to the role of the *darughachi*, see
   Endicott-West 1989b.

this proposed institutional infrastructure of schools, granaries, and agricultural improvement projects was widely realized.[74]

In 1279 Qubilai's armies completed the conquest of South China. Absorbing the Southern Song territories, with a population more than six times greater than that of the "Han lands" of North China, posed enormous fiscal and logistical challenges to the fledgling imperial government at Dadu. Qubilai relied on a series of merchant advisors – notably the notorious Ahmad, a Persian who dominated fiscal administration between 1262 and his execution in 1282, and the more judicious Tibetan minister Sangha, who wielded supreme influence at the Yuan court during the last years of Qubilai's reign – to reorganize the fiscal administration.[75] Ahmad and Sangha turned to the commercial sector, especially the salt monopoly, to generate new revenues. Taxing salt was by no means new; the Mongols had instituted a salt monopoly even before their final victory over the Jin. Under Sangha's direction, however, a vastly expanded salt monopoly, with 140 salt depots across the empire, became the financial backbone of the Mongol regime. In 1285 the salt monopoly generated two-thirds of the Yuan state's cash revenues, and commercial taxes supplied an additional 17 percent. In later years the salt monopoly contributed as much as 80 percent of state revenue.[76]

Following the incorporation of the Southern Song into the Yuan Empire, the Mongols were largely content to maintain the existing Song taxation system rather than bring the south into conformity with the institutional framework developed in the north. Thus the twice-a-year tax system was retained in the south, in contrast to the array of household taxes imposed on the "Han lands." Apart from several conspicuous cases of confiscation of lands for the support of its armies and gifts to the Mongol nobility, the Mongols generally interfered very little in the private economy of South China. Liberated from the restrictive policies of the traditional Confucian state, rich families and entrepreneurs amassed massive landholdings and invested their wealth in lucrative commercial and industrial ventures. These wealthy magnates also took the initiative in founding or expanding market towns that gave further impetus to commercial growth.[77] The Mongols were keen to tap the agricultural resources of the south, however. The Mongol overseers applied the principles of tax-farming to agrarian revenues as well, relying on the great landowners to collect and deliver the statutory quotas of grain taxes.[78]

The continuing prosperity of Jiangnan's agricultural and commercial economy was reflected in the allocation of the tax burden. According to figures from 1328, Jiangnan was assigned 37 percent of the total grain tax quota as

---

[74] On the *she* institution, see Nakajima 2001.
[75] On Sangha's career and policies, see Petech 1980; Uematsu 1983.
[76] Schurmann 1956b: 166–73.   [77] Von Glahn 2003b.   [78] Uematsu 1996: 338–39.

well as equal or higher proportions of the salt, wine, and commercial taxes.[79] In addition to building new canals to connect Dadu to the Grand Canal network, Sangha also instituted ocean-going convoys to deliver tribute grain from the Yangzi Delta to the capital. The significant savings in time and cost persuaded Qubilai to divert all of the grain revenue from the south from the Grand Canal to the maritime route in 1287.[80]

Integration of the Southern Song economy into the Yuan paper currency system proved more difficult. The new paper currency issued by Qubilai in 1260, while freely exchangeable with silver, was intended to displace metallic currencies, both bronze coin and silver. In 1263 Qubilai's government began to commute the *baoyin* silver tax to payments in paper currency. Bronze coin largely disappeared from circulation, except in petty trade in some parts of South China. Ahmad's administration vastly increased the amount of paper currency in circulation, resulting in severe depreciation and a sizable deficit. Sangha restored some stability by devaluing the paper money in circulation and limiting further expansion of the money supply.

Apart from a disastrous and short-lived attempt to introduce a new paper currency linked to bronze coin in 1309–10, Yuan finance ministers prudently maintained monetary stability until the 1340s, when popular uprisings against Mongol rule precipitated grave political and fiscal crises.[81]

The formation of a pan-Asian Mongol empire under Chinggis and his successors had revived the overland trade network of Central Asia and touched off a new boom in East–West trade. Initially, the Uighur caravaners were the prime beneficiaries of the *Pax Mongolica* and the Mongols' ardent patronage of commerce, but over time the *ortoq* merchants, acting as agents for the Mongol leaders, came to dominate trans-Eurasian trade. As noted above, the *ortoq* merchants shipped immense sums of silver from China to the Islamic world, severely depleting China's stock of silver. But in the early fourteenth century the Florentine merchant Pegolotti wrote of foreign merchants carrying silver to Dadu and Hangzhou to purchase silks and other goods.[82]

The incorporation of the Southern Song into the Yuan realm at a time when internecine conflict had erupted among the rival Mongol khanates once again prompted a reorientation of China's foreign trade toward the maritime world.[83] In 1285 the Yuan court imposed a government monopoly on maritime trade, which it reserved for its *ortoq* agents. But Sangha reopened maritime trade to

---

[79] Schurmann 1956b: 80; Matsuda 2000: 139. The figures for Jiangnan also included Fujian, since the two regions were subsumed into Jiangzhe 江浙 province under the Yuan.
[80] Matsuda 2000: 146–51. The amount of grain shipped by the maritime route rose from 1.5 million *shi* (143 million liters) in 1290 to 3.5 million *shi* (333 million liters) in 1329. Ibid.: 147.
[81] On the development of the multiple paper currencies during the Yuan, see von Glahn 2010.
[82] Pegolotti 1914: 154–55.
[83] On maritime trade policies under the Yuan, see Yokkaichi 2006.

private merchants. Quanzhou became one of the greatest ports in the world, home to numerous colonies of foreign merchants. Marco Polo, who left for home from Quanzhou in 1292, claimed that "for one shipload of pepper that goes to Alexandria or elsewhere, destined for Christendom, there comes a hundred such to this haven [Quanzhou]; for it is one of the two greatest havens in the world for commerce."[84] Similarly, the Muslim traveler Ibn Battuta, visiting the pepper-growing regions of southwestern India in 1341, reported that Chinese ships dominated the sea routes from India to China. These junks, Battuta tells us, "carried a complement of a thousand men" and were equipped with "four decks with rooms, cabins, and saloons for merchants; a cabin has chambers and a lavatory, and can be locked by its occupant, who takes along with him slave girls and wives."[85] Ceramics from Jingdezhen and Fujian flowed out through Quanzhou to Southeast Asia, the Islamic world, and eastern Africa. The development of Jingdezhen's renowned blue-white porcelain was made possible by the import of cobalt pigments from Persia known to the Chinese as "Muslim blue."[86] Maritime commerce with Japan, fueled by the brisk export of bronze coin, continued to flourish once the turbulence caused by Qubilai's unsuccessful attempts to invade the Japanese archipelago dissipated. Chinese bronze coin also became the standard currency of the Majapahit kingdom in Java by the beginning of the fourteenth century.[87]

Although international trade flourished under Mongol rule, the Yuan dynasty failed to establish a stable fiscal infrastructure. The attempt to assimilate Mongol institutions with the norms of Chinese imperial governance during the fourteenth century engendered multiple and conflicting political hierarchies rather than bureaucratic order. Qubilai and his strong-willed financial advisors succeeded in asserting central control over revenues, but fiscal discipline disintegrated after Qubilai's death. The entanglement of the state's fiscal administration with the spendthrift habits of the imperial family and the Mongol nobility left the government mired in debt. Agricultural production faltered with the onset of the shift in the global climate toward cooler temperatures, which some historians have dubbed "the Little Ice Age."[88] The government's response to crises, such as the devastating floods that altered the course of the Yellow River in 1344 and the rampant inflation that set in afterwards, proved wholly inadequate. By the 1350s much of the Chinese population of the Yuan Empire was in open revolt, and in the end the Mongols abandoned China for the safety and security of their steppe homeland.

[84] Polo 1929, 2: 351.   [85] Ibn Battuta 1929: 235.   [86] Finlay 2010: 139–40.
[87] Wicks 1998: 290–97.
[88] On the onset of a long-term cooling trend in China beginning in the mid-thirteenth century, see Liu Zhaomin 1992: 17–25, 130–35. On the "Little Ice Age" as a global phenomenon in the northern hemisphere, see Grove 1990.

The early Ming reversal

The disintegration of Yuan rule in the 1340s ushered in two decades of fierce civil wars. By the time Zhu Yuanzhang (Emperor Hongwu, r. 1368–98) vanquished the last of his rivals and founded the Ming dynasty in 1368, millions had died and the economy was in ruins. Hongwu was determined to eradicate what he regarded as the pernicious influence of Mongol customs and to restore the institutions and values of the agrarian society enshrined in the Confucian Classics. In so doing Hongwu repudiated not only the Mongol heritage but also the market economy that had developed during the Tang-Song transition. The early Ming period thus marked a sharp rupture in the evolution of economic life and livelihood in China, especially in Jiangnan.

Although Hongwu's policies evolved over his thirty-year reign, his basic goals remained constant: to restore the autarkic village economy of the idealized past as envisioned by Mencius and other Confucian philosophers and to minimize (if not eliminate) the market economy and the inequalities it fostered. In pursuit of this agenda the emperor formulated fiscal policies predicated on a return to unilateral in-kind payments to the state, conscripted labor service, self-sufficient military farms, and payments to officials and soldiers in goods rather than money. From the outset Hongwu established strong personal control over the bureaucracy, but beginning in 1380 he launched a series of purges against officials of his own government and enacted sweeping institutional changes intended to concentrate power in the hands of the emperor. The early Ming model of government was characterized by strong autocratic rule at the top and the delegation of many of the functions of civil governance to village leaders at the bottom. In spirit, if not precisely in institutions, Hongwu's regime harked back to the military-physiocratic state of the early empires.

Apart from his ideological principles, Hongwu's policies also were motivated by a practical objective: commandeering the wealth of Jiangnan to rebuild an empire ravaged by decades of war and destruction. Demographic historians estimate that China's population fell by at least 15 percent, and perhaps as much as a third, between 1340 and 1370.[89] This population loss coincided with the Black Death that ravaged Europe and much of the Islamic world in 1347–52. However, there is a conspicuous lack of evidence for pandemic disease on the scale of the Black Death in China at this time. War

---

[89] Wu Songdi (2000: 387, 391) estimates the total population of Yuan China at 75 million in 1290 and 90 million *c.* 1340, whereas Cao Shuji (2000a: 464) gives lower figures of 68 million and 82.5 million respectively. Estimates of the total population around the time of the Ming founding fall in the range of 60–65 million, and Cao (2000a: 465) posits a total population of 72.7 million for 1393.

and famine – and the diseases that typically accompanied them – probably were the main causes of mortality in the final decades of Mongol rule.[90] In any event, the Jiangnan region emerged from the late Yuan civil wars relatively unscathed and suffered no serious population loss. Indeed, the destruction borne most heavily by the northern and western provinces only enhanced Jiangnan's preeminent position in the national economy. Hongwu's decision to establish his capital at Nanjing reflected the economic reality that the resources needed to consolidate his rule and establish military and political control could only come from the Jiangnan region.

Initially Hongwu sought the cooperation of the local elite of Jiangnan in his imperial project. The revenue system he enacted in 1371 designated the wealthiest landowners in each county as tax captains (*liangzhang* 糧長) with responsibility for collecting and delivering tax grain to the capital. By 1380, however, Hongwu became convinced that the Jiangnan elite, both as government officials and private citizens, were thwarting his plans. He then reversed course, purging thousands of officials and confiscating the property of many of Jiangnan's great landowners. Hongwu refined his vision of social reform: the greatest priority, as he now saw it, was to free peasant farmers from exploitation by wealthy landowners and corrupt officials and clerks as well as the vicissitudes of the money economy. By the end of Hongwu's reign more than half of Jiangnan's arable land had been seized by the state.[91]

Many of the tax captains had been swept up in Hongwu's campaigns against corruption. Although the tax captain system was retained, in 1381 Hongwu introduced a new institutional framework of rural control known as *lijia* 里甲. The *lijia* system organized rural society into groups (*li* 里) of 110 households (usually based on existing villages, or combining smaller hamlets into *li* units) under the leadership of ten Elders who served in rotation as head of the *li* over a ten-year period. The *li* headmen were entrusted with broad responsibility for local governance, including policing the village, adjudicating legal disputes, collecting taxes, and assigning duties for communal public works projects such

---

[90] It has long been recognized that the highlands of southwestern China and Southeast Asian were a "disease reservoir" for the bacillus that causes bubonic plague. In his pioneering study of the history of epidemics, William McNeill (1976: 171–73) postulated that Mongol horseriders who invaded Burma in 1252–53 became the agents of transmission of the flea-borne plague bacillus to the Eurasian steppe and thence both to Europe and to China. Recent genetic research (Morelli *et al.* 2010) has discovered DNA evidence that the great pandemics of bubonic plague that swept across the Mediterranean in the sixth century and the Black Death of the fourteenth century originated in China (i.e., the territory of the modern PRC). But the genetic evidence is silent on the question of whether China suffered a Black Death-type pandemic in the fourteenth century. The absence of evidence for a bubonic plague pandemic in China in the mid-fourteenth century militates strongly against McNeill's assertion that the mortality experienced in China was linked to the Black Death. See Sussman 2011.

[91] Mori 1967; 1988: 45–196; Danjō 1995: 229–66; von Glahn 2007b.

as flood control and irrigation systems as well as statutory labor services owed to the state. Despite Hongwu's antipathy for the Mongols, his government also followed the Yuan precedent of registering the population into hereditary occupational groups. Civilian households, the great majority of the population, were liable for taxes levied in grain and other goods as well as statutory labor service; military households (about one-fifth of the total population in the early fifteenth century) were stationed at garrisons and given lands to farm when not engaged in military duties; artisan and saltern households were obligated to provide either labor services or goods to the government.[92] Land and population surveys carried out in 1387 and 1393 provided the benchmarks for refining the *lijia* system and establishing permanent tax quotas. *Lijia* registration and tax quotas remained unchanged after 1393, and thus bore increasingly little resemblance to social and economic reality over time.[93]

In keeping with Hongwu's intention to reduce the logistical and administrative costs of government, the Ming fiscal system generated a low level of income compared to the Song. The land tax, collected in grain, amounted to no more than 5–10 percent of yields.[94] No revenue was earmarked for military expenditures, since the military garrisons were expected to be self-supporting. After a brief attempt to restore a sound bronze currency, Hongwu instituted a new type of inconvertible paper currency (*baochao* 寶鈔) while simultaneously banning the use of gold and silver (and for a period of time even state-issued bronze coin) as money. But from the outset the paper currency suffered from steep depreciation; in 1394 *baochao* were circulating at a discount of nearly 80 percent. By 1425 paper notes were worth only 2 percent of their face value and essentially had ceased to function as viable currency.[95] The Ming state also throttled the flourishing maritime commerce that had developed during the Song and Yuan periods. In 1374 Hongwu prohibited private merchants from engaging in overseas trade, although some trade was allowed under a highly regulated system of tributary relations with foreign rulers.[96] The ban on private maritime trade would last until the late sixteenth century.

Although the early Ming fiscal system succeeded in reducing the burden of administrative expenses, it reverted to a heavy reliance on agrarian sources of

---

[92] Registration of military households varied widely in different regions, and Hongwu-era statistics for military personnel are considered unreliable. Cao Shuji (2000a: 377) believes that in the mid-fifteenth century period military households comprised 19 percent of the total population and that this estimate is valid for the Yongle era as well.
[93] Kuribayashi (1971) remains the classic study of the *lijia* system. See also Tsurumi 1984; Farmer 1995; Heijdra 1998: 459–81.
[94] Ray Huang 1974: 88.   [95] Von Glahn 1996a: 70–73.
[96] Danjō 1997. One of the motivations (and perhaps the primary one) for the ban on private maritime trade was to prevent the flight of precious metals and coin to foreign countries at a time when the Ming was trying to establish a purely fiduciary paper money. See Ōsumi 1990.

state income. Fixed land tax quotas severely limited the state's ability to capture new revenue as the agricultural economy recovered and expanded. Moreover, weak and ineffective fiscal institutions squandered much of the revenue received by the central government. Unlike earlier dynasties, the Ming failed to separate state revenues from the personal income of the emperor, resulting in rampant abuses, especially at the hands of the eunuch cadre that dominated the palace administration.

The operation of the salt monopoly typified the Ming approach to economic management. The Ming resurrected the Northern Song frontier delivery (renamed *kaizhong* 開中) system, under which merchants who delivered grain to the armies stationed along the northern frontier were rewarded with lucrative salt trading privileges. However, the central government starved the salt monopoly by failing to provide adequate financial support to producers while disbursing excessive quantities of salt certificates. Saltern households often went unpaid, and merchants found that they had to wait years, or even decades, to redeem their certificates. Consequently salt smuggling soared, further reducing the amount of salt available to the government. By the end of the fifteenth century the frontier delivery system had broken down, to be replaced by new procedures under which frontier merchants sold their certificates to salt merchants in Yangzhou and other major salt-producing centers. The Yangzhou salt merchants, mostly comprised of Huizhou men, had the ample capital resources needed to survive the vicissitudes of what had become a highly unstable business. The final resolution to the problems of erratic supplies and endemic mismanagement came in 1617, when the government instituted a franchise system that awarded exclusive and permanent salt trading rights to syndicates of Yangzhou merchants. Subsequently the Yangzhou salt merchants became the wealthiest men in the empire, yet the state reaped only meager income from the salt monopoly, which in 1578 (the only year for which we have complete national accounts) generated a mere 10 percent of the revenue obtained from the land tax.[97]

Emperor Yongle (r. 1402–25), who overthrew his brother and usurped the throne in 1402, was more inspired by the Mongol vision of world empire than his virulently anti-Mongol father. Yongle invaded and occupied northern Vietnam in 1407, launched repeated sallies against the Mongols, and dispatched massive armadas to the South Seas under the leadership of his close confidante, Admiral Zheng He. Zheng He's seven expeditions between 1405 and 1433, which journeyed as far as the coasts of Arabia and Africa, were driven by imperial ambition rather than economic enterprise, however, and drained the state's treasuries.[98]

---

[97] Ray Huang 1974: 180–225; Puk 2006.   [98] On Zheng He and his voyages, see Dreyer 2007.

Yongle did not alter the basic fiscal policies and institutions laid down by Hongwu, but his foreign adventures greatly increased state expenditures, further eroding the value of paper currency. Although tax levies remained unchanged, demands for statute labor service soared. Yongle's most enduring initiative was his decision to move the capital from Nanjing in the south to the site of the old Yuan capital (renamed Beijing) in the north. The relocation of the capital to Beijing created new logistical problems: the Grand Canal transport system had to be refurbished and extended, and the cost of delivering the grain tribute rose precipitously. These costs fell most heavily on the tax captains and *lijia* heads, further undermining the foundations of the revenue system.

The rigid system of fiscal administration instituted by the early Ming emperors could not be sustained. By the 1430s the Ming government abandoned its paper money system, and halted minting of bronze coin as well. The state was forced to accept the uncoined silver that had deeply infiltrated the private economy as its new monetary standard. In 1436 the grain tribute delivered to Beijing from Jiangnan was commuted to payments of silver, bringing considerable relief to taxpayers. The *lijia* and hereditary occupational household systems largely collapsed over the course of the fifteenth century, which had the virtue of freeing up productive energies. Eventually these and many other service obligations were commuted to payments in silver as well.[99]

The anti-commercial policies of the early Ming state, coupled with its expropriation of the wealth of the Jiangnan elite, wreaked havoc on the flourishing market economy of the Jiangnan region and arrested the commercial and urban growth that had continued with little disruption throughout the era of Mongol rule.[100] Commerce and industry foundered, hampered by mismanagement of the monetary system, a sharp decline in overseas trade, and a system of hereditary artisan households that impeded the rational allocation of labor. Urban population fell, and many market towns were abandoned. The economic malaise that resulted from the traumatic transition from Mongol to Ming rule persisted for more than a century.

Nonetheless, the restoration of domestic peace enabled the agrarian economy to recover and even prosper. Resettlement of the northern provinces – especially in the Central Plain – devastated by war, famine, and disease was a major priority of the new regime. The government forcibly relocated large numbers of people to these areas, where new villages were formed under the framework of the *lijia* system. The central Yangzi valley (Hunan and Hubei provinces) also experienced substantial immigration during the Ming period.

---

[99] Ray Huang 1974: 109–12; Tsurumi 1984: 268–73. On the conversion of *lijia* duties into silver payments, see Kuribayashi 1971: 79–142.
[100] Von Glahn 2003b: 205–11, 2007b.

Ming demographic trends are difficult to discern, given the absence of any national censuses after 1393. The meager evidence available has led scholars to produce widely divergent estimates of the magnitude of population growth over the course of the dynasty. While precise measurement remains elusive, the general impression is one of sustained increase until the 1630s. The most reliable data pertains to the Jiangnan region, where the population seems to have risen from roughly 9 million in 1393 to 16.5 million by 1620, an increase of more than 80 percent. In fast-growing provinces on the southern frontiers such as Hunan and Guangdong the population probably tripled during the Ming dynasty.[101]

In the view of some scholars, by mid-Ming times many regions of the empire were beginning to show symptoms of overpopulation. In Jiangnan, the size of the average small farm declined from 40 *mu* to 20 *mu*. At the same time, though, family size decreased (from six to five persons per household) while yields rose significantly. Thus increases in labor productivity offset the decline in farm size. Farming practices changed little in the north, but farmers continued to make important advances in the south. During the Ming period the large polders constructed during the Southern Song were divided into smaller enclosures that could be more easily drained, which greatly improved the fertility of paddy land. Better-drained soils also could be planted in winter crops such as wheat, beans, and rape. Application of nitrogen-rich fertilizers such as bean cake and rapeseed cake also appeared during this period. By the end of the Ming period yields from Jiangnan rice farming had doubled compared to the Southern Song, indicating that output per household had not diminished.[102]

The tax captain system collapsed during the fifteenth century, and tax collection was absorbed into the tasks of the *li* headmen. The onerous burden of *lijia* duties, rising tenancy, and the revival of towns accelerated a trend toward absentee landlordism in Jiangnan. Village society became overwhelmingly comprised of smallholders and tenant farmers, with few landowners of substantial means able to fulfill the duties of the *li* headmen. Local experiments in commuting service duties to money payments culminated in 1488 with the establishment of a national program of "equalized service" (*junyao* 均徭) that converted many forms of statutory labor to silver payments. While the "equalized service" reform was warmly welcomed, it had the effect of further eroding the solidarity of the village community. Labor service, like the land tax,

---

[101] Ho Ping-ti's (1959: 264) pioneering study concluded that Ming population grew steadily from 65 million in 1368 to a peak of 150 million c. 1600. Cao Shuji (2000a: 452, 464–65) proposes an increase from 73 million in 1393 to a peak of 192 million in 1630. Heijdra's (1998: 438) revisionist hypothesis that postulates a population in the range of 268–353 million by the end of the Ming is severely flawed and cannot be considered credible.

[102] Li Bozhong 2003.

became an individual rather than collective responsibility, and the *lijia* system was reduced to a mere paper relic.[103]

Despite the political shocks that disrupted the commercial dynamism of Jiangnan during the first century of the Ming, the rural economy remained enmeshed in markets for land, labor, and goods. Hongwu's campaigns against Jiangnan's great landowners had a leveling effect on village society, but his effort to uproot the money economy foundered. The restless currents of economic change are fully evident in the oldest surviving set of Ming household registers, which pertain to the household of Li Shu, from Qimen county in Huizhou, Anhui province (the basic facts of the registers are summarized in Table 7.7).[104] A mountainous region with limited rice agriculture, Huizhou had become a major supplier of tea, lumber, and paper to Jiangnan markets in the Song, and its entrepreneurial merchants achieved unparalleled national prominence in the mid-late Ming era (see Chapter 6, pp. 251–52, and Chapter 8, pp. 303–6). The Li Shu case illustrates how routinely – at least in the more commercialized regions of the empire – farm families bought and sold land to adjust to changes in economic fortunes and household composition.

Li Shu died in 1398, leaving his four-year-old son Wuben as sole heir. Li's widow, Xie Rongniang, age 22 at the time of her husband's death, remarried by bringing in a "foster father" (*yifu* 義父), with whom she had two daughters.[105] But by the time of the 1412 census the situation had radically changed: both Rongniang's second husband and her son Li Wuben had died, and a distant cousin, Li Jingxiang (a mere two years old), had been adopted into the patriline to serve as heir. However, the toddler Li Jingxiang was only nominally a member of the Li Shu household; he continued to live with his parents. Although Jingxiang remained the titular head of the household in the 1422 census, subsequently Xie Rongniang filed suit to have him removed on both ritual grounds (not being the same generation as Li Wuben) and because the absent Jingxiang, then 22 years old, made no contribution to the household's maintenance. In 1432 the magistrate agreed with Rongniang's petition and removed Jingxiang as head of the household, instructing

---

[103] Yamane 1984. Based on Huizhou archival records, Nakajima (2002) has shown that before 1450 nearly all property disputes were handled by *li* headmen; between 1450 and 1520 about half of disputes were decided in magistrates' courts; and after 1520 the *lijia* system had ceased to play any role in dispute resolution.

[104] The following paragraphs are based on Luan Chengxian 2007: 121–42. The primary document is a copy of the family's household registers (known in the Ming as "yellow registers," *huangce* 黃冊) for four consecutive decennial censuses from 1403 to 1432. We also possess land sale contracts, property affidavits, and legal petitions pertaining to the Li Shu household.

[105] This was an instance of the common practice of uxorilocal marriage, whereby a widow "invited in" a second husband who took up residence with the widow, supported the household, and if needed provided an heir to continue the husband's line of descent. See Waltner 1990: 99–110; Ebrey 1993: 235–40.

Table 7.7 *Li Shu household and its landholdings, 1391–1432*

Census	Household members				Landholdings (mu)		
	Head of household	Adult males	Females	Total	Arable	Non-arable	Total
1391	Li Shu	Li Shu	Xie Rongniang	2	16.34	2.19	18.53
1403	Li Wuben	None	Xie Rongniang	2	35.58	2.19	37.77
1412	Li Jingxiang	None	Xie Rongniang and two daughters	4	0	0	0
1422	Li Jingxiang	None	Xie Rongniang and two daughters	4	32.27	0.17	32.39
1432	Xie Rongniang	None	Xie Rongniang	1	5.43	0	5.43

Source: Luan Chengxian 2007: 131, table 4.1.

Rongniang to find a new heir. Thus the household register from that same year listed Rongniang, then age 59, as head of the household. The Li family launched a countersuit against the Xie for having reneged on the payment for timberland purchased from the Li. But at that point the documentary record ends, and the ultimate outcome of the feud remains unknown.

According to the household registers, the household estate held 37.8 *mu* of land in 1403, half of which Li Shu had purchased from five different members of his wife's lineage. Three sales contracts from 1406–10 show that the widow Rongniang sold off all of this land, mostly to her brother Xie Nengjing, an enterprising landowner and local notable.[106] But Xie Nengjing returned 11 *mu* in 1414, and the household purchased 7 other parcels by the time of the 1422 census. According to a property affidavit of 1431, the Li Shu household also possessed 20 *mu* of timberland (exempt from taxation, and therefore not included on the household register) that was cultivated mostly with hired laborers (six in all). Most likely Rongniang hired laborers to farm the arable paddy land as well. In sum, over a forty-year period the Li Shu household engaged in eighteen separate land transactions (involving dozens of parcels) with thirteen different individuals, and at its peak owned 50-odd *mu* of arable and timberland. From notations on the documents it is clear that some of the transfers were made to avoid labor service assessments; for example

---

[106] Xie's once-august lineage had fallen on hard times in his father's generation, but Xie Nengjing resurrected the family's fortunes and acquired substantial landholdings. See Luan Chengxian 1990; Nakajima 2002: 113–48.

Xie Nengjing had transferred at least 3 parcels to the Li Shu household in 1403 when the head of the household, Li Wuben, was still a minor, and then bought these lands back in 1410, when Wuben turned sixteen. The documents also trace a decades-long struggle between Li Shu's kinsmen and the powerful Xie family over control of the household's property, most of which originally had belonged to members of the Xie lineage. Despite some unusual features, the history of the Li Shu household – a modestly prosperous rural family – reveals the instability of landownership, the competitive economic environment, and the profound impact of the market even in an age of relative stasis at the macroeconomic level.

Conclusion

The commercial efflorescence of the Southern Song period touched virtually all quarters of Chinese society. Farming families produced their own staple foods, but many items of daily consumption were obtained through market exchange. Monetization of taxes and the procurement of military supplies through market mechanisms became even more pronounced in the Southern Song compared to the New Policies era. Unable to sustain the massive output of bronze coin achieved in the eleventh century, the Southern Song state still managed to maintain flexibility in the money supply through new paper currencies and increasing resort to silver as a monetary medium. A panoply of institutional innovations in financial services – including commercial brokers, credit financing, bills of exchange, advance sale contracts, *commenda* partnerships, and joint-capital enterprises – facilitated the expansion of interregional and overseas trade. Apart from seaport regions such as Quanzhou, dynamic growth fostered by cross-sectoral integration was most evident in Jiangnan, which solidified its stature as the center of gravity in the Chinese economy.

The Jurchen and Mongol conquests inflicted heavy blows on the economy of North China. In contrast, Jiangnan continued to prosper under Mongol-Yuan rule. The onerous demands for tribute that the Mongols imposed on the former Jin territories in North China were ameliorated after Qubilai's conquest of the Southern Song. The great landowners of Jiangnan attained extraordinary strength during the Yuan, thanks to the Mongol court's lax attitude toward the concentration of private wealth, its avid encouragement of domestic and foreign commerce, and its reliance on tax farmers for revenue collection. But a sharp reversal set in after the founding of the Ming dynasty. The first Ming emperor, Hongwu, spurned not only the Mongol heritage and the extreme inequities in wealth and landownership that had festered under Yuan rule, but also the very premises of the market economy. Hongwu's program of social reform envisioned restoring a simple, village-based agrarian society unbesmirched by venality, ostentation, and exploitation. His fiscal strategies, such as his attempt to create a purely fiat paper currency, were motivated by a desire to replace the market with a command economy subservient to imperial will. Along with his draconian expropriation of the landholdings of the Jiangnan elite, Hongwu's policies had a stifling effect on Jiangnan's market economy, a setback that took more than a century to overcome.

8   The maturation of the market economy (1550 to 1800)

Emperor Hongwu's project of social and economic reformation delivered a shocking blow to China's commerce and industry, especially in Jiangnan, the empire's economic heartland. The author of a Suzhou gazetteer published in 1506 acidly observed that Hongwu's campaigns against Suzhou's landowners, the forced removal of wealthy families to the capital, and the conscription of artisans into hereditary service to the state, had severely retarded the city's population growth and economic recovery even a century afterward.[1] But by the end of the fifteenth century Hongwu's key institutional innovations – the *lijia* village household organization and the *liangzhang* tax headmen – were essentially defunct, and the system of hereditary occupational households inherited from the Yuan had atrophied as well. The ban on private maritime trade was still in force, although Fujian seafarers easily evaded the lax net of enforcement. By the early decades of the sixteenth century commercial growth was beginning to revive, despite lingering obstacles such as a stagnant money supply following the closure of the Ming mints in the 1430s.

Economic developments in the sixteenth century utterly erased Emperor Hongwu's vision of village autarky and self-sufficiency. Steady gains in agricultural production and the formation of national markets for industrial goods such as cotton, silk, and porcelain stimulated regional specialization. The growing allure of overseas trade following the abrupt influx of silver imports – first from Japan, and later from Spain's American colonies – beginning in the 1540s galvanized agitation against the interdiction of foreign trade, which was repealed in 1567. Massive infusions of foreign silver stoked the fires of commercial and industrial growth during the last century of the Ming, especially in coastal regions with ready access to foreign markets. The expansion of the money economy, the growth of rural industries, the increasing spatial range of markets, the greater volume of foreign trade, the disappearance of bound labor, and the ascendancy of private enterprise over state economic management all contributed to what some scholars have

---

[1] *GSZ*: 14.2a-b. See von Glahn 2007b: 124–25.

referred to as a "second economic revolution" (after the first "economic revolution" of the Tang-Song transition) beginning *c*. 1550.[2]

Commercial revival in the late Ming

Hongwu's campaigns against the entrenched landowning elite of Jiangnan resulted in a leveling of rural society and more fragmented landholdings. Individual farms typically consisted of a number of plots spread over a wide area; the properties of large landowners often were scattered over several counties. The dispersed nature of landholding and the intensive cultivation techniques necessary for wet-rice agriculture militated against capital-intensive managerial farming in this region. Rather than directly engaging in farming using hired labor, landowners preferred to lease their land to tenants. Tenant farmers often owned some land of their own, but their plots were too small to support their own subsistence. Sharecropping – under which the landlord and the tenant divided the harvest equally, or the landlord took an even larger share if he provided tools, draft animals, and seed – was the norm, but in some cases tenants paid fixed rents in silver.

The sixteenth century witnessed a renewed trend toward concentration of landownership in Jiangnan, especially in hands of patrician families and lineage trusts, and increasing incidence of bondservitude. The Confucian patrician elite – active or retired government officials and those who held advanced degrees from the civil service examinations, broadly encompassed under the designation *shi* 士 – were entitled to generous exemptions from labor services. The onerous liabilities of labor service (especially *li* headmen, who had broad liability for tax arrears) encouraged many commoners of middling wealth to commend (*touxian* 投獻) their lands to privileged patricians. In most Jiangnan counties, the minimum standard for assignment of *li* headmen duties was 300–400 *mu*, but in some areas landowners with as few as 230 *mu* were impressed into service as *li* headmen.[3] Those who commended their property nominally became bondservants (legally defined as members of the master's household) and continued to work their land as tenant farmers. Wealthy families also acquired bondservants through purchase, adoption, and debt bondage, chiefly for domestic work rather than agricultural labor. Bondservitude typically entailed forms of service or tribute specified by contract, not unconditional or hereditary submission.[4] In this respect, the status of bondservants was akin to that of long-term hired laborers, over whom employers enjoyed certain legal privileges and paternalist responsibilities. Still, the prevalence of large landed estates and bound labor in agriculture has been

---

[2] Rowe 1985.   [3] Hamashima 1982: 263–335.   [4] McDermott 1981.

unduly exaggerated.[5] According to Ray Huang, apart from a few extremely wealthy families that may have owned 10,000 *mu* or more, the largest landowners possessed combined holdings of 500 to 2,000 *mu*.[6] Such landowners typically resided in towns and cities rather than the countryside, entrusting management of their holdings and rent collection to overseers – often trusted bondservants. Tenant farmers and bondservants remained economically independent of their landlords, absentee or not.

During the sixteenth century rising output and the revival of long-distance trade had begun to foster renewed regional specialization in agricultural production and handicrafts. Jiangnan and perpetually land-hungry Fujian became reliant on rice imports to feed populations that earned their living from cash crops and handicraft industry (sericulture and cotton manufacture in Jiangnan, sugar, tea, and ceramics in Fujian). The central Yangzi valley provinces of Hunan and Hubei shipped surplus rice downriver to Jiangnan, while oceangoing ships carried rice from the Pearl River Delta to Fujian. Before 1550 nearly all major commercial cities were located along the two major arteries of interregional trade, the Yangzi River and the Grand Canal. In the second half of the sixteenth century, however, the pace of commercialization began to accelerate, transforming the economic structure of the Chinese empire. The proliferation of periodic markets in many parts of China, including the North China Plain, testified to the steady expansion of the market into rural life.[7]

The demise of the early Ming systems of labor service duties and hereditary artisan households paved the way for more efficient allocation of labor. The twenty-five imperial silk textile factories established in the early Ming were reduced to three, located in the major silk-producing centers of Nanjing, Hangzhou, and Suzhou. The output of private silk manufacturing vastly exceeded that of state-run factories. In the early seventeenth century, Suzhou

---

[5] Virtually no scholars today – apart, perhaps, from some Marxist historians in China – would agree with Mark Elvin's (1973: 235) characterization of late Ming society as a "manorial order with serfdom and serf-like tenancy." Even Ōyama Masaaki, whose earlier work (1984; originally published in 1957–58) portrayed late Ming agriculture as based on slave labor, later (1974) adopted a much more reserved position, conceding that servile labor constituted no more than a quarter of the agricultural labor force, a figure that most scholars today would still regard as far too high. McDermott (2013a: 253) estimates that in Huizhou, a region that traditionally had a high incidence of bondservitude, bondservants comprised less than 1 percent of the agricultural labor force in the late Ming. Land registers from 1582 cadastral survey for She and Xiuning counties in Anhui show that nearly all land was owned by locals, and 70 percent of all households owned some land. Landownership was fairly evenly dispersed, with landlords (a mere 0.3 percent of the population) owning less than 20 percent of all land. See Zhang Youyi 1984: 9.

[6] Ray Huang 1974: 158. Kang Chao (1986: 107–28) argues that increasing competition for land effectively deterred the formation of large landed estates.

[7] For studies of long-term market development on the local/regional level, see Shiba (1977) on Ningbo and Marks (1999) on Guangdong. Little investigation of periodic market systems has been conducted for North China, but a noteworthy study is Ishihara 1973.

boasted several thousand "loom households" engaged in silk weaving, along with thousands more employed in dyeing and other specialized tasks, compared to 300 looms at the imperial silk factory. The concentration of silk manufacture continued in the Qing. It has been estimated that the total number of silk-weaving looms in operation in Jiangnan cities rose from 15,000 in the late Ming to 80,000 by the early nineteenth century.[8] At Jingdezhen, by far the largest porcelain manufacturing center, a highly complex division of labor developed that divided the manufacturing process into more than twenty specialized tasks. The imperial factory at Jingdezhen initially relied on three-month service rotations of hereditary artisans before shifting to hired labor and eventually suspending its own manufacturing altogether in favor of contracting out consignments to private firms. By the late Ming more than 200 private kilns, each employing about 30 workers, were operating in Jingdezhen as well as thousands of smaller pottery workshops producing both fine pieces for the imperial court and the international market and a wide range of wares for ordinary consumers.[9]

Impressive as the growth of urban manufacturing was, in many respects the major development in the late Ming period was the rise of rural handicraft industries, above all cotton manufacture. Introduced to the Yangzi Delta at the end of the Song, cotton flourished in the sandy soils near the seacoast. During the fifteenth century cotton spinning and weaving, spurred by technological borrowing from silk manufacture, boomed in the delta. Songjiang prefecture (the vicinity of modern Shanghai) became the center of cotton manufacture, producing cloth sold throughout the empire (Map 8.1). Cotton cultivation, ginning, spinning, and weaving became specialized tasks within the rural economy, while dyeing and calendaring became urban industries. Since Jiangnan could not produce sufficient cotton to meet the rising demand for cloth, merchants imported raw cotton from the Central Plain and Guangdong. Merchant capital regularly intervened at each step in the manufacturing process. Many rural spinners and weavers, the vast majority of whom were women, became full-time cottage handicraft workers earning piece-rate wages. Brokers based in market towns delivered ginned cotton to spinners and yarn to weavers on credit, purchasing the finished product at a discounted price. Scholarly opinion remains divided on the degree to which merchants controlled the labor process in cotton manufacture, but there is little doubt that many rural households depended on the sale of domestic handicraft goods to meet their subsistence needs.[10]

---

[8] Fan Jinmin and Jin Wen 1993: 200–4.
[9] Xu Dixin and Wu Chengming 2000: 308–26. On the formation of a global market for Ming – and especially Jingdezhen – porcelain wares, see Finlay 2010; Pierson 2013.
[10] Nishijima 1984 remains the most detailed study in English of the Ming cotton industry; for a brief and more current synopsis, see Zurndorfer 2013: 77–83. Most scholars (e.g., Fan Jinmin 1998; Xu Dixin and Wu Chengming 2000: 222–23; Zurndorfer 2013: 82) agree with

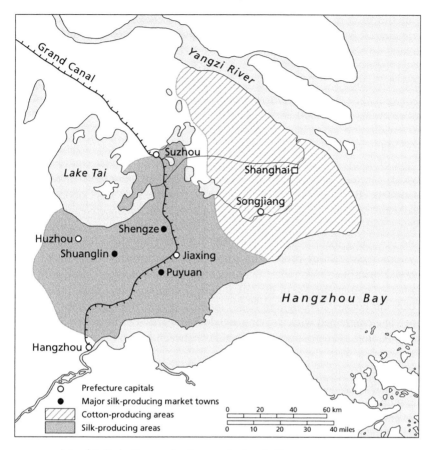

Map 8.1 Sericulture and cotton production in Jiangnan

Local specialization in rural industry also developed in other parts of Jiangnan. For example, rural households in Shaoxing began to specialize in brewing rice wine, creating a brand identity that by the eighteenth century dominated the national market while remaining almost entirely a rural industry. Half of the rice fields in Shaoxing were planted with the high-gluten

Nishijima's argument that merchants did not have a direct role in the manufacture of cotton cloth. Li Bozhong (2000: 77–85), in contrast, argues that merchants became involved in the production process – for example, by enforcing quality standards. Ch'iu Peng-sheng's study (2004) of the judicial treatment of contracts and dispute resolution in the Suzhou cotton finishing industry supports Li's analysis.

varieties used in brewing.[11] As more rural households were drawn into the commercial economy, small towns, most having only 500–2,000 inhabitants, sprang up across the Jiangnan countryside. These towns served as intermediaries between rural producers and regional and national markets. Market towns that flourished as centers of silk and cotton manufacture such as Shengze, Nanxun, Zhenze, Wuqing, Puyuan, Xinshi, and Jiangwan grew into substantial cities of 20,000–50,000 inhabitants.[12]

A variety of labor arrangements were practiced in the urban textile industry. Many weavers were independent artisans who relied exclusively on the labor of family members. The larger weaving workshops were equipped with twenty or more looms and employed artisans on long-term hired labor contracts. But even many skilled workers worked as day laborers who gathered at specified bridges or teashops to await prospective employers. Some merchants practiced a putting-out system, renting looms to weavers and providing them with raw materials.[13] In the Qing dynasty a multitiered system of contracting production emerged in the Jiangnan textile trades that served to diffuse risk rather than concentrate control of production in the hands of entrepreneurs. In the silk industry, wholesale merchants known as "account houses" (*zhangfang* 賬房) purchased yarn from merchant middlemen and contracted with weaving and dyeing workshops to weave and finish the silk cloth. The contract arrangements between account houses and workshops often were mediated by intermediaries (*chengguan* 承管) who bore responsibility for fulfillment of orders and losses of goods.[14] A similar arrangement existed in the cotton textile manufacture, where the wholesale merchants – known as "trademark firms" (*zihao* 字號), since they marketed the finished cloth under their own brand labels – relied on contractors for dyeing and calendaring. The cotton calendaring industry in Suzhou, which employed more than 10,000 workers in the 1730s, was controlled by a group of 300 contractors who owned their own equipment, received cloth on consignment from wholesale merchants, and took their fees out of the wages paid to laborers hired on a piece-rate basis.[15]

Artisanal organization remained weak. While urban merchants and shopkeepers began to form guilds in the seventeenth century, the imperial state suppressed labor combination and collective action by journeymen workers. In the calendaring industry, for example, government officials prohibited workers from collectively negotiating wage increases and granted contractors

---

[11] Yōgi 1997.   [12] Liu Shiji 1987; Fan Shuzhi 1990.   [13] Lillian Li 1981: 45–52.
[14] Ibid.: 51–56; Fan Jinmin and Jin Wen 1993: 220–35. Fan and Jin assert that the account house system was the dominant form of organizing silk production in Jiangnan by the beginning of the nineteenth century.
[15] Terada 1972a. On the role of middlemen (known as *gushi* 賈師) and their relationship to *zihao* firms in the Jiangnan cotton industry, see Ch'iu 2012.

the right to use coercion to enforce discipline.[16] In adjudicating disputes over contracts, debts, and work stoppages, magistrates gave firm support to standard contractual procedures and "the established rules of the trade" (*xianding zhangcheng* 現定章程). But magistrates also strove to strike a balance by preventing merchants' monopolization of the market on one hand and protecting the livelihood of the laboring classes on the other.[17]

The expansion of long-distance trade and regional specialization of production during the late Ming period promoted new developments in economic organization and management. Most commercial enterprises were family firms, but the expanding scale of commerce often demanded capital and personnel resources well beyond the capacity of individual households. Entrepreneurs seeking to recruit partners and employees still looked to their kinsmen and countrymen, however. The development of lineage institutions, and especially the creation of corporate lineages, provided the means to transform the family firm into a quasi-corporate business institution. In addition, long-distance traders who sojourned or settled in distant cities formed cooperative alliances with other merchants from their home areas. These alliances based on native place association not only facilitated long-distance trade but led to the creation of veritable trading empires by the two most successful groups: the Huizhou and Shanxi merchants.

One of the most far-reaching social transformations occurring during the Song-Yuan-Ming transition was the invention of localized corporate lineages. Initially, corporate lineages were rooted in ritual practice and group solidarity rather than common economic interests; each patriline (*jia*) remained a separate economic and fiscal unit. Neo-Confucian kinship norms were institutionalized through ritual practices and legal changes that strengthened patrilineal descent and agnatic bonds. Ancestral sacrifices, common graveyards, and the compilation of genealogies further fostered collective kinship identity.[18] The creation of corporate lineages resulted from divergent strategies, in some cases promoting exclusive membership while in other cases adopting liberal principles of inclusion (not restricted to demonstrated common descent) in order to build alliances. In many areas, especially in South China, local lineages superseded the defunct *lijia* groupings as the basic units of local society and governance. A crucial turning point in the formation of corporate lineages came in the early sixteenth century, when the Ming state condoned the building of ancestral halls by the general public. This dispensation

---

[16] Yokoyama 1962.
[17] Ch'iu 2004. The Qing Code formally proscribed "manipulation of the market" (*bachi hangshi* 把持行市), which could refer either to merchants acting as cartels to exert oligopolistic power or to collective action by workers to extract concessions on wages and working conditions.
[18] Ebrey 1986b. On the codification of Neo-Confucian patrilineal principles in formal family, marriage, and inheritance laws during the Yuan and Ming, see Birge 2002.

triggered a boom in the construction of ancestral halls, which often displaced communal rites and shrines dedicated to local deities as the focal sites of social solidarity. This trend also encouraged the proliferation of single-lineage villages, in which lineage membership conferred legal privileges and land-ownership rights. Incorporation of lineage trusts created permanent entities to manage common assets – the ancestral hall; endowments for ritual expenses, upkeep of the ancestral hall, and charitable relief and subventions for marriages and burials for lineage members; and landed estates that yielded income to provide for these expenses – that were not subject to partible inheritance rules.[19]

In Huizhou (Anhui), lineage trusts began to proliferate already in the fifteenth century. In this region, timber-yielding forest lands were valuable assets and the economic mainstay of many households (as we saw in the case of the Li Shu household in Chapter 7). It was common practice for lineage trusts to accumulate timber lands, which required the kind of patient invest-ment that permanent corporations could best afford (evergreen oaks required thirty years to mature). Management of lineage assets – and the tenant farmers and woodcutters, sometimes numbering in scores – typically devolved to the wealthiest or most socially prominent branch within the lineage. Private trusts – in which groups of lineages or individuals acquired joint ownership (divided into shares) of forest tracts – also appeared in the fifteenth century. Both owners and tenants sought to mitigate risks by purchasing or cultivating dispersed plots. Tenants, who typically leased plots from multiple owners, acquired considerable control over their tenancies, and by the sixteenth century tenants commonly transferred their cultivation rights (also divided into shares) to others through sales and subleases.[20]

In the coastal regions of Guangdong and Fujian, which experienced surges in agricultural productivity, population increase, and commercial growth after 1550, corporate lineages exerted an especially powerful influence over social and economic life. In the Pearl River Delta lineage trusts became profit-driven institutions that dominated the local economy. Single-lineage villages quickly became the norm in much of this region, and in some counties lineage corpor-ations owned as much as 60 percent of the arable land in the early twentieth century.[21] The Liugengtang lineage estate in Panyu (Guangzhou), which originated with an endowment of a mere 14 *mu* in 1587, saw its landholdings swell to 2,144 *mu* by the end of Ming and 27,852 *mu* in 1786. Lineage estates

---

[19] The formation of corporate lineages in the Ming has been studied in greatest detail for Fujian and Guangdong; see Zheng Zhenman 2001; Szonyi 2002; Faure 2007. But similar trends have been observed for other parts of South China. See Dardess 1996: 112–38; McDermott 2013a: 235–368. Lineage trusts were commonly designated as *tang* 堂, in reference to the ancestral halls that constituted their institutional core.

[20] McDermott 2013a: 409–20.   [21] Ye Xian'en and Tan Dihua 1985b: 26–27; 34–35, table 1.

in the delta vied with one another for control of marketplaces as well as landholdings. The Guan lineage in Nanhai county originally invested its funds – contributed by 212 donors – in moneylending. In 1637 the trust purchased a shop in a local market town. By 1800, the Guan owned twelve of the town's twenty-three shops. Credit associations (*yinhui* 銀會), which exclusively lent their funds to lineage members, generated income not only for ritual activities but also for business investments.[22] In the city of Foshan, the largest iron-manufacturing center in China, four powerful lineage trusts owned and operated foundries, pottery kilns, wharves, ferries, and warehouses.[23]

Of course, kinship bonds did not shield lineage trusts from internecine conflicts, and entrepreneurs often struck out on their own, unencumbered by family ties and obligations. The Huizhou merchant Fang Tingke, for example, refrained from business alliances with kinsmen or other Huizhou merchants. Fang started off in the late fifteenth century as an itinerant peddler who struggled for twenty years to build up capital for investment. Fang then settled in Kaifeng, where he traded in cotton and linen goods and acquired a sizable fortune before eventually retiring to Huizhou. Fang brought his son, grandson, and nephews into his business, but otherwise kept his distance, financially speaking, from his brothers and kinsmen. Although the Fang lineage prospered during the economic boom of the late Ming – it encompassed six branches and more than a thousand adult members around 1550 – only members of Fang Tingke's branch ventured into long-distance trade. With only one son, Fang Tingke did not have to divide his wealth and business operations among multiple heirs as most successful merchants did. But his descendants went their separate ways, eschewing the risks of trade for the more certain profits of moneylending, either in Kaifeng or at home in Huizhou. The Fang lineage remained weakly integrated despite its prosperity; many shunned Fang Tingke's appeal for funds to construct an ancestral hall, and its poorer members turned to individual patrons, not the lineage, for loans and charity.[24]

The Taitang Cheng lineage of Huizhou, in contrast, relied heavily on lineage organization to develop a far-flung business empire. Members of the Kezhou branch of the Taitang Cheng lineage appear to have first engaged in money-lending in the textile centers of Suzhou and Songjiang in the early years of the Ming, and then invested their profits in the lucrative salt monopoly. The Cheng also obtained bulk raw materials in Hubei such as cotton, timber, coal, and tung oil for sale in Jiangnan, and in return brought salt and cotton textiles to Hubei. By the end of the fifteenth century the Kezhou branch had established trading colonies in Yangzhou (the main salt trade center), Jiangnan, and two localities in southern Hubei, each populated by immigrants from a different

---

[22] Faure 2007: 222–29.   [23] Ye Xian'en and Tan Dihua 1985a: 146–48.
[24] McDermott 2013b: 235–49.

segment of the home lineage in Huizhou. The leaders of the Kezhou branch exercised strong centralized control over their diverse business interests (like the Fang, the Cheng also invested heavily in moneylending wherever they went), but divided their geographic spheres of operations outside Huizhou among the branch's four segments. The internal organization of the Cheng partnership is unknown, but like long-distance traders elsewhere they clearly preferred to deal with kinsmen and fellow countrymen rather than strangers with whom they shared little beyond the thirst for profit.[25]

By the late Ming period the Huizhou merchants had become fixtures of China's commercial landscape. In this respect they were preceded by the so-called "Shanxi merchants," a loose geographical label for merchants from Shanxi and Shaanxi provinces in northwestern China (Map 8.2). The Shanxi merchants first achieved prominence in the early Ming delivering provisions to frontier armies through the *kaizhong* system, whereby the government repaid merchants with salt monopoly privileges. Consequently many Shanxi merchants settled in Yangzhou and Huai'an, the principal salt depots in eastern China, which gave them ready access to Jiangnan markets. In addition to their dominant position in the grain and salt trades, Shanxi merchants marketed cotton cloth from Jiangnan across North China.[26] The Shanxi and Huizhou merchants became fierce competitors throughout the cities and market towns of Jiangnan, and each group utilized native place ties to build alliances and extend their networks of partners, agents, and clients. The scholar-official Xie Zhaozhe, a native of Fujian, expressed widely shared sentiments in singling out the conspicuous wealth of the Huizhou and Shanxi merchants in a work published in 1616:

If we were to name those recognized as the richest families of all, one would have to propose the Huizhou merchants in the south, and the Shanxi merchants in the north. The great merchants of Huizhou trade in fish and salt, amassing fortunes measured in the millions of silver taels; those worth 200,000–300,000 taels could only be considered merchants of middling rank. Shanxi merchants deal in salt and silk, some traveling afar to peddle their goods while others pile up stocks of grain. Their wealth exceeds that of the Huizhou merchants, because while the latter are spendthrift, the Shanxi merchants are frugal.[27]

One year later, in 1617, the Huizhou merchants scored a decisive triumph with the inauguration of the franchise system that awarded salt monopoly rights to syndicates of wealthy merchants based in Yangzhou (see Chapter 7). The

[25] Ibid.: 249–60. The standard reference on the Huizhou merchants is Zhang Haipeng and Wang Tingyuan 1995.
[26] The pioneering study by Terada (1972) remains the classic account of Shanxi merchants in the Ming. On the formation of regionally based merchant networks and their activities in Jiangnan, see Fan Jinmin 1998: 184–309.
[27] *WZZ*: 4.96.

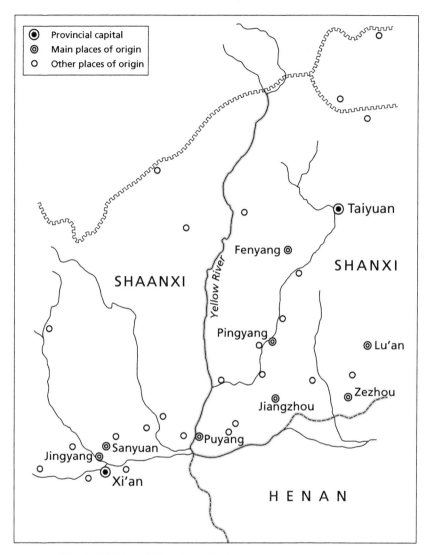

Map 8.2 Origins of Shanxi merchants

franchise system enabled the Huizhou merchants to wrest control of the salt trade from their Shanxi rivals.[28] Merchants from other regions, such as Guangdong and Fujian, likewise developed their own commercial networks based on native-place ties. But it was above all in Huizhou that, in the

[28] Zhang Haipeng and Wang Tingyuan 1995: 159–84.

306 The Economic History of China

words of a local gazetteer published in 1609, "Gold's decrees rule heaven, while the god Money looms over the earth."[29] The commercial efflorescence of the late Ming undermined customary ideas about class, status, and social order.[30] Wealth conveyed social power, and poverty no longer was deemed, as it often was in the past, a mark of virtue. The power of wealth erased its moral stigma; a growing share of the patrician elite arose from mercantile backgrounds, and the image of the wise and virtuous entrepreneur who manifests diligence, frugality, and magnanimity began to supplant hoary caricatures of greedy and miserly swindlers.[31] Ironically, the erosion of social boundaries aroused new efforts to delineate legal discriminations between "honorable" (liang 良) and "mean" (jian 賤) statuses. Mean statuses traditionally had been defined in terms of disreputable occupations, ranging from actors and prostitutes to barbers, butchers, and sedan-bearers. Yet although these groups continued to suffer social ostracism, economic improvement commonly led to social acceptance.[32] Bondservitude, of course, conferred mean status, but hired laborers no longer were treated as such. As the definition of mean statuses narrowed – and would be abolished altogether by imperial decree in 1723 – the "poor" eclipsed the "mean" as a social category. Growing recognition of poverty as not simply the natural condition of a broad swath of society but as a social problem bred by the remorselessly competitive market economy resulted in the proliferation of social welfare institutions to succor orphans, widows, and the "deserving poor."[33] Much ink was spilt to clarify the ethical status of the poor as older, morally neutral views gave way to deepening suspicions that poverty resulted from improvidence and sloth. Less ambiguously, charity for the poor provided an avenue for the honorable use of wealth and justified its accumulation.[34]

Fluid social mobility spurred social climbing and status anxiety. Emulation of the patrician lifestyle encouraged the commercialization of literati culture and ostentatious spending on art, antiques, books, and furnishings for the home and the scholar's studio. "Fashion" and "taste" emerged as the guiding principles for the acquisition and display of material goods expressing one's pedigree (or aspirations for higher status). Unsurprisingly, "taste" itself became a highly contested arena of status competition, and supercilious patricians derided the shallow pretensions of the nouveaux riches. With rising incomes, mass consumption of tea, sugar, rice wine, porcelain, silk and cotton goods, books, lacquerwares, and furniture rose, as well as expenditures on

---

[29] SZ: 5, fengtu 風土, 12a.   [30] This theme is explored at length in Brook 1998.
[31] Yu Yingshi 1987.   [32] Liang Qizi 1993.
[33] There is a very substantial literature on the rise of private philanthropy in the late Ming and Qing periods. See Fuma 1997; Liang Qizi 1997; Handlin Smith 2009.
[34] Liang Qizi 1993: 151–57.

entertainment, religious and ritual activities, leisure, and travel. Consumer demand – and increasingly differentiated consumer tastes – exerted more pervasive influence in shaping the production of goods for both luxury and ordinary purposes.[35]

The silver economy and the seventeenth-century crisis

One of the key constraints on economic growth in Ming China was the monetary disorder bequeathed by the disastrous fiscal policies of the early Ming emperors. The Ming attempt to repeat the Mongol Yuan success in instituting an inconvertible paper money system proved an abject failure. By the 1430s the Ming *baochao* notes were worthless, and shortages of copper had forced the government to shutter its mints. For nearly a century afterward the Ming issued no new bronze coin. Beginning with the commutation of the Jiangnan rice tribute levy in 1436, the Ming state gradually shifted from in-kind payments to taxes collected in uncoined silver, which circulated in the private economy in the form of ingots that varied widely in weight and fineness. This trend culminated in the "Single Whip" reforms of the late sixteenth century, which converted numerous labor services into silver payments assessed on landholdings rather than individuals. These changes marked a concession to the reality of a *de facto* silver monetary standard in the private economy. Bronze coin, produced in modest quantities after 1527, supplemented silver as a fractional currency for everyday transactions, but the commercial revival of the late Ming era was fueled by silver.

Nonetheless, China produced little silver to meet this burgeoning need. After a spurt in output from domestic mines in the early fifteenth century, Ming silver mining dwindled to insignificant levels. Illicit private maritime trade probably brought in some silver, but the crucial breakthrough came in the 1530s, when silver strikes at Iwami in western Honshū touched off a prodigious mining boom. The Ming court had suspended all intercourse with Japan in 1523, but by 1540 large quantities of Japanese silver were being smuggled into the coastal provinces of southeastern China.[36] In addition, the first Portuguese merchant ships arrived on the coast of China in 1522. European traders purchased cargoes of Chinese porcelains and silks with silver from Spain's fledgling empire in the New World. The Ming allowed the Portuguese to establish a trading base at Macau in 1557, and the Spanish founded their own colonial outpost at Manila in 1571, opening a direct channel across the

---

[35] On the impact of rising demand for luxury goods on consumption and cultural values, see Wu Renshu 2007; Clunas 1991; Brook 1998.
[36] Von Glahn 1996a: 113–18.

Pacific between Mexico and China that gave birth to the first truly global circuit of economic exchange.[37]

The irresistible demand for silver undermined the Ming founder's long-standing prohibition against private overseas trade. Friction between the Ming state and clandestine traders (dubbed Wokou 倭寇 or "Japanese pirates," although most were Chinese) erupted into outright warfare in the 1540–50s. Devastating Wokou attacks on coastal areas and pressure from merchant and official constituencies in the southeastern provinces finally persuaded the Ming court to relax the trade ban in 1567. The Ming created a new licensing system to regulate the volume of private trade, but left in force the prohibition against direct trade with Japan. Nonetheless commercial exchange with Japan flourished through Portuguese intermediaries or mutual trade between Chinese and Japanese merchants at neutral ports such as Hoi-an in Vietnam. Japanese customers were no less eager than Europeans to acquire Chinese goods.

The influx of foreign silver after 1570 was a crucial catalyst for the explosive commercial growth of the late Ming period. Although silver still circulated in uncoined form, the huge expansion of the money supply eliminated a key bottleneck constraining the market economy. In southern Fujian, the region most directly tied to the boom in foreign trade, cash crops such as sugar and tobacco (the latter an import from the Americas) squeezed out rice farming.[38] Surging demand for silk and sugar also encouraged many farmers in the Pearl River Delta to abandon rice cultivation in favor of planting mulberry and sugar cane; after 1600 the region became dependent on rice imports, especially from Guangxi province to the west, to sustain its food supply.[39]

The Chinese hunger for silver exerted a powerful influence on the emerging global economy. Silver was the principal commodity of global trade in the early seventeenth century. Silver fetched a higher price in China than anywhere else, and European traders rushed to deliver silver to the Chinese market. As a retired Portuguese merchant wrote in a book published in Lisbon in 1621, "silver wanders throughout all the world in its peregrinations before flocking to China, where it remains, as if at its natural center."[40] In the second half of the sixteenth century China imported at least 50 tons of silver per year. I estimate that in the first four decades of the seventeenth century China's annual silver imports soared to 115 tons or more; some scholars have suggested much higher figures (see Table 8.1). Roughly half of this silver came from Japan, and the rest originated in Peru and Mexico. The handsome profit

---

[37] Flynn and Giráldez 1995.

[38] Rawski 1972: 48–49. Fujian quickly became the main tobacco-growing region within China. On the diffusion of tobacco throughout the highlands of South China after its introduction in the late sixteenth century, see Tajiri 1999; Benedict 2011: 15–60.

[39] Marks 1999: 130–31.   [40] Cited in Godinho 1969: 531.

Table 8.1 *Estimates of silver imports to China, 1550–1645*
(all figures in metric tons)

	From Japan	From Americas (Pacific)	From Americas (Atlantic)	Total
Liang (1939)	2,795	948		3,743
Yamamura and Kamiki (1983)	7,350–9,450	1,320		8,670–10,780
Zhuang (1995)	6,527	2,250	1,013	9,800
Li (2005)	6,375	4,688		11,250
Von Glahn (2013)	3,634–3,825	2,481	1,230	7,345–7,536

Sources: Liang Fangzhong 1939: 173–79; Yamamura and Kamiki 1983: 351–53; Zhuang Guotu 1995: 3; Li Longsheng 2005: 165; von Glahn 2013: 32, 41.

Table 8.2 *Grain and money revenues in Ming China*

	c. 1435–49	1612
Taxes in grain (*shi*)	26,871,152	28,369,247
Equivalent in silver (*liang*)	6,717,783	18,069,584
Value of textile revenues in silver (*liang*)	239,385	370,002
Value of paper money revenues in silver (*liang*)	4,379	–
Taxes in silver (*liang*)	2,430,000	4,000,000
Total income in silver equivalent (*liang*)	9,391,552	22,439,586
Percentage of total paid in silver	25.9	17.8

Source: Wu Hui 1990: 41.

European and Japanese traders earned from silver imports financed purchases of Chinese silks and porcelain wares, giving further impetus to China's industrial output.

The growth of the commercial economy did not strengthen the Ming state, however. Although the Ming replaced many in-kind taxes with silver payments, tax rates remained tied to the quotas established in the early years of the dynasty. The Ming government failed to capture revenue from the expansion of agriculture and commerce, and thus suffered from chronic underfunding. Indeed, given the falling purchasing power of silver as imported silver flooded China's domestic market, the value of silver revenues actually declined compared to the fifteenth century (Table 8.2). Moreover, commercial and urban growth engendered not only prosperity, but also greater economic volatility, pools of poverty, and deepening social rifts. Beginning in the 1590s many cities suffered from sharp social conflict and outbreaks of violence.[41] Beset by social turmoil and political strife, the Ming state was ill-prepared for the Manchu invasion of 1618, which inflicted a crushing defeat on Ming armies. During the next two decades the Ming suffered repeated military reversals. Desperate to stave off utter collapse of its defenses, the court enacted a rapidly escalating series of emergency taxes that quadrupled its silver revenues between 1617 and 1637. War expenditures still far outran state income, however, while the tax increases fanned popular discontent. Poor harvests in the mid-1630s sparked large-scale rebellions in North China, prompting the central government to raise taxes another 50 percent between 1637 and 1639.[42] Finally, devastating floods, famines, and outbreaks of epidemic disease during 1638–42 crippled both the national economy and the Ming state. In 1644 a peasant rebel army seized Beijing, followed several months later by the Manchu occupation of the capital and the founding of a new conquest dynasty, the Qing (1644–1911).

In the view of some scholars, the fall of the Ming dynasty in 1644 was linked to a set of general economic and political crises that churned up social turmoil and popular protests against ruling authorities across Eurasia. The idea of a "general crisis of the seventeenth century" originated in scholarship on Europe and has remained central to interpretations of the transition to modernity in European historiography. These interpretations vary widely, but there is general agreement that Europe experienced a prolonged economic crisis from late sixteenth to early eighteenth century that was manifested in population decline, falling agricultural and industrial production, a recession in international trade, and price deflation.[43] Some historians of Asia have argued that the disruptions in international trade, and especially a decline in the flow of bullion to Asian markets, led to a devastating economic contraction.[44] According to William Atwell, after decades of rampant economic growth the flow of silver into China suddenly fell sharply in the late 1630s as a result of Japan's seclusion policies (*sakoku* 鎖国), Spain's curtailment of Philippine trade with China, and the dissolution of Portugal's alliance with Spain in 1640, severing trade between Manila and Macau. In addition, the Ming government's escalating tax demands extracted

---

[41] Yuan 1979; von Glahn 1991.   [42] Tang Wenji 1990.
[43] On the economic dimensions of "the general crisis of the seventeenth century," see de Vries 1976.
[44] These views were advanced by specialists in Chinese, South Asian, and Southeast Asian history in a thematic issue of the journal *Modern Asian Studies*. See Atwell 1990; Reid 1990; Richards 1990. However, in the same issue Niels Steensgaard (1990) disputed claims for a "general crisis" in seventeenth-century Asia, concluding that apart from environmental disruptions, the economic trends in different parts of Asia (and their political consequences) diverged substantially.

a sizable quantity of silver from the private economy, resulting in a slowing of commerce and industrial production that spread to the agrarian economy as well. The appreciation of silver raised the real cost of taxes and loans, bankrupting family farms. Thus a severe commercial depression ultimately became a crisis in production as well.[45]

The hypothesis that a scarcity of silver resulting from the disruption of international trade caused widespread economic depression in China does not stand up to theoretical or empirical scrutiny, however. China's foreign trade and silver imports remained vibrant down to 1642.[46] Grain prices soared in the late 1630s, but prices for land, industrial goods such as cotton and silk textiles, and exports remained stable. Moreover, the decline in silver imports in the 1640s was far too small to have a dramatic effect on the total stock of money in China, and the fall of the gold price of silver in China to the international level precisely at this time also undermines the claim of a dire shortage of silver. The evidence of trade flows, prices, and exchange ratios all point instead toward an acute subsistence crisis precipitated by catastrophic harvests and popular rebellions.[47] Atwell is much more persuasive in attributing the harvest failures of 1638–42 to the climatic disturbances and cold weather experienced across the whole of the northern hemisphere during the seventeenth century.[48] War, natural disasters, and epidemics wrought a terrible toll of devastation and death, resulting in severe population losses estimated at 20 percent of China's total population.[49]

The Manchu conquest of China itself was relatively bloodless, but economic recovery proved elusive. The persistent spell of cold and wet weather from the 1620s to the 1690s hindered agricultural recovery. The grave subsistence crisis of the last years of the Ming continued into the early Qing, sharply curtailing demand for textiles and other manufactured goods. Prices for manufactured goods plummeted, dragging down industry and commerce (Figure 8.1). In the late 1650s grain prices also fell sharply, inaugurating a prolonged deflation that would last until the 1690s. The "Kangxi depression" of 1660–90 – named after the reigning Manchu emperor, Kangxi (r. 1661–1722) – was marked by a general decline in prices, wages, rents, and land values.[50]

The economic doldrums were aggravated by policies undertaken in 1661 by the Manchu regime to isolate the renegade regime of Zheng Chenggong, a Fujian merchant prince who had taken refuge on Taiwan. The Manchus sought

---

[45] Atwell 1982, 1986, 1990, 2006.   [46] Li Longsheng 2005.
[47] Von Glahn 1996b, 2013: 31–39.   [48] Atwell 1986, 1990. See also Marks 2012: 187–89.
[49] The demographic historian Cao Shuji (2000b: 451–52, table 11.1) has estimated that Ming China attained a maximum population of 192 million by 1630, and suffered a population loss of 40 million (21 percent) between 1630 and 1644. Other scholars (e.g., Marks 2012: 187) have proposed population declines of similar magnitude.
[50] Kishimoto-Nakayama 1984; von Glahn 1996a: 207–33.

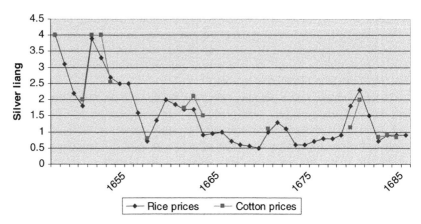

Figure 8.1 Rice and cotton prices in Jiangnan, 1644–84
Source: Rice prices (per *shi*): Wang Yeh-chien 1992: 40, table 1.1; cotton
cloth prices (per bolt): Kishimoto 1997: 151, table 4.7.

to impose an economic blockade on Zheng by renewing the ban on overseas
trade and forcing much of the population along the southeast coast to move
inland. The Zheng regime continued to hold out thanks to its control of the
thriving clandestine trade between China and Japan until the Qing mounted a
successful invasion and takeover of Taiwan in 1683. But the embargo and the
relocation policy clearly wounded southeastern China's commercial economy.
    By 1683 the Qing had quelled all armed resistance to its rule. In the
following year the ban on maritime trade ended, and record numbers of
Chinese ships flocked to Nagasaki. The slow recuperation of population and
agricultural recovery brought an end to the Kangxi depression. A long era of
domestic peace and prosperity began that would endure until the final years
of the eighteenth century.

Fiscal governance under Manchu rule

By 1683 the Manchus had secured control of the former Ming territories,
although the Manchu Empire was greatly enlarged during the eighteenth
century through conquests of Mongolia, Tibet, and the "New Frontier"
(Xinjiang 新疆) carved out of Uighur- and Mongol-populated Central Asia
(Map 8.3). Like earlier Chinese dynasties, the first priority of the Qing state was
to restore a stable agricultural base. The Qing government sponsored migration
and agricultural development in frontier regions, mobilized labor for major
flood control projects, and sharply curtailed the tax exemptions and other
privileges of the patrician elite. Like the Ming before it, the Qing state was

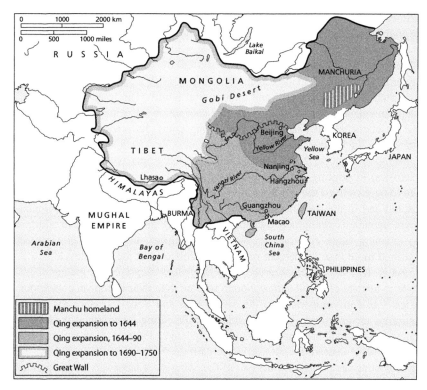

Map 8.3 Territorial expansion of the Qing state

ideologically committed to easing the burden of state exactions while relying on direct taxation of land as the mainstay of its fiscal system. The Qing state can perhaps be described as a *provisioning state*, one dedicated to improving the people's livelihood through, for example, investments in famine relief and flood control. Yet in contrast to the activist conception of the state that prevailed in the Song, Qing governance was predicated on minimal intervention in the economic life of its subjects. Much of the actual responsibility for popular welfare was ceded to local public and private initiative. The laissez-faire policies toward commerce adopted by the Qing rulers encouraged Smithian dynamics of market expansion, division of labor, and regional specialization. But at the same time the limited fiscal capacity of the Qing state deterred investments in public goods that would help sustain economic growth.

The Manchus introduced a number of new political institutions derived from their own heritage, but by the eighteenth century the Qing state had largely become assimilated to Chinese forms of bureaucratic governance. Manchu rule in China initially depended heavily on military control based on standing armies known as banners (twenty-four altogether, separated into Manchu, Mongol, and Han Chinese divisions) stationed at strategic points throughout the empire. Sizable tracts of land were set aside to support the banners. The Manchus also created a new agency staffed by Chinese bondservants, the Imperial Household Department (Neiwufu 內務府), to manage the affairs and finances of the emperor and the imperial family. The Imperial Household Department was intended to curb the usurpation of imperial authority by palace eunuchs that had plagued the Ming court. Its activities ranged from managing the banner lands and various monopolies (such as salt, Manchurian ginseng, the copper trade with Japan, and the imperial silk and porcelain factories) to printing official editions of scholarly works.[51] For the most part the Qing preserved the governmental structure of the Ming dynasty both at the capital and in the provinces. But the Ministry of Revenue and its provincial-level intendants strengthened central control over fiscal resources; in addition to enacting more rigorous accounting procedures, the central government claimed more than 80 percent of revenues collected at the local level.[52]

As R. Bin Wong has observed, the Qing rulers displayed far greater solicitude in matters of social and economic welfare than their European contemporaries.[53] But in comparison to the earlier Han and Song dynasties the state's presence at the village level was minimal. The Qing government never conducted a universal land survey, nor did it update earlier records in any comprehensive way. Instead, it continued to rely on the Ming land survey of 1581–82 in allocating tax quotas. By the end of the Ming most labor service obligations had been converted to payments in silver, although these payments continued to be assessed on individual adult males (*ding*). In 1712 the Qing established permanent quotas for the *ding* labor service levy based on the 1711 census returns, and in 1713 the Kangxi emperor, in an act of imperial magnanimity, declared that the land tax quotas would be permanently frozen at the level of the 1711 assessments.[54] In 1729 the *ding* levy was formally merged into the land tax on an empire-wide scale. Henceforth individual landowners paid a single lump-sum tax in silver. This step completed the process of shifting taxation (and by extension the state's control over local society) from persons to land. At the time the Qing enjoyed substantial budget surpluses. By the end of the eighteenth century, however, the inability of the state to capture new revenues greatly weakened its ability to respond to political and economic crises.

The early Qing tax reforms obviated the need to compile detailed information about the composition of households. Indeed, the family as a social unit no longer was a unit of taxation. In 1668 the Qing suspended the compilation of yellow registers, which had served as the basis of the Ming land and labor

---

[51] Torbert 1977.   [52] Zelin 1984: 26–46.   [53] Wong 1997.
[54] Yeh-chien Wang 1973: 20–31.

taxes. In their place local officials were expected to conduct quinquennial surveys known as *bianshen* 編審. Unlike the yellow registers, which included data on all members of the household, the *bianshen* surveys merely gathered information on those liable for the *ding* labor service levy. The merging of the *ding* levy into the land tax in 1729 rendered the *bianshen* surveys obsolete, although they were formally ended only in 1772.[55] Although the conjugal family remained the fundamental socio-economic institution in Chinese society, it had achieved unprecedented autonomy from the attenuated reach of the imperial state.

Lijia units continued to exist in name under the Qing dynasty, but the primary mechanism of rural social control was a revamped *baojia* system of local policing modeled on the earlier Song institution. As in the Song, the Qing *baojia* system gradually absorbed tax collection duties and other civil responsibilities, such as famine relief. In 1740 the government officially transferred responsibility over population registration from the *lijia* units to the *baojia* headmen. But since the population registers no longer had any fiscal purpose, compiling population data became an empty bureaucratic exercise. As G. William Skinner has shown, from the early nineteenth century local officials simply adjusted older figures with routine additions (since a growing population was taken as a sign of prosperity), leading to vastly inflated population statistics by the end of the century.[56]

In 1766 the land tax generated nearly three-quarters of state income, with 16 percent coming from the salt monopoly and inland customs excises (Table 8.3). Nominally voluntary "contributions" (*juanna* 捐納) were a unique feature of the Qing revenue system. These funds derived from three sources: officials who were obliged to remit a portion of their salaries to provincial governments; individuals who purchased examination degrees and titles (and, on some occasions, actual offices) to secure higher social status; and wealthy merchants who received special favors bestowed by the state (primarily the cartels of salt merchants and the Cohong merchants who from 1757 gained monopoly privileges to trade with European merchants at Guangzhou).[57] Although the Qing state, like the Ming, derived the bulk of its revenues from land taxes, it had converted most of the land revenues formerly assessed in grain to money payments.[58] Moreover, the population boom of the eighteenth century, following the freezing of land tax quotas in 1713, sharply reduced the

---

[55] Hsiao 1960: 88–91. Tables 8.7 and 8.8 below are based on data collected from these *bianshen* surveys.
[56] Skinner 1986.
[57] Yeh-chien Wang: 8–9. For details on the *juanna* system, see Xu Daling 1974.
[58] It should be noted that although tax assessments were denominated in silver, a substantial portion of these taxes were paid in bronze coin, especially following the sharp increase in mint output in the mid-eighteenth century. See Yeh-chien Wang 1973: 59–61.

Table 8.3 *Central government revenues, 1766*
(all revenue figures in millions of silver taels)

Revenue source		Revenue	Percent
Land taxes, rents, and grain tribute	田賦, 田租, 漕糧	31.06	73.8
		20.31*	
Salt gabelle	鹽課	5.75	8.2
Internal and maritime customs	關稅	5.42	7.7
Tax surcharges	耗羨	3.50	5.0
Regular contributions	常例捐輸	2.00	2.9
Miscellaneous local taxes	落地雜稅	0.86	1.2
Stamp taxes	契稅	0.19	0.3
Brokerage and pawnshop licenses	牙當等稅	0.16	0.2
Marshes and fishing excises	蘆課魚課	0.15	0.2
Mining excises	礦課定額	0.08	0.1
Tea excise	茶課	0.07	0.1
Total		69.55	

*Portion of land tax collected in grain, converted to silver based on 1753 rates in Yeh-chien Wang 1973: 70.
Sources: Chen Feng 2008: 369, table 6–3.

per capita burden of taxation. In 1766 the real per capita land tax levy – measured in grain – was 70 percent below the modest level of the mid-fifteenth century (Table 8.4). Although estimating total national income for any period of imperial Chinese history is necessarily speculative given the limitations of our sources, it seems likely that during the Qing period the proportion of government revenue as a share of the national economy was substantially lower than in the Song, which relied heavily on taxation of commerce and consumption, and perhaps below the Ming level as well.

Compared to its predecessors, the Qing state exercised a relatively light hand in managing the domestic commercial economy. Apart from the salt monopoly, operated under the franchise system inherited from the Ming, the government interfered little in the production and distribution of goods. Even in the case of the salt monopoly, merchants handled the production, transport, and sale of salt, while the state merely collected an excise levy. Merchants and craftsmen assumed a greater degree of self-governance. Guilds, typically organized on the basis of native place identity rather than trade before the nineteenth century, proliferated in commercial cities throughout the empire. While guilds had broad authority to regulate membership fees and duties, wages and prices, and the terms of apprenticeship, they were forbidden to restrict access to their trade.[59] A few great merchants, such as the Huizhou salt

[59] Golas 1977; Ch'iu 1990; Moll-Murata 2008.

Table 8.4 *Grain and money revenues in Ming and Qing China*

	Land tax revenue					Total revenue			
	Land (millions of *mu*)	Grain (millions of *shi*)	Silver (millions of taels)	Grain (*shi*) per *mu*	Silver (taels) per *mu*	Population (millions)	Grain (*shi*) per capita	Silver (taels) per capita	Total per capita in grain
c. 1435–49	424.7	26.87	1.0	0.063	0.002	53.7	0.49	0.019	0.56
1766	741.4	8.32	29.92	0.011	0.040	208.1	0.04	0.233	0.17

Source: Wu Hui 1990: 45.

merchants in Yangzhou, amassed enormous fortunes thanks to their monopoly privileges.[60] But the vast majority of merchants and artisans inhabited a highly competitive market economy.

The Qing approach to economic management was exemplified by the brokerage system. Since the Song dynasty the government licensed brokers (*yahang*) who served as intermediaries between local merchants and long-distance traders, assisting the latter in finding customers, negotiating deals, acting as guarantors, and arranging transportation, lodging, credit, and ware-housing services. In the Qing period, brokers increasingly acted in lieu of magistrates in recording transactions, policing trade, adjudicating disputes, and collecting various commercial taxes. In return the government restricted the number of licenses within a locality, guaranteeing brokers a comfortable income. The state charged only nominal fees for brokerage licenses; its chief interest was to ensure the smooth operation of commerce, not to raise revenue.[61] In some areas (notably in Shandong) local notables, lineage leaders, or merchants obtained rights to create "free markets" (*yiji* 義集) by paying the requisite commercial tax quotas out of private funds (for example, a lineage bursary or guild assessments). The ostensible reason behind "free markets" was to eradicate nettlesome exactions by predatory brokers, but the institution readily allowed entrenched elites to exert power and patronage over local commerce.[62] Both the brokerage system and the "free markets" essentially became forms of tax-farming that limited the reach of the state into local commerce. The common practice whereby taxpayers used intermediaries to deliver payments to the authorities, known as "proxy remittance" (*baolan* 包攬), also constituted a form of tax-farming.[63]

The Qing government also assumed a laissez-faire posture towards foreign trade, severing the link between tributary diplomacy and commercial privileges devised by the Ming founder. The Qing banned maritime trade in 1662 as part of its campaign against the outlaw Zheng regime in Taiwan. Following the conquest of Taiwan in 1683, the Kangxi emperor repealed the imperial proscription, reopening Chinese ports to foreign merchants and allowing Chinese merchants to venture overseas, which they did in great numbers.[64] A vigorous trade between China and Japan recommenced, but by this time the Tokugawa regime had implemented stringent restrictions on the export of silver, prompting Chinese merchants to shift to purchasing large quantities of Japanese copper (2,600 tons annually in 1685–1715) to supply the Qing

---

[60] On the economic power and social influence of the Huizhou salt merchants in Yangzhou, see Finnane 2004; Wang Zhenzhong 2014.

[61] Mann 1987.   [62] Katō 1952a: 545–52; Mann 1987: 70–93.   [63] Hsiao 1960: 132–39.

[64] The evolution of early Qing policies leading to greater liberalization of maritime trade is detailed in Gang Zhao 2013.

mints. In 1715, however, the Japanese authorities enacted even more rigid controls on foreign trade that sharply reduced copper exports. During the eighteenth century trade between China and Japan tailed off sharply. Japanese demand for silk fabrics, porcelain wares, and sugar was increasingly satisfied by domestic producers who displaced Chinese imports with native products.[65]

Trade with European merchants also revived after 1683, but in the early eighteenth century the bulk of China's maritime trade was conducted with Southeast Asia. The value of cargoes carried by Chinese ships to Southeast Asia in the first half of the eighteenth century has been estimated at 6–14 million taels (equivalent to 22–52 metric tons) annually.[66] Emigrant Chinese from Fujian and Guangdong settled in Thailand, the Malay Peninsula, Java, and the Philippines, creating a web of trade networks spanning South China and Southeast Asia and turning the seas around the Indonesian archipelago into, in the words of one historian, "a Chinese Mediterranean."[67] By the second half of the eighteenth century, émigré Chinese merchants, laborers, and financiers had become the dominant force in the commercial economy of Southeast Asia (see Chapter 9).

Direct trade between Europeans and Chinese was relatively modest around 1700, but grew steadily throughout the eighteenth century. In 1757 the Qing court, in retaliation against European merchants' complaints about customs officials, restricted European traders' access to the Chinese market to the single port of Guangzhou. Furthermore, European merchants were required to conduct business through a cartel of twenty-odd Chinese merchant houses who became known as the Cohong.[68] These restrictions slowed the growth of trade with the Europeans, which stagnated for several decades. In the 1780s, however, Sino-Western trade again surged, fueled by explosive growth in exports of tea, which was becoming the staple beverage of the English population, and massive imports of Spanish silver coin from Mexico. Unable to sell European manufactured goods in the Chinese market, British merchants turned to

---

[65] Technology transfer enabled Tokugawa Japan to pursue a policy of "import substitution," developing its domestic industries such as silk manufacture and sugar processing in order to sever its dependence on imported goods from China. See Kawakatsu 1991.

[66] Kishimoto 1997: 186. During 1716–29, at the instigation of the Kangxi Emperor (who feared that the diaspora population harbored seditious elements), the Qing suspended maritime trade with Southeast Asia. Gang Zhao (2013: 153–68) sees this episode as an aberrant political decision that deviated from what he describes as the "open-door policy" that prevailed after 1683.

[67] Lombard 1990, 1: 13. On the trade network linking Xiamen (Amoy) in Fujian with Taiwan and Southeast Asia, see Ng 1983. For an overview of Chinese emigration to Southeast Asia, see Kuhn 2008.

[68] Gang Zhao (2013: 169–86) contends that the restriction of European traders to Guangzhou in 1757 to a significant degree was promoted by provincial interests in Guangzhou who feared competition from other Chinese ports. On commercial institutions and the conduct of foreign commerce at Guangzhou, see Van Dyke 2005.

importing cotton and opium obtained from its colonial empire in India into China. After gaining independence from the English East India Company's monopoly on commerce with Asia, merchants from the fledgling United States also rushed to tap into the China trade and became the principal suppliers of silver to the Chinese market.

At times – chiefly at the instigation of the Yongzheng Emperor (r. 1722–36) – the Qing state aggressively pursued an activist agenda of tax reform, public investment, and expansion of the state's presence at the local level.[69] But Yongzheng's long-lived successor Qianlong (r. 1736–95) rescinded or retreated from many of his father's initiatives. Under the rubric of "storing wealth among the people" (cangfu yu min 藏富於民), Qianlong's government strove to ensure that any increase in the wealth of the empire accumulated in the hands of the people rather than be siphoned off by the state and its agents.[70] Scholars have characterized Qianlong's regime as "non-interventionist," or even as a turning point toward the emergence of "economic liberalism" in Chinese fiscal ideology, if not policy.[71] Certainly Qing policymakers displayed a more positive attitude toward the benefits of market forces in enabling a more optimal distribution of goods and resources, and by extension in protecting popular welfare. But it is surely an overstatement to claim, as William Rowe does in his study of the influential minister Chen Hongmou (1696–1771), that "storing wealth among the people ... meant first and foremost doing every-thing possible to augment their per capita economic productivity."[72] Not only was the idea of continuous growth in output and productivity inconceiv-able within the intellectual milieu of Qing political economy, but Qing officials remained resolutely focused on the efficient use of land and labor resources, the elimination of waste (especially in the form of luxury con-sumption), and largely rhetorical efforts to promote the diffusion of best practices in agriculture. The non-interventionist stance that prevailed at Qianlong's court left little scope for the state to promote economic development.[73]

Consequently, the Qing imperial government wielded at best indirect con-trol over local society, relying on mediation by local elites. Since the final decades of the Ming dynasty, local patricians had steadily expanded their responsibilities in managing many aspects of local governance and social

---

[69] On Yongzheng's effort to rationalize tax collection and place local government finance on sounder footing, see Zelin 1984.

[70] Rowe 2001: 45–51, 251–52. To the best of my knowledge the idea of "storing wealth among the people" was coined by the fifteenth-century statecraft theorist Qiu Jun. See *DXYYB*: 20.2b.

[71] See, respectively, Kishimoto 1997: 309–21; Dunstan 1996: 6–9, 2006: 91–95.

[72] Rowe 2001: 287.

[73] On these points I find Will's (1994) characterization of eighteenth-century Chinese political economy more persuasive than those of Rowe (2001) or Dunstan (2006).

welfare, including public works, irrigation projects, public security, famine and poor relief, schools, and temples.[74] This trend accelerated during the eighteenth century. The Qing period also witnessed the proliferation of a wide range of new intermediate social institutions – including corporate lineages, merchant and artisan guilds, native-place associations, communal water control leagues, and an array of religious, fraternal, and philanthropic societies – to which the imperial state entrusted managerial responsibilities within local society. Although local leaders operated independently of magistrates and the state bureaucracy, they often held examination degrees and many were retired officials. State officials and local patricians shared essentially similar agendas of social control, popular welfare, and moral leadership. Thus R. Bin Wong has argued that the expanded role of local elites in civil governance constituted a delegation, not a devolution, of public power that may have limited the imperial state's range of action but did not erode its authority.[75] Still, the managerial roles assumed by local elites allowed freer rein to the pursuit of private interests in the guise of public welfare.

Water control epitomized the struggle between private and public interests. For example, rice farmers in South China steadily encroached upon and enclosed low-lying lakes to reclaim land for cultivation. But deforestation, dike construction, and the loss of reservoirs intensified the flow of rivers and increased sedimentation, raising the risks of catastrophic flooding. In late Ming Jiangnan local officials sought to establish rules that would apportion the responsibilities for dike maintenance and repair equitably among tenant cultivators (who provided labor) and landowners (who contributed money, supplies, and provisions for laborers). In the Middle Yangzi region, however, private initiative held sway, and cooperation was more difficult to achieve. The government attempted to intercede more forcefully in managing water control with the aim of restricting poldering and rehabilitating the natural ecology. But Qing officials expected local communities to bear the costs of water control. Not surprisingly, private interests vested in maximizing land reclamation – buoyed by population growth and sharply rising food prices – usually triumphed. The fragility of the region's ecology was exposed in the nineteenth century, when the Middle Yangzi repeatedly suffered devastating floods.[76]

One arena of public welfare in which the Qing government did vigorously intervene was food supply and famine relief. The Qing established a comprehensive network of "ever-normal granaries" (*changpingcang* 常平倉) in each county whose reserves were used not only to provide famine relief but also to

---

[74] Shigeta 1984; Elvin 1977; Rowe 1990; Rankin 1990, 1994.   [75] Wong 1997.
[76] Will 1985; Perdue 1987: 164–233; Marks 2012: 208–13.

Table 8.5 *Population of Qing China*

	Population (in millions)
1680	150
1776	311
1820	383
1850	436

Source: Cao Shuji 2000b: 704, table 16–2.

stabilize grain prices at affordable levels.[77] The state's target for ever-normal granary stockpiles reached as high as 58 million *shi* (enough to feed 85 million adults for a month) in 1740. State purchases and stores directed the flow of grain supplies from surplus to deficit areas, but officials recognized the limits of bureaucratic intervention in grain markets and generally were disinclined to interfere with the private grain trade. Evidence from the mid-eighteenth century suggests that the state's famine relief policies achieved success in moderating the volatility of grain prices and containing subsistence crises during years of dearth.[78] The efficient operation of the state granary system and famine relief policies no doubt contributed to China's sustained prosperity and demographic growth during the eighteenth century.

The economic boom of the eighteenth century

Between the pacification of Taiwan in 1683 and the outbreak of the White Lotus rebellion in 1796, China enjoyed a century of remarkable domestic tranquility. The economic boom of the eighteenth century rested on a foundation of steady growth in population and agricultural output. By the end of the seventeenth century, China's population had returned to its Ming peak of 150 million. Over the course of the eighteenth century the empire's population doubled, with the most pronounced increase occurring during the first half of the eighteenth century (Table 8.5). While economic growth in the late Ming had been concentrated in the southeastern coastal provinces, during the early and middle Qing period the most striking increases in population and agricultural production were found in the interior provinces of the south (Hunan, Hubei, and especially Sichuan), the Central Plain, and the southwestern frontier provinces. Much of this increase resulted from the advance of Chinese settlement and agriculture into the remote upland regions of the interior.

---

[77] On famine relief policies and the operation of the Qing granary system, see Will 1990; Will and Wong 1991; Rowe 2001: 250–87; Dunstan 2006.

[78] Lillian Li 2007: 221–49.

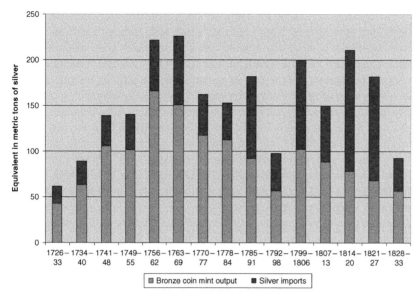

Figure 8.2 Growth of the money supply, 1726–1833
Source: bronze coin mint output: Vogel n.d.: 606–40, appendix D.4; silver imports: Dermigny 1964, 2: 735; coin:silver exchange ratios: Vogel 1987: 17–23, appendix 3.

The sustained commercial expansion of the eighteenth century was also facilitated by a substantial rise in the money supply. As rural and interior areas became more integrated into the market economy, the demand for media of exchange intensified. Although silver imports in the early eighteenth century had fallen from their peak level of a century earlier, imports of Japanese copper and the rapid development of copper mining in Yunnan from the 1730s to the 1790s enabled the Qing state to raise the output of state mints nearly ten-fold compared to the late seventeenth century.[79] During the period 1740–85 the average annual output of bronze coin was equivalent in value to 125 tons of silver at a time when silver imports averaged 50 tons per year (Figure 8.2). In contrast to the Ming, which operated mints only in Beijing and Nanjing, the Qing established mints in every province. Still, the demand for bronze coin was most acute in highly commercialized regions such as Jiangnan, where bronze coin displaced silver as the monetary standard in the mid-eighteenth century.[80]

[79] From 1738 to 1810 Yunnan copper mines produced an average of 6,000 tons of copper annually, reaching a peak of 9,000 tons in 1764. Vogel 1987: 32–33.
[80] On the return to a bronze coin monetary standard in Jiangnan in the mid-eighteenth century, see Kuroda 1987; Kishimoto 1997: 353–63.

The agrarian regime of the Qing period represented a culmination of the post-Song trend toward labor-intensive, small-scale farming based on legally free households with strong tenurial rights. In the early years of the Qing, a large percentage of cultivated land was owned by the state, members of the imperial household, and the banner garrisons. By the early eighteenth century, however, most of these lands had reverted to private ownership.[81] A competitive and highly dynamic market for land already existed at the beginning of the dynasty. Some restrictions limited the full alienability of land: the law recognized the household, not the individual, as the unit of ownership, and both legal statutes and customary practices granted kinfolk certain proprietary rights. The long-standing principle of equal inheritance ensured that private landholdings would be dispersed among surviving sons, inhibiting the concentration of landownership over time.

One of the most important institutions affecting the alienability of land was the development of permanent rights of tenancy. Rice cultivation required substantial investment in building and maintaining irrigation systems, investments that tenant farmers would not make without some guarantee that they would reap the long-term benefits. Tenancy contracts did not specify the length of tenancy, and usufruct rights were conventionally regarded as hereditary. The widespread practice of conditional sales of land reserving the right of redemption (*dianmai*; also known as *huomai* 活賣, or "live sale") rather than outright sale also fostered permanent tenurial rights. The multiple tiers of ownership resulting from the practice of landowners selling usufruct rights (known as the "bones" of the soil [*tiangu* 田骨]) while retaining legal ownership (the "skin" [*tianpi* 田皮]) – known as "one field, two masters" (*yitian liangzhu*) – had already appeared in the Song (see Chapter 7). The holders of usufruct rights also might sublease the land to tenant farmers, creating a third tier of possession rights. By ensuring security of tenure, multitiered landownership created incentives for cultivators to preserve and enhance the productivity of the land. This arrangement also allowed ready transfer of ownership rights (both "skin" and "bones") within a competitive market economy, providing farming families greater flexibility to expand or contract their holdings in response to changes in their labor force or other economic circumstances. Although multiple ownership was found in almost every corner of the Qing Empire, it flourished most abundantly in the coastal regions of Fujian, Guangdong, and the Yangzi Delta, areas characterized by absentee landlordism, strong demand for land, and high overhead costs of farming.

---

[81] Shi Zhihong (1994: 25) reports that public lands constituted only 7 percent of the total cultivated land in 1724. Li Wenzhi and Jiang Taixin (2005: 296) give figures of 10.6 percent in 1812 and 12.9 percent in 1887; the higher figures in the nineteenth century resulted from the expansion of school lands and inclusion of more categories of public lands in the later data.

For example, of a total of 418 contracts from Quanzhou in Fujian dating from 1600 to 1900, 23 percent involved sale of rights within multitiered landowner-ship. Similarly, in Huizhou – a more remote but highly commercialized region – 30 percent of land sale contracts and 29 percent of tenancy contracts from the Qing period involved transfers of either "bones" or "skin."[82] The prevalence of trading in multitiered landownership rights was much higher in cases of entrepreneurial landowners who frequently bought and sold land. Of forty-two land transactions contracted by the Sun family in Huizhou between 1662 and 1795, two-thirds involved multitiered rights, and twenty of thirty-nine land transfers contracted by the Wang family between 1710 and 1843 involved multitiered rights.[83] Multitiered landownership thus accommo-dated the interests of both investors seeking a reliable source of income and farmers desiring secure claims to the land they cultivated.[84]

Tenurial systems varied significantly from region to region in eighteenth-century China. The most striking trend was the shift from sharecropping arrangements to fixed rents, whether paid in grain or money. Fixed rents in grain predominated in all regions except North China, which had a much higher incidence of rents paid in money (Table 8.6). This high proportion of money rents perhaps reflected the prevalence of absentee owners of noble and banner estates in Hebei and Shandong.[85] Overall, rates of tenancy were much lower in North China than in the south, and in contrast to the trend toward permanent tenancy in the south, in North China tenancy contracts were short, often only for one year. The *bianshen* survey records from Huolu county, a relatively poor region near modern Shijiazhuang in Hebei, display a pattern of extremely fragmented landholding among numerous small farms. Four-fifths

---

[82] Li Wenzhi and Jiang Taixin 2005: 274–79.   [83] Ibid.: 278–79.

[84] It has been argued (see, e.g., Philip Huang 1990: 102–14, Taisu Zhang 2011) that conditional sales and multitiered landownership diminished incentives to acquire land or make capital investments, and thus impeded the development of managerial farming. But the discounted price for conditional sales more than compensated for the possibility of future redemption or the practice of seeking supplemental payments (*zhaojia* 找價) beyond the original sale price. See Pomeranz 2008b. As Pomeranz observes, conditional sales and permanent tenancy were most prominent in the regions (Jiangnan, Fujian, and Pearl River Delta) where agricultural product-ivity was highest. The preliminary study of the corpus of 8,000 land documents from the village of Shicang on the Zhejiang-Fujian border by Cao *et al.* (2010) shows that residual property rights themselves became alienable commodities. Such rights promoted agricultural develop-ment by, for example, encouraging cultivation of undeveloped land owned by others through conferral of partial ownership known as "labor share" (*gongben* 工本) rights. In Shicang, alienation of land proceeded through three steps, each of which was documented by contract: sale (*mai*) or "ceding" (*tui* 退) of land, conveyance of tax responsibility, and supplemental payment (*zhaojia*). The supplemental payment – which in 95 percent of Shicang cases occurred within one year of the original sale – rendered the sale final and irrevocable. Cao and his collaborators conclude that the language of land rights in Shicang was very precise, and that the flexibility of transactional instruments promoted the orderly functioning of the land market.

[85] Philip Huang 1985: 102.

Table 8.6 *Regional variation in tenancy systems*

	Number	In-kind sharecropping (%)	Fixed in-kind rents (%)	Money rents (%)
North China	168	23.2	29.2	47.6
South/Southeast	506	7.9	71.9	20.2
Hunan/Hubei	97	7.2	57.7	35.1
Southwest	110	10.0	56.4	33.6
Total	881	11.0	60.3	28.7

Source: Data from legal cases in the Ministry of Justice archives from the Qianlong era (1736–95) reported in Shi Zhihong 1994: 77, table 2.3.

Table 8.7 *Registered households and landholdings, Huolu county (Hebei), 1706–1771*
(figures in percentages except for last column)

		None	0–10 *mu*	11–20 *mu*	21–50 *mu*	51–100 *mu*	100+ *mu*	Totals
1706	Households	18	37	23	16	5	1.2	7,520
	Landholdings	–	12	22	29	17	20	114,882
1726	Households	22	42	18	11	5	1.5	5,592
	Landholdings	–	13	17	22	22	26	79.867
1746	Households	26	38	16	12	6	1.8	11,713
	Landholdings	–	11	15	23	25	26	177,847
1771	Households	16	45	17	16	5	1.8	1,483
	Landholdings	–	12	16	23	29	20	22,417

Source: Li Wenzhi and Jiang Taixin 2005: 304–05, tables 7–9, 7–10.

of all households in Huolu owned less than 20 *mu* (in a region where an adult male could cultivate 20–30 *mu*) and even large landowners owned only 200–400 *mu* on average. The distribution of landholdings in Huolu remained highly stable throughout the eighteenth century, despite the demographic surge of this era. The only significant changes were the steady declines in the percentage of patricians among the large landowners and in the size of the largest landholdings as the century wore on (Tables 8.7 and 8.8). Scattered data from other regions likewise depict highly dispersed landownership, with most farming families owning some land and relatively few large holdings.[86]

[86] Li Wenzhi and Jiang Taixin 2005: 302–32.

Table 8.8 *Patrician and Plebeian large landowners in Huolu County, 1706–1771*

		Number of households	Percent	Landholdings	Percent	Average landholding
1706	Patrician	54	61	17,837	16	330
	Plebeian	35	39	5,294	29	151
1726	Patrician	48	56	14,902	11	310
	Plebeian	38	44	5,848	22	154
1746	Patrician	78	36	24,293	12	311
	Plebeian	137	64	22,636	23	165
1771	Patrician	5	19	1,224	16	245
	Plebeian	22	81	3,196	23	145

Source: Li Wenzhi and Jiang Taixin 2005: 304–05, tables 7–9, 7–10.

Regional differences in agrarian regimes remained pronounced. In North China, landownership was more universal and more uniform, with few great landowners and few tenant farmers. A substantial class of poor and landless men worked as hired laborers. Although subsistence farming was prevalent in much of the north, new cash crops such as sorghum (distilled to make liquor), cotton, tobacco, and peanuts adapted well to the region's ecology and drew farming households into commodity production. In some parts of the Central Plain 20–30 percent of the land was planted in cotton, although cotton did not account for as large portion of the region's total agricultural production as has been sometimes suggested.[87]

Although high rates of tenancy prevailed in Jiangnan and southern coastal provinces such as Fujian and Guangdong, many tenant farmers owned some land of their own. As Table 8.6 shows, the trend toward fixed rents that developed during the late Ming accelerated, ensuring that tenants would reap the rewards of improved productivity – and bear greater risk in the event of harvest failure. Since rents generally were calculated on the basis of the expected yield of the autumn rice crop, tenants also had strong incentive to practice double-cropping. The double-cropping regime combining winter crops (wheat, beans, and oil-seed plants) with paddy rice became much more widespread, and in the tropical parts of Fujian and Guangdong farmers could plant two or even three rice crops in a single year.

In Jiangnan, the intensive labor invested in rice farming was augmented by new fertilizers such as soybean cake, resulting in a 50 percent increase in yields compared to the late Ming. But overall rice production in Jiangnan

---

[87] Lillian Li 2007: 100–1. Claims that 20–30 percent of *all* agricultural land in North China was planted in cotton (Naquin and Rawski 1987: 143) are wildly exaggerated.

diminished as rural households devoted more of their labor to sericulture, cotton cultivation and manufacture, and other cottage handicrafts. Textile manufacture, performed almost exclusively by women and children, generated a substantial share – and perhaps even the largest portion – of household income. In the mid-eighteenth century rural households in Jiangnan cultivated only 10 or fewer *mu* of land, but household income rose thanks to the proceeds of cottage industry (for more details on Jiangnan agriculture in this period, see Chapter 9).[88]

Commercial agriculture also accelerated in the coastal regions of Fujian and Guangdong. The Pearl River Delta in Guangdong experienced a dramatic surge in agricultural productivity, population increase, and commercial growth after 1550. Reclamation of the delta's swamps and sandy coastal lands through the construction of polders and irrigation channels greatly expanded the amount of arable land. Ready access to domestic and overseas markets encouraged market-oriented production. Many delta farmers forsook rice cultivation to plant sugar-cane as a cash crop. Already in the early seventeenth century Guangdong was exporting sugar to Japan and other parts of maritime East Asia, and even – before the takeoff of the Caribbean sugar economy – to Europe. In contrast to the colonial sugar plantations in the Americas, which were both capital-intensive and dependent on slave labor, sugar cultivation in Guangdong and Fujian remained in the hands of small-scale family farmers. Growers typically negoti-ated advance contracts with mill owners from whom they borrowed capital. In some cases sugar cultivators leased mills, or formed cooperatives to operate a mill collectively.[89] After processing and refining the sugar, merchants sold it in Jiangnan and returned with raw cotton to supply rural spinners and weavers.

By the early eighteenth century, according to one estimate, half of the cultivated land in Guangdong was planted in commercial crops.[90] The intro-duction of American food crops facilitated the conversion of rice paddies to cane fields in Guangdong and Fujian. Peanuts complemented sugar cultivation by restoring fertility to soils sorely depleted of nitrogen by sugar cane, and peanut meal also could be used as fertilizer. Extraction of peanut oil involved similar milling technology as crushing sugarcane, and mill owners often combined sugar and peanut oil refining.[91] Sweet potatoes, like peanuts, flourished in the sandy soils of the delta and required only minimal labor. A gazetteer published in 1612 observed that sweet potatoes had been intro-duced to southern Fujian from Guangdong only five or six years before, but already had become the main staple food of the poor.[92]

The interior provinces of southern China and the new frontier regions of Taiwan and the southwestern provinces of Guizhou, Guangxi, and Yunnan

---

[88] Li Bozhong 1998.   [89] Mazumdar 1998: 84–86, 323–31.   [90] Marks 1999: 184.
[91] Mazumdar 1998: 254–60.   [92] Cited in Fu Yiling 1982: 125.

experienced substantial immigration and new settlement. The expansion of farming into the rugged terrain of these regions was made possible by the introduction of American food crops such as maize and sweet potato along with timber cutting and tea planting. In many areas entrepreneurs acquired titles to large tracts of virgin land and then recruited tenants to clear the forests for cultivation. But the rapid agricultural development of the interior provinces exacted substantial ecological costs. Deforestation and erosion increased the risk of floods in lowland areas. As noted earlier, the central basins of the Yangzi valley around Lake Dongting and Lake Poyang, where farmers had constructed polders to reclaim the fertile soil of the lakebeds for rice cultivation, became especially vulnerable to flooding. Landowners and tenant farmers combined their resources to build elaborate dike and drainage systems to redirect the flow of rivers that previously fed into the now shrunken lakes.[93]

Sichuan typified this pattern of rapid population growth and agricultural expansion in the interior. Much of Sichuan, a key economic region in earlier times, had been laid waste by the Mongol invasions in the thirteenth century and peasant rebellions in the seventeenth century. Laws granting homesteaders perpetual rights to lands they brought into cultivation, the subjugation and relocation of non-Han peoples, and poor harvests and natural disasters in the 1740–50s that particularly afflicted the central Yangzi region encouraged migrants from Hunan and Hubei to move westward. Sichuan probably experienced the highest rate of demographic growth in the eighteenth century: a six-fold increase in population from 3 million in 1673 to 17 million in 1776, rising to over 23 million by 1820.[94] The resettlement of Sichuan also initiated a gradual shift in the region's commercial core away from its traditional center in the Chengdu Plain to Chongqing in the Yangzi River valley.[95]

The surge in China's population that began in the late seventeenth century continued uninterrupted down to 1850 (Figure 8.3). As Figure 8.4 shows, between 1776 and 1820 the rate of increase was significantly higher in the sparsely inhabited provinces in the west (Sichuan and Shaanxi above all), and yet even densely populated Jiangnan recorded impressive growth. Contemporary observers fully recognized this remarkable population increase, and as early as 1748 leading statesmen expressed fears that population growth – which had always been seen as a sign of good governance – was outstripping food production, creating a disequilibrium that drove up prices and posed an endemic threat to subsistence and survival.[96] Certainly, the eighteenth century

---

[93] Will 1985; Perdue 1987.
[94] Cao Shuji 2000b: 324–25. On state encouragement of immigration to Sichuan, see Chen Feng 2008: 299–317.
[95] Paul J. Smith 1988.
[96] Will 1994: 866–68; Marks and Chen 1995: 141–42; Dunstan 2006: 307–462.

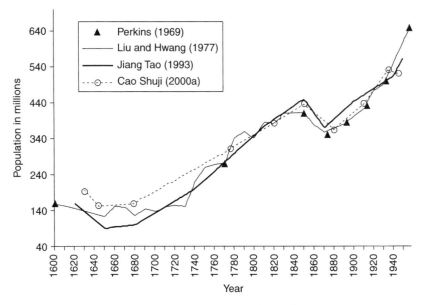

Figure 8.3 Population change in China, 1660–1850
Source: Peng Kaixiang 2006: 148, figure A2.1.

also was marked by a secular rise in the price level. The sharpest increases occurred in rice-deficit areas such as Jiangnan and Guangdong in 1730–58; but prices moderated thereafter, and even fell in the 1790s.[97] The most comprehensive evidence for price inflation comes from rice prices (Figure 8.5), but the prices of other grains, cotton, silk, and various consumer goods (clothing, fuel, liquor, medicine, and paper) also exhibit similar trends during the eighteenth century.[98] Thus relative prices remained fairly stable. Data from Guangdong show that rice prices denominated in bronze coin and silver remained closely synchronized between 1740 and 1780. Subsequently silver prices trended lower, no doubt because of the surge in imports of foreign silver (Figure 8.6). The price inflation of the eighteenth century most likely reflected the substantial growth of the total money supply (Figure 8.2) rather than the stress of overpopulation.[99] China did not yet face a Malthusian subsistence crisis.

[97] For Jiangnan prices, see Yeh-chien Wang 1992; for Guangdong, see Marks and Chen 1995. Wheat prices in Zhili (Lillian Li 1992) and rice prices in Hunan (Wong and Perdue 1992) rose very gradually from 1740 to 1790.
[98] Kishimoto 1997: 138–53; Peng Kaixiang 2006: 34–36; Chen Chunsheng 2005: 158–61.
[99] This is the conclusion in Peng Kaixiang 2006, the most sophisticated study of Qing price history.

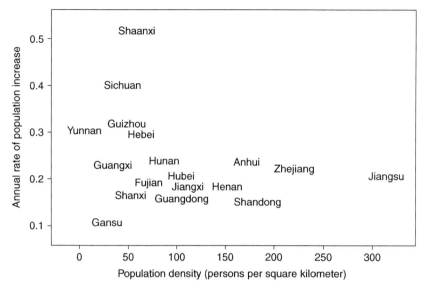

Figure 8.4 Population density and rates of growth, 1776–1820
Source: Peng Kaixiang 2006: 61, figure 4.4.

Population pressure on the food supply was mitigated by the flow of grain through long-distance trade networks. Suzhou emerged as the hub of a well-integrated rice marketing system that encompassed the entire Yangzi River drainage basin, and to some degree extended northward along the Grand Canal corridor as well.[100] In the second half of the eighteenth century, on average 17 million *shi* of rice (over 3 million tons) passed each year through Fengqiao, the great rice emporium on the outskirts of Suzhou, more than a quarter of the total of 62 million *shi* estimated to have entered long-distance trade (Map 8.4).[101] Separate grain trade networks supplied chronically rice-deficient areas along the southern coast: Guangdong imported 3 million *shi* yearly, mostly from Guangxi to the west, while Fujian imported 1 million *shi* from Taiwan, where Chinese settlement spread rapidly in the eighteenth century.[102]

---

[100] Numerous studies of price correlations have confirmed the existence of a highly integrated interregional rice market centered on Suzhou: see Ch'üan and Kraus 1975; Peng Kaixiang 2006; Shiue and Keller 2007; Cheung 2008.

[101] Zheng Yibing 1994: 90–91. Zheng Yibing's estimate for the magnitude of the interregional grain trade is double that (30 million *shi*) proposed for 1840 by Wu Chengming (1985: 255–59) in his influential study. Certainly the evidence points to a decline in the scale of interregional trade in grain beginning in the 1790s. But most scholars now regard Wu's figures as too low. See Peng Kaixiang 2006: 6; Fang Xing *et al.* 2007, 2: 733.

[102] Chen Chunsheng 2005: 45–46; Yeh-chien Wang 1985: 90–95.

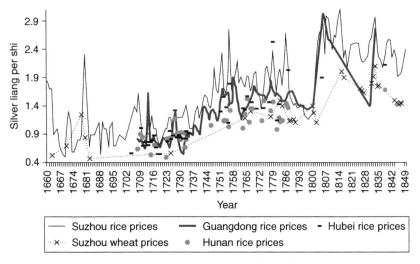

Figure 8.5 Grain prices in South China, 1660–1850
Source: Peng Kaixiang 2006: 33, figure 3.1.

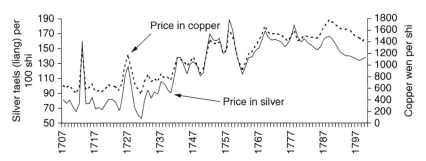

Figure 8.6 Silver and copper prices of rice in eighteenth-century Guangdong
Source: Marks and Chen 1995: 122, figure 5.

The Grand Canal artery supplied Beijing and its environs with 1 million tons of rice per year (half of which was delivered as tribute rice), and also served as the route for shipping large quantities of wheat and soybeans to the Yangzi Delta.[103] Because of these integrated regional and interregional grain markets, harvest failures had only modest impact on grain prices, at least in urban

---

[103] The degree of integration between grain markets in north and central China is disputed. Cheung (2008: 23–25) argues that grain prices at major Shandong commercial cities such as Linqing and Ji'nan display only weak correlation with Suzhou prices. Lillian Li (2007: 217–19), in contrast, finds a strong correlation in grain prices between Zhili (Hebei) and Suzhou.

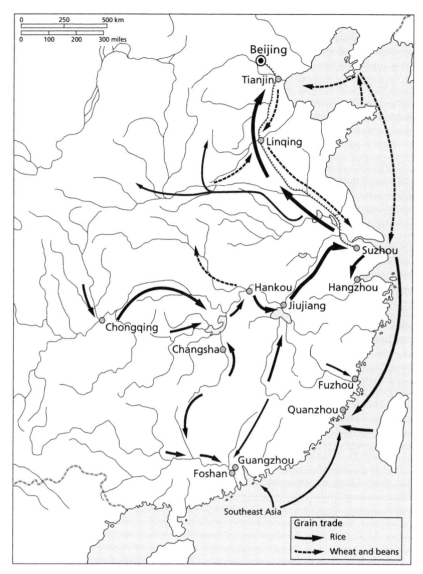

Map 8.4 Flow of grain trade along major commercial routes in eighteenth-century China
Source: Zheng Yibing 1994.

areas.[104] The state's granary stores also helped to minimize supply shocks on grain prices; but after 1750 the state shifted away from maintaining large stockpiles and instead supplied funds to ever-normal granary administrators to purchase grain on the open market. Recent comparative study of grain prices in the late eighteenth century indicates that long-distance trade in China operated more efficiently than in Europe. Although the Yangzi Delta region lagged behind England in overall market efficiency, it achieved levels comparable to or surpassing continental Western Europe.[105]

The sophisticated commercial networks that linked major commercial centers and most cities in eighteenth-century China bypassed rural communities in many areas, however. Rural periodic markets proliferated during the Qing – by one estimate, there were more than 22,000 local markets by the end of the eighteenth century – but the great majority of these markets handled only petty merchandise, with few or no wholesale traders and little connection to interregional trade networks.[106] High transport costs hindered integration of town and countryside. In parts of North China that lacked access to water transport, no trend toward market integration can be discerned, and indeed the degree of integration appears to decline after 1800.[107] G. William Skinner, drawing on nineteenth-century data, argued that before the advent of railroads and steamships the Chinese economy was only weakly integrated at the national level. Instead, Skinner proposed that the economic structure of the Chinese empire conformed to a series of eight physiographic macroregions principally defined by water transport routes. Each macroregion engendered its own hierarchy of cities, trade routes, and patterns of resource extraction. Commercial development was concentrated in the core areas of the macroregions, while population, exchange, and wealth increasingly thinned in peripheral areas (Map 8.5).[108] Skinner's model is flawed, especially in its slighting of the powerful centripetal effects of interregional trade. But the impressive degree of interregional trade and market integration achieved in the early Qing began to wane by the final decade of the eighteenth century. The onset of political and economic crises in the nineteenth century reversed the impetus toward integration on an empire-wide scale. As the century

---

[104] This conclusion was reached by Marks (1999: 268–74) for Guangdong and Lillian Li (1992: 88–95) for Hebei.

[105] Shiue and Keller 2007. Marks (1999: 271) found that there was less volatility in the yield–price ratio in eighteenth-century Guangdong than in seventeenth-century England.

[106] For the estimate of periodic markets, see Fang Xing et al. 2007, 2: 778.

[107] Lillian Li 2007: 207–13. Xu Tan (2000) has been the staunchest proponent of the view that an integrated national market penetrated deeply into the countryside in the Qing. But Li's skeptical view is much more solidly grounded.

[108] Skinner 1977a, 1977b.

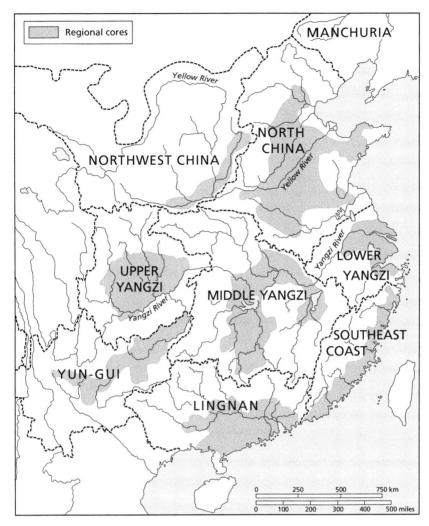

Map 8.5 Macroregional structure of late imperial China
Source: Skinner 1977.

wore on, the economic structure of the Qing Empire increasingly resembled Skinner's macroregional construct.

In sum, the efficiency of domestic markets, regional specialization of production, and an expanding money supply stimulated economic and demographic expansion in early Qing China. The steady rise in prices across the eighteenth century corresponded closely to the increase in population, suggesting that agricultural and industrial output kept pace with rapid population growth without any appreciable decline in per capita income. Yet the prosperity engendered by the quantitative growth in output masked the lack of significant innovation in productive technologies.

Business organization and credit markets

In Chinese agriculture, independent family farms persisted as the basic units of production, even when landownership was aggregated in the hands of large landowners. Commercial enterprises also primarily took the form of family firms that drew exclusively on the family's labor, capital, and technical expertise. Nonetheless, in Ming-Qing times it became increasingly common for multiple investors to form partnerships to pool resources, reduce risks, and extend the spatial range of their commercial activities. Many of these ventures, such as the *commenda* type of partnership, were short-lived. But new forms of partnership that institutionalized the enterprise as a permanent corporation independent of its individual investors also emerged. The lineage trust, as we have seen, developed from the sixteenth century as a permanent, incorporated business entity. In addition, joint-share partnerships began to evolve beyond the constraints of the family firm. The development of permanent partnership firms was facilitated by the emergence of share capital. Some scholars have argued that share capital enterprises already appeared in the Song, but conclusive evidence is available only from the sixteenth century. Dividing a partnership into shares contributed to the longevity of firms by enabling investors to withdraw without jeopardizing the firm's capital assets and by allowing multiple heirs (a frequent occurrence under imperial China's legal principle of equal inheritance) to preserve their individual stakes. It also facilitated the formation of partnerships in which managers provided only their expertise and labor but no capital. By the eighteenth century there is ample testimony to the buying and selling of shares. However, no stock market emerged from this trading in shares, which rested largely on personal relationships and contacts.

In conventional practice, partnerships (*hehuo* 合夥, 合伙) could take a variety of forms, such as: (1) the *commenda* arrangement; (2) joint-share partnerships (also known as *heben* 合本 or *hegu* 合股); and (3) agency partnerships. Under the *commenda* partnership, one partner invested a sum of money as capital while the "active" partner undertook the actual work of traveling to distant markets and negotiating transactions. The active partner contributed his skills – his expertise in evaluating the quality and value of goods; his knowledge of clients, brokers, and shippers; and his familiarity with markets and trade routes – as well as his time. The investor, by placing his capital at the disposal of the active partner, assumed even greater risk, and usually reaped the greater share of the profit, although in many cases the partners divided their profit equally. *Commenda* partnerships usually endured only for a single trading venture.

In joint-share ventures, multiple investors contributed capital and received shares (*fen* 分) in proportion to the amount they invested. Managerial authority was retained by one or more principal partners, while common partners had no role in decision-making. In agency partnerships, professional managers – like the active partner in the *commenda* – and in some cases other managerial staff received partnership shares (their expertise and labor earned them certain equity rights). In contrast to the *commenda*, joint-share and agency partnerships were intended to be long-term arrangements.[109]

No strict legal definition of partnerships existed in imperial China, nor was there a body of civil law that governed their organization and activities.[110] Partnerships were established through the use of contracts, which as we have seen were essential to economic life in imperial China.[111] Customary commercial practices embedded in contracts were sanctioned and enforced by magistrates as long as they did not conflict with the provisions of statutory law.[112] To be sure, murky areas remained, especially since imperial law recognized only households, not individuals, as bearers of property rights (and, by extension, debts). Business disputes generally were settled through private mediation rather than in a court of law. Bankruptcy proceedings, for example, typically operated outside the formal legal system through customary forms of negotiation; magistrates intervened only to compel parties to cooperate in mediation or to punish fraud.[113]

The lineage trust, as we have seen, provided one mechanism for establishing a permanent business corporation. Of course, lineage trusts differed from modern capitalist corporations in significant ways. The purposes of lineage trusts were fundamentally ritual and moral ones: to maintain the ancestral hall and gravesites and sustain the bonds of solidarity among kinsmen. Their resources derived from contributions of members, who became shareholders in the trust. Although lineage members obtained income from their shares in such trusts, they exercised no ownership rights and could not freely dispose of their shares. David Faure likens the lineage trust to a holding corporation rather than a commercial partnership.[114] Faure insists that the

---

[109] All three types of business organization were employed by Shanxi and Huizhou merchants, although the agency type was more common in Shanxi and the joint-share enterprise in Huizhou. See Terada 1972: 265–83; Zhang Haipeng and Wang Tingyuan 1995: 68–82.

[110] The Chinese terms (*hehuo*) broadly encompassed all of these types of partnership, and even were used to refer to cases where a proprietor hired salaried employees. See Liu Qiugen 2007: 187–89.

[111] On the role of contracts in securing property rights and establishing business partnerships, see Zelin 2004; Kwan 2004; Gardella 2004.

[112] Zelin 2004: 27–30; Kwan 2004: 292–93.   [113] Dykstra 2013: 413–20.

[114] Faure 2007: 230.

ritual character of lineage trusts sharply distinguished them from profit-driven corporations.[115] Nonetheless, lineage trusts displayed a keen interest in profit maximization. Faure mentions a 1745 contract whereby fifty-five households from a single lineage each contributed 55 taels to establish a marketplace in the Pearl River Delta. The pooled funds were used to construct walls, gateways, a pier, a temple, and thirty-eight shops. The property was divided into eleven shares held by groups of five families. The shareholders themselves were responsible for finding tenants and negotiating leases for the commercial real estate. In Faure's words, "the close involvement of lineages in business activities renders meaningless any hard distinction between merchants and gentry."[116]

The joint-share partnership provided the means not only to raise additional capital but also to establish an enterprise on permanent footing independent of its founders or investors. It became common practice for the principal investors to exercise managerial authority and responsibilities. Common investors were limited partners with no voice in day-to-day business decisions, but could readily join or withdraw from the partnership at will (at the time of the annual settlement of accounts on the eve of the New Year holiday). Given the constraints of the capital market, this relative ease of entry and exit gave the firm flexibility to raise new investments. But it also could cause serious financial difficulties if investors withdrew precipitously.[117]

The potential for a firm to assume a permanent corporate existence is well illustrated by the case of the Wanquantang medicine shop, founded in Beijing at the turn of the eighteenth century by Yue Fengyi, scion of a family of physicians.[118] Yue Fengyi and his successors managed the Wanquantang as a family business, but in the 1740s the shop encountered financial difficulties and fell into debt. In 1746, the Yue were obliged to bring in a certain Suo to manage the store under an agency partnership (Table 8.9).[119] The firm's fortunes revived under Suo's guidance and the Yue were able to clear their debts, but in 1751 Suo received an official appointment and resigned from the business. After a fire damaged the shop in 1755 the Yue enlisted four new partners – all proprietors of their own medicine shops – under a fifteen-year

---

[115] Faure 2006: 33–44. Despite the durability of lineage institutions, these kin groups often were beset with internal conflict. As McDermott (2013a: 366–68) observes, the main long-term problem confronting lineage trusts was sustaining control and cooperation among increasingly numerous and distantly related members.
[116] Faure 2007: 231–32.   [117] Liu Qiugen and Xie Xiuli 2005.
[118] Liu Yongcheng and He Zhiqing 1983. Yue Fengyi's elder brother had opened his own medicine shop in 1702; Fengyi's shop probably opened for business not long afterwards (certainly it was in existence by 1709).
[119] In 1742 a branch store was transferred to a pair of businessmen in a conditional sale that netted 2,000 taels. The Yue continued to operate the branch store, but after several attempts to find a suitable partner failed they subleased the store to new managers.

Table 8.9 *Ownership changes in the Wanquantang medicine shop*

	Original owner	Contribution	New investor(s)	Contribution	Profit share
1746	Yue family	Shop, inventory, brand name	Suo	2,724 tls.	Equal
1751	Yue Yulin	3,251 tls.	Jian	2,490 tls.	Equal
1755	Yue, Jian	Brand name	Jiang, Sun	5,000 tls.	Yue, Jian: 30% Jiang, Sun: 70%
1772	Yue, Jian, Jiang, Sun				Sun *et al.*: 60% Yue: 20% Jian: 20%
1810	–	–	Jiang Chengzhai, Han Jintang	Jiang: 8,200 tls. Han: 12,000 tls.	Equal
1817	Han Jintang, Jiang Shengyuan	Han: 15,000 tls. Jiang: 5,000 tls.			?

Source: Liu Yongcheng and He Zhiqing 1983.

partnership agreement with Yue Yulin as general manager. The partnership was renewed in 1772 with Yue Yulin's brother Yuxiu as manager, but following Yue Yuxiu's death in 1792 the general manager position passed to one of the outside investors.

In 1810, for reasons left unexplained, the Wanquantang partnership was dissolved. The five partners sold the business and their stock to new owners, a partnership created by two Shanxi merchant consortia from the Jiang and Han families, putting an end to the Yue family's century-long association with the firm.[120] The partnership between fellow countrymen was by no means an amicable one, however. In 1817 the Jiang withdrew from the partnership, complaining that Han family members, who held the majority of the shares, allowed them little voice in decision-making. The Han resorted to a conditional sale of the shop to make up the deficit in capital funds. Shortly afterward, the Han persuaded Jiang Shengyuan (who was related to the Han by marriage) to resume the partnership, although with a more modest investment, only one-quarter of the total. Thereafter the partnership remained under Han family control. Although its fortunes rose and fell and new investors

[120] The new shareholders were groups of kinsmen operating, as David Faure said of lineage trusts, as a holding company.

Table 8.10 *Equity shareholders in the Wanquanhao cotton goods store*

1724–45	Hua branch	B branch	C branch					
1746–48				Mingzhou, Kanghou	Junli	Zuochen		
1748–51						Four branches (Feng, Jun, Mu, Li)		
1752–55								
1756–59							Jia sub-branch	Feng sub-branch

Source: Liu Qiugen 2007: 432–33, appendix table 8.

joined and left, the Wanquantang enterprise flourished in the early twentieth century prior to the nationalization of enterprises under the People's Republic of China.[121]

The 250-year history of the Wanquantang medicine shop demonstrates the flexibility of the business partnership form of enterprise. It allowed firms to expand their capital resources and recruit expert managers and to obtain a permanent existence that did not depend on the interests, skills, or personal financial condition of the founders or their heirs.[122] The relative ease of entry and exit in such partnerships can also be seen in the account books of the Wanquanhao silk goods shop, which was owned by members of the Ma lineage of Huizhou (Table 8.10). Our information largely comes from the ledgers held by one branch of the lineage (the Hua), and thus is incomplete.[123] Initially the firm was jointly owned by three branches of the Ma lineage. In 1746 two members of the Hua branch, Ma Mingzhou and Ma Kanghou, became independent shareholders, holding one share between them (these two individuals also appear as general managers of the firm, a position that rotated annually). After 1748 two of the original branches (designated B and

---

[121] The Tongrentang medicine shop founded by Yue Fengyi's elder brother in 1702 also acquired outside investors over time, but in 1820 the Yue family recovered sole ownership. Unlike the Wanquantang, the Tongrentang granted dividend shares to its managerial personnel. In 1818 the twenty-one equity shareholders (with a total investment of 43,800 taels) held 36.5 shares, while the managers and personnel held 10 shares (21.5 percent of the total). See Liu Yongcheng and He Zhiqing 1983: 12.

[122] Pomeranz (1997) finds a similar evolution from a family firm to a multiple partnership relying on professional managers in the history of the Yutang processed foods company, founded in Jining (Shandong) in 1779. But in 1905 one of the two principal investors – whose predecessors had been partners dating back to 1807 – bought out his partner and the common investors and reestablished Yutang as a family-owned firm, which it remained until it was nationalized in 1956.

[123] Liu Qiugen 2007: 415–47.

C here, since their actual names are unknown) exited the partnership. The B branch and Ma Junli shifted their investments to a separate silk goods shop, the Rishengtang. At the same time four new segments of the Hua branch jointly obtained one share in the Wanquantang. By 1756 the firm began to suffer losses, and the partnership was reorganized with four shareholders who agreed to cover its debts: the Hua branch, two of its segmented sub-branches (the Jia and Feng), and Ma Mingzhou and Ma Kanghou again as joint shareholders. Although the Wanquanhao was wholly owned by members of the Ma lineage, it was not rigidly bound to the lineage organization, and the ownership structure could readily adjust to the changing economic priorities of its shareholders.

We lack details on the earnings of these firms, but such business partnerships usually paid its shareholders annual fixed dividends, with the managing shareholder receiving a supplemental payment. If the firm had an especially prosperous year, bonuses were paid both to investors and managerial staff. In general the dividends were proportional to the investors' share in the firm's equity, but in some cases (as happened with the Wanquantang in 1746, 1751, and 1810; see Table 8.9) partners received equal shares even though they invested unequal amounts of capital. In the case of the Wanquanhao, shareholders generally received identical annual dividends even though their equity shares were unequal.[124] In addition, both the Wanquantang and Wanquanhao firms followed the common practice of granting investors the right to withdraw funds for alternative purposes, which could range from wedding and funeral expenses to purchases of real estate or brevet official titles. Such withdrawals, which eroded the firm's equity and posed a significant threat to its long-term financial health, reveal that – from an investor's perspective, at least – there was little distinction between the firm's capital and their personal assets. The freedom of investors to exit the firm or withdraw capital at will hindered the capacity of firms to accumulate capital over the long term, and often was the cause of bankruptcy.[125]

The lack of a formal market for trading shares and the endemic problem of peremptory withdrawals of capital – even though contracts routinely forbid such withdrawals – imposed constraints on the long-term viability of individual firms. Business partnerships often remained vulnerable to the whims of individual investors. The trend toward agency partnerships based on professional managers in the Qing period reduced the role of investors in business operations. At the same time, since professional managers often received a substantial equity stake, their interests coincided with those of the investors.

---

[124] Liu Qiugen 2007: 424–25, appendix table 3.   [125] Liu Qiugen and Xie Xiuli 2005.

342   The Economic History of China

Another feature of business organization in late imperial China – one that has attracted scant notice by scholars – was the formation of "linked-firm" (*lianhao* 聯號) enterprises. Successful firms often expanded through the multiplication of branch firms under independent management rather than centralized control. This loose structure allowed branch managers to exercise operational autonomy, and probably also served to limit the financial liability of the parent firm. Pawnbrokerages widely employed this type of organization, but it also was adopted by commercial firms, as we can see in the case of the Cai merchant empire in Fujian and Taiwan.

In 1723, Cai Daguang, a silversmith by trade, persuaded various Cai families who previously lacked any formal kinship organization to create a single Cai lineage to pool their resources for the purpose of building – in concert with other local lineages – port facilities at Dongshigang (near Quanzhou in Fujian).[126] The new port featured a 2-kilometer harbor channel lined with sixteen wharves (most belonging to individual lineages, including six wharves owned by the Cai, with one large public wharf) and warehouses. At its peak in the late nineteenth century Dongshigang numbered more than fifty shipping firms who deployed over 200 ships. The Cai family alone owned thirty of these firms, the largest of which had over thirty ships.

At the time the Dongshigang port was first developed, the upstart Cai lineage organized itself into three branches and ten sub-branches.[127] In the 1730s–40s, many members of the Cai family joined the wave of migration to Taiwan, including Cai Jizhao's two brothers. The Taiwan immigrants became farmers, but kept close ties with their mainland relatives. Cai Jizhao, who continued to manage a shipping business in Dongshigang, formed three separate partnerships with his relatives in Taiwan to develop fish farms, while his commercial fleet expanded to twenty-one ships, each of which was independently financed (one ship was underwritten by women of the Cai family who pooled together their dowries). Eventually Cai Jizhao's commercial empire included rice paddies, salterns, oil presses, pawnbrokerages, and retail stores. Other branches of the Cai lineage likewise flourished by investing in the Fujian–Taiwan trade, developing correspondence relationships and linked-firm partnerships with their migrant kinsmen in Taiwan to trade in Taiwan exports such as grain, sugar, leather, maritime products, sulfur, wax, camphor, bezoar, rattan, and fruits while importing Fujian goods such as medicine, tobacco, paper, tea, porcelain, and construction materials.

Despite the prosperity of the Cai family businesses – which lasts to this day – they were not immune to the vicissitudes of business cycles, such as the

---

[126] On the Cai lineage's business activities, see Chen Zhiping 2009: 32–116.
[127] On this type of lineage formation in which previously unrelated families invented a lineage to secure property rights or combine resources, see Szonyi 2002.

economic depression of the 1820s–40s (see Chapter 9). During periods of commercial expansion, the Cai sought to consolidate ownership by buying out partners, especially when fresh capital investment was needed. But household division as well as adverse market conditions resulted in the dissolution of partnerships and dispersal of assets. (Because ships were substantial assets, property division testaments often divided them into shares to be distributed among heirs.) Even as the social distances among geographically dispersed kin grew over time, family connections proved invaluable to continued business success. Linked-firm enterprises provided a crucial institutional mechanism for maintaining these family-based business networks.

A common feature of the partnerships discussed above was their reliance on equity investments rather than credit markets as a source of capital. Indeed, the proprietors of the Wanquantang prided themselves on their financial independence from pawnbrokers and creditors. The frequent resort to partnerships in commercial enterprise itself attested to the absence of well-developed credit markets as an alternative source of capital. Despite the development of transfer banking through bills of exchange since the Song dynasty, banks – in the sense of institutions providing long-term credit – did not emerge before the nineteenth century.

As the examples of the Wanquantang and Wanquanhao show, debt-ridden commercial firms – like family farms – often turned to conditional sales of real property assets. In these cases the firm leased back the shop from the new owner, but retained the right to redeem the property within a specified period, although it was common to grant extensions. For example, when the Han family sold the Wanquantang shop via conditional sale in 1817 the contract called for redemption (i.e., repayment of the principal) within two years, although in fact the shop was redeemed only in 1830. Shareholders were another source of short-term capital. The ledgers of the Cheng-Wu dyeworks (operated by a partnership of seven Huizhou merchants) dating from 1591 to 1604 show that on average only 48 percent of the firm's capital came from equity investments by the partners; the remainder was obtained through short-term loans from partners, kinfolk, pawnbrokerages, and credit associations. The return on investments – both for partners and outside investors – was in the range of 1.2–1.5 percent per month, or roughly 20 percent per year.[128] It remains unclear how widely this type of financing was practiced.

The principal sources of credit in late imperial China, of course, were pawnbrokers. In the countryside pawnbrokers mostly made short-term loans (one to six months) to farmers, either to provide funds for purchases of seed, tools, and draft animals or for subsistence purposes. Credit from

---

[128] Fan Jinmin 2001; see also Liu Qiugen 2007: 447–60.

pawnbrokerages was vitally important to the sericulture industry in Jiangnan, where rural silk producers depended on such loans to finance purchases of mulberry leaves or raw silk.[129] Pawnbrokerages charged high rates of interest and required substantial collateral – typically 50 percent of the loan value – when issuing loans, reflecting the poor creditworthiness of borrowers and the high frequency of defaults. In addition, a wide range of groups – including lineage trusts, mutual aid societies, and religious associations – also engaged in moneylending, either as a service to members of the group or as a profit-making activity through loans to the public at large.

Pawnbroking was very much a growth industry in the early Qing period. The number of pawnbrokerages rose from 7,695 in 1685 to 23,139 in 1812.[130] As in commerce in general, the regional merchant groups from Shanxi and Huizhou dominated pawnbroking in North and South China respectively. Shanxi and Huizhou merchants drew on their substantial profits from the salt trade and other commercial ventures to capitalize pawnshops in both urban and rural areas. Pawnbrokerages also accepted interest-bearing deposits from individuals, lineage and temple trusts, and charitable foundations; in addition, during the Qing dynasty government officials occasionally deposited monies such as payroll funds in pawnshops. Pawnbroking was a retail enterprise: large commercial cities often had more than 100 pawnbrokerages (Beijing c. 1740 had more than 200), and individual merchants might own a dozen or more pawnbrokerages in the same city through a linked-firm network. Capital assets varied considerably – 1,000 taels sufficed for pawnshops in rural areas, while those in major cities generally required at least 5,000–10,000 taels, and 20,000 taels was considered the minimum requirement in Beijing.

Qing law decreed that lenders charge no more than 3 percent interest per month and total accrued interest not exceeding the amount of principal. Actual interest rates were lower than the law permitted, but still relatively high: in the range of 20–30 percent per annum (Table 8.11). Loans contracted in silver generally charged interest rates of 1.5–2 percent per month (with some rising to the legal maximum of 3 percent). Interest rates on loans of grain fluctuated more erratically (based on price trends), but on average carried lower nominal rates than loans in silver, reflecting greater confidence that farming families could produce the grain needed to repay the loans. The broad trend shows that annualized interest rates offered by pawnbrokers declined from roughly 30 percent in the seventeenth century to 20 percent by the nineteenth century.[131] The decline in interest rates was most marked in Jiangnan, where in the late eighteenth century reputable borrowers could obtain commercial loans for 0.8–1 percent per month, or 10–12 percent on an annualized basis.[132]

---

[129] Ming-te Pan 1996.   [130] Liu Qiugen 2000: 80–81.   [131] Liu Qiugen 2007: 176–204.
[132] Hiyama 1996: 80.

Table 8.11 *Pawnbrokerage interest rates, seventeenth–twentieth centuries*

	Huizhou, Anhui (1617–1936)		Zhangzhou, Fujian (1665–1935)		Baxian, Sichuan (1756–1850)		Xinzhu, Taiwan (1816–1895)	
	Silver	Grain	Silver	Grain	Silver	Grain	Silver	Grain
Number of contracts	469	272	20	184	153	0	46	29
Average annual interest rate	18.92	25.34	30.40	19.13	24.23	–	26.50	16.36
Median interest rate	20.00	20.30	30.00	14.35	24.00	–	24.00	13.00
Standard deviation	6.03	19.99	6.00	18.52	10.88	–	7.67	10.71

Source: Peng Kaixiang *et al.* 2008: 152, table 1.

Still, the costs of capital as reflected by the interest rates charged by pawnbrokers and other lending institutions remained high, far higher than in Europe. As the above examples show, merchant and kinship networks functioned as internal credit markets, dampening the demand for commercial credit.[133] The tardy development of banking in China also reflected the absence of sovereign debt – in contrast to European states, the Chinese government never borrowed money, but instead financed itself entirely through current tax revenues. But the growth of long-distance trade in eighteenth-century China did generate new demands for capital. At the end of the eighteenth century there was a proliferation of local banks known as *qianzhuang* 錢莊 that financed commercial ventures through short-term loans. From the 1820s large-scale remittance banks (*piaohao* 票號) – a consortium of twenty-odd banks based in Shanxi province – provided a range of financial services to private merchants and the imperial government (see Chapter 9).

Conclusion

By the sixteenth century, long-lasting domestic peace and stability had engendered rising agricultural production and a revival of trade. From 1550, the pace of commercial expansion quickened. Expanding international markets for

---

[133] Rosenthal and Wong 2011: 153. As these authors point out, comparisons of interest rates on short-term loans charged by Chinese pawnbrokers with the rates on the types of long-term borrowing common in Europe such as mortgages, annuities, and sovereign debt confuse two entirely different types of credit. Disputing claims that interest rates in China were ten to twenty times greater than in Europe, they conclude (ibid.: 139) that the real cost of capital for creditworthy commercial borrowers in China was perhaps twice that of Europe – still a significant difference, to be sure.

Chinese silks and porcelains stimulated industrial production, and the massive inflow of Japanese and New World silver lubricated the wheels of commerce. Urban growth was most conspicuous in the flourishing Jiangnan cities of Suzhou, Hangzhou, and Nanjing, whose inhabitants engaged in hundreds of artisanal crafts to sate the swelling hunger for luxury goods and new consumer staples. The gravitational pull of these great cities radiated throughout the Jiangnan countryside, where hundreds of satellite market towns emerged that linked rural industries – chiefly, but not exclusively, textiles – to urban markets both near and far. In the eyes of contemporary patricians, the growth of cities and towns, and the wealth that accumulated in them, bode ill for public morality and social order. "In my father's day," wrote Ma Yilong (1499–1571) in the preface to his treatise on husbandry, "people subsisted on the fruits of their own labor, and tradesmen and shopkeepers were spread across the countryside ... Nowadays people live off the toil of others, and rural inhabitants have flocked to the towns and marketplaces, scurrying to and fro without stable employment, palms open and tongues jabbering, resorting to any chicanery to sell their wares."[134] The insinuation of money into all spheres of social life indeed would have profound cultural as well as economic repercussions. The military and political crises that ushered in the abrupt collapse of the Ming dynasty in 1644 and the Manchu conquest of China dealt only a short-term setback to the economic forces unleashed during the last century of the Ming, which continued to prevail well into the nineteenth century.

The maturation of the market economy was the signal feature of the economic history of the late imperial era. Long-distance trade networks extended to every corner of the empire, even though the circulation of commodities bypassed large swaths of rural China. The growth of long-distance trade was made possible by the development of a wide range of institutional innovations, including lineage trusts, native-place networks and trade specialization, joint-share partnerships, and linked-firm enterprises. In contrast to the Song period, when state procurement was a key catalyst in the creation and articulation of long-distance trade networks, private enterprise was the dynamic force fostering market growth in the late imperial era. Unfettered development of private commerce promoted a pattern of "Smithian growth" in which greater economic efficiency was achieved through market expansion and specialization of labor.

By the same token, the fiscal role of the state diminished compared to the Song dynasty. The commutation of taxes to silver payments and the elimination of nearly all labor service duties in the early Qing period reduced the relationship between the state and the household to a monetary transaction.

---

[134] Cited in *MSC*: 100.9a.

But the Qing state, like the Ming before it, remained dedicated to the Confucian principle of minimal taxation, which constricted its capacity to make infrastructural investments or provide public welfare. The aggressive state activism promoted by the Yongzheng Emperor in the 1720s–30s receded under his successor Qianlong, who favored benign laissez-faire policies. Even if they had the will to do so, Qing leaders lacked the fiscal resources to stimulate economic development.

Beginning in the late seventeenth century, China underwent a surge in demographic growth – a tripling of the population between 1680 and 1850 – virtually unprecedented in the history of the premodern world. This remarkable demographic expansion was propelled by prolonged domestic peace and a sustained rise in economic output made possible by the efficiency of markets, regional specialization of production, and an expanding money supply.

Yet the prosperity engendered by the quantitative growth in output masked the lack of significant innovation in productive technologies that would have lessened the pressure on increasingly scarce resources – land, water, food, and energy. Even contemporary Chinese statesmen were alarmed by the rapid pace of population growth and the mounting pressures on the agricultural base of the economy. The outbreak of the White Lotus rebellion in western China in 1796 not only shattered domestic tranquility but also starkly exposed the state's unpreparedness to subdue civil disorder. In the following decades the Chinese economy tumbled into a lengthy economic depression that would fan the flames of social discontent. At the same time Qing sovereignty came under siege by industrializing Western powers seeking to throw open Chinese markets.

9   Domestic crises and global challenges: restructuring the imperial economy (1800 to 1900)

In the first half of the nineteenth century, China descended into a prolonged economic depression. Although population growth continued uninterrupted down to 1850, signs of economic malaise already were visible by 1820. The "Daoguang Depression" (named after the reigning Daoguang Emperor, r. 1820–50) coincided with grave political challenges and social turmoil. China's defeat at the hands of Great Britain in the Opium War (1839–42) led to the forcible opening of China to foreign trade on terms dictated by the British. The Taiping rebellion (1851–64) posed an even more dire threat to the survival of the Qing Empire. Although the Qing ultimately succeeded in suppressing the insurrection, it devastated the richest provinces of China and caused the deaths of tens of millions. In retrospect, the Opium War fiasco and the ruin left in the wake of the Taiping rebellion fostered the conventional portrait of nineteenth-century China – one that largely persists today – as a poor and backward country.

The sharp contrast between the "prosperous age" (*shengshi* 盛世) – as many contemporaries described it – of the eighteenth century and the apparent poverty and stagnation of the nineteenth century has long compelled scholars to ask what forces had brought about such a drastic change in China's fortunes. Many historians have focused on structural explanations: the inherent constraints of the smallholder peasant economy, the limits of premodern technology, and the absence of systems of knowledge that would promote technological and scientific innovation to overcome those limits. Others have proposed more historically contingent factors, especially China's integration into a global economy dominated by Western imperialist powers, resulting in the drain of wealth abroad, deindustrialization in traditional sectors such as cotton manufacture, and the peripheralization of China as a producer of cheap raw materials for the industrializing West.

Questions about the nature of the premodern Chinese economy and its modern fate have been thrust into new perspectives in recent debates about "the Great Divergence" in global economic history, which we examined briefly in the Introduction. It had been commonplace assumption that the onset of the Industrial Revolution in Europe was premised on institutional

348

foundations – urban development, mercantile capitalism, demographic behavior, and a liberal-democratic political culture – established in medieval or early modern times. The "California School" scholarship challenged staid assumptions about the causal relationships between these institutions and the Industrial Revolution and the equally untested postulation that China was mired in economic torpor induced by a despotic state. Most notably, Kenneth Pomeranz marshaled copious new evidence to support his theoretically rigorous argument that the "Great Divergence" in productivity and living standards between the most economically advanced regions of Europe and Asia did not occur until after 1800.[1]

During the past fifteen years the question of the "Great Divergence" has generated energetic and constructive debate across the field of economic history.[2] Not the least of its contributions – further enhanced by the simultaneous flowering of world history scholarship – is the growing recognition that economic historians must situate their work within broad temporal and world-historical perspectives that consider not only comparisons but also the connections among economic institutions and behavior. Before examining the struggles of the Chinese economy in the nineteenth century, it is worth considering how well the Chinese economy was performing in 1800, especially in comparison with the advanced economies of Western Europe on the verge of the Industrial Revolution, the epochal transformation that would engender sustained, capital-intensive economic growth.

Measuring economic performance in late imperial China

The economy of eighteenth-century China was remarkably free compared to contemporary Europe. Competitive markets existed for land, labor, and goods. The Qing state actively encouraged the expansion of private commerce: free markets prevailed for virtually all commodities apart from salt and copper; the state taxed domestic trade only lightly, and did not impose any tariffs on foreign imports; urban guilds exercised only limited powers; and rural industry remained entirely free of guild regulation. The growth of rural industry enabled households to make more intensive use of the underutilized labor power of women and children. This pattern – which historians designate "protoindustrialization" – appeared in many parts of Europe in the eighteenth century, and in Japan as well. As families devoted more of their labor to

---

[1] Pomeranz 2000.
[2] Critiques of Pomeranz's analysis are legion; some of the more noteworthy examples include Vries 2002; Brenner and Isett 2002; Broadberry and Gupta 2006; van Zanden 2009; Rosenthal and Wong 2011; Parthasarathi 2011; and Brandt, Ma, and Rawski 2014. See also the special issue of *Economic History Review*, "Asia in the Great Divergence" (vol. 64, suppl. 1), published in 2011.

production for the market, many goods they formerly produced for their own use – including foodstuffs, clothing, shoes, candles, and tools – were purchased instead.[3]

By many standards the economic well-being of China's population in the eighteenth century was unsurpassed by any other contemporary society. Life expectancy – averaging 35–40 years for males (somewhat lower for females) who survived infancy among relatively well-off populations – was roughly comparable to Western European societies and Japan.[4] Income inequality was probably less severe in China than in Europe, given that ownership of land, the most important form of wealth, was spread much more evenly in China. A comprehensive study of household consumption in Jiangnan has estimated that the typical family spent 56 percent of its household budget on foodstuffs, a ratio almost identical to that (53 percent) for lower-class English families in the 1790s (Table 9.1).[5] Consumption of what for ordinary households were luxury goods – sugar, tea, and tobacco – also seems to have been roughly equal in China and Western Europe. Estimated per capita consumption of sugar in China in 1800 was well behind that of England, but double the level of the rest of Europe. Of course, in contrast to Europe, sugar, tea, and tobacco were not exotic imports in China, but rather domestic goods produced by family farms and distributed through highly competitive markets that yielded little revenue for the state.[6] Quantitative evidence for the consumption of durable consumer goods such as housing, furniture, and clothes is more exiguous; the earliest surveys of household consumption of such goods in China date from the 1920s. But assuming that consumption levels were no lower in the eighteenth century (the data in Table 9.1 point toward a slight decline in non-food consumption in the twentieth century), Jiangnan families maintained standards of household consumption comparable to the advanced regions of Western Europe.[7]

Nonetheless, a substantial body of scholarship depicts the agrarian economy of Qing China as caught in an economic impasse in which, for the sake of

---

[3] "Protoindustrialization" refers to rural, household-based manufacture (mainly by women and children) for extra-local markets (principally textiles, but also other consumer goods). Proto-industry absorbed the underutilized labor of landless or land-poor households, providing a means to enhance family income and increase its consumption potential. On protoindustrialization in Europe, see Ogilvie and Cerman 1996; de Vries 2008; for Japan, see Hayami 1979; Saitō 1983; Sugihara 2003.

[4] Pomeranz 2000: 36–38. For data on life expectancy, see Lee and Wang 1999: 54–55, tables 4.1, 4.2.

[5] Fang Xing (1996) arrived at virtually an identical figure (55 percent) for household expenditures on staple foods in eighteenth-century Jiangnan. The comparison with England is from Pomeranz 2000: 137.

[6] Pomeranz 2000: 116–24.

[7] Pomeranz 2000: 143–46. On household consumption in eighteenth-century Europe, see de Vries 2008.

Table 9.1 *Household consumption expenditures of Jiangnan farming families,*
eighteenth century to 1930s
(percentages of household expenditures)

	Mid-eighteenth century	Mid-nineteenth century	1930s
Food	56.6	59.8	60.2
Grain	39.7	45.0	41.8
Vegetables, fish, meat, eggs	11.2	9.5	12.1
Oil, salt, sugar, condiments	5.7	5.4	6.3
Clothing	11.2	8.0	9.7
Fuel and lighting	7.4	7.0	5.1
Rent	3.8	5.8	3.9
Household goods	0.6	0.6	0.6
Transport	1.9	2.1	2.0
Ritual and religion	9.7	8.1	8.7
Entertainment	0.4	0.5	0.4
Education	1.0	0.8	1.0
Medicine and health	2.9	2.3	2.7
Tea, alcohol, tobacco	4.6	4.8	4.8

Source: Huang Jingbin 2009: 307–08, table 8.1.

sheer survival, farming families expended ever greater labor only to glean steadily diminishing returns. It has often been argued that Chinese agriculture suffered from technological stasis after the Song dynasty, resulting in what Mark Elvin has described – speaking of the Chinese economy as a whole – as "quantitative growth, qualitative standstill."[8] In his pioneering quantitative assessment of Chinese agriculture, Dwight Perkins concluded that per capita grain production remained stagnant from 1400 to the 1950s: increases in grain output due to expansion in cultivated land and rising yields merely kept pace with population growth.[9] But others suggest that even this scenario is too optimistic. Kang Chao has asserted that after the Song population growth outran grain production despite increasingly intensive cultivation; the worsening labor/land ratio drove down wages and increased the price of land, thwarting any incentive to enhance productivity through labor-saving techno-logical innovation.[10] Chao and Philip Huang both contend that ready access to markets for land, labor, and goods enabled households to intensify their work in farming and handicrafts to secure a subsistence income despite sharply diminishing returns (as measured by daily wages). The result was an "involutionary" pattern of labor-intensive, small-scale farming that crowded out managerial farms which relied on greater capital investment, wage labor,

[8] Elvin 1973: 285–316.   [9] Perkins 1969: 13–26.   [10] Chao 1986.

Table 9.2 *Work days per* mu *in Jiangnan agriculture*

c. 820	9.48
c. 1630	11.5
c. 1830	10+
1936	13.75
1941	11.25
1957	15

Source: Li Bozhong 2002: 116, table 3–5.

and economies of scale.[11] In Huang's view, rather than raising real wages, commercialization encouraged greater exploitation of family labor and resulted in falling rather than rising returns to labor.

In contrast, Li Bozhong's studies of Jiangnan agriculture have found substantial improvements in land utilization, capital investment, and labor productivity during the Ming-Qing era that raised agricultural output well beyond Song levels.[12] The shrinking size of farms in Jiangnan – from an average of 40 *mu* in the Song to 25 *mu* in the Ming and 10 *mu* by 1800 – was offset, Li believes, by smaller families, higher yields, universal adoption of double-cropping of rice with winter crops, larger shares of land devoted to mulberry and cotton cultivation, and the shift of domestic female labor from agriculture to textile production. Li points to the revived use of oxen (prevalent in the Song, oxen virtually disappeared from Jiangnan farms in the Ming) and the large-scale application of soybean cake fertilizer as examples of labor-saving capital investments that belied Chao's claims of severe population pressure and labor surpluses. Labor intensity in rice agriculture changed little during the late imperial period compared to earlier times, although it increased in the twentieth century (Table 9.2). By Li's calculation, net household income in Jiangnan increased by 15 percent from the sixteenth to the eighteenth century, largely because of the contribution of women's work in textile manufacture (Table 9.3).

The debate over the vigor of the Jiangnan rural economy thus largely turns on the question of the income yielded by women's labor in textile production. The limited data available to measure this income even at particular moments – let alone track changes over time – defies definitive assessment. Cotton spinning, all agree, generated meager income – barely enough to support the

[11] Ibid.; Philip Huang 1990.
[12] Li Bozhong 2000, 2002, 2003. It should be noted that Li's estimates for Song rice yields almost certainly are too low; see the critiques in Ge Jinfang and Gu Rong 2000; Liu Guanlin 2013.

Table 9.3 *A model of family income in Jiangnan, sixteenth to eighteenth centuries*

	Sixteenth century		Eighteenth century	
	Farming	Cotton cloth	Farming	Cotton cloth
Inputs				
Land (*mu*)	25	–	10	–
Male labor (days/year)	275	25	217	83
Female labor (days/year)	163	37	0	200
Income (grain equivalent, in *shi*)	18.7	1.4	15.7	7.1
Total income (in *shi*)	20.1		22.8	

Source: Li Bozhong 1998: 151–53.

spinner – and thus was largely performed by young girls. Households that combined weaving with spinning – which was the dominant pattern in Jiangnan – fared considerably better, as Li Bozhong's figures indicate.[13] But rising rice and raw cotton prices after 1750 – and falling cotton cloth prices after 1800 – eroded the returns to cotton manufacture. Pomeranz suggests that real earnings from cotton spinning and weaving declined by a third from 1750 to 1840.[14] The silk industry fared much better. The most careful reconstruction, Zhang Li's analysis of sericulture in Wuxi *c.* 1873, shows that in this period – when escalating foreign demand was making sericulture highly lucrative – the net income per *mu* per workday in mulberry cultivation was more than eight times greater than rice agriculture.[15] Silk-reeling likewise generated two to four times greater income per workday than rice farming.[16] Extrapolating backward from Zhang's findings, the returns to labor in sericulture surely also had been high throughout the early nineteenth century, when silk prices remained buoyant. As we shall see, by 1800 Jiangnan's dominance of the domestic cotton market encountered stiff competition from cheaper (albeit coarser) cottons produced in the interior provinces, but silk producers faced no such rivals.

As Zhang Li persuasively argues, farming families in Wuxi (where sericulture had not been practiced in the past) reallocated their land and labor

[13] Pomeranz (2000: 319–20) arrives at a figure of 7.2 tls for the contribution of women's labor to the household based on 1750 prices, sufficient for the subsistence needs of 1.9 adult male workers. Philip Huang (1990: 86) concedes that one weaver could support two adult male workers, but describes this as "no more than a barely adequate subsistence, with virtually no possibility for enrichment."
[14] Pomeranz 2000: 326.
[15] Zhang Li 2010: 171–81. Philip Huang's (1990: 79, 126–27) calculations for returns to labor in sericulture are based on flawed data, as Zhang (ibid.: 35–61, 155–71) shows.
[16] Zhang Li 2010: 190, table 24.

resources from rice cultivation to sericulture in response to market incentives. Combining her findings with those of Li Bozhong and Kenneth Pomeranz, we must conclude that for Jiangnan, at least, the "involutionary" model of economic behavior described by Philip Huang is invalid.[17] Instead, the Jiangnan rural economy displayed a pattern of labor-absorbing intensification of both agriculture and manufacture that raised household and per capita incomes, much as we see in Tokugawa Japan at the same time.[18] Of course, Huang's involution model may have application in other regions where the returns to labor investment in textile or other cottage industrial production were more limited.

Kenneth Pomeranz's bold assertion that income levels in eighteenth-century Jiangnan were on a par with the most advanced economic regions of Europe (England and the Netherlands) has prompted historians of China to give renewed attention to the role of economic institutions – for example, property rights, contracts, dispute resolution mechanisms, credit markets, merchant associations, kinship practices, and corporate governance – in facilitating or impeding economic growth.[19] In addition, economic historians have made a concerted effort to develop quantitative measures for evaluating the economic performance of late imperial China in comparison with other advanced economies in Europe and Asia. The two principal measures utilized in making such comparisons have been gross domestic product (GDP) estimates and real wage rates. To be sure, there are significant theoretical and empirical problems both with calculating GDP and real wages and their utility as measures of comparison, and the results of such exercises must be viewed with caution.[20]

The late Angus Maddison was the pioneer in developing GDP estimates to measure and compare long-term economic performance on a global scale. Maddison estimated that China's per capita GDP had reached a high level ($600 in 1990 international dollars) in 1700 – slightly less than two-thirds of the level of Europe, but ahead of both Japan and India. Maddison also asserted that aggregate GDP growth in China outpaced Europe between 1700 and 1820,

[17] Huang Jingbin (2009: 318–19) also describes sericultural households in eighteenth-century Jiangnan as "affluent," and further concludes that the decline in the level of household consumption in the nineteenth century was fairly modest (see Table 9.1 above).

[18] Sugihara Kaoru (1996, 2003) has described this common pattern as the "East Asian path of development."

[19] See, for example, Zelin et al. 2004; Goetzmann and Köll 2005; Ch'iu 2008; Rosenthal and Wong 2011; Debin Ma 2011; Zurndorfer 2011; So 2013a; Brandt, Ma, and Rawski 2014.

[20] For an incisive argument asserting the fallacy of GDP as a measure of economic productivity in premodern societies, see Du Xuncheng and Li Jin 2011. GDP is intended to measure all goods, labor, and services that entered the marketplace, but much of the gross product of premodern societies was not marketed. Conversion of values into universal measures for purposes of comparison such as 1990 US dollars also requires a standard index for prices (usually gold, which had no monetary function in China) that may not actually reflect real market values. On the technical problems of price calculations for GDP estimates, see Peng Kaixiang 2011.

with the result that in 1820 China's share of global GDP reached 33 percent, eclipsing that of Europe (27 percent). But this increase was a consequence of China's huge population expansion, not economic development; on a per capita basis, China's GDP had stagnated since 1700, in contrast to sustained improvement in Europe. By Maddison's calculation, China's per capita GDP in 1820 had sunk to only 55 percent of the European level.[21]

Apart from the very rough estimates proposed in the 1980s by Albert Feuerwerker, most efforts to quantify the size of the economy in late imperial China have been responses to Maddison's methods and results. Maddison's technique, it should be noted, was relatively crude and presumed that per capita output remained unchanged from the end of the Song to the nineteenth century (Table 9.4). Feuerwerker's methodology, too, assumed a fixed per capita grain output from the Song to modern times. Recent studies have sought more nuanced historical specification. Liu Guanglin derived his estimates – which show a very high per capita GDP in the Song that fell precipitously in the Ming and only partially recovered in the Qing – from calculations of soldiers' real wages as a proxy for per capita income. Guan Hanhui and Li Daokui have attempted to apply national accounting analysis to the exiguous Ming data, and like Liu Guanglin find a low and stagnant level of per capita GDP in the Ming, equivalent to only half of Maddison's estimate. Guan and Li admit that their method does not adequately capture industrial output, and their calculation that agriculture generated 88 percent of national income (a percentage that was increasing in the late Ming!) seems scarcely tenable.[22] Guan and Li's estimate that Ming per capita GDP ranged between $220–$239 (1990 US$) is well below what is usually regarded as the minimum level of survival, and indeed the authors conclude that Ming China was ensnared in a Malthusian trap in which population growth outran the available food supply, culminating in the positive checks of famine, war, and epidemic in the 1620–40s.

Liu Ti also has utilized the national accounting method, but arrives at strikingly different results. Liu concludes that agriculture generated a mere 54 percent of GDP in 1600, in contrast to 34 percent produced by industry and construction. By Liu's calculation nominal GDP grew five-fold between

---

[21] Maddison 2001: 42–48, 2007: 44, tables 2.1–2.2c.

[22] The authors propose far lower figures for handicraft manufacture than those proposed by other scholars. For example, Guan and Li (2010: 800) estimate total cotton cloth production in the late Ming at 5 million bolts, only one-quarter of Wu Chengming's (2001a: 131) estimate of 20 million bolts for Songjiang alone. Their calculation (Guan and Li 2010: 808) that per capita GDP peaked in the middle of the fifteenth century and steadily declined thereafter (with a slight rise – but still below the 1450 peak – in 1600–26) certainly defies all other assessments of the Ming economy. In their more recent collaboration with Stephen Broadberry (Broadberry, Li, and Guan 2014), these authors have revised their late Ming estimate to four times the level asserted in their 2010 article.

Table 9.4 *Estimates of Chinese GDP*

Feuerwerker 1984			Maddison 2007		Liu Guanglin 2005			Guan Hanhui and Li Daokui 2010			Liu Ti 2009			Broadberry, Guan, and Li 2014	
Year	GDP (million tls.)	p.c. GDP (tls.)	Year	p.c. GDP (1990 $)	Year	GDP (million tls.)	p.c. GDP (shi)	Year	GDP (million tls.)	p.c. GDP (shi)	Year	GDP (million tls.)	p.c. GDP (1990 $)	Year	p.c. GDP (1990 $)
1080	381	4.2	960	450	1120s	764	7.5							1090	1,204
			1300	600	1420s	62–81	2.9–3.8	1402	150	6.0–6.3				1400	960
1550	635–847	4.2–5.6			1580s	346–576	3.95	1578	325	5.2–5.4				1570	968
								1626	290–300	5.5–6.0	1600	900	388	1600	977
1750	952–1,713	3.5–6.3	1700	600	1770s	2,009	5.28				1750	1,664	340	1750	685
1880s	3,339	8.3	1820	600	1880s	2,781	5.96				1840	4,480	318	1850	594
1908	3,032–6,063	7.1–14.2	1952	538											

Sources: Feuerwerker 1984: 300, table 1; Maddison 2007: 44, tables 2.1–2.2c; Liu Guanglin 2005: 338, table D.5; Guan Hanhui and Li Daokui 2010: 807; Liu Ti 2009: passim; Broadberry, Guan, and Li 2014: 34, table 4.

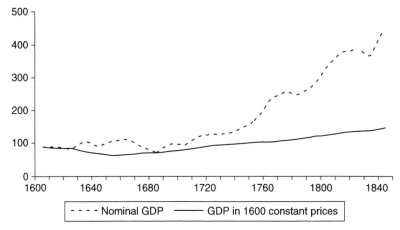

Figure 9.1 Nominal and real GDP estimates, 1600–1840
1600 = 100
Source: Liu Ti 2009: 151, figure 2.

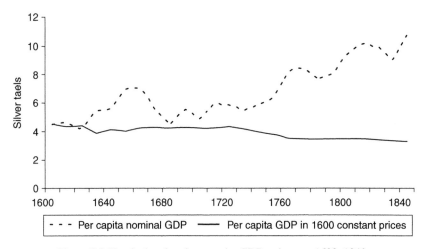

Figure 9.2 Nominal and real per capita GDP estimates, 1600–1840
Source: Liu Ti 2009: 151, figure 3.

1600 and 1840, but the increase in real terms (constant prices) was far more modest, and per capita real GDP declined by roughly 20 percent (Figures 9.1 and 9.2). Part of this decline is explained by the reduced share of the industrial sector, which declined by nearly half, to 20 percent, by 1840 (agriculture, in contrast, rose to 69 percent). The size of the service sector remained constant (around 11–12 percent of the total), but its composition changed radically:

Liu concludes that finance comprised a third of the service sector in 1840 compared to only 4 percent in 1600, while government spending's share of the service economy fell from 45 to 22 percent. Like Guan and Li, however, Liu Ti arrives at the conclusion that China's per capita GDP already was far below European levels: 40 percent of Britain's per capita GDP in 1600, and less than 20 percent of the British level by 1840.[23] Liu Ti's absolute figures for per capita GDP surely are too low as well, but his analysis of the composition of GDP and the long-term trend in per capita GDP seems more plausible.

Finally, the recent analysis of long-term changes in China's per capita GDP by Stephen Broadberry and his collaborators shows a continuous decline from a peak in the Northern Song period. Their figures indicate a steady equilibrium throughout the Ming period at roughly 80 percent of the late Northern Song level, followed by a steep plunge in the Qing period. By their calculation, population growth had sharply curtailed per capita GDP already by 1750, with a further decline by 1850 to a level half that of the Song peak. These findings largely reflect the failure of grain yields to keep pace with population growth from the Song period onward (thus echoing Kang Chao's analysis). The authors conclude that their analysis confirms Huang's involution thesis.[24]

Given the severe limitations of the data and the necessity of making very large and tentative assumptions, these efforts to analyze the size and structure of GDP in premodern China can only be regarded as heuristic exercises. This caveat is all the more true as one moves back in time, as the wide discrepancies in estimates indicate. Liu Guanglin's assertion that per capita GDP peaked in the Northern Song affirms the conclusion of Robert Hartwell, who – also on the basis of a calculation of soldier's real wages – posited a GDP equivalent to 908 million taels in 1077.[25] Peter Golas, working from Feuerwerker's figures, instead arrived at a far lower figure of 413 million taels for the Song, although he conceded that this figure is implausibly low, since it would suggest that government revenues consumed 24 percent of GDP.[26] According to Hartwell's estimates, government revenues comprised 11–12 percent of GDP during the Song, a figure that seems reasonably aligned with our knowledge of the highly activist Song state. For the late imperial era, Liu Ti's results strike me as

[23] Liu Ti 2009.

[24] Broadberry, Guan, and Li (2014): 20. Shi Zhihong et al. (2014) arrive at slightly lower (by roughly 10 percent) per capita GDP figures from 1661 to 1850 than Broadberry et al., but the trend they chart is virtually identical. The key new argument proposed by Shi Zhihong et al. is that the decline in GDP largely resulted from the relative decline in the high-income service sector (especially government) from 1650 to 1900.

[25] Hartwell 1988: 78–79. Unlike Liu, however, Hartwell did not provide the data underlying his estimates for soldier's real wages.

[26] Golas 1988: 93–94.

providing the best approximation – at least of the trend, if not the absolute level – in per capita GDP, based on present knowledge.

Of course, as Pomeranz has persuasively argued, comparing the whole Chinese empire, with its vast disparities in economic development, to European countries such as Britain mixes together highly dissimilar and unequal units of analysis. Instead, Pomeranz has insisted on the necessity of comparing the most advanced economic regions of roughly equal size, such as England, the Netherlands, Jiangnan, and the Kantō Plain in Japan. This principle is the cornerstone of the collaborative study by Li Bozhong and Jan Luiten van Zanden, which compares GDP and labor productivity in the Netherlands and two counties (Huating and Lou) in Songjiang in the 1820s.[27] The geography of the two regions is similar (low-lying plains with ready access to both inland and overseas water transport), and they both were characterized by high rates of urbanization and commercialization (Li estimated that 80 percent of output and 67 percent of consumption in Hua-Lou passed through the marketplace). But the regional economies differed in significant ways: Hua-Lou, the heart of Songjiang's cotton industry, had a much higher proportion of the workforce engaged in manufacture, whereas commerce and banking employed a much greater share of the Netherlands's population. Li and van Zanden find that labor productivity in agriculture was very high in both regions, but wages from artisanal and industrial work in Hua-Lou were far lower than in the Netherlands, reflecting the fact that Hua-Lou's industrial workforce consisted overwhelmingly of women spinners and weavers. Consequently, there was a large disparity in per capita income between the two regions: the Dutch level was 81 percent higher (86 percent higher when measured in purchasing power parity [PPP] terms) than in Hua-Lou. The authors attribute this gap to greater Dutch capital investment in labor-saving technologies in industrial production, transport, and to some extent agriculture. Low wage rates and high interest rates and capital costs acted as brakes on such investment in Hua-Lou. Based on Maddison's estimate of Dutch per capita GDP in 1820 of $1,838 (1990 US$), Li and van Zanden calculate that Hua-Lou's per capita GDP in 1820 was $988, or about 83 percent of the level of Western Europe as a whole. In contrast to Pomeranz and studies that have focused on consumption, Li and van Zanden find a large gap in GDP between Jiangnan and advanced economic regions in Europe. But Li and van Zanden's estimate for Hua-Lou's per capita GDP is 70–80 percent higher than the estimates of Broadberry *et al.* ($598) and Shi Zhihong *et al.* ($545) for China as a whole in 1850.[28]

---

[27] Li and Van Zanden 2012. The 1820s were a period of economic torpor, if not depression, in both regions.

[28] Debin Ma (2008) calculates that per capita GDP in Jiangsu-Zhejiang in the early twentieth century was roughly 50 percent higher than the average for China as a whole. He also points out

Economic historians commonly utilize real wages as an index of the standard of living, based on the logic that since wage earners occupied a marginal niche within premodern economies their wages can serve as a proxy for marginal labor productivity in general. Robert Allen's comparison of real wages in China and Europe has found that wage-rates in Ming-Qing China were substantially lower than in England and the Netherlands, although comparable to other parts of Europe such as Germany and Italy.[29] Drawing primarily on Li Bozhong's data (with adjustments) and converting income data to purchasing power parity (PPP) exchange rates, Allen concluded that the labor productivity of Jiangnan farmers was already high in 1600 and remained unchanged in 1800 at a level comparable to the richest agricultural regions in England. Farm work was vastly more intensive in Jiangnan: labor intensity (days worked per unit of land) was eight times greater in Jiangnan than England, but output in Jiangnan was nine times higher. In the early seventeenth century, Jiangnan's farming families earned substantially higher incomes than English farm workers. But net income (measured in rice) of female textile workers fell by half between the seventeenth and nineteenth centuries. By Allen's calculation, family income in Jiangnan declined by 42 percent from 1620 to 1820, largely due to falling prices for textiles and the sharp reduction in farm size. To be sure, the income of Jiangnan farming families c. 1820 was no worse than that of English farm workers. But Allen concludes that population growth and the worsening land/labor ratio had resulted in growing impoverishment even in Jiangnan.[30]

In another study, Allen and a group of collaborators have sought to compare the real wages of unskilled workers in Beijing, Suzhou, and Guangdong with other European and Asian cities.[31] They conclude that real wages in Chinese cities already were far below (barely half) the level of London and Amsterdam already in the first half of the eighteenth century, although on a par with central and southern European cities well into the nineteenth century.[32] But the utility of such comparisons is questionable. Compared to Europe, a far smaller percentage of the Jiangnan workforce consisted of full-time wage

that per capita tax revenue (which perhaps can be taken as a rough proxy for income) was also 50 percent higher in Jiangsu-Zhejiang during the eighteenth century.

[29] Allen 2009.
[30] Allen concludes that the golden age for Jiangnan farming/weaving families came in the early seventeenth century, but of course his study skips over the intervening two centuries. If one substitutes the much higher cotton cloth prices that prevailed in the late eighteenth century in place of the extremely depressed prices of the 1820s I suspect that the golden age continued down to 1800 irrespective of population growth.
[31] Allen et al. 2011.
[32] It is also worth noting – especially because the authors make no mention of it – that the gap in real wages between Beijing and London–Amsterdam narrowed considerably over the course of the eighteenth century before rising sharply in the nineteenth century.

laborers – perhaps 10–15 percent, in contrast to more than half in England and the Netherlands. Wage laborers in Jiangnan earned only 30–40 percent of the income of tenant farmers with security of tenure, and even less compared to smallholders.[33] The earnings of such wage laborers – the vast majority of whom were single men – barely sufficed for their own upkeep and could not support a family (hence the epithet by which they were commonly known: "bare sticks" [*guanggun* 光棍]). The disparity in proletarian wages adduced by Allen and his collaborators is not incompatible with closer parity in family incomes and living standards in general.

Nonetheless, the economic growth of the eighteenth century could not be sustained indefinitely. There is considerable evidence that the Chinese economy had seriously begun to exhaust its productive capacities by 1800. Despite the impressive economic expansion of the early Qing, no new institutions, public or private, were developed to mitigate these pressures. By 1820 China was sinking into an economic depression that would last for more than three decades.

Economic depression in early nineteenth-century China

The first signs of economic deterioration were revealed abruptly at the close of the eighteenth century by the outbreak of what became known as the White Lotus rebellion. Heavy-handed attempts by the Qing government to suppress religious dissidents suspected of sedition in western Hubei ignited a popular uprising in 1796. The stubborn resistance of the rebels shocked the court and exposed the deterioration of the Qing armies' preparedness. Quelling the White Lotus insurrection, which spread to the neighboring provinces of Sichuan and Henan, took ten years and erased the treasury surpluses that had accumulated during the previous half-century (Figure 9.3).

Scholars commonly point to the White Lotus rebellion as the crucial turning point marking the end of the "High Qing" period of dynastic vigor and economic prosperity in the eighteenth century and the onset of the protracted political and institutional decline that culminated in the fall of the dynasty in 1911.[34] The uprising epitomized the deep-seated political and social problems that sapped the vigor of the Qing order. The rebellion erupted in the Han River highlands in western China, an "internal frontier" that had absorbed a great influx of migrants during the second half of the eighteenth century. The wave of settlement soon overwhelmed the productive resources of this peripheral region.[35] Economic hardship and the state's crackdown

---

[33] Pomeranz 2008a: 84–85. Xu Dixin and Wu Chengming (2000: 37) estimated that only 1–2 percent of the Ming population were wage laborers.

[34] The classic statement is Mann Jones and Kuhn 1978.

[35] Vermeer 1991; Wensheng Wang 2014: 61–70.

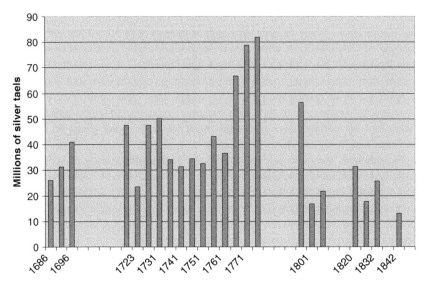

Figure 9.3 Ministry of revenue silver treasury reserves, 1686–1842
Source: Shi Zhihong 2008: 104, table 1.31, 253–55, table 2.28.

against sectarian religious groups galvanized dissent among a broad swath of the Han highlands population, which harbored bandits, salt smugglers, and hardscrabble "shack people" (*pengmin* 棚民) practicing crude swidden farming amid the rugged hills. Corruption, bureaucratic malaise, and the debilitated condition of the Qing armed forces stymied the state's response to the insurgency – a prelude to a pattern that would recur during the vastly more devastating rebellions of the mid-nineteenth century.

In the wake of the White Lotus rebellion the Jiaqing Emperor (r. 1796–1820) instituted a range of political reforms to uproot corruption and make the state more prepared to resolve political and economic crises. Recent scholarship has accentuated the positive influence of Jiaqing's reforms in establishing a stable footing for "sustainable political development" that moderated the ambitions of the Qing state and arrested dynastic decline.[36] However, these political reforms did little to enhance the state's infrastructural capacity. The rigid revenue base, tethered to the land tax rates frozen by imperial decree in 1713, hampered its ability to respond to military emergencies and natural disasters. The intrusion of Chinese settlers into frontier regions inhabited by non-Chinese minorities in the southwest and northwest

---

[36] Wensheng Wang 2014 (see ibid: 6–9 for his definition of "sustainable political development"). On the recent trend in scholarship toward a more positive evaluation of the Jiaqing reign and its political reforms, see Rowe 2011.

aggravated ethnic and religious tensions that flared into violence with increasing frequency. Recurring famines in the early decades of the nineteenth century, especially after the colossal Tambora volcanic eruption of 1815 caused climatic anomalies that ruined harvests worldwide for several years, depleted the state's granary reserves. The onset of the Daoguang Depression marked the definitive end to the prosperity of the "long eighteenth century."

Many scholars have cited population growth and the pressure it imposed on resources as one of the most – if not the most – dire problems confronting the Qing state in the late eighteenth and early nineteenth centuries.[37] The population boom of the eighteenth century continued uninterrupted down to the eve of the calamitous Taiping rebellion in the 1850s (Figure 8.3). Intensifying pressure on the land exhausted many vital resources – especially the loss of forests that supplied fuel and building materials – and pushed China to the brink of ecological crisis. The internal colonization of upland regions in the Yangzi River watershed by the "shack people," who planted maize as their principal food crop, resulted in massive deforestation. Although maize required less labor than sweet potatoes, it rapidly depleted soil fertility, forcing the shack people to move to virgin forests every few years. Deforestation triggered erosion, which worsened the problem of flooding and water control in lowland areas.[38] Planting tea on hillsides mitigated but did not halt environmental degradation. In 1824, the silting of the Yellow River overwhelmed the elaborate system of dikes, locks, revetments, dredging equipment, and overspill reservoirs maintained by the Qing government, flooding vast areas of the Central Plain and the Huai River valley. Despite the enormous funds and labor expended by the central government to bring the flood under control, the Yellow River had altered its course, and devastating floods recurred over the next several decades until a new course, to the north of the Shandong Peninsula, was reestablished in 1855.[39]

Although the strain imposed on the environment and productive resources by population growth became increasingly severe, the evidence does not

---

[37] Mann Jones and Kuhn 1978: 108–10; Wensheng Wang 2014: 23–6.

[38] Marks 2012: 205–15. Similar ecological problems emerged in the upland periphery of Jiangnan as well. See Osborne 1994, 1998. According to Marks (2012: 206), the Hakka who settled in the highlands of southeastern China had a more muted environmental impact than the shack people because they relied on sweet potatoes for subsistence and preserved the forest cover by cultivating Chinese fir as a commercial crop.

[39] During the collapse of the Yellow River water control system in 1824–26, the state was forced to resort to seaborne transport of tribute grain from the Yangzi Delta to Beijing. Although the alternative proved more efficient than the Grand Canal route, political pressures compelled the court to return to canal shipment once the waterways were stabilized. Leonard (1996) gives a positive spin to this episode, regarding it as evidence of the administrative competence of the Daoguang Emperor and his advisors. But as Leonard concedes (1996: 233), at this time the Qing state was capable only of "small-scale ameliorative actions" and had abandoned "grandiose schemes."

suggest that China had reached the point of a Malthusian demographic crisis. To be sure, sharp spikes in mortality occurred on a regular basis. In 1813–14, a severe drought caused grain prices in Hebei to double and culminated in a genuine mortality crisis, with the state powerless to relieve starvation and suffering. Hebei again suffered severe harvest failures in the early 1820s.[40] Demographic research on rural Liaoning (Manchuria) has demonstrated definite correlations between vitality and short-term price movements: marriages and births declined during years of high food prices and increased when prices were low, while conversely deaths rose and fell in tandem with the rise and fall of grain prices.[41] Population growth certainly exacerbated the economic pressure on the poor. Long-term trends in Liaoning show no increase in male mortality during 1800–50, but household formation, marriages, and births declined, suggesting a society under demographic stress. Female infanticide was a prevalent means of controlling family size and husbanding its economic resources. Ruthless as sex-specific infanticide was as a technique of population control, it showed that families altered their reproductive strategies in the face of changing economic circumstances.[42]

But long-term correlations between prices and population change are less evident. Following the steady increase in grain prices across the eighteenth century, prices plunged in the 1790s, and then rose after 1800. Grain prices spiked sharply in both north and south in the 1810s, but abated in most areas in the 1820s (the main exception was in Suzhou, where rice prices remained high down to the 1840s).[43] According to the ledgers of the Tongtaisheng, a general goods merchandising firm based in Ningjin, Hebei, the nominal prices of both agricultural and manufactured goods rose in the 1810s and then trended downward in the 1820s (with a sharp drop in the early 1830s) before returning to their previous level (Figure 9.4).[44] But in silver prices (converted from

[40] Lillian Li 2007: 255–66.   [41] Lee and Campbell 1997: 31–39.
[42] Lee and Campbell (1997: 65–70, 81–82) argue that female infanticide was practiced at the upper echelons of Qing society, including within the imperial clan, and not only by the poor and desperate. But other scholars emphasize that infanticide was far more prevalent among the poor (which the Lee-Campbell data also shows), and thus serves as an index of the growing immiseration of the Chinese population. See Wolf 2001; Lillian Li 2007: 315–16. There is general agreement that despite the Chinese predilection for marriage at an early age, fertility was lower in China than in Europe. But whereas Lee et al. attribute this low fertility to birth control, Wolf attributes it to poverty and malnutrition. A recent study of the Que lineage in Songyang county, on the Zhejiang-Fujian border, shows that fertility rose during the lineage's rise to prosperity in 1730–1830, then steadily diminished as its economic fortunes deteriorated from 1830 onward. The authors conclude that Que households actively adjusted their family size in tandem with changing economic circumstances, although the pronounced reduction in fertility after 1830 did not halt the lineage's economic decline. See Che Qun and Cao Shuji 2011.
[43] For grain prices in South China, see Figure 8.5; for grain prices in the north, see Lillian Li 2007:196–220; Lee and Campbell 1997: 27–39.
[44] For an introduction to the Tongtaisheng ledgers and their utility for economic history, see Yuan Weipeng and Ma Debin 2010.

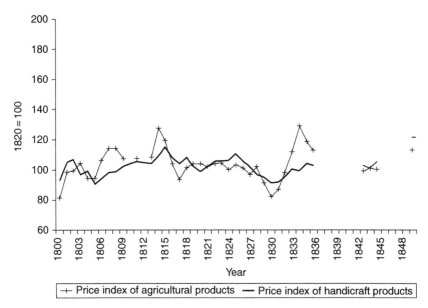

Figure 9.4 Prices of agricultural and manufactured goods in Ningjin (Hebei), 1800–50
Source: Ningjin Tongtaisheng ledgers; Peng Kaixiang 2006: 90, figure 5.4.

prices originally recorded in coin), the prices of both agricultural and manufactured products as well as wages deteriorated steadily from 1815 to 1850, apart from a brief recovery in the mid-1830s (Figure 9.5). Other data corroborate these trends. For example, real wages (measured in grain) of unskilled laborers were relatively stable in Beijing during 1807–1838. Nominal daily wages paid in coin (the typical practice in Beijing) rose slightly during this period, but purchasing power measured in silver fell significantly (Figure 9.6).

The Daoguang Depression years of 1820–50 thus witnessed static or declining real prices and wages – and in silver terms, steep deflation – even as China's population continued to grow at a steady rate. It has been argued that the chief cause of this deflation of silver prices was the massive outflow of silver during these years, a reversal of the centuries-long pattern of silver flowing into China, as a result of surging opium imports.[45] This argument traces back to contemporary Chinese officials and statesmen: as early as 1820 the influential policy advisor Bao Shichen warned that opium smuggling by foreign merchants was causing 100 million silver taels to drain out of China every year.[46] In fact, it was

---

[45] Mann Jones and Kuhn 1978: 130; Peng Zeyi 1983: 25–26.
[46] Rowe 2010: 72. Needless to say, Bao's hyperbolic figures are hardly credible.

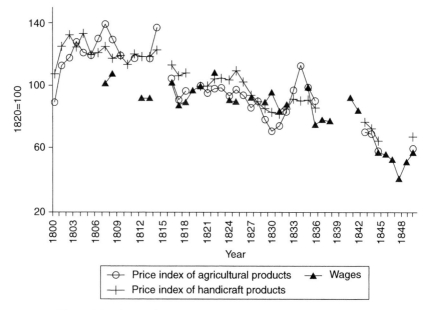

Figure 9.5 Prices and wages (silver equivalents) in Ningjin (Hebei), 1800–50
Source: Ningjin Tongtaisheng ledgers; Peng Kaixiang 2006: 37, figure 3.5.

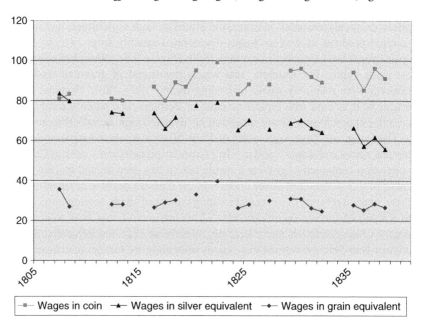

Figure 9.6 Daily wages of unskilled laborers in Beijing, 1807–38
Source: Li Longsheng 2010: 174, table 3.17.

Table 9.5 *Net flow of silver from China, 1818–54*
(all figures in millions of pesos)

	A Silver imports	B Silver exports	Net flow of silver (A−B)
1818–20	19.31	9.42	+9.89
1821–25	26.13	5.12	+21.01
1826–30	12.72	25.68	−12.96
1831–35	5.17	24.98	−19.81
1836–40	2.77	32.26	−29.49
1841–45	2.34	53.67	−51.33
1846–50	0.24	30.82	−30.57
1851–54	0.82	21.51	−20.69
Total	69.51	203.46	−133.95

Source: von Glahn 2013: 50, table 2.10.

only after 1827 that China experienced a net outflow of silver, which reached its peak level during 1840s (Table 9.5).

Some scholars, myself included, have cast a more skeptical eye on these assessments of the role of opium as the principal cause in the reversal of the flow of silver. Louis Dermigny long ago pointed out that opium imports alone accounted for no more than half of the total amount of silver that China exported during the 1830s–40s. Dermigny instead attributed the net outflow of silver from China to the rising value of silver in international markets.[47] In a recent study, Lin Man-houng likewise disputes the opium import thesis, emphasizing that silver began to flow back into China in substantial quantities after 1857 even though opium imports reached unprecedentedly high levels and accounted for even a greater proportion of China's imports. Instead, Lin contends that falling global production of silver and stagnant or shrinking European markets for tea and silk, China's principal exports, caused a reversal of China's trade balance and the net outflow of silver during the first half of the nineteenth century. With the revival of gold and silver production and rapid growth of tea and silk exports in the 1850s silver once again began to flow into China.[48]

Although Lin Man-houng's analysis shifts the focus away from opium, she still views the outflow of silver as the proximate cause of economic depression in China. But I believe this thesis is untenable. Indeed, each component of her analysis is unpersuasive.[49] Contrary to Lin's claims, there was no crisis of silver

---

[47] Dermigny 1964: 3, 1342–43.   [48] Lin Man-houng 1991, 2006: 87–114.
[49] For my critique of Lin's analysis, see von Glahn 2013: 49–58. In her 2006 book Lin presented figures that showed the outflow of silver beginning as early as 1808. However, her data had

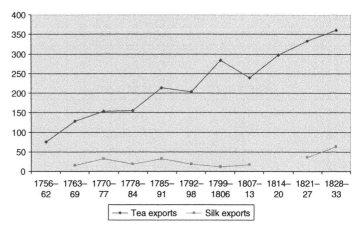

Figure 9.7 Tea and silk exports, 1756–1833 (annual averages; tea exports in thousands of piculs; silk exports in hundreds of piculs)
Source: Dermigny 1964: 2, 549–53.
NB: Silk data is incomplete, and no silk data is available for 1756–62 and 1814–20.

production following the demise of Spanish colonial rule in Latin America in the 1810s. Coin output in Mexico did decline from the historical high of 18 million pesos minted in 1810, but by 1827, when the outflow of silver from China began, output had returned to a minimum of 10 million pesos per year.[50] Nor is it true that China's exports of tea and silk declined during this period. On the contrary, exports of tea and silk reached an unprecedented high level in the early 1830s (Figure 9.7). Chinese exports then leveled off until the dramatic surge to far higher levels that occurred in the 1850s.

The principal evidence for a shortage of silver in China during the first half of the nineteenth century is the sharp appreciation of silver (relative to bronze coin) beginning in the mid-1830s (Figure 9.8). Contemporary Chinese statesmen attributed the falling value of bronze coin to the widespread use of foreign silver pesos as a means of exchange and exhorted the court to halt the circulation of foreign coin. Undoubtedly the greater utility of a silver coin of

major defects, as has been shown by Kishimoto 2009: 93–95. Correcting for these errors, Lin's figures, like mine, show the outflow beginning in the late 1820s.

[50] Von Glahn 2013: 47, figures 2.15, 2.16. As I (von Glahn 2007a) and Irigoin (2009) have argued, the crucial change was not a decline in the output of coin but a marked deterioration in the quality of the coins minted by the new Latin American republics, which sharply decreased their value in the eyes of Chinese. In other words, slackening Chinese demand rather than a shortfall in the global supply contributed to the cessation of Chinese imports of American silver.

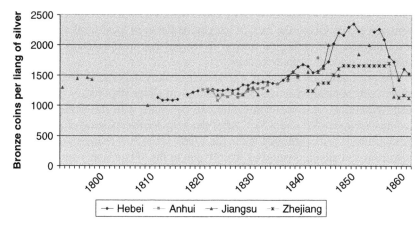

Figure 9.8 Silver:bronze coin exchange ratios, 1790–1860
Source: von Glahn 2013: 55, figure 2.20.

standard weight and purity such as the Spanish peso contributed to the diminished value of bronze coin, but bronze coin also depreciated relative to uncoined sycee silver. Debasement of the bronze coin issued by the state – confirmed by numismatic evidence – encouraged widespread private minting of heavily adulterated coin.[51] Thus the increasingly inferior quality of bronze coin contributed to its fall in value. Another new development that contributed to the depreciation of bronze coin was the growing issue of bronze coin-denominated paper notes (*qianpiao* 錢票) by the private banks (*qianzhuang* and *yinhao*) that began to proliferate from the end of the eighteenth century, especially in North China.[52]

Surprisingly, Figure 9.8 reveals that the depreciation of bronze coin appears to have been significantly more severe in North China, traditionally a region more dependent on bronze coin, rather than in Jiangnan, where silver was in more common use and Spanish peso coins had become widely employed as means of exchange. Oscillations in the silver:bronze coin exchange ratios reflected the differential demand for each type of currency, and not simply a shortage of silver. As Kuroda Akinobu persuasively argues, the fragmentary structure of currency circulation in late imperial China and the high seasonality of monetary demand resulted in a disproportionate demand for means of payment, especially bronze coin, within local markets. In the Qing period this demand was increasingly satisfied by money substitutes

---

[51] Burger 2015; Wang Yejian 2003: 196–99.
[52] Wang Yejian 2003: 180–84. Provincial officials roundly blamed the excess of *qianpiao* notes for contributing to the depreciation of bronze coin. See von Glahn 2013: 55–57.

such as *qianpiao*. In Kuroda's view, China suffered from shortages of bronze coin, not silver. Given the lack of integration between local-level and upper-level markets, the influx of foreign silver did not fundamentally alter the autonomy of local currency circuits.[53]

The price deflation of the early nineteenth century thus cannot be correlated either with population trends or fluctuations in silver imports (or in foreign trade generally). A closer correlation can be found with the money supply (compare Figures 8.2 and 8.5).[54] After the long secular increase of the eighteenth century, prices abruptly fell in the 1790s, when new infusions of money, both coin and silver, contracted sharply due to the White Lotus uprising and the curtailment of European overseas trade following the French Revolution and the outbreak of the Napoleonic Wars. But the correlation is inexact, especially during 1818–27, when silver prices fell even as silver imports peaked. The deflationary trend that commenced c. 1815 cannot be explained by variations in the money supply. Moreover, the standard estimates of money supply fail to account for the spreading use of paper substitutes such as *qianpiao* and the "silver notes" (*yinpiao* 銀票) that were widely used in South China. Li Longsheng has gone so far as to propose that the volume of silver notes in circulation (which he estimates at 61 million taels) fully replaced the net outflow of silver (62 million taels, by his estimate) during 1820–51.[55] In the absence of more explicit evidence for the volume of notes in circulation, however, this hypothesis remains speculative.

As the pronounced dip in grain prices in the 1790s – often dismissed as a statistical anomaly – indicates (and the outbreak of the White Lotus rebellion confirmed), China's domestic economy was displaying signs of serious strain.[56] We lack data to measure changes in output and trade with any precision, but reports from inland and maritime customs depots are revealing. Table 9.6 shows the revenues reported by the four largest customs depots. The data indicates that trade volume peaked in domestic commercial centers such as Huai'an (linchpin of the Grand Canal, and the salt trade in particular), Suzhou (hub of the national rice market), and Jiujiang (a major Yangzi River port and gateway to the Middle Yangzi tea-producing regions) in the 1770s–90s and declined thereafter. In contrast, maritime trade at Guangzhou soared in the late eighteenth century; beginning in 1802, the maritime customs revenue of Guangzhou surpassed the total revenues of the three largest inland customs stations, testifying both to the vitality of overseas trade and the torpor into which domestic trade had descended. More

[53] Kuroda 2000, 2008:187–98.   [54] This is the major conclusion of Peng Kaixiang 2006.
[55] Li Longsheng 2010: 179–80, table 3.20.
[56] Cheung (2013) argues that the deflationary episode in the 1790s was caused by the sharp contraction in silver imports.

Table 9.6 *Customs revenues, 1725–1831*
(thousands of silver taels)

Huai'an inland		Xupu (Suzhou) inland		Jiujiang inland		Guangzhou maritime	
1725	84	1727	353	1727	91		
1736	484	1738	382	1739	352	1742	310
1753	325	1753	495	1753	354	1753	515
1773	557	1764	542	1776	662	1765	600
1818	441	1791	583	1801	539	1804	1,642
1828	302	1818	427	1820	585	1812	1,375
1831	324	1831	391	1829	600	1831	1,462

Source: Wu Chengming 2001b: 271, table 18.

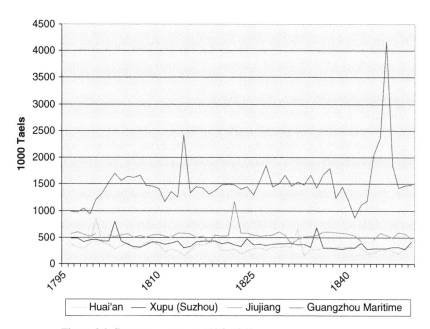

Figure 9.9 Customs revenues, 1796–1850
Source: Ni Yuping 2010: 153–56, table 5.1.

complete domestic customs data for the first half of the nineteenth century confirms these trends (Figure 9.9). Customs revenues at Guangzhou and Jiujiang held relatively steady from the turn of the century down to the Opium War (although the Jiujiang receipts remained below their eighteenth-century peak). Customs revenue figures at Suzhou and Huai'an reveal a downward trend across the first half of the nineteenth century well below late eighteenth-century levels.[57]

Although the economic expansion of the eighteenth century initially fostered a more integrated national market centered on Jiangnan, by the end of the century a strong centrifugal trend toward regionalization had emerged. Migration to the marginal agricultural regions of the interior arrested growth in labor productivity. Crop yields continued to improve in Jiangnan, but overall agricultural productivity probably declined. In North China, production of cotton and other non-food crops fell after 1750, reflecting a shift toward subsistence farming to meet the needs of the region's still rapidly growing population.[58] The population of the great commercial emporia of Suzhou and Guangzhou soared past 500,000, and industrial cities such as Jingdezhen (porcelain) and Foshan (iron and textiles) developed into major metropolises of 200,000 or more inhabitants. But the prodigious size of these cities obscured the reality that the share of the national population of the eight core prefectures of Jiangnan had shrunk from 14 percent in 1391 to 7.6 percent in 1776.[59] The proportion of the total population living in cities declined to about 5 percent in the mid-nineteenth century, less than half the urbanization rate of the Southern Song.[60]

Jiangnan's preeminent role in the national economy diminished as well. For example, rural households in Hubei began to manufacture coarse cotton cloth which they exchanged for rice from the more productive agricultural regions of Hunan and Sichuan. Subsequently Sichuan developed its own "native cloth" (tubu 土布) industry that marketed its products within Sichuan and in the outlying frontier provinces of Yunnan and Guizhou. The growth of rural industry in the interior came at the expense of core areas such as Jiangnan, which produced better-quality but more expensive cloth. As the market for Jiangnan textiles in the interior dried up, the flow of rice, timber, and other raw materials down the Yangzi River ebbed.[61]

---

[57] To be sure, Ni Yuping himself (2010: 150–61) argues that total revenue figures for all thirty-four customs stations remained roughly constant around 5 million taels throughout the first half of the nineteenth century and therefore refute the notion of a "Daoguang Depression." But the great majority of customs stations every year reported the exact same figure (based on their quota) for customs revenues; only the largest stations (the four tabulated here invariably accounted for 50–60 percent of total annual customs revenue) show annual variations.

[58] Pomeranz 2000: 140–41.

[59] For population data for the eight core prefectures for 1391, see Li Bozhong 2003: 142, table 4.3; for the 1776 data, see Cao Shuji 2000b: 87–88, table 3–5, 113, table 3-15. Pomeranz (2000: 288, 2008: 88) asserts that Jiangnan's population stagnated between 1750 and 1850, but Cao's data indicates that the region's population grew at roughly the same rate as the national population during this period.

[60] Skinner (1977b: 229) estimated China's urbanization rate in 1843 at 5.1 percent.

[61] Yamamoto 1991, 1997, 2002, esp. ch. 1 and 3; Pomeranz 2000: 242–49.

This pattern of domestic "import substitution" curtailed interregional trade (as we see in Table 9.5), resulting in greater regional autarky and the displacement of national markets by the macroregional structure delineated by G. William Skinner.

Jiangnan, China's most commercially developed region, was thus particularly vulnerable to the structural changes in the Chinese economy. By the early nineteenth century the economy of Jiangnan bore little resemblance to the agrarian order that prevailed throughout most of China. According to Li Bozhong's reconstruction of the Hua-Lou local economy in the 1820s, manufacturing employed 56 percent of adult workers and generated 33 percent of total added value, in contrast to 27 percent and 31 percent respectively for agriculture. The Hua-Lou area had an urbanization rate as high as 40 percent, and nearly 30 percent of its gross product (consisting almost entirely of cotton goods) was exported to external markets.[62] But the cotton industry was by no means flourishing. According to Li's figures, cotton manufacture absorbed 43 percent of total employment in Hua-Lou, but generated only 9 percent of its aggregate product. Price data for the cotton industry is extremely fragmentary, but the few figures that do exist suggest a substantial decline compared to the eighteenth century. Data on Chinese cotton exports show that in the early 1830s the price of cotton cloth (predominantly Songjiang "nankeens") at Guangzhou had fallen 28 percent compared to the average price of the 1810s.[63] A treatise on Songjiang agriculture published in 1834 observed that the market for Songjiang cloth had been distressed for more than a decade, and poor cotton harvests since 1829 had made raw cotton prohibitively expensive.[64]

In his synoptic overview of the Daoguang Depression, Wu Chengming has emphasized the multiple causes of the protracted slump in the Chinese economy, including population pressure on the land and the inherent limitations of the Chinese mode of peasant family production. Wu primarily stressed endogenous causes, such as the weak purchasing power of Chinese consumers, for the persistent deflation.[65] Li Bozhong likewise has underscored the diverse causes of the Daoguang Depression, drawing attention especially to climatic disruptions that resulted in catastrophic harvest failures. As Li observes, complaints of economic distress and widespread impoverishment of rich and poor alike already were being aired by 1820, well before bronze coin depreciation had become severe.[66] There is little doubt that the steep depreciation of bronze coin in the 1830s–50s was highly disadvantageous to peasants and artisans whose earnings and savings mostly consisted of bronze coin.

---

[62] Li Bozhong 2010, 2013.   [63] Wu Chengming 2001b: 267.
[64] Cited in Li Bozhong 2010: 492.   [65] Wu Chengming 2001b: 241–42, 287–88.
[66] Li Bozhong 2007.

But the reversal of the flow of silver that commenced *c*. 1827 and the subsequent depreciation of bronze coin appear to have been consequences, not causes, of an economic decline that traces back to the final decade of the eighteenth century.

Fiscal and economic strategies of the late Qing state

By the early decades of the nineteenth century, then, population growth (concentrated in the poorest regions), resource constraints, and waning domestic trade had fomented economic malaise and social unrest. After 1815 natural disasters increasingly escalated into social crises: food riots and grain blockages multiplied, and resistance to payment of tax and rent arrears intensified. The messianic rebels of the Taiping Heavenly Kingdom tapped into this swelling tide of dissent. Incubated in the highlands of remote Guangxi in the late 1840s, the Taiping movement burst into violent revolt in 1851, and its early military triumphs attracted the allegiance of the poor and disaffected. Subsequently the Taiping armies marched unchecked through Central China to the Yangzi Delta. From 1853 to its final defeat in 1864, the Taiping Heavenly Kingdom, with its capital at Nanjing, controlled much of the economic heartland of the Middle and Lower Yangzi River Basins. Total loss of life during the fifteen-year duration of this massive civil war has been estimated at a minimum of 20–30 million, and perhaps as many as 73 million, people.[67] The economic toll of the Taiping rebellion was concentrated in what had been the most prosperous provinces of the empire. The Taiping conquests left the great cities of Nanjing, Suzhou, and Hangzhou in ruins and inflicted enormous damage to the region's manufactures, especially silk textiles. Moreover, the weakened dynasty also had to cope with insurrections in other regions, including the Nian rebels in east-central China (1851–68), the uprising of the indigenous Miao peoples in the southwest (1854–73), and Muslim separatist rebels in Xinjiang (1875–84) (Map 9.1).

Devastating as the Taiping rebellion was, it was the confrontation with the Western imperialist powers that ultimately led to the downfall of the Qing dynasty. Qing efforts to interdict the illegal import of opium – a trade that had become vitally important to financing British rule in India – provoked armed retaliation by the British. The Opium War (1839–42) ended in humiliating military defeat for the Qing. Under the terms of the Treaty of Nanjing (1842), the Qing were forced to open five ports to trade and settlement by Western merchants, end the Cohong monopoly on foreign trade, tolerate the import of opium, and pay a sizable indemnity to the British Crown. Britain obtained

---

[67] The high estimate of 73 million lives lost during the Taiping rebellion is from Cao Shuji 2000b: 445–53.

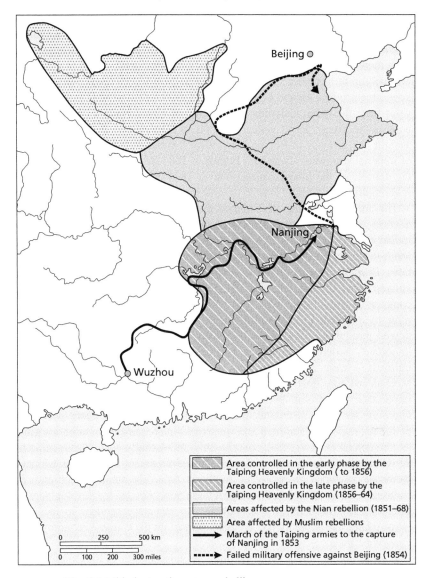

Map 9.1 Mid-nineteenth-century rebellions

Hong Kong as a colonial territory and imposed what would become known as
the "treaty port" system, whereby the Chinese allowed European powers to
carve out territories (known as "concessions") at major ports subject to foreign
rather than Chinese rule. But the prediction of Henry Pottinger, the author of

the Treaty of Nanjing, that "all the mills in Lancashire could not make stocking stuff sufficient for one of its provinces" proved wholly erroneous.[68] Although opium imports soared during the next two decades, Chinese exports of tea rose even more precipitously, while British manufactured goods failed to make any headway in the Chinese market. Disgruntled British merchants prodded their government into a second Opium War (1856–60) that wrested more concessions from the Qing, including the opening of nine additional "treaty ports," notably the Yangzi River valley entrepôts of Hankou and Jiujiang as well as Tianjin, the gateway to Beijing (Map 9.2).[69] Subsequent defeats at the hands of imperialist powers – war with France in 1884–85 and, most momentously, the debacle of the Sino-Japanese War in 1894–95 – further eroded Chinese sovereignty.

The forcible opening of Chinese markets had mixed economic consequences, stimulating some sectors of domestic economy (notably the traditional exports, tea and silk) and undermining others (homespun cotton yarn was soon replaced by machine-made products), and its effects changed over time. Despite the end of the Cohong monopoly, Western merchants were obliged to use Chinese intermediaries (compradors) to gain access to domestic commercial and financial networks. Only after 1895 did foreign firms gain the right to establish manufacturing facilities in China. Foreign trade largely flowed through existing channels of commercial exchange, but strategically important modern technologies – shipbuilding, armaments, mining, and railroads – were monopolized by government-run or licensed companies. Mechanized consumer-goods industries such as cotton textiles had negligible importance before the twentieth century. Although new external market opportunities arose in coastal areas, especially around the treaty ports, the peripheral regions of northern and western China became even more marginal to commercial exchange and, consequently, increasingly poor. The opening of the treaty ports also accelerated the rapid development of overseas Chinese merchant networks, especially in Southeast Asia. The streams of migration, commerce, and remittances throughout these networks and the development of port facilities, steamships, and banking and insurance services to facilitate intra-Asian trade arguably had a greater impact on the Chinese economy than East–West trade.

Most profound, surely, were the political consequences of the Opium Wars. British military might posed a blunt challenge not only to the self-confidence of the Qing leadership, but also to their most deeply cherished notions of

---

[68] Quoted in A. J. Sargent, *Anglo-Chinese Commerce and Diplomacy* (Oxford: Clarendon Press, 1907): 106.

[69] For the argument that the Second Opium War (also known as the *Arrow* War) was motivated by economic considerations, see J. Y. Wong 1998.

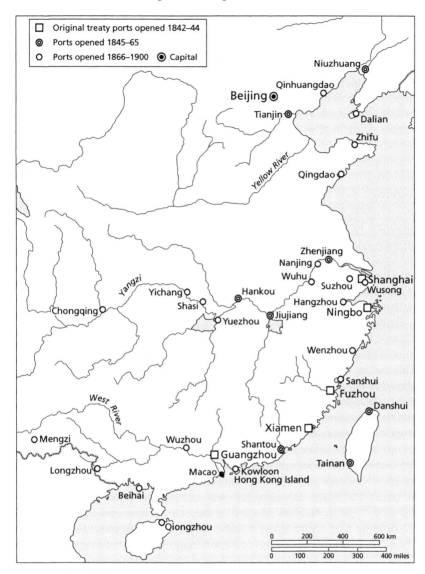

☐	Original treaty ports opened 1842–44
◉	Ports opened 1845–65
○	Ports opened 1866–1900 ◉ Capital

Map 9.2 The treaty port network

Confucian governance. In stark contrast to Confucian principles, the Western imperialist regimes aggressively promoted the wealth and power of their nation through military conquest and economic domination. Relinquishing its time-honored values and commitments did not come easily to the Qing court. But the crippling blow inflicted by the Taiping insurrection and the occupation of Beijing by a foreign army in 1860 roused the Qing leaders to embark on their own program of national "self-strengthening." The immediate objective was to modernize the Qing military by building arsenals and shipyards utilizing Western industrial technologies. The results were dismal. Despite employing Western technical advisers, the rifles, artillery, and warships produced by the government-run enterprises were poorly made and exorbitantly expensive. Coordinating the new military forces also proved a vexing problem. The court had ceded broad military and fiscal authority to regional military viceroys charged with suppressing the Taiping rebels and other insurrections. The viceroys mustered new provincial armies and built industrial facilities to supply them with modern armaments by relying on patronage networks and the personal loyalty of the military officers and civilian staff under their command. But this reliance on patronage inhibited long-term planning and development, and the new armaments projects foundered for lack of dedicated support and funding.[70] The rout of the Qing navy by a smaller Japanese force in 1894 exposed the inadequacy of the Qing's efforts at military modernization, driving home the lesson that rather than catching up with the imperialist powers, China had fallen much farther behind.

By the 1870s, Chinese statesmen had begun to speak not merely of guarding China's territorial integrity but also of waging "commercial warfare" (*shangzhan* 商戰) to recover its economic sovereignty (*liquan* 利權) as well.[71] This fusion of political strategy with economic development was best displayed in the creation in 1872 of the China Merchant Steamship and Navigation Company (CMC) at the instigation of Li Hongzhang, the governor of Zhili and the most powerful official of his day. The CMC was conceived as a joint-stock company under government patronage. To a certain degree the CMC had its origins in the venerable precedents of the salt monopoly: the state granted the company monopoly privileges (e.g., delivering tribute rice to Beijing) to attract private capital and give it a competitive advantage against foreign rivals, in return for which the company was expected to generate revenues for the state.[72] Since their introduction in the late 1850s – and especially after the opening of the Suez Canal in 1869, which halved the travel time between China and Europe – steamships had revolutionized China's foreign trade. The

---

[70] Provincial officials were loath to support costly enterprises over which they lacked personal control, and the Beijing government proved too feeble to compel them to fund such projects. The fledgling Qing navy and the Fuzhou shipyard in particular were plagued by this lack of reliable financing. See Pong 1994; Wenkai He 2013: 159–63.

[71] Yen-p'ing Hao 1986: 166–67; Pong 1985.

[72] Feuerwerker 1958: 10–11. Ownership of CMC shares was restricted to Qing subjects. There was no modern-style stock market, but shares could be traded publicly through licensed brokers.

leading Western firms in the China trade began to form joint-stock steamship companies – with much of their capital raised from Chinese investors – in the early 1860s, and the CMC was intended to ensure that the profits of the lucrative shipping business in Chinese coastal and inland waterways accrued to Chinese, not foreigners.[73] The CMC also sought to capture new sources of private capital, especially from compradors who acted as agents of foreign trading companies and had acquired substantial fortunes. Li arranged for government loans (which later became outright subsidies) as start-up funds for the new company, which offered private investors a guaranteed annual dividend of 10 percent. After the company was placed under the management of two merchants in 1873 it achieved impressive success in attracting private capital, amounting to nearly 500,000 taels by the end of 1874. In 1877 CMC was operating thirty-one steamships on seven routes (its two main foreign competitors together had fourteen ships on five routes), and by 1883 its capital stock had increased to 2 million taels.

Although the prodigious early success of CMC induced a number of Qing officials to propose a state takeover of the company by converting its outstanding government debt into stock shares, Li Hongzhang staunchly protected its independence. But the financial panic of 1883 drastically altered the company's fortunes. The success of CMC spurred provincial governors to launch joint-stock mining companies, unleashing a fever of stock-buying speculation fueled by reckless borrowing from native banks (*qianzhuang*). The overheated bubble burst (in part because of the impending war with France) in August of 1883, causing the bankruptcy of eighty-nine of Shanghai's ninety-nine native banks. Share prices plummeted, and many shareholders were wiped out.[74]

In the wake of the 1883 crisis, CMC was reorganized into what became known as a "state supervised and merchant managed" (*guandu shangban* 官督商辦) enterprise, in which government bureaucrats replaced merchants as chief executives. During the Sino-French War Li Hongzhang diverted resources from CMC to the navy, and after 1885 the government routinely raided CMC capital, causing private investors to flee. Bereft of knowledgeable leadership and private capital, the company stagnated, steadily losing its share of the steamship business. Inevitably, CMC and other *guandu shangban* enterprises, tasked with irreconcilable political and economic goals, were doomed to failure.[75] Fearing government interference and expropriation, private investors shunned the *guandu shangban* companies in favor of foreign-

---

[73] On the prominent role of Chinese investment in Western-managed steamship companies, see Zhang Zhongmin 2002: 111–26.

[74] Liu Guangzhi 1983; Yen-p'íng Hao 1986: 323–29.

[75] Feuerwerker 1958; Yen-p'íng Hao 1986: 202–11, 330–34; Chi-kong Lai 1992.

controlled joint-stock enterprises. Chinese shareholders provided nearly half of the total capital of the foreign-run banks, warehouses, silk filatures, and steamship, insurance, and light and power companies that operated in the treaty ports.[76] But apart from rampant speculation in railway stocks in the first decade of the twentieth century, Chinese investors had little appetite for shareholding in publicly traded domestic companies.

Expansion of the state's fiscal powers was indispensable to overcoming the mid-century rebellions and bolstering imperial rule. But to a significant degree, control over fiscal resources devolved to the military viceroys and provincial governors. Although the central government retained formal supervisory powers (and, even more importantly, the loyalty of its provincial officials), the initiative for restructuring the state's fiscal apparatus passed to regional leaders in strategically important provinces. During the anti-Taiping campaigns, out of fiscal expediency, the military viceroys developed two new sources of commercial revenues: (1) the *lijin* tariffs on domestic trade (inaugurated in 1853), and (2) the Imperial Maritime Customs, established in 1861, which collected duties on foreign trade.[77] After the defeat of the Taipings the *lijin* and maritime customs revenues became crucial sources of revenue, generating more than a third of the state's income in the 1880s–90s. Total state revenues more than doubled between 1849 and 1893, almost entirely as a result of new (and old) taxes on commerce and consumption (Table 9.7). The land tax – which had generated 74 percent of government revenues in the mid-eighteenth century (Table 8.3) – dwindled in importance. Although this shift toward indirect taxation departed from the model of the Confucian provisioning state that had been the foundation of Ming-Qing fiscal policy, the Qing state did not waver from the principle of light direct taxation on agricultural production enshrined in Kangxi's decision in 1713 to freeze the land tax. The dramatic leap in nominal revenues in 1908 to a large degree reflected a doubling of the price level since 1893; measured in real terms (in rice), the increase was about 65 percent (and probably less, since Yeh-chien Wang's estimate of miscellaneous revenues is surely too high).

The massive increase in state revenues in the last half-century of Qing rule did not necessarily enhance the central government's fiscal power, however. Neither the new sources of revenue nor the self-strengthening industrial and communications enterprises were truly integrated into the management structure of the Ministry of Revenue. Instead, revenue collection and fiscal decision-making became more dispersed to the regional/provincial or even local level. In

---

[76] Yen-p'ing Hao 1986: 245–58; Motono 2000: 119.
[77] The *lijin* in principle was an ad valorem tax on commodities in transit, but often it became a form of tax-farming in which merchant guilds, brokers, and local magistrates negotiated lump-sum payments for each trade.

Table 9.7 *Government revenues in the late Qing*
(figures in millions of silver taels)

	1849		1893		1908	
Land tax	32.8	77%	35.6	40%	102.4	35%
Miscellaneous taxes			6.5	7%	65.0*	22%
Salt tax	5.0	12%	15.3	17%	45.0	15%
Domestic customs	4.7	11%	1.1	1%	6.7	2%
Maritime customs			14.7	17%	32.9	11%
Lijin	–		17.1**	19%	40.0**	14%
Total	42.5		89.0		292.0	

NB: The 1893 figures are averages for the three years 1892–94.
*Wang's miscellaneous tax figure for 1908 was derived by extrapolating from a detailed record for Guangdong province, where two-thirds of the miscellaneous revenues came from a tax on gambling (the rest from a variety of commercial taxes and fees). I am skeptical that such large gambling revenues were realized on an empire-wide basis.
**Includes the *lijin* excise on the domestic opium trade instituted in 1891, which generated 2.2 million taels in 1893.
Sources: 1849 and 1893: Chen Feng 2008: 397–98, tables 6-12, 6-14. 1908: Yeh-chien Wang 1973: 74, table 4.3.

the post-Taiping era, local elites were brought in more formally into tax collection as well as reconstruction and economic development efforts.[78] But the profusion of new fiscal institutions at the regional and local levels rendered central coordination more difficult. The *lijin* excise and the maritime customs were managed by commissioners who were not directly subject to central oversight. There was no unified treasury, and only in the 1880s did the Ministry of Revenue succeed in establishing centralized accounting of provincial finances. Although expenditure of revenues collected at the local and regional levels such as the *lijin* excises in principle required the ministry's approval, provincial governors often rebuffed central directives by claiming other urgent priorities.[79] In the final decades of the nineteenth century the Beijing government gradually asserted control of maritime customs revenue (which was deposited in foreign banks for transfer to Beijing), salt revenues, and much of the *lijin* revenue as well. But even then Beijing retained direct administrative control of no more than half of total state income. Feuerwerker estimated that the Qing state's total revenue of 292 million taels in 1908 represented 7.5 percent of GDP, although the central government's share was only 3 percent.[80] Yeh-chien

[78] Mann 1987: 110–12; Bernhardt 1992: 117–60.
[79] Bastid 1985: 59–68. For more positive assessments of the fiscal capacity of the late Qing state, see R. Bin Wong 2012: 372–77; Wenkai He 2013: 157–72.
[80] Feuerwerker 1980: 64.

Wang proposed that state revenues comprised a much smaller proportion of the total economy, a mere 2.4 percent of GDP in 1908.[81] Per capita government expenditures doubled between 1849 and the first decade of the twentieth century, but even this level of government spending was far below that of the Russian and Ottoman Empires, let alone the Western powers.[82]

Moreover, despite innovations in private finance (see below, pp. 385–90), the Qing state was unable to place the monetary system on stable footing. During the depression years of the 1820s–40s, when bronze coin depreciated sharply against silver, statesmen and scholars debated the feasibility of reintroducing paper money, but the majority opinion remained firmly opposed to a fiat currency.[83] But the fiscal crisis precipitated by the Taiping rebellion forced the court to resort to desperate measures. Given the urgent need to pay its armies at a time when it was cut off from its main sources of revenue in the south, in 1853 the Beijing government issued inconvertible paper notes (denominated both in coin and silver) and overvalued large copper coins as well as adopting other fiscal expediencies such as a greatly expanded program of selling titles and offices.[84] The new paper monies and large coins were shunned in the marketplace, resulting in a vicious spiral of price inflation. In the early 1860s, acknowledging that the new currencies were an abject failure, the government withdrew them from circulation and reverted to minting standard copper coins, but only in modest quantities.

The most important expansion of the money supply in the second half of the nineteenth century came with the renewed surge in imports of silver coin from Mexico. The international flow of silver reversed again in China's favor in the 1850s, and the influx of foreign silver reached new highs in the 1870s after most of China's trading partners adopted the gold standard. The Mexican silver dollar became sufficiently prevalent in commercial exchange that it constituted a new de facto monetary standard, known as *yuan* (圓, 元).[85] In 1889 the provincial administration in Guangdong began to issue *yuan* silver coins (and also subsidiary copper coins) that the Qing court recognized

---

[81] Yeh-chien Wang 1973: 133.
[82] For real rates of fiscal expenditure and comparison with other states, see Brandt, Ma, and Rawski 2014: 66–70. State revenues comprised 15–16 percent of national income in Russia in 1895–1910, and more than 10 percent in the Ottoman Empire during the same time period. See Gattrell 2012: 207; Pamuk 2012: 325.
[83] On this debate see Lin Man-houng 2006: 147–79; Rowe 2010.
[84] On the monetary experiments of the 1850s–60s, see King 1965; Wenkai He 2013: 131–52; Kaske 2015. The important role of office-selling in stabilizing Qing finances in the late nineteenth century is underscored in Kaske 2011. In addition, various provinces distributed a kind of paper scrip known as "pay bills" (*xiangpiao* 餉票) to their troops. Purchase of official titles required payment partly in silver but mostly in pay bills, so in principle the soldiers could tender the bills for silver from potential purchasers of titles. In practice, though, the bills were heavily discounted. See Kaske 2015.
[85] Von Glahn 2007a.

Table 9.8 *Estimates of China's money supply* c. *1910*
(figures in millions of silver dollars)

	Value in silver dollars	Percentage of total	Totals	Percentage of total
New forms of money			1,629	65
Silver coins	1,320			
Domestic coins	240	10		
Imported coins	1,080	43		
Copper coins	149	6		
Paper money	160			
Silver dollar notes	50	2		
Foreign banknotes	110	4		
Old forms of money			862	35
Silver taels	347	14		
Copper cash	373	15		
Silver tael notes	42	2		
Copper cash notes	100	4		
			2,491	

Sources: Peng Xinwei 1965: 888–89; Yen-p'ing Hao 1986: 68, table 5.

as legal tender. However, the Beijing government, stung by the dismal miscarriage of its fiat currency experiment in the 1850s, resisted appeals to reintroduce paper money.[86] Both foreign and domestic banks issued their own banknotes, but these bills had only limited range of circulation. By the end of the Qing dynasty China still depended heavily on silver coin as its principal currency, while the various types of paper money in circulation altogether comprised only 12 percent of the total money supply (Table 9.8).[87]

The most dramatic change in public finance came in the 1890s, when the Qing state broke with long-standing tenets of governance and resorted to deficit financing to meet its fiscal obligations. Since the Taiping emergency, provincial and later central authorities had begun in a modest way to borrow from foreign lenders, chiefly for military exigencies. Over a forty-year period these loans totaled only 46 million taels (Table 9.9). In the mid-1890s, however, the Qing court was forced to seek loans from foreign banks to fund the war effort against Japan and subsequently to pay the massive indemnity (230 million taels)

[86] A state-sponsored bank, the Imperial Bank of China, was established in Shanghai in 1898 and licensed to issue currency, but the Qing did not grant IBC notes and coins the status of legal tender. As of 1907 the IBC had only put 3.3 million *yuan* of paper notes into circulation, a tiny fraction of the amount of private banknotes. See Feuerwerker 1958: 225–41. In 1908, shortly before the fall of the dynasty, the Qing finally created a state bank, the Board of Revenue Bank, that was given exclusive privilege to issue legal tender. See Linsun Cheng 2003: 25–32.
[87] For overviews of monetary conditions in the late nineteenth century, see King 1965: 189–228; Yen-p'ing Hao 1986: 34–71; Chen Feng 2008: 615–66.

Table 9.9 *China's Foreign Debt, 1853–94*

	Debt (millions of silver taels)	Percentage
Military expenses	34.3	75
Industrial development	4.7	10
Imperial household expenditures	4.5	10
Water conservancy projects	2.3	5
Other	0.2	< 1
Total	46.0	

Source: Chen Feng 2008: 434, table 7–12.

imposed by the Japanese after their victory, resulting in the *de facto* creation of national debt as a mainstay of public finance. The Qing state relied chiefly on maritime customs and *lijin* revenues to repay these loans, but it also assigned portions of the debt to individual provinces. It did not, however, create a central bank to issue bonds in order to meet its debt obligations. In 1898 the central government unveiled a plan to issue 100 million taels of twenty-year bonds paying 5 percent interest. Rather than market these bonds directly, the Beijing government distributed them to individual provinces, which became responsible for interest payments and finding buyers. Only 10 million taels of bonds were sold before the experiment was aborted.

Because the Qing state did meet its debt obligations in timely fashion, Wenkai He has concluded that there was a genuine possibility for the Qing to create a modern fiscal state funded through long-term public borrowing.[88] But this assessment fails to consider the purposes of state expenditures. Burdened with crushing debt obligations, the Qing dedicated little of its spending to economic development, education, or public welfare. This was even more true after the Boxer rebellion fiasco in 1900 saddled the Qing court with onerous indemnities totaling 450 million taels. During 1894–1911 the Qing state amassed a staggering debt of 746 million taels in foreign loans, mostly to service indemnity payments; of the remainder, 331 million taels were intended for railway construction and a mere 26 million taels for other industrial purposes. The Qing paid an annual average of 30 million taels in principal and interest on its indemnity obligations, an amount twice as great as the total initial capitalization of all foreign and Chinese manufacturing enterprises established during these years.[89] Although the structure of state finance had been irrevocably transformed, the Qing regime lacked the fiscal resources to undertake a meaningful program of economic development.

---

[88] Wenkai He 2013: 177–79. In He's view the reason why this potential went unfulfilled was because the Qing did not faced a credit crisis sufficiently dire to compel such radical reform.
[89] Feuerwerker 1980: 65–68.

The new institutional matrix in finance and commerce

Despite China's growing integration into global trade networks, movement toward an industrial revolution was almost wholly absent before the twentieth century. Nonetheless, significant institutional developments were underway that would lay the foundations for a relatively rapid transition toward a modern economy after 1900. New banking and credit institutions lowered the cost of credit, regulated commercial exchange, and facilitated the linkages between domestic markets and foreign trade. The merchant networks that had become a conspicuous feature of long-distance trade in China since the Ming dynasty evolved into more formal institutions, shedding some of their parochial character. Although native-place ties remained important (especially in the high-risk world of banking), trade guilds increasingly displaced native-place associations as the principal institutional mechanism for regulating commercial practices and resolving business disputes. In addition, more sophisticated forms of business partnership emerged that enabled entrepreneurs to raise capital for long-term industrial investment on a much larger scale than in the past. These institutional innovations certainly were stimulated by growing integration into the international economy, and to a limited degree they borrowed from Western precedents. But for the most part they consisted of adaptations of existing institutions to meet diverse new demands for commercial services.

Beginning in the eighteenth century, a range of new financial institutions emerged to facilitate commercial exchange. The earliest of these new kinds of banks were the "account agencies" (*zhangju* 賬局) created to finance trade – especially in tea – with Russia, which boomed following the Treaty of Kyakhta in 1727. The first account agency was established by a Shanxi firm at the border market town of Zhangjiakou in 1736. Shanxi merchants traditionally dominated long-distance commerce in North China, and Shanxi firms quickly asserted control of Sino-Russian trade as well. The account agencies, which were chiefly located in Beijing and Zhangjiakou, issued loans to commercial clients, generally for five to six months up to one year. Reportedly there were over 110 account agencies in Beijing alone in 1852, with total capital assets of more than 10 million taels. But their operations remained fairly small; most had assets of no more than 40,000–50,000 taels, roughly the size of the capital's typical pawnbrokerage.[90]

The so-called native banks (*qianzhuang* 錢莊) were institutionally similar to the account agencies, although the *qianzhuang* became active in foreign trade only in the treaty port era. The origins of *qianzhuang* are obscure, but they were already active in Shanghai in the 1770s, and by 1796 nearly a hundred

---

[90] Huang Jianhui 1987.

qianzhuang had formed a guild in Shanghai. The *qianzhuang* accepted deposits, made short-term loans to merchants, exchanged currency, and issued various types of commercial paper, including bills of exchange and promissory notes known as *zhuangpiao* 莊票. The growth of foreign trade after the opening of the treaty ports spurred a surge in demand for the financial services *qianzhuang* provided. Lacking access to provincial producers of tea and silk, foreign firms depended on the brokerage services of their Chinese agents, known as compradors. Many compradors established their own *qianzhuang* to funnel financing from foreign firms to domestic clients. *Qianzhuang* also became outlets for surplus funds held by foreign firms and banks. From the 1860s *qianzhuang* commonly borrowed money from foreign firms using only their own *zhuangpiao* notes as security – a form of call loans known as "chop loans" (*chaipiao* 拆票) – to make short-term loans to Chinese merchants. Given the modest capital assets of *qianzhuang* (generally in the range of 20,000–60,000 taels), the chop loans greatly extended their credit resources. But since chop loans could be called on only one to two days' notice and *qianzhuang* kept small cash reserves, this practice rendered them highly vulnerable to sudden economic fluctuations. Financial crises in 1873 and again in 1883 bankrupted more than half of Shanghai's *qianzhuang*, although new firms quickly sprang up in their place. In 1890 Shanghai's *qianzhuang* bankers' guild established its own clearinghouse where members met daily to clear accounts and set interest rates. Foreign firms came to rely on this clearinghouse to settle accounts with the various native banks with whom they did business. The clearinghouse proved to be a great boon to the larger *qianzhuang* who dominated the finance guild, especially those operated by entrepreneurs from Ningbo and Shaoxing.[91]

Since *qianzhuang* mostly issued unsecured loans and faced unlimited liability, success in business relied heavily on personal trust and connections. Familiarity bred through native-place ties affirmed the creditworthiness of partners, correspondents, and clients – what one scholar has dubbed "fiduciary communities."[92] Proprietors of Shanghai's *qianzhuang* overwhelmingly were sojourner immigrants from the cities of Ningbo and Shaoxing in Zhejiang, 100 miles south of Shanghai. The close personal ties among the Ning-Shao banking network undergirded the practice of account transfers (*guozhang* 過帳) that enabled merchants to settle debts without resort to exchanging hard currency. Thanks to the dominance of the Ning-Shao bankers' "fellowship" (*bang* 幫) in Shanghai, their fellow countrymen achieved success in garnering the lion's share of financial business in inland export entrepôts

---

[91] McElderry 1976; on the role of *qianzhuang* in financing foreign trade, see also Yen-p'ing Hao 1986: 72–111. In some regions (e.g., Guangzhou and Tianjin) these institutions were known instead as *yinhao* 銀號.

[92] McElderry 1995: 28.

such as Hankou. The linked-firm (*lianhao*) form of business organization, which dispersed risk and enabled managers to cultivate intimate personal relationships with clients, was especially common in the finance industry. The Fang family of Ningbo alone owned forty-two *qianzhuang*, including twenty-five in Shanghai. Ning-Shao bankers also dominated the top executive positions of the late Qing state banks, and of the modern private banks that proliferated after 1908.[93]

Despite their crucial role in financing the export trade, the *qianzhuang* remained essentially local institutions. In this respect they differed significantly from the so-called Shanxi banks (*piaohao* 票號), which initially focused on facilitating long-distance trade and ultimately devoted the bulk of their business to government finance.[94] In 1823, Li Daquan, the owner of a dyestuffs business in Beijing and other cities, began to offer remittance services to other merchants. Li invested 300,000 taels to establish a separate firm, Rishengchang, with branches in Tianjin, Hankou, and his native Pingyao (Shanxi), to handle the remittance business. The Rishengchang also accepted interest-bearing deposits and made commercial loans. Other Shanxi merchants quickly imitated Li's initiative. By 1850, there were 15 *piaohao* banks in existence with approximately 150 branches in nearly 30 cities; at that time the *piaohao* banks held an estimated 6–7 million taels in deposits and handled a total volume of 47 million taels of remittances.

After the outbreak of the Taiping rebellion, the central government turned to *piaohao* to remit provincial tax revenues to Beijing. The enormous infusion of funds from tax receipts (during the 1870s–90s the Shanxi banks handled 30 percent of total government revenues) provided the *piaohao* with the resources to broaden their portfolio. By the 1880s there were 28 *piaohao* with a total of 446 branches that held aggregate deposits of 114 million taels (Table 9.10). By the first decade of the twentieth century, the *piaohao* issued currency (148 million taels of silver-denominated notes issued by *piaohao* were in circulation *c.* 1910), offered personal loans (notably to officials awaiting lucrative appointments), provided advances to government agencies, and brokered loans from foreign banks for enterprises such as railway construction.[95] The *piaohao* banks thus mobilized capital on a vastly greater scale than the *qianzhuang* native banks. But as the dependence of the *piaohao* on their lucrative business with the imperial government grew, their welfare became inseparable from the fiscal health of the Qing state.

---

[93] On the Ning-Shao bankers' business network, see Mann Jones 1972, 1974.
[94] *Piaohao* (lit., "remittance firms") became known as "Shanxi banks" because all of these banks were headquartered in the three Shanxi towns of Pingyao, Taigu, and Qixian.
[95] Liu Jiansheng 2007: 235.

Table 9.10 *Estimated financial resources of Shanxi Banks, 1850s–1910s*

	Number of banks	Total number of branches	Total value of remittances (millions of taels)	Deposits (millions of taels)	Loans (millions of taels)	Share capital (millions of taels)	Net profit (millions of taels)	Total assets (millions of taels)
1850s	15 (5)*	150	46.6	6.4	7.8	0.7	0.5	53.7
1870s–80s	28 (17)	446	118.8	114.0	48.6	38.6	1.3	236.6
1900–11	26 (22)	500	588.7	173.5	128.4	52.5	2.1	767.4
1913	20 (8)	320	–	36.2	45.4	?	(net loss)	?
c. 1917	12 (6)	120	–	27.6	4.4	30.7	(net loss)	?

*The estimates are extrapolated from the average figures for individual banks (number in parentheses) for which data is available during the designated period.

Source: Yan Hongzhong 2007: 131, table 3.

Despite the instability of certain sectors of the financial system – particularly in the case of *qianzhuang* – the development of new financial institutions in the nineteenth century significantly lowered the cost of commercial credit. Account agencies in Beijing offered monthly interest rates of 0.38–0.5 percent in 1844, which corresponded to annual rates of 5–6 percent.[96] *Piaohao* reportedly paid 5 percent annualized interest on deposits, while charging 10 percent on loans.[97] These rates were roughly twice as much as the cheapest interest rates – 4–4.5 percent for letters of exchange and discount rates on government bonds – available in England and France at that time.[98] Foreign mercantile houses generally offered private loans to their Chinese customers in the range of 10–15 percent per year.[99] Although the costs of capital certainly were higher in China than in Europe, the magnitude of the difference was much smaller than is often supposed. Nonetheless, outside the foreign trade sector most commercial firms relied on their own capital resources to finance expansion of their business.

The footprint of foreign banks, whose activities remained restricted to treaty ports, was relatively modest. The dozen foreign banks that established branches in Shanghai between 1848 and 1872 dominated international remittances and foreign trade, but they had tangential influence on China's domestic finance apart from issuing banknotes that circulated widely among the treaty port cities from the late 1870s.[100] Chinese valued the safety and security of foreign banks, which received most of their deposits from Chinese customers. Even so, foreign banks accounted for only 29 percent of all bank deposits in 1912.[101]

In the aftermath of the Sino-Japanese War, advocates of political reform prevailed upon a reluctant Qing court to establish quasi-public banks funded by the state. China's first modern bank, the Imperial Bank of China (IBC), was founded in Shanghai in 1897. Organized as a limited liability joint-stock company, the IBC was modeled after the Hong Kong and Shanghai Bank, the largest foreign-owned bank operating in China. In addition to financing commercial ventures and *guandu shangban* self-strengthening enterprises, the IBC received licenses to mint coin and issue paper currency on behalf of the imperial state, but it made only minor inroads into the currency and commercial finance markets. In 1905 the Qing government replaced the IBC with the Da Qing ("Great Qing") Bank, which was based in Beijing and intended to function as a central bank. In addition to its public financing, the

[96] Huang Jianhui 1987: 117.　[97] Liu Jiansheng 2007: 235.
[98] Rosenthal and Wong 2011: 139.　[99] Yen-p'ing Hao 1986: 107.
[100] Ibid.: 52–55. Horesh's (2009) study of foreign banknote issuance generally concedes this conclusion.
[101] Rawski 1989: 134.

Da Qing Bank sold shares by public subscription and accepted deposits. The Da Qing Bank received exclusive privilege to issue currency (although this was largely an empty gesture) and to manage the state treasury, and it also took over most of the remittances from the *piaohao*.[102]

The fall of the Qing dynasty in 1911 had a devastating effect on China's financial system. A violent run on the Da Qing Bank's reserves forced it to close its doors. Even more notable casualties of 1911 were the *piaohao* banks, already reeling from the deep erosion of their core tax remittance business to the Da Qing Bank. Within a few years nearly half of the *piaohao* (including most of the largest ones, with a total of 222 branches) had gone out of business (see Table 9.10). Although the *piaohao* institution largely disappeared, many of its managerial personnel went on to found modern private banks in the early Republican era.

Because *qianzhuang* and *piaohao* mostly supplied unsecured credit, they carefully scrutinized both their customers and employees and relied heavily on personal trust, long-standing business relations, and guarantors. Personal credit loans remained a substantial portion of the loan portfolios among modern banks as well down to the 1930s.[103] *Qianzhuang* did business locally and knew their customers; the *piaohao* shirked the inherent risks of financing private enterprise by focusing on the guaranteed profits of handling government remittances. Neither type of institution paid much attention to attracting deposits to build up capital. The Chinese financial industry remained focused on short-term commercial lending and government finance. Even during the Republican era China's modern banks made little contribution to industrial capital formation; most of their funds were invested in government bonds and personal lending, and as late as 1936 banks supplied only 12 percent of industrial financing.[104]

Another crucial – but often overlooked – development in the nineteenth-century Chinese economy was the dramatic growth of intra-Asian trade, especially after 1780. After the Qing rescinded its ban on maritime trade and travel in 1683, merchants from Guangdong and Fujian rushed to exploit new commercial opportunities throughout Southeast Asia, especially in the Philippines, the Mekong Delta, the Gulf of Siam, and Java. Emigration took off after 1754, when the Qing court lifted its restrictions on sojourning abroad. The influx of Chinese into Southeast Asia conformed to the classic pattern of a "trade diaspora."[105] Chinese merchants cultivated close relations with local rulers and the Dutch colonial regime in Batavia by providing services as purveyors of goods, revenue farmers, and administrators. Chinese ships and

---

[102] On the short-lived IBC and Da Qing banks, see Linsun Cheng 2003: 25–32.
[103] Ibid.: 157.   [104] Ibid.; Rawski 1989: 137.
[105] For the classic statement of the concept of "trade diaspora," see Curtin 1984.

traders dominated maritime commerce within Southeast Asia as well as trade with China, displacing long-established merchant communities from South and West Asia.[106] Chinese merchants even founded their own independent city-states, such as Hatien on the coast of Cambodia. (To be sure, the commercial efflorescence of this era also stimulated entrepreneurship among some indigenous communities, such as the Bugis of Sulawesi and the Sulu Sea islanders.)

In contrast to other seafaring communities, Chinese merchants also pushed beyond the port cities to develop commercial links with hinterland areas in the interior. In lightly populated areas such as the Malay Peninsula, the Mekong Delta, and Kalimantan (Borneo), local rulers welcomed Chinese settlers, miners, and planters. The pervasive insinuation of Chinese capital and labor into the region's political economy has prompted historians to refer to the period between 1740 and 1840 as the "Chinese Century" in Southeast Asian history.[107]

The success of the Chinese in Southeast Asia has been attributed to their ability to construct cohesive social and economic communities across this "water frontier."[108] Chinese immigrants mostly came from a few homeland territories in Guangdong and Fujian, but they were sharply divided by ethnic and linguistic boundaries. Social solidarity was built among these immigrants through the ritual and religious bonds fostered by the institutions of temple associations and surname clans. Temple associations combined the culture of sworn brotherhoods with common worship of familiar tutelary deities from the homeland regions. Surname clans provided a form of fictive kinship for unrelated people sharing a common surname, utilizing the forms of lineage organization (such as worship of common ancestors) to establish quasi-familial ties.[109] The Hakkas – an embattled ethnic minority in South China, long inured to frontier life in inhospitable environments – were a conspicuous presence among the overseas Chinese pioneers, especially in the mining camps. Gold and tin miners in Kalimantan and Malaysia formed syndicates known in Hakka as *kongsi* (in Mandarin, *gongsi* 公司) through which they pooled funds to cover their expenses until they received payment for the minerals they extracted. These syndicates – strongly

---

[106] For a digest of these trends, see Kwee 2013.
[107] Reid 1997b, 2004; Blussé (1999) refers to the eighteenth century as the "Chinese century."
[108] The term "water frontier" was coined to refer to the estuarial lowlands of the Mekong Delta and adjacent areas from the central coast of Vietnam to Cambodia. See Li Tana 2004. But the term – which was intended to connote the fluid population, absence of state power, and reliance on maritime commerce characteristic of this region – is equally applicable to other parts of Southeast Asia where Chinese merchants and miners established beachheads, such as the Malay Peninsula and Kalimantan (although less true of Siam and Java, also magnets for Chinese immigration).
[109] Kwee 2007.

tinged with the ethos of sworn brotherhoods – later evolved into more formal and hierarchically organized joint-stock companies dominated by merchant capitalists that reduced the miners' remuneration to simple wages.[110] Chinese planters in Malaysia also formed share partnerships on the *kongsi* model.[111] In the nineteenth century the word *kongsi* /*gongsi* entered the common Chinese vernacular as the standard designation for a joint-stock corporation after initially being applied to foreign companies doing business in the Chinese treaty ports.[112]

From the 1780s, intra-Asian commerce flourished, driven primarily by exponential growth in trade in bulk commodities such as rice, opium, pepper, and gambier (a tree gum that was consumed with the betel nut, a ubiquitous stimulant throughout Southeast Asia). Kaoru Sugihara estimates that on the eve of the Opium War intra-Asian maritime trade was roughly a third greater in value than East–West trade.[113] Grain-deficient areas of South China began to import large quantities of rice from Luzon, Siam, and the Mekong Delta. Chinese entrepreneurs established pepper and gambier plantations in Malaysia and Brunei, with the result that Southeast Asia's share of the global pepper market surpassed that of India. Chinese merchants also played the leading role in the formation of a multilateral intra-Asian trade network centered on Southeast Asia's new commercial capitals of Bangkok – capital of the Chakri dynasty of Siamese kings, founded in 1782 – and Singapore, which became the hub of Britain's commercial empire in Asia after 1819.[114] After 1850, Chinese trading houses and shopkeepers displaced indigenous merchants from wholesale and retail trade alike across much of maritime Southeast Asia. Chinese entrepreneurs also established processing firms such as rice mills, sugar refineries, sawmills, tin smelting works, and pineapple canneries, often utilizing *gongsi* syndicates to raise capital.[115] Chinese-owned remittance houses in Hong Kong not only financed much of overseas Chinese trade, but also became a crucial source of investment capital in Southeast Asia (e.g., for rubber plantations and tin mines in Malaysia) during the second half of the nineteenth century.[116]

The opening of the treaty ports and growing integration in global markets created new opportunities for Chinese entrepreneurs. Silk and tea exports surged. Although subject to sharp cyclical fluctuations, silk exports rose thirty-fold from 2,000 piculs in 1844 to over 60,000 piculs annually by the

---

[110] Kwee 2013: 20–21; Somers Heidhues 1993.   [111] Trocki 1990.
[112] Efforts to find the origins of the term *kongsi/gongsi* in the Chinese homeland have thus far proved fruitless, despite much later claims that it was indigenous to Fujian or perhaps can be traced back to the Zheng family thalassocracy in Taiwan in the seventeenth century. For a review of the evidence, see Zhang Zhongmin 2002: 40–57.
[113] Sugihara 2009: 265, table 1.   [114] Reid 1997a.   [115] Kwee 2013: 23–27.
[116] Hamashita 2008a: 155–57.

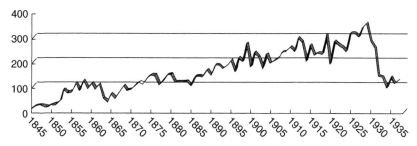

Figure 9.10 Chinese silk exports, 1844–1937
Source: Zhang Li 2010: 98, table 1.

late 1850s, and surpassed 100,000 piculs per year in the 1890s (Figure 9.10).[117] Tea exports also boomed from the 1850s, reaching a peak level of 280 million pounds in 1880, when tea accounted for more than half of China's total exports. However, in the final decades of the nineteenth century China's tea exports fell precipitously as Indian tea seized most of the international market.[118] Chinese entrepreneurs also expanded into East Asian markets, just as they had in Southeast Asia. Following the opening of Japan and Korea to foreign traders (as in China, on terms imposed by the Western powers), Chinese merchants quickly established themselves in the new treaty ports of Kobe (from 1868) and Inchon (from 1883). Down to the 1890s Chinese merchants handled nearly all British cotton textiles imported to Kobe (via Shanghai) in addition to raw cotton imports from China.[119] Chinese dominance over the Korean import trade at Inchon has been attributed to their better access to capital and credit through *piaohao* banks that established overseas branches in both Korea and Japan.[120]

The treaty port system also solidified Shanghai's position as the hub of an international trading network that dominated not only China's domestic and foreign trade but also the flow of Western manufactured goods as well as Chinese products to Korea and Japan.[121] In 1874, more than 70 percent of total imports and nearly 50 percent of exports passed through Shanghai.[122]

---

[117] Zhang Li 2010: 84, table 10, 92–96, table 14.
[118] In 1880, India's tea exports amounted to only 15 percent of Chinese exports; by 1920 those proportions had reversed, and in 1920 tea accounted for a mere 1.6 percent of China's total exports. See Gardella 1994: 111, table 13.
[119] Furuta 2005; Kagotani 2005. After 1890 the Chinese merchants' position in Kobe sharply deteriorated as Japanese-made cotton goods displaced foreign imports. But they remained dominant at Inchon until Japan's annexation of Korea in 1910.
[120] Hamashita 2008b, 2008c: 94–110.   [121] Furuta 2000.
[122] Ibid.: 152–59, tables 6-1, 6-2.

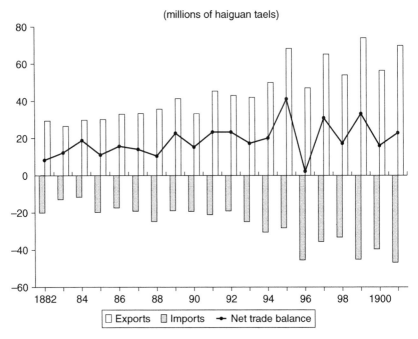

Figure 9.11 Shanghai's trade balance, 1882–1901
Source: Furuta 2000: 170, figure 6.4.

Shanghai's share of foreign trade diminished as the number of treaty ports proliferated, but the city still accounted for roughly half of both imports and exports in 1900. In contrast to other treaty ports, where both domestic and international imports tended to be consumed locally, Shanghai reexported the vast majority of its imports.[123] Moreover, although China's foreign trade balance turned negative after 1880, Shanghai itself maintained a strong trade balance except during the Sino-Japanese War (Figure 9.11).

The rapid rise of Shanghai as the linchpin of the East Asian international trade network owed far more to the entrepreneurial energies of Chinese merchants than to the intrusion of Western capitalism. Although foreign firms continued to dominate exports, the import trade (and reexports abroad) largely gravitated to Chinese firms. After 1880, in the face of stiff competition and diminishing profits, many venerable foreign trading firms failed or withdrew from the Chinese market; others redirected their business interests toward

---

[123] Keller, Li, and Shiue 2012: 161–67. But it is also true that the per capita consumption of foreign goods was far higher in Shanghai than in other regions (ibid.).

finance, shipping, and insurance.[124] The success of Chinese merchants in capturing the lion's share of the growth in foreign trade has been attributed to their business networks, which created backward linkages into production and credit and forward linkages into marketing and distribution into trades such as rice imports from Southeast Asia and handicraft cotton textile manufacture (using imported yarn) for both domestic and foreign markets.[125]

The growth of domestic trade in the nineteenth century was accompanied by the expansion of merchant networks based on native place ties. But in the post-Taiping era of reconstruction, merchants tended to form new guilds based on trade or business (known as *gongsuo* 公所, or "public halls") instead of exclusive native place ties. The older *huiguan* native place associations also became internally differentiated, with separate *bang* fellowships for individual trades.[126] Trade guilds also began to perform quasi-governmental functions such as collecting *lijin* taxes, leading to more formal recognition by the state that gave them an unprecedented voice in commercial affairs.[127] Through their guilds Chinese merchants exerted more direct influence not only in regulation of trade and finance, but also in municipal governance. In Hankou, a treaty port populated by recently arrived immigrants, merchant leaders collaborated across parochial native-place boundaries to form citywide institutions such as militias, fire-fighting brigades, and philanthropic societies. Under the leadership of the so-called "Eight Great Guilds," Hankou's merchant elite exercised broad authority in municipal governance, public security, and public works. The Eight Great Guilds became the institutional foundation for the chamber of commerce founded in 1898.[128] Merchant elites in other commercial centers formed similar citywide leadership circles – for example, the Eight Provincial Associations in Chongqing and the Big Eight Families in Tianjin – to mediate commercial disputes and increasingly, after 1850, to assume leadership roles within the urban community.[129]

Still, family ties, personal relationships, and native-place affiliations continued to carry great weight in defining one's place within the "fiduciary community," as the continuing dominance of Shanxi and Ningbo firms in

---

[124] Furuta 2005: 41.
[125] Brown 1995: 7–9; Furuta 2000; Hamilton and Chang 2003: 199–202; Sugihara 2005: 5–6.
[126] Peng Zeyi 1983: 177–81; Rowe 1984: 264–82.
[127] Mann 1987: 121–44. Motono (2000: 7–10) contends that the right to collect *lijin* duties was instrumental in strengthening the monopoly control of Chinese guilds over crucial sectors of trade in the late nineteenth century.
[128] Rowe 1984: 323–34.
[129] For Chongqing, see Zhou Lin 2011; for Tianjin, see Kwan 2001. Because the salt monopoly overwhelmingly dominated Tianjin's economy before 1900, the merchant elite there (the Big Eight Families, whose membership fluctuated with their individual fortunes) consisted entirely of salt merchants rather than a consortium of guilds or native place associations. In Chinese popular culture the number eight has the auspicious connotation of "striking it rich."

finance demonstrates.[130] The salient place of social networks and kinship institutions such as lineage trusts in Chinese business often has been regarded as favoring a "patronage economy" that hindered the development of impersonal, professional management, the adoption of modern corporations, or indeed the emergence of capitalism itself.[131] Of course, Chinese entrepreneurs were well aware of the constraints imposed by kinship obligations. For example, native-place ties were essential to gaining employment in the Shanxi *piaohao* banks, but as a rule these firms did not hire kinsmen, to avoid nepotism and entanglements that could compromise effective decision-making and the firm's best interests. Moreover, the agency partnership (see Chapter 8, pp. 336–41), in which shareholders entrusted decision-making to professional managers, was widely practiced even among family firms.[132] Lineage trusts, like individual entrepreneurs, often invested their funds in a diverse portfolio of commercial enterprises as well as real estate assets to balance profit-seeking with security. Before the development of mechanized industry, few enterprises required the large-scale, long-term capital accumulation and investment for which the modern corporation is well-suited. Mining was one industry that did have significant and growing capital and technical requirements. In the Zigong salt yards in Sichuan, it became common for diverse investors – including local landowners, lineages trusts, and Shanxi merchants, often brought together by what we might call venture capitalists – to form partnerships run by professional managers that integrated exploration, production, refining, and marketing.[133] We also see that the leading industrial enterprises in early twentieth-century China typically combined features of both social networks and hierarchical corporate management, and foreign corporations such as British American Tobacco and Standard Oil flourished by developing partnerships with local agents, suppliers, and merchandising networks rather than strictly relying on vertically controlled corporate organizations.[134] Although it is true that at the end

---

[130] On the continued importance of social networks in the formation of chambers of commerce in twentieth-century Jiangnan, see Chen Zhongping 2011.

[131] The characterization of imperial China as a "patronage economy" is expressed in Brandt, Ma, and Rawski 2014: 79. For influential statements on kinship ties, social networks, and business organization as obstacles to a breakthrough to modern capitalism, see Feuerwerker 1984: 319–20; Eastman 1988: 153; Faure 2006: 37–44. Motono (2000) is particularly critical of traditional guilds in this regard. On the resistance – because of "organizational structures and values rooted in networks of family and regional ties" – of Chinese firms to adopting the publicly traded and regulated limited liability corporation as a form of enterprise after such entities were given legal standing in 1904, see Kirby 1995 (quotation from p. 46). Goetzmann and Kröll (2005) attribute the slow development of corporate ownership in China even after the adoption of the 1904 commercial code to the stultifying effects of political patronage, social networks, the lack of capital markets, and the weakness of shareholder rights.

[132] Pomeranz 1997; Zelin 2009: 624–25.   [133] Zelin 2005.

[134] Cochran 2000; Zelin 2009: 633–35.

of the Chinese empire – just as in today's capitalist world – many firms and business leaders staunchly opposed innovations that threatened their self-interest, others displayed adaptability and an openness to new modes of doing business.

Conclusion

China's defeats in the Opium Wars compromised the imperial court's sovereign powers, and the devastation wrought by the mid-century rebellions undermined its sway over the economy. The Qing fiscal system – rooted in the Confucian ideals of supporting agriculture as the economic base of society, minimal taxation, and an unwavering commitment on the part of the state to protect and preserve the people's livelihood – was shattered. Under the rubric of "self-strengthening," the Qing government adopted a new model of political economy, enlarging its revenues by shifting from direct to indirect taxation and investing in enterprises such as arsenals, steamships, mines, and telegraph services requiring imported technologies. But these initiatives failed to harness private entrepreneurship or to develop the managerial skills necessary to put them on a sound financial footing. Provincial and local authorities frequently imposed arbitrary and often exploitative exactions, further weakening the fiscal foundations of the empire. New tensions emerged between the imperial government and local elites who saw their interests as increasingly detached from those of the Qing dynasty. The failure of the Qing modernization efforts was painfully revealed in China's humiliating defeat in its war against Japan in 1894–95.

The debacle of the Sino-Japanese War finally prompted fundamental change in economic policy. The Treaty of Shimonoseki of 1895 granted foreign firms rights to operate manufacturing ventures in the thirty-plus treaty ports and to form joint ventures to invest in railroad construction. For the first time foreign capital and mechanized industry began to exert a significant impact on the Chinese economy. The treaty also saddled the Qing court with an enormous indemnity, which forced the state to seek private financing and foreign loans to service its debt. Serious contemplation of substantive political change inspired a movement for political reform that temporarily won imperial endorsement in 1898, but proved abortive. The Boxer rebellion fiasco of 1900, in contrast, made reform imperative. During the first decade of the twentieth century tentative steps were taken toward reinventing the Qing empire as a constitutional monarchy and grafting new institutions of public finance, commercial law, banks, and schools borrowed from the West onto a revamped bureaucracy. But the new economy that began to emerge at the close of the nineteenth century only hastened the final collapse of the empire in 1911.

China's gradual incorporation into an increasingly globalized economy created both challenges and opportunities. Foreign trade, which rose dramatically after 1860, was a crucial catalyst for change. China's share of world merchandise exports was twice as great as that of Japan in 1913, and still 50 percent greater in 1929 (although in per capita terms China's share was far lower).[135] By the 1880s, more than half of total silk output was exported.[136] The terms of trade (measured in import and export prices) also improved by 25 percent in China's favor between 1870 and 1913.[137] But the economic changes set in motion by new commercial and industrial forces exacerbated existing regional inequalities. Coastal regions fared better than the interior. Hinterland areas increasingly fell behind the coastal areas in real incomes and social welfare.[138] The state's capacity to transfer resources from richer to poorer areas – long a staple feature of the imperial political economy and a crucial fulcrum of social stability – waned. Ecological fragility, already evident in 1800, precipitated natural disasters that escalated into profound human tragedies, such as the devastating North China famine of 1876–79, which claimed ten million or more lives.[139]

By many measures, China achieved impressive economic growth in the early decades of the twentieth century. Yet the pace of economic change appeared to be more dramatic than actually was the case. The phenomenal transformation of Shanghai, where 40 percent of China's modern industry was located in 1933, masked the more gradual and uneven degree of economic development elsewhere. Modern industry grew rapidly, at a rate of more than 8 percent per year between 1912 and 1936, but still accounted for only 2.5 percent of GDP in 1933, while handicraft industries held steady at 7.5 percent of GDP throughout this period. Although exports increased nearly five-fold between 1870 and 1929, China's share of global merchandise exports remained constant at 2 percent.[140] The extractive power of the state – now fractured into regional warlord regimes, a debilitated national government, and increasingly autonomous local powerholders – increased, thanks in large part to modern transport and weaponry. Yet China's new political leaders provided little in the way of services, public investment, or social welfare. Local governments and economic elites exercised greater influence on economic development than the national state. The permeability of a region to new product, currency, and credit markets also was often determined by local interest groups.[141] But the inability to fulfill

---

[135] Keller, Li, and Shiue 2013: 36, table 1.   [136] Lillian Li 1981: 65–76.
[137] Richardson 1999: 46.   [138] Pomeranz 1993; Lillian Li 2007: 310–40.
[139] Pomeranz 2008a: 90–1; Edgerton-Tarpley 2008.
[140] Richardson 1999: 63; Maddison 2007: 54, table 2.5, 88, table 3.25.
[141] Pomeranz 1993: 268–74.

traditional commitments to welfare or to ameliorate the economic reversals and distress that afflicted China during these turbulent years of unremitting warfare, social turmoil, and ultimately global depression vitiated the legitimacy of China's rulers. In the wake of this failure to refashion political economy to meet the demands of the modern era, political authority was ceded to the upstart Communist leaders who would launch China onto a path of radical economic experimentation.

Bibliography

Primary sources cited

BS: *Bei shi* 北史. Beijing: Zhonghua shuju, 1974.

DXYYB: *Daxue yanyi bu* 大學衍義補. *Qiu Jun* 邱濬. *Wenyuange siku quanshu* edition. Taipei: Taiwan shangwu yinshuguan, 1983.

FXZ: *Faxian zhuan jiaozhu* 法顯傳校注. Ed. Zhang Xun 章巽. Faxian 法顯. Beijing: Zhonghua shuju, 2008.

GSZ: *Gu Su zhi* 姑蘇志. 1506.

GY: *Guoyu jijie* 國語集解. Ed. Xu Yuangao 徐元誥. Rev. ed.; Beijing: Zhonghua shuju, 2002.

GZ: *Guan Zi jiaozhu* 管子校注. Ed. Li Xiangfeng 黎翔風. Beijing: Zhonghua shuju, 2004.

HFZ: *Han Fei Zi jishi* 韓非子集釋. Ed. Chen Qiyou 陳奇猷. Taipei: Hanjing wenhua shiye gongsi, 1983.

HHS: *Hou Han shu* 後漢書. Fan Ye 范曄. Beijing: Zhonghua shuju, 1965.

HS: *Han shu* 漢書. Ban Gu 班固. Beijing: Zhonghua shuju, 1962.

LJ: *Li ji* 禮記. *Shisanjing zhijie* 十三經直解 edition. Nanchang: Jiangxi renmin chubanshe, 1993.

LSCQ: *Lüshi chunqiu jiaoshi* 呂氏春秋校釋. Ed. Chen Qiyou 陳奇猷. Shanghai: Xuelin chubanshe, 1994.

MSC: *Ming shan cang* 名山藏. He Qiaoyuan 何喬遠. Chongzhen ed.; Rpt. Beijing: Ming Qing shiliao congbian weiyuanhui, 1993.

NS: *Nong shu* 農書. Chen Fu 陳尃. Beijing: Zhonghua shuju, 1956.

QL: *Qianfu lun jian jiaozheng* 潛夫論箋校正. Ed. Wang Jipei 王繼培. Wang Fu 王符. Beijing: Zhonghua shuju, 1985.

QMJ: *Minggong shupan qingming ji* 名公書判清明集. Beijing: Zhonghua shuju, 1987.

QMYS: *Qimin yaoshu jinshi* 齊民要述今釋. Ed. Shi Shenghan 石聲漢. Jia Sixie 賈思勰. Beijing: Kexue chubanshe, 1957–58.

SDPQJ: *Su Dongpo quanji* 蘇東坡全集. Su Shi 蘇軾. Taipei: Shijie shuju, 1982.

ShJ: *Shijing* 詩經. *Shisanjing zhijie* 十三經直解 edition. Nanchang: Jiangxi renmin chubanshe, 1993.

SJ: *Shi ji* 史記. Sima Qian 司馬遷. Beijing: Zhonghua shuju, 1959.

SJS: *Shangjun shu zhuizhi* 商君書錐指. Ed. Jiang Lihong 蔣禮鴻. Beijing: Zhonghua shuju, 1986.

SoS: *Song shu* 宋書. Beijing: Zhonghua shuju, 1974.

400

SS: *Sui shu* 隋書. Beijing: Zhonghua shuju, 1973.

SZ: *She zhi* 歙志. 1609.

TD: *Tongdian* 通典. Du You 杜佑. *Shitong* 十通 edition. Shanghai: Shangwu yinshuguan, 1935.

TLD: *Tang liudian* 唐六典. Ed. Li Linfu 李林甫. Beijing: Zhonghua shuju, 1982.

TPYL: *Taiping yulan* 太平御覽. Ed. Li Fang 李昉. 1199 ed.; rpt. Taipei: Dahua shuju, 1980.

WDJ: *Wudi ji* 吳地記. Lu Guangwei 陸廣微. Nanjing: Jiangsu guji chubanshe, 1999.

WS: *Wei shu* 魏書. Beijing: Zhonghua shuju, 1974.

WXZ: *Jiatai Wuxing zhi* 嘉泰吳興志. 1201.

WZZ: *Wu za zu* 五雜俎. Xie Zhaozhe 謝肇淛. Taipei: Weiwen chubanshe, 1977.

XCB: *Xu zizhi tongjian chang bian* 續資治通鑑長編. Li Tao 李燾. Beijing: Zhonghua shuju, 1992.

XL: *Huan Zi Xin lun* 桓子新論. Huan Tan 桓譚.

XYJ: *Da Tang Xiyu ji* 大唐西域記. Xuanzang 玄奘. Shanghai: Shanghai renmin chubanshe, 1977.

XZ: *Xun Zi jishi* 荀子集釋. Ed. Li Disheng 李滌生. Taipei: Xuesheng shuju, 1979.

YSJX: *Yanshi jiaxun jijie* 顏氏家訓集解. Ed. Wang Liqi 王利器. Yan Zhitui 顏之推. Shanghai: Shanghai guji chubanshe, 1980.

YSSF: *Yuanshi shifan* 袁氏世範. Yuan Cai 袁采. *Wenyuange siku quanshu* edition. Taipei: Taiwan shangwu yinshuguan, 1983.

YTL: *Yantie lun jiaozhu* 鹽鐵論校注. Ed. Wang Liqi 王利器. Huan Kuan 桓寬. Beijing: Zhonghua shuju, 1992.

YZS: *Yi Zhou shu huijiao jizhu* 逸周書彙校集注. Ed. Huang Huaixin 黃懷信 *et al.* Shanghai: Shanghai guji chubanshe, 2007.

ZGZH: *Zhanguo zongheng jiashu* 戰國縱橫家書. Ed. Mawangdui Hanmu boshu zhengli xiaozu 马王堆汉墓帛书整理小组. Beijing: Wenwu chubanshe, 1976.

ZhL: *Zheng lun zhushi* 政論注釋. Ed. Shanghai diba gangtiechang gongren lilun xiaozu 上海第八钢铁厂工人理论小组. Cui Shi 崔寔. Shanghai: Shanghai renmin chubanshe, 1976.

ZL: *Zhou li zhijie* 周禮直解. *Shisanjing zhijie* 十三經直解 edition. Nanchang: Jiangxi renmin chubanshe, 1993.

ZS: *Zhou shu* 周書. Beijing: Zhonghua shuju, 1971.

ZZ: *Zuozhuan* 左傳. *Shisanjing zhijie* 十三經直解 edition. Nanchang: Jiangxi renmin chubanshe, 1993.

Secondary scholarship cited

Abe Takeo 安部健夫. 1972. "Gen jidai no hōginsei no kōken" 元時代の包銀制の考研. In Abe, *Gendaishi no kenkyū* 元代史の研究, 75–232. Tokyo: Sōbunsha.

Acemoglu, Daron, and James A. Robinson. 2012. *Why Nations Fail: The Origins of Power, Prosperity, and Poverty*. London: Profile.

Adachi Keiji 足立啓二. 1985. "Sōdai Ryōsetsu ni okeru suitōsaku no seisanryoku suijun" 宋代両浙における水稲作の生産力水準. *Kumamoto daigaku bungakubu ronsō* 熊本大学文學部論叢 17: 80–100.

Allen, Robert C. 2009. "Agricultural Productivity and Rural Incomes in England and the Yangtze Delta, *c.* 1620–*c.* 1820." *Economic History Review* 62.3: 525–50.

Allen, Robert C., Jean-Pascal Bassino, Debin Ma, Christine Moll-Murata, and Jan Luiten Van Zanden. 2011. "Wages, Prices, and Living Standards in China, 1738–1925: In Comparison with Europe, Japan, and India." *Economic History Review* 64, supplement 1: 8–38.

Allsen, Thomas T. 1987. *Mongol Imperialism: The Policies of the Grand Qan Möngke in China, Russia, and the Islamic Lands, 1251–1259.* Berkeley: University of California Press.

1989. "Mongol Princes and their Merchant Partners, 1200–1260." *Asia Major,* 3rd series, 2.1: 83–126.

Amano Motonosuke 天野元之助. 1967. "Kō Kan Sai Shi 'Shimin getsuryō' ni tsuite" 後漢蔡 寔 '四民月令' について. *Kansai daigaku keizai ronshū* 関西大学経済論集 16.4–5: 361–86.

1979. *Chūgoku nōgyōshi kenkyū* 中国農業史研究. Revised edn. Tokyo: Ochanomizu shobō.

Aoki Atsushi 青木敦. 2006. "Kaihatsu, chika, minjiteki hōki: 'Seimeishū' ni mieru jakkan tochi tenbai kankeihō o megutte" 開発, 地価, 民事的法規:「清明集」に見える若干土地 典売関係法をめぐって. *Machikaneyama ronshū (shigaku hen)* 待兼山論集 (史学篇) 40: 1–47.

2013. "Sōdai teitōhō no suii to 'nōdenchoku' – yōso shijō ni okeru shihō to shūkan" 宋代抵当法の推移 と「農田勅」–要素市場における司法と習慣. In *Chūgoku no shijō chitsujo – jūshichi seiki kara nijū seiki zenhan o chūshin ni* 中国の市場秩序:十七 世紀から二十世紀前半を中心に, pp. 19–47. Ed. Furuta Kazuko 古田和子. Tokyo: Keio daigaku shuppankai.

Arrighi, Giovanni, Takeshi Hamashita, and Mark Selden, eds. 2003. *The Resurgence of East Asia: 500, 150, and 50 Year Perspectives.* London: Routledge.

Atwell, William S. 1982. "International Bullion Flows and the Chinese Economy circa 1530–1650." *Past and Present* 95: 68–90.

1986. "Some Observations on the 'Seventeenth-Century Crisis' in China and Japan." *Journal of Asian Studies* 45.2: 223–44.

1990. "A Seventeenth-century 'General Crisis' in East Asian History?" *Modern Asian Studies* 24.4: 661–82.

2006. "Another Look at Silver Imports into China, *c.* 1635–1644," *Journal of World History* 16.4: 467–89.

Bagley, Robert. 1999. "Shang Archaeology." In M. Loewe and E. L. Shaughnessy, eds. *The Cambridge History of Ancient China: From the Origins of Civilization to 211 BC,* 124–231. Cambridge University Press.

Bai Yunxiang 白云翔. 2010. "Qin Han shiqi juluode kaogu faxian ji chubu renshi" 秦汉时期聚 落的考古发现及初步认识. In *Handai chengshi he juluo kaogu yu Han wenhua* 汉代城 市和聚落考古与汉文化, pp. 44–55. Ed. Bai Yunxiang and Sun Xinmin 孙新民. Beijing: Kexue chubanshe.

Bairoch, Paul. 1976. *Commerce éxterieur et développement économique de l'Europe au XIXe siècle.* Paris: Mouton.

Balazs, Etienne. 1964a. "Evolution of Land Ownership in Fourth- and Fifth-century China." In E. *Balazs, Chinese Civilization and Bureaucracy,* 101–12. New Haven: Yale University Press.

1964b. "Political Philosophy and Social Crisis at the End of the Han Dynasty." In E. Balazs, *Chinese Civilization and Bureaucracy*, 187–225. New Haven: Yale University Press.

Bao Weimin 包伟民. 2001. *Songdai difang caizheng shi yanjiu* 宋代地方财政史研究. Shanghai: Shanghai guji chubanshe.

Barbieri-Low, Anthony. 2007. *Artisans in Early Imperial China*. Seattle: University of Washington Press.

Barbieri-Low, Anthony, and Robin D. S. Yates. Forthcoming. *Law, State, and Society in Early Imperial China: Translation and Study of the Zhangjiashan Legal Texts*. Leiden: Brill.

Barfield, Thomas. 1989. *Perilous Frontiers: Nomadic Empires and China*. Cambridge, MA: Blackwell.

Bastid, Marianne. 1985. "The Structure of the Financial Institutions of the State in the Late Qing." In S. R. Schram, ed. *The Scope of State Power in China*, 51–79. London: School of Oriental and African Studies.

Benedict, Carol. 2011. *Golden-Silk Smoke: A History of Tobacco in China, 1550–2010*. Berkeley: University of California Press.

Bernhardt, Kathryn. 1992. *Rents, Taxes, and Peasant Resistance: The Lower Yangzi Region, 1840–1950*. Stanford University Press.

Bielenstein, Hans. 1986. "Wang Mang, the Restoration of the Han Dynasty, and Later Han." In D. Twitchett and M. Loewe, eds. *The Cambridge History of China, vol. 1: The Ch'in and Han Empires, 221 BC–220 AD*, 223–90. Cambridge University Press.

Birge, Bettine. 2002. *Women, Property and Confucian Reaction in Sung and Yüan China (960–1368)*. Cambridge University Press.

Blake, Robert P. 1937. "The Circulation of Silver in the Moslem East down to the Mongol Epoch." *Harvard Journal of Asiatic Studies* 2.3–4: 291–328.

Blussé, Leonard. 1999. "Chinese Century: The Eighteenth Century in the China Sea Region." *Archipel* 58.2: 107–29.

Bol, Peter. 2008. *Neo-Confucianism in History*. Cambridge: Harvard University Asia Center.

Bonney, Richard J. 1999. "Introduction." In Richard J. Bonney, ed. *The Rise of the Fiscal State in Europe, c. 1200–1815*, 1–17. New York: Oxford University Press.

Brandt, Loren, Debin Ma, and Thomas G. Rawski. 2014. "From Divergence to Convergence: Reevaluating the History Behind China's Economic Boom." *Journal of Economic Literature* 52.1: 45–123.

Bray, Francesca. 1979–80. "Agricultural Technology and Agrarian Change in Han China." *Early China* 5: 3–13.

1984. *Science and Civilisation in China, vol. 6: Biology and Biological Technology, part 2: Agriculture*. Joseph Needham, ed. Cambridge University Press.

1997. *Technology and Gender: Fabrics of Power in Late Imperial China*. Berkeley: University of California Press.

Brenner, Robert, and Christopher Isett. 2002. "England's Divergence from China's Yangzi Delta: Property Relations, Microeconomics, and Patterns of Development." *Journal of Asian Studies* 61.3: 609–22.

Broadberry, Stephen N., and Bishnupriya Gupta. 2006. "The Early Modern Great Divergence: Wages, Prices, and Economic Development in Europe and Asia, 1500–1800." *Economic History Review* 59.1: 2–31.

Broadberry, Stephen, Hanhui Guan, and David Daokui Li. 2014. "China, Europe, and the Great Divergence: A Study in Historical National Accounting, 980–1850." Paper presented at the Fourth Asian Historical Economics Conference, Istanbul. Available at www.lse.ac.uk/economicHistory/pdf/ Broadberry/China8.pdf.

Brook, Timothy. 1998. *The Confusions of Pleasure: Commerce and Culture in Ming China*. Berkeley: University of California Press.

Brown, Rajeswary Ampalavanar. 1995. "Introduction: Chinese Business in an Institutional and Historical Perspective." In R. A. Brown, ed. *Chinese Business Enterprise in Asia*, 1–26. London: Routledge.

Burger, Werner. 2015. "Silver is Expensive, Cash is Cheap: Official and Private Cash Forgeries as the Main Cause for the 19th Century Monetary Turmoil." In J. K. Leonard, and U. Theobald, eds. *Money in Asia (1200–1900): Small Currencies in Social and Political Contexts*, 141–54. Leiden: Brill.

Cao Lüning 曹旅宁. 2002. *Qinlü xintan* 秦律新探. Beijing: Zhongguo shehui kexue chubanshe.

Cao Shuji 曹树基. 2000a. *Zhongguo renkou shi* 中國人口史, vol. 4: *Ming shiqi* 明时期. Shanghai: Fudan daxue chubanshe.

2000b. *Zhongguo renkou shi: Qing shiqi* 中国人口史, vol. 5: 清时期. Shanghai: Fudan daxue chubanshe.

Cao Shuji 曹树基, Li Nan 李楠, and Gong Qisheng 龚启圣. 2010. "'Canque chanquan' zhi zhuanrang: Shicang 'tuiqi' yanjiu (1727–1949)" 「残缺产权」之转让:石仓「退契」研究. *Lishi yanjiu* 历史研究 3: 118–31.

Cao Wei 曹玮. 2002. "Wei ding" 衛鼎. In *Jijin zhuguo shi: Zhouyuan chutu Xi Zhou qingtongqi jingcui* 吉金鑄國史: 周原出土西周青銅器精粹, pp. 237–241. Ed. Beijing daxue kaogu wenbo xueyuan. Beijing: Wenwu chubanshe.

Cartier, Michel. 1976. "Sapèques et tissus à l'époque des T'ang: remarques sur la circulation monétaire dans la Chine medievale." *Journal of the Economic and Social History of the Orient* 19.3: 323–44.

Chang, Kwang-chih. 1977. "Ancient China." In K. Chang, ed. *Food in Chinese History: Anthropological and Historical Perspectives*, 23–52. New Haven: Yale University Press.

Chao, Kang. 1986. *Man and Land in Chinese History: An Economic Analysis*. Stanford University Press.

Che Qun 车群 and Cao Shuji 曹树基. 2011. "Qing zhongye yijiang Zhenan xiangcun jiazu renkou yu jiazu jingji: jian lun fei-Maersasi shide Zhonguo shengyu moshi" 清中叶以降 浙南乡村家族人口与家族经济:兼论非马尔萨斯式的中国生育模式. *Zhongguo renkou kexue* 中国人口科学 2011.3: 42–53.

Chen Chunsheng 陳春聲. 2005. *Shichang jizhi yu shehui bianqian: 18 shji Guangdong mijia fenxi* 市場機制與社會變遷:18 世紀廣東米價分析. 2nd edn. Taipei: Daoxiang chubanshe.

Chen Feng 陈锋. 2008. *Qingdai caizheng zhengce yu huobi zhengce yanjiu* 清代财政政策与货币政策研究. Wuhan: Wuhan daxue chubanshe.

Chen Jie 陈絜. 2009. "Liye 'hujijian' yu Zhanguo moqide jiceng shehui" 里耶 "户籍简" 与战 国末期的基层社会. *Lishi yanjiu* 历史研究 5: 23–40.

Ch'en, Kenneth. 1956. "The Economic Background of the Hui-Ch'ang Suppression of Buddhism." *Harvard Journal of Asiatic Studies* 19.1–2: 67–105.

Chen Mingguang 陈明光. 1997. *Liuchao caizheng shi* 六朝财政史. Beijing: Zhongguo caijing jingji chubanshe.

Chen Qiaoyi 陈桥驿. 1962. "Gudai Jianhu xingfei yu Shan Gui pingyuan nongtian shuili" 古代 鉴湖兴废与山会平原农田水力. *Dili xuebao* 地理学报 3: 187–201.

Chen, Shen. 2003. "Compromises and Conflicts: Production and Commerce in the Royal Cities of Eastern Zhou, China." In M. L. Smith, ed. *The Social Construction of Ancient Cities*, pp. 290–310. Washington, DC: Smithsonian Institution.

Chen Shuang 陈爽. 1998. *Shijia dazu yu beichao zhengzhi* 世家大族与北朝政治. Beijing: Zhongguo shehui kexue chubanshe.

Chen Zhengxiang 陈正祥. 1982. *Zhongguo wenhua dili* 中國文化地理. Taibei: Muduo chubanshe.

Chen Zhiping 陈支平. 1993. "Song Yuan Ming Qing shiqi Jiangnan shizhen shehui" 宋元明清 时期江南市镇社会. *Zhongguo shehui jingji shi yanjiu* 中国社会经济史研究 1: 33–8.

    2009. *Minjian wenshu yu Ming Qing dongnan zushang yanjiu* 民间文书与明清 东南族商研究. Beijing: Zhonghua shuju.

Chen, Zhongping. 2011. *Modern China's Network Revolution: Chambers of Commerce and Sociopolitical Change in the Early Twentieth Century*. Stanford University Press.

Cheng, Linsun. 2003. *Banking in Modern China: Entrepreneurs, Professional Managers, and the Development of Chinese Banks, 1897–1937*. Cambridge University Press.

Cheng Minsheng 程民生. 1984. "Lun Bei Song caizhengde tedian yu jipin de jiaxiang" 论北宋 财政的特点与积贫的假象. *Zhongguo shi yanjiu* 中国史研究 3: 27–40.

Cheung, Sui-Wai. 2008. *The Price of Rice: Market Integration in Eighteenth-century China*. Bellingham, WA: Western Washington State University Press.

    2013. "Copper, Silver, and Tea: The Question of Eighteenth-Century Inflation in the Lower Yangzi Delta." In B. K. L. So, ed. *The Economic History of Lower Yangzi Delta in Late Imperial China: Connecting Money, Markets, and Institutions*, 118–32. London: Routledge.

Chia, Lucille. 2003. "Commercial Publishing in Jianyang from the Song to the Ming." In P. J. Smith and R. von Glahn, eds. *The Song-Yuan-Ming Transition in Chinese History*, 284–328. Cambridge: Harvard University Asia Center.

Chien, Cecilia Lee-fang. 2004. *Salt and State: An Annotated Translation of the Songshi Salt Monopoly Treatise*. Ann Arbor: University of Michigan Center for Chinese Studies.

Chin, Tamara T. 2014. *Savage Exchange: Han Imperialism, Chinese Literary Style, and the Economic Imagination*. Cambridge: Harvard University Asia Center.

Ch'iu, Peng-sheng (Qiu Pengsheng 邱澎生). 1990. *Shiba shijiu shiji Suzhouchengde xinxing gongshangye tuanti* 十八,十九世紀蘇州城的新興工商業團體. Taipei: Guoli Taiwan daxue chubanshe.

    2004. "You fangliao dao gongchang: Qingdai qianqi Suzhou mianbu zihaode jingji yu falü fenxi" 由放料到工厂: 清代前期苏州棉布字号的经济与

法律分析. In Li Bozhong 李伯重 and Zhou Shengchun 周生春, eds. *Jiangnande chengshi gongye yu difang wenhua, 960–1850* 江南的城市工业与地方文化, *960–1850*, 66–94. Beijing: Tianjin daxue chubanshe.

2008. *Dang falü yushang jingji: Ming Qing Zhongguode shangye falü* 當法律遇上經濟:明清中國的商業法律. Taipei: Wunan tushu gongsi.

2012. "Shiba shiji Su-Song mianbuyede guanli jiagou yu falü wenhua" 十八世纪苏松棉布业的管理架构与法律文化. *Jianghai xuekan* 江海学刊 2: 143–57.

Chittick, Andrew. 2009. *Patronage and Community in Medieval China: The Xiangyang Garrison, 400–600 CE.* Albany, NY: State University of New York Press.

Ch'üan, Han-sheng, and Richard A. Kraus. 1975. *Mid-Ch'ing Rice Markets and Trade: An Essay in Price History.* Cambridge, MA: Council on East Asian Studies, Harvard University.

Clark, Hugh D. 2009. "The Southern Kingdoms between the T'ang and the Sung, 907–979." In D. Twitchett and P. J. Smith, eds. *The Cambridge History of China, vol. 5: The Sung Dynasty and its Precursors, 907–1279*, 133–205. Cambridge University Press.

Clunas, Craig. 1991. *Superfluous Things: Material Culture and Social Status in Early Modern China.* Urbana: University of Illinois Press.

Cochran, Sherman. 2000. *Encountering Chinese Networks: Western, Japanese, and Chinese Corporations in China, 1880–1937.* Berkeley: University of California Press.

Cook, Constance A. 1997. "Wealth and the Western Zhou." *Bulletin of the School of Oriental and African Studies* 60.2: 253–94.

Cox, Cheryl Anne. 1998. *Household Interests: Property, Marriage Strategies, and Family Dynamics in Ancient Athens.* Princeton University Press.

Crowell, William G. 1990. "Northern Émigrés and the Problems of Census Registration under the Eastern Jin and Southern Dynasties." In A. E. Dien, ed. *State and Society in Early Medieval China*, 171–209. Stanford University Press.

Curtin, Philip D. 1984. *Cross-Cultural Trade in World History.* Cambridge University Press.

Dai Jianguo 戴建国. 2001. "Songdaide tianzhai jiaoyi toushui pingyou he guanyin tianzhai qishu" 宋代的田宅交易投税凭由和官印田宅契书. *Zhongguo shi yanjiu* 中国史研究 3: 97–111.

2011. "Songdaide mintian dianmai yu 'yitian liangzhu zhi'" 宋代的民田典卖与「一田两主制」. *Lishi yanjiu* 历史研究 6: 99–117.

Daniels, Christian. 1996. "Agro-Industries: Sugarcane Technology." In J. Needham, ed. *Science and Civilisation in China, vol. 6: Biology and Biological Technology, part 3: Agro-Industries and Forestry*, 1–539. Cambridge University Press.

Danjō Hiroshi 壇上寬. 1995. *Minchō sensei shihai no shiteki kōzō* 明朝専制支配の史的構造. Tokyo: Kyūko shoin.

1997. "Minsho no kaikin to chōkō: Minchō sensei shihai no rikai ni yosete" 明初の海禁と朝貢: 明朝専制支配の理解に寄せて. In Mori Masao 森正夫 *et al.* eds. *Min Shin jidaishi no kihonteki mondai* 明清時代史の基本的問題, 203–34. Tokyo: Kyūko shoin.

Dardess, John W. 1996. *A Ming Society: T'ai-ho County, Kiangsi, in the Fourteenth to Seventeenth Centuries.* Berkeley: University of California Press.

De la Vaissière, Étienne. 2005. *Sogdian Traders: A History.* Leiden: Brill.

Deng, Gang. 1999. *The Premodern Chinese Economy: Structural Equilibrium and Capitalist Sterility*. London: Routledge.

Deng, Kent G. 2012. "The Continuation and Efficiency of the Chinese Fiscal State, 700 BC–AD 1911." In B. Yun-Casalilla and P. K. O'Brien, eds. *The Rise of Fiscal States: A Global History, 1500–1914*, 335–52. Cambridge University Press.

Dermigny, Louis. 1964. *La Chine et l'occident: le commerce à Canton au XVIIIe siècle*. Paris: S.E.V.P.E.N.

De Vries, Jan. 1976. *The Economy of Europe in an Age of Crisis*. Cambridge University Press.

1984. *European Urbanization, 1500–1800*. Cambridge: Harvard University Press.

2008. *The Industrious Revolution: Consumer Behavior and the Household Economy, 1650 to the Present Day*. Cambridge University Press.

Di Cosmo, Nicola. 2002. *Ancient China and its Enemies: The Rise of Nomadic Power in East Asian History*. Cambridge University Press.

Ding Bangyou 丁邦友. 2009. *Handai wujia xintan* 汉代物价新探. Beijing: Zhongguo shehui kexue chubanshe.

Dong Guodong 冻国栋. 2002. *Zhongguo renkou shi* 中国人口史, vol. 2: *Sui Tang Wudai shiqi* 隋唐五代时期. Shanghai: Fudan daxue chubanshe.

Dreyer, Edward L. 2007. *Zheng He: China and the Oceans in the Early Ming Dynasty, 1405–1433*. New York: Pearson/Longman.

Du Xuncheng 杜恂诚 and Li Jin 李晋. 2011. "Zhongguo jingji shi 'GDP' yanjiu zhi wuqu" 中国经济史 "GDP" 研究之误区. *Xueshu yuekan* 学术月刊 43.10: 74–81.

Du Zhengsheng 杜正勝. 1990. *Bianhu qimin: chuantong zhengzhi shehui jiegou zhi xingcheng* 編戶齊民: 傳統政治社會結構之形成. Taipei: Lianjing chuban gongsi.

Dunstan, Helen. 1996. *Conflicting Counsels to Confuse the Age: A Documentary Study of Political Economy in Qing China, 1644–1840*. Ann Arbor: University of Michigan Center for Chinese Studies.

2006. *State or Merchant? Political Economy and Political Process in 1740s China*. Cambridge: Harvard University Asia Center.

Dykstra, Maura. 2013. "Beyond the Shadow of the Law: Firm Insolvency, State-Building, and the New Policy Bankruptcy Reform in Late Qing Chongqing." *Frontiers in Chinese History* 8.3: 406–33.

Eastman, Lloyd. 1988. *Family, Fields, and Ancestors: Constancy and Change in China's Social and Economic History, 1550–1949*. New York: Oxford University Press.

Ebrey, Patricia Buckley. 1974. "Estate and Family Management in the Later Han as Seen in *The Monthly Instructions for the Four Classes of People*." *Journal of the Economic and Social History of the Orient* 17.2: 173–205.

1978. *The Aristocratic Families of Early Imperial China: A Case Study of the Po-ling Ts'ui Family*. Cambridge University Press.

1984a. "Conceptions of the Family in the Sung Dynasty." *Journal of Asian Studies* 43.2: 219–45.

1984b. *Family and Property in Sung China: Yüan Ts'ai's Precepts for Social Life*. Princeton University Press.

1986a. "The Economic and Social History of Later Han." In D. Twitchett and M. Loewe, eds. *The Cambridge History of China, vol. 1: The Ch'in and Han Empires, 221 BC–220 AD.*, 608–48. Cambridge University Press.

1986b. "Early Stages in the Development of Descent Group Organization." In P. Ebrey and J. L. Watson, eds. *Kinship Organization in Late Imperial China, 1000–1940*, 16–61. Berkeley: University of California Press.

1993. *The Inner Quarters: Marriage and the Lives of Chinese Women in the Sung Period*. Berkeley: University of California Press.

Edgerton-Tarpley, Kathryn. 2008. *Tears from Iron: Cultural Responses to Famine in Nineteenth-Century China*. Berkeley: University of California Press.

Elvin, Mark. 1973. *The Pattern of the Chinese Past*. Stanford University Press.

1977. "Market Towns and Waterways: The County of Shang-hai from 1480 to 1910." In G. W. Skinner, ed. *The City in Late Imperial China*, 441–73. Stanford University Press.

Emura Haruki 江村治樹. 2005. *Sengoku Shin Kan jidai no toshi to kokka: kōkogaku to bunken shigaku kara no appuroochi* 戦国秦漢時代の都市と国家:考古学と文献史学からの アップローチ. Tokyo: Hakuteisha.

2011. *Shunshū Sengoku jidai seidō kahei no seisei to tenkai* 春秋戦国時代青銅貨幣の生成と展開. Tokyo: Kyūko shoin.

Endicott-West, Elizabeth. 1989a. "Merchant Associations in Yüan China: The Ortoγ." *Asia Major*, 3rd series, 2.1: 127–54.

1989b. *Mongolian Rule in China: Local Administration in the Yuan Dynasty*. Cambridge: Harvard Council on East Asian Studies.

Epstein, S. R. 2000. *Freedom and Growth: The Rise of States and Markets in Europe, 1300–1750*. London: Routledge.

Fan Jinmin 范金民. 1998. *Ming Qing Jiangnan shangyede fazhan* 明清江南商业的发展. Nanjing: Nanjing daxue chubanshe.

2001. "Mingdai Huishang randiande yige shili" 明代徽商染店的一个实例. *Anhui shixue* 安徽史学 2001.3: 2–4.

Fan Jinmin 范金民 and Jin Wen 金文. 1993. *Jiangnan sichou shi yanjiu* 江南丝绸史研究. Beijing: Nongye chubanshe.

Fan Shuzhi 樊树志. 1990. *Ming Qing Jiangnan shizhen tanwei* 明清江南市镇探微. Shanghai: Fudan daxue chubanshe.

Fan Zhaofei 范兆飞 and Zhang Mingming 张明明. 2011. "Shiliuguo Bei Wei shiqide wubao jingji" 十六国北魏时期的坞堡经济. *Zhongguo shehui jingjishi yanjiu* 中国社会经济史 研究 2: 14–21.

Fang Gaofeng 方高峰. 2009. *Liuchao zhengquan yu changjiang zhongyou nongye jingji fazhan* 六朝政权与长江中游农业经济发展. Tianjin: Tianjin guji chubanshe.

Fang Xing 方行. 1996. "Qingdai Jiangnan nongminde xiaofei" 清代江南农民的消费. *Zhongguo jingji shi yanjiu* 中国经济史研究 3: 91–8.

Fang Xing 方行, Jing Junjian 经君健, and Wei Jinyu 魏金玉, eds. 2007. *Zhongguo jingji tongshi: Qing* 中国经济通史:清. 2nd edn. Beijing: Jingji ribao chubanshe.

Farmer, Edward L. 1995. *Zhu Yuanzhang and Early Ming Legislation: The Reordering of Chinese Society Following the Era of Mongol Rule*. Leiden: Brill.

Farris, William Wayne. 1998. *Buried Texts and Sacred Treasures: Issues in the Historical Archaeology of Ancient Japan*. Honolulu: University of Hawai'i Press.

Faure, David. 2006. *China and Capitalism: A History of Business Enterprise in Modern China*. Hong Kong: Hong Kong University Press.

2007. *Emperor and Ancestor: State and Lineage in South China*. Stanford University Press.

Feuerwerker, Albert. 1958. *China's Early Industrialization: Sheng Hsuan-huai (1844–1916) and Mandarin Enterprise*. Cambridge: Harvard University Press.

1980. "Economic Trends in the Late Ch'ing Empire, *c.* 1870–1911." In J. K. Fairbank, ed. *The Cambridge History of China*, vol. 10: *Late Ch'ing, 1800–1911*, 2: 1–69. Cambridge University Press.

1984. "The State and the Economy in Late Imperial China." *Theory and Society* 13.3: 297–326.

Findlay, Ronald, and Kevin H. O'Rourke. 2007. *Power and Plenty: Trade, War, and the World Economy in the Second Millennium*. Princeton University Press.

Finlay, Robert. 2010. *The Pilgrim Art: Cultures of Porcelain in World History*. Berkeley: University of California Press.

Finley, M. I. 1973. *The Ancient Economy*. Berkeley: University of California Press.

Finnane, Antonia. 2004. *Speaking of Yangzhou: A Chinese City, 1550–1850*. Cambridge: Harvard University Asia Center.

Flynn, Dennis O., and Arturo Giráldez. 1995. "Born with a 'Silver Spoon': World Trade's Origins in 1571." *Journal of World History* 6.2: 201–22.

Fogel, Joshua. 1984. *Politics and Sinology: The Case of Naitō Kōnan (1866–1934)*. Cambridge: Harvard University Council on East Asian Studies.

Frank, Andre Gunder. 1998. *ReOrient: Global Economy in the Asian Age*. Berkeley: University of California Press.

Fu Yiling 傅依凌. 1982. "Mingmo Qingchu Jiangnan ji dongnan yanhai diqu 'funong jingying' de chubu kaocha" 明末清初江南及东南沿海地区 '富农经营' 的初步考察. In Fu, *Ming Qing shehui jingji shi lunwenji* 明清社会经济史论文集, 121–44. Beijing: Renmin chubanshe.

Fujiie Reinosuke 藤家礼之助. 1989. *Kan Sangoku Ryō Shin Nanbokuchō no densei to zeisei* 漢 三国両晋南北朝の田制と税制. Tokyo: Tōkai daigaku shuppankai.

Fuma Susumu 夫馬進. 1997. *Chūgoku zenkai zendō shi kenkyū* 中国善会善堂史研究. Kyoto: Dōhōsha.

Furuta Kazuko 古田和子. 2000. *Shanhai nettowaaku to kindai Higashi Ajia* 上海ネットワークと近代東アジア. Tokyo: Tokyo daigaku shuppankai.

2005. "Kobe Seen as Part of the Shanghai Trading Network: The Role of Chinese Merchants in the Re-Export of Cotton Manufactures to Japan." In K. Sugihara, ed. *Japan, China, and the Growth of the Asian International Economy, 1850–1949*, 23–48. Oxford University Press.

Gale, Esson M. 1931. *Discourses on Salt and Iron: A Debate on State Control of Commerce and Industry in Ancient China, Chapters I-XIX*. Leiden: E. J. Brill.

Gansusheng wenwu kaogu yanjiusuo 甘肃省文物考古研究所, ed. 1989. *Qin Han jiandu lunwenji* 秦汉简牍论文集. Lanzhou: Gansu renmin chubanshe.

Gao Congming 高聪明. 1999. *Songdai huobi yu huobi liutong yanjiu* 宋代货币与货币流通研究. Baoding: Hebei daxue chubanshe.

Gao Dalun 高大伦. 1998. "Yinwan Hanmu mujian 'Jibu' zhong hukou tongji ziliao yanjiu" 尹湾汉墓木简《集簿》中户口统计资料研究. *Lishi yanjiu* 历史研究 5: 110–23.

Gao Min 高敏. 1986. *Qin Han Wei Jin Nanbeichao tudi zhidu yanjiu* 秦汉魏晋南北朝
土地制度研究. Zhengzhou: Zhongzhou guji chubanshe.
    1987. "Bei Wei juntian faling jiaoshi" 北魏均田法令校释. In Gao Min, *Wei Jin
Nanbeichao shehui jingji shi tantao* 魏晋南北朝社会经济史探讨, 186–219.
Beijing: Renmin chubanshe.
    1989. "Shin Kan jidai no kanshi shukōgyō" 秦漢時代の官私手工業. *Chūgoku:
shakai to bunka* 中国：社会と文化 4: 103–22.
    2004. "Yinwan Hanjian 'Jibu' de shidu, zhiyi yu yiyi tantao: du Yinwan Hanjian
zhaji zhi er" 尹湾汉简《集簿》的释读, 质疑与意义探讨: 读尹湾汉简札记之
二. In Gao Min, *Qin Han Wei Jin Nanbeichao shi lunkao* 秦汉魏晋南北朝史论
考, 94–104. Beijing: Zhongguo shehui kexue chubanshe.
    2006. "Cong 'Changsha Zoumalou Sanguo Wujian zhujian (yi)' kan Sun Quan
shiqide kouqian suanfu zhidu" 从《长沙走马楼三国吴简。竹简 (壹)》看孙权
时期 的口钱算赋制度. *Shixue yuekan* 史学月刊 4: 24–27.
Gardella, Robert. 1994. *Harvesting Mountains: Fujian and the China Tea Trade,
1757–1937.* Berkeley: University of California Press.
    2004. "Contracting Business Partnerships in Late Qing and Republican China:
Paradigms and Patterns." In M. Zelin, J. K. Ocko, and R. Gardella, eds. *Contract
and Property in Early Modern China*, 327–47. Stanford University Press.
Gatrell, Peter. 2012. "The Russian Fiscal State, 1600–1914." In B. Yun-Casalilla
and P. K. O'Brien, eds. *The Rise of Fiscal States: A Global History, 1500–1914*,
191–212. Cambridge University Press.
Ge Jianxiong 葛剑雄. 2000. "Guanyu Qindai renkou shuliangde xin guji" 关于秦代人
口数量 的新估计. In Ge Jianxiong, *Ge Xianzhong zixuanji* 葛剑雄自选集,
16–25. Guilin: Guangxi shifan daxue chubanshe.
    2002. *Zhongguo renkou shi* 中国人口史, vol. 1: *Daolun, Xian Qin zhi Nanbeichao
shiqi* 导论、先秦至南北朝时期. Shanghai: Fudan daxue chubanshe.
Ge Jinfang 葛金芳 and Gu Rong 顾蓉. 2000. "Songdai Jiangnan diqude liangshi
muchan jiqi gusuan fangfa bianxi" 宋代江南地区的粮食亩产及其估算方法辨
析. *Hubei daxue xuebao (zhexue shehui kexue ban)* 湖北大学学报(哲学社会科
学版) 27.3: 78–83.
Geng Yuanli 耿元骊. 2007. "Bei Song zhongqi Suzhou nongminde tianzu fudan he
shenghuo shuiping" 北宋中期苏州农民的田租负担和生活水平. *Zhongguo
jingji shi yanjiu* 中国经济史研究 1: 150–58.
Gernet, Jacques. 1995. *Buddhism in Chinese Society: An Economic History from the
Fifth to the Tenth Centuries.* New York: Columbia University Press.
Giele, Enno. 2010. "Excavated Manuscripts: Context and Methodology." In M. Nylan
and M. Loewe, eds. *China's Early Empires: A Re-appraisal*, 114–34. Cambridge
University Press.
Godinho, Vitorino Magalhães. 1969. *L'Économie de l'empire portugais au XVe et XVIe
siècles.* Paris: S.E.V.P.E.N.
Goetzmann, William, and Elisabeth Köll. 2005. "The History of Corporate Ownership
in China: State Patronage, Company Legislation, and the Issue of Control." In
R. K. Morck, ed. *A History of Corporate Governance around the World: Family
Business Groups to Professional Managers*, 149–81. University of Chicago Press.
Golas, Peter J. 1977. "Early Ch'ing Guilds." In G. W. Skinner, ed. *The City in Late
Imperial China*, 555–80. Stanford University Press.

1980. "Rural China in the Song." *Journal of Asian Studies* 39.2: 291–325.
1988. "The Sung Economy: How Big?" *Bulletin of Sung-Yuan Studies* 20: 89–94.
Goldstone, Jack A. 1998. "The Problem of the 'Early Modern' World." *Journal of the Economic and Social History of the Orient* 41.3: 249–84.
2002. "Efflorescences and Economic Growth in World History: Rethinking the 'Rise of the West' and the Industrial Revolution." *Journal of World History* 13.3: 323–89.
Graff, David A. 2002. *Medieval Chinese Warfare, 300–900*. London: Routledge.
Grove, Jean M. 1990. *The Little Ice Age*. London: Routledge.
Guan Hanhui 管汉晖 and Li Daokui 李稻葵. 2010. "Mingdai GDP ji jiegou shitan" 明代 GDP 及结构试探. *Jingjixue jikan* 经济学季刊 9.3: 787–828.
Guo Zhengzhong 郭正忠. 1985. "Nan Song zhongyang caizheng huobi suishou kaobian" 南宋 中央财政货币岁收考辨. In Zhongguo shehui kexueyuan lishi yanjiusuo Song Liao Jin Yuan shi yanjiushi, 宋辽金史论丛1: 168–91.
1990. *Songdai yanye jingji shi* 宋代盐业经济史. Beijing: Renmin chubanshe.
1997. *Liang Song chengxiang shangpin huobi jingji kaolüe* 两宋城乡商品货币经济考略. Beijing: Jingji guanli chubanshe.
Guy, John. 2010. "Rare and Strange Goods: International Trade in Ninth Century Asia." In R. Krahl *et al.*, ed. *Shipwrecked: Tang Treasures and Monsoon Winds*, 19–27. Washington, DC: Smithsonian Institution.
Hall, Kenneth R. 2011. *A History of Early Southeast Asia: Maritime Trade and Societal Development, 100–1500*. Lanham, MD: Rowman and Littlefield.
Hamashima Atsutoshi 濱島敦俊. 1982. *Mindai Kōnan nōson shakai no kenkyū* 明代江南農村 社会の研究. Tokyo: Tokyo daigaku shuppankai.
Hamashita, Takeshi. 2008a. "China and Hong Kong in the British Empire in the Late Nineteenth and Early Twentieth Centuries." In T. Hamashita, *China, East Asia, and the Global Economy: Regional and Historical Perspectives*, 146–66. London: Routledge.
2008b. "Maritime Asia and Treaty Port Networks in the Era of Negotiation: Tribute and Treaties, 1800–1900." In T. Hamashita, *China, East Asia, and the Global Economy*, 85–112. London: Routledge.
2008c. "Overseas Chinese Financial Networks: Korea, China, and Japan in the Late Nineteenth Century." In T. Hamashita, *China, East Asia, and the Global Economy*, 167–78. London: Routledge.
Hamilton, Gary, and Wei-an Chang. 2003. "The Importance of Commerce in the Organization of China's Late Imperial Economy." In G. Arrighi, T. Hamashita, and M. Selden, eds. *The Resurgence of East Asia: 500, 150, and 50 Year Perspectives*, 173–213. London: Routledge.
Handlin Smith, Joanna. 2009. *The Art of Doing Good: Charity in Late Ming China*. Berkeley: University of California Press.
Hansen, Valerie. 1995. *Negotiating Daily Life in Traditional China: How Ordinary People Used Contracts, 600–1400*. New Haven: Yale University Press.
2012. *The Silk Road: A New History*. New York: Oxford University Press.
Hao, Yen-p'ing. 1986. *The Commercial Revolution in Nineteenth-Century China*. Berkeley: University of California Press.
Hartwell, Robert M. 1962. "A Revolution in the Chinese Iron and Coal Industries during the Northern Sung, 960–1126 AD." *Journal of Asian Studies* 21.1: 153–62.

1966. "Markets, Technology, and the Structure of Enterprise in the Development of the Eleventh-century Chinese Iron and Steel Industry." *Journal of Economic History* 26.1: 29–58.

1967. "A Cycle of Economic Change in Imperial China: Coal and Iron in Northeast China, 750–1350," *Journal of the Economic and Social History of the Orient* 10: 102–159.

1971. "Financial Expertise, Examinations, and the Formulation of Economic Policy in Northern Sung China." *Journal of Asian Studies* 30.2: 281–314.

1982. "Demographic, Political, and Social Transformation of China, 750–1550," *Harvard Journal of Asiatic Studies* 42.2: 365–442.

1988. "The Imperial Treasuries: Finance and Power in Song China." *Bulletin of Sung-Yuan Studies* 20: 18–89.

1989. "Foreign Trade, Monetary Policy, and Chinese 'Mercantilism.'" In *Ryū Shiken hakase shōju kinen Sōshi kenkyū ronshū* 劉子健博士頌寿記念宋史研究論集, pp. 454–88. Kinugawa Tsuyoshi 衣川強, ed. Kyoto: Dōbunsha.

Hashimoto Takashi 橋本健史. 2007. "Tōichi Shin ni okeru gō no kinō: kokka to zaichi shakai no setten" 統一秦における郷の機能:国家と在地社会の接点. In Ōta Yukio 太田幸男 and Tada Kensuke 多田狷介, eds. *Chūgoku zenkindai shi ronshū* 中国前近代史論集, 111–45. Tokyo: Kyūko shoin.

Hayami Akira 速水融. 1979. "Kinsei Nihon no keizai hatten to 'Industrious Revolution.'" 近世 日本の経済発展と 'Industrious Revolution.' In Shinbō Hiroshi 新保博and Yasuba Yasukichi 安場保吉, eds. *Kindai ikōki no Nihon keizai* 近代移 行期の日本経済, 3–14. Tokyo: Nihon keizai shimbunsha.

He Bingdi 何炳棣. 1988. *Zhongguo gujin tudi shuzide kaoshi he pingjia* 中國古今土地數字的 考釋和評價. Beijing: Zhongguo shehui kexue chubanshe.

He Qinggu 何清谷. 2003a. "Qin Shihuang shidaide siying gongshangye" 秦始皇時代的私 營工商業. In He Qinggu, *Qinshi tansuo* 秦史探索, 326–35. Taipei: Liantai chubanshe.

2003b. "Qinbi chunqiu" 秦幣春秋. In He Qinggu, *Qinshi tansuo* 秦史探索, 300–25. Taipei: Liantai chubanshe.

He Shuangquan 何双全. 1989. "'Hanjian xiangli zhi' jiqi yanjiu"《汉简。乡里志》及其研究. In Gansusheng wenwu kaogu yanjiusuo 甘肃省文物考古研究所, ed. *Qin Han jiandu lunwenji* 秦汉简牍论文集, 145–235. Lanzhou: Gansu renmin chubanshe.

He, Wenkai. 2013. *Paths toward the Modern Fiscal State: England, Japan, and China.* Cambridge: Harvard University Press.

Heckscher, Eli F. 1955. *Mercantilism.* Rev. edn, London: George Allen and Unwin.

Heijdra, Martin. 1998. "The Socio-Economic Development of Rural China during the Ming." In D. C. Twitchett and F. W. Mote, eds. *The Cambridge History of China, vol. 8: The Ming Dynasty, 1368–1644, part 2,* 417–578. Cambridge University Press.

Heng, Derek. 2009. *Sino-Malay Trade and Diplomacy from the Tenth through the Fourteenth Century.* Athens, OH: Ohio University Press.

Higashi Ichio 東一夫. 1970. *Ō Anseki shimpō no kenkyū* 王安石新法の研究. Tokyo: Kazama shobō.

Higo Masaki 肥後政紀. 1990. "Zen Kanchō no jinkōsū ni tsuite: ōkoku-kōkoku no kosū tōkei shori o chūshin to shite" 前漢朝の人口数について:王国・侯国の戸数統計処理を中 心として. *Shūkan tōyōgaku* 集刊東洋学 64: 115–31.

Hino Kaisaburō 日野開三郎. 1980. *Hino Kaisaburō Tōyō shigaku ronshū*日野開三郎東洋史 学論集, vol. 2: *Godai shi no kichō* 五代史の基調. Tokyo: Sanichi shobō.

1982. *Hino Kaisaburō Tōyō shigaku ronshū, vol. 5: Tō Godai no kahei to kinyū* 唐五代の貨幣と金融. Tokyo: Sanichi shobō.

1984. *Hino Kaisaburō Tōyō shigaku ronshū*, vol. 10: *Hokutō Ajia kokusai kōryū shi no kenkyū* 北東アジア国際交流史の研究. Tokyo: Sanichi shobō.

1988. *Hino Kaisaburō Tōyō shigaku ronshū*, vol. 11: *Kokō mondai to tekibaihō* 戸口 問題と糴買法. Tokyo: Sanichi shobō.

Hiyama Miko 日山美子. 1996. "Shindai tentōgyō no rishiritsu ni kan suru ichi kōsatsu: Kōki-Kenryū ki no Kōnan o chūshin toshite 清代典当業の利子率に関する一考察:康熙—乾隆期の江南を中心として. *Tōhōgaku* 東方学 91: 76–89.

Ho, Chuimei. 2001. "The Ceramic Boom in Minnan during Song and Yuan Times." In A. Schottenhammer, ed. *The Emporium of the World: Maritime Quanzhou, 1000–1400*, 237–81. Leiden: Brill.

Ho, Ping-ti. 1959. *Studies on the Population of China, 1368–1953*. Cambridge: Harvard University Press.

Holcombe, Charles. 2001. *The Genesis of East Asia, 221 BC–AD 907*. Honolulu: University of Hawai'i Press.

Holmgren, Jennifer. 1983. "The Harem in Northern Wei Politics, 398–498 AD: A Study of T'o-pa Attitudes towards the Institutions of Empress, Empress-Dowager, and Regency Governments in the Chinese Dynastic System during Early Northern Wei." *Journal of the Economic and Social History of the Orient* 26.1: 71–96.

Honda Osamu 本多治. 2000a. "Chūgoku nōgyō shi no sōron" 中国農業史の総論. In Matsuda Kōichi 松田孝一, ed. *Higashi Ajia keizaishi no shomondai* 東アジア経済史の 諸問題, 3–16. Kyoto: A'unsha.

2000b. "Chūgoku suiri kaihatsu shi: Kōnan" 中国水利開発史—江南. In Matsuda Kōichi 松田孝一, ed. *Higashi Ajia keizaishi no shomondai* 東アジア経済史の 諸問題, 38–55. Kyoto: A'unsha.

Hong Yi 弘一. 1974. "Jiangling Fenghuangshan shihao Hanmu chutu jiandu kaoshi" 江陵凤凰 山十号汉墓出土简牍考释. *Wenwu* 文物 6: 78–84.

Horesh, Niv. 2009. *Bund and Beyond: British Banks, Banknote Issuance, and Monetary Policy in China, 1842–1937*. New Haven: Yale University Press.

Hori Toshikazu 堀敏一. 1975. *Kindensei no kenkyū: Chūgoku kodai kokka no tochi seisaku to tochi shoyūsei* 均田制の研究:中国古代国家の土地政策と土地所有制. Tokyo: Iwanami shoten.

1994. "Chūgoku kodai no henkosei: tokuni shūryaku no hensen" 中国古代の編戸制:特に集落の変遷. In Hori, *Chūgoku kodaishi no shiten* 中国古代史の視点, 271–303. Tokyo: Kyūko shoin.

1996. *Chūgoku kodai no ie to shūryaku* 中国古代の家と集落. Tokyo: Kyūko shoin.

Hou Xudong 侯旭东. 2005. *Beichao cunminde shenghuo shijie: chaoting, zhouxian, yu cunli* 北朝村民的生活世界:朝廷,州县,与村里. Beijing: Shangwu yinshuguan.

Hsiao, Kung-ch'üan. 1960. *Rural China: Imperial Control in the Nineteenth Century*. Seattle: University of Washington Press.

Hsieh, Ming-liang. 2010. "The Navigational Route of the Belitung Shipwreck and the Late Tang Ceramic Trade." In R. Krahl *et al.*, ed. *Shipwrecked: Tang Treasures and Monsoon Winds*, 137–43. Washington, DC: Smithsonian Institution.

Hsu, Cho-yun. 1980. *Han Agriculture: The Formation of Early Chinese Agrarian Economy (206 BC–AD 220)*. Seattle: University of Washington Press.

Hsu, Cho-yun and Kathryn M. Linduff. 1988. *Western Chou Civilization*. New Haven: Yale University Press.

Hu Jichuang 胡寄窗. 1962. *Zhongguo jingji sixiang shi* 中國經濟思想史. Shanghai: Shanghai renmin chubanshe.

Huang Chunyan 黄纯艳. 2003. *Songdai haiwai maoyi* 宋代海外贸易. Beijing: Shehui kexue wenxian chubanshe.

Huang Jianhui 黄鉴晖. 1987. "Qingdai zhangju chutan" 清代帐局初探. *Lishi yanjiu* 历史研究 1: 111–24.

Huang Jingbin 黄敬斌. 2009. *Minsheng yu jiaji: Qingchu zhi Minguo shiqi Jiangnan juminde xiaofei* 民生与家计:清初至民国时期江南居民的消费. Shanghai: Fudan daxue chubanshe.

Huang Jinyan 黄今言. 2005. *Qin Han shangpin jingji yanjiu* 秦汉商品经济研究. Beijing: Renmin chubanshe.

Huang, Philip C. C. 1985. *The Peasant Economy and Social Change in North China*. Stanford University Press.

1990. *The Peasant Family and Rural Development in the Yangzi Delta, 1350–1988*. Stanford University Press.

Huang, Ray. 1974. *Taxation and Governmental Finance in Sixteenth-century Ming China*. New York: Cambridge University Press

Huang Shengzhang 黄盛璋. 1974a. "Jiangling Fenghuangshan Hanmu jiandu jiqi zai lishi dili yanjiu shangde jiazhi" 江陵凤凰山汉墓简牍及其在历史地理上的价值. *Wenwu* 文物 6: 66–77.

1974b. "Shilun San Jin bingqide guobie he niandai jiqi xiangguan wenti" 试论三晋兵器的国别和年代及其相关问题. *Kaogu xuebao* 考古学报 1: 13–43.

1977. "Guanyu Fenghuangshan yiliuba hao Hanmude jige wenti" 关于凤凰山一六八号汉墓的几个问题. *Kaogu* 考古 1: 43–50.

1982. "Qingchuan xinchu Qin tianlü mudu jiqi xiangguan wenti" 青川新出秦田律木牍及其相关问题. *Wenwu* 文物 9: 71–75.

2001. "Qin bingqi fenguo duandai yu youguan zhidu yanjiu" 秦兵器分国断代与有关制度研究. *Gu wenzi yanjiu* 古文字研究 21: 227–85.

Hulsewé, Anthony. 1981. "The Legalists and the Laws of Ch'in." In W. L. Idema, ed. *Leyden Studies in Sinology*, 1–22. Leiden: Brill.

1985a. "The Influence of the 'Legalist' Government of Qin on the Economy as Reflected in the Texts Discovered in Yunmeng County." In S. Schram, ed. *The Scope of State Power in China*, 211–35. London: School of Oriental and African Studies.

1985b. *Remnants of Ch'in Law: An Annotated Translation of the Ch'in Legal and Administrative Rules of the 3rd Century BC Discovered in Yun-meng Prefecture, Hu-pei Province, in 1975*. Leiden: Brill.

Hymes, Robert P. 1993. "Moral Duty and Self-Regulating Process in Southern Sung Views of Famine Relief." In R. P. Hymes and C. Schirokauer, eds. *Ordering the World: Approaches to State and Society in Sung Dynasty China*, 280–309. Berkeley: University of California Press.

Ibn Battuta. 1929. *Travels in Asia and Africa, 1325–1354*. Trans. H. A. R. Gibbs. London: Routledge and Kegan Paul.

Iida Sachiko 飯田祥子. 2004. "Zen Kan kōhanki ni okeru gunken min shihai no henka: naigun to hengun no bunka kara" 前漢後半期における郡県民支配の変化:内群と辺群の分 化から. *Tōyō gakuhō* 東洋学報 86.3: 1–36.

Iio Hideyuki 飯尾秀幸. 2007. "Shin-Zen Kan shoki ni okeru ri no uchi to soto: rōgoku seiritsu zenshi" 秦・前漢初期における里の内と外:牢獄成立前史. In Ōta Yukio 太田幸男 and Tada Kensuke 多田狷介, eds. *Chūgoku zenkindai shi ronshū* 中国前近代史論集, 147–72. Tokyo: Kyūko shoin.

Ikeda On 池田温. 1973. "T'ang Household Registers and Related Documents." In A. F. Wright and D. Twitchett, eds. *Perspectives on the T'ang*, 121–50. New Haven: Yale University Press.

1979. *Chūgoku kodai sekichō kenkyū: gaikan, rokubun* 中国古代籍帳研究:概観, 録文. Tokyo: Tokyo daigaku shuppankai.

1988. "Shinryū sannen Kōshōken Sūkagō tensekiyō ni tsuite" 神竜三年高昌県崇化郷点籍様について. In *Kurihara Masuo sensei koki kinen ronshū Chūgoku kodai no hō to shakai* 栗原益男先生古希記念論集中国古代の法と社会, 245–70. Tokyo: Kyūko shoin.

Ikeda Yūichi 池田雄一. 2008a. "Ri Kai no 'Hōkyō'" 李悝の「法経」. In Ikeda, *Chūgoku kodai no ritsuryō to shakai* 中国古代の律令と社会, 76–146. Tokyo: Kyūko shoin.

2008b. "Ryogō 'Ninen ritsuryō' o meguru shomondai" 呂后「二年律令」をめぐる諸問題. In Ikeda, *Chūgoku kodai no ritsuryō to shakai* 中国古代の律令と社会, 446–511. Tokyo: Kyūko shoin.

Inaba Ichirō 稲葉一郎. 1978. "Shin Shikō no kahei tōichi ni tsuite" 秦始皇の貨幣統一について. *Tōyōshi kenkyū* 東洋史研究 37.1: 59–85.

1984. "Kandai no kazoku keitai to keizai hendō" 漢代の家族形態と経済変動. *Tōyōshi kenkyū* 東洋史研究 43.1: 88–117.

2007. "Nan-gun no kensetsu to Sengoku Shin no kahei seido" 南郡の建設と戦国秦の貨幣制度. *Shirin* 史林 90.2: 239–67.

Irigoin, Alejandra. 2009. "The End of a Silver Era: The Consequences of the Breakdown of the Spanish Peso Standard in China and the United States, 1780s–1850s." *Journal of World History* 20.2: 207–43.

Ishihara Jun 石原潤. 1973. "Kahokushō ni okeru Min Shin Minkoku jidai no teikiichi bunpu kaisō oyobi chūshin shūraku no kankei ni tsuite" 河北省における明清民国時代の定期市分 布階層および中心聚落の関係について. *Chirigaku hyōron* 地理学評論 46.4: 245–63.

Itō Michiharu 伊藤道治. 1975. *Chūgoku kodai ōchō no keisei: shutsudo shiryō o chūshin to suru In Shū shi no kenkyū* 中国王朝の形成: 出土史料を中心とする殷周史の研究. Tokyo: Sōbunsha.

1978. "Kyūei shoki kō: Sei Shū-ki tochi shoyū keitai ni kansuru shiken" 裘衛諸器 考: 西周期土地所有形態に関する私見. *Tōyōshi kenkyū* 東洋史研究 37.1: 35–58.

1987. *Chūgoku kodai kokka no shihai kōzō: Sei Shū hōken seido to kinbun* 中国古代国家の支配構造: 西周封建制度と金文. Tokyo: Chūō kōronsha.

Jia Daquan 贾大泉. 1981. "Songdai fushui jiegou chutan" 宋代赋税结构初探. *Shehui kexue yanjiu* 社会科学研究 3: 51–8.

Jiang Fuya 蔣福亞. 2005. *Wei Jin Nanbeichao shehui jingji shi* 魏晋南北朝社会经济史. Tianjin: Tianjin guji chubanshe.

2008. "Wujian suojian Wuguo qianqi mintian tuntian – jianlun Wei Wu mintunde qubie" 吳簡所見吳國前期民田屯田 – 兼論魏吳民屯的區別. *Zhonghua wenshi luncong* 中華文史論叢 89: 13–57.

Jiang Tao 姜涛. 1993. *Zhongguo jindai renkou shi* 中国近代人口史. Hangzhou: Zhejiang renmin chubanshe.

Jiang Xidong 姜锡东. 2002. *Songdai shangren yu shangye ziben* 宋代商人与商业资本. Beijing: Zhonghua shuju.

Kagotani, Naoto. 2005. "The Chinese Merchant Community in Kobe and the Development of the Japanese Cotton Industry, 1890–1941." In Sugihara Kaoru, ed. *Japan, China, and the Growth of the Asian International Economy, 1850–1949*, 49–72. Oxford University Press.

Kakinuma Yōhei 柿沼陽平. 2010. "Shindai kahei keizai no kōzō to sono tokushitsu" 晋代貨幣経済の構造とその特質. *Tōhōgaku* 東方学 120: 18–33.

2011. *Chūgoku kodai kahei keizai shi kenkyū* 中国古代貨幣経済史研究. Tokyo: Kyūko shoin.

Kamei Meitoku 亀井明徳. 1992. "Tōdai tōji bōeki no tenkai to shōnin" 唐代陶磁貿易の展開と商人. In Arano Yasunori 荒野泰典 et al., ed. *Ajia no naka no Nihonshi* アジアのなかの日本史, vol. 3: *Kaijō no michi* 海上の道, 115–45. Tokyo: Tokyo daigaku shuppankai.

Kamiya Masakazu 紙屋正和. 1994. "Ryō Kan jidai no shōgyō to ichi" 両漢時代の商業と市. *Tōyōshi kenkyū* 東洋史研究 52.4: 655–82.

Kanaya Osamu 金谷治. 1987. *Kanshi no kenkyū* 管子の研究. Tokyo: Iwanami shoten.

Kaske, Elisabeth. 2011. "Fund-Raising Wars: Office-Selling and Interprovincial Finance in Nineteenth Century China." *Harvard Journal of Asiatic Studies* 71.1: 69–141.

2015. "Silver, Copper, Rice, and Debt: Monetary Policy and Office Selling in China during the Taiping Rebellion." In J. K. Leonard and U. Theobald, eds. *Money in Asia (1200–1900): Small Currencies in Social and Political Contexts*, 343–97. Leiden: Brill.

Katō Shigeshi 加藤繁. 1937. "On the Hang or the Association of Merchants in China, with Special Reference to the Institution in the T'ang and Sung Periods." *Memoirs of the Research Department of the Tōyō Bunko* 8: 45–83.

1952a. "Shindai ni okeru sonchin no teikiichi" 清代に於ける村鎮の定期市. In Katō Shigeshi 加藤繁. *Shina keizai shi kōshō* 支那経済史考証, vol. 2: 505–56. Tokyo: Tōyō bunko.

1952b. "Sōdai ni okeru toshi no hattatsu ni tsuite" 宋代に於ける都市の発達に就いて. In Katō Shigeshi 加藤繁. *Shina keizai shi kōshō* 支那経済史考証, vol 1: 299–346. Tokyo: Tōyō bunko.

1952c. "Sōdai no shōshūkan 'sha' ni tsuite" 宋代の商習慣「賒」に就いて. In Katō Shigeshi 加藤繁. *Shina keizai shi kōshō* 支那経済史考証, vol. 1: 222–34. Tokyo: Tōyō bunko.

1952d. "Tō Sō jidai no ichi" 唐宋時代の市. In Katō Shigeshi 加藤繁. *Shina keizai shi kōshō* 支那経済史考証, vol. 1: 347–79. Tokyo: Tōyō bunko.

1952e. "Tō Sō jidai no shōen no soshiki narabini sono shūraku to shite hattatsu ni tsuite" 唐宋時代の庄園の組織並に其の聚落として発達に就いて. In Katō Shigeshi 加藤繁. *Shina keizai shi kōshō* 支那経済史考証, vol. 1: 231–60. Tokyo: Tōyō bunko.

Katsari, Constantina. 2011. *The Roman Monetary System: The Eastern Provinces from the First to the Third Century AD*. Cambridge University Press.

Kawakatsu Heita 川勝平太. 1991. *Nihon bunmei to kindai seiyō: "sakoku" saikō* 日本文明 と近代西洋:《鎖国》再考. Tokyo: NHK bukkusu.

Kawakatsu Yoshio川勝義雄. 1982. *Rikuchō kizokusei shakai no kenkyū* 六朝貴族制社 会の研究. Tokyo: Iwanami Shoten.

Kawazoe Shōji 川添昭二. 1993. "Kamakura makki no taigai kankei to Hakata: Shin'an chinbotsusen mokkan · Tōfukuji · Jōtenji" 鎌倉末期の対外関係と博多:新安沈没船 木簡 · 東福寺 · 承天寺. In Ōsumi Kazuo 大隅和雄, ed. *Kamakura jidai bunka denpan no kenkyū* 鎌倉時代文化伝 播の研究, 301–30. Yoshikawa kōbunkan.

Kegasawa Yasunori 気賀澤保規. 1999. *Fuheisei no kenkyū: fuhei heishi to sono shakai* 府兵 制の研究:府兵兵士とその社会. Tokyo: Dōhōsha.

Keller, Wolfgang, Ben Li, and Carole H. Shiue. 2012. "The Evolution of Domestic Trade Flows When Foreign Trade is Liberalized: Evidence from the Chinese Maritime Customs Services." In Masahiko Aoki, Timur Kuran, and Gérard Roland, eds. *Institutions and Comparative Economic Development*, 152–72. Houndmills: Palgrave Macmillan.

2013. "Shanghai's Trade, China's Growth: Continuity, Recovery, and Change since the Opium War." *IMF Economic Review* 61.2: 336–78.

Khazanov, Anatoly. 1989. *Nomads and the Outside World*. Cambridge University Press.

Kidder, J. Edward, Jr. 2007. *Himiko and Japan's Elusive Chiefdom of Yamatai: Archaeology, History, and Mythology*. Honolulu: University of Hawai'i Press.

Kidder, Tristram R., Haiwang Liu, and Minglin Li. 2012. "Sanyangzhuang: Early Farming and a Han Settlement Preserved Beneath Yellow River Flood Deposits." *Antiquity* 86.331: 30–47.

Kieschnik, John. 2003. *The Impact of Buddhism on Chinese Material Culture*. Princeton University Press.

King, Frank H. H. 1965. *Money and Monetary Policy in China, 1845–1895*. Cambridge: Harvard University Press.

Kirby, William C. 1995. "China Unincorporated: Company Law and Business Enterprise in Twentieth-Century China." *Journal of Asian Studies* 54.1: 43–63.

Kishimoto Mio 岸本美緒. 1997. *Shindai Chūgoku no bukka to keizai hendō* 清代中国の物価 と経済変動. Tokyo: Kembun shuppan.

2007. "Tochi shijō to 'sōka kaishoku' mondai: Sōdai kara Shindai no chōkiteki dōkō" 土地市場と「找価回贖」問題: 宋代から清代の長期的動向. In Ōshima Ritsuko 大島 立子, ed. *Sō – Shindai no hō to chiiki shakai* 宋 – 清代の法と地域社会, pp. 213–62. Tokyo: Tōyō bunko.

2009. "New Studies on Statecraft in Mid- and Late-Qing: Qing Intellectuals and their Debates on Economic Policies." *International Journal of Asian Studies* 6.1: 87–102.

2011. "Property Rights, Land, and Law in Imperial China." In D. Ma and J. L. van Zanden, eds. *Law and Long-Term Economic Change: A Eurasian Perspective*, 68–90. Stanford University Press.

Kishimoto-Nakayama, Mio. 1984. "The Kangxi Depression and Early Qing Local Markets." *Modern China* 10.2: 226–56.

Knoblock, John. 1988. *Xunzi: A Translation and Study of the Complete Works.* Stanford University Press.

Knoblock, John, and Jeffrey Riegel, trans. 2000. *The Annals of Lü Buwei.* Stanford University Press.

Kong Xiangjun 孔祥军. 2012. "Juyan xinjian 'Jianwu sannian shieryue hou Su jun suo ze Kou En shi' ceshu fuyuan yu yanjiu" 居延新简《建武三年十二月候粟君所责寇恩事》册 书复原与研究. *Xiyu yanjiu* 西域研究 4: 76–86.

Kroll, J. L. 1978–79. "Toward a Study of the Economic Views of Sang Hung-yang." *Early China* 4: 11–18.

Kuhn, Dieter. 2009. *The Age of Confucian Rule: The Song Transformation of China.* Cambridge: Harvard University Press.

Kuhn, Philip A. 2008. *Chinese Among Others: Emigration in Modern Times.* Lanham, MD: Rowman and Littlefield.

Kumamoto Takashi 熊本崇. 1983. "Ō Anseki no shiekihō to shōnin" 王安石の市易法と商人. *Bunka* 文化 46.3–4: 168–88.

Kuribayashi Norio 栗林宣夫. 1971. *Rikasei no kenkyū* 里甲制の研究. Tokyo: Bunri shoin.

Kurihara Masuo 栗原益男. 1964. "Fuheisei no hōkai to shin heishu: zenhanki Tōchō shihai no hōkai ni kansuru jakkan no kōsatsu o fukumete" 府兵制の崩壊と新兵種:前半期唐朝 支配の崩壊に関する若干の考察をふくめて. *Shigaku zasshi* 史学雑誌 73.2: 121–46, 73.3: 269–95.

Kuroda Akinobu 黒田明伸. 1987. "Kenryū no senki" 乾隆の銭貴. *Tōyōshi kenkyū* 東洋史研 究 45.5: 692–723.

    2000. "Another Monetary Economy: The Case of Traditional China." In A. J. H. Lathan and H. Kawakatsu, eds. *Asia-Pacific Dynamism, 1500–2000,* 187–98. London: Routledge.

    2008. "Concurrent but Non-Integrable Currency Circuits: Complementary Relationships among Monies in Modern China and Other Regions." *Financial History Review* 15.1: 17–36.

    2009. "The Eurasian Silver Century (1276–1359): Commensurability and Multiplicity." *Journal of Global History* 4: 245–69.

Kusano Yasushi 草野靖. 1996. "Nōgyō tochi mondai" 農業土地問題. In Satake Yasuhiko 佐竹靖彦 et al., eds. *Sō Gen jidaishi no kihon mondai* 宋元時代史の基本問題, 303–31. Tokyo: Kyūko shoin.

Kwan, Man Bun. 2001. *The Salt Merchants of Tianjin: State Making and Civil Society in Late Imperial China.* Honolulu: University of Hawai'i Press.

    2004. "Custom, the Code, and Legal Practice: The Contracts of Changlu Salt Merchants in Late Imperial China." In M. Zelin, J. K. Ocko, and R. Gardella, eds. *Contract and Property in Early Modern China,* 269–97. Stanford University Press.

Kwee, Hui Kian. 2007. "Pockets of Empire: Integrating the Studies on Social Organizations in Southeast China and Southeast Asia." *Comparative Studies of South Asia, Africa, and the Middle East* 27.3: 616–32.

    2013. "Chinese Economic Dominance in Southeast Asia: A Longue Durée Perspective." *Comparative Studies in Society and History* 55.1: 5–34.

Lai, Chi-kong. 1992. "The Qing State and Merchant Enterprise: The China Merchants' Company, 1872–1902." In J. K. Leonard and J. R. Watt, eds. *To Achieve Security and Wealth: The Qing Imperial State and the Economy, 1644–1911,* 139–55. Ithaca, NY: Cornell University East Asia Program.

Lai Ming-chiu (Li Mingzhao) 黎明釗. 2009. "Liye Qinjian: huji dangande tantao" 里耶
秦簡: 户籍档案的探讨. *Zhongguoshi yanjiu* 中国史研究 2: 5–23.
Lamouroux, Christian. 1991. "Organisation territorial et monopole du thé dans la
Chine des Song (960–1059)." *Annales: Économies, Sociétés, Civilisations* 46.5:
977–1008.
  2002. "Commerce et bureaucratie dans la Chine des Song." *Études rurales* 161–62:
183–213.
  2003. *Fiscalité, comptes publics et politiques financières dans la Chine des Song:
Le Chapitre 179 du Songshi.* Paris: Institut des hautes études chinoises.
  2007. "Bureaucratie et monnaie dans la Chine du XIe siècle: les désordes monétaires
au Shaanxi." In B. Théret, ed. *La Monnaie dévoilée par ses crises, vol. 1, Crises
monétaires d'hier et d'aujourd'hui*, 171–204. Paris: École des hautes études en
sciences sociales.
Landes, David S. 1998. *The Wealth and Poverty of Nations: Why Some are so Rich and
Some so Poor.* New York: Norton.
Lee, James Z., and Cameron Campbell. 1997. *Fate and Fortune in Rural China: Social
Organization and Population Behavior in Liaoning, 1774–1873.* Cambridge
University Press.
Lee, James Z., and Wang Feng. 1999. *One Quarter of Humanity: Malthusian
Mythology and Chinese Realities, 1700–2000.* Cambridge: Harvard University
Press.
Leonard, Jane Kate. 1996. *Controlling from Afar: The Daoguang Emperor's
Management of the Grand Canal Crisis, 1824–1826.* Ann Arbor: University of
Michigan Center for Chinese Studies.
Lewis, Mark Edward. 1990. *Sanctioned Violence in Early China.* Albany, NY:
State University of New York Press.
  1999. "Warring States Political History." In M. Loewe and E. L. Shaughnessy, eds.
*The Cambridge History of Ancient China: From the Origins of Civilization to
211 BC*, 587–650. Cambridge University Press.
  2000a. "The City-State in Spring-and-Autumn China." In Mogens Herman Hansen,
ed. *A Comparative Study of Thirty City-State Cultures*, 359–73. Copenhagen:
Kongelige Danske Videnskabernes Selskab.
  2000b. "The Han Abolition of Universal Military Service." In Hans van de Ven, ed.
Warfare in Chinese History, 33–75. Leiden: Brill.
  2006. *The Construction of Space in Early China.* Albany, NY: State University of
New York Press.
  2009. *China between Empires: The Northern and Southern Dynasties.* Cambridge:
Harvard University Press.
Li Bozhong 李伯重. 1990. *Tangdai Jiangnan nongyede fazhan* 唐代江南农业的发展.
Beijing: Nongye chubanshe.
  1998. *Agricultural Development in Jiangnan, 1620–1850.* London: Macmillan.
  2000. *Jiangnande zaoqi gongyehua* 江南的早期工业化. Beijing: Shehui kexue
wenxian chubanshe.
  2002. *Fazhan yu zhiyue: Ming Qing Jiangnan shengchanli yanjiu* 發展與制約:
明清江南生產力研究. Taipei: Lianjing chubanshe.
  2003. "Was There a 'Fourteenth-Century Turning Point? Population, Land,
Technology, and Farm Management." In P. J. Smith and R. von Glahn, eds.

The Song-Yuan-Ming Transition in Chinese History, 135–75. Cambridge: Harvard University Asia Center.

2007. "Daoguang xiaotiao yu guiwei dashui" 道光萧条与癸未大水. *Shehui kexue* 社会科学 6: 173–78.

2010. *Zhongguode zaoqi jindai jingji: 1820 niandai Huating-Louxian diqu GDP yanjiu* 中国的早期近代经济: *1820年代华亭—娄县地区 GDP 研究*. Beijing: Zhonghua shuju.

2013. "An Early Modern Economy in China: A Study of the GDP of the Huating-Lou Area, 1823–1829." In B. K. L. So, ed. *The Economic History of Lower Yangzi Delta in Late Imperial China: Connecting Money, Markets, and Institutions*, 133–45. London: Routledge.

Li, Bozhong 李伯重 and Jan Luiten van Zanden. 2012. "Before the Great Divergence? Comparing the Yangzi Delta and the Netherlands in the Beginning of the Nineteenth Century." *Journal of Economic History* 72.4: 956–89.

Li, Feng. 2006. *Landscape and Power in Early China: The Crisis and Fall of the Western Zhou, 1045–771 BC*. Cambridge University Press.

2008. *Bureaucracy and the State in Early China: Governing the Western Zhou, 1045–771 BC*. Cambridge University Press.

Li Huarui 李华瑞. 1995. *Songdai jiude shengchan he zhengque* 宋代酒的生产和征榷. Baoding: Hebei daxue chubanshe.

Li Li 李力. 2007. *"Lichenqie" shenfen zaiyanjiu* 「隶臣妾」身份再研究. Beijing: Zhongguo fazhi chubanshe.

Li, Lillian M. 1981. *China's Silk Trade: Traditional Industry in the Modern World, 1842–1937*. Cambridge: Council on East Asian Studies, Harvard University.

1992. "Grain Prices in Zhili Province, 1736–1911: A Preliminary Study." In T. G. Rawski and L. M. Li, eds. *Chinese History in Economic Perspective*, 69–99. Berkeley: University of California Press.

2007. *Fighting Famine in North China: State, Market, and Environmental Decline, 1690s–1990s*. Stanford University Press.

Li Ling 李零. 1998. "Xi Zhou jinwen zhongde tudi zhidu" 西周金文中的土地制度. In *Li Ling zixuan ji* 李零自选集, 85–111. Guilin: Guangxi shifan daxue chubanshe.

Li Longsheng 李隆生. 2005. *Wan Ming haiwai maoyi shuliangde yanjiu: jian lun Jiangnan sichou chanye yu baiyin liurude yingxiang* 晚明海外贸易数量的研究：兼論江南絲綢 產業與白銀流入的影響. Taibei: Xiuwei zixun keji.

2010. *Qingdaide guoji maoyi: baiyin liuru, huobi weiji he Wan Qing gongyehua* 清代的國際貿易：白銀流入,貨幣危機和晚清工業化. Taipei: Xiuwei zixun keji.

Li, Min. 2003. "Ji'nan in the First Millennium BC: Archaeology and History." *Journal of the Economic and Social History of the Orient* 46.1: 88–126.

Li Ping 李凭. 2000. *Bei Wei Pingcheng shidai* 北魏平城时代. Beijing: Shehui kexue wenxian chubanshe.

Li, Tana. 2004. "The Water Frontier: An Introduction." In N. Cooke and T. Li, eds. *Water Frontier: Commerce and the Chinese in the Lower Mekong Region, 1750–1880*, 1–17. Lanham, MD: Rowman and Littlefield.

Li Weiguo 李伟国. 2007. "Songdai jingji shenghuo zhongde shikuai" 宋代经济生活中的市侩. In Li, *Songdai caizheng he wenxian kaolun* 宋代财政和文献考论, 123–47. Shanghai: Shanghai guji chubanshe.

Li, Wenying. 2012. "Silk Artistry of the Northern and Southern Dynasties." In Dieter Kuhn, ed. *Chinese Silks*, 167–201. New Haven: Yale University Press.

Li Wenzhi 李文治 and Jiang Taixin 江太新. 2005. *Zhongguo dizhuzhi jingji lun: fengjian tudi guanxi fazhan yu bianhua* 中国地主制经济论: 封建土地关系发展与变化. Beijing: Zhongguo shehui kexue chubanshe.

Li Xueqin 李学勤. 1982. "Qingchuan Hejiaping mudu yanjiu" 青川郝家坪木牍研究. *Wenwu* 文物 10: 68–72.

1999. "Qinjian yu Zhouli" 秦简与周礼. In Li Xueqin, *Jianbo dieji yu xueshu shi* 简帛迭籍与学术史, 110–18. Nanchang: Jiangxi jiaoyu chubanshe.

Li, Xueqin and Xing Wen. 2001. "New Light on the Early-Han Code: A Reappraisal of the Zhangjiashan Bamboo-Slip Legal Texts." *Asia Major*, 3rd series, 14.1: 125–46.

Li, Yung-ti. 2006. "On the Function of Cowries in Shang and Western Zhou China." *Journal of East Asian Archaeology* 5.1–4: 1–26.

Li Zhi'an 李治安. 1992. *Yuandai fenfeng zhidu yanjiu* 元代分封制度研究. Tianjin: Tianjin guji chubanshe.

Liang Fangzhong 梁方仲. 1939. "Mingdai guoji maoyi yu yinde shuchuru" 明代國際貿易與銀的輸出入. Rpt. in Liang, 1990. *Liang Fangzhong jingji shi lunwen ji* 梁方仲經濟史論文集, 132–179. Beijing: Zhonghua shuju,

ed. 1980. *Zhongguo lidai hukou tiandi tianfu tongji* 中国历代户口 田地田賦统计. Shanghai: Shanghai renmin chubanshe.

Liang Gengyao 梁庚堯. 1984. *Nan Songde nongcun jingji* 南宋的農村經濟. Taipei: Lianjing chuban shiye gongsi.

1997. "Nan Song chengshide fazhan" 南宋城市的發展. In Liang, *Songdai shehui jingji shi lunji* 宋代社會經濟史論集, 2: 481–590. Taipei: Yunchen wenhua.

Liang Qizi 梁其姿. 1993. "Pinqiong yu qiongren guannian zai Zhongguo sushi shehui zhongde lishi yanbian" 貧窮與窮人觀念在中國俗世社會中的歷史演變. In Huang Yinggui 黃應貴, ed. *Renguan, yiyi, yu shehui* 人觀, 意義, 與社會, 129–62. Taipei: Zhongyang yanjiuyuan minzuxue yanjiusuo.

1997. *Shishan yu jiaohua: Ming Qingde cishan zuzhi* 施善與教化:明清的慈善組織. Taipei: Lianjing chuban shiye gongsi.

Lianyungang shi bowuguan 连云港市博物馆. 1996. "Yinwan Hanmu jiandu shiwen xuan" 尹湾汉墓简牍释文选. *Wenwu* 文物 8: 26–31.

Lin Man-houng (Lin Manhong) 林滿紅. 1991. "Zhongguode baiyin wailiu yu shijie jinyin jianchan, 1814–50" 中國的白銀外流與世界金銀減產1814–50. In Wu Jianxiong 吳劍雄, ed. *Zhongguode haiyang fazhan shi lunwenji* 中國的海洋發展史論文集, 6: 1–44. Taipei: Academia Sinica.

2006. *China Upside Down: Currency, Society, and Ideologies, 1808–1856.* Cambridge: Harvard University Asia Center.

Lin Wenxun 林文勋. 2011. *Tang Song shehui biange lungang* 唐宋社会变革论纲. Beijing: Renmin chubanshe.

Liu Guangjing 刘广京. 1983. "Yibabasan nian Shanghai jinrong fengchao: yangwu yundong zhuanti zhi er" 一八八三年上海金融风潮: 洋务运动专题之二. *Fudan daxue xuebao (shehui kexue ban)* 复旦大学学报 (社会科学版) 3: 94–102.

Liu Guanglin 劉光臨. 2008. "Shichang, zhanzheng, he caizheng guojia: dui Nan Song fushui wentide zai sikao" 市場,戰爭,和財政國家: 對南宋賦税問題的再思考. *Taida lishi xuebao* 臺大歷史學報 42: 221–85.

2012. "Lingnan zhoufu Song Yuan Ming zhi ji liangshui zhengshoude bijiao yanjiu" 岭南州府宋元明之际两税征收的比较研究. *Beida shixue* 北大史学 17: 68–105.

Liu, Guanglin William. 2005. *"Wrestling for Power: The State and Economy in Later Imperial China, 1000–1700."* PhD dissertation, Harvard University.

2013. "Agricultural Productivity in Early Modern Jiangnan." In B. K. L. So, ed. *The Economic History of Lower Yangzi Delta in Late Imperial China: Connecting Money, Markets, and Institutions*, 99–117. London: Routledge.

Liu Jiansheng 刘建生. 2007. "Shanxi piaohao yewu zongliang zhi guji" 山西票号业务总量之估计. *Shanxi daxue xuebao (zhexue shehui kexue ban)* 山西大学学报 *(哲学社会科学版)* 6: 233–39.

Liu, Paul K. C., and Kuo-shu Hwang. 1979. "Population Change and Economic Development in Mainland China since 1400." In Chi-ming Hou and Tzong-shian Yu, ed. *Modern Chinese Economic History*, 61–90. Taipei: Academia Sinica.

Liu Qiugen 刘秋根. 2000. *Ming Qing gaolidai ziben* 明清高利贷资本. Beijing: Shehui kexue wenxian chubanshe.

2007. *Zhongguo gudai hehuozhi chutan* 中国古代合伙制初探. Beijing: Renmin chubanshe.

Liu Qiugen 刘秋根 and Xie Xiuli 谢秀丽. 2005. "Ming Qing Huishang gongshangye pudian hehuozhi xingtai: sanzhong Huishang zhangpude biaomian fenxi" 明清徽商 工商业铺店合伙制形态: 三种徽商帐簿的表面分析. *Zhongguo jingji shi yanjiu* 中国经济史研究 3: 79–87.

Liu Shiji 刘石吉. 1987. *Ming Qing shidai Jiangnan shizhen yanjiu* 明清时代江南市镇研究. Beijing: Zhongguo shehui kexue chubanshe.

Liu Shufen 劉淑芬. 1992. *Liuchaode chengshi yu shehui* 六朝的城市與社會. Taipei: Xuesheng shuju.

2001. "Jiankang and the Commercial Empire of the Southern Dynasties: Change and Continuity in Medieval Chinese Economic History." In S. Pearce, A. Spiro, and P. Ebrey, eds. *Culture and Power in the Reconstitution of the Chinese Realm, 200–600*, 35–52. Cambridge: Harvard University Asia Center.

Liu Ti 刘逖. 2009. "1600–1840 nian Zhongguo guonei shengchan zongzhi gusuan" 1600–1840 年中国国内生产总值估算. *Jingji yanjiu* 经济研究. 10: 144–55.

Liu, William Guanglin. 2015. "The Making of a Fiscal State in Song China, 960–1279." *Economic History Review* 68.1: 48–78.

Liu, Xinru. 1988. *Ancient India and Ancient China: Trade and Religious Exchanges, 1–600 AD*. Delhi: Oxford University Press.

1996. *Silk and Religion: An Exploration of Material Life and the Thought of People, AD 600–1200*. Delhi: Oxford University Press.

Liu Yang 刘杨 and Zhao Ronghua 赵荣华. 2001. *Jizhou yaoci* 吉州窑瓷. Nanchang: Jiangxi meishu chubanshe.

Liu Yongcheng 刘永成 and He Zhiqing 赫治清. 1983. "Wanquantang de youlai yu fazhan" 万全堂的由来与发展. *Zhongguo shehui jingji shi yanjiu* 中国社会经济史研究 1: 1–16.

Liu Zhaomin 劉昭民. 1992. *Zhongguo lishishang qihou zhi bianqian* 中國歷史上氣候之變遷. Taipei: Taiwan shangwu yinshuguan.

Loewe, Michael. 1967. *Records of Han Administration*. Cambridge University Press.

1974. *Crisis and Conflict in Han China, 104 BC to AD 9*. London: George Allen and Unwin Ltd.

2006. *The Government of the Qin and Han Empires, 221 BCE–220 CE*. Indianapolis, IN: Hackett Publishing.

2010a. "The Laws of 186 BCE." In M. Nylan and M. Loewe, eds. *China's Early Empires: A Re-appraisal*, 253–65. Cambridge University Press.

2010b. "Social Distinctions, Groups, and Privileges." In M. Nylan and M. Loewe, eds. *China's Early Empires: A Re-appraisal*, 296–307. Cambridge University Press.

Lombard, Denys. 1990. *Le Carrefour javanais: essai d'histoire globale*. Paris: École des hautes études en sciences sociales.

Long Denggao 龙登高. 2009. "The Diversification of Land Transactions in Late Imperial China." *Frontiers of History in China* 4.2: 183–220.

Lu, Weijing. 2004. "Beyond the Paradigm: Tea-Picking Women in Imperial China." *Journal of Women's History* 15.4: 19–46.

Luan Chengxian 欒成显. 1990. "Mingchu dizhu jilei jianbing tudi tujing chutan: yi Xie Nengjing hu wei li" 明初地主积累兼并土地途经初探: 以谢能静户为例. *Zhongguo shi yanjiu* 中国史研究 3: 101–11.

2007. *Mingdai huangce yanjiu* 明代黄册研究. Rev. edn. Beijing: Shehui kexue chubanshe.

Luo Xizhang 罗西章. 1998. "Zai Shou gui ming lüekao" 宰兽簋铭略考. *Wenwu* 文物 8: 83–87.

Luo, Yinan. 2005. "A Study of the Changes in the Tang-Song Transition Model." *Journal of Song-Yuan Studies* 35: 99–127

Ma Chengyuan 馬承源, ed. 1988. *Shang Zhou qingtongqi mingwen xuan* 商周青銅器銘文選. Vol. 3. Beijing: Wenwu chubanshe.

1990. "Xi Zhou jinwenzhong youguan 'zhu' zi ciyude ruogan jieshi" 西周金文中有關《貯》字辭語的若干解釋. *Shanghai bowuguan jikan* 上海博物館集刊 5: 82–91

2000. "Kang ding mingwen: Xi Zhou zaoqi yong beibi jiaoyi yuqi de jilu" 亢鼎銘文: 西周早期用貝幣交易玉器的記錄. *Shanghai bowuguan jikan* 上海博物館集刊 8: 120–23.

Ma Daying 马大英. 1983. *Handai caizheng shi* 汉代财政史. Beijing: Zhongguo caizheng jingji chubanshe.

Ma, Debin. 2008. "Economic Growth in the Lower Yangzi Region of China in 1911–1937: A Quantitative and Historical Analysis." *Journal of Economic History* 68.2: 355–92.

2011. "Law and Economy in Traditional China: A 'Legal Origin' Perspective on the Great Divergence." In D. Ma and J. L. van Zanden, eds. *Law and Long-Term Economic Change: A Eurasian Perspective*. 46–67. Stanford University Press.

Ma Feibai 馬非百. 1979. *Guan Zi qingzhongpian xinquan* 管子輕重篇新詮. Beijing: Zhonghua shuju.

Macfarlane, Alan. 2000. *The Riddle of the Modern World: Of Liberty, Wealth, and Equality*. Basingstoke: Macmillan.

Maddison, Angus. 2001. *The World Economy: A Millennial Perspective*. Paris: OECD Publications.

2007. *Chinese Economic Performance in the Long Run, 960–2030 AD*. Rev. edn. Paris: OECD Publications.

Magnusson, Lars. 1994. *Mercantilism: The Shaping of an Economic Language*. London: Routledge.

Mann, Michael. 1986. *The Sources of Social Power, vol. 1: A History of Power from the Beginning to AD 1760*. Cambridge University Press.

Mann, Susan. 1987. *Local Merchants and the Chinese Bureaucracy, 1750–1950*. Stanford University Press.

Mann Jones, Susan. 1972. "Finance in Ningbo: the 'Ch'ien Chuang,' 1750–1880." In W. E. Willmott, ed. *Economic Organization in Chinese Society*, 47–77. Stanford University Press.

1974. "The Ningbo Pang and Financial Power in Shanghai." In Mark Elvin, ed. *The Chinese City Between Two Worlds*, 73–96. Stanford University Press.

Mann Jones, Susan, and Philip Kuhn. 1978. "Dynastic Decline and the Roots of Rebellion." In John K. Fairbank, ed. *The Cambridge History of China, vol. 10: Late Ch'ing, 1800–1911*, 1: 107–62. Cambridge University Press.

Mao Hanguang 毛漢光. 1990a. "Jin Sui zhiji Hedong diqu yu Hedong dazu" 晉隋之際河東地 區與河東大族. In Mao, *Zhongguo zhonggu zhengzhi shilun* 中國中古政治史論, 99–130. Taipei: Liangjing chuban shiye gongsi.

1990b. "Xi Wei fubing shilun" 西魏府兵史論. In Mao, *Zhongguo zhonggu zhengzhi shilun*, 167–280. Taipei: Liangjing chuban shiye gongsi.

Marks, Robert B. 1999. *Tigers, Rice, Silk, and Silt: Environment and Economy in Late Imperial South China*. Cambridge University Press.

2012. *China: Its Environment and History*. New York: Rowman and Littlefield.

Marks, Robert B. and Chunsheng Chen. 1995. "Price Inflation and its Social, Economic, and Climatic Context in Guangdong Province, 1707–1800." *T'oung Pao* 81.1–3: 109–52.

Maruhashi Mitsuhiro 丸橋充拓. 2001. "Tō Sō henkakushi kenkyū kinkyō" 唐宋変革史研究近況. *Chūgoku shigaku* 中國史学 11: 149–68.

Matsuda Kōichi 松田孝一. 2000. "Chūgoku kōtsū shi: Gen jidai no kōtsū to nanboku butsuryū" 中國交通史: 元時代の交通と南北物流. In Matsuda Kōichi 松田孝一, ed. *Higashi Ajia keizaishi no shomondai* 東アジア経済史の諸問題. 135–57. Kyoto: A'unsha.

Matsui Yoshinori 松井嘉徳. 2002. *Shūdai kokusei no kenkyū* 周代国制の研究. Tokyo: Kyūko shoin.

Matsumaru Michio 松丸道雄. 1984. "Sei-Shū kōki shakai ni mieru henkaku no hōga: Koteimei kaishaku mondai no shohoteki kaiketsu" 西周後期社会にみえる変革の萌芽:召銘解 釈問題の初歩的解決. In *Higashi, Ajia shi ni okeru kokka to nōmin* 東アジア史における 国家と農民, 29–74. Tokyo: Yamakawa shuppankai.

Matsumaru Michio 松丸道雄 and Takeuchi Yasuhiro 竹内康浩. 1993. "Sei-Shū kinbunchū no hōsei shiryō" 西周金文中の法制史料. In Shiga Shūzō 滋賀秀三, ed. *Chūgoku hōseishi: kihon shiryō no kenkyū* 中国法制史: 基本史料の研究, 3–55. Tokyo: Tokyo daigaku shuppankai.

Mazumdar, Sucheta. 1998. *Sugar and Society in China: Peasants, Technology, and the World Market*. Cambridge: Harvard University Asia Center.

McDermott, Joseph P. 1981. "Bondservants in the T'ai-hu Basin during the Late Ming: A Case of Mistaken Identities." *Journal of Asian Studies* 40.4: 675–701.

1984. "Charting Blank Spaces and Disputed Regions: The Problem of Sung Land Tenure." *Journal of Asian Studies* 44.1: 13–41.

1991. "Family Financial Plans of the Southern Sung." *Asia Major* 3rd series 4.2: 15–52.

2013a. *The Making of a New Rural Order in South China,* vol. 1: *Village, Land, and Lineage in Huizhou, 900–1600.* Cambridge University Press.

2013b. "The Rise of Huizhou Merchants: Kinship and Commerce in Ming China." In B. K. L. So, ed. *The Economic History of Lower Yangzi Delta in Late Imperial China: Connecting Money, Markets, and Institutions,* 233–66. London: Routledge.

McElderry, Andrea Lee. 1976. *Shanghai Old-Style Banks (Ch'ien-chuang), 1800–1935.* Ann Arbor: Michigan Papers in Chinese Studies.

1995. "Securing Trust and Stability: Chinese Finance in the Late Nineteenth Century." In R. A. Brown, ed. *Chinese Business Enterprise in Asia,* 27–44. London: Routledge.

McKnight, Brian E. 1971. *Village and Bureaucracy in Southern Sung China.* University of Chicago Press.

McKnight, Brian E. and James T. C. Liu, eds. 1998. *The Enlightened Judgments, Ch'ing-ming Chi: The Sung Dynasty Collection.* Albany, NY: State University of New York Press.

McNeill, William H. 1976. *Plagues and Peoples.* New York: Anchor Press.

Mehendale, Sanjyot. 1996. "Begram: Along Ancient Central Asian and Indian Trade Routes." *Cahiers d'Asie centrale* 1/2: 47–64.

Mihelich, Mira Ann. 1979. "*Polders and the Politics of Land Reclamation in Southeast China during the Northern Sung Dynasty (960–1126).*" PhD dissertation, Cornell University.

Miu Kunhe 繆坤和. 2002. *Songdai xinyong piaoju yanjiu* 宋代信用票據研究. Kunming: Yunnan daxue chubanshe.

Miyakawa, Hisayuki. 1955. "The Naitō Hypothesis and its Effects on Japanese Studies of China." *Far Eastern Quarterly* 14.3: 533–52.

1956. "Rikuchō jidai no mura" 六朝時代の村. In Miyakawa, *Rikuchō shi kenkyū: seiji shakai hen* 六朝史研究:政治社会篇, 437–71. Tokyo: Nihon gakujutsu shinkōkai.

Miyazaki Ichisada宮崎市定. 1943. *Godai Sōsho no tsūka mondai* 五代宋初の通貨問題. Kyoto: Hoshino shoten.

1950. *Tōyōteki kinsei*東洋的近世. Osaka: Kyōiku taimusu sha.

Miyazawa Tomoyuki 宮澤知之. 1998. *Sōdai Chūgoku no kokka to keizai* 宋代中國の国家と 経済. Tokyo: Sōbunsha.

2000. "Gi Shin Nanbokuchō no kahei keizai 魏晋南北朝の貨幣経済. *Ōryū shigaku* 鷹陵史学 26: 41–82.

2007. *Chūgoku dōsen no sekai: senka kara keizaishi e* 中国銅銭の世界: 銭貨から経済史へ. Kyoto: Shibunkaku shuppan.

2008. "Godai Jūkoku jidai no tsūka jōkyō" 五代十国時代の通貨状況. *Ōryō shigaku* 鷹陵史学 34: 1–35.

Mizuno Masaaki 水野正明. 2000. "Tō Sō jidai no sangyō to chagyō no hattatsu" 唐宋時代の 産業と茶業の発達. In Matsuda Kōichi 松田孝一, ed. *Higashi Ajia keizaishi no shomondai* 東アジア経済史の 諸問題. 82–100. Kyoto: A'unsha.

Moll-Murata, Christine. 2008. "Chinese Guilds from the Seventeenth to the Twentieth Centuries: An Overview." *International Review of Social History* 53, supplement 16: 213–47.

Morelli, Giovanni, *et al.* 2010. "Yersinia pestis Genome Sequencing Identifies Patterns of Global Phylogenetic Diversity." *Nature Genetics* 42.12: 1140–43.

Mori Masao 森正夫. 1967. "Jūyon-seki kōhanki Sessai chihō jinushisei ni kansuru oboegaki" 十四世紀後半期浙西地方地主制に関する覚書. *Nagoya daigaku bungakubu kenkyū ronshū* 名古屋大学文学部研究論集 44: 67–88.

———. 1988. *Mindai Kōnan tochi seido no kenkyū* 明代江南土地制度の研究. Kyoto: Dōhōsha.

Mori Masao 森正夫, Noguchi Tetsurō 野口鐵郎, Hamashima Atsutoshi 濱島敦俊, Kishimoto Mio 岸本美緒, and Satake Yasuhiko 佐竹靖彦, eds. 1997. *Min Shin jidaishi no kihonteki mondai* 明清時代史の基本 的問題. Tokyo: Kyūko shoin.

Mostern, Ruth. 2011. *"Dividing the Realm in Order to Govern": The Spatial Organization of the Song State (960–1276 CE)*. Cambridge: Harvard University Asia Center.

Motono, Eiichi. 2000. *Conflict and Cooperation in Sino-British Business, 1860–1911: The Impact of the Pro-British Commercial Network in Shanghai*. Houndmills, UK: Macmillan.

Musgrave, R. A. 1992. "Schumpeter's Crisis of the Tax State: An Essay in Fiscal Sociology." *Journal of Evolutionary Economics* 2.2: 89–113.

Muthesius, Anna. 2002. "Essential Processes, Looms, and Technical Aspects of the Production of Silk Textiles." In Angeliki E. Laiou, ed. *The Economic History of Byzantium, from the Seventh through the Fifteenth Century*, 1:147–68. Washington, DC: Dumbarton Oaks Research Library and Collection.

Myers, Ramon. 1991. "How did the Chinese Economy Develop? A Review Article." *Journal of Asian Studies* 50.3: 604–28.

Nagai Chiaki 長井千秋. 1992. "Waitō Sōryōjo no zaisei unei" 淮東総領所の財政運営. *Shigaku zasshi* 史学雑誌 101.7: 1235–66.

———. 2000. "Chūka teikoku no zaisei" 中華帝国の財政. In Matsuda Kōichi 松田孝一, ed. *Higashi Ajia keizaishi no shomondai* 東アジア経済史の 諸問題, 101–34. Kyoto: A'unsha.

Nakagawa Manabu 中川学. 1962. "Tōdai no tōko, fukyaku, kyakko ni kansuru oboegaki" 唐代 の逃戸, 浮客, 客戸に関する覚書. *Hitotsubashi ronsō* 一橋論叢 50.3: 339–45.

Nakajima Gakushō 中島楽章. 2001. "Gendai shasei no seiritsu to tenkai" 元代社制 の成立と 展開. *Kyūshū daigaku tōyōshi ronshū* 九州大学東洋史論集 29: 116–46.

———. 2002. *Mindai gōson no funsō to chitsujo* 明代郷村の紛争と秩序. Tokyo: Kyūko shoin.

Naquin, Susan, and Evelyn S. Rawski. 1987. *Chinese Society in the Eighteenth Century*. New Haven: Yale University Press.

Ning Ke 宁可. 1982. "Guanyu 'Han Shiyanli fulao dan maitian yueshu shiquan'" 关于《汉侍 延里父老僤买田约束石券》. *Wenwu* 文物 12: 21–7.

Needham, Joseph. 1971. *Science and Civilisation in China,* vol. 4: *Physical Technology,* part 3: *Civil Engineering and Nautics.* Cambridge University Press.

Neimenggu zizhiqu bowuguan gongzuodui 内蒙古自治区博物馆文物工作队. 1978. *Helinge'er Hanmu bihua* 和林格尔汉墓壁画. Beijing: Wenwu chubanshe.

Ng, Chin-keong. 1983. *Trade and Society: The Amoy Network on the China Coast, 1683–1735.* Singapore University Press.

Ni Yuping 倪玉平. 2010. *Qingchao Jia Dao guanshui yanjiu* 清朝嘉道关税研究. Beijing: Beijing shifan daxue chubanshe.

Niida Noboru 仁井田昇. 1937. *Tō Sō hōritsu monjo no kenkyū* 唐宋法律文書の研究. Tokyo: Tōhō bunka gakuin Tōkyō kenkyūjo.

Nishijima Sadao 西嶋定産. 1966. *Chūgoku keizai shi kenkyū* 中国経済史研究. Tokyo: Tokyo daigaku shuppankai.

1984. "The Formation of the Early Chinese Cotton Industry." In L. Grove and C. Daniels, eds. *State and Society in China: Japanese Perspectives on Ming-Qing Social and Economic History,* 17–77. University of Tokyo Press.

Nishioku Kenji 西奥健志. 2004. "Sōdai shiteki seido no zaiseiteki haikei: chobi no kakutoku o chūshin to shite" 宋代市糴制度の財政的背景: 儲備の獲得を中心として. *Shakai keizai shigaku* 社会経済史学 70.3: 331–45.

Ōba, Osamu. 2001. "The Ordinance on Fords and Passes Excavated from Han Tomb Number 247, Zhangjiashan." *Asia Major,* 3rd series, 14.2: 119–42.

O'Brien, Patrick. 1982. "European Economic Development: The Contribution of the Periphery." *Economic History Review* 35.1: 1–18.

2012. "Fiscal and Financial Preconditions for the Formation of Developmental States in the West and the East from the Conquest of Ceuta (1415) to the Opium War (1839)." *Journal of World History* 23.3: 513–53.

Ogilvie, Sheilagh C. and Markus Cerman, ed. 1996. *European Proto-Industrialization.* Cambridge University Press.

Okada Isao 岡田功. 1990. "Shunshū sengoku Shin Kan jidai no taishaku kankei o meguru ichikōsatsu" 春秋戦国秦漢時代の貸借関係をめぐる一考察. *Sundai shigaku* 駿台史学 78: 69–91.

Okamoto Takashi 岡本隆司, ed. 2013. *Chūgoku keizai shi* 中国経済史. Nagoya daigaku shuppankai.

Ōkushi Atsuhiro 大櫛敦弘. 1985. "Kandai no 'chūka no san' ni kan suru ichi kōsatsu: Kyoen Kankan shoken no 'ko' 'choku' o megutte" 漢代の『中家の産』に関する一考察:居延漢簡所見の『賈・直』をめぐって, *Shigaku zasshi* 史学雑誌 94.7: 1172–94.

Onodera Ikuo 小野寺郁夫. 1966. "Sōdai ni okeru toshi no shōnin soshiki 'kō' ni tsuite" 宋代における都市の商人組織「行」について. *Kanazawa daigaku hōbun gakubu ronshū shigakuhen* 金沢大学法文学部論集史学篇 13: 42–74.

Ōsawa Masaaki 大澤正昭. 1996. *Tō Sō henkakuki nōgyō shakai shi kenkyū* 唐宋変革期農業社会史研究. Tokyo: Kyūko shoin.

Osborne, Anne. 1994. "The Local Politics of Land Reclamation in the Lower Yangzi Highlands." *Late Imperial China* 15.1: 1–46.

1998. "Highlands and Lowlands: Economic and Ecological Interactions in the Lower Yangzi Region under the Qing." In M. Elvin and Ts'ui-jung Liu, eds. *Sediments of Time: Environment and Society in Chinese History* 203–34, Cambridge University Press.

Ōshima Ritsuko大島立子. 1980. "Gendai no kokei no yōeki" 元代の戸計と徭役. *Rekishigaku kenkyū* 歴史学研究 484: 23–32.

1983. "The *Chiang-hu* in the Yüan." *Acta Asiatica* 45: 69–95.

Ōsumi Akiko 大隅晶子. 1990. "Mindai Kōbutei no kaikin seisaku to kaigai bōeki" 明代洪武帝 の海禁政策と海外貿易. In *Yamane Yukio kyōju taikyū kinen Mindai shi ronsō* 山根幸 夫教授退休記念明代史論集, vol. 1, 497–519. Tokyo: Kyūko shoten.

Otagi Matsuo 愛宕松男. 1973. "Addatsusen to sono haikei: Jūsan-seiki Mongoru Genchō ni okeru gin no dōkō" 斡脱銭とその背景: 十三世紀モンゴル元朝にお ける銀の動向. *Tōyōshi kenkyū* 東洋史研究 32.1: 1–27, 32.2: 163–201.

1987. *Otagi Matsuo Tōyō shigaku ronshū* 愛宕松男東洋史学論集, *vol. 1: Chūgoku tōshi sangyō shi* 中國陶瓷産業史. Tokyo: San'ichi shobō.

Ōtsu Tōru 大津透. 1986. "Tō ritsuryō kokka no yosan ni tsuite: Gihō sannendo sōshō yonnen kinbu shifu shishaku" 唐律令国家の予算について: 儀鳳三年度奏抄 四年金部旨符 試釈. *Shigaku zasshi* 史学雑誌 95.12: 1831–79.

Ōyama Masaaki 大山正明. 1974. "Mindai no daitochi shoyū to doboku" 明代の大土地所 有と奴僕. *Tōyō bunka kenkyūjo kiyo* 東洋文化研究所紀要 62: 77–131.

1984. "Large Landownership in the Jiangnan Delta Region during the Late Ming-Early Qing Period." In L. Grove and C. Daniels, eds. *State and Society in China: Japanese Perspectives on Ming-Qing Social and Economic History*, 101–63. University of Tokyo Press.

Pamuk, Şevket. 2012. "The Evolution of Fiscal Institutions in the Ottoman Empire, 1500–1914." In B. Yun-Casalilla and P. K. O'Brien, eds. *The Rise of Fiscal States: A Global History, 1500–1914*, 304–31. Cambridge University Press.

Pan, Ming-te. 1996. "Rural Credit in Ming-Qing Jiangnan and the Concept of Peasant Petty Commodity Production." *Journal of Asian Studies* 55.1: 94–117.

Parthasarathi, Prasannan. 2011. *Why Europe Grew Rich and Asia Did Not: Global Economic Divergence, 1600–1850*. Cambridge University Press.

Pearce, Scott. 1991. "Status, Labor, and Law: Special Service Households under the Northern Dynasties." *Harvard Journal of Asiatic Studies* 51.1: 89–138.

Peerenboom, R. P. 1993. *Law and Morality in Ancient China: The Silk Manuscripts of Huang-Lao*. Albany, NY: State University of New York Press.

Pegolotti, Francesco. 1914. *Notices of the Land Route to Cathay and Asiatic Trade in the First Half of the Fourteenth Century*. In Henry Yule and Henri Cordier, eds. *Cathay and the Way Thither: Being a Collection of Medieval Notices of China*, vol. 3. London: Hakluyt Society.

Peng Kaixiang 彭凱翔. 2006. *Qingdai yilaide liangjia: lishixuede jieshi yu zaijieshi* 清代以来 的粮价:历史学的解释与再解释. Shanghai: Shanghai renmin chubanshe.

2011. "Lishi GDP gusuan zhongde jijia wenti chuyi" 历史 GDP 估算中的计价 问题刍议. *Zhongguo jingji shi yanjiu* 中国经济史研究 4: 53–60.

Peng Kaixiang 彭凱翔, Chen Zhiwu 陈志武, and Yuan Weipeng 袁为鹏. 2008. "Jindai Zhongguo nongcun jiedai shichangde jizhi – jiyu minjian wenshude yanjiu" 近代中 国农村借贷市场的机制—基于民间文书的研究. *Jingji yanjiu* 经济研究 5: 147–59.

Peng Wei 彭卫. 2010. "Guanyu xiaomai zai Handai tuiguangde zaitantao" 关于小麦在汉代推 广的再探讨 *Zhongguo jingji shi yanjiu* 中国经济史研究 4: 63–71.

Peng Xinwei 彭信威. 1965. *Zhongguo huobi shi* 中國貨幣史. 2nd edn. Shanghai: Shanghai renmin chubanshe

Peng Zeyi 彭泽益. 1983. *Shijiu shiji houbanqide Zhongguo caizheng yu jingji* 十九世纪后半期的中国财政与经济. Beijing: Renmin chubanshe.

Perdue, Peter C. 1987. *Exhausting the Earth: State and Peasant in Hunan, 1500–1850.* Cambridge, MA: Council on East Asian Studies, Harvard University.

Perkins, Dwight H. 1969. *Agricultural Development in China, 1368–1968.* Chicago: Aldine.

Petech, L. 1980. "Sang-ko, a Tibetan Statesman in Yuan China." *Acta Orientalia Academiae Scientiarum Hungaria* 34.1–3: 193–208.

Pierson, Stacey. 2013. *From Object to Concept: Global Consumption and the Transformation of Ming Porcelain.* Hong Kong University Press.

Pirazzoli-t'Serstevens, Michèle. 2010. "Urbanism." In M. Nylan and M. Loewe, eds. *China's Early Empires: A Re-appraisal,* 168–85, Cambridge University Press.

Polo, Marco. 1929. *The Book of Ser Marco Polo the Venetian concerning the Kingdoms and Marvels of the East.* Henry Yule and Henri Cordier, eds. 3rd edn. London: John Murray.

Pomeranz, Kenneth. 1993. *The Making of a Hinterland: State, Society, and Economy in Inland North China, 1853–1937.* Berkeley: University of California Press.

1997. "'Traditional' Chinese Business Forms Revisited: Family, Firm, and Financing in the History of the Yutang Company of Jining, 1779–1956." *Late Imperial China* 18.1: 1–38.

2000. *The Great Divergence: China, Europe, and the Making of the Modern World Economy.* Princeton University Press.

2008a. "Chinese Development in Long-Run Perspective." *Proceedings of the American Philosophical Society* 152.1: 83–100.

2008b. "Land Markets in Late Imperial and Republican China." *Continuity and Change* 23.1: 101–50.

Pong, David. 1985. "The Vocabulary of Change: Reformist Ideas of the 1860s and 1870s." In David Pong and Edmund S. K. Fong, eds. *Ideal and Reality: Social and Political Change in Modern China, 1860–1949,* 25–61. Lanham, MD: University Press of America.

1994. *Shen Pao-chen and China's Modernization in the Nineteenth Century.* Cambridge University Press.

Puk, Wing Kin. 2006. "Salt Trade in Sixteenth-Seventeenth Century China." PhD dissertation, Oxford University.

Qi Xia 漆侠. 1979. *Wang Anshi bianfa* 王安石变法. Shanghai: Shanghai renmin chubanshe.

1999. *Zhongguo jingji tongshi: Songdai jingji juan* 中国经济通史: 宋代经济卷. Beijing: Jingji ribao chubanshe.

Qiu Xigui 裘锡圭. 1974. "Hubei Jiangling Fenghuangshan shihao Hanmu chutu jiandu kaoshi" 湖北江陵凤凰山十号汉墓出土简牍考释. *Wenwu* 文物 1974.7: 49–62.

1979. "Xin faxiande Juyan Han jiande jige wenti" 新发现的居延汉简的几个问题. *Zhongguo shi yanjiu* 中国史研究 4: 103–10.

Quan Hansheng 全漢昇. 1935. *Zhongguo hanghui zhidu shi* 中國行會制度史. Shanghai: Shanghai xinshengming shuju.

1972. "Tang Song shidai Yangzhou jingji jingkuang de fanrong yu shuailuo" 唐宋時代揚州經濟境況的繁榮與衰落. In Quan, *Zhongguo jingji shi luncong* 中國經濟史 論叢, 1: 1–28. Hong Kong: Xianggang zhongwen daxue Xinya shuyuan Xinya yanjiusuo.

Rankin, Mary Backus. 1990. "The Origins of a Chinese Public Sphere: Local Elites and Community Affairs in the Late Imperial Period." *Études chinoises* 9.2: 13–60.

1994. "Managed by the People: Officials, Gentry, and the Foshan Charitable Granary, 1795–1845." *Late Imperial China* 15.2: 1–52.

Raschke, Manfred G. 1978. "New Studies in Roman Commerce with the East." In Hildegard Temporini and Wolfgang Haase, eds. *Ufstieg und Niedergang der Römischen Welt: Geschichte und Kultur Roms im Spiegel der Neueren Forschung*, 2: 604–1363. Berlin: Walter de Gruyter.

Rawski, Evelyn Sakakida. 1972. *Agricultural Change and the Peasant Economy of South China*. Cambridge: Harvard University Press.

Rawski, Thomas. 1989. *Economic Growth in Prewar China*. Berkeley: University of California Press.

Rawson, Jessica. 1999. "Western Zhou Archaeology." In M. Loewe and E. L. Shaughnessy, eds. *The Cambridge History of Ancient China: From the Origins of Civilization to 211 BC*, 352–449. Cambridge University Press.

Reid, Anthony. 1990. "The Seventeenth-century Crisis in Southeast Asia." *Modern Asian Studies* 24.4: 639–59.

1997a. "A New Phase of Commercial Expansion in Southeast Asia, 1760–1850." In Anthony Reid, ed. *The Last Stand of Asian Autonomies*, pp. 57–81. Houndmills, UK: Macmillan.

1997b. "Introduction." In Anthony Reid, ed. *The Last Stand of Asian Autonomies*, pp. 1–25. Houndmills, UK: Macmillan.

2004. "Chinese Trade and Economic Expansion in Southeast Asia in the Later Eighteenth and Early Nineteenth Centuries: An Overview." In N. Cooke and Li Tana, eds. *Water Frontier: Commerce and the Chinese in the Lower Mekong Region, 1750–1880*, 21–34. Lanham, MD: Rowman and Littlefield.

Reinert, Eric S. 1999. "The Role of the State in Economic Growth." *Journal of Economic Studies* 26.4/5: 268–326.

Reinert, Eric S. and Sophus A. Reinert. 2005. "Mercantilism and Economic Development: Schumpeterian Dynamics, Institution-Building, and International Benchmarking." In K. S. Jomo and Eric S. Reinert, eds. *The Origins of Development Economics: How Schools of Thought Have Addressed Development*, 1–23. London: Zed Books.

Richards, John F. 1990. "The Seventeenth-century Crisis in South Asia." *Modern Asian Studies* 24.4: 624–38.

Richardson, Philip. 1999. *Economic Change in China, c. 1800–1950*. Cambridge University Press.

Rickett, W. Allyn. 1985. *Guan Zi: Political, Economic, and Philosophical Essays from Early China*, vol. 1. Princeton University Press.

1998. *Guan Zi: Political, Economic, and Philosophical Essays from Early China*, vol. 2. Princeton University Press.

Rosenthal, Jean-Laurent, and R. Bin Wong. 2011. *Before and Beyond Divergence: The Politics of Economic Change in China and Europe*. Cambridge: Harvard University Press.

Rossabi, Morris. 1988. *Khubilai Khan: His Life and Times*. Berkeley: University of California Press.

Rowe, William T. 1984. *Hankow: Commerce and Society in a Chinese City, 1796–1889*. Stanford University Press.

1985. "Approaches to Modern Chinese Social History." In Olivier Kunz, ed. *Reliving the Past: The Worlds of Social History*, 236–96. Chapel Hill: University of North Carolina Press.

1990. "The Public Sphere in Modern China." *Modern China* 16.3: 309–29.

2001. *Saving the World: Cheng Hongmou and Elite Consciousness in Eighteenth-Century China*. Stanford University Press.

2010. "Money, Economy, and Polity in the Daoguang-Era Paper Currency Debates." *Late Imperial China* 31.2: 69–96.

2011. "Introduction: The Significance of the Qianlong-Jiaqing Transition in Chinese History." *Late Imperial China* 32.2: 74–88.

Sagawa Eiji 佐川英治. 1999. "Hoku-Gi no henkosei to chōhei seido" 北魏の編戸制と徴兵制度. *Tōyō gakuhō* 東洋学報 81.1: 1–35.

2001a. "Hoku-Gi kindensei kenkyū no dōkō 北魏均田制研究の動向." *Chūgoku shigaku* 中国史学 11: 131–47.

2001b. "Hoku-Gi kindensei no mokuteki to tenkai: dohi kyūden o chūshin to shite" 北魏均田制の目的と展開: 奴婢給田を中心として. *Shigaku zasshi* 史学雑誌 110.1: 1–38.

Sahara Yasuo 佐原康夫. 2002a. *Kandai toshi kikō no kenkyū* 漢代都市機構の研究. Tokyo: Kyūko shoin.

2002b. "Kōryō Hōōzan Kankan saikō" 江陵鳳凰山漢簡再考. *Tōyōshi kenkyū* 東洋史研究 61.3: 405–33.

Saitō, Osamu. 1983. "Population and the Peasant Family Economy in Proto-Industrial Japan." *Journal of Family History* 8: 30–54.

Satake Yasuhiko 佐竹靖彦. 1996. "Zōsetsu" 総説. In Satake Yasuhiko 佐竹靖彦, Shiba Yoshinobu 斯波義信, Umehara Kaoru 梅原郁, Uematsu Tadashi 植松正 and Kondō Issei 近藤一成, eds. *Sō Gen jidaishi no kihon mondai* 宋元時代史の基本問題, 3–42. Tokyo: Kyūko shoin.

Satō Taketoshi 佐藤武敏. 1962. *Chūgoku kodai kōgyō shi no kenkyū* 中国古代工業史の研究. Tokyo: Yoshikawa Kōbunkan.

1967. "Kandai no jinkō chōsa" 漢代の人口調査. *Shūkan tōyōgaku* 集刊東洋学 18: 1–27.

Schaberg, David. 2010. "The *Zhouli* as Constitutional Text." In Benjamin Elman and Martin Kern, eds. *Statecraft and Classical Learning: The Rituals of Zhou in East Asian History*, 33–66. Leiden: Brill.

Scheidel, Walter. 2009. "The Monetary Systems of the Han and Roman Empires." In Walter Scheidel, ed. *Rome and China: Comparative Perspectives on Ancient Empires*, 137–207. New York: Oxford University Press.

Schifferli, Christoph. 1986. "Le système monétaire au Sichuan vers la fin du Xe siècle." *T'oung Pao* 72.2: 269–90.

Schirokauer, Conrad, and Robert P. Hymes. 1993. "Introduction." In R. P. Hymes and C. Schirokauer, eds. *Ordering the World: Approaches to State and Society in Sung Dynasty China*, 1–58. Berkeley: University of California Press.

Schmoller, Gustav. 1967. *The Mercantile System and Its Historical Significance*. Rpt. New York: A.M. Kelley.

Schoppa, Keith. 1989. *Xiang Lake – Nine Centuries of Chinese Life*. New Haven: Yale University Press.

Schottenhammer, Angela. 2001. "The Role of Metals and the Impact of the Introduction of *Huizi* Paper Notes in Quanzhou on the Development of Maritime Trade in the Song Period." In Angela Schottenhammer, ed. *The Emporium of the World: Maritime Quanzhou, 1000–1400*, 95–176. Leiden: Brill.

Schumpeter, Joseph A. 1954. *History of Economic Analysis*. New York: Oxford University Press.

1991. "The Crisis of the Tax State." In Richard Swedborg, ed. *The Economics and Sociology of Capitalism*, 99–140. Princeton University Press.

Schurmann, Herbert Franz. 1956a. *Economic Structure of the Yüan Dynasty: Translation of Chapters 93 and 94 of the Yüan shih*. Cambridge: Harvard University Press.

1956b. "Mongolian Tributary Practices of the Thirteenth Century." *Harvard Journal of Asiatic Studies* 19.3–4: 304–89.

Scogin, Hugh. 1990. "Between Heaven and Man: Contract and the State in Han Dynasty China." *Southern California Law Review* 63: 1325–1404.

Sen, Tansen. 2003. *Buddhism, Diplomacy, and Trade: The Realignment of Sino-Indian Relations, 600–1400*. Honolulu: University of Hawai'i Press.

Shaughnessy, Edward L. 1991. *Sources of Western Zhou History: Inscribed Bronze Vessels*. Berkeley: University of California Press.

1999. "Western Zhou History." In M. Loewe and E. L. Shaughnessy, eds. *The Cambridge History of Ancient China: From the Origins of Civilization to 211 BC*, 292–351. Cambridge University Press.

Shi Junzhi 石俊志. 2009. *Banliangqian zhidu yanjiu* 半两钱制度研究. Beijing: Zhongguo jinrong chubanshe.

Shi Yang 石洋. 2012. "Ryō Kan yōka hensen kōshō" 両漢傭価変遷考証. *Tōyōshi kenkyū* 東洋史研究 71.2: 191–218.

Shi Zhihong 史志宏. 1994. *Qingdai qianqide xiaonong jingji* 清代前期的小农经济. Beijing: Zhongguo shehui kexue chubanshe.

2008. *Qingdai hubu yinku shouzhi he kucun tongji* 清代户部银库收支和库存统计. Fuzhou: Fujian renmin chubanshe.

Shi, Zhihong, Xuyi, Ni Yuping, and Bas van Leeuwen. 2014. "Chinese National Income, c. 1661–1933." Centre for Global Economic History (Utrecht University) Working Paper Series, no. 62. Available at: www.cgeh.nl/sites/default/files/WorkingPapers/CGEHWP62_ShiXuyiNiVanLeeuwen.pdf.

Shiba Yoshinobu 斯波義信. 1968. *Sōdai shōgyō shi kenkyū* 宋代商業史研究. Tokyo: Kazama shobō.

1970. *Commerce and Society in Sung China*. Trans. Mark Elvin. Ann Arbor: University of Michigan Center for Chinese Studies.

1975. "Urbanization and the Development of Markets in the Lower Yangtze Valley." In John Winthrop Haeger, ed. *Crisis and Prosperity in Sung China*, 13–48. Tucson: University of Arizona Press.

1977. "Ningbo and its Hinterland." In G. W. Skinner, ed. *The City in Late Imperial China*, 391–439. Stanford University Press.

1983. "Sung Foreign Trade: Its Scope and Organization." In Morris Rossabi, ed. *China Among Equals: The Middle Kingdom and its Neighbors, 10th–14th Centuries*, 80–115. Berkeley: University of California Press.

1988. *Sōdai Kōnan keizai shi no kenkyū* 宋代江南経済史の研究. Tokyo: Tokyo daigaku shuppankai.

1998. "Environment versus Water Control: The Case of the Southern Hangzhou Bay Area from the Mid-Tang through the Qing Period." In Mark Elvin, ed. *Sediments of Time: Environment and Society in Chinese History*, 135–64. Cambridge University Press.

Shigechika Keiju 重近啓樹. 1990. "Shin Kan no shōnin to sono futan" 秦漢の商人とその負担. *Sundai shigaku* 駿台史学 78: 27–59.

Shigeta, Atsushi. 1984. "The Origins and Structure of Gentry Rule." In L. Grove and C. Daniels, eds. *State and Society in China: Japanese Perspectives on Ming-Qing Social and Economic History*, 335–85. University of Tokyo Press.

Shimasue Kazuyasu 島居一康. 1990. "Ryōzei setsunō ni okeru nōzei kagaku to shijō kagaku" 両税折納における納税価額と市場価額. In Chūgokushi kenkyūkai, ed. *Chūgoku sensei kokka to shakai tōgō* 中国専制国家と社会統合, 333–86. Tokyo: Bunrikaku.

Shiue, Carol H., and Wolfgang Keller. 2007. "Markets in China and Europe on the Eve of the Industrial Revolution." *American Economic Review* 97.4: 1189–1216.

Si Weizhi 斯维至. 1978. "Lun shuren" 论庶人. *Shehui kexue zhanxian* 社会科学战线 2: 103–10.

Sima Qian. 1993. *Records of the Grand Historian: Han Dynasty II*. Trans. Burton Watson. New York: Columbia University Press.

Skaff, Jonathan Karam. 1998. "Sasanian and Arab-Sasanian Silver Coins from Turfan: Their Relationship to International Trade and the Local Economy." *Asia Major*, 3rd series, 11.2: 67–115.

2003. "The Sogdian Trade Diaspora in East Turkestan during the Seventh and Eighth Centuries." *Journal of the Economic and Social History of the Orient* 46.4: 475–524.

Skinner, G. William, 1977a. "Cities and the Hierarchy of Local Systems." In G. W. Skinner, ed. *The City in Late Imperial China*, 276–351. Stanford University Press.

1977b. "Regional Urbanization in Nineteenth-Century China." In G. W. Skinner, ed. *The City in Late Imperial China*, 212–49. Stanford University Press.

1986. "Sichuan's Population in the Nineteenth Century: Lessons from Disaggregated Data." *Late Imperial China* 7.2: 1–76.

Smith, Paul J. 1988. "Commerce, Agriculture, and Core Formation in the Upper Yangzi, 2 AD to 1948." *Late Imperial China* 9.1: 1–78.

1992. *Taxing Heaven's Storehouse: Horses, Bureaucrats, and the Destruction of the Sichuan Tea Industry, 1074–1224*. Cambridge: Council on East Asian Studies, Harvard University.

1993. "State Power and Economic Activism during the New Policies, 1068–1085: The Tea and Horse Trade and the 'Green Sprouts' Loan Policy." In Robert P. Hymes and Conrad Schirokauer, eds. *Ordering the World: Approaches to*

State and Society in Sung Dynasty China, 76–127. Berkeley: University of California Press.

2009. "Shen-tsung's Reign and the New Policies of Wang An-shih, 1067–1085." In D. Twitchett and P. J. Smith, eds. *The Cambridge History of China, vol. 5: The Sung Dynasty and its Precursors, 907–1279*, 347–483. Cambridge University Press.

So, Billy K. L. 2000. *Prosperity, Region, and Institutions in Maritime China: The South Fukien Pattern, 946–1368.* Cambridge: Harvard University Area Center.

2013. "Institutions in Market Economies of Premodern Maritime China." In B. K. L. So, ed. *The Economic History of Lower Yangzi Delta in Late Imperial China: Connecting Money, Markets, and Institutions*, 208–32. London: Routledge.

So, Jenny F. and Emma C. Bunker. 1995. *Traders and Raiders on China's Northern Frontier.* Seattle: Smithsonian Institution and University of Washington Press.

Sogabe Shizuo曾我部静雄. 1941a. "Nan Sō no wabaiken oyobi setsuhakusen no kenkyū" 南宋の和買絹及び折帛銭の研究. In Sogabe, *Sōdai zaisei shi* 宋代財政史, 333–92. Tokyo: Seikatsusha.

1941b. "Sōdai no zaisei ippan" 宋代の財政一般. In Sogabe, *Sōdai zaisei shi* 宋代財政史, 3–85. Tokyo: Seikatsusha.

Somers Heidhues, Mary. 1993. "Chinese Organizations in West Borneo and Bangka: Kongsis and Hui." In David Ownby and Mary Somers Heidhues, eds. *"Secret Societies" Reconsidered: Perspectives on the Social History of Modern South China and Southeast Asia*, 68–88. Armonk, NY: M.E. Sharpe.

Steensgaard, Niels. 1990. "The Seventeenth-Century Crisis and the Unity of Asian History." *Modern Asian Studies* 24.4: 683–97.

Su Jilang 苏基朗. 2004. "Liang Song Minnan Guangdong Zhedong waimao ciye kongjian moshide yige bijiao fenxi" 两宋闽南广东浙东外贸瓷业空间模式的一个比较分析. In Li Bozhong 李伯重 and Zhou Shengchun 周生春, eds. *Jiangnande chengshi gongye yu difang wenhua, 960–1850* 江南的城市工业与地方文化, *960–1850*, 141–92. Beijing: Tianjin daxue chubanshe.

Sudō Yoshiyuki周藤吉之. 1954a. "Godai ni okeru kinzeihō" 五代に於ける均税法. In Sudō, *Tō Sō tochi seido shi kenkyū* 唐宋土地制度史研究, 405–27. Tokyo: Tokyo daigaku shuppankai.

1954b. "Nan Sō matsu no kōdenhō" 南宋末の公田法. In Sudō, *Tō Sō tochi seido shi kenkyū* 唐宋土地制度史研究, 537–92. Tokyo: Tokyo daigaku shuppankai.

1954c. "Sōdai shōensei no hattatsu" 宋代庄園制の発達. In Sudō, *Tō Sō tochi seido shi kenkyū* 唐宋土地制度史研究, 195–288. Tokyo: Tokyo daigaku shuppankai.

Sugihara, Kaoru 杉原薫. 1996. "Agriculture and Industrialization: The Japanese Experience." In Peter Mathias and John A. Davis, eds. *Agriculture and Industrialization from the Eighteenth Century to the Present Day*, 148–66. Oxford: Blackwell.

2003. "The East Asian Path of Economic Development: A Long-Term Perspective." In G. Arrighi, T. Hamashita, and M. Selden, eds. *The Resurgence of East Asia: 500, 150, and 50 Year Perspectives*, 78–123. London: Routledge.

2005. "An Introduction." In K. Sugihara, ed. *Japan, China, and the Growth of the Asian International Economy, 1850–1949*, 1–19. Oxford University Press.

2009. "19 seiki zenhan no Ajia kōekiken: tōkeiteki kōsa" 19世紀前半のアジア交易圏: 統計的考察. In Kagotani Naoto 篭谷直人 and Wakimura Kōhei 脇村孝平, eds. *Teikoku to Ajia nettowaaku: chōki no 19 seiki* 帝国とアジアネットワーク: 長期の19世紀, 250–81. Kyoto: Seikai shisōsha.

Sugiyama Masaaki 杉山正明. 2004. *Mongoru teikoku to Dai Gen urusu* モンゴル帝国と大元 ウルス. Kyoto: Kyoto daigaku gakujutsu shuppankai.

Sumiya Tsuneko 角谷常子. 1994. "Kyoen Kan kan ni mieru baibai kankei kan ni tsuite ichi kōsatsu" 居延漢簡にみえる売買関係簡について一考察. *Tōyōshi kenkyū* 東洋史研究 52.4: 545–65.

Sun, Zhouyong. 2008. *Craft Production in the Western Zhou Dynasty (1046–771 BC): A Case Study of a Jue-Earrings Workshop at the Predynastic Capital Site, Zhouyuan, China*. Oxford, UK: Archaeopress.

Sussman, George D. 2011. "Was the Black Death in India and China?" *Bulletin of the History of Medicine* 85.3: 319–55.

Suzuki Naomi 鈴木直美. 1990. "Hōōzan jūgō Kanbotsu shutsudo shiryō kara mita Kōryō shakai" 鳳凰山一〇号漢墓出土史料から見た江陵社会. *Sundai shigaku* 駿台史学 80: 39–76.

Swann, Nancy Lee. 1950. *Food and Money in Ancient China: The Earliest Economic History of China to AD 25*. Princeton University Press.

Szonyi, Michael. 2002. *Practicing Kinship: Lineage and Descent in Late Imperial China*. Stanford University Press.

Tada Kensuke 多田狷介. 1964. "Go-Kan gōzoku no nōgyō keiei: kasaku, yōsaku, dorei rōdō" 後漢豪族 の農業経営: 仮作, 傭作, 奴隷労働. *Rekishigaku kenkyū* 歴史学研究 286: 13–21.

1965. "Kandai no chihō shōgyō ni tsuite: gōzoku to shonōmin no kankei o chūshin toshite" 漢代の地方商業について:豪族と小農民の関係を中心として. *Shichō* 史 潮 92: 36–49.

Tajiri Tōru 田尻利. 1999. "Shindai tabako kenkyūshi oboegaki" 清代タバコ研究史覚書. In Tajiri, *Shindai nōgyō shōgyōka no kenkyū* 清代農業商業化の研究, 284–312. Tokyo: Kyūko shoin.

Takahashi Yoshirō 高橋芳郎. 2001. "Sō Gen dai no dohi, kōyōjin, demboku no mibun" 宋元 代の奴婢, 雇傭人, 佃僕の身分. In Takahashi, *Sō–Shin mibunhō no kenkyū* 宋―清身 分法の研究, 1–84. Sapporo: Hokkaidō daigaku toshokan kōkai.

Takenami Takayoshi 竹浪隆良. 1984. "Hoku-Gi ni okeru jinshin baibai to mibunsei shihai: enshō sannen (514) jinshin baibai rongi o chūshin to shite" 北魏における人身売買と身 分制支配: 延昌三年 (五一四) 人身売買論議を中心として. *Shigaku zasshi* 史学雑 誌 93.3: 279–312.

Tanaka Katsuko 田中克子 and Satō Ichirō 佐藤一郎. 2008. "Bōeki tōjiki no sui'i" 貿易陶磁 器の推移. In Ōba Kōji 大庭康時, ed. *Chūsei toshi Hakata o horu* 中世都市博多を掘る, 112–28. Fukuoka: Kaichōsha.

Tanaka, Masatoshi. 1984. "Rural Handicraft in Jiangnan in the Sixteenth and Seventeenth Century." In L. Grove and C. Daniels, eds. *State and Society in China: Japanese Perspectives on Ming-Qing Social and Economic History*, 79–100. University of Tokyo Press.

Tang Changru 唐長孺. 1954. "Nanchaode tun, di, bieshu ji shanze zhanling" 南朝的
    屯, 邸, 別墅及山澤占領. *Lishi yanjiu* 歷史研究 1954.3: 95–113.
1955. "Wei Jin hudiaozhi jiqi yanbian" 魏晉戶調制及其演變. In Tang, *Wei Jin
    Nanbeichao shi luncong* 魏晉南北朝史論叢, 59–84. Beijing: Sanlian shudian.
1961. "Guanyu Wu Zetian moniande futaohu" 关于武则天末年的浮逃户. *Lishi
    yanjiu* 歷史研究 6: 90–95.
1990. "Clients and Bound Retainers in the Six Dynasties Period." In A. E. Dien, ed.
    State and Society in Early Medieval China, 111–38. Stanford University Press.
Tang Wenji 唐文基. 1990. "Sanxiang jiapai: Mingmo fandongde caizheng" 三餉加派:
    明末反動的財政. In *Yamane Yukio kyōju taikyū kinen Mindai shi ronsō* 山根幸
    夫教授退休 記念明代史論叢, 2: 979–1001. Tokyo: Kyūko shoten.
Tang Yongtong 汤用彤. 2006. *Han Wei Liang Jin Nanbeichao fojiao shi* 汉魏两晋南
    北朝佛教 史. Rev. edn. Beijing: Kunlun chubanshe.
Tanigawa, Michio. 1985. *Medieval Chinese Society and the Local "Community."*
    Berkeley: University of California Press.
Terada Takanobu 寺田隆信. 1972. *Sansei shōnin no kenkyū; Mindai ni okeru shōnin
    oyobi shōgyō shihon* 山西商人の研究:明代における商人および商業資本.
    Kyoto: Tōyōshi kenkyūkai.
1972a. "Soshū senfugyō no keiei keitai" 蘇州踹布業の経営形態. Rpt. in *Sansei
    shōnin no kenkyū; Mindai ni okeru shōnin oyobi shōgyō shihon* 山西商人の研究:
    明代における商人および商業資本, 337–410. Kyoto: Tōyōshi kenkyūkai.
Thierry, François. 1993. "Sur les monnaies sassanides trouvées en Chine." In Groupe
    pour l'Étude de la Civilisation du Moyen-Orient, ed. *Circulation des monnaies,
    des marchandises et des biens*, 89–139. Leuven: Peeters Press.
Tianchangshi wenwu guanlisuo天长市文物管理所. 2006. "Anhui Tianchang Xi
    Hanmu fajue jianbao" 安徽天长西汉墓发掘简报. *Wenwu* 文物 11: 4–21.
Torbert, Preston M. 1977. *The Ch'ing Imperial Household Department: A Study of its
    Organization and Principal Functions, 1662–1796*. Cambridge, MA: Council on
    East Asian Studies, Harvard University.
Trocki, Carl A. 1990. *Opium and Empire: Chinese Society in Colonial Singapore,
    1800–1910*. Ithaca: Cornell University Press.
Trombert, Éric. 1995. *Le Crédit à Dunhuang: vie matérielle et société en Chine
    medievale*. Paris: Collège de France/Institut des Hautes Études Chinoises.
2000. "Textiles et tissus sur la route de la soie." In Jean-Pierre Drège, ed. *La Sérinde,
    terre d'échanges*, 107–20. Paris: La Documentation française.
Tsien, Tsuen-hsiun. 1985. *Science and Civilisation in China*, vol. 5: *Chemistry and
    Chemical Technology*, part 1: *Paper and Printing*. Cambridge University Press.
Tsurumi, Naohiro. 1984. "Rural Control in the Ming Dynasty." In L. Grove and
    C. Daniels, eds. *State and Society in China: Japanese Perspectives on Ming-Qing
    Social and Economic History*, 245–77. University of Tokyo Press.
Twitchett, Denis. 1954. "The Salt Commissioners after An Lu-shan's Rebellion."
    Asia Major, new series, 4.1: 60–89.
1963. *Financial Administration under the T'ang Dynasty*. Cambridge University
    Press.
1966. "The T'ang Market System." *Asia Major*, new series, 12.2: 202–48.
1969–70. "Local Financial Administration in Early T'ang Times." *Asia Major*,
    new series, 15: 82–114.

1973. "The Composition of the T'ang Ruling Class: New Evidence from Tun-huang." In A. F. Wright and D. Twitchett, eds. *Perspectives on the T'ang,* 47–85. New Haven: Yale University Press.

1979. "Hsuan-tsung (reign 712–56)." In Denis Twitchett, ed. *The Cambridge History of China,* vol. 3: *Sui and T'ang China, 618–907,* part 1, 333–463. Cambridge University Press.

Twitchett, Denis and Janice Stargardt. 2002. "Chinese Silver Bullion in a Tenth-Century Indonesian Wreck." *Asia Major,* third series, 15.1: 23–72.

Uematsu Tadashi 植松正. 1983. "The Control of Chiang-nan in the Early Yüan." *Acta Asiatica* 45: 49–68.

1996. "Genchō shihai shita no Kōnan chiiki shakai" 元朝支配下の江南地域社会. In Satake Yasuhiko 佐竹靖彦 *et al.,* eds. *Sō Gen jidaishi no kihon mondai* 宋元時代史の基 本問題, 333–58. Tokyo: Kyūko shoin.

Underhill, Anne P., *et al.* 2008. "Changes in Regional Settlement Patterns and the Development of Complex Societies in Southeastern Shandong, China." *Journal of Anthropological Archaeology* 27: 1–29.

Uno Nobuhiro 宇野伸浩. 1989. "Ogodei han to Musurimu shōnin: Orudo ni okeru kōeki to Nishi Ajiasan no shōhin" オゴデイ・ハンとムスリム商人:オ ルドにおける交易と 西アジア産の商品. *Tōyō gakuhō* 東洋学報 70.3–4: 71–104.

Utsunomiya Kiyoyoshi 宇都宮清吉. 1955. *Kandai shakai keizai shi kenkyū* 漢代社会 経済史 研究. Tokyo: Kōbundō shōbō.

Vaggi, Gianni, and Peter Groenewegen. 2003. *A Concise History of Economic Thought: From Mercantilism to Monetarism.* Basingstoke, UK: Palgrave Macmillan.

Van de Mieroop, Marc. 2004. *A History of the Ancient Near East c. 3000–323 BC.* Oxford: Blackwell.

Van Dyke, Paul A. 2005. *The Canton Trade: Life and Enterprise on the China Coast, 1700–1845.* Hong Kong University Press.

van Zanden, Jan Luiten. 2009. *The Long Road to the Industrial Revolution: The European Economy in a Global Perspective, 1000–1800.* Leiden: Brill.

Vermeer, Eduard B. 1991. "The Mountain Frontier in Late Imperial China: Economic and Social Developments in the Bashan." *T'oung Pao* 77.4–5: 300–29.

Vogel, Hans Ulrich. 1987. "Chinese Central Monetary Policy, 1644–1800." *Late Imperial China* 8.2: 1–52.

n.d. "Chinese Central Monetary Policy and Yunnan Copper Mining, 1644–1800." Unpub. ms.

von Falkenhausen, Lothar. 1999a. "Late Western Zhou Taste." *Études Chinoises* 18: 143–78.

1999b. "The Waning of the Bronze Age." In M. Loewe and E. L. Shaughnessy, eds. *The Cambridge History of Ancient China: From the Origins of Civilization to 211 BC,* 450–544. Cambridge University Press.

2005. "The E Jun Qi Metal Tallies: Inscribed Texts and Ritual Contexts." In Martin Kern, ed. *Text and Ritual in Early China,* 79–123. Seattle: University of Washington Press.

2006. *Chinese Society in the Age of Confucius (1000–250 BC): The Archaeological Evidence.* Los Angeles, CA: Cotsen Institute of Archaeology, University of California.

von Glahn, Richard. 1987. *The Country of Streams and Grottoes: Expansion, Settlement, and the Civilizing of the Sichuan Frontier in Song Times.* Cambridge: Harvard University Council on East Asian Studies.

1991. "Municipal Reform and Urban Social Conflict in Late Ming China." *Journal of Asian Studies* 50.2: 280–307.

1993. "Community and Welfare: Chu Hsi's Community Granary in Theory and Practice." In R. P. Hymes and C. Schirokauer, eds. *Ordering the World: Approaches to State and Society in Sung Dynasty China*, 221–54. Berkeley: University of California Press.

1996a. *Fountain of Fortune: Money and Monetary Policy in China, 1000–1700.* Berkeley: University of California Press.

1996b. "Myth and Reality of China's Seventeenth-Century Monetary Crisis." *Journal of Economic History* 56.2: 429–54.

2003a. "Imagining Pre-modern China." In P. J. Smith and R. von Glahn, eds. *The Song-Yuan-Ming Transition in Chinese History*, 35–70. Cambridge: Harvard University Asia Center.

2003b. "Towns and Temples: Urban Growth and Decline in the Yangzi Delta, 1200–1500." In P. J. Smith and R. von Glahn, eds. *The Song-Yuan-Ming Transition in Chinese History*, 176–211. Cambridge: Harvard University Asia Center.

2004. "Revisiting the Song Monetary Revolution: A Review Essay." *International Journal of Asian Studies* 1.1: 159–178.

2005. "Origins of Paper Money in China." In K. Geert Rouwenhorst and William N. Goetzmann, eds. *Origins of Value: The Financial Innovations that Created Modern Capital Markets*, 65–89. New York: Oxford University Press.

2007a. "Foreign Silver Coin in the Market Culture of Nineteenth Century China." *International Journal of Asian Studies* 4.1: 51–78.

2007b. "Zhu Yuanzhang *ex nihilo*?" *Ming Studies* 55: 113–141.

2010. "Monies of Account and Monetary Transition in China, Twelfth to Fourteenth Centuries." *Journal of the Economic and Social History of the Orient* 53.3: 463–505.

2013. "Cycles of Silver in Chinese Monetary History." In B. K. L. So, ed. *The Economic History of Lower Yangzi Delta in Late Imperial China: Connecting Money, Markets, and Institutions*, 17–71. London: Routledge.

2014. "The Ningbo-Hakata Merchant Network and the Reorientation of East Asian Maritime Trade, 1150–1300." *Harvard Journal of Asiatic Studies* 74.2: 251–81.

von Redden, Sitta. 2010. *Money in Classical Antiquity.* Cambridge University Press.

von Verschuer, Charlotte. 2006. *Across the Perilous Sea: Japanese Trade with China and Korea from the Seventh to the Sixteenth Centuries.* Ithaca, NY: Cornell University East Asia Program.

Vries, Peer H.H. 2002. "Are Coal and Colonies Really Crucial? Kenneth Pomeranz and the Great Divergence." *Journal of World History* 12.2: 407–46.

2015. *State, Economy, and the Great Divergence: Great Britain and China, 1680s–1850s.* London: Bloomsbury Academic.

Wade, Geoff. 2009. "An Early Age of Commerce in Southeast Asia, 900–1300 CE." *Journal of South East Asian Studies* 40.2: 221–65.

Wagner, Donald B. 2001a. "The Administration of the Iron Industry in Eleventh-century China." *Journal of the Economic and Social History of the Orient* 44.2: 175–97.

2001b. *The State and the Iron Industry in Han China.* Copenhagen: Nordic Institute of Asian Studies.

2008. *Science and Civilisation in China,* vol. 5: *Chemistry and Chemical Technology,* part 11: *Ferrous Metallurgy.* Cambridge University Press.

Waltner, Ann. 1990. *Getting an Heir: Adoption and the Construction of Kinship in Late Imperial China.* Honolulu: University of Hawai'i Press.

Wang, Helen. 2004. *Money on the Silk Road: The Evidence from Eastern Central Asia to AD 800.* London: British Museum Press.

Wang Shengduo 汪圣铎. 1995. *Liang Song caizheng shi* 两宋财政史. Beijing: Zhonghua shuju.

Wang Su 王素. 2011. "Changsha Wujian zhongde dianke yu yishike – jianlun Xi Jin hudiao shizhongde 'Nanchaohua' wenti" 長沙吳簡中的佃客與衣食客 – 兼論西晉戶調式中的 '南朝化' 問題. *Zhonghua wenshi luncong* 中華文史論叢 101: 1–34.

Wang Wencheng 王文成. 2001. *Songdai baiyin huobihua yanjiu* 宋代白银货币化研究. Kunming: Yunnan daxue chubanshe.

Wang, Wensheng. 2014. *White Lotus Rebels and South China Pirates: Crisis and Reform in the Qing Empire.* Cambridge: Harvard University Press.

Wang Yanhui 王彦辉. 2006. "Lun Handaide fenhu xichan" 论汉代的分户析产. *Zhongguoshi yanjiu* 中国史研究 4: 19–38.

Wang, Yeh-chien. 1973. *Land Taxation in Imperial China, 1750–1911.* Cambridge, MA: Harvard University Press.

1985. "Food Supply in Eighteenth-Century Fukien." *Late Imperial China* 7.2: 80–117.

1992. "Secular Trends of Rice Prices in the Yangzi Delta, 1638–1935." In T. G. Rawski and L. M. Li, eds. *Chinese History in Economic Perspective,* 35–68. Berkeley, CA: University of California Press.

Wang Yejian 王業鍵. 2003. "Zhongguo jindai huobi yu yinhangde yanjin (1644–1937)" 中國 近代貨幣與銀行的演進. In Wang, *Qingdai jingji shi lunwenji* 清代經濟史論文集, 161–274. Taipei: Daoxiang chubanshe.

Wang Yichen 王怡辰. 2007. *Wei Jin Nanbeichao huobi jiaoyi he faxing* 魏晉南北朝貨幣交易 和發行. Taipei: Wenjin chubanshe.

Wang, Yi-t'ung. 1953. "Slaves and Other Comparable Social Groups during the Northern Dynasties (386–618)." *Harvard Journal of Asiatic Studies* 16.3/4: 293–364.

Wang Zengyu 王曾瑜. 1985. "Songchaode fangguohu" 宋朝的坊郭户. In Zhongguo shehui kexueyuan lishi yanjiusuo Song Liao Jin Yuan shi yanjiushi, *Song Liao Jin shi Luncong* 宋辽金史论丛 1: 64–82.

Wang, Zhenping. 2006. *Ambassadors from the Islands of the Immortals: China-Japan Relations in the Han-Tang Period.* Honolulu: University of Hawai'i Press.

Wang Zhenzhong 王振忠. 2014. *Ming Qing Huishang yu Huai-Yang shehui bianqian* 明清徽 商与淮扬社会变迁. Rev. edn. Beijing: Sanlian shudian.

Wang, Zhongshu. 1982. *Han Civilization.* Yale University Press.

Wang Zijin 王子今. 2005. "Xi Han 'Qi san fuguan' bianzheng" 西汉'齐三服官'辨证. *Zhongguo shi yanjiu* 中国史研究, 35–40.

Washio Yūko 鷲尾祐子. 2009. *Chūgoku kodai no sensei kokka to minkan shakai: kazoku, fūzoku, kōshi* 中国古代の専制国家と民間社会: 家族, 風俗, 公私. Kyoto: Ritsumeikan tōyōshi gakkai.

Watanabe Shinichirō 渡辺信一郎. 1986. *Chūgoku kodai shakai ron* 中国古代社会論. Tokyo: Aoki shoten.

   1989. "Kandai no zaisei un'ei to kokkateki butsuryū" 漢代の財政運営と国家的物流. *Kyōto furitsu daigaku gakujutsu hōkoku (jinbun)* 京都府立大学学術報告 (人文) 41: 1–20.

   2010. *Chūgoku kodai no zaisei to kokka* 中国古代の財政と国家. Tokyo: Kyūko shoin.

Watson, Burton. 1967. *Basic Writings of Mo Tzu, Hsün Tzu, and Han Fei Tzu*. New York: Columbia University Press.

Weber, Max. 1978. *Economy and Society*. Guenther Roth and Claus Wittick, eds. Berkeley, CA: University of California Press.

Wicks, Robert S. 1998. *Money, Markets, and Trade in Early Southeast Asia: The Development of Indigenous Monetary Systems to AD 1400*. Ithaca, NY: Cornell University Southeast Asia Programs Publications.

Wilbur, C. Martin. 1943. *Slavery in the Former Han Dynasty, 206 BC–AD 25*. Chicago: Field Museum of Natural History.

Will, Pierre-Étienne. 1985. "State Intervention in the Administration of a Hydraulic Infrastructure." In S. R. Schram, ed. *The Scope of State Power in China*, 295–347. London: School of Oriental and African Studies.

   1990. *Bureaucracy and Famine in Eighteenth-Century China*. Stanford University Press.

   1994. "Développement quantitatif et développement qualitatif en Chine à la fin de l'époque impériale." *Annales: Histoire, Sciences Sociales* 49.4: 863–902.

Will, Pierre-Étienne and R. Bin Wong. 1991. *Nourish the People: The State Civilian Granary System in China, 1650–1850*. Ann Arbor: University of Michigan Center for Chinese Studies.

Wolf, Arthur P. 2001. "Is There Evidence of Birth Control in Late Imperial China?" *Population and Development Review* 27.1: 133–54.

Wong, J. Y. 1998. *Deadly Dreams: Opium and the Arrow War (1856–1860) in China*. Cambridge University Press.

Wong, R. Bin. 1997. *China Transformed: Historical Change and the Limits of European Experience*. Ithaca: Cornell University Press.

   2012. "Taxation and Good Governance in China, 1500–1914." In B. Yun-Casalilla and P. K. O'Brien, eds. *The Rise of Fiscal States: A Global History, 1500–1914*, 353–77. Cambridge University Press.

Wong, R. Bin, and Peter Perdue. 1992. "Grain Markets and Food Supplies in Eighteenth-Century Hunan." In T. G. Rawski and L. M. Li, eds. *Chinese History in Economic Perspective*, 126–44. Berkeley: University of California Press.

Wright, Arthur F. 1978. *The Sui Dynasty: The Unification of China, AD 581–617*. New York: Knopf.

Wu Chengming 吳承明. 1985. "Lun Qingdai qianqi woguo guonei shichang" 论清代前期我国国内市场. In Wu, *Zhongguo ziben zhuyi yu guonei shichang* 中国资本主义与国内市场, 247–65. Beijing: Zhongguo shehui kexue chubanshe.

2001a. "Lun Mingdai guonei shichang he shangren ziben" 论明代国内市场和商人资本. In Wu, *Zhongguode xiandaihua: shichang yu shehui* 中国的现代化: 市场与社 会, 111–43. Beijing: Sanlian shudian.

2001b. "Shiba yu shijiu shiji shangyede Zhongguo shichang" 18 与19 世纪上叶的中国市场. In Wu, *Zhongguode xiandaihua: shichang yu shehui* 中国的现代化: 市场与社 会, 238–88. Beijing: Sanlian shudian.

Wu Hui 吴慧. 1990. "Ming Qing (qianqi) caizheng jiegouxing bianhuade jiliang fenxi" 明清 (前期) 财政结构性变化的计量分析. *Zhongguo shehui jingji shi yanjiu* 中国社会经济 史研究 3: 39–45.

Wu Renshu 巫仁恕. 2007. *Pinwei shehua: Wan Mingde xiaofei shehui yu shidafu* 品味奢華: 晚明的消費社會與士大夫. Taipei: Zhongyang yanjiuyuan/Lianjing chubanshe.

Wu Songdi 吴松弟. 2000. *Zhongguo renkou shi* 中国人口史, vol. 3: *Liao Song Jin Yuan shiqi* 辽宋金元时期. Shanghai: Fudan daxue chubanshe.

2007. *Nan Song renkou shi* 南宋人口史. Shanghai: Shanghai guji chubanshe.

Xie Guihua 谢桂华. 1989. "Hanjian he Handaide quyong daixu zhidu" 汉简和汉代的取庸代 戍制度. In Gansusheng wenwu kaogu yanjiusuo 甘肃省文物考古研究所, ed. *Qin Han jiandu lunwenji* 秦汉简牍论文集, 77–112. Lanzhou: Gansu renmin chubanshe.

Xie Yanxiang 谢雁翔. 1974. "Sichuan Pixian Xipu chutude Dong Han canbei' 四川郫县犀浦 出土的东汉残碑. *Wenwu* 文物 4: 67–71.

Xiong, Victor Cunrui. 1993. "Sui Yangdi and the Building of Sui-Tang Luoyang." *Journal of Asian Studies* 52.1: 66–89.

1999. "The Land Tenure System of Tang China: A Study of the Equal Field System and the Turfan Documents." *T'oung Pao* 85.4–5: 328–90.

2000. *Sui-Tang Chang'an: A Study in the Urban History of Medieval China.* Ann Arbor: University of Michigan Center for Chinese Studies.

Xu Daling 許大齡. 1974. *Qingdai juanna zhidu* 清代捐納制度. Taipei: Wenhai chubanshe.

Xu, Dixin and Wu Chengming. 2000. *Chinese Capitalism, 1522–1840*. London: Macmillan.

Xu Hong 许宏. 2000. *Xian Qin chengshi kaoguxue* 先秦城市考古学. Beijing: Beijing yanshan chubanshe.

Xu Tan 许檀. 2000. "Ming Qing shiqi chengxiang wangluo tixide xingcheng ji yiyi" 明清时期 城乡网络体系的形成及意义. *Zhongguo shehui kexue* 中国社会科学 3: 191–202.

Xu Yihua 徐义华. 2007. "Xin chutu 'Wunian Zhousheng zun' yu Zhousheng qiming shixi" 新 出土《五年瑞生尊》与瑞生器铭试析. *Zhongguo shi yanjiu* 中国史研究 2: 17–27.

Xu Yueyao 徐乐尧. 1989. "Juyan Hanjian suojiande shi" 居延汉简所见的市. In Gansusheng wenwu kaogu yanjiusuo 甘肃省文物考古研究所, ed. *Qin Han jiandu lunwenji* 秦汉简牍论文集, 49–69. Lanzhou: Gansu renmin chubanshe.

Yamada Katsuyoshi 山田勝芳. 1975. "Ō Mō dai no zaisei" 王莽代の財政. *Tōyōshi kenkyū* 東洋史研究 33.1: 63–85.

1979. "Chūgoku kodai no shōnin to shiseki" 中国古代の商人と市籍. In *Kaga hakase taikan kinen Chūgoku bun shi tetsugaku ronshū* 加賀博士退官記念中国文史哲 学論集, 175–96. Tokyo: Kodansha.

1981. "Hōōzan jūgōbotsu monjo to Kansho no shōgyō" 鳳凰山一〇号墓文書と
漢初の商業. *Tōhoku daigaku kyōyōbu kiyō* 東北大学教養部紀要 33:
172–92.

1987. "Shin Kan jidai no dainai to shōnai" 秦漢時代の大内と少内. *Shūkan
tōyōgaku* 集刊東洋学 57: 19–39.

1988. "Chūgoku kodai no shō to ko: sono imi to shisōshiteki haikei" 中国古代の 商
と賈: その意味と思想史的背景. *Tōyōshi kenkyū* 東洋史研究 47.1: 1–29.

1990. "Offices and Officials of Works, Markets, and Lands in the Ch'in Dynasty."
Acta Asiatica 58: 1–23.

1993. *Shin Kan zaisei shūnyū no kenkyū* 秦漢財政収入の研究. Tokyo: Kyūko
shoin.

1998. "Shin Kan dai shukōgyō no tenkai: Shin Kan dai kōkan no hensen kara
kangaeru" 秦漢代手工業の展開: 秦漢代工官の変遷から考える. *Tōyōshi
kenkyū* 東洋史研究 56.4: 701–32.

2000. *Kahei no Chūgoku kodaishi* 貨幣の中国古代史. Tokyo: Asahi shinbunsha.

2007. "Zen Kan Buteidai no chiiki shakai to josei yōeki: Ankishō Tenchōshi
Anrakuchin jūkyūgō mokutoku kara kangaeru" 前漢武帝代の地域社会と女性
徭役: 安徽省天長市安楽鎮十九号木牘から考える. *Shūkan tōyōgaku* 集刊東
洋学 97: 1–19.

Yamamoto Susumu 山本進. 1991. "Shindai Shisen no chiiki keizai: inyū daitai
mengyō no keisei to Ha-ken gagyō" 清代四川の地域経済: 移入代替棉業の形
成と巴県牙行. *Shigaku zasshi* 史学雑誌 100.12: 2005–35.

1997. "Shōhin seisan kenkyū no kiseki" 商品生産研究の軌跡. In Mori Masao
森正夫, Noguchi Tetsurō 野口鐵郎, Hamashima Atsutoshi 濱島敦俊,
Kishimoto Mio 岸本美緒, and Satake Yasuhiko 佐竹靖彦, eds. *Min Shin
jidaishi no kihonteki mondai* 明清時代史の基本 的問題, 79–101. Tokyo:
Kyūko shoin.

2002. *Shindai no shijō kōzō to keizai seisaku* 清代の市場構造と経済政策. Nagoya:
Nagoya daigaku shuppankai.

Yamamura, Kōzō and Kamiki Tetsuo. 1983. "Silver Mines and Sung Coins." In John
F. Richards, ed. *Precious Metals in the Late Medieval and Early Modern Worlds*,
329–62. Durham, NC: Carolina Academic Press.

Yamane, Yukio. 1984. "Reforms in the Service Levy System in the Fifteenth and
Sixteenth Centuries." In L. Grove and C. Daniels, eds. *State and Society in China:
Japanese Perspectives on Ming-Qing Social and Economic History*, 279–310.
University of Tokyo Press.

Yamazaki Riichi 山崎利一. 1978. *Shisan no shōgai to shisō* 子産の生涯と思想.
Osaka: Maeda shoten.

Yamazaki Satoshi 山崎覚士. 2010a. "Mikan no kaijō kokka: Go-Etsu koku no
kokoromi" 未完 の海上国家: 呉越国の試み. In Yamazaki, *Chūgoku Godai
kokka ron*中國五代国家 論, 230–267. Kyoto: Bukkyo daigaku.

2010b. "Kyūseiki ni okeru Higashi Ajia kaiiki to kaishō – Jo Kōchoku to Jo Kōyū"
九世紀における東アジア海域と海商—徐公直と徐公裕. In Yamazaki, *Chūgoku
Godai kokka ron*中國五代国家 論, 171–204. Kyoto: Bukkyo daigaku.

Yan Hongzhong 燕红忠. 2007. "Shanxi piaohao ziben yu lirun zongliang zhi guji"
山西票号资 本与利润总量之估计. *Shanxi daxue xuebao (zhexue shehui kexue
ban)* 山西大学学报 (哲学社会科学版) 30.6: 128–31.

Yanagida Setsuko 柳田節子. 1963. "Sōdai tochi shoyūsei ni mirareru futatsu no kata: senshin to henkyō" 宋代土地所有制に見られる二つの型: 先進と辺境. *Tōyō bunka kenkyūjo kiyō* 東洋文化研究所紀要 29: 95–130.

1973. "Sōdai tenkosei no saikentō: saikin no Kusano Yasushi shi no kenkai o megutte" 宋代佃戸制の再検討:最近の草野靖氏の見解をめぐって. *Rekishigaku kenkyū* 歴史学研究 395: 24–33.

1986. *Sō Gen gōsonsei no kenkyū* 宋元郷村制の研究. Tokyo: Sōbunsha.

1995. "Sōdai nōka keiei to eiun" 宋代農家経営と営運. In Yanagida, *Sō Gen shakai keizai shi kenkyū* 宋元社会経済史の研究, 85–105. Tokyo: Sōbunsha.

Yang Dequan 杨德泉. 1982. "Tang Song hanghui zhidu zhi yanjiu" 唐宋行会制度之研究. In Deng Guangming 邓广铭 and Cheng Yingliu 程应镠, eds. *Songshi yanjiu lunwenji* 宋史研究论文集, 204–40. Shanghai: Shanghai guji chubanshe.

Yang Jiping 杨际平. 2003. *Beichao Sui Tang juntianzhi xintan* 北朝隋唐均田制新探. Changsha: Yuelu shushe.

2006. "Xi Changsha Zoumalou Sanguo Wujian zhongde 'diao': jian tan hudiaozhide qiyuan" 析长沙走马楼三国吴简中的《调》: 兼谈户调制的起源. *Lishi yanjiu* 历史研究 3: 39–58.

Yang Jiping 杨际平 and Li Qing 李卿. 2003. "Li Xianfu ji zhu Li kai Liyuchuan shishi kaobian – jian lun Wei Shou suoweide Taihe shinianqian 'wei li zongzhu duhu' 李显甫 集诸李开李鱼川史事考辨 – 兼论魏收所谓的太和十年前 '唯立宗主督护'". *Xiamen daxue xuebao (zhexue shehui kexue)* 厦门大学学报 (哲学社会科学) 3: 93–102.

Yang Kuan 杨宽. 1998. *Zhanguo shi* 战国史. Rev. edn. Shanghai: Shanghai renmin chubanshe.

Yang Liansheng 楊聯陞. 1934. "Cong Simin Yueling suo jiandaode Handai jiazu shengchan" 從四民月令所見到的漢代家族生產. *Shihuo banyuekan* 食貨半月刊 1.6: 8–11.

Yang, Lien-sheng. 1956. "Great Families of Eastern Han." In E-tu Zen Sun and John DeFrancis, eds. *Chinese Social History: Translations of Selected Studies*, 103–34. New York: American Council of Learned Societies.

1961. "Notes on the Economic History of the Chin Dynasty." In Yang, *Studies in Chinese Institutional History*, pp. 119–97. Cambridge: Harvard-Yenching Institute.

Yang Ying 杨英. 1996. "Shilun Zhoudai shurende shehui shenfen he shehui diwei" 试论周代 庶人的社会身份和社会地位. *Zhongguo lishi bowuguan guankan* 中国历史博物馆馆 刊 2: 10–21.

Yang Zhenhong 杨振红. 2003. "Qin Han 'mingtianzhai zhi' shuo: cong Zhangjiashan Hanjian kan Zhanguo Qin Han de tudi zhidu" 秦汉「名田宅制」说: 从张家山汉简看战国秦 汉的土地制度. *Zhongguoshi yanjiu* 中国史研究 3: 49–72.

2009. *Chutu jiandu yu Qin Han shehui* 出土简牍与秦汉社会. Guilin: Guangxi shifan daxue chubanshe.

2010. "Songbo Xi Han mu buji du kaoshi" 松柏西汉墓簿籍牍考释. *Nandu xuebao (renwen shehui kexue xuebao)* 南都学报 (人文社会科学学报) 30.5: 1–8.

Yates, Robin D. S. 1987. "Social Status in the Ch'in: Evidence from the Yün-meng Legal Documents. Part One: Commoners." *Harvard Journal of Asiatic Studies* 47.1: 197–237.

2002. "Slavery in Early China: A Socio-Cultural Approach." *Journal of East Asian Archaeology* 3.1–2: 283–331.

2013. "The Qin Slips and Boards from Well No. 1, Liye, Hunan: A Brief Introduction to the Qin Qianling County Archives." *Early China* 35: 291–329.

Yazawa Tadayuki 矢沢忠之. 2008. "Sengokuki San Shin chiiki ni okeru kahei to toshi: hōsokufu・sensokufu o chūshin ni" 戦国期三晋地域における貨幣と都市: 方足布・尖足布を中心に. *Kodai bunka* 古代文化 60.3: 37–54.

Ye Xian'en 叶显恩 and Tan Dihua 谭棣华. 1985a. "Fengjian zongfa shili dui Foshan jingjide kongzhi jiqi chanshengde yingxiang" 封建宗法势力对佛山经济的控制及其产生的影响. In Guangdong lishi xuehui 广东历史学会., ed. *Ming Qing Guangdong shehui jingji xingtai yanjiu* 明清广东社会经济形态研究, 144–64. Guangzhou: Guangdong renmin chubanshe.

1985b. "Lun Zhujiang sanjiaozhoude zutian" 论珠江三角洲的族田." In Guangdong lishi xuehui 广东历史学会., ed. *Ming Qing Guangdong shehui jingji xingtai yanjiu* 明清广东社会经济形态研究, 22–64. Guangzhou: Guangdong renmin chubanshe.

Ye Yuying 叶玉英. 2005. "Lun Zhangjiashan Hanjian 'Suanshushu' de jingji shiliao jiazhi 论张家山汉简《算数书》的经济史料价值, *Zhongguo shehui jingjishi yanjiu* 中国社会经济史研究 1: 38–45.

Yinqueshan hanmu zhujian zhengli xiaozu 银雀山汉墓竹简整理小组. 1985. "Yinqueshan zhushu 'Shoufa,' 'Shouling' deng shisan pian" 银雀山竹书《守法》《守令》等十三篇. *Wenwu* 文物 4: 27–38.

Yōgi Yoshimi 要木佳美. 1997. "Minmatsu Shōkō ni okeru jōzōgyō no tenkai to beikoku ryūtsū" 明末紹興における醸造業の展開と米穀流通. In Ono Kazuko 小野和子, ed. *Minmatsu Shinsho no shakai to bunka* 明末清初の社会と文化, 277–313. Kyoto: Kyoto daigaku jimbun kagaku kenkyūjo.

Yokkaichi Yasuhiro 四日市康博. 2006. "Genchō nankai kōeki keiei kō: monjo to senka no nagare kara" 元朝南海交易経営考: 文書と銭貨の流れから. *Kyūshū daigaku tōyōshi ronshū* 九州大学東洋史論集 34: 133–56.

Yokoyama Suguru 横山英. 1962. "Shindai ni okeru hōtōsei no tenkai" 清代における包頭制の展開. *Shigaku zasshi* 史学雑誌 71.1: 45–71, 71.2: 185–98.

Yoneda Kenjirō 米田賢次郎. 1989. *Chūgoku kodai nōgyō gijutsu shi kenkyū* 中國古代農業技術史研究. Tokyo: Dōhōsha.

Yoshimoto Michimasa 吉本道雅. 1986. "Shunshū kokujin kō" 春秋国人考. *Shirin* 史林 69.5: 631–72.

You Biao 游彪. 2003. *Songdai siyuan jingji shigao* 宋代寺院经济史稿. Baoding: Hebei daxue chubanshe.

Yu Yaohua 余耀华. 2000. *Zhongguo jiage shi: Xian Qin-Qing chao* 中国价格史: 先秦—清朝. Beijing: Zhongguo wujia chubanshe.

Yü, Ying-shih. 1967. *Trade and Expansion in Han China: A Study in the Structure of Sino-Barbarian Economic Relations*. Berkeley, CA: University of California Press.

Yu Yingshi 余英時. 1987. *Zhongguo jinshi zongjiao lunli yu shangren jingshen* 中國近世宗教倫理與商人精神. Taipei: Lianjing chubanshe.

Yu Zhenbo 于振波. 2004a. "Zhangjiashan Hanjian zhongde mingtianzhi jiqi zai Handaide shishi qingkuang" 张家山汉简中的名田制及其在汉代的实施情况. *Zhongguo shi yanjiu* 中国史研究 1: 29–40.

2004b. *Zoumalou Wujian chutan* 走馬樓吳簡初探. Taipei: Wenjin chubanshe.

Yuan, Tsing. 1979. "Urban Riots and Disturbances during the Late Ming and Early Ch'ing Period." In Jonathan D. Spence and John E. Wills, Jr., eds. *From Ming to Ch'ing: Conquest, Region, and Continuity in Seventeenth-Century China*, 277–320. New Haven: Yale University Press.

Yuan Weipeng 袁为鹏 and Ma Debin 马德斌. 2010. "Shangye zhangbu yu jingjishi yanjiu: yi Tongtaisheng hao shangye zhangbu wei zhongxin (1798–1850)" 商业账簿与经济 史研究: 以统泰升号商业账簿为中心. *Zhongguo jingji shi yanjiu* 中国经济史研 究 2: 50–60.

Yun-Casalilla, Bartolomé. 2012. "Introduction: The Rise of the Fiscal State in Eurasia from a Global, Comparative, and Transnational Perspective." In B. Yun-Casalilla and P. K. O'Brien, eds. *The Rise of Fiscal States: A Global History, 1500–1914*, 1–35. Cambridge University Press.

Zelin, Madeleine. 1984. *The Magistrate's Tael: Rationalizing Fiscal Reform in Eighteenth-Century Ch'ing China*. Berkeley, CA: University of California Press.

2004. "A Critique of Property Rights in Prewar China." In M. Zelin, J. K. Ocko, and R. Gardella, eds. *Contract and Property in Early Modern China*, 17–36. Stanford University Press.

2005. *The Merchants of Zigong: Industrial Entrepreneurship in Early Modern China*. New York: Columbia University Press.

2009. "The Firm in Early Modern China." *Journal of Economic Behavior and Organization* 71.4: 623–37.

Zelin, Madeleine, Jonathan K. Ocko, and Robert Gardella, eds. 2004. *Contract and Property in Early Modern China*. Stanford University Press.

Zhang Guogang 张国刚. 2006. "Tangdai bingzhide yanbian yu zhonggu shehui bianqian" 唐代 兵制的演变与中古社会变迁. *Zhongguo shehui kexue* 中国社会科学 4: 178–89.

2012. "Tangdai nongye jiating shengji tanlüe" 唐代農業家庭生計探略. *Zhongguo wenshi luncong* 中國文史論叢 98: 1–51.

Zhang Haipeng 张海鹏 and Wang Tingyuan 王廷元. 1995. *Hui shang yanjiu* 徽商研究. Hefei: Anhui renmin chubanshe.

Zhang Jinguang 张金光. 2007. "Pubian shoutianzhide zhongjie yu siyou diquande xingcheng – Zhangjiashan Hanjian yu Qinjian bijiao yanjiu zhi yi" 普遍授田制的终结与私有地权的 形成 – 张家山汉简与秦简比较研究之一. *Lishi yanjiu* 历史研究 5: 49–65.

Zhang Jinling 张金岭. 2001. *Wan Song shiqi caizheng weiji yanjiu* 晚宋时期财政危机研究. Chengdu: Sichuan daxue chubanshe.

Zhang Jinpeng 张锦鹏. 2003. *Songdai shangpin gongji yanjiu* 宋代商品供给研究. Kunming: Yunnan daxue chubanshe.

Zhang Li 张丽. 2010. *Feipinghenghua yu bupingheng: cong Wuxi jindai nongcun jingji fazhan kan Zhongguo jindai nongcun jingjide zhuanxing (1840–1949)* 非平衡化与不平衡: 从 无锡近代农村经济发展看中国近代农村经济的转型. Beijing: Zhonghua shuju.

Zhang Rongqiang 张荣强. 2005. "'Ernian lüling' yu Handai keyi shenfen" 《二年律令》与汉 代课役身分. *Zhongguo shi yanjiu* 中国史研究 2: 25–41.

Zhang, Taisu. 2011. "Property Rights in Land, Agricultural Capitalism, and the Relative Decline of Pre-Industrial China." *San Diego International Law Journal* 13: 129–200.

Zhang Xunliao 张勋燎 and Liu Panshi 刘磐石. 1980. "Sichuan Pixian Dong Han canbei de xingzhi he niandai" 四川郫县东汉残碑的性质和年代. *Wenwu* 文物 4: 72–3.

Zhang Youyi 章有义. 1984. *Ming Qing Huizhou tudi guanxi yanjiu* 明清徽州土地关系研究. Beijing: Zhongguo shehui kexue chubanshe.

Zhang Zhongmin 张忠民. 2002. *Jiannande bianqian: jindai Zhongguo gongsi zhidu yanjiu* 艰难的变迁:近代中国公司制度研究. Shanghai: Shanghai shehui kexueyuan chubanshe.

Zhao, Gang. 2013. *The Qing Opening to the Ocean: Chinese Maritime Policies, 1684–1757*. Honolulu: University of Hawai'i Press.

Zhao Guangxian 赵光贤. 1979. "Cong Qiu Wei zhu qiming kan Xi Zhoude tudi jiaoyi" 从裘卫 诸器铭看西周的土地交易. *Beijing shifan daxue xuebao (shehui kexue ban)* 北京师范 大学学报 (社会科学版) 6: 16–23.

Zhao Ming 昭明 and Ma Liqing 马利清. 2007. *Zhongguo gudai huobi* 中国古代货币. Tianjin: Baihua wenyi chubanshe.

Zhao Ping'an 赵平安. 2004. "Zhanguo wenzi zhongde yan zi jiqi xiangguan wenti yanjiu" 战 国文字中的盐字及其相关问题研究. *Kaogu* 考古 8: 728–33.

Zheng Binglin 郑炳林. 2004. "Wan Tang Wudai Dunhuang shangye maoyi shichang yanjiu" 晚唐五代敦煌商业贸易市场研究. *Dunhuangxue jikan* 敦煌学楫刊 1: 103–18.

Zheng Yibing 郑亦兵. 1994. "Qingdai qianqi neilu liangshi yunshuliang ji bianhua qushi" 清代 前期内陆粮食运输量 及变化趋势. *Zhongguo jingji shi yanjiu* 中国经济史研究 3: 80–92.

Zheng Zhenman. 2001. *Family Lineage Organization and Social Change in Ming and Qing Fujian*. Honolulu: University of Hawai'i Press.

Zhongguo shehui kexueyuan lishi yanjiusuo Song Liao Jin Yuan shi yanjiushi 中国社 会科学院历史研 究所宋辽金元史研究室, ed. 1985. *Song Liao Jin shi lunji* 宋辽 金史论集. Beijing: Zhonghua shuju.

Zhou Junmin 周俊敏. 2003. *Guanzi jingji lunli sixiang yanjiu* 管子经济伦理思想研究. Changsha: Yuelu shushe.

Zhou Lin 周琳. 2011. "Chengshi shangren tuanti yu shangye zhixu: Qingdai Chongqing basheng kezhang tiaochu shangye jiufen huodong wei zhongxin" 城市 商人团体与商业秩 序: 清代重庆八省客长调处商业纠纷活动为中心. *Nanjing daxue xuebao (zhexue renwen kexue shehui kexue ban)* 南京大学学报 (哲学人文 科学社会科学版) 2:80–99.

Zhou Xiaolu 周晓陆 and Lu Dongzhi 路东之. 2005. "Xincai gucheng Zhanguo fengnide chubu kaocha" 新蔡古城战国封泥的初步考察. *Wenwu* 文物 1: 51–61.

Zhou Ziqiang 周自强. 1987. "Chonglun Xi Zhou shiqide 'gongtian' he 'sitian" 重论西周时期 的『公田』和『私田』. *Shilin* 史林 1: 1–10.

    ed. 2007. *Zhongguo jingji tongshi: Xian Qin* 中国经济通史:先秦. 2nd edn. Beijing: Jingji ribao chubanshe.

Zhu Fenghan 朱风瀚. 2004. *Shang Zhou jiazu xingtai yanjiu* 商周家族形态研究. Rev. edn. Tianjin: Tianjin guji chubanshe.

Zhu Honglin 朱紅林. 2008. *Zhangjiashan Hanjian "Ernian lüling" yanjiu* 张家山汉 简《二年律令》研究. Haerbin: Heilongjiang renmin chubanshe.

Zhu Ruixi 朱瑞熙. 2006. "Songdai tudi jiage yanjiu" 宋代土地價格研究. *Zhonghua wenshi luncong* 中華文史論叢 82: 97–157.

Zhu Shaohou 朱绍侯. 1985. *Qin Han tudi zhidu yu jieji guanxi* 秦汉土地制度与阶级 关系. Zhengzhou: Zhongzhou guji chubanshe.

Zhuang Guotu 庄国土. 1995. "16–18 shiji baiyin liuru Zhongguo shuliang gusuan" 16–18世纪白银流入中国数量估算. *Zhongguo qianbi* 中国钱币 5: 3–10.

Zurndorfer, Harriet. 2011. "Contracts, Property, and Litigation: Intermediation and Adjudication in the Huizhou Region (Anhui) in Sixteenth-Century China." In D. Ma and J. L. van Zanden, eds. *Law and Long-Term Economic Change: A Eurasian Perspective*, 91–114. Stanford University Press.

2013. "Cotton Textile Production in Jiangnan during the Ming-Qing Era and the Matter of Market-Driven Growth." In B. K. L. So, ed. *The Economic History of Lower Yangzi Delta in Late Imperial China: Connecting Money, Markets, and Institutions*, 72–98. London: Routledge.

Index

agriculture
  as share of GDP, 355
  commercialization of, 242, 297, 308,
    327–28, 350–54, 359
  crop rotation, 131, 191, 219, 221, 224, 327
  double-cropping, 220, 224, 327, 352
  farm size, 225, 265, 290, 352
  fertilizer, 132, 191, 290, 327–28
  in Dunhuang, 219–20
  in Han, 130–34, 139–41
  in Ming, 290
  in Period of Disunion, 191–94
  in Qin, 97
  in Qing, 327–29
  in Song, 223–25, 273–74
  in Tang, 219–23
  in Warring States era, 61
  in Zhou, 28–32
  per capita production, 351, 358
  plow, 130–34, 191
  plow oxen, 61, 131, 140, 173, 191, 270
  polders, 223–25, 256, 273, 290, 321, 328
  ridge-and-furrow cultivation, 131, 133
  swidden, 131
  terraced fields, 223
Ahmad, 282–83
Allen, Robert, 360
alum, 227, 245
An Lushan rebellion, 170, 207–8, 210–21, 226,
    236, 253
Angkor, 272
appointment inscriptions, 22, 38
Arabia, 271–72, 288
archer lords, 15, 17, 19, 25, 38, 42
aromatics, 154, 197–99, 227, 271
arsenals, 89, 97, 106, 115, 378, 397
artisans
  as hereditary occupation, 172, 280
  as occupational category, 13, 49, 56, 59, 68,
    76, 78, 91, 287
  bronze, 28, 37, 163
  conscription of, 106, 280, 295, 297–98

in state workshops, 72, 91, 147
lacquer, 106
legal discrimination against, 92
private, 149, 318
regulation of, 216
relocation of, 170
servile, 13, 25
silk, 106
stone, 36
taxation of, 59, 114, 147, 287
textiles, 146, 150, 246–47, 300
types of, 201
urban, 74, 266, 346
wages, 373
Asiatic mode of production, 1
Atwell, William, 310–11
autocratic state, 2, 13, 46, 55, 59, 75, 78, 82,
    86–87, 91, 101
  in Qin, 55–58
  in Wei, 55

Bai Gui, 64, 70
Ban Gu, 142
Bangkok, 392
banking
  account transers (*guozhang*), 386
  and economic development, 385–90
  and government loans, 384
  bank notes, 383, 387, 389
  chop loans (*chaipiao*), 386
  deposit, 216, 267, 344, 386–88
  foreign banks, 383, 389
  guild, 386
  overseas remittances, 376, 389, 392
  piaohao remittance banks, 345, 387–90,
    393, 396
  qianzhuang, 345, 369, 379, 385–87, 390
  state banks, 389, 397
  yinhao, 369
  zhangju (account agencies), 385
Bao Shichen, 365
baojia militias, 237

in Northern Wei, 172
in Qin, 87
in Qin-Han, 85
in *Rituals of Zhou*, 88
in Sui, 184
in Tang, 206
in Warring States period, 81
in *zu-yong-diao* system, 186, 188
monetization of, 236, 240, 314
under Mongols, 279–80
women, 104
lacquer
artisans, 37, 106
consumption, 306
manufacture, 65, 148, 154, 242
trade, 64, 154, 225, 245, 251
wares, 37, 70, 74, 146–47, 156, 193, 200
workshops, 150
land
commendation (*touxian*), 296
inheritance of, 27, 92, 94, 201, 275, 277, 302, 324
reclamation, 161, 223–44, 321, 328–29
state confiscation of, 277, 286, 294
state-owned, 97, 133, 218, 278, 314, 324
surveys, 54, 227, 276, 287, 314
land allocations
in Han, 93–94, 110, 128
in Northern Qi, 180
in Northern Wei, 173–76
in Northern Zhou, 181
in Qin, 91
in Sui, 183
in Tang, 185
land tenure
in Han, 138
in Northern Wei, 173–76
in Qin, 58
in Song, 274
in Spring and Autumn era, 58
in Zhou, 28, 41–42
privatization of, 218
land transactions
in Han, 92, 139
in Ming, 291–93
in Qing, 324–25
in Song, 268, 273–78
in Zhou, 26–29, 39–42
landownership
concentration of, 111, 114, 127, 134–39, 175, 180, 183, 205–6, 218, 282, 296, 302
dispersal of, 225, 273, 296, 324, 326
multiple, 277, 302
of Buddhist institutions, 202

law
and bankruptcy, 337
and dispute resolution, 277, 301, 354
and interest rates, 344
code of Li Kui, 55
code of Shang Yang, 56
code of Zichan, 51
commercial, 397
discrimination against tenants, 219
Qin Code, 91
Wei Code, 55, 91
leather, 26–27, 37, 40, 65, 148, 216, 270, 342
Legalism, 55, 76, 81, 85, 90, 95, 127
Lewis, Mark, 52
Li (Zhou king), 19–20
Li Bing, 61
Li Bozhong, 4, 219, 221, 352–54, 359–60, 373
Li Daokui, 355
Li Daquan, 387
Li Hongzhang, 378–79
Li Kui, 55–57, 61, 70, 75–76, 78
Li Linfu, 205
Li Ling, 41
Li Longsheng, 370
Li Shimin (Emperor Taizong of Tang), 185
Li Shu, 291, 302
Li Si, 96, 105
Li Xianfu, 171
Li Yuan (Emperor Taizu of Tang), 184, 207
Liang, fiscal administration in, 165
liangren (free subjects), 174, 306
lichenqie (penal servitude), 59
life expectancy, 350
Lin, Man-houng, 367
lineage
corporate, 301–4, 321
in Spring and Autumn era, 49
in Zhou, 13, 25–27, 41–42
trusts, 296, 302–4, 336–44, 346, 396
linked-firm (*lianhao*) enterprises, 342–44, 346, 387
Linzi, 40, 68, 71, 109, 146
Little Ice Age, 284
liturgic governance, 12
Liu Bang (Emperor Gaozu of Han), 85, 100–2, 105, 108, 127
Liu Guanglin, 355, 358
Liu Pi, 107
Liu Ti, 355, 358
Liu Xiu (Emperor Guangwu of Han), 135, 137, 158
Liu Yan, 212
Liu Yu (Emperor Wu of Song), 160
loess, 28, 131
Loulan, 197

Qiu Wei, 26–27, 37, 39
Quanzhou, 248, 250, 271–72, 284, 293, 325, 342
qubchir (tax), 279–80
Qubilai Khan, 255, 280–84, 293

railroads, 376, 380, 384, 397
ramie, 186–87, 194, 222
Renzong, emperor of Song, 232
rice
  Champa, 223
  consumption, 266
  cultivation, 130–31, 220–44, 324, 327
  double-cropping, 327
  for brewing, 299
  imports, 392, 395
  trade, 164, 297, 308, 333, 370, 372, 392
  transplanting, 132, 220
  yields, 221, 290, 327, 352
Rituals of Zhou, 39, 86, 88–89, 136
Roman Empire, 120, 154–55
Rowe, William, 320
rubber, 392

safflower, 193
salt
  certificates, 238, 254, 264, 267
  consumption, 266
  levies, 213, 227
  licenses, 230, 232–33
  merchants, 65, 148, 288, 316
  mining, 396
  monopoly, 117, 121, 123–26, 146, 212–13, 230, 237, 243, 254, 282, 288, 303–6, 314–16, 349, 378
  production, 172, 227
  smuggling, 362
  trade, 65, 163, 198, 216, 225, 270, 272, 342, 344, 370, 396
Salt and Iron Debates, 123–26
Samarkand, 199
Sang Hongyang, 116–21, 123–26, 148, 155, 253
Sangha, 282–84
sangha households (*sengqihu*), 202–3
Schmoller, Gustav, 9
Schumpeterian growth, 9–10
self-strengthening, 378, 380, 389, 397
sericulture, 132, 140, 192, 216, 223, 231, 246, 297, 328, 344, 354
sesame, 131, 140, 164
settlements
  bang, 23
  dispersed, 133
  elite, 47

fortified villages, 157, 170
li, 23, 89, 109
single-lineage villages, 302
villages, 138, 153, 171, 193, 281, 286, 290
walled cities, 44–47, 66–71, 73
xian towns, 54, 56, 71
yi, 22–23, 42, 46, 48
seyi (specialized service), 186–87, 206
shack people (*pengmin*), 363
Shang Yang, 54–59, 62, 76, 87, 90–91, 94, 96–98
Shangfang workshops, 145, 147
Shanghai
  and foreign trade, 392–95
  banking in, 379, 385–86, 389
Shanxi merchants, 301, 304–6, 344, 387, 395–96
Shaoxing, 161–63, 223–24, 228, 248, 266, 299, 386
she (advance sale contracts), 268
Shenzong, emperor of Song, 236–37, 240, 242
shi
  as aristocracy, 157
  as officials, 88
  as ruling class, 78
  lesser nobility in Zhou, 46, 59
  patricans, 296
Shi Zhihong, 359
Shiba Yoshinobu, 2–4
shipbuilding, 215, 242, 244–45, 271, 376, 378
shuren (commoners), 34, 58–59, 93–95
Sikou (Minister of Public Works), 72
silk
  "account houses" (*zhangfang*), 300
  and Silk Road, 154, 198
  as domestic industry, 133, 246
  clothing, 32, 36
  consumption, 306
  exports, 197, 271, 319, 346, 353, 367–68, 376, 386, 392–93, 398
  filatures, 380
  in tax payments, 158, 175, 190, 214, 280
  manufacture, 65, 106, 132, 140, 194–96, 216, 242, 246, 252, 297, 300, 314, 353
  middlemen (*chengguan*), 300
  rural industry, 344
  state purchases, 231
  trade, 64, 116, 141, 164, 216, 239, 245, 247, 270, 283, 295, 308
  tribute, 155, 229
  yarn, 36, 154–55, 175, 194, 197, 266, 280, 300
Silk Road, 113, 154–56, 187, 196–201, 217, 270
Silla, 184, 205